BTEC NATIONAL

Public Services (Uniformed)

Book 2

Debra Gray, David Stockbridge

Heinemann Educational Publishers
Halley Court, Jordan Hill, Oxford OX2 8EJ
Part of Harcourt Education

Heinemann is the registered trademark of
Harcourt Education Limited

First published 2004

08 07 06 05 04
10 9 8 7 6 5 4 3 2 1

British Library Cataloguing in Publication Data is available
from the British Library on request.

ISBN 0 435 45658 X

Websites
Please note that the examples of websites suggested in this book were up to date at the time of writing. It is essential for tutors to preview each site before using it to ensure that the URL is still accurate and appropriate. We suggest that tutors bookmark useful sites and consider enabling students to access them through the school or college intranet.

Edited by Rosalyn Bass
Designed by Artistix
Typeset and illustrated by J&L Composition

Cover design by Wooden Ark

Printed by The Bath Press Ltd.

Cover photo: © Photofusion

Picture research by Bea Ray

Acknowledgements
Every effort has been made to contact copyright holders of material reproduced in this book. Any omissions will be rectified in subsequent printings if notice is given to the publishers.

Tel: 01865 888058 www.heinemann.co.uk

Contents

Acknowledgements

I would like to thank the following:

My colleagues at Dearne Valley College: Christine Rawson, Barry Pinches, Paul Meares, Geoff Smales, Lynn Harris, John Vause, Boris Lockyer and Dave Stockbridge. You make going to work a pleasure and as far as I am concerned you are the finest public services team in the country. Long live the Dark Lords!

Members of the public services and others who have contributed their knowledge to this book: PC Surinder Dev, Inspector Ian Cox, Inspector Mick Venables, Sgt Paul Sherridan, Signaller Kelly Stevens, 124 Army Youth Team and all of the members of the public services who have given their time and energy to support the public services programme at DVC.

Thanks to Debbie Rowe for her typing skills, Pen Gresford and Rosalyn Bass at Heinemann for their patience and support, Bridie Murphy whose kickboxing tuition kept me sane for 90% of this project until I got so enormously pregnant that the thought of a jump reverse spinning crescent kick made me want to sit down and have a cup of tea.

Special thanks are due to my husband Ben and daughter India who make everything I do worthwhile – yes I can come out and play now!

Finally a special mention to all the students who have attended DVC Public Services over the last eight years – in many ways you have taught me more than I taught you.

Debra Gray

I wish to thank everyone at Dearne Valley College, in particular Christine Rawson for her support and mentoring over the years that has moulded me into the lecturer I am today and Debra, 'the iron maiden' Gray for her professional help, her right hook and spinning back kick. I also wish to thank Kerry Wilson for teaching me the most important lesson in life, to laugh and smile again. Finally I wish to thank myself for all my hard work and patience.

David Stockbridge

Photo acknowledgements

We are grateful to the following for permission to reproduce photographs:

Alamy Images page 21, 79
Corbis, pages 30, 43, 46, 69, 70, 81, 93, 101, 112, 117, 151, 157, 164, 166, 183, 184, 185, 187, 215, 228, 237, 244, 250, 270, 289, 315, 323, 344
Defence Picture Library page 51, 93
Dr Belbin page 253
Dr Margerison page 257
Dr McCann page 257
Empics page 67
Getty Images UK/PhotoDisc page 305
Getty News and Sport pages 23, 183, 184
Getty News and Sport/Tom Shaw page 249
Harcourt Education Ltd/Gareth Boden page 37, 308, 311
Harcourt Education Ltd/Gerald Sunderland page 76
Harcourt Education Ltd/Peter Gould page 310
Harcourt Eduation Ltd/Trevor Clifford page 308
PA Photos pages 7, 32, 44, 81, 97, 105, 149, 156
PA Photos/Andrew Parsons page 263
PA Photos/Ben Curtis page 16
PA Photos/EPA page 90
PA Photos/Mathew Fearn page 148
Rex Features page 41, 76, 78, 107, 155
Topham Picturepoint page 64

INTRODUCTION

This textbook is designed to help you achieve the National Certificate and Diploma in Public Services.

These qualifications are equivalent to A-levels and will help you achieve your goal of joining a public service and also will provide you with the opportunity to go to university to study for a HND or a degree if you want to.

Structure of the Public Services National Qualifications		
Award – 6 units	**Certificate – 12 units**	**Diploma – 18 units**
Core – All 3 units must be studied: 03 – Leadership 08 – The Uniformed Services 09 – Physical Preparation for Uniformed Services	**Core – All 5 units must be studied:** 01 – Understanding the Public Sector 02 – Law and the Legal System 03 – Leadership 04 – Citizenship and Contemporary Issues 08 – The Uniformed Services	**Core – All 8 units must be studied:** 01 – Understanding the Public Sector 02 – Law and the Legal System 03 – Leadership 04 – Citizenship and Contemporary Issues 05 – Diversity and the Public Services 06 – International Perspectives 07 – Data Interpretation 08 – The Uniformed Services
Options – 3 units must be studied from the following list: 02 – Law and the Legal System 11 – Expedition Skills 14 – Understanding Discipline 16 – Dealing with Accidents 22 – Signals and Communication Systems 24 – Major Incidents	**Options – 7 units must be studied from the following list:** 07 – Data Interpretation 09 – Physical Preparation for Uniformed Services 10 – Democratic Processes 11 – Expedition Skills 12 – Human Behaviour 13 – Media and the Public Services 14 – Understanding Discipline 15 – Public Services in Europe 16 – Dealing with Accidents 17 – Teamwork in the Public Services 18 – Health and Fitness 19 – Nautical Studies 20 – Outdoor Activities 21 – Criminology 22 – Signals and Communication Systems	**Options – 10 units must be studied from the following list:** 09 – Physical Preparation for Uniformed Services 10 – Democratic Processes 11 – Expedition Skills 12 – Human Behaviour 13 – Media and the Public Services 14 – Understanding Discipline 15 – Public Services in Europe 16 – Dealing with Accidents 17 – Teamwork in the Public Services 18 – Health and Fitness 19 – Nautical Studies 20 – Outdoor Activities 21 – Criminology 22 – Signals and Communication Systems 23 – Custodial Care 24 – Major Incidents

Structure of the Public Services National Qualifications

If you are studying the National Certificate or Diploma, you will need to use this book in tandem with Book One in this series. Each textbook covers a different set of units:

Book One – Award
Leadership The Uniformed Services Physical Preparation for the Uniformed Services Law and the Legal System Expedition Skills Understanding Discipline Signals and Communications Systems Major Incidents
Book Two – Certificate
Understanding the Public Sector Citizenship and Contemporary Issues Diversity and the Public Services International Perspectives Democratic Processes Human Behaviour Media and the Public Services Health and Fitness Criminology

In addition, Unit 7 Data Interpretation and Unit 23 Custodial Care are available in a web-based format.

How to use this book

This book is designed to operate on a unit by unit basis which means you don't need to read all of the book in order to find the information you need. Simply look in the contents, choose the unit you need and go to the appropriate page. If you are looking for a specific topic within a unit then go to the index and find the topic with its appropriate page number. Sometimes if a unit has strong links with another you may find information is cross referenced. Examples of units with strong links are:

04 Citizenship and Contemporary Issues and Unit 05 Diversity in the Public Services

18 Health and Fitness and Book 1 Unit 09 Physical Preparation for the Uniformed Services.

You can use this book for a whole range of purposes including background reading for a particular unit, help with your assignments, understanding a topic that you missed or didn't understand in class, completion of the activities to reinforce what you already know or to improve your broader general public service knowledge so that you are a better employment prospect for the public services.

This book is written at the level of an A-level textbook as the National Certificate is equivalent to an A-level qualification. However, it is written in a friendly and accessible style.

How this book is designed to help you

Each chapter contains many or all of the following elements.

Think about it

These are points designed to provoke classroom discussion or discussion in your study group or even just to get your mind working by considering something from a different point of view. This is important because many of the public services could ask you spot questions in your interviews and prior discussion will ensure you will be much better prepared to tackle them if and when they occur.

Case studies/Simulations

The case studies in the chapters are a mixture of real life events and realistic simulations. They are designed to give you an insight into potential problems or controversial issues which can arise in the public services.

Completing the case studies may involve you critically considering the actions or inactions of the public services, commenting on their positive and negative conduct and putting yourself in the shoes of serving officers and deciding what you would have done in their place. The use of role-play and case studies is on the increase in public service recruitment procedure and is seen as a valuable tool in assessing your potential.

Case studies also allow you to put the subject knowledge you have learned in the chapters to practical application. This will ensure you retain more of the information you need to learn.

Theory into practice

Activities are included throughout the units to provide you with the opportunity to work with others and implement the knowledge you will learn during the chapter.

Assessment activities

Throughout each unit you will find a series of assessment activities which are based around the assessment criteria set by EDEXCEL. Any assessment you are set by your own college will be based around exactly the same questions, so if you complete the assessment activities provided you will have a head start on how to approach your real assignment. In addition, each assessment activity tells you how to obtain the higher grades of merit and distinction as well as the basic pass criteria. Each assessment activity starts with the unit number and then Pass (P), Merit (M) or Distinction (D) for each part of the evidence required to pass that unit.

Completing your assignments

As the National Certificate and Diploma are based on coursework it is extremely important that you are disciplined and organised with your time, to enable you to meet deadlines and have a better chance of getting higher grades.

It is important that you understand and comply with the key words specified in the grading criteria. An understanding of the key words will enable you to achieve merits and distinctions with greater ease. Below is a description of some of the most common action words found in your assignments.

Analyse – this means to examine something in great detail or to break something down into its essential parts. For example, if you were asked to analyse the role of a police officer, you would not just say that a police officer was someone who wore a uniform. This is not an analysis – it is one particular feature and a feature that fits many other professions. To analyse the role of a police officer you must state everything that fulfils the role of being a police officer and in doing so separates a police officer from other professions.

Identify – this means to recognise, select or establish something. For example, if you were asked to identify three qualities needed for self-discipline, then you would merely state what they are, just as you would state that a certain item belonged to you.

Describe – if you were asked to describe three qualities needed for self-discipline, then you would give a descriptive account of them just as you would an item of property that belonged to you.

Examine – this means to look at something very closely and in detail – to subject something to close scrutiny. It differs from 'analyse,' though it is very similar in meaning, in that you are not necessarily breaking it down into its essential parts. For example, a doctor may examine a patient to see what is wrong with them but he or she doesn't have to analyse the patient in order to do so.

Investigate – this is similar to 'examine' in that they both involve studying something very carefully, though they do have different meanings. To investigate something is to ask questions and have an inquiring mind so that we may find answers to the questions or put forward a theory based on the information that has been gathered. For example, when a police officer investigates a crime, he or she gathers clues and information so that he or she can form a picture (or a theory) of why and how the crime was committed. However, if we examine something, we do not necessarily have to ask questions about something, we merely give a true account of what happens to be the case. For example, a scene of crime or a fingerprint could be examined without the need for forming an opinion.

Evaluate – this means to assess something or to appraise it – to balance the good points against the bad points and then give a reasoned opinion. It does not mean, merely, to describe or summarise something, though you may have to do this before you evaluate it. For example, if you were asked to evaluate the role of discipline in the public services, you would firstly have to say why discipline was necessary and what its effects were. This could include the negative and positive effects of blind obedience. You would then have to weigh up the positive effects against the negative effects and give an opinion as to whether discipline was, overall, a good or bad thing.

What can I do with a National Award/Certificate/ Diploma in Public Services

The course you have chosen to study is not only a superb introduction to the working and organisation of the public services, it is also an excellent general education course as well. If you complete the National Diploma in Public Services you will have studied eighteen different subjects and gained the equivalent of three A-levels. This means that in addition to joining a public service or any other form of employment you also stand a very good chance of being accepted into higher education institutions such as universities and HE colleges. As many public services such as the police prefer recruits to have some life experience and be a little older than the lowest age of entry which is eighteen, many students feel that a university education makes them more employable to the services and provides them with life experience such as living independently.

If you want to go to university your college will be able to advise you on the procedure and help you select the right course for your career aspirations. See your tutor or careers advisor if you feel this is the right option for you. If you want to join a public service straight away the main thing to remember is that the majority of the services are highly competitive and they have more people applying than they can take on. This means that if you want to be employed, you must be better than the other candidates. This is not easy when you consider you could be up against people who have more experience and qualifications than you do. However, there are some things you can do to make yourself more attractive to the services.

Complete your public services qualification

The services like to see commitment to a project as they are not looking for people who change their minds frequently about what is right for them. It costs a great deal of money to train a public service recruit and they will not be willing to spend that money on someone with a track record of not completing tasks they have undertaken.

Be punctual and reliable at college

Your public service application could depend on the reference of a tutor who has known you for a long period of time. Your tutor must be honest in any reference they give, which means that if you have repeated absence, sickness and lateness your reference will not make particularly good reading. The services require you to be punctual and reliable so it is best to get into the habit at college and allow your tutors to be able to pass on your good conduct to the service of your choice.

Hand your coursework in on time

Once again, this is directly related to references. If you regularly fail to meet set deadlines it does not speak well of your management and organisational skills and your tutor will write this in a reference. The services will be less likely to recruit someone who has a track record of poor self discipline.

Take part in college and community activities

Many students simply attend college and go home which does not add to their CV or their value to the services. All public service employers want team players who show an active interest in their community. If you are serious about a public service career then join some college clubs such as sports or martial arts clubs or consider giving a couple of hours voluntary work to a local charity. Not only will this make you much more employable, it will also help you understand your public services qualification to better effect.

Wear your uniform smartly

Many public services courses have a uniform as a requirement, such as a college tracksuit, a particular colour polo shirt or a full police style uniform with epaulettes. Uniforms are worn to get you into the habit of being different from other students (just as you will be different from members of the public if you join a service) and it is also used to teach you self discipline. If your uniform is untidy, it does not give a good impression and if you can't take this small amount of discipline in college are you likely to be able to cope with a large amount of discipline in the line of duty?

UNDERSTANDING THE PUBLIC SECTOR

Introduction to Unit 1

This unit is fundamental to anyone considering a career within the uniformed or non-uniformed public services. The unit gives you an understanding of how the public sector has grown to become what it is today and how its structure has changed over time. Throughout this unit, knowledge of the issues affecting public service work will be identified along with trends of employment and expenditure within the public sector.

The unit also looks at the main differences between the public, private and voluntary sector and how internal environments such as organisational structure and culture and external factors such as the European Union have affected the public sector. It also analyses how changing political ideology and economic policy have affected public services in recent years.

It also considers how demographic social and technological change have affected the provision of public services.

Assessment

Throughout the unit, activities and tasks will help you to learn and remember information. Case studies are included to add industry relevance to the topics and learning objectives. You are reminded that when you are completing activities and tasks, opportunities will be created to enhance your key skills evidence.

After completing this unit you should be able to achieve the following outcomes.

Outcomes

1 Describe the **development and structure** of the public sector

2 Explain the effects of the **internal and external** environment on the public sector

3 Analyse the effects of **political and economic** policy on public sector organisations

4 Analyse the effects of **socio-cultural and technological** changes on the public sector organisations.

Development and structure

Development of the public sector

The public sector has developed and changed radically since its emergence in Victorian Britain and we probably could not imagine a country without public services. Today the public sector accounts for around 40 per cent of the government's total expenditure in Britain.

The public sector consists of Government–run services such as the Armed Forces, the police service, the National Health Service (NHS), the education system and the fire service

Therefore public services are all those services which are paid for through government taxation. The public sector also includes central government, local government, and public corporations, for example nationalised industries and National Health Service Trusts. Public sector organisations are publicly owned services which offer goods and services to the public and are controlled directly by the government or local authorities. One of the reasons for publicly owned services is to ensure that the public are not exploited and these services are run properly at an affordable price or even free of charge. They meet some of our most important needs as members of society.

Think about it

Discuss why the services offered by the police force, NHS and fire service are so vital to our well being.

Theory into practice

Although the public sector is now seen as essential to the well-being of society, there are disadvantages as well as advantages. For each of the following advantages and disadvantages, find an example to illustrate the points.

Advantages of public sector
Essential services will be provided.
Wasteful duplication of services is eliminated.
Planning can be coordinated through central control.
Disadvantages of public sector
Political interference can occur.
Lack of incentive for employees to perform.
The taxpayer must meet inefficiency costs if a service is failing.

Development of the public services

The concept of public services is relatively new as in the past individuals had to provide for these needs themselves. It was gradually recognised that communities needed to pay for these services collectively and the first public services came into being. Here are a few examples of early public service development.

- **In 1829 Robert Peel (Home Secretary) established the police service** that replaced local parish constables and night watchmen. At first it was not very popular as people were very concerned that the police service would be like the military and therefore great care was taken to ensure that police constables did not look like soldiers. This is why police officers wore top hats instead of helmets and carried truncheons instead of rifles and their focus was on preventing crime, rather than punishing criminals. The success of the Metropolitan Police Force led other parts of the country to set up their own police service. However, it did not become compulsory for counties and boroughs to have a police service until 1856.
- **In 1824 The Edinburgh Fire Brigade** was established. It consisted of 80 part time fire fighters who had building trade experience and the formation of the service came about through the pressures of insurance companies who wanted to protect themselves against claims.
- **In 1948 The National Health Service** was created because the country was suffering the effects of a world war and the NHS was intended to help the millions of families who could not afford medical treatment when they became ill.

The public sector was initially developed through local authorities who were delegated powers by Central Government to provide services but this was done in a piecemeal fashion.

Self-government dates back to the 13th century, as many of the bigger communities would have mayors which is a term used still today to describe the leader of the council. To have a mayor meant that the town had been given a royal privilege to form a borough. Parish councils also existed and one of the earliest reforms was that parishes had the responsibility of offering relief to the poor through the **Poor Law of 1601.**

Little changed until the industrial revolution, when many cities expanded out of the control of the people who ran the cities. This meant that a great number of reforms took place to help address the problems:

A Victorian policeman

- **The Municipal Corporations Act 1835** created 78 multi purpose authorities and required all boroughs to have elected councils and for all meetings to be open to the public.
- **The Public Health Act 1872** created health authorities throughout England and Wales with the primary function of improving sanitary conditions.
- **The Local Government Act 1888** created county councils with responsibilities for looking after the highways, water, sewage and the fire service to name a few.
- **The Local Government Act 1894** created urban district councils and rural districts councils for those areas within county council jurisdiction that did not have *enough* people for borough status (less than 50,000 population)

These local councils had limited responsibility at first but by 1902 county councils were given the power to run schools, which is still today the councils' biggest responsibility and certainly the most expensive. This was followed by the power to build low-cost housing and the power over land development (planning). The local authorities also acquired a share of the public utility market (gas, electricity and water) and had the responsibility of supplying it to the community they served.

These reforms were by no means static as in the **1940–50s** many of the councils responsibilities formed in the Victorian era were taken away. For example, the creation of the NHS meant that the health functions of the council were lost. Electricity was nationalised in 1948 along with gas in 1949 and water supply was transferred to water authority control in the 1970s. Water and sewerage and drainage services were removed from local government control in 1974 and privatised in 1982. Public transport was deregulated and in effect, privatised in 1986.

During the **1960s** and **1970s** there was constant reform with regard to county boundaries, which created many of the modern counties and district councils that we have today.

The **1980s** saw the first move towards contracting out services to private contractors as a way of saving money and in The Local Government Act of 1988, the term compulsory competitive tendering was created which meant that local authority services such as refuse collection, catering for schools and leisure and grounds management could be provided by private companies and paid by the local authorities. Contracts were awarded to companies who could provide the best value for money. This provision was expanded in the **1990s** to include other services such as housing, IT and finance and administration services.

Ultimately this has meant that more functions and services have been privatised and local authorities have become more accountable for their actions. They also now also have to collaborate with both public, private and voluntary organisations to ensure that policies and services are maintained.

Theory into practice

Create a time line of the key stages of development for the local councils including the main pieces of legislation.

The following chart identifies the main roles and responsibilities of local authorities in modern Britain.

In very large urban areas and some rural areas, there are authorities called 'unitary authorities' which have the responsibility for looking after all the services outlined in the chart below. Big cities such as Birmingham, Bristol and Manchester are metropolitan authorities

Structure and role of the public services

Local government and public services

The importance of local authorities in the development of public services is outlined above and they still play a key role today. Local authorities provide the majority of public services we use in our everyday lives.

County councils (tier 1)	District councils (tier 2)	Town/parish councils (tier 3)
Responsible for matters requiring planning and administration of substantial resources. Each county covers a population of 500,000 – 1,500,000. Examples: Nottinghamshire, East Sussex. There are 32 county councils in England.	Responsible for administering functions of local significance. There are between 4–14 within each County Council area, each covering a population of about 100,000. Example: Nottinghamshire has 7 district Councils including Broxtowe Borough Council and Mansfield District Council.	Responsible for managing very local affairs for populations up to 3,000 such as limited environmental improvements. There are 10,376 parishes in England, 867 in Wales and about 1,200 in Scotland. In Nottinghamshire there are: ● 152 Parish Councils ● 8 Town Councils These cover about half the population of the county, including all of rural Nottinghamshire and some of its towns. They range in size from 20 residents to nearly 25,000.
Responsibilities include: ● strategic planning ● transport planning ● highways ● traffic regulation ● education and libraries ● consumer protection ● refuse disposal ● fire and rescue ● personal social services ● residential and children's homes ● meals on wheels and home helps ● country parks ● trading standards ● registrars for births, deaths and marriages. ● magistrates courts.	Responsibilities include: ● environmental health – pest control ● housing ● planning ● refuse collection ● collection of council tax ● parking ● parks and leisure centres.	Responsibilities include: ● car parking ● parks and gardens ● tourist information

Figure 1.1 Roles and responsibilities of local authorities

Local councils are responsible for supplying various services to the local community and are elected by that community. The day-to-day running of local authorities is provided by appointed salaried managers often referred to as council officials. Elected councillors are responsible for the overall policy and they are not usually paid for their services.

Differences between councils

Metropolitan councils, for example Birmingham City council; Unitary councils, such as Newport Borough council and London Boroughs, for example London Borough of Lewisham deliver all the local government services in their area such as housing and social services. However, Local Authority services which are not metropolitan or unitary split their functions between county councils and district councils. Police and fire services are run separately – but they do have local councillors on their governing bodies and their civilian employees are often employed by one of the nearby local councils.

Council composition in England	
1 Tier	**2 Tier**
46 Unitary authorities 32 Metropolitan borough councils 32 London borough councils	238 Borough & district councils 34 County councils

Theory into practice

- Find out whether the area you live in has a 2 tier or unitary structure. If it is a 3 tier structure, find out how many district and town councils it has.
- Find out which political party runs your local council.

Case study

Central Government is responsible to the Crown for the smooth and efficient running of the fire service in Great Britain.

Responsibilities are delegated from that point:

- Office of the deputy prime minister
- Local fire authorities (Metropolitan, County councils and Combined Unitary authorities
- Fire brigade committees
- Chief fire officers

Local government through county councils have the responsibility of offering a standard of fire cover that is in line with Home Office guidelines. One of the local authorities functions is to check premises such as offices, factories and hotels and issue them with fire certificates if they are safe or enforce improvements before they issue a certificate.

1 Why is this important?
2 What more could county councils do?

Financing of local government

Local governments spend around 25% of all government expenditure.

Their money comes from:

- grants from central government of around £90 billion per year
- council taxes which generate around £70 billion per year.

The biggest expense of local authorities is education which receives £24 billion or 15% of the total local authority budget.

Local authority current spending can broadly be divided into two categories: main local services which local authorities have some discretion over and which are partly financed by local taxation and other spending which is financed wholly by central government specific grants. This means that local authorities have considerable discretion to determine the level, pattern, and standard of the main services.

Think about it

Why do we pay Council tax?

What are the key expenditures for the local council with regard to services?

If we didn't pay taxes would anybody else offer these services?

Public corporations

Public corporations are organisations which are not directly controlled by local authorities or central government but are still funded by government money. NHS Trusts and police authorities are examples of public corporations.

Public corporations are established to carry out state-owned activities, but are financially independent of the state and are run by a board. The first public corporation to be formed in the UK was the Central Electricity Board in the 1920s. After World War II, a number of industries were nationalised and new public corporations were established. However, since the late 1970s there has been a growing incidence of privatisation which will be discussed later in this chapter and many previously nationalised activities have been returned to the private sector, becoming public limited companies.

Case study

The police are not directly accountable to local authorities. It is the police authority that creates policy and runs the police services in England and Wales at regional level. These are made up of committees which include local county councillors to allow the council to question police duties, policies and actions.

The local authorities have little control over the budget, the only power they have is to approve the budget and the operational side is run by the senior police officers. London is slightly different as the Metropolitan police is the responsibility of the Home Secretary.

1 Should local authorities have more control?
2 Should the community have more of a say?

Public corporations are financed by:

- general taxation given in the form of Treasury grants
- borrowing from the Treasury
- trading surpluses retained profits which the corporations make from their trading activities.

In the 1970s public corporations were not expected to make a profit. At best, they were expected to cover all costs or break even. If an organisation did not do so, the government would usually keep it in the black by giving it a subsidy or a grant from public funds to keep it going. More recently, subsidies have been abolished except for some essential services and public sector organisations are expected to meet strict financial targets to break even.

Central government

Both local authorities and public corporations are ultimately answerable to central government.

You will find detailed information on central government in the Democratic Processes unit. If you require further information please turn to page 132.

Central government has the job of managing the country. It is made up of different departments run by Ministers and is headed by the Prime Minister who is the leader of the elected party and whose responsibility it is to appoint the ministers from the elected MPs.

The Prime Minister chooses his/her most senior ministers to help him run the country through the cabinet. The cabinet is made up of 20 MPs who each run one of the key departments. As a group they propose government policy for approval by Parliament and co-ordinate the work of the different government departments. The cabinet meets each week at 10 Downing Street. Every government's cabinet has met in this room in Downing Street since 1856 and at present, a cabinet meeting is held weekly on Thursday mornings. They mainly discuss the making and controlling of government policy.

A cabinet meeting

The government departments that are relevant to the public sector are the following.

Secretary of State for the Home Department responsible for police, prisons, fire and Customs and Excise.

Secretary of State for Defence responsible for the Armed Forces – Army, Navy and RAF.

Secretary of State for Health responsible for the NHS – ambulance service.

Home Office: This is the government department which looks after the police, prisons, Customs and Excise and the fire service by allocating adequate funding for each of the services. Apart from this it has wider responsibilities such as building a safer and more tolerant society by reducing crime and the fear of crime, ensuring the effective delivery of justice and delivering effective custodial and community sentences to protect the public and reduce re-offending.

Department of Health: This is the government department responsible for the National Health Service in England. It looks after hospitals, local social services and matters of public health. The Secretary of State has overall strategic responsibility for NHS improvement including delivery, reform, finance and resources as well as the responsibility for funding the ambulance service throughout England and Wales. The ambulance service plays a vital role as they help millions of patients get to hospital to receive healthcare each year.

Case study

Foundation Hospitals are one of the latest proposals made by the labour government to help modernise the National Health Service. Foundation trusts will be owned and controlled by local communities, rather than central government or shareholders. They will be not-for-profit organisations, part of the NHS and subject to NHS standards and inspections, but no longer directed from Whitehall.

The first 10 hospitals will be given foundation status on April 1st 2004 with another 13 hospitals aiming to become foundation trust on July 21st 2004.

The main elements are:

- the formation of foundation hospitals in England, providing free care to NHS patients but without Whitehall's direct control.
- foundation hospitals will be not-for-profit 'public interest corporations'. Governors will be elected by local people, but decisions will be closely supervised by an independent regulator.
- they will not be allowed to reduce their commitment to the NHS by taking on more private patients.

1 Are foundation hospitals the way forward?

2 What are the advantages and disadvantages of such hospitals?

The **Ministry Of Defence:** This department employs over 300,000 people and has an annual budget of £23.7 billion which is about 6% of the government's overall budget and approximately half of the amount spent on education. The Secretary of State for Defence is ultimately responsible for all elements of defence along with making and executing defence policy, budgetary issues, deployment of Armed Forces including supporting NATO and delivery of modernisation to the Armed Forces such as equal opportunities.

The purpose of the Ministry of Defence and the Armed Forces is to defend the United Kingdom by strengthening international peace and security. This is why defence remains crucial to the current government as it has deployed troops to Afghanistan and more recently to Iraq. Troops are also needed closer to home as the increased threat of terrorism hangs over us.

Think about it

What are the other government departments and their roles? Who are their ministers?

Relationship between central and local government

The powers and responsibilities of local government derive from Parliamentary Acts and the responsibility for the overall administration of the country rests with Cabinet ministries. Local authorities are legally independent of central government (Local Government Act 1972) but they have the role of offering many of the key services within England and Wales. Central government pays grants to local authorities to provide many of the services and financially the government has power over local authorities. However, local authorities also raise their own revenue through council taxes as discussed earlier.

Scale of public sector

Current government expenditure

Public expenditure is spending by central government, local government, and nationalised industries. The government's expenditure in the UK for 2001/2002 was £394 billion.

In 1996 for every pound of public spending:

- central government spent 74p
- local authorities spent 25p
- public corporations spent 1p.

Government expenditure is vital for the efficient running of the economy:

- Much of the government expenditure arises from the fact that some goods would either not be provided are under-provided if the market was run completely by the private sector as some goods and services would not be profitable. These are known as 'merit goods'.

  Merit goods are things such as healthcare and education or any service which benefits society when consumed and costs the government greatly. However, demerit goods are goods such as tobacco and alcohol which although are heavily taxed they are in demand so profit is made by the government when they are consumed and this money is often re-allocated to fund merit services in the next budget.
- Some government expenditure provides a safety net for the less well off in society ensuring that they are able to survive.
- Some government expenditure is on providing services necessary to maintain our economy, for example roads, education and training.

Theory into practice

Give examples of benefits which the government provides for the less well off.

Think about it

Can you think of services which might not exist if the government did not provide expenditure for them?

The government expenditure in 2001/02 was as follows.

Department	Expenditure (£bn)
Social security	£109
Health	£72
Housing and environment	£18
Defence	£24
Education	£50
Law and order	£23
Transport	£10
Industry, agriculture and employment	£16
Debt interest	£23
Other	£49

Figure 1.2 Government expenditure in 2001/02 (Source: Treasury)

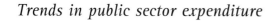

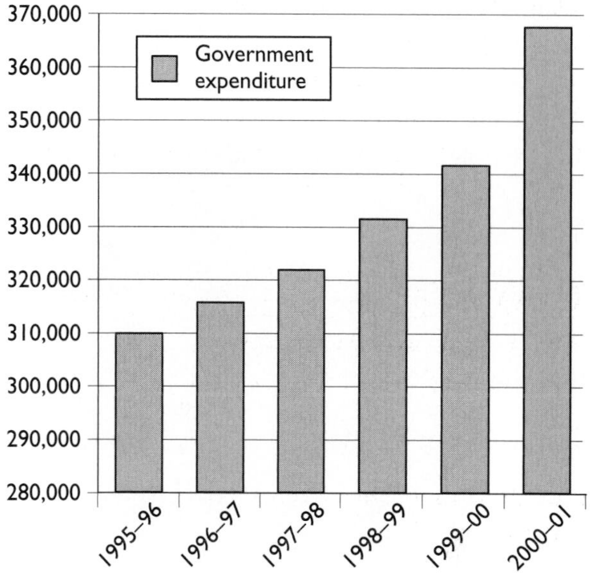

Figure 1.3 Public sector expenditure (Source: Treasury)

Theory into practice

Using figure 1.3, calculate the percentage increase in government expenditure from 1995–2001.

Trends in public sector expenditure

Before 2002, public sector expenditure in Britain was as follows. The amounts are very large and involve **billions** of pounds. To read all the figures accurately, you need to add six noughts.

Not all areas of public sector expenditure have seen greater investment. For example, transport has seen a fall in investment from 11.5 billion to 9.1 billion. This area includes roads, local transport, ports and shipping, national rail services and DVLA. Housing has also seen a decrease in investment from 5 billion to 3.4 billion which includes all council and social housing throughout England and Wales.

Theory into practice

Study Figures 1.3 and 1.4 and then answer the following questions:

- Do any of the figures surprise you?
- Which government department receives the largest amount of funding?
- List what this department is spending its money on.
- Calculate which department has seen the biggest percentage rise in its budget between 1995 and 2001.

Year	Social security	Health	Education	Defence	Law and order
95–96	92,754	39,401	35,573	21,631	15,737
96–97	96,453	40,772	36,143	22,249	16,207
97–98	97,381	42,542	37,174	21,611	16,861
98–99	99,415	44,746	38,761	22,606	17,340
99–00	103,214	48,737	40,889	22,507	18,754
00–01	105,634	54,236	45,865	23,581	20,560

Figure 1.4 Key areas of public sector expenditure (Source: Treasury)

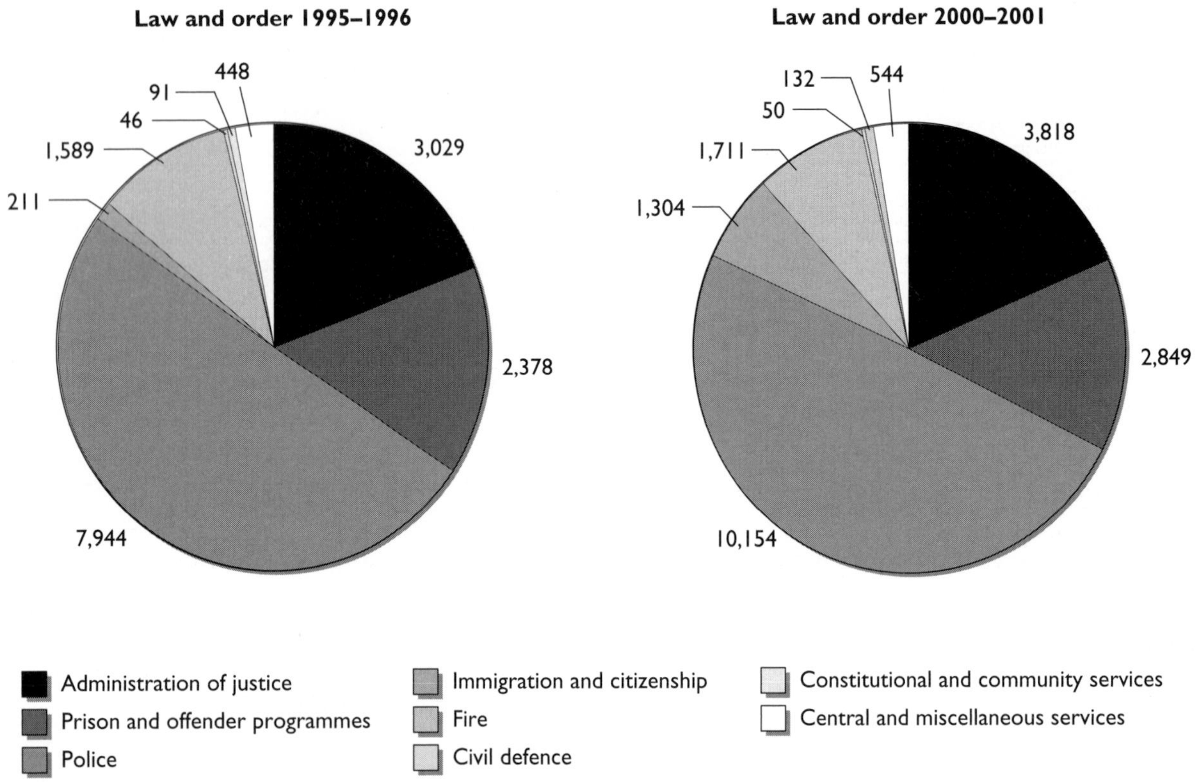

Figure 1.5 Breakdown of expenditure within the law and order budget

These overall patterns of expenditure can be broken down further. For example, the budget for law and order covers a wide variety of areas which have all seen greater investment from 1995–2001. One area of substantial growth in expenditure in this department is immigration and citizenship which has seen an increase of more than 500%. The breakdown of expenditure on law and order is shown in Figure 1.5.

Sources of government income

The government needs money to pay for all the public expenditure looked at throughout this chapter. The revenue is raised in a number of ways including taxation, national insurance contributions, borrowing, charging for services or by selling off state-owned assets.

The Chancellor of the Exchequer is in charge of government finances. The Chancellor announces how much the government is going to spend through the budget and states how it is going to raise the money to pay for the expenditure through various taxes and charges.

Taxes collected	£bn
Income tax	118
National insurance	65
Value added tax	64
Excise duties	38
Corporation tax	33
Business rates	19
Council tax	16
Other	55
TOTAL	418

Figure 1.6 Revenue collected in 2001 (Source: *Treasury 2002*)

Theory into practice

Calculate how much was spent in 2001/2 and compare it with the revenue raised (see above table). What kind of budget (from the 3 types shown below) was introduced in that year?

- **deficit budget** where government spending is greater than government income
- **surplus budget** where government income exceeds expenditure
- **neutral budget** where government income and spending are the same.

The aims of taxation are not only to raise money to pay for government spending but also to redistribute income from the rich to the poor. Also some taxes are in place to discourage people from buying harmful goods such as cigarettes and alcohol.

Main types of taxation

- **Income tax**: everyone is given a tax-free personal allowance (amount) above which additional earnings are taxed at an increasing rate.

  Income tax is very familiar by all who work, but many people do not understand fully how it is charged. It is an important tax to the government as it is its main revenue-raising tax, though despite that it only represents just over a quarter of total tax revenue. National Insurance and VAT come fairly close on the list in terms of importance.

  Over 25 million individuals pay income tax in the UK, but not all income incurs tax. The main kind of income upon which income tax is levied are pay, pension payments upon retirement, unemployment benefit, profits from business, income from property, bank and building society interest and dividends on shares.

- **Value added tax**: (VAT) is a tax on spending: 17.5% is added onto the selling price of most non-essential goods and services.
- **Duties**: are taxes on the sale of luxury goods. A fixed amount is added to the selling price.
- **Council tax**: is a local tax on property. All properties are valued and the amount of council tax paid depends on the value band which the property falls into.
- **Corporation tax**: is a tax on company profits.
- **Petroleum revenue tax**: is a tax on oil taken from the North Sea.

Employment trends in the public sector

The public sector is a major employer in the UK so a major part of government expenditure is on wages and salaries. There were 29.4 million jobs in the UK in 2001 of which 5.2 million were in the public sector.

Since the 1980s, attempts have been made to reduce the number of public sector employees. Over the last 10 years employment has decreased by over 1.5 million. However, in 1999 the number of jobs in the public sector increased for the first time since 1979. The biggest rise within local government was in education, an increase of 48,000 jobs (3.7 per cent) between 2000 and 2001.

Income tax allowances 2001/2002	£	Income tax rates 2001/2002	£ of taxable income
Personal allowance (under 65)	4,535	Lower rate – 10%	0–1,880
Personal allowance (65–74)	5,990	Basic rate – 22%	1,881–29,400
Personal allowance (over 75)	6,260	Higher rate – 40%	Over 29,400

Figure 1.7 Tax-free personal allowances

Jobs in the public sector increased by 91,000 between 2000 and 2001 whilst private sector jobs rose by 115,000 over the same period, The increase in public sector jobs was mainly due to education and the National Health Service.

Theory into practice

Answer the following questions based on Figure 1.8 below.

1 Have any of the sectors increased levels of employment since 1992? If not, why do you think this is the case?
2 Which sector has reduced its employment numbers by the most?
3 Which sector has decreased the largest in percentage terms?
4 Why do you think the government is now spending more money on the NHS and education?

Employees salaries in the public sector

In the public sector the salaries of its employees are varied (see figure 1.9 overleaf). Unequal pay structures in the public sector have led to a growing resentment and unrest amongst public service workers, when they compare there salaries and yearly pay increases with the private sector and in some cases with other public sector workers. For example, recent substantial increases in London allowances for police officers – in response to recruitment and retention difficulties – have put them some distance ahead of other key workers. This has meant that employees of the fire service and ambulance service have been out on strike recently to try and gain a substantial pay rise. The main problem is that pay increases for public sector workers usually mean higher taxes.

Year + Service	Education	Social services	Fire-fighters	Police service	Traffic wardens	Magistrates court	Probation officers
1992	835,800	232,200	34,300	120,800	4,900	10,000	6,900
1993	712,100	225,800	34,200	121,400	4,900	10,000	7,100
1994	692,800	233,300	33,900	121,000	4,700	9,900	7,200
1995	698,400	234,300	33,800	118,800	4,500	10,000	7,200
1996	691,800	230,600	33,600	118,400	4,300	9,900	6,900
1997	691,800	227,300	33,300	118,500	4,100	9,200	6,900
1998	693,900	221,300	33,100	119,200	3,500	8,900	6,200
1999	707,300	215,900	34,000	119,200	3,300	9,000	6,800
2000	731,500	213,000	33,800	117,000	2,800	8,900	7,100
2001	768,200	213,300	34,500	118,600	2,600	9,100	7,100
2002	781,700	206,600	35,200	120,100	2,200	9,300	7,200

Figure 1.8 Employment trends in selected public sector services

Theory into practice

Answer the following questions using Figure 1.9 below to help you.

1 Which group of workers achieve the highest salaries?
2 Do you think the pay differences are justified?
3 Find out what the current average income is in England and Wales. How well off are public service workers compared with this?
4 Why do public service workers in London receive more money?

Case study

In 2003, a lengthy industrial dispute by ambulance workers in Sussex came to an end after they agreed to accept a new pay offer. As part of the dispute, ambulance crews began working to rule which included limited cover for neighbouring stations and not recording call-out times.

The breakthrough came after their union, Unison, found two-thirds of those taking action were in favour of accepting a new offer on pay and conditions.

The deal put forward by Sussex Ambulance management included an average pay rise of 4.2% and two extra days off each year for staff with more than ten years' service.

Management also agreed to look at the ways crews work, specifically in connection to the way they base themselves at strategic points around the country rather than at ambulance stations.

Do you believe that public service workers should be able to strike when the safety and lives of others depends on their help and assistance?

Case study – newspaper article

Firefighters demands for a 40% pay rise will open the floodgates and lead to big tax rises, say their employers. The Local Government Association issued the warning ahead of the result of the Fire Brigade Union's strike ballot on Friday.

More than 50,000 firefighters are being asked to vote on whether to stage their first national strike for 25 years. The Fire Brigades' Union is seeking a 40% pay rise, which would see salaries for fully qualified firefighters rise to about £30,000.

Employers are offering 4% as an interim deal, plus whatever an independent government review recommends should be linked to new ways of working.

If union members reject the deal, strike action could begin by the end of October.

BBC News Article – Thursday, 17 October, 2002

1 What is your view about the pay of the firefighters? Are they being unreasonable?
2 Should public sector workers be allowed to strike in support of a pay claim?

2002	National (E&W)		London	
Occupation	**Starting pay £pa**	**After 5 years £pa**	**Starting pay £pa**	**After 5 years £pa**
Firefighter	17,208	21,531	20,280	24,603
Nurse	16,005	17,670	19,873	21,605
Police officer	19,842	23,037	25,953	31,148
Social worker	16,734	19,770	21,060	24,345
Teacher	17,628	22,806	20,733	25,911

Note: under the terms of a recently-agreed package of changes to their pay and conditions, police officers' salaries will rise by £402 from 1 April 2003, in addition to any increases arising from the normal September 2002 pay review.

Figure 1.9 Employees salaries in the public sector in 2002

Assessment activity 1-P1, 1-M1, 1-D1

The labour government are reviewing the funding structures of the main public sector organisations and have consulted you for advice. To help them prepare their recommendations for parliament in the form of a white paper they have asked you to provide detailed answers to the following:

To achieve a **pass** you need to demonstrate a basic understanding of the development, structure and scale of the public sector

To achieve a **merit** you need to demonstrate a sound knowledge of the development, structure and scale of the public sector

To achieve a **distinction** you need to demonstrate a comprehensive knowledge of the development, structure and scale of the public sector

Key points

This section has helped give an overview of:

- the nature of the public sector
- how it has developed historically
- the way services are organised nationally and locally
- how public services are financed and how they spend their money
- trends in employment in the public sector.

Internal and external environment

In recent years there have been many changes in the way that public services are provided. Private companies now provide some of them, for example, in the prison service some private security companies have been given contracts to manage prisons

Main differences between public and private sectors

There are differences in the way private companies and public services work as shown in Figure 1.10 overleaf.

Private goods

Private goods are ones for which the benefit is restricted to an identifiable consumer (individual or organisation) and for which a market price is easily established between the consumer and producer. Therefore the new owners can then consume it themselves and get the full benefit from consumption.

Public goods

Public goods are ones delivered for the benefit of the wider community at large such as street lighting, parks and leisure facilities. These are often provided for by the state to ensure that the optimal level and quality of the goods/service is provided. Public goods can be identified through two characteristics 'non excludable' and 'non-rival'.

- **Non-rivalry** means that by one person consuming the goods it does not reduce the amount available for other people. For example, if person A needs a police officer then this should not prevent person B from obtaining the same level of assistance when he requires a police officer. This means that each constabulary through government funding should have enough police officers to meet community demand.
- **Non-excludability** means once the good has been provided it is not possible to prevent people consuming it whether they have paid for it or not. An example of a public good is legal aid. In a sense legal aid is available to everyone even though they may not have paid for it. It is also true that one person relying on legal aid does not reduce the amount others can receive.

Main differences between the public and private sector	
Private	**Public**
Money is raised through selling at a profit.	Public sector is funded through taxation etc.
Firms compete to offer goods/services.	Often monopolies – there is no choice of provider.
Private goods/services are purchased by people/ organisations for their own use.	Public goods/services are provided as they are essential to the well being of society.
Companies are not accountable to public.	Organisations are accountable to the public.
Main motive of organisation is to make a profit.	A public service ethos exists as the aim is to provide a good service.

Figure 1.10 Differences between the public and private sector

Differences in funding

Funding is an obvious difference between the public and private sector as most public sector organisations are funded substantially by central government whilst private sector organisations have to rely on profits made from the sale of their goods and services. Government expenditure will be looked at later on in this chapter.

Monopoly provision

Many public service organisations are statutory monopolies which means the government insists only that organisation can provide the service. In the private sector, monopolies are considered unacceptable as they could lead to excessive profit. The monopoly position of many public services have been challenged in recent years as state monopolies can lead to a lack of choice for the public. For example, few people have a real choice about medical treatment on the NHS. The NHS will treat you when and where it can which often means a long wait and no choice of hospital. A lack of competition has led others to argue that state monopolies have become wasteful.

Theory into practice

What are the advantages and disadvantages of having only one public funded police force in a given area?

To counteract rising costs and dissatisfaction with the quality of some public service monopolies, some private companies have been allowed to compete with state provided services. For example, the introduction of private companies into waste disposal and the introduction of Private Finance Initiatives (PFIs) – some new hospitals are being built by private companies who rent out the hospital to the health trusts. This is known as privatisation. **(see later in the chapter)** It is debatable whether these will improve efficiency or are simply cost cutting exercises.

Marketisation

In the 1970s the public sector was not expected to make a profit. At best, it was expected to cover all costs or break even. If it did not do so, the government would usually keep the organisation in the black by giving it a subsidy or a grant from public funds to keep it going. However, since the Thatcher era subsidies have now been abolished, except for some essential services. These days' public sector organisations are expected to meet strict financial targets to break even.

Differences in accountability

As the public is paying for public services through their taxes, these services are accountable to the public whereas private organisations providing they keep within the law, are not.

Think about it

How are public services made accountable to the public?

Powers to ensure compliance

Public sector organisations work to a strict framework, often created by central government. These produce systems of accountability for every public service employee as they will be directly accountable to higher ranked person or a body.

Traditionally in Britain, the chain of 'accountability' in the public services ends with the relevant Secretary of State. For example, all civil servants are accountable to the minister in charge of that particular ministry and every fire-fighter is ultimately responsible to the Home Secretary who is accountable for the fire service. Government is also accountable to the public and the public will express their opinions through the ballot box at local and general elections.

Many public sector organisations are responsible for enforcing laws and regulations, such as public health regulations. Infringement could mean a financial penalty or even imprisonment. No private companies have these powers.

Different ethos in public and private sector

A key difference between the public and private sectors lies in the different ethos or attitude of each sector.

The public service ethos represents impartiality, accountability, honesty and trust. However, this ethos seems under threat because of the pressure on the public sector to make a profit and the creation of private/public partnerships by the current Labour government. To many in the public sector, the Labour government appears to be attacking this ethos through cutting back staff, privatisation and criticism, which has meant poor morale in many public sector areas.

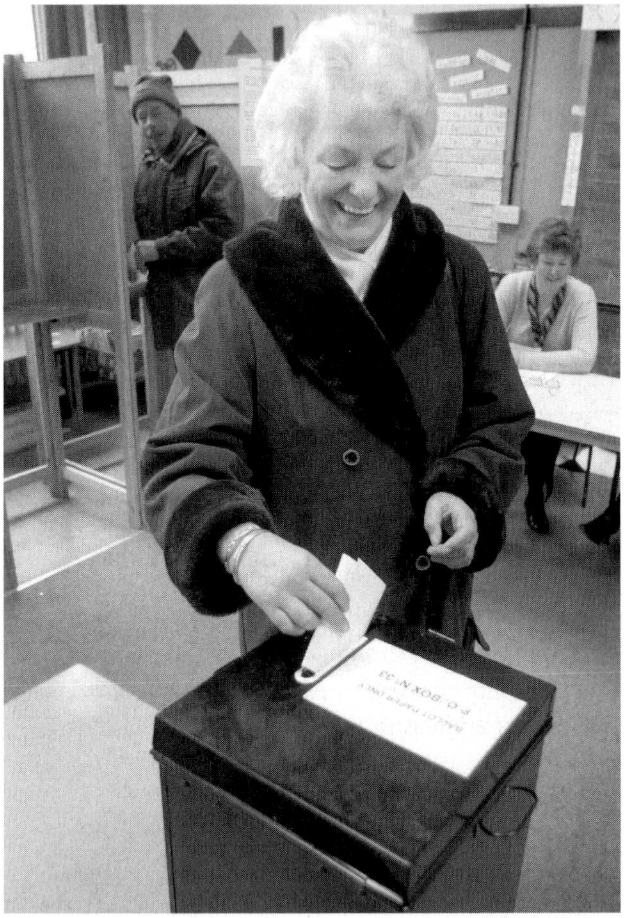

The public can express opinions at local and general elections

The Neill committee 2001 (a government review into public services) stated that public service ethos had seven principles:

- selflessness
- integrity
- objectivity
- accountability
- openness
- honesty
- leadership.

To protect the public service ethos the Commons Select Committee on Public Administration suggested that a public service code of conduct (see opposite) be created to re-establish these traditional values and all public sector staff should be trained to ensure that they understood it.

Public service code of conduct

- Observe at all times the ethical standards expected of public servants and public service bodies.
- Make themselves accountable for their policies and performance and ensure that they maintain a high standard of openness and transparency in their job.
- Aim to deliver public services that match in quality the best private equivalents, including standards of customer care. Where there is no private sector equivalent, best practice in the public sector should be matched.
- Treat public service workers and users fairly and equitably, and involve them as much as possible in service issues.
- Respect at all times the right of the citizen to good administration as set out in the Charter of Fundamental Rights of the European Union, and his or her right to safe, reliable public services. Proper redress should be made where maladministration has taken place.
- Remember at all times that public service means serving the public, not serving the interests of those who provide the service, and work collaboratively with others to this end.

A section of the public service code of conduct presented by the Neill committee 2001

Think about it

Using the key words below to help you, discuss what your own code of conduct would include:

- accountability
- high quality service
- fair treatment
- good administration
- serve the public
- well being of community
- performance and practises.

Internal environment

Organisational structure

The structure of an organisation refers to the way in which its activities are grouped or arranged. In any organisation it is sensible for people who do similar types of work to be grouped together. Big organisations such as the local councils or uniformed public services are completely unmanageable unless they are structured.

The structure of an organisation will depend on whether it is in the manufacturing or service sector, whether it is a local, national or international organisation and the type of work with which it is involved.

Public sector and private sector organisations are very different in structure. To determine the structure of an organisation they will often have an organisational chart which will show the hierarchical levels, where individuals fit in and how departments are structured.

Think about it

Do you work part time? If so, how is your place of work structured? Create your own organisational chart and use it to identify what type of organisational structure your company has.

Almost all organisations consist of a combination of these basic parts:

- The **executive** are the people responsible for the administration of a business and are often the most senior members such as directors and managers.
- The **operating core** which consists of the people who perform the basic work.
- a **middle line** of managers which creates a hierarchy of authority.
- a group of people called **analysts** which are people with expert knowledge when specialist skills are needed.
- **support staff** such as administrative workers, catering staff etc.

Theory into practice

Identify each of the basic parts outlined above for 2 chosen public services.

Public sector structure: The public sector mainly offers services so often these services will be grouped into divisions for housing, education and leisure. This divisional structure is similar to colleges as they will have educational divisions such as humanities, business and performing arts. This is known as a divisional structure.

Private sector structure: In the private sector, middle to large organisations are largely performing functions so they will often be sub-divided to allow certain types of people to work together who may have completely different functions within a company. For example, sales and marketing, personnel and finance. This is called a functional structure.

Culture

Every organisation also has its own culture and ideology. This encompasses tradition, values and beliefs and infuses a distinctive life into the structure.

Schein (1985) argued that culture consists of three dimensions – assumptions, values and artefacts. Assumptions are widely held views of human nature that are taken for granted, values represent preferences for alternative outcomes as well as means of achieving those outcomes and artefacts are the physical representation of culture that includes rituals, slogans, traditions and myths.

Organisational culture is the basic personality of the organisation and this culture reflects the shared social beliefs, values and acquired patterns of behaviour which developed during the development and growth of the organisation and which is manifested through the physical elements of the organisation. This culture is shared by all members of the organisation and can be defined as some underlying structure of meaning that persists over time, constraining people's perception, interpretation and behaviour.

Influences on the evolution of organisational culture are:

- size
- location
- goals and objectives
- the market they serve.

There are often many visible manifestations of these cultural values, including the type of buildings occupied by the organisation and the image projected in its publicity and public relations. Different organisations will have different cultures. For example, the culture of a large private corporation is quite different than that of a public hospital.

Furthermore new employees to an organisation will very quickly sense the particular culture of an organisation and work hard to fit in whilst new leaders may shape and change the existing organisation culture.

Think about it

Think of the differences in culture between a local authority and a multi national corporation such as McDonalds.

Organisational culture is important as it will affect the type of people employed, the career aspirations of its employees and their status in society. Some members of the organisation may find it easier to fit in with the culture than others. This may be influenced by the age, sex, and educational background of the individual.

Types of organisational culture

According to Handy (1993) there are 4 types of organisational culture:

Type	Characteristics of the culture
Role culture	Classical structure; bureaucratic nature; roles more important than the people who fill them. This culture serves the cause of structure.
Task culture	The focus is on completing the job; individuals' expertise and contribution are highly valued; the unifying force of the group is manifested in high levels of collaboration.
Power culture	Power emanates from the centre; very political and entrepreneurial. This culture serves the leader.
Person culture	A loose collection of individuals – usually professionals – sharing common facilities but pursuing own goals separately; members are experts in their own right. This type of culture serves the individual.

Figure 1.11 There are 4 types of organisational structure

- **Role culture** is perhaps the most readily recognised and common of all the cultural types. Often referred to as a bureaucracy, it is based around the job or role rather than the personalities and develops what we tend to think of as the traditional hierarchical structure. Role cultures tend to develop best in relatively stable environments and are common in public organisations such as local government and the civil service.
- **Task culture** is very much organised around a small team with a network of people co-operating together to deliver a project. For example, a team of police officers working on a big enquiry will work in this type of group. This is known as a matrix organisation. The emphasis of this culture is on results and getting things done. Performance is judged in terms of results and problems solved. Although a structure exists, it is flexible and capable of being formed and reformed depending upon the task in hand.
- **Power culture** tends to rely on a central figure for its strength. This culture is often found in small entrepreneurial organisations. In relation to the public sector, this type of culture may grow up around a particular manager, for example a charismatic Army officer, but as he or she is constrained by other regulations, the power of the 'leader' is limited.
- In a **person culture,** the individual is the central point. If there is a structure, it exists only to serve the individuals within it. If a group of individuals decide to band together to do his or her own thing it is a person culture. A person culture may exist within freelance or organisational consultants, workers co-operatives and barristers' chambers.

Theory into practice

Using Handy's model which of the cultures is likely to fit the Armed Forces, the fire service and local councils? Give a reason for each of your answers.

External environment

We have so far looked at how the central government and local government shape the public services but they are affected on a wider scale from Europe and in particular the European Union.

Effects of the European Union

As a member of the European Union, the UK is bound by EU Treaties and Directives and this affects public services through central government. By joining the European union in 1973, it means that the policies and treaties are created in Europe and have to be applied through our own legislation and democratic process.

These are some of the ways public services have been affected by the European Union.

- **Court of Justice**: this can add another dimension to the British legal system as individuals can also bring proceedings against EU institutions before the Court and can ask for judgements on whether British Law is in keeping with EU law. This is, in theory, the highest court in the British legal system as the House of Lords can refer cases that question the interpretation or implementation of EU law. Also other countries can use this court to take another country to court.

Case study – newspaper article

Spain is to take Britain to court over a new law which allows Gibraltarians and some members of the Commonwealth to vote in European elections, according to reports yesterday.

According to the newspaper El Mundo, José María Aznar's conservative People's party government is so fed up with Britain's refusal to listen to complaints about the new law that it intends to take the case to the European Court of Justice.

Spain will claim that the law is illegal because only European Union citizens should be allowed to vote. 'We cannot allow non-European citizens to have a vote,' a diplomatic source explained to the paper.

A foreign ministry spokesman in Madrid said. 'We have nothing to say on the matter.'

A Foreign Office spokesman said Britain had expected Spain to drop the matter after the European commission last year declared it had acted 'within the margin of discretion presently given to member states by EU law'.

'We are quite surprised by this. It was the first we had heard that Spain was still considering taking it to court,' the spokesman said.

'We have had no official confirmation that this is what they intend to do. If they do decide to go to court we are confident of our case and will defend it robustly.'

Gibraltarians won the right to vote in Europe only as part of a British constituency after taking their own case to the European Court of Justice.

Britain passed a new law last year incorporating Gibraltar's 20,000 voters into the combined south-west of England constituency.

Extract from the Guardian – Wednesday February 18, 2004

Does this go against peoples fundamental rights?

- **Education**: the EU does not decide what you learn at college but it does work towards ensuring that your educational and professional qualifications are properly recognised in other EU countries.
- **Free movement and the single market**: all people can work and travel wherever they want in the 15 European Union countries including working in any of the various public services abroad. This has led to greater co-operation with European police and customs.
- **Keeping the peace**: EU is now increasingly involved in preserving peace and creating stability in neighbouring countries, for example the peace keeping force which was sent into Croatia was from Europe. The EU is developing this area further to create a common foreign and security policy to ensure a more co-operative approach to defence.
- **Security and justice**: EU are tackling the problems of international terrorism, drug trafficking and abuse, trafficking in human beings and the illegal exploitation of foreign women for prostitution. The EU countries have adopted common policies and procedures, which are being enacted by the police, customs and law courts. EU also ensures that people have rights to asylum through their asylum and migration policy.
- **Home affairs**: apart from common rules on asylum the EU introduced rules on immigration applicable to nationals of non-member countries. There are also rules ensuring that there is police cooperation to combat cross-border crime and it is looking to create more harmonisation in the areas of civil and criminal law.

- **Social policy protocol**: the Maastricht Treaty ensures that the following aspects should be available to all citizens who live within the EU: free movement, fair pay, better working conditions, social security protection, freedom of association and collective bargaining, vocational training, equal treatment for men and women, health protection and safety at the workplace and protection of children, the elderly and the disabled.

Stakeholders effect on the public services

A stakeholder is someone who has a share or an interest in a particular service or business. Stakeholders can be groups of people, organisations, institutions and sometimes even individuals. To identify who is a stakeholder within the public sector you need to identify the particular public service you are focusing on and ask yourself who is involved and who are their customers. For example, a hospital will have amongst its stakeholders the following: patients, doctors, nurses, hospital staff and the local authority.

Stakeholders have a great deal of influence on public service organisations as they are, in a way, clients of the public service in question. They are therefore important in shaping public services.

Theory into practice

You are a stakeholder in the police service and will have views on what their role is in society. Write down what you believe is the role of the police service within society and compare your views with the views of your friends. Do you have the same opinions?

Check your answers by referring to a mission statement for the police service or find their aims and objectives.

Now identify who you believe are their stakeholders and create a list which gives a reason for each one you have chosen. Consider the following to help you:

- local authorities
- central government
- pressure groups
- community
- trade unions
- crown prosecution service.

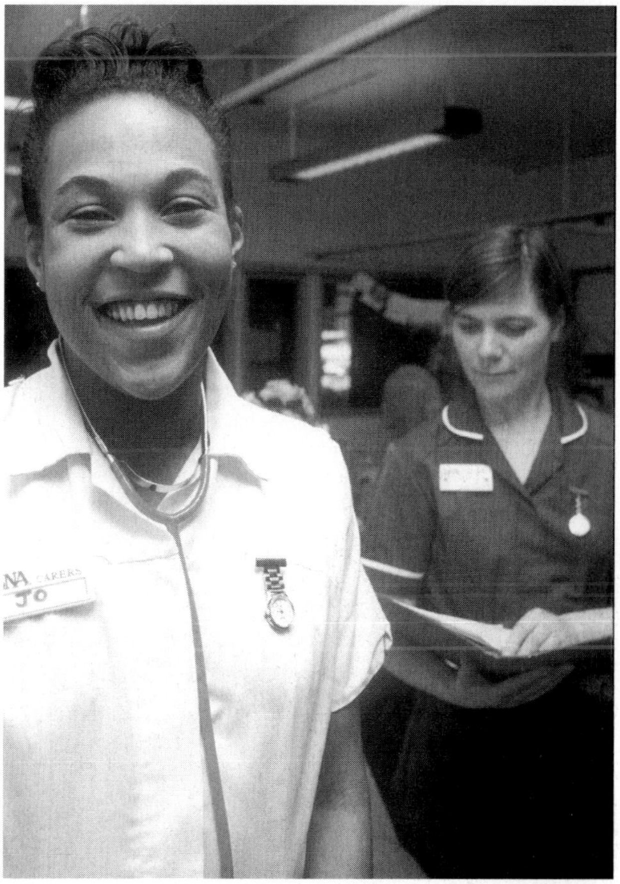

Nurses are stakeholders in a hospital

There are different types and levels of stakeholders as follows.

- **Active stakeholders** are those who affect or determine a decision or action in the organisation.
- **Passive stakeholders** are those who are affected by decisions or actions of others.
- **Key stakeholders** are those who have a significant influence on the success of an organisation.
- **Primary stakeholders** are the intended beneficiaries of the organisation.

- **Secondary stakeholders** are those who benefit indirectly from the organisation. For example, a better understanding by police officers to the needs of victims of crime will help charitable organisations such as Victim Support reach out to these victims and offer them support.

Theory into practice

Stakeholders include all those who affect and are affected by policies, decisions or actions of a public service. Create a list of stakeholders for the following two public service organisations – there will be some overlap:

- Armed Forces
- Health service – NHS

Once you have created a list, identify what type of stakeholder they are, for example key, primary or secondary.

Assessment activity 1-P2, 1-M2, 1-D2

A friend of yours has just gained employment as a nurse and has asked you to help him understand the pressures faced by public service workers by answering the following questions:

To achieve a **pass** you need to provide a limited explanation of the effects of the internal and external environment on public sector organisations

To achieve a **merit** you need to provide detailed explanation of the effects of the internal and external environment on public sector organisations

To achieve a **distinction** you need to provide a detailed evaluation of the effects of the internal and external environment on public sector organisations

Political and economic policy

Political ideologies

Political ideology comes from Greek meaning 'idea'. Today, ideology is a system of ideas or a vision of how life should be organised. Figure 1.12 maps the different political ideologies which have in different degrees shaped public services in Britain.

- **Anarchism**: a political theory proposing that all forms of governmental authority are unnecessary and undesirable and society is based on voluntary co-operation and free association of individuals and groups.
- **Capitalism**: an economic system characterised by private ownership of all goods and services. All investment, prices, production, and distribution is determined by private decisions and everyone is entitled to compete in a free market (survival of the fittest). In a capitalist society the wealth is unequally distributed.
- **Communism**: based on the idea of eliminating private property. This is a system in which goods are owned in common and are available

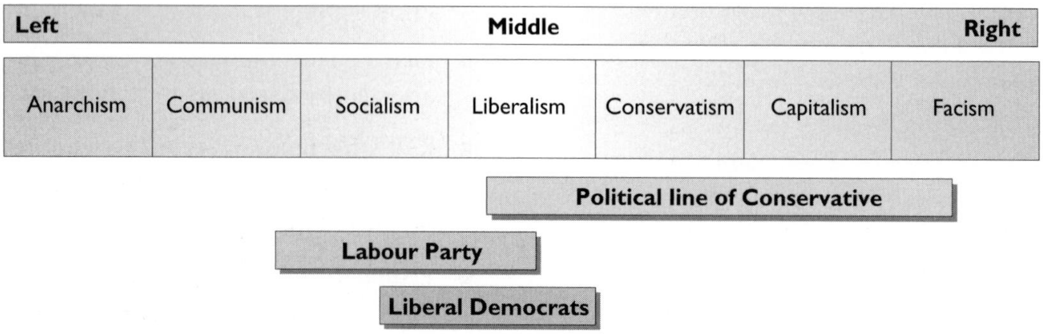

Figure 1.12 Political ideologies in Britain

to all as needed. This theory was strongly influenced by Karl Marx and Vladimir Lenin made it the official ideology of the USSR (Russia). It produced a totalitarian system of government in which a single party controlled state-owned production. In theory, the government then distributed these economic goods fairly and equally. In practice, Communism led to economic stagnation in Russia which finally led to the overthrow of the USSR and its replacement with the Federation of Russian States in the late 1980s.

- **Conservatism**: the traditional principles and policies of the Conservative party are based on tradition and social stability and seek to conserve tradition and ways of the past, stressing established institutions and preferring gradual development to abrupt change. They defend traditional institutions and practices and believe in the principals of community, continuity, law and order. They look to preserve traditions such as states' rights, family values, individual initiative and free enterprise.
- **Fascism**: a political regime based on a centralised autocratic government headed by a dictatorial leader. This leader is responsible for all economic production and distribution and all social decisions. Frequently based on racial divisions as in Nazi Germany. To ensure continual control the leader will forcibly suppress the opposition, for example Saddam Hussein.
- **Liberalism**: this is an economic theory that focuses on individual freedom from restraint. It is based on free competition, the self-regulating market (the freedom of the individual to buy and sell goods and services without any controls), it emphasises choice and competition and is the philosophy underlying capitalism. It is also a political philosophy based on a belief in progress; the essential goodness of the human race, the autonomy of the individual and it stands for the protection of political and civil liberties.

Margaret Thatcher, leader of the Conservative party from 1979–1990

- **Socialism**: this is an economic and political theory based on advocating collective or governmental ownership and administration of the means of production and distribution of goods, particularly in key industries. It involves nationalising companies and running them for the benefit of the country as a whole. It aims to ensure that everyone enjoys a sound basic standard of living and does this by redistributing income through the tax system. It emphasises gradual change and key ideas are collective responsibility and social justice. Socialist ideals have been important in the development of the Labour Party.

Theory into practice

Using information in this section and through your own research, create a fact-sheet based on political ideology that could be given to a person that knows nothing about political ideologies. Consider using relevant images to demonstrate your understanding.

Changing political ideology in the UK

In summary, these have been the basic political positions of the 3 main parties in the UK:

> **Conservatives**: favour Conservatism, capitalism and liberalism and are generally seen as right wing
>
> **Labour**: favour socialism and are traditionally left wing
>
> **Liberal Democrats**: promote the individualistic themes of Liberalism

World War II resulted in great human loss and an increased national debt. It also cost Britain its status as a world power as it was struggling economically. To tackle this economic problem the nation's two largest political parties ditched their traditional strategies for economic development, providing for the population and improving living conditions. They created a joint consensus to help Britain recover again.

The foundations of this consensus were based upon John Maynard Keynes (1883–1946) theory and focused on expanding the welfare state. This meant that the 2 parties worked towards the development of a state-financed system of social security accessible to all citizens and state responsibility for the economy.

The Labour Party nationalised many key areas of the economy including public utilities, airlines, public transport and the steel industry (even though these services today are denationalised and run privately) to help growth and recovery. This joint consensus lasted until the mid 1970s and many elements are still present today such as the NHS and social security benefits.

During the 1970s, the economy began to stagnate and unemployment began to increase which led to disillusion with the consensus and the rise of the new right.

The new right

1979 saw the election victory of the Conservative Party under the leadership of Margaret Thatcher. While the Labour Party continued to hold on to out-dated ideals about a welfare state, the Conservative Party moved away from it.

Margaret Thatcher set about completely re-organising the economy into a private market-based economy through a comprehensive program of privatisation. The new benchmark for social policy was not whether services were required, but whether they could be financed. Unemployment was to be regarded as the fate of the individual rather than the responsibility of the state. Those affected were to bear the main responsibility for finding new work and wherever possible, the state withdrew itself out of social policy. The aim of this policy was to rid Britain of uncompetitive structures, to encourage entrepreneurial spirit and to break a mentality among some sections of society that they have a right to receive benefits without doing anything themselves to improve their situation (dependency culture).

While these policies improved the economy, the problems caused by these changes included growing homelessness and the widening gap between rich and poor. This in turn led to disillusion with the capitalistic ideas underpinning Thatcherism.

New Labour

The Labour Party was successfully elected in 1997. They argued that while it was not returning to the failed policies of the 70s, it could not accept a situation in which large regions of Britain outside of the booming South East were shut out from Britain's economic successes. The Prime Minister, Tony Blair, was keen to point out that he too would like to use the efficiency of the private businesses but any successes should be linked to achieving social justice and conciliation between the classes.

The aim of the New Labour party was to create an efficient education system and a situation in which every one, regardless of background, has an equal chance in society, and to ensure that all who are willing to work are allowed to share in the nation's success. In contrast to the old welfare state, New Labour did not guarantee comprehensive social security unless individuals are prepared to work and take responsibility for their lives.

Government economic policy

Government spending

The Labour government has insisted on keeping a tight control of public spending. It has continued with the trend to privatise public services (see below) and has attempted to keep the budget in balance. (see earlier in the chapter). The last year or two has seen an increase in expenditure on health and education to meet government pledges to improve these services.

It has also attempted to redistribute income in line with its focus on social justice and has had a target of reducing child poverty. It has introduced systems of tax credits to benefit families.

Privatisation

Since the 1980s, the influence of right wing ideas has increased and this has led to a reversal of the trend to nationalise key industries and services in the 1940s and 1950s.

The last two decades have seen a battle for the control of public services. On the one hand we have the post-war tradition of state-owned, state-run services and on the other hand we have privatisation. It appears apparent that the Labour government like it predecessors are opting for the privatisation route.

Privatisation is the sale of government owned businesses to the private sector. This can be done by a sale of the entire business or selling a controlling share in a business to a single company.

Towards the end of the 1970s, the British economy was suffering under the strain of unprofitable monopolistic national industries such as the coal and steel industry. It was thought by some that it was time for a change and time to make Britain more competitive. This was a legacy of the Thatcher administration as she sold many state owned business in the 1980s such as:

- council housing
- British Telecom
- gas
- Jaguar
- local bus companies
- British Airways.

Reasons for privatisation

There are a number of reasons for privatisation including:

- failure of nationalised industries to be economically successful
- need to compete in global markets
- political policy and ideology
- EU competition rules.

There is no going back on privatisation. It has successfully improved the services offered by many previously government controlled companies and some of these have succeeded in establishing a world presence. However, there have been costs such as job losses and continued subsidies to some industries, most notably the railways. Even so, privatisation is now an adopted policy of governments the world over. It has also affected people on a wide scale in Britain as over 650,000 workers have changed from the public sector to the private sector, over 1 million council houses have been sold and over 9 million people have become shareholders of these established companies.

Advantages	Disadvantages
• Improved quality of service and competitive prices. • Created a more open and free market both domestically and internationally. • Reduced government spending. • Increased government revenues from sale of assets (between 1991–1993 the government received 8 billion a year through privatisation). • Lower taxation levels or redirection of tax to other services. • Government still has a role in controlling prices in other industries through regulatory bodies such as Ofwat and Oftel. • Firms operate more efficiently because they are trying to maximise profits. • Ordinary people can become involved by being shareholders.	• Success of these businesses has come through huge redundancies to ensure profits. • Control of some industries has moved abroad. • There is a growth of 'fat cat' directors as wealth is achieved by a few. • Very little to stop these companies becoming private monopolies. • These services are necessary to society, so it is dangerous passing ownership to the private sector as they may be mismanaged. • Can lead to strikes as people fear for there jobs.

Figure 1.13 Advantages and disadvantages of privatisation

Case study

Over 2 million council properties have been sold to tenants over the last 20 years under Tory 'right to buy' policies. The current labour party continue to privatise council homes by mass transfer of whole housing estates, and in some cases the whole housing stock of a city, into the housing association sector.

Privatisation usually takes the form of creating local housing companies – an arrangement whereby public housing estates are sold to and funded through housing associations and managed by a body made up of the association, the council and tenants' representatives.

What implications are there for public service workers of privatising council housing?

Public-private partnerships (PPPs) and privately financed projects (PFPs)

Recent years have seen the Government's push for greater private sector involvement in the delivery of public services, providing new opportunities for industry through programs to attract private sector investment and participation in the provision of major public infrastructure. For example, building a new hospital or school and related ancillary services such as providing maintenance staff.

This has led to public-private partnerships (PPPs) and privately financed projects (PFPs), which have helped to build new schools or facilities onto existing schools and through new hospitals. The Government's economic program relies on private agencies and since 1997 more than £35 billion of investment has been committed to completed and projected PPP/PFI projects, including 40 major hospital projects and work at 550 schools.

The PFI debate

PFI are starting to occur throughout the public sector in relation to the construction of hospitals, prisons and schools to name a few.

Problems with PFIs: Some people argue that PFI are a bad idea and threaten the whole ethos of the public services when private companies become involved in the development and running of various services. The introduction of PFI by national government is seen by many as a money saving way of getting finance for new hospitals and schools.

The problem with this is that PFI schemes cost much more than conventionally funded projects. The private sector borrows at higher rates than the public sector since governments can borrow at much lower rates. This means that the private sector demands high returns and despite very low risks, profits from PFI are extremely high. As well as the huge returns made by private companies they are refinancing their deals and yielding huge profits at the expense of the public sector.

Thought for reflection: There is a growing use of the private finance initiative or public private partnerships to allow private companies to raise money for major public service projects. However, it costs more for private companies to raise money than it would for the government or local government and the only way private companies will make their money back is to cut either services or staffing costs. That means public service workers and users pay the real costs.

What do the labour government say: They believe its about relieving the government of a tiresome bureaucratic burden.

By allowing private firms to design, construct and maintain the thousands of state-owned roads, schools and hospitals, it allows government to concentrate on what it should really be doing – formulating and implementing policy.

Chancellor Gordon Brown thinks the PFI is the quickest way of building new schools, hospitals, transport schemes. He also believes that, in the long run, he can make the government's money stretch further, by spreading necessary spending over many years.

Think about it

Discuss the advantages and disadvantages to the government of public services and of private firms being involved in providing buildings and related services in the education and health sector.

Compulsory competitive tendering

Compulsory competitive tendering ensures that work to be carried out by public organisations is open to bids from private companies. It was first introduced for construction, maintenance and highways work by the Planning and Land Act 1980 and now exists in local government in the following areas:

- refuse collection
- ground maintenance
- sports and leisure management
- some white-collar work such as finance and marketing and IT services.

The idea is to create a competitive environment and break down public sector monopolies by opening up services to private sector organisations. It is also hoped that this will save money by services being run more effectively as the providers will be looking to make a profit.

A local authority can carry out certain defined activities in-house only if the work has first gone out to tender and been won in open competition.

Drawbacks

Barriers to competitive tendering is that it can alter the organisational culture, the market can be restricted as the private firm will only offer services or goods that are profitable and the whole issue of who carries the risk is in question.

Trade unions argue that this regime has not been easy for some authorities and it has led to changing practices, job losses, poor working conditions, poor standards and depressed pay in unpopular service areas (the areas where it is hard for a supplier to make a profit). We must also remember that the focus of the private sector is often to produce a basic product/service at a minimum price and not to create a quality product/service.

Assessment activity 1-P3, 1-M3, 1-D3

You are to attend a youth forum with your local MP to discuss politics in general. Before you go you need to prepare answers for the following areas:

To achieve a **pass** you need to display an understanding of the effects of political ideology and the government economic policy on a public sector organisation

To achieve a **merit/distinction** you need to show a detailed understanding/analysis of the effects of political ideology and the government economic policy on a public sector organisation

Socio-cultural and technological changes

From 3.03 billion in 1960, the population has more than doubled to 6.23 billion. By the end of this century it is likely to be over 10 billion. This explosive rate of population growth is due to improved sanitation, medicine, and nutrition, reduced mortality rates, increased longevity and high fertility rate.

Demographic changes

The main problem with population growth is the threat of increased poverty. About thirty years ago, there were about one billion people living at a level above poverty and 2.5 billion people living in poverty. Now, after some great technological advances there are only 1.2 billion people that are living above poverty and 4.1 billion people living in poverty. Absolute poverty is defined as people who suffer from or are more susceptible to malnutrition, disease, squalid surroundings, high infant morality and lower life expectancy.

Other consequences of population growth include:

- children starve to death every day in different places around the world
- wrecks economies and social structures
- depletes natural resources quicker
- increases rate of pollution and global warming
- destruction of natural ecosystems
- land issues – erosion, desertification
- cheap labour for developed countries
- no sustainable development of underdeveloped countries
- increased world conflict (oil)
- international migration (net immigration)
- disease and famine
- increase in illicit activities such as drug farming, urban crime; poaching of exotic animals, and plant life.

Theory into practice

What effects is population growth going to have on the following agencies.

- central government
- local councils
- police service
- Armed forces
- fire service.

UK population

The population of the UK is over 59 million and is still growing. This means that the UK population has grown nearly 20% since 1950. If it continues to rise at its current annual rate (2001) of 0.4 per cent a year (236,000), it will reach 63.47 million in 2020 and 71.55 million in 2050.

Britain claims to be a multi-cultural society in structure and there is a good argument that this is the case. In 2001 there were 4.5 million people from ethnic minorities in the UK – 7.6% of the total population. There were also over 1.5 million Islamic followers within Britain which is about 3% of the population

Think about it

How are the following affected by population growth?

- education
- health/hospitals
- housing
- economy
- pollution
- employment
- public services – demand for services and recruitment
- prisons.

Societal pressures

The police have a difficult job in balancing their role within society with the needs of the community they serve.

The general expectations of the police are often said to be a quick response and friendly contact, a quality service, proactive policing (taking action before it happens), visible patrolling to deter criminals and general advice. The police service must cater for these needs against their own financial restraints and performance indicators. The police are also more likely to influence the views of, and demand for policing if they have a strong and productive relationship with the public (see the diversity chapter for further information on how this can be achieved).

Every group in society seeks competent policing that addresses the concerns and threats it members perceive. However these needs and perceptions vary between different age groups.

- **Young (14–25)** – perceive the police as rude and dismissive to there needs and often feel they are out of touch with their culture.
- **Mid-life adults (25–45)** – perceive the police as a service that doesn't treat the members of its community equally and feel that often officers can be arrogant and act in a superior manner. One of their main concerns of this group is the lack of interest in victims of crime.
- **Older adults (45–60+)** – As people get older they seem to be more positive and appreciative of the job of the police service and are very sympathetic and trusting towards them. They are more likely to support local police initiatives and recognise that the police cannot operate independently of society.

Apart from the perceptions of different age groups, people from the ethnic minorities have very different perceptions from the majority group within the UK.

Some of the main perceptions of ethnic minority groups are that they are treated differently than the majority group. They feel that the police service in particular are unreliable and only contact them when they need something from them, which has meant that they believe them to be reactive and not proactive towards their needs. Many people from ethnic minority groups believe that racism towards them still exists within the police service by some officers, but this is an issue that is a continual priority of the police following the Stephen Lawrence case and negative media over the last decade.

Pressure groups

Public participation is essential to effective policy-making. A high level of public involvement means that policies made by the government or at grass roots level by the public services can be developed with the benefit of a wide range of different opinions and evidence. A pressure group can be described as an organised group that seeks to influence government policy or legislation. They are sometimes referred to as 'interest groups', 'lobby groups' or 'protest groups'.

The aim of all pressure groups is to influence the people who actually have the power to make decisions. Pressure groups do not look for the power themselves, but do seek to influence the decisions made by those who do hold this power.

Public services and the local community

In order for the police to increase their profile and meet the needs of the communities they serve they should:

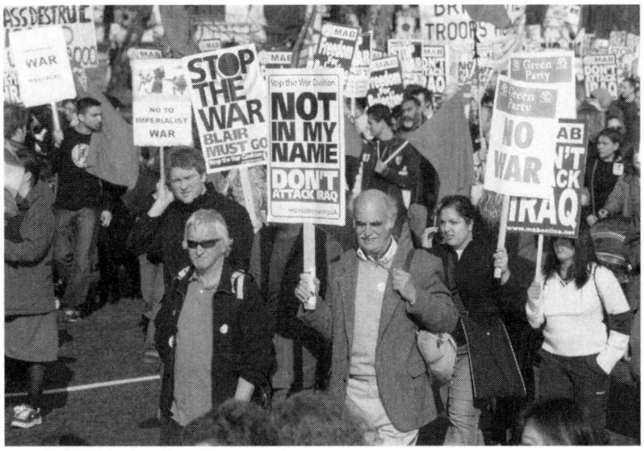

A pressure group

- provide an equal quality of service to all by responding to the varying needs of society
- demonstrate a depth of understanding of varying social situations and service needs
- be aware of crime levels in the area so appropriate police initiatives can be put in place to tackle the problems
- offer free advice on crime prevention and target hardening
- publish their crime rates to show success and achievement.

Like all police constabularies, South Yorkshire police service believes that they can help meet the expectations of the public by:

- knowing what local people need and expect through consultation and community forums
- offering equality of service by considering the impact of their services on all sections of the community. This element also includes additional recruitment of minority groups
- aiming to be the best by setting performance indictors
- being accountable for their actions to the local community

Theory into practice

List these ten expectations in order of importance to your community.

- increased recruitment of minority groups
- more visible policing
- reduced crime levels
- more CCTV coverage of town/city centres
- using political correct language
- hold and be involved in community forums
- deal with racial incidents quickly
- increase the number of police officers
- introduce community wardens to help police problem areas
- make police officers aware of the aims and objectives of the police service

Lifestyle changes

The life we live is very different from the lives of people living in 1903. These changes in lifestyle are down to a variety of reasons, which include the fact that we live longer as the life expectancy for men is 75 and 80 for women, where hundred years ago it was 45 and 49.

The pace of life has certainly accelerated and we all have more leisure time and money to spend which has meant greater demands of the community on many types of facilities including the public services.

Think about it

List the ways in which our lifestyles have changed with regard to the following areas since 1903

- sickness
- entertainment and leisure
- jobs
- food and drink
- holidays and travel
- communication
- transportation
- science and technology.

One of the biggest lifestyle change which affect the public services is drug and alcohol use. Apart from being a cause of crime and a reason for anti-social behaviour it also affects the following:

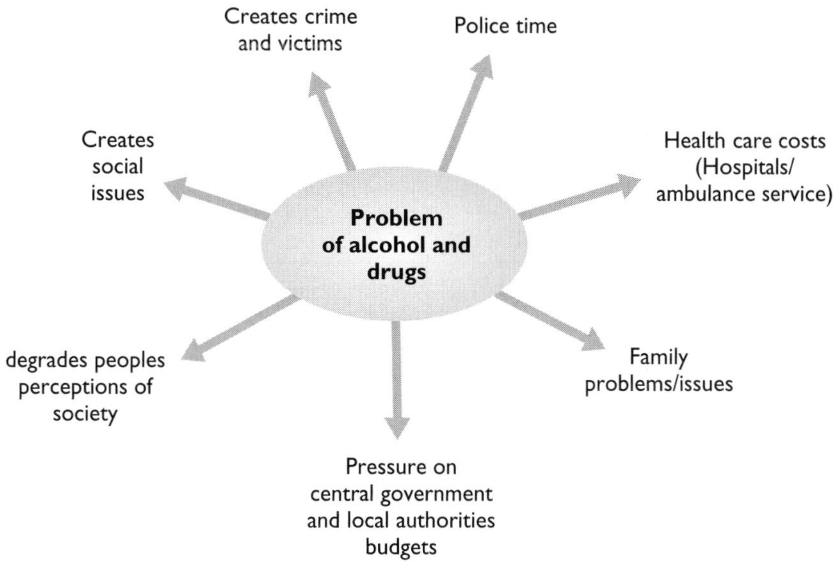

Figure 1.14 Affects of drugs and alcohol

Think about it

How has the job of a police officer, fire-fighter or soldier improved because of lifestyle changes over the last 100 years?

Assessment activity 1-P4, 1-M4, 1-D4

You have been asked by the Home Secretary to discuss the effects of socio, cultural and technological changes to one public service of your choosing.

To achieve a **pass** you need to display an understanding of the effects of socio-cultural and technological changes on a public sector organisation.

To achieve a **merit/distinction** you need to show a detailed understanding/analysis of the effects of socio-cultural and technological changes on a public sector organisation.

Technological changes

The role of the public services has changed due to the increased use of technology including:

- satellite and global positioning system to locate people or employees
- improved transport and more advanced transport such as helicopters
- CCTV coverage and the use of speed cameras enabling police and other public services to monitor and react quickly to violations or likely violations of the law
- many police officers also carry basic equipment such as mobile phones so they can be contacted by victims of crimes directly when on duty
- updated communication networks enabling contact to all the public services through the Internet
- helicopters which have the latest equipment to help track law breakers such as thermo imaging and heat seeking devices
- the uniforms worn by the uniformed services are constantly improved using technology as the fire-fighters uniform is designed to give them maximum possible protection in dangerous situations and the police service use specially designed body armour and equipment such as pepper spray and fasers in high risk situations.
- technology is also used by the public services especially the police to investigate crimes and collect evidence such as DNA, sampling, ballistics and voice pattern analysis.

Marriage	Nowadays, 40 per cent of births are outside marriage. Marriage is on the decline and co-habiting is on the up.
Education	The number of pupils at school has risen from 4.7 million just after the Second World War to a peak of 8.4 million in the mid 1970s.
Employment	Employment has changed dramatically with the rise of two-income families. Flexible working is also on the rise.
Income and expenditure	Men's income still outstrips that of women of all ages, but the growth in average earnings is on the increase for both sexes.
Health	Healthcare, more than anything else over the past 100 years, has improved our lifestyle and quality of life as people today live much longer and more fruitful lives.
Transportation	70 per cent of households have at least one car.
Housing	In 2002 the average house price in the UK was £96,800, whilst the average price in 1952 was £1,890. Also houses bought by first-time buyers cost just 60 per cent of the amount spent by a former owner-occupier. The number of houses with a home computer almost doubled between 1988 and 1998, from 18 per cent to 34 per cent.

Figure 1.15 Lifestyle changes

Think about it

Can you think of any other examples of how the public services use technology to carry out their job more effectively

Video identification parade electronically recorded (VIPERS)

This is a virtual identity parade sanctioned by the Home Office. The database includes over 10,000 look-alikes which allows any police force to create its own virtual identity parade within a matter of hours rather than a real parade which can take a number of weeks to organise. In addition, a real parade can cost between £600 and £1,250 whilst a virtual parade costs as little as £150. The system will be able to handle up to 200 virtual parades a day within the next few years. As a method of gathering evidence this method is likely to increase as there is less stress on the victim as they need not come to face to face with their attacker and it is conducted in more relaxed circumstances.

Mobile wireless system

The introduction of a new mobile wireless system will help officers deal with incidents much more quickly. The system will provide officers with mobile data links and allow them to file reports remotely, rather than returning to the station.

This mobile technology includes the use of handheld personal digital assistants and in-vehicle computers with pocket PCs. This will create mobile officers in the field through the use of wireless

Police helicopter helps track law breakers

technology and may mean the end of traditional police stations. Officers will also be able to receive and send text messages and make enquiries whilst on the streets. It is estimated that the time officers will spend out of the station will increase by over 15% which is the equivalent to approximately 150 extra officers in each constabulary.

Automatic number plate recognition (ANPR)

This technology recognises car number plates and has been used to help arrest people whose vehicles have been involved in a crime or to help prevent terrorism. The system scans registration plates and checks them against police databases to identify the owner and see if the car has been used in a crime or has been reported stolen.

Assessment activity 1-P6, 1-M6

As part of your assessment for this unit, you must demonstrate the use of a range of specialist terminology. Find out what the following terms mean:

1. Public sector
2. Expenditure
3. Public and private goods
4. Public accountability
5. Monopoly provision
6. Organisational culture
7. Stakeholders
8. Political ideologies
9. New right
10. Taxation
11. Competitive tendering
12. Privatisation
13. Merit and demerit goods

End of unit questions

1. What agencies fall within the public sector?
2. How do they differ from private sector agencies?
3. What is the role of the local authorities with regard to the public services?
4. What is the role of central government with regard to the public services?
5. What is the job of the Chancellor of the Exchequer?
6. In what ways are taxed collected?
7. Should the public sector be allowed to have monopolies when the private sector can't?
8. What are the different types of stakeholders found in the public sector and which are the most important?
9. Why do you think that Britain is not a communist state?
10. Are private finance initiatives and public private partnerships the way forward?
11. How can pressure groups bring about change in society?
12. How is technology used to make the job of the fire service easier?

Resources

Anderton A, *Economics*, Ormskirk Lancashire 1991

Blundell and Murdock, *Managing in the public sector*, Butterworth–Heinemann, 1995

Marsh I et al, *Sociology: Making sense of society 2nd ed.* Prentice Hall, London, 1996

Rose A and Lawton A, *Publice Service Management*, Pearson Education, 1999

Websites

www.number-10.gov.uk – 10 Downing Street

www.hm-treasury.gov.uk – HM Treasury

www.homeoffice.gov.uk –Home Office

www.met.police.uk – Metropolitan Police

CITIZENSHIP AND CONTEMPORARY ISSUES

Introduction to Unit 4

This chapter is designed to help you develop an understanding of citizenship and current issues which you will be required to know when you join a public service. It is important to understand the need for public services personnel to demonstrate citizenship and civic duty in their professional and personal lives. In addition, it is important that you understand the rights and responsibilities of both the state and the citizen and be aware of what may happen when these rights and responsibilities come into conflict.

Assessment

It is important that you use the material and activities in this unit not only to expand your learning, but to prepare for assessment.

Throughout the unit activities and tasks will help you to learn and remember information. Case studies will be included to add industry relevance to the topics and learning objectives. This unit is externally assessed and guidance on preparing for your IVA is included on page 356. You are reminded that when you are completing activities and tasks, opportunities will be created to enhance your key skills evidence. After completing this unit you should be able to achieve the following outcomes which will be assessed on your IVA.

Outcomes

1 Explain how at least three public services define **'citizens'** and citizenship.

2 Identify the qualities associated with a **'good' citizen** and the effect of this on the individual, the environment and the work of at least two public services.

3 Define **equal opportunities**, human and **individual rights** of citizens.

4 Differentiate between local, statutory and non-statutory public services and describe the **role of the services to individuals and groups of citizens**.

Citizenship

Citizenship is concerned with many issues that are important to the public services today. It involves questioning rather than accepting your role in society and trying to understand complex topics such as:

- your role as a citizen
- your influence on society and how much power you have to change things
- what is going on in society and how will it affect you personally and in your professional life
- the role and functions of the major institutions in society.

Citizenship and contemporary issues is concerned with debates, discussions and evaluation of evidence. An understanding of these issues will make you more socially and politically aware which is a vital skill for any potential public service recruit and one you should be actively seeking to develop.

The meaning of citizenship is difficult to define. Legal citizenship lays down legal requirements which enable you to claim nationality and citizenship in a particular nation. The moral and political view of citizenship centres around how a person should operate within society. There is not a great deal of debate to be had about legal requirements in this context because they are created by parliament and are relatively fixed and static. However, the rights and responsibilities of the citizen and the state are constantly changing and developing therefore it is important for you to understand your rights and responsibilities in order to play an effective role in society at local, national and international level.

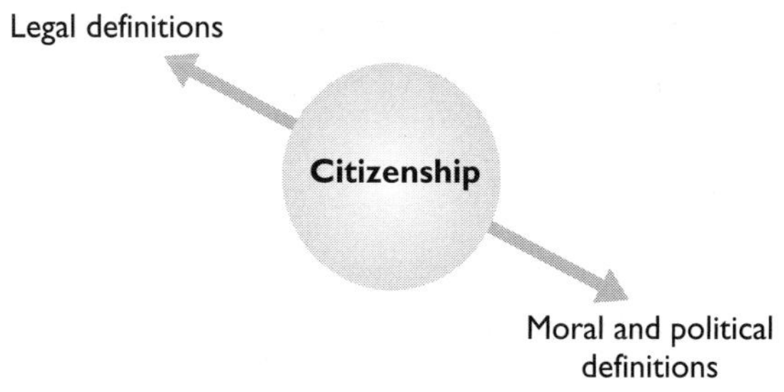

Figure 4.1 Two main areas of citizenship

Type	Detail
British citizen	People who gained British nationality because they are connected with the UK through: • birth • descent • registration • naturalisation. This is the only group of people who have the right to live permanently in the UK and enjoy freedom of movement throughout the EU. This is called the right of abode.
British dependent territories citizen (BDTC)	People who live in dependent British Colonies, such as • Gibraltar • British Virgin Islands.
British overseas citizen (BOC)	Groups of individuals who do not qualify in either of the previous two categories. These groups are mainly ethnic minorities from East Africa or Malaysia and have a relationship with a former British colony. It is currently under discussion whether to give this group the right of abode in the UK.
British nationals (overseas) (BNO)	People from Hong Kong were given the chance to acquire this status as many were unhappy at the thought of losing British Nationality when Hong Kong was returned to China in 1997.
British protected persons (BPP)	Individuals who had a connection with a former British Protectorate.
British subjects	Individuals who were British Subjects under the 1948 British Nationality Act were allowed to keep their status under the 1981 Act. Applies mainly to Citizens of Eire and India. These people do not have a specific connection with the UK.

Figure 4.2 Different types of British nationality

Think about it

What rights and responsibilities do you think a citizen might have?

Legal citizenship

The British Nationality Act 1981 created six types of British nationality as shown in Figure 4.2.

If a person does not fall into one of the categories shown in the table, for example, they may have settled here because of work or as an asylum seeker, they may wish to apply for British nationality. In order to apply for British nationality, a person must be:

- 18 or over
- of sound mind
- of good character
- have sufficient knowledge of a UK language (Welsh, Gaelic, English)
- intend to have your main home in the UK
- resident in UK for 5 years to register or naturalise.

Alternatively, a person may be married to a British citizen who already has the right of abode. People who have right of abode have the right to live in the UK permanently and leave and re-enter as they see fit. To join the public services you must be a British citizen although some public services such as the police extend this to include citizens of the British Commonwealth and citizens of the Irish Republic.

The Commonwealth

One of the most common places where people apply for British Citizenship from are member countries of the British Commonwealth, such as India, Canada and Pakistan. The commonwealth is a group of closely linked countries that evolved from the UK's imperial past. It is made up primarily of nations who were colonised by Britain and when these nations were decolonised they wished to remain on friendly terms with the UK. The Commonwealth contains 1.7 billion people in 54 nations, equivalent to 30% of the world's population. It is made up of a diverse group of nations ranging from the very tiny such as Vanuatu and Malta to the large and populous such as Australia and South Africa.

Political/moral aspects of citizenship

Who are citizens?

In the moral and political definition of citizenship all of us are citizens, even if we are not old enough to vote. We all have a variety of roles that make us citizens, (see Figure 4.3 overleaf).

All of these roles help support the nation and ensure that we are economically stable and socially aware. Without them, society could not function as taxes need to be paid in order to fund public services, students need to learn in order to take on a specialised role such as a doctor or barrister and families need to raise the next generation in order to ensure the continuation of society. They provide a support network so that as we give more to the state it can provide more for us. The citizen and the state are completely interdependent, one cannot exist without the other.

Non-legal definitions of citizenship

Non-legal definitions of citizenship revolve around 3 main components as shown in Figure 4.4 overleaf.

Social and moral responsibility

This is the development of behaviour that shows respect towards others including peers and those in authority. It also includes the understanding of the concept of civic duty, which is the responsibility you have towards helping the people in your community and their responsibility towards you. It could include acts such as checking on the welfare of elderly neighbours or reporting a crime that you witnessed against a

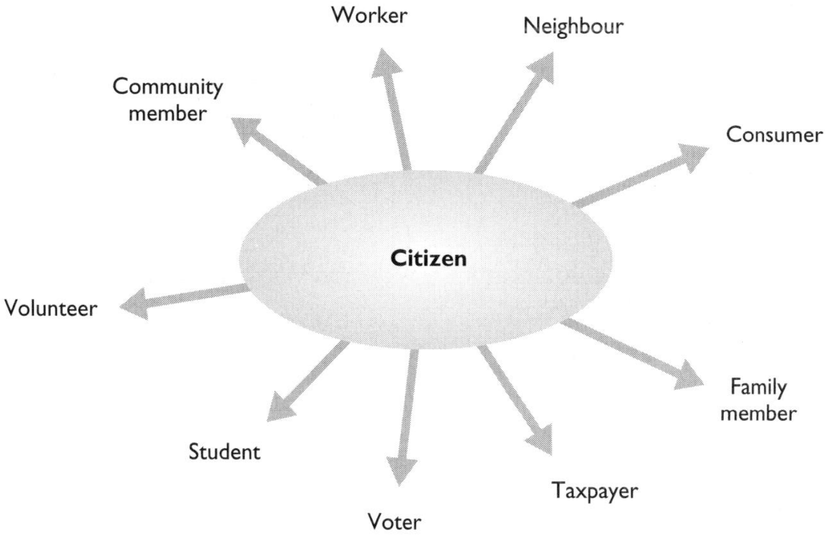

Figure 4.3 There are many roles that make everyone citizens

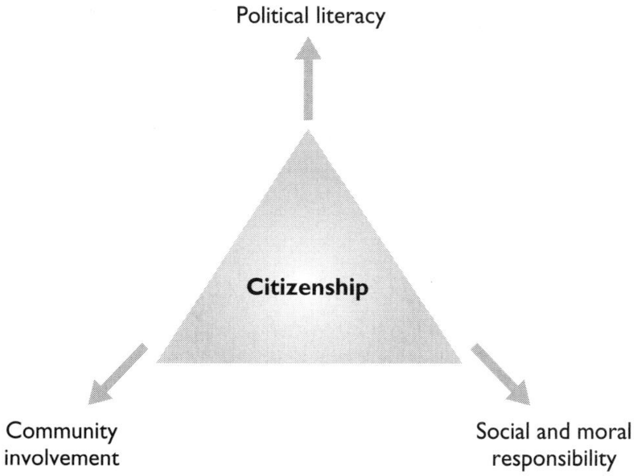

Figure 4.4 There are three components to non-legal citizenship

community member's property. It is about treating others as you would wish to be treated by them.

Community involvement

This is about taking an active interest in your community by becoming involved with the life and concerns of your neighbourhood through giving service to it. This can include things like volunteer work in your area, taking part in community initiatives like Neighbourhood Watch or becoming involved in environmental issues which may have an impact on your community.

Community involvement is an important part of citizenship

Political literacy

This is about understanding the political life of society locally, regionally and nationally. It involves knowing about the way local and national governments work and being clear on the role you can play in democracy in terms of participation in political issues and encouraging social change which may benefit your community. This may involve speaking to your local MP or councillors about a variety of issues or it may involve you becoming politically active yourself. At the very least it involves understanding how your vote in an election works and why it is important to use it.

Theory into practice

Research the political issues that are of current importance to your local area. It might be issues such as speed cameras, school closures or crime. What role could you play in encouraging change on these issues?

Theory into practice

A survey conducted by MORI in 1998 on public attitudes to citizenship found that 95% of people considered themselves to be good citizens but it also found out that:

- 75% of people didn't really know how their local council worked
- 83% of people didn't really know how the European Union worked
- 25% of people considered themselves to be poor neighbours.

How politically literate are you? Answer the following questions:

1 How often are general elections held?
2 Who is the current Home Secretary?
3 How many countries are currently in the European Union?
4 How does your local council work?
5 Who must approve the appointment of the Prime Minister after a general election?
6 What does the EU do?
7 What is the role of the House of Lords?
8 What electoral system does the UK use to appoint MPs?
9 What is devolution?
10 Who is your local MP?

Active citizenship

All of these components stress that to be a full and effective member of our society your citizenship must be 'active'. You must be participating in community life rather than observing from a distance. An active citizen is therefore an individual who understands that the responsibility for improving community conditions and addressing social problems lies with them. They understand that democracy demands the contributions of all community members are valued and they accept that social change can be made through group and community action.

Case study

Tom Hurndall was a 22 year-old British peace activist who died nine months after being shot by an Israeli soldier while working in a refugee camp in the Gaza strip in Palestine. His death in January 2004 brought to the fore the danger that peace workers are in when they enter disputed territories. Tom worked with an agency called International Solidarity Movement which campaigns against the Israeli occupation of Palestine using non-violent means. At the time of the shooting he was said to be escorting Palestinian children to safety to protect them from the violence.

1 How did Tom display the qualities of an active citizen?
2 What do you feel strongly enough about that you would be prepared to become active in promoting change?
3 Tom's actions could be considered heroic. Are heroes simply good citizens who are prepared to compromise their own safety for the benefit of a greater good? Explain the reasons for your answer.

Active v passive citizenship

- **Passive citizenship**

  This view sees rights as being provided for us by a democratic government who wishes to ensure our participation. As these rights are arbitrarily granted rather than fought for they evoke little emotional response in a citizen.

- **Active citizenship**

  The fundamental concept of active citizenship is that the rights of citizens were won from ruling governments through political struggle and demonstrations. In this view, citizenship is very precious and must be used by all citizens to demand quality services from their government.

Different nations have differing philosophies on active and passive citizenship. Desmoyers-Davis (2001) sums up this difference in philosophy between France and the UK perfectly:

> *"This could be the explanation to the frequently asked question as to 'why UK citizens are more likely to moan about the standard of their services whilst the French are more likely to go out and demonstrate about them."*
>
> Desmoyers-Davis (2001)
> Chpt 2 – p. 18

Case study

The French government is secular (non religious) in nature and at the end of 2003 it passed a law which states that all overt religious symbols should be banned in schools. This has meant that there is a ban on Muslim girls wearing traditional headscarves to cover their hair and a ban on the use of skullcaps for the Jewish faith as well as a ban on crucifixes and other religious symbols. This sparked widespread protests across France particularly among the Islamic community, who feel that freedom to worship and follow Islam is a fundamental citizenship right that they are now being denied. The protests have mainly taken the form of public demonstrations and marches and the application of political pressure to the French government.

1. Is banning religious symbols in schools compatible with the idea of a free and democratic society?
2. Do you think protests are an effective tool of change that citizens can use?
3. What do you think the reaction of British citizens would have been to a similar law imposed here?
4. Why do you think different nations seem to have different ways for their citizens to express displeasure with the government.

Think about it

Do you think it is true that the British tend to be more passive citizens?

Remember that communities do not just exist in the place we live, there are other kinds of communities:

- **School/college communities**: including you, your colleagues, your tutors, senior management, caretakers, etc. This is a group of people who share the same working and learning environment and may have the same concerns about it.
- **Workplace communities**
- **Interest based communities:** such as drama groups, music clubs, outdoor activity clubs.
- **Virtual communities**: which are found on the Internet or in virtual classrooms where people from all over the world meet in cyberspace to exchange ideas and meet new people.

Think about it

What communities do you belong to? Can you think of any other sorts of communities that citizens may belong to?

The 'good' citizen

Good or active citizens often fulfil a variety of roles such as:

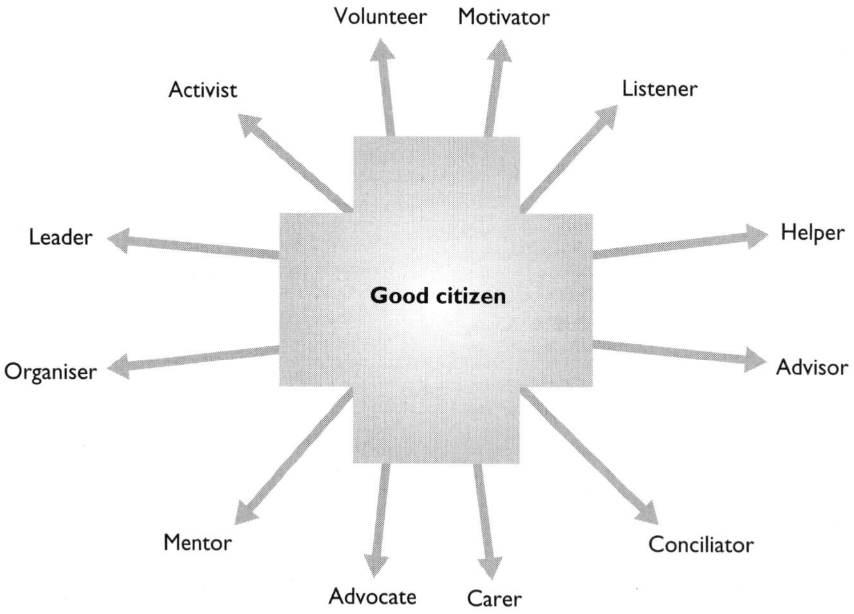

Figure 4.5 The roles of a 'good' citizen

Think about it

Look at Figure 4.5 which describes some of the roles good citizens may fulfil. Explain how each of the roles could contribute to the well being of your local community. In addition, consider how many of these roles you personally fulfil in your everyday life.

An active citizen may take part in some or all of the following activities:

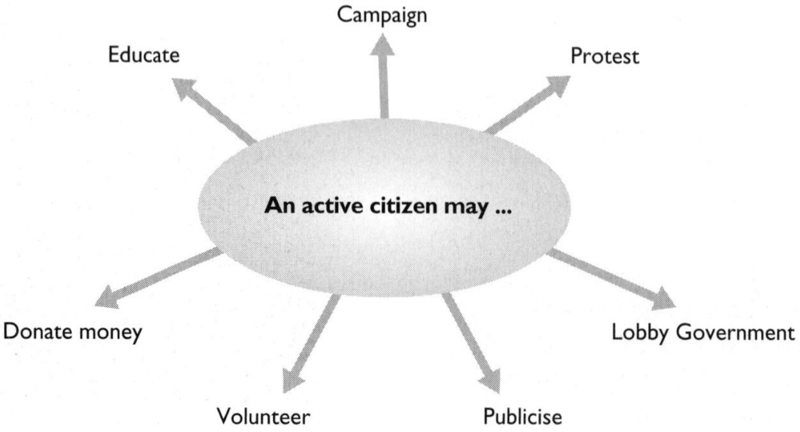

Figure 4.6 Roles of an active citizen

Public service definitions of moral and political citizenship

The public services definition of moral and political citizenship revolves around the following responsibilities.

- community involvement
- taking responsibility for the safety of others
- taking responsibility for the safety of the environment
- a commitment to continually develop life skills
- a positive attitude which welcomes challenges.

Although the Armed Services and emergency services perform different tasks in society, their definitions of citizenship are very similar. All of them require active citizens to fulfil the above points, it is important that the services set a good example of citizenship to civilians due to the power and influence they have.

Citizenship qualities required for entry into the public services

Many young people aspire to join a uniformed service, so you must remember that you will have a much better chance of being recruited if you are an active citizen. In addition, you need to be able to demonstrate many key citizenship qualities in order to be considered suitable for entry in the first place. These key qualities underpin the training recruits receive making it more effective. So what citizenship qualities do the public services look for? Consider the following case studies.

Case study

The British Transport Police has responsibility for policing Britain's railway infrastructure. They deal with over 100,000 offences each year including all major crimes such as murder and rape and minor crimes such as graffiti and theft. The BTP also deals with specific railway issues such as trains being obstructed, the transport of sports fans and issues of safety on tracks and at stations. The force has over 2000 officers in 8 operational areas. The key citizenship qualities they look for in potential recruits are:

- diplomacy
- management
- decisiveness
- flexibility
- versatility
- determination
- personal responsibility and discretion
- good communication skills
- excellent interpersonal skills
- teamwork
- initiative
- good sense and balanced judgement.

A British Transport police officer

Only about 5% of potential recruits actually become BTP Officers which demonstrates the rigorous nature of the recruitment process and highlights the importance of possessing good citizenship qualities before you apply.

1 How do you think The British Transport Police would define citizenship based on the information described above?
2 How could you improve your citizenship skills if you wanted a career in the BTP?
3 How would the skills listed above make you an asset to your community and to a service?
4 Are good citizenship skills the same as having good interpersonal and leadership skills? Explain your answer.

Case study

The British Army are the largest single employers in the UK and they have approximately 15,000 vacancies to fill annually. Qualities of good citizens are very important to them both for soldiers and officers. Important qualities for the Army are:

Soldier

- enthusiasm
- stamina
- self discipline
- teamwork
- leadership
- mental & physical agility

Officer

- decision making
- negotiation
- self confidence
- communication skills
- management

Remember that although many people have these skills in abundance, the mark of a good citizen is that they are prepared to use these skills for the benefit of others and to promote and effect change for the better in a society rather than use them solely for self-gain.

1 One of the main roles of The British Army today is to deliver humanitarian aid and act as a peacekeeping force. Why is the idea of good or active citizenship important for these roles?
2 How do you think the Army would define citizenship based on the information above?
3 Do you need to be a good citizen to go into combat? Explain your reasons.
4 The Army are actively involved in promoting citizenship education in schools and colleges. Why do you think this is?

Case study

The fire service has a varied role including emergency response to fires, responding to other emergency situations which threaten life or property, inspection/safety matters and fire prevention education. As their role is varied and demanding, good citizenship skills are naturally very important. Qualities in potential recruits include:

- teamwork
- community involvement
- reliability
- flexibility
- understanding
- ability to act quickly.

Fire-fighters go to work every day with the knowledge that they may be required to compromise their own safety to ensure the safety of others. The mark of a good/active citizen is that they are prepared to compromise their own needs for the greater good of the society or community they live in.

1 Why are good citizenship qualities important to the role of a firefighter?
2 How do you think the fire service would define citizenship based on the roles they fulfil?
3 Do you think you have the necessary citizenship skills to become a fire-fighter? Justify your answer.

Assessment activity 4-P1

The public services value citizenship qualities in potential and serving recruits and each service deals with a wide variety of different groups of citizens in the course of their day-to-day operations, each with very specific needs and requirements. Produce an A3 poster which identifies the differing groups of individuals found in society. Make your poster as colourful and engaging as you can.

In addition, define what a citizen is and research how the following organisations define 'citizenship':

- fire service
- police
- Army.

Careers Offices and websites are a good place to start as well as visiting speakers who visit your college from any of the services. Produce your definitions in an A5 leaflet to accompany your poster.

Assessment activity 4-P2

It is important that you know and understand how citizenship qualities can improve the work of the public services. Conduct and record a discussion with a colleague where you identify the qualities of a good citizen and explain how these qualities would make a positive contribution to the work of an individual in your chosen public service.

Local and national citizenship

Environmental issues

Environmental issues can affect the public services in two main ways. One is that they may have to deal with the consequences of the changing environment, for example when dealing with flooding which many believe is linked to global warming or bridge collapses which might be linked to acid rain. Secondly, the police may have to deal with protests by environmental pressure groups such as Greenpeace or Friends of the Earth who object to certain courses of action being taken by governments and corporations regarding the well-being of the environment.

Protest by an environmental pressure group

Global warming: This is a change in climate, which is predicted to happen because human activities are changing the chemical make up of the atmosphere, making global temperatures rise. We are changing the make up of the atmosphere by releasing 'greenhouse gases' into the environment such as carbon dioxide, methane and nitrous oxide. They are called greenhouse gases because they trap heat just like the panes of glass in a greenhouse.

This process is a normal and natural part of keeping the Earth warm, but since the industrial revolution there has been a huge increase in the amount of greenhouse gases in the atmosphere. Some estimates claim that carbon dioxide has increased by 30%, methane by 50% and nitrous oxide by 15%. This increase coincides with the burning of fossil fuels and industrial growth and the dramatic change in transport from horses to locomotives and eventually to cars.

Over the last century sea levels have risen 4–8 inches and the overall temperature of the Earth has increased by 0.5–10°F. Increasing concentrations of greenhouse gases are likely to accelerate this warming with disastrous consequences including:

- increased global rainfall leading to flooding which naturally has an impact on the public services in terms of emergency rescue of people and protection of property
- large rise in sea levels resulting in loss of land for agriculture potentially leading to famine and widespread poverty which has implications on the public services in terms of delivering humanitarian aid

- rise in infectious diseases such as malaria, dengue fever and cholera because of the spread of mosquitoes and rodents from warmer areas, which has implications on the health service and also the services who are most likely to deliver humanitarian aid to areas of need.

There are several ways to reduce the amount of greenhouse gases which are being expelled into the atmosphere but progress is slow. You can do your part as an active citizen by considering the following ways to reduce the problem:

- control/reduce emissions from cars
- phasing out coal and oil fired power plants and changing them to other cleaner sources such as natural gas
- being more energy efficient by using energy efficient lighting and heating
- increase the use of renewable energy sources such as wind.

Effect of global warming on the public services: Flooding seems to have become an annual winter problem in the UK due to heavy rainfall causing rivers and streams to burst their banks. This increase in flooding may be a direct consequence of the process of global warming which has direct consequences for the emergency services. For example, the fire service and police often co-ordinate and carry out rescues and evacuations as well as the Army who are often called upon to build and reinforce flood defences where a flood is anticipated. If there is a continuous increase in flooding due to global warming, this will stretch the resources and personnel of the public services.

Rescue services operating in floods

In addition to the strain on the emergency and armed services, the rise of water borne and infectious diseases will place the health services and ambulance services in a position of having to recognise and control diseases which are currently unknown in the UK.

Think about it

How have individuals and groups of citizens tried to bring about changes to reduce global warming?

Genetically modified crops: Genetic modification (GM) is used in order to make crops disease and pest resistant to help them survive extreme weather conditions such as frost, to improve their nutritional value and to improve their yields. Trials of GM crops here have provoked a negative public reaction with protesters destroying trial GM crops over concerns such as:

- crops in neighbouring fields may be modified by accident due to cross pollination
- unknown long term health impact of GM foods
- the 'terminator' gene which prevents crops producing seeds which means that poor and third world farmers must buy new seeds from the seed companies every year rather than collecting the previous year's seeds
- the development of 'super pests' which feed on GM crops
- GM crops are disturbing the natural balance of the ecosystem.

Think about it

Find 2 newspaper articles dealing with some of the issues raised by GM crops and share them with your group. Debate the pros and cons of GM crops and come up with your own personal conclusions on the issue.

Effects on the police: The GM crops issues have an effect on the police as GM protesters have previously damaged property and caused disturbances which the police have been called in to deal with. The offence that GM protesters are often charged with is aggravated trespass which is an offence under Section 68 of the Criminal Justice and Public Order Act 1994. Controversial environmental issues such as this can sometimes lead to highly charged situations in which the police must balance sensitivity to public feelings with the execution of their duty.

Assessment activity 4-P3

Using the information above write a 200-word report which explains how environmental issues may affect the work of the public services.

Social and economic issues

Unemployment and poverty

Both unemployment and poverty can produce problems the public services have to cope with. There are currently around 1.5 million people registered as unemployed but some consider this underestimates the real number of unemployed considerably while others argue many of the unemployed may be working illegally in the informal economy.

Unemployment often leads to poverty although by no means are all the poor unemployed as the

Consequences to society of unemployment and poverty	Implications for public services
Crime	There are implications here on policing strategies. There is some evidence that unemployment and poverty leads to increased crime levels.
Political unrest	Unemployment and poverty can cause anger in the population towards the governing political parties who they believe to be responsible for the situation. The anger can lead to mass public demonstrations which need to be policed effectively and sensitively. It can also mean that extremist political views rise in prominence, which can lead to violence – again with implications for the police in terms of protecting vulnerable groups.
Inner city tensions	Unemployment can cause poverty and disillusionment, which can create tensions between different groups in communities who perceive that one group receives more favourable treatment than another. The police and public services need to ensure they are not treating groups differently and the emergency services need to be ready to respond to inner city riots such as those in Oldham in 2001 (see case study overleaf).
Cost	There are significant costs to the government and public services in terms of paying for benefits to the poor and funding additional policing and public services provision in times of high unemployment.
Racism	In conditions of economic depression and unemployment there is often an increase in racist attitudes as ethnic minority populations are scape-goated and blamed for the economic position of some of the ethnic majority. This has direct implications for the public services in terms of dealing with racist attacks and incidents.

Figure 4.7 The impact of poverty and unemployment on the public services

elderly and children are among the poorest groups in society. There are different ways of defining poverty. In Britain, the main type is relative poverty which is being poor by comparison with the standard of living of the majority. In some parts of the world however, absolute poverty exists which means an absence of the basic necessities of life such as food, water or shelter.

Poverty is a major social contemporary issue across the globe although there are distinct differences in the types of poverty that each nation suffers. Poverty and unemployment can have a substantial impact on the public services in the UK (see Figure 4.7 on page 45).

Case study

The combination of economic disadvantage combined with feelings that the public services discriminate against you can lead to an explosive situation as occurred in the North of England in 2001.

Racial violence broke out in the Northern towns of Burnley, Oldham and Bradford in the summer of 2001. In May 2001, 3 days of running battles caused tremendous damage to property, business and ethnic relations in Oldham. In June, the troubles moved to Burnley where gangs of Asian and white youths clashed with each other and the police over a three-day period. The government initiated specialist task forces to go into these economically deprived areas to find out the difficulties which exist in multi-ethnic communities and the best ways of preventing their reoccurrence. Some of the problems were caused by the perceptions of the Asian minorities that they receive poorer services from the police and local authorities than the white population.

Independent reports into the reasons behind the riots blamed the following groups:

- extremists such as the BNP who exploited the prejudicial fear of local residents
- poor leadership from the local councils with regard to promoting racial equality and addressing the causes of racial division

Violent disturbances in the North of England

- communities suffering from deep rooted segregation and with little sense of citizenship
- policing policies in these areas are not community focused
- government failure to solve poverty and deprivation in these areas by funding regeneration projects.

1 How can poverty and unemployment lead to racial tensions?
2 What can the public services do to reduce racial tensions?
3 What is the evidence that some sections of the community receive a poorer service from the public services than others?
4 Are violent protests an extension of active citizenship or not? Explain your answer.

On a global scale, poverty can number among the causes of armed conflict and it can also be a direct consequence of armed conflicts. Poverty caused like this often results in aid and humanitarian missions to assist the poverty stricken population of nations and communities. Often it is the armed and voluntary public services such as The British Red cross and the Army who respond to these needs. Unemployment and poverty have a profound impact on almost every nation on the planet.

Race and ethnicity

The fact that Britain is a society made up of many different groups and could be called a multicultural society has many implications for the public services in carrying out its duties to all citizens. The public services have frequently been accused of treating members of ethnic minority communities unfairly (see unit on Diversity for full discussion of the nature of ethnic minority groups) and there have been times when the public services have been accused of not responding effectively to the needs of these groups.

It is clear that the cultural background of citizens can range widely and this has led some people to feel that the majority ethnic culture is under some sort of threat. Although this view is not true it has been reflected through our political system and has undoubtedly fed aspects of institutional racism in the public services.

Think about it

"If we went on as we are, then by the end of the century there would be four million people of the New Commonwealth or Pakistan here. Now that is an awful lot and I think it means that people are really rather afraid that this country might be swamped by people with a different culture".

Margaret Thatcher,
The Guardian 31st January 1978

The above quote highlights the concerns some people have about cultural diversity and how these concerns might have been manipulated by politicians for their own reasons and to suit their own political agendas. These concerns stem from a british national identity that many would see as racist and intolerant.

Think about it

Consider the quote above by Margaret Thatcher. Mrs Thatcher was voted in as conservative Prime Minister in 1979 and served until 1991. What effect do you think comments like this have on the public in general and how the public services might interact with members of ethnic minority communities.

The reality of cultural diversity in Britain poses problems for many of our public services, particularly in terms of recruitment and community relations. It is true to say that the public services of a society should reflect the communities that they serve. Unfortunately many public services do not truly reflect the range of diversity in Britain today which can lead to misunderstanding, intolerance, prejudice and racism.

Racism and the police: The police in particular have had to deal with issues surrounding diversity since the Macpherson report on the murder of Stephen Lawrence. The report highlighted the racist attitudes of police officers that led to a very poor operational investigation of a serious crime (see Unit 5 Diversity for a full account of the issues surrounding the Macpherson report). Clearly issues such as this can lead to very poor relationships between public services and diverse ethnic and cultural groups who may feel that the public services operate only for the benefit of the ethnic majority.

The Macpherson report accused the Metropolitan police of institutional racism and policing practices have had to change as a consequence (see Diversity unit for an account of how the police have responded).

Citizens rights and responsibilities

Citizens and the state

There are broadly speaking two main approaches to citizenship taken by political parties which reflect different views of the partnership between the citizen and the state:

1 **Individualistic approach**: the role of the state is reduced and the individual enjoys greater freedom of action and the environment in which to pursue self interest.

2 **Communitarian approach**: this has much greater emphasis on the role of the state and its duties and responsibilities. Shared goals of a community are seen as much more important than an individual's self interest.

The UK has varied in its approach to citizenship. According to Desmoyers-Davis (2001) the last century saw two waves of communitarian action. Firstly that taken by the Liberal government in the years before World War I and the actions taken by the Labour government in the post World War II era. Both of these periods saw participation in the state being actively encouraged by a series of welfare reforms in education, housing and health. The individualistic approach took precedence in the Conservative governments of the 1980s and 1990s, when attempts were made to reduce the role of the state and citizens were forced to take more responsibility for themselves.

Case study

The early 1980s was a period of high unemployment in the UK and expenditure on unemployment was rising. The Conservative government argued that it was not the state's responsibility to go on paying generous unemployment benefits, which the taxpayer continued to fund. They argued that those in work should not be expected to dip into their pockets forever to support those who were unwilling to take responsibility for finding a job. As a result, they introduced a range of cuts in benefits to the unemployed and introduced measures to ensure only those actively looking for work would receive benefits. They also pioneered schemes such as Neighbourhood Watch arguing that crime prevention was as much the responsibility of the citizen as the police.

Individualists (right wing) supported these measures as they saw them as encouraging responsibility and reducing unnecessary waste. However, communitarians (left wing) saw this as the state denying full rights to the unfortunate people who were unemployed through no fault of their own and in general blaming victims of misfortune to some extent. They saw the measures as a cynical way of hiding the real aim which was to cut taxes.

1 Does the state have a responsibility to take care of those who for one reason and another cannot currently take care of themselves?

2 Do you support the left wing or right wing approach to this argument? Explain your reasons.

3 Should state benefits provide a good standard of living for the unemployed? Explain your reasons.

4 Should the payment of benefits be conditional on the actions and behaviour of the claimant?

Since 1997, the Labour government has tried to bring about a change in the political attitude to citizenship, but eighteen years of individualistic focus cannot be changed overnight. A whole generation of adults had grown up under individualistic notions of citizenship and a wholesale move towards communitarianism would have been unacceptable to them. The approach New Labour took in the face of these difficulties was to try and reintegrate excluded sections of society back into the mainstream and encourage greater tolerance and greater equality of opportunity for all sections of society. From this developed the notion of a citizen becoming a 'stakeholder' in society – taking an interest because they have a stake in the future. The New Labour approach attempted to solve the problem of changing the public's attitude towards citizenship by combining the personal achievement of the individualistic approach with the social justice of the collectivist view. They built on the notions of 'active citizenship' developed from the policies and ethos of the Conservative government in the 1980s. The government was searching for cost effective and realistic ways to reduce crime and cut public spending which the government could implement with minimum involvement. One of the ways it did this was to promote the idea that responsibility for community problems did not lie with the government alone, it rested with every British citizen. In effect, rather than citizenship simply earning you rights in society you had to pay for those rights by taking responsibility for making society better.

Citizenship became a two way street between you as an individual and the state. In 1991 John Major's Conservative government published 'The Citizens Charter' which outlined this dual nature of citizenship and made it available to the whole country. Tony Blair strengthened this concept of rights and responsibilities by providing British citizens with more rights under The Human Rights Act 1998 (see also Unit 6 International Perspectives).

The above discussion shows that the balance between the rights given to you and the responsibilities expected from you can change depending on the circumstances a society finds itself in. For instance, in war a society may expect duties from you that outweigh the rights you have. This includes things such as being forced to enlist in the armed services in order to defend the nation or having to pay higher taxes in order to fund a war.

Citizens rights

Here in the UK, we do not have a written document that sets out all of the rights that a citizen is entitled to. A document that does set out such rights is called a constitution or a bill of rights, for example the US constitution. The rights of citizens in the UK come from a variety of sources such as:

- Acts of Parliament
- common law and judicial precedent
- customs and tradition
- international organisations such as the United Nations and European Union.

Rights are entitlements which citizens can legally and morally expect to receive from the society they live in, although the government can change the rights of any and all citizens simply by passing an Act of Parliament.

Individual human rights

Individual human rights are set out in documents such as:

- The United Nations Declaration of Human Rights (see chapter on International Perspectives)
- The European Convention on Human Rights (see chapter on International Perspectives)
- The Human Rights Act 1998 – this law was brought in to effect on 1st October 2000. It was intended to make the European Convention on Human Rights law in this country. It outlines and protects a variety of rights such as freedom of religion and a right to family life and privacy. More importantly, it makes clear that an individual is entitled to these rights regardless of sex, race, colour, language, religion, national or social origin, political affiliation or any other status. The act is therefore a crucial piece of legislation which confirms in law the rights that British citizens have long been entitled to and in some cases extending these rights further.
- Freedom of Information Act.

Documents such as those described above cover issues such as:

1 **The right to privacy:** this protects an individuals right to have a private life that is uninvaded by others. This would include celebrities or even people who are being stalked.

2 **Freedom of speech:** this is the right to say whatever you feel is appropriate whether or not it is considered popular or politically correct to do so. There are limits to this power in most Western nations. Comments which incite racial or religious hatred for example are not tolerated publically in the UK.

3 **Freedom of movement:** this refers to the ability of a citizen to freely move within the borders of their own nation.

4 **The right to a fair trial:** this refers to the provision of due process in trial to ensure that the law is followed and in theory only the guilty are convicted.

Equal opportunities

Equal opportunities include a right to decent health, education and a certain minimum standard of living. The right to equal opportunities is a relatively modern development and has resulted in legislation such as:

- Sex Discrimination Act 1975
- The Race Relations Act 1976
- The Equal Pay Act 1970 and 1983
- The Disability Discrimination Act 1995.

The Sex Discrimination Act 1975: this act makes it unlawful to discriminate on the grounds of sex or marital status in recruitment, promotion and training. It includes both direct discrimination where a person is treated less favourably than another person of the opposite sex in the same circumstances and indirect discrimination where a condition is applied equally to both sexes but the proportion of one sex meeting the condition is considerably higher than the proportion of the other sex. This has certainly been an issue in the fire service fitness recruitment tests.

The Race Relations Act 1976: this act performs similar functions to the Sex Discrimination Act. It outlaws discrimination on the grounds of race, colour, nationality or ethnic origin and like the Sex Discrimination act it covers important issues to the public services such as recruitment, promotion and training and deals with both direct and indirect discrimination. Racism in the public services is an ongoing problem and the Macpherson report into the Stephen Lawrence inquiry is likely to highlight only the tip of the iceberg in its assessment of institutional racism within our public services.

Think about it

What is the difference between discrimination and disadvantage? To what extent do you think the disadvantage of some groups is due to discrimination and to what extent is it due to poverty or lack of qualifications? Why might minorities feel the police discriminate against them?

Race Relations (Amendment) Act 2000: in response to the Stephen Lawrence inquiry the government extended the 1976 act to cover the activities of the police and other public bodies. This means that public authorities are required to promote racial equality and tackle racial discrimination within the service, encourage equality of opportunity and good relations with the community they serve, ensure that their services are fair, consult with the public about policies and plans to ensure they don't have a negative effect on minority groups, ensure that their employment practices are fair and publish reports about what they have done to meet the afore mentioned requirements.

The Equal Pay Acts (1970 and 1983): this legislation was created and implemented in order to eliminate discrimination in pay between men and women who did the same work. In 1983 it was improved to include work of equal value as well as the same work. It is an important piece of legislation as it recognises the equal contribution of women in the workplace and in the public services. In spite of these acts, women still receive on average 85% of the pay earned by men.

The Disability Discrimination Act 1995: this is a particular issue for the public services as currently they can exclude people with disabilities on the grounds of operational effectiveness. However, it is difficult to see how they will be able to maintain this stance as increasing technological advances mean that a great deal of public service work can be done from a computer or can be office based. As public services rely increasingly on technology rather than 'able-bodied' personnel to perform efficiently and effectively they may need to be more progressive and less traditional in their recruitment practices.

The Act itself became incorporated into UK law on 2nd December 1996 and operates much as the Sex Discrimination and Race Relations Acts do. In addition, it places a duty on employers to make reasonable adjustments to premises or working practices which would facilitate the employment of a person with a disability.

The Royal Navy

The Navy states in its equal opportunities policy that there shall be no discrimination against any person on the grounds of sex unless it is necessary to maintain combat effectiveness. There will be no discrimination on the grounds of marital status and no discrimination on the grounds of race, ethnic origin or religion.

The Royal Navy's equal opportunities goal is to achieve universal acceptance and a working environment free from harassment, intimidation, and unlawful discrimination. Its aim is to ensure all individuals have equality of opportunity in contributing to the maintenance and enhancement of operational effectiveness.

Figure 4.8 overleaf shows some of the measures taken by the Royal Navy to ensure equal opportunities in the workplace.

During the period from the mid 1980s to the mid 1990s the recruitment of women in the Royal Navy doubled and 20% of officers are now female.

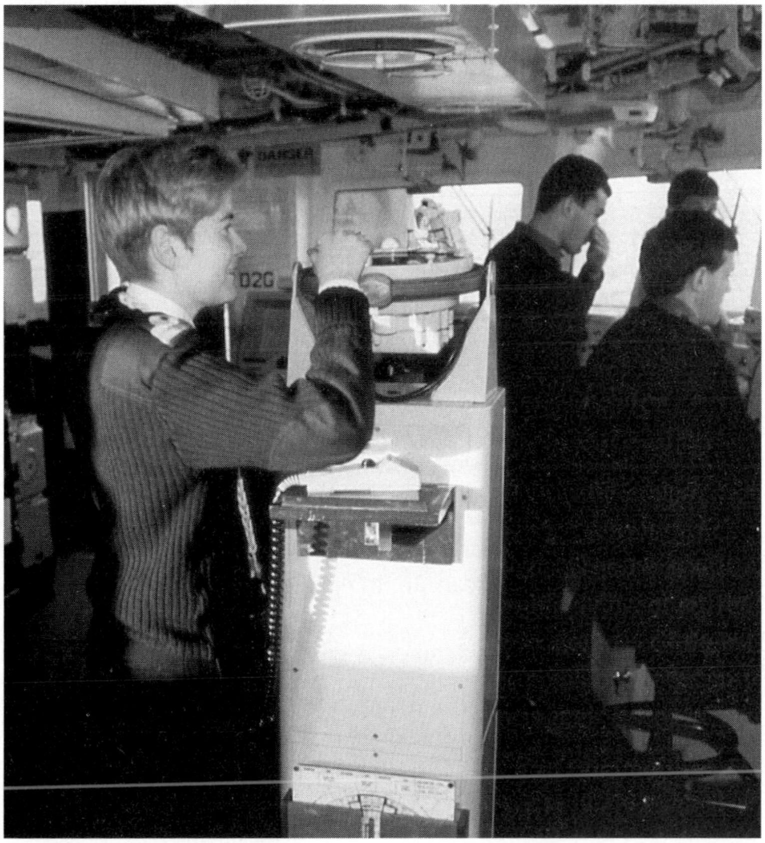

A female Royal Navy officer

However there are some restrictions imposed on female naval recruits as only about 75% of jobs are open to women. For instance, women are not allowed to serve as submariners or mine clearance divers as well as frontline ground combat roles such as those fulfilled by the Royal Marines.

Theory into practice

1. Do you think the Royal Navy does enough to address the issues of equal opportunities in the service?
2. What else could the Royal Navy do to support equal opportunities?
3. Why do you think there are restrictions posed on women in the Royal Navy? Do you believe these restrictions to be fair?
4. Are the Armed Services a career that women and ethnic minorities are traditionally drawn to? Why do you think this is?

Think about it

Is discrimination against females on the grounds of combat effectiveness justified. What are the arguments for and against?

The British Army

The Army has taken many steps to eliminate discrimination. In 2001, the head of the Army; General Sir Roger Wheeler outlined the Army's commitment to diversity and its improvements in dealing with harassment, intimidation and discrimination in its ranks.

The Army believes that an effective equal opportunities policy is crucial for operational effectiveness. Article 2 of the Equal Opportunities Policy for the Army (2000) states:

> *"Equality of opportunity is a critical factor in delivering the human element of fighting power and is, therefore, directly linked to operational effectiveness. All commanders have a duty not only to comply with the law, but also to foster an environment, both on and off duty, which attracts high quality recruits from the broadest possible societal base, and to maximise the potential and teamwork of all soldiers serving under them."*

The initiatives in place to implement this policy into the organisation are shown in Figure 4.9 overleaf.

Area	Measures taken
Dress	• Sikh men may wear turbans for general service. • Muslim women may wear long sleeves.
Recruitment	• Increased recruitment of ethnic minority applicants at both officer level and other ranks.
Gender issues	• 75% of roles in the Royal Navy are open to women. • Doubled recruitment of women from mid 1980s to mid 1990s. • 20% of officer entrants are female.
Religion	• Adequate provision must be made for spiritual and moral needs. • Commanding officers are to encourage religious observance by those under them. • Sympathetic consideration is given to officially recognised non-Christian faiths.
Food	• Halal, kosher and vegetarian foods available in the Royal Navy and the Royal Marines.
Naval swimming test	• This test may be carried out with a female only staff.

Figure 4.8 Equal opportunitiy measures in The Royal Navy

Area	Measures taken
Recruitment	• An ethnic minorities recruitment campaign. • The establishing of an ethnic minorities recruitment team. • Ethnic minority recruitment target setting to be increased annually. • Recruitment monitored by the Commission for Racial Equality (CRE) and partnership undertaken with CRE in implementing and developing policy.
Religion	• Commitment to allowing individuals the opportunity to practice their religion where possible. • Regularly seeks advice from religious leaders on matters of non Christian faith. • Every effort is made to allow the celebration of religious festivals. • Arrangement can normally be made for daily prayer where practical.

Dress	• Sikhs can wear turbans and the 5 K's as long as operational effectiveness is not compromised:
	  • Kara – steel bangle
	  • Kesh – uncut hair
	  • Kanga – small comb
	  • Kaccha – knee length undergarment
	  • Kirpan – small sword.
	• A Jewish male may wear a dark yarmulke when not wearing another headgear.
	• All females may wear trousers as part of their uniform or jogging bottoms for sport.
	• There are no current regulations which allow Muslim women to wear a headscarf.

Food	• Halal, Kosher and vegetarian foods are available.

Figure 4.9 Equal opportunity measures in The British Army

The Army recognises that in the past it has not always placed equal opportunities at the forefront of its policy making provision, but it has made a new beginning and has forged partnerships with the Commission for Racial Equality and religious groups in order to ensure that prejudice and discrimination is eliminated from the modern Army.

Theory into practice

1. Which of the Armed Services you have examined is more proactive in supporting equal opportunities?
2. What other measures would you recommend the Army takes to support its ongoing work in the field of equal opportunities?
3. Should the army and other public services be promoting recruitment to ethnic minority communities? Explain your answer.
4. What are the implications for the Army in promoting equal opportunities?

Effects of policies

Across all three Armed Services, ethnic minority recruitment stood at around 1.4% in the late 1990s compared with an ethnic minority population in the UK of around 9%. Clearly ethnic minorities are not fully represented in our fighting forces. However, The Ministry of Defence has set challenging targets for ethnic minority recruitment, with an aim that 5% of the Armed Services will be from an ethnic minority group by the end of 2002.

The situation with female recruitment shows similar trends. According to the MOD about 8% of the armed services are female compared with around 50% in the general population. However, recruitment of females into the services is continually rising and many more job roles are now open to women than ever before. Although women do not serve in land based frontline combat, they can and do serve in frontline air and sea combat.

Think about it

Do you think women are disadvantaged in the Armed Services because of the limitations imposed on them as front line combatants?

Theory into practice

Research and conduct a debate with your colleagues describing the arguments for and against women acting as front line combatants.

Assessment activity 4-P4, 4-M2, 4-D2

Working in pairs produce a 10-minute presentation which describes the main features of the Human Rights act and other equal opportunities legislation such as the Race Relations Act and the Equal Pay Act. In addition explain how two public services implement equal opportunities and human rights policies into their organisations.

To get a **merit** grade, produce a supporting handout which shows how your two public services are addressing the main issues associated with equal opportunities and human rights policies.

To get a **distinction**, include a closing statement on your handout which evaluates, compares and justifies the approaches used by your two public services to the main issues of equal opportunities and human rights.

Restriction on our rights

All of these pieces of legislation ensure that the rights and freedoms of individuals are maintained and protected, but it must also be acknowledged that the law can be a double edged sword guaranteeing rights in some legislation, but restricting it in others.

Freedom of speech and expression

Freedom of speech and expression are restricted by:

- Libel Acts
- Censorship
- Official Secrets Act
- Public Order Act.

Freedom of Association

Freedom of Association is restricted by:

- Prevention of Terrorism Act
- Public Order Act.

Freedom of Assembly

Freedom of Assembly is restricted by:

- Public Order Act 1986
- Criminal Justice and Public Order Act 1996.

Think about it

Why might it be necessary to restrict our rights as citizens?

Responsibilities of citizens

Rights are offset by corresponding responsibilities. For every right the UK confers on its citizens, the citizen has a corresponding responsibility to the state. In this approach the business of government is a two way process.

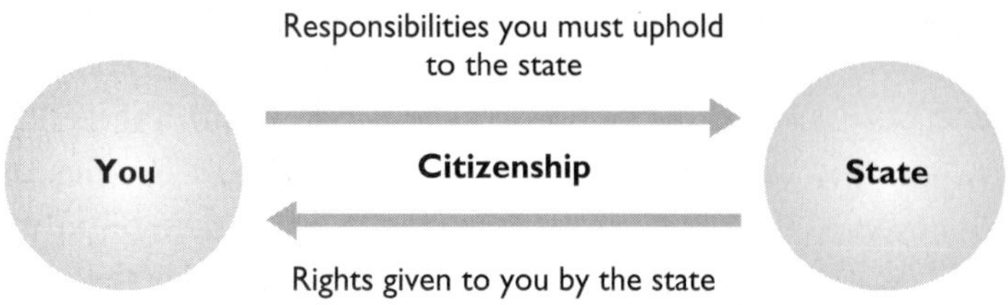

Figure 4.10 Relationship of citizen to the State

Right	Responsibility
The right to state welfare when you are unemployed.	You must pay taxes to help fund welfare when you are employed.
The right to live in peace and security.	You must take up arms to defend your nation if it is demanded of you.
Freedom of speech.	To use it sensibly and not to incite hatred or violence. Also to speak up for people who may be denied a voice in society.
Freedom of association.	To avoid association with those who may seek to harm society such as terrorists.
The right to a fair trial.	To form part of the mechanism for a fair trial by serving as a lay magistrate or on a jury.
The right to free education.	To use your education for the greater good of society by working or passing on your knowledge to others.
The right to be a parent.	To care for your children and ensure they are raised as good citizens.

Figure 4.11 Rights and responsibilities of citizens

Theory into practice

Discuss how the rights of the individual may come into conflict with the needs of the community. If such a conflict did arise whose rights should take precedence?

Case study

Diane Blood gave birth to her first son in 1998. What is remarkable about this story is that the baby's father and Diane's husband Stephen Blood contracted meningitis in 1995 and died shortly after. During Stephen's illness two samples of his sperm were placed with medical authorities for safekeeping. After his death, Diane had to fight her way through the courts to gain access to the sperm samples so that she could conceive and raise the family that she and Stephen had planned for. The Human Fertilisation and Embryology Authority (HFEA) refused to allow her to try to conceive, saying a dead man's sperm can only be used if he had given written consent. The HFEA also refused to give Diane permission to take the samples abroad so that she could be treated in a less restrictive country. In 1997 The Court of Appeal ruled that The High Court had breached

Diane Blood

Diane's rights by refusing to allow her to be treated abroad. This is because European Law gives EU citizens the right to access medical services in another member state unless there are overriding reasons to prevent it.

Diane was able to give birth to a second son in 2002 and her fight to have her deceased husband named on the birth certificates of both boys led to a change in the law and created The Human Fertilisation and Embryology (Deceased Fathers) Act 2003 which now allows children conceived after their father's death to have the correct details recorded on their birth certificate.

1 How did Mrs Blood's rights conflict with the directives of the state?
2 Do you think Mrs Blood's rights should have taken precedence over the state? Explain your answer.
3 Did Mrs Blood have the right to conceive her late husband's children? Who do you think his sperm deposits belonged to?
4 Why would the courts try to prevent Mrs Blood having her husband's children?

Assessment activity 4-M1, 4-D1

Research and organise your own early morning chat show along the lines of Trisha. Discuss with your 'guests' how the rights of the individual may conflict with the needs of the community. To get a **distinction** give a closing speech to the audience which evaluates the need to protect the right of the individual against the need to maintain the working of society as a whole.

Asylum seekers

The issue of asylum is a local, regional, national and international subject, which is often misunderstood by both the general public and the public services alike.

Asylum seekers are individuals and families who have to flee from their homes in the face of persecution, war, religious intolerance, racial hatred or any number of other factors, which may harm them or their children. Being an asylum seeker means that your life may be under threat in your home country. Currently these people have very few rights on England and will be deported unless they can prove their lives are in danger. Initially they may be given 'right to remain' status: and only after some time will they be given full refugee status.

Government statistics published in 2002 show that despite some fluctuations, the year on year total of people seeking asylum in the UK is falling. New legislation introduced in early 2003 now requires asylum seekers to register as soon as they arrive in England.

It is also important to understand that most asylum seekers are kept in detention centres, which operate along the lines of prisons, and those that are not kept in such centres have a very restricted standard of living. The basic allowances in 2003 for asylum seekers were as follows:

Person aged 18–24	£28.95 per week
Person aged 25+	£36.54 per week
Couple	£57.37 per week

Only £10 a week of this money is available as cash, the rest is provided in voucher form. In addition, asylum seekers are not allowed to seek employment for 6 months and when they are able to, most asylum seekers will struggle to get a job due to language, transport and literacy difficulties.

Some people have argued that rather than asylum seekers being unwelcome and unwanted in society, they are necessary for it to survive. We should be taking in more asylum seekers not less. The UK's population is getting older and the birth rate is getting lower, meaning that at some point there may not be enough young people working to support the public services which take care of those who do not work, such as the very young and the very old. A Study by the University of Swansea has suggested that we need to increase immigration by a fifth if we are to prevent population decline and avert an economic crisis.

Think about it

- What are the main arguments for and against allowing asylum seekers into Britain?
- How do you feel about the current treatment of asylum seekers by the government?
- Why do you think people feel so threatened by asylum seekers?
- How are the rights of asylum seekers balanced by the responsibilities of the state.

Roles of the public services to individuals and groups of citizens

Statutory and non-statutory public services

In general, public services fall into two categories – statutory and non-statutory. Statutory public services are required to exist by law and are funded by the government and non-statutory public services are not required to exist by law and are often charities or self-funded. See the table below for some examples:

Statutory public services	Non-statutory public services
The police service	Victim Support
The fire service	Help the Aged
The ambulance service	Trade Unions
The RAF	Alcoholics Anonymous
The Royal Navy	The Samaritans
The Education Service	The NSPCC
The NHS	The Salvation Army
The Probation Service	Church groups
The local Council	

Some services that are funded by the government do not wear a uniform, such as the probation service and some services which are not funded by the government do wear a uniform, such as The Salvation Army.

All statutory public services are government funded in one way or another, but non-statutory public services may need to rely on charitable donations or seek alternative methods of funding such as bidding for government or European funds and lottery money. All public services whether uniformed or non uniformed perform a crucial role for the public. The roles and responsibilities of the statutory public services are outlined in Unit 8 The Uniformed Services, so they will not be repeated here, but it is crucial to remember that the term 'service' is of vital importance. Public services should exist to serve the citizen and members of the public services should always remember that they have a duty towards the public, which should be conducted with fairness, respect and impartiality.

However, there are many non-statutory public services which are not covered in Unit 8 and it is important that you understand the services they provide to individuals and their role in effecting change if you are to successfully complete your assessment.

Non-statutory public services

As previously described these agencies tend to be charitable in nature, but they are no less valuable to the nation than statutory public services. In fact, they often fill gaps in provision to the public that the government funded public services cannot offer.

Victim Support: as a registered charity, Victim Support has a low political profile and does not seek to agitate the criminal justice system into change. Instead it focuses on helping victims of crime in terms of emotional support and practical tasks, such as helping with insurance or compensation claims. As a result of its apolitical stance it receives support from the police and funding from central government, but this funding is by no means guaranteed. Victim Support relies on the police to notify them of people who need their aid, but the police do not refer every victim to them, which means that many victims receive no help at all.

The Witness Service: the witness service exists to ensure that the process of giving evidence in court is as comfortable an experience as possible. It was established in 1989 and is managed and organised by its parent charity Victim Support. There is a witness service in every Crown Court in England and Wales and it performs several functions:

- to provide information on courtroom procedure to witnesses
- to accompany witnesses into the courtroom
- to help and reassure victims and witnesses.

Many witnesses may be very intimidated at the thought of giving evidence, but without their testimony many prosecutions would fail and offenders would be able to continue to commit crime without fear of punishment. It is therefore in the governments interests to encourage the growth of the witness service since better supported witnesses can lead to more convictions which may in turn lead to fewer active criminals on the street. The witness service is not permitted to discuss the case itself or discuss the evidence the witness will give as this can only be discussed with the police or legal representatives. Cases of witness intimidation happen regularly and there are a range of methods which can be used if the witness or victim might be in danger, for example

- screens between witness and accused
- live TV link to give evidence
- giving evidence privately.

This is particularly important in the case of child witnesses who may feel much more frightened than an adult would in the same circumstances. When the child is a witness to or victim of physical or sexual abuse the measures such as those described above are compulsory.

The witness service can arrange for a victim or witness to visit the court in advance and be briefed about what to expect. When a witness gives evidence they will be expected to take an oath to tell the truth. This can be sworn on a holy book such as the bible or Q'uran or a non-religious person will simply affirm to tell the truth. They will then be examined by the prosecuting lawyer if they are a prosecution witness and then cross examined by the defence. If the person is a defence witness then the order will be reversed.

Women's Aid Federation: this organisation supports the survivors and families of domestic violence by providing them with a place to live in a refuge with others in similar situations and offering practical and emotional support through volunteers and trained support workers. As with all charities, they have limited funds and often struggle to cope with the demand for their services:

- providing refuges and support for women and dependent children who have experienced domestic violence or who are in fear of domestic violence
- to raise awareness of the issues surrounding domestic violence
- to lobby government for changes in law and policy to protect victims of domestic violence
- to train outreach workers to support victims and act as advocates for them
- to share knowledge and techniques with other public services such as the police.

Women's aid provides over 400 refuges nationally, which provide a place of safety for abused women and children. It was created in 1974 in response to a desperate need for battered women and children to be able to have a safe environment to escape to.

The police traditionally did not take issues of domestic violence seriously and women had little support from the law if they were victimised by their husbands or partners. The overwhelming aim of the Women's Aid Federation is to empower victims of domestic violence and enable them to determine their own lives and the lives of their children. Each year over 50,000 women and children seek safety in women's aid refuges and many more seek help through telephone support lines such as the National Domestic Violence Help-line, which is also part of the Women's Aid

Federation. Women's Aid is a charity and consequently it must rely on the goodwill of volunteers if it is to survive. This also extends to its funding as it must rely on charitable donations, grants and fundraising for all of its income.

Citizens Advice Bureau: another non-statutory volunteer agency which seeks to help victims of crime, amongst others, is the Citizens Advice Bureau (CAB). The CAB began as an emergency measure during the second world war and has now evolved into a much relied upon national agency. The CAB deals with around six million queries per year on a wide range of issues such as:

- benefits
- debt
- consumer issues
- legal issues
- homelessness
- immigration.

There are over 2,000 CABs in England, Wales and Northern Ireland staffed with almost 25,000 workers of whom 20,000 are unpaid volunteers. Like many other agencies in the non-statutory sector they are almost entirely dependent on government grants and charitable donations for their continued survival. The CAB also acts as a social policy lobby group. As the CAB sees so many problems faced by the public each year they are well placed to advise the government on changes to law and policy which would make the lives of citizens easier. They can help victims of crime by referring them to legal agencies such as the police or helping them find a civil or criminal solicitor to help represent them. They can also refer people to the witness service and victim support and give expert advice to victims on their legal rights.

Rape Crisis: the first rape crisis centre was established in London in 1976 as a response to the fact that female victims of rape and sexual assault were often treated unfairly by the police and criminal justice system, even to the extent of being blamed for causing the attack upon them. There are now many rape crisis centres around the country operating 'drop in' centres and telephone support and providing legal and medical information in a safe and emotionally supportive environment.

Statutory public services

In your assignment you are required to discuss statutory public services, such as the emergency and armed services and detail the services they provide to groups of citizens. You are also required to explain the roles and responsibilities of these services. You will find this information in Unit 8 The Uniformed Services which should be combined with the information detailed above on non-statutory public services to provide you with the information you need to complete your assessment.

Assessment activity 4-P5, 4-M3 and 4-D3

You have been asked to produce a magazine for your local community which is colourful and engaging and describes the services provided to individuals and groups of citizens by statutory and non-statutory public services. You must also detail the roles and responsibilities of the services and make a note of the differences between them in terms of their relationships with the public and each other, the consequences of what they do and the influence they have.

In order to get a **merit** your magazine must *analyse* the services provided to individuals and groups and the need for such services to exist.

In order to get a **distinction** your magazine must *critically analyse* the services provided to individuals and groups and *justify* the need for these services.

How citizens can effect change

Citizens acting individually and as groups can effect change at local, national and international levels. This may involve campaigning against the construction of a communications mast in a local area, protesting against unfair taxes nationally or taking action to halt the third world debt internationally.

Citizens who are over the age of 18 and who are not long term prisoners also have the right to vote in local, national and European elections. Political parties offer voters a manifesto every five years. The manifesto contains details of what the political party aims to do if they are elected to office. The main UK parties are:

- Labour
- Conservative
- Liberal Democrat.

Theory into practice

Log on to one of the political party's web sites and see if you can find their most recent manifesto. What were their main promises for the last election and how would these promises have effected change?

An informed citizen can effect change by reading the manifestos of the parties and voting according to whom they think will build the best society for them. In addition, political parties play a vital role in preserving democracy because they are constantly in opposition to each other and monitoring and commenting on each other's performance.

Pressure groups

Citizens bonding together to promote social change can often develop into official reform or pressure groups as described earlier. Some of the most prominent pressure groups in the UK today are shown in Figure 4.12 below.

Theory into practice

As a group try to find a poster or flyer about as many of the groups listed in Figure 4.12 as you can. Create a wall display with what you collect.

Although individuals can and do effect change across the world, citizens often have more success when they team together to work towards a particular goal. It is easier for a government or an organisation to ignore an individual than a group with hundreds or thousands of members (or in the case of Amnesty International over 1,000,000). Social and economic change has to start somewhere and usually it begins with concerned citizens.

Function	Organisation
Animal Rights	Hunt Saboteurs Association Compassion in World Farming Countryside Alliance
Civil Liberties and Human Rights	Amnesty International Liberty Campaign for Freedom of Information Human Rights Commission
Constitutional Reform Groups	Charter 88 Direct Votes
Disability	Mind Royal National Institute for Blind
Environment	Greenpeace Friends of the Earth
Sexual Orientation	Stonewall Outrage

Figure 4.12 Pressure groups in the UK

How the public services can effect change

Statutory and voluntary public services can be just as effective as individuals and groups in changing society for the better and improving the lives of citizens. They do this in a variety of ways:

- they fulfil the roles and responsibilities that are allocated to them and by doing this they help and support the community.
- they can act as a pressure group to change government policy or influence how the government approaches a particular social issue.
- they can campaign for more resources to be deployed in dealing with particular issues.
- they can influence and advise governments on changes to the law or the introduction of new laws.
- they have a closer relationship with the public and are often very well informed about what the public want or need – this information can be passed on to the government who can use the information to best effect.
- they have specialist knowledge and skills which may be used by the state to secure change.
- they can bring to light hidden issues which wouldn't otherwise be known about.

Case study

The 'just one click' report issued by the non-statutory public service Barnardo's in February 2004 highlighted the sexual abuse of children taking place on the Internet, including children being sold to paedophiles and being forced to engage in sexual conduct for the purposes of being watched on the Internet. The report calls on the government to trace the children involved in such abuse so that they can be protected and offered support and counselling to help them deal with the consequences of their ordeal. It also calls upon third generation mobile phone companies to regulate how their phones are used to pass digital images.

1. How have Barnardo's effected change in this instance?
2. How likely is it that the 'just one click' report will be actioned by the government and phone companies? Explain your answer.
3. Why are Barnardo's well placed to find out about issues such as this?
4. Why are Barnardo's more concerned with finding the victims of abuse than finding the offenders?

Case study

The 43 UK police services in England and Wales effect change every day simply by fulfilling their day-to-day operational roles and responsibilities. However, sometimes they are forced to deal with an incident which has wide reaching repercussions across the services, such as the loss of 19 cockle pickers in Morecambe Bay in February 2004. The incident and subsequent police investigation highlighted the use of illegal migrant labour and the dangerous conditions these people are forced to endure in order to earn a wage.

1. How could the police bring about changes in the way migrant labour is used as a result of their investigation?
2. Why does it take an incident like this to bring to the government's attention issues which are potentially dangerous?
3. What other ways will the police have changed the situation by conducting an investigation?

Assessment activity 4-P6

Produce a 200-word report which explains how the statutory and non-statutory public services effect change and the roles of groups, personnel and information on the changes that take place. Provide two case studies which support your report and show how the public services bring about change.

End of unit test

1 What is legal citizenship?

2 What are the types of legal citizenship available to be applied for?

3 What is the right of abode?

4 What is political literacy?

5 What is social and moral responsibility?

6 Describe two political views on citizenship?

7 Describe the kinds of rights which an individual is entitled to.

8 What is the difference between statutory and non-statutory public services?

9 What qualities do good citizens display?

10 What is the difference between an active and a passive citizen?

11 What are the main provisions of the Human Rights Act 1998?

12 How do the Army define citizenship?

13 What is the role of the individual in bringing about change?

14 What is the role of the public services in bringing about change?

15 How do the services promote respect for equal opportunities?

16 How do environmental issues such as global warming have an impact on the public services?

17 How do social issues such as unemployment and poverty have an impact on the public services?

18 What types of groups in society are the public services likely to encounter in their day-to-day operations?

19 Why is it important that the public services respect different cultural and ethnic groups in society?

20 Why are good citizens prized by the public services as potential recruits?

Resources

Desmoyers-Davis T *Citizenship in Modern Britain* 2001 London: Cavendish Publishing

Steele P *Citizenship* 2002 London: Evans Brothers

Mason D *Race and Ethnicity in Modern Britain* 2000 2nd ed Oxford: Oxford University Press

Gray D et al *National Diploma in Public Services –* Book 1 2004 London: Heinemann

Foster S *Citizenship in Focus – Democracy in Action* 2003 London: Harper Collins

Foster S *Citizenship in Focus – Global Concerns* 1999 London: Harper Collins

Foster S *Citizenship in Focus – Human Rights* 1999 London: Harper Collins

West K *Citizenship in Focus – The Citizens and the Law* 1999 London: Harper Collins

Dobson A *Citizenship and the Environment* 2003 Oxford: Oxford University Press

Heater D *What is Citizenship* 1999 London: Polity Press

Holden-Rowley T and Blewitt J *AS Citizenship* 2004 London: Hodder Arnold H&S

Thorpe T (ed) *Young Citizens Passport 9th ed* 2004 London: Hodder Headline

DIVERSITY IN THE PUBLIC SERVICES

Introduction to Unit 5

This chapter is essential to anyone considering a career in the public services as a key focus of the public services is to reflect an awareness of equality and diversity, not only in employment and recruitment of new employees but also in all their dealing with the public. This unit will give you an insight into how Britain became a multicultural society and an understanding of the different religions found in Britain and across the world. It will help you understand why people have different beliefs and values and why these people have completely different lifestyles, which include the things they eat and the way they dress. You will also explore the kinds of support groups found in your local area which can offer services to a diverse range of people and interests.

You will explore discrimination and stereotyping and see how the law tries to prosecute those who do discriminate. The final focus of the unit is how the public services deal with the legal requirements of these acts and how they promote good practice through work policies and procedures and ultimately what they are doing to create a diverse workforce.

Assessment

Throughout the unit, activities and tasks will help you to learn and remember information. Case studies are included to add industry relevance to the topics and learning objectives. You are reminded that when you are completing activities and tasks, opportunities will be created to enhance your key skills evidence. After completing this unit you should have an understanding of the following outcomes.

Outcomes

1 Investigate **multiculturalism** in the public services
2 Investigate the term **diversity** in the context of the local community
3 Describe the **role of public services** and its duty to provide equality of service to all members of the community
4 Explore the **policies and procedures** that have been introduced to address cultural issues.

Multiculturalism

Multiculturalism has two meanings. The first is simply that society is composed of people with a variety of cultural backgrounds. Secondly, it means that it is desirable that people from different backgrounds are treated equally.

Equality of treatment means not necessarily treating people the same but treating people with an equal level of respect. This means that people should have equal access to services such as education and training, employment, housing and protection from crime.

Think about it

1 List as many different groups who live in modern Britain as you can.
2 Identify some of the differences in lifestyle between the white majority and some of the groups you have identified.
3 Think of examples of how 'treating people the same' could lead to unfairness.

Britain is a very diverse society (diverse simply means composed of people from many different groups.) It is composed of people who have many different cultures. Britain has always been a racially and culturally mixed society. It is a nation populated by people from different countries and who immigrated as long ago as the Bronze Age (5,000 years ago). This early immigration was followed by invasions and occupation by Romans, Celts, Saxons, Vikings and Normans who have all settled in Britain to live. Immigration still continues in Britain today with refugees from Eastern Europe and Africa arriving steadily.

Many groups of people in modern Britain do not share the same physical characteristics, values, customs or beliefs as the dominant white English groups who are descended from a mixture of races and groups from centuries of migration. Minority groups are often seen negatively by the dominant group which has led to disadvantage and discrimination for these groups. In recent years, successive governments have passed laws to make Britain a more inclusive society, which celebrates the cultural differences between its citizens and ensures all citizens enjoy equal opportunity. The public services need to reflect this commitment to equal opportunities for all citizens in all aspects of their work

Development of a multi-cultural Britain

The main cause of cultural diversity has been immigration into the UK. Key periods of migration to Britain are:

- from 1933–1939 3,960,000 European Jews settled in the United Kingdom along with 80,000 refugees from central Europe due to the rise of Adolf Hitler and the development of the Nazi state in Germany.
- mid 1950s to early 1960s saw the immigration of non-white people from the Commonwealth, in particular the Caribbean, India and Pakistan, due to labour shortages in the UK as a result of the economic boom during the post war period.
- 1990s wars and persecution have seen new group of immigrants fleeing from countries such as Afghanistan and Croatia. They have come to seek political asylum in the UK.

Immigrants from Germany arriving in the UK in the 1930s

Theory into practice

1. In what way were the reasons for coming to the UK different for the groups listed above?
2. From the 1930s–1990s, many people have emigrated from the UK. Which countries have many people gone to and why have they left the UK?
3. Find a copy of Social Trends or look up figures on a Government web site and discover what the net migration is (numbers entering/leaving each year) at the current time.

After the Second World War, there was a general feeling of goodwill between Britain and the Commonwealth countries due to the war effort made by citizens of the Commonwealth. This was further reflected in the 1948 British Nationality Act, which stated that all Commonwealth citizens were free to enter Britain, to find work and settle with their families. This meant that by the late 1950s, hundreds of thousands of people from black commonwealth countries had settled in Britain to try and gain a better standard of living. They came to fill mainly low paid jobs such as cleaning, catering and transport which were seen as undesirable jobs to many existing white citizens.

The arrival of large numbers of people who were physically and culturally different led to fear among the white population and race riots broke out in Notting Hill in London in 1958. This led to a series of Immigration Acts designed to strictly control the number of immigrants who are racially and culturally different from the white majority:

- Commonwealth Immigrants Act 1962 reduced the migrants from the commonwealth by only allowing in people who had skills in short supply.
- Immigration Act 1981 tightened up conditions further by limiting rights of families and partners to automatically enter the UK.
- 1991 saw the beginning of stringent checks on people claiming refugee status.
- Asylum and Immigration Appeals Act 1993 led to asylum seekers being held in detention centres until their claim was processed.
- fines in 2000 were introduced for lorry drivers smuggling asylum seekers into Britain.

These Acts reflect the problems our society has had in accommodating people from different cultures. In the 1960s, Enoch Powell, a conservative MP, made his famous 'rivers of blood' speech which he believed summed up the concerns of the people at that time. He called for the repatriation (return to the country of birth, citizenship, or origin) of all coloured immigrants who had settled in Britain.

Think about it

Do you think immigration controls are designed to control the numbers entering the UK or to exclude certain types of immigrants?

Theory into practice

Identify some of the problems in the following countries of origin which have caused asylum seekers to flee. What are your views about asylum seekers?

- Iraq
- Afghanistan
- Somalia
- Zimbabwe
- China
- Sri Lanka
- Turkey
- Pakistan
- Federal Republic of Yugoslavia
- Czech Republic

Cultural diversity in Britain today

As a result of the patterns of immigration discussed above, the government now collects data on people of ethnic minority origin. The main ethnic categories used by the Home office are outlined in the figures below.

1991 Census shows the UK population as follows:

White	93.3%
Black Caribbean	0.9%
Black African	0.7%
Indian	1.6%
Pakistani	1.2%
Bangladeshi	0.5%
Chinese	0.2%
Other groups	1.1%

Source: *Crown copyright material is reproduced with the permission of the Controller of HMSO and the Queen's Printer for Scotland.*

Time line of immigration since First World War

Roots of the Future; Ethnic Diversity in the Making of Britain – Commission for Racial Equality, 1996

1914–8	First World War. Influx from dominions, colonies and occupied Belgium. German businesses in Britain are confiscated and all German residents interned.
1920	Greek-Cypriot settlement begins.
1933	Hitler becomes Chancellor in Germany. Persecution of German Jews begins.
1936	Spanish Civil War brings refugees.
1938	Government tightens controls on emigrates.
1939	Second World War. Soldiers and workers from all over the Empire are stationed in Britain, including US troops, and 100,000 Poles fighting under British command. All Germans resident in Britain are interned or deported.
1940	Mussolini declares war against the UK on 10 June and all Italians resident in Britain are interned or deported.
1943	There are 114,000 refugees in Britain.
1945	End of the war. Polish refugees and their families choose to settle in Britain.
1947	European Volunteer Workers Scheme introduced to help with post-war reconstruction.
1948	SS Empire Windrush brings the first West Indian immigrants to Britain.
1950	Immigration from the Commonwealth begins. Encouragement of immigration from Ireland, West Indies, South Asia, Italy and Cyprus.
1962	Commonwealth Immigrants Act.
1968	British Asians are expelled from Kenya and many settle in Britain.
1972	British Asians are expelled from Uganda, many settle in Britain.
1974	Turkish invasion of Cyprus brings refugees to Britain.
1976	Race Relations Act passed and the Commission for Racial Equality established. British Asians from Malawi settle in Britain.
1979	Vietnamese refugees arrive in Britain.
1981	British Nationality Act is passed.
1980s	Somali, Kurdish and Tamil refugees arrive in Britain.
1993	Asylum and Immigration Appeals Act is passed.

This means that around 7% of the population may be categorised as an ethnic minority. Well over half of these groups are people who have been born in the UK and many of them have made a substantial contribution to the life of Britain and have enriched areas such as industry and commerce (textiles), sport and music.

Think about it

How many of your favourite performers and sportsmen are black or Asian?

Case study

Nasser Hussain made his debut against the West Indies in 1989 at the age of 21 years and his highest batting score was against Australia when he blasted a double century. Since taking over from Alec Stewart in July 1999, Hussain established himself as one of the most successful captains in British History. Under Hussain, England won four Test series in a row for the first time since Mark Brearley and rose to third place in the ICC Test Championship table after being ninth.

Nasser Hussain

Case study

Sulzeer Jeremiah (Sol) Campbell made his debut against Republic of Ireland in February 1995 at the age of 20 and has since made over 50 appearances for England most of which have been in the starting line up and has been impressive in all major championships since the World Cup in France in 1998. He is deemed by many to be the best defender in English Football along with his England team-mate Rio Ferdinand. In his first season at Arsenal, he helped Arsenal to win both the league championship and FA Cup.

Sol Campbell

Think about it

In spite of their considerable contribution to society, members of ethnic minority groups are sometimes seen as inferior citizens who don't quite 'belong'. Consider the following 2 examples:

- the Cantle report which looked into the causes of the Burnley, Bradford and Oldham riots recommended that all immigrants be required to swear an 'oath of allegiance' to Britain.
- Home Secretary David Blunkett in response to the above race riots suggest that immigrants should be required to speak English and ethnic minorities should be encouraged to become 'more British'.

These comments seem to suggest that minorities should become more integrated into the society and appear less different. Do your think these suggestions are reasonable? How might these requirements affect the identity of minorities?

Assessment activity 5-P1

Summarise the history which has made Britain a multicultural society

Religious and cultural beliefs

While the first part of this unit has focused on the reason for Britain being a multicultural society, there are other forms of diversity which link with ethnicity and cut across these divisions. Being a multicultural society means recognising other religious and cultural differences as well as ethnic differences.

Each society has its own culture which includes the beliefs, customs, norms (or rules for behaviour) and values. While these are influenced by religion, they are also influenced by our national or even local culture. Cultural differences range from language to rules on marriage and from attitudes to women to the clothes people wear.

The UK supports freedom of worship with many religions crossing ethnic and cultural barriers. An understanding of religion in all its forms will help the public services address cultural issues which may cause conflict and misunderstanding in society both in the public at large and damage the relationship between the services and the public. The main faiths in Britain today are:

- Christianity
- Hindu
- Islam
- Sikh
- Jewish
- Jain
- Buddhist
- Zoroastrian
- Baha'I

The UK of the 21st century is a modern dynamic environment in which the public services must be equipped to deal with a variety of faiths, beliefs, religion and culture. Not only in their official capacity in dealing with the public but also as employers who must comply with the law and should have the best interests of their employees at heart.

It is vitally important that the cultural and religious diversity in the UK is understood and appreciated by the public services as it can have a tremendous impact on their day-to-day operation. This is because religion is a major influence on people's lives and has a profound impact on lifestyle, dress, diet and celebrations.

Christianity

Christianity developed in the Middle East and is in excess of 2,000 years old. Christians believe in one God and that God revealed himself to mankind through the bible and through his son Jesus Christ, who was crucified as part of God's plan for redeeming the sins of all mankind. Our day-to-day lives are affected by the Christian calendar as Christian festivals often reflect the holiday periods and school calendar.

Christianity is worshipped in a church

Christianity is divided into 4 principal denominations each with unique practices and differences:

- Orthodox
- Pentecostal
- Protestant
- Catholic

There are approximately 2 billion Christians globally and in the UK around 40 million people claim an allegiance with the Christian faith (Weller 1997).

Hinduism

Hinduism is used to describe the ancient religious culture of India. The word Hindu was first used by the Arabs to describe people who lived beyond the River Indus valley. It has about 750 million followers and is dominant in areas such as India and Nepal. It is over 5,000 years old but has neither a single founder, nor a single scripture. It has the Bhagavad Gita (the lords song) and Hindus worship many gods. They believe in the notion of reincarnation and that behaviour in life determines your status in the next world.

Islam

Islam has links with Christianity and Judaism. Islam means 'submission' or 'surrender' and followers of Islam are called Muslims. Muslims who adhere to the Islamic faith believe that Allah is the unique and only God, and that the prophet Muhammad was Allah's final messenger on Earth (born in Mecca about 570 years AD). The Qur'an and Sunnah together provide an authoritative source for Muslim law. Their faith also demands that they bear witness to their faith, pray 5 times daily, fast in the holy month of Ramadan, pay alms to the poor annually and take a pilgrimage to Mecca (the Hajj) once in their lifetime.

Muslims must abide by a restricted dress code. Both males and females are required to dress modestly and from puberty women are required to cover their hair and wear loose clothing which conceals the shape of their body. Islam also imposes dietary restrictions. Only halal food may

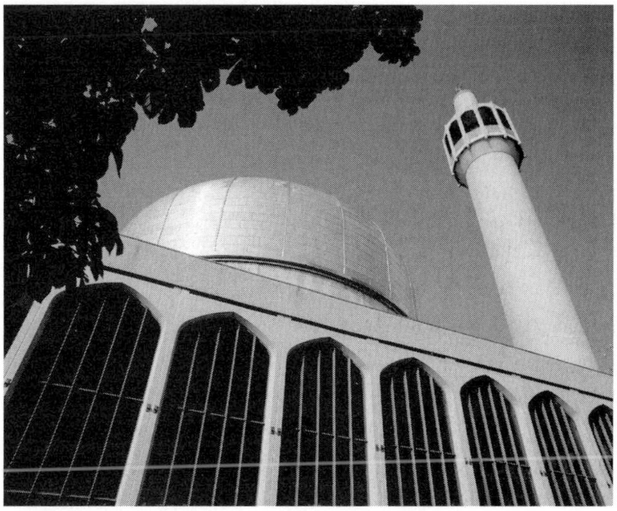
The Islamic place of worship is in a mosque

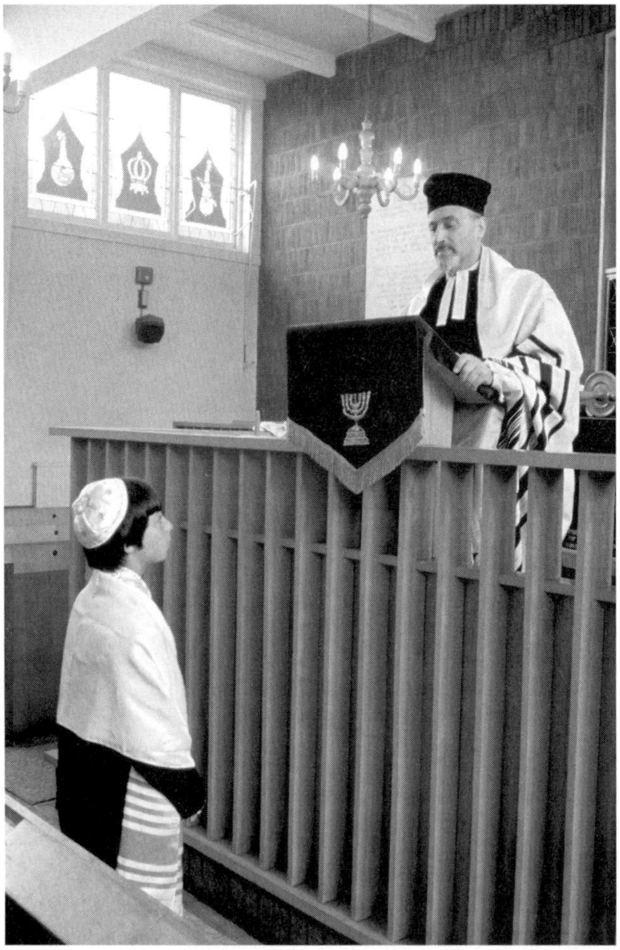

Judaism is practiced in a synagogue

be eaten by Islamic law which requires that animals are slaughtered by a trained person in the name of God. In addition, pork and alcohol are strictly prohibited.

Judaism

This is the oldest monotheistic religion (belief in one God) which originated in the Middle East. Christianity developed from a Jewish sect based in Jerusalem.

According to the Torah, the central scripture for Jews, God is holy and unmitigated. The rules and traditions an observant Jew follows are known as the Halakha (the path), which come from the first five books in the Bible (the Pentateuch or Torah). These were given to Moses on Mount Sinai over three thousand years ago. They contain the famous 'ten commandments' and another 603 dealing with the rules for living and sharing society with others.

Jews have specific dietary requirements. They must eat 'kosher' food which means that only certain kinds of meat and fish are available to them and meat must be prepared in a ritually accepted manner. As with Islam and Sikhism, pork is strictly forbidden. The dress code for practising Jews require that women dress modestly and that men keep their head covered at all times with a skull cap (often called a kippah or yarmulke).

Sikhism

Sikhism is around 500 years old and emerged as a result of the teachings of Guru Nanak in India 1469 CE. Guru Nanak's aim was to encourage all people to faithfully worship one god with the idea of individuals helping humanity. The ultimate aim of a practising Sikh is to build a close and loving relationship with God. Like Hindus, Sikh's also believe in the eternal cycle of rebirth. The nine gurus who succeeded him then further developed the fundamental aims of the religion. The last Guru declared that after him, there would be no other gurus as the Sikh holy book would be viewed as the eternal guru.

Sikh dietary restrictions forbid smoking and the consumption of alcohol and many Sikhs are vegetarian although it is not compulsory. If Sikhs do choose to eat meat, the cow is considered to be sacred and is not eaten and the pig is considered unclean and therefore not fit for human consumption. The dress code for Sikhs is very specific. Men must wear a turban to cover their uncut hair and the 'five k's' must be worn about their person:

1 kesh – uncut hair covered by a turban
2 kangah – comb
3 kacha – shorts
4 kara – metal bracelet
5 kirpan – ceremonial dagger

Buddhism

Buddhism is more than 2,500 years old and has more than 2,000 sects with around 655 million practicing Buddhists worldwide. It is a major cultural influence in China and about ¾ of Japanese people are Buddhists. It developed in North India around the 6th century BC, when Siddharthe Gautama attained 'enlightenment' – the ultimate truth by which people are freed from the cycle of re-birth. He became the Buddha (enlightened one).

> **Theory into practice**
>
> Choose a religion that has been mentioned during this chapter and create a fact sheet that highlights how the religious and cultural beliefs and norms may differ from your own. Consider the following areas of research for your fact sheet: dietary requirements, hygiene, prayer, dress/jewellery, names, festivals, religious signs and symbols and origin and their beliefs.

Religion	Membership	Deity	Holy text	Main holidays	Diet	Dress	Place of worship
Christianity	2 billion	God (monotheistic)	Bible New Testament	• Easter • Christmas	No specific restrictions	No specific restrictions	Church
Islam	1 billion +	Allah (monotheistic)	Qur'an	• Eid-Ul-Fitr • Eid-Ul-Adha	• Halal food • No pork • No alcohol	Modest dress, women must cover hair with head scarf	Mosque
Hinduism	750 million	Brahman (polytheistic)	Holy scriptures Mahabarata Vedas Upanishadas	• Deepawal	• Beef forbidden • Many Hindus are vegetarian	No specific restrictions	No specific place – worship is a private matter but there are Hindu temples
Sikhism	22.5 million	God (9 gurus)	Granth Sahib	• Divali • Vaisakhi Birth of: • Guru Nanak • Guru Gobind • Singh	• Tobacco and alcohol are forbidden • Pork banned	Men must wear turban 5 K'S	Gurdwara
Judaism	18 million	God (monotheistic)	Old Testament Talmud	• Yom kippur • Passover • Rosh Hashana	• Kosher food • Pork forbidden	Modest dress Skull cap for men	Synagogue
Buddhism	665 million	No deity Worship of Buddha – the Enlightened one	Buddha's teachings	• Wiesak • Dharma Day • Sangha Day • Parinirvana Day	• No specific rules	No specific rules	Temple

Figure 5.1 A summary of the main faiths and their cultures

Think about it

For each of the main ethnic groups listed below, make a simple chart in order to identify the following:

Country/ies of origin, religion and any other feature of their lifestyle of which you are aware is different from mainstream white culture.

- Black Caribbean
- Black African
- Indian
- Pakistani
- Bangladeshi
- Chinese
- Other groups

Think about it

Think of one other European country. Identify as many differences in culture as you can between that country and Britain.

Think about it

Are there any special customs or celebrations which take part regularly in your local community?

Are there any special foods associated with your area?

Lack of knowledge

In a multi cultural society, we are encouraged to respect differences in culture, providing the behaviour is not against the law. However, many people lack knowledge about the customs and norms of other cultures which can lead to stereotyping, prejudice and even discrimination.

Stereotyping

Stereotyping involves making assumptions about people based purely on superficial characteristics such as appearance. Groups of people are perceived to have common characteristics, which are often negative. For example, young men in groups are likely to be looking for trouble or blondes are dumb. Stereotyping is often negative but not always, as in the common assumption that black people are good at sport. Stereotypes are commonly made when we have very little understanding of the group of people in question and are frequently used in the media to whip up feelings about a group. For example, skinheads may be portrayed as violent right wing fascists and hooligans.

Prejudice

Prejudice means to prejudge. Prejudices usually come from stereotypes which lead people to believe something about another on no sound basis. Prejudice is a way of dehumanising others who are different from ourselves. Probably all of us are prejudiced about some group but not all of us discriminate against that group – treat people differently because of our views.

Discrimination

Discrimination means behaving differently, usually unfairly, to a group of people. Discrimination is the result of a prejudice combined with a power. It can lead to problems for those who are discriminated against in every area of life, for example, obtaining a decent education, obtaining a job and even receiving the right medical attention.

Think about it

Man A and Man B share the same prejudice that female drivers are poor drivers when compared with men. Man A works as a lawyer in the city and often shares this opinion with his colleagues over lunch. Man B is a driving examiner and has a very low pass rate for female drivers as he sets a higher test standard for them. While both are prejudiced, Man B has a power to turn his prejudice into discrimination.

What effect may discrimination have on those who experience it?

Think about it

What groups in modern Britain are likely to be the subject of prejudice?

Discrimination law

In order to prevent racism, sexism and other forms of prejudice taking hold and creating injustice and social division, the law has changed over the last fifty years. The government has introduced a series of acts to try to prevent various forms of discrimination and to try to ensure all members of society have equal opportunities in key areas. While it is impossible to legislate against prejudice, it is possible to try and prevent people acting on their prejudices and acting unfairly. The law aims to protect social groups that have historically been less able than others to obtain a fair share of opportunities, rewards and benefits that society has to offer. These groups that suffer from inequality are women, minority ethnic groups, gays and lesbians and the disabled.

Turn to page 50 in the Citizenship unit for details of Equal Opportunities legislation.

Cross cultural communication

Given the cultural diversity of Britain, public service workers need to be aware of the basics of good communication whether face to face, by telephone or by email.

Language

Language is an obvious barrier for minorities for whom English is not their first language but even when people are speaking English, there can be problems with terminology used (slang words and phrases), body language and different levels of directness. There are a number of other languages spoken in Britain such as, Chinese, Hindu or Punjabi, Urdu and Bengali. One of the ways the public services can communicate with a diverse community is through specialised multilingual publications such as posters, leaflets and multi media.

Think about it

You will be unlikely to be expected to learn another language to be a member of the public services but think about which services employ translators and interpreters to help communicate effectively with non–English speakers.

Theory into practice

As a group, visit your local council offices or other public service building and collect examples of multilingual publications. Create a display board that can be placed in a public area of your college to make other students aware of the ways we communicate with others.

Non verbal communication

Non verbal communication involves all actions which accompany communication. Many of these have a recognised meaning and are used intentionally to send meaning through signs. In addition, deaf people often use sign language to communicate.

When we are communicating with others we should be aware of the gestures we make, our tone of voice, our movement and facial expressions.

Think about it

How would you convey the following through body signals:

- amusement
- surprise
- shock
- disbelief
- anger.

Body language refers to the whole way in which a person's body is behaving and can tell us a great deal about someone's state of mind. For example, a nervous person is likely to fidget, pinch or tug their flesh and a defensive person is likely to cross their arms and avoid eye contact. These can be valuable signs for a police officer to look out for when interviewing a person they suspect of a crime.

Some people estimate that between 60–80% of a communicated message is communicated through non-verbal communication.

Other examples of non-verbal communication include:

Making direct eye contact	Friendly, sincere, self-confident, assertive.
Shaking head	Disagreeing, shocked, disbelieving.
Smiling	Contented, understanding, encouraging.
Biting the lip	Nervous, fearful, anxious.
Folding arms	Angry, disapproving, disagreeing, defensive, aggressive.
Leaning forward	Attentive, interested.
Shifting in seat	Restless, bored, nervous, apprehensive.
Having erect posture	Self-confident, assertive.

Diversity

So far, we have established that Britain is a diverse community and we will shortly look at the compositions of a local community. Firstly, we will look at what diversity means to the public services and why it is important.

The word diversity to the public services simply means 'difference'. This difference is not only about racial and gender differences, but all differences found in a community and all the differences that affect the delivery of a quality service.

This means the public services must acknowledge differences and apply flexibility when fulfilling their duties to meet the relevant needs of all the community.

How the local community is made up

Communities in Britain vary considerably in their composition in terms of age, class, ethnicity and employment. A good way of finding out about the composition of your local area is by looking at the national census. This is carried out every 10 years and the last one was completed in April 2001. The national census is the only survey which provides a detailed picture of the entire population and covers the following areas: population, health, housing, employment, transport and ethnic groups. The following example shows you the type of information you will need to find out.

Profile of a local community

Rotherham in South Yorkshire

- The population of Rotherham has decreased by 2.2% over the last ten years whilst the UK population has risen by 2.4%.
- The average age of the population of Rotherham is 38.6 years of age.
- There are 248,179 people living in the Rotherham borough, 120,694 are male whilst 127,482 are female.
- 55.1% of the local population over 16 are either married or re-married whilst 25.71% have never been married.
- 36.78% of the population of Rotherham do not have any formal qualifications whilst the national average is 29.1%.
- 11.5% of the population of Rotherham have degrees whilst the national average is 19.8%.
- The unemployment rate for Rotherham is 3.9% whilst the national average is 3.4%. When broken down further the unemployment rate for men is 5.2% and the unemployment rate for women is 2.8%.

- 14.5% of the population in Rotherham are retired whilst the national average is 13.6%.
- The top 3 industries for employment in Rotherham are manufacturing 20.2%, wholesale and retail trade 18.8% and health and social work 11.42%.
- The percentage of people in Rotherham born within the UK is 97.40% and the size of Rotherham's ethnic minority communities is 3.1% (7,712 people) whilst the national average is 8.7%.
- The largest ethnic group within Rotherham is Pakistani at 1.9% (4,704 people) and the next largest is Indian at 0.2% (497 people).
- 79.4% of the population are Christians, whilst 10.22% stated that they were not religious and next was Muslim with 2.18%.
- There are 1,234 people in nursing homes or residential care.
- 49.03% of the people in Rotherham live in semi-detached houses and 20% live in either terraced or detached houses.
- 65.35% of people own their own house and 34.65% rent.
- lone parent households make up 6.8% of the housing market.
- 13.1% of the population travel to work by public transport, whilst 71.3% of households in Rotherham own one or more cars.

Source: *National Census 2001*

Theory into practice

Using your research skills, compare Rotherham with your local area. How does the composition of your area differ from Rotherham?

Assessment activity 5-P2

Conduct research on your local community to establish its composition such as ethnicity, age, gender and present your findings in graph format. Identify their needs and the support available to them.

Support groups

The following support groups you will find in most communities as they have many branches spread across the country. However, these are just a few of the agencies that support the needs of various groups. There are many more including unique local services in your area which meet the needs of a certain group of people or to tackle an issue in your local community.

Citizens Advice Bureau

Citizens Advice Bureau (CAB) is an advice-giving agency but it is also attempts to identify the underlying issues which may give rise to problems. The aims of CAB are to ensure that individuals do not suffer, through lack of knowledge, loss of their rights and responsibilities in all areas of life or suffer through an inability to express their needs effectively and equally.

The most common issues that a CAB advice worker is likely to deal with are employment issues, housing problems, immigration laws, consumer debt and matrimonial disputes. The service they offer is independent and confidential advice, which is impartial and free. A CAB advice worker mainly gives information or advice, but may negotiate or represent a client, could act as a mediator in a dispute or refer the client to expert advice, for example a solicitor.

Age Concern

Age Concern is concerned with the needs and aspirations of older people and is the leading authority on age related issues. Age Concern helps older people to continue living independent lives, promotes the role of older people to enable them

Age Concern helps older people to continue living independently

to influence the issues that directly affect them and highlights the experience and skills older people can still offer local communities and society as a whole.

Age Concern also conduct a range of activities/ services to meet the need of older people such as information, advice and advocacy services, day centres and lunch clubs, shops, drop-in and leisure centres, IT and other training activities, home visits and a national call centre. The aim of Age Concern is to ensure that the voices of older people are heard by policy makers and to make certain that the diverse needs of older people are reflected in its services.

Victim Support

Victim Support is the national charity for people affected by crime. It is a completely independent organisation, offering a free and confidential service to over 1 million people a year. Their staff and volunteers are trained to provide emotional support, information and practical help to people who have suffered the effects of crime ranging from burglary to the murder of a relative.

Staff and volunteers are also trained to provide support and information about the court process to witnesses, victims and their families, before, during and after the trial. The service also runs a witness service to support witnesses in every criminal court in England and Wales.

Victim Support has the following primary objectives: to provide support and assistance to individual victims, witnesses, their families and friends and to raise public awareness and recognition of the effects of crime and promote victim's rights.

Scope

Scope is a charity whose focus it is to support people with cerebral palsy. Their aim is to help disabled people achieve equality in a society so that they are valued and have the same rights as everyone else.

Scope's services focus on four main areas where disabled people face the greatest inequality: early years, education, daily living and work. They also provide local support services, which respond to the needs identified by disabled people in their areas. The local support service will offer information, advice and support to disabled people and their families and work with local groups to encourage the development of new and existing services which meet needs identified locally.

Sure Start

Sure Start is a government funded scheme to improve the health and well-being of families and children before and after birth. It does this by setting up local programmes to improve services for families with children and is the cornerstone of

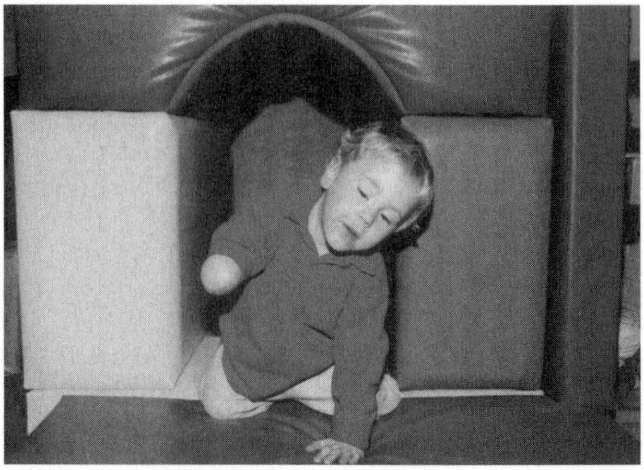
Scope is a charity which supports people with special needs

the Government's drive to tackle child poverty and social exclusion. Sure Start programmes are concentrated in neighbourhoods where a high proportion of children are living in poverty.

By 2004, there will be over 500 Sure Start programmes helping up to 400,000 children living in disadvantaged areas. Local programmes work with parents and parents-to-be to provide better access to family support and advice on nurturing, health services and early learning. They also provide support for children and parents with special needs.

Mind

Established in 1946, Mind has grown into the leading mental health charity in England and Wales. Mind works to provide a better life for everyone with experience of mental distress by: boosting the ambitions of people with experience of mental distress; promoting inclusion by challenging discrimination; influencing policy through campaigning and education and achieving equal civil and legal rights through campaigning and education.

On a local level they offer many services around the country including supported housing, crisis helplines, drop-in centres, counselling, befriending, advocacy, employment and training schemes.

Samaritans

The role of the Samaritans is to offer support in any way they can. There are 203 branches across the country for people to come in and talk face-to-face with trained volunteers about their problems as well as 24-hour telephone support where people are allowed to explore their feelings by being listened to in confidence without prejudice.

> ***Theory into practice***
>
> Visit your nearest town and list 10 agencies that can be found in the locality that offer support to the local community.

Role of public services

As the public services are providing essential support to the communities they serve, it is essential that they provide equality of service to the diverse groups within the communities they serve. For example, at the 1998 Labour Party Conference in Blackpool the former Home Secretary Jack Straw set out his vision for the police service: 'a police service which was representative of the community, working in partnership with the community, for the benefit of all sections of the community. A service, which is part of the community, not apart from it'. He said that he 'wanted Government to be a beacon of racial equality and opportunity' and that he would be 'bringing forward recruitment targets for the police, fire, prison and probation services and the Home Office itself.'

Racism in the police force

While all branches of the public services need to strive to provide an equally good service to all sections of society, the police are probably the best example of how strategic aims and objectives are being used to meet the needs of the communities. This is partly because the Macpherson report accused the police of being 'institutionally racist'. This report was produced in response to the mishandling by the police of the murder of a black teenager, Stephen Lawrence.

As long ago as the early 1980s, the police have been aware that they need to tackle racism. After the Brixton and Toxteth Riots in 1981, The Scarman Report of 1982 stated that: 'there is widespread agreement that the composition of our police force must reflect the makeup of the society they serve. A police force which fails to reflect the ethnic diversity of our society will never succeed in securing the full support of all its sections.'

Case study

Late on 22 April in 1993 an 18-year-old A-level student called Stephen Lawrence and his friend Duwayne Brooks were making their way home after spending the day together.

The boys were rushing to catch a bus in the southeast London suburb of Eltham when they were confronted by a gang of white youths. The gang set upon Stephen while a stunned and helpless Duwayne briefly watched in paralysed silence before he was chased off by one of the white youths.

Driven by fear and adrenaline, Stephen managed to scramble free as Duwayne urged him to 'just run' but he had been beaten badly and was bleeding profusely. He collapsed after 200 yards in a pool of blood and died.

Source: *Extract from A fight for justice: The Stephen Lawrence story – Monday, 22 February 1999, BBC News*

Stephen Lawrence

The Police investigation into the murder of Stephen Lawrence and the Lawrence family's fight for justice highlighted how the police failed to investigate the crime properly and how their failure led to the actual release of the suspects.

Some of the key events that led to the release of the suspects were as follows:

- The Crown Prosecution Service refused to prosecute the five suspects because they didn't have enough evidence.
- Doreen and Neville Lawrence (Stephen's parents) brought about a private prosecution, which was unprecedented at the time. This prosecution failed because of a lack of witnesses. Although many local people came forward with information about the suspects, they were scared of recriminations.
- Duwayne Brooks, who was with Stephen at the time of his murder, was deemed an unreliable witness.

Find out the answers to the following questions:

1. Why were the main suspects never convicted of the murder of Stephen Lawrence?
2. Do you believe that the police were incompetent and racist?
3. How can this be avoided in future?

The Macpherson report

The Macpherson report into police conduct during the murder investigation of the teenager Stephen Lawrence devised a series of 70 recommendations through which society could show a zero tolerance attitude to racism and racist attacks. The report demanded changes across all public bodies such as the police, the judiciary, the NHS and education. The recommendations made by the report revolve around several key areas:

- openness, accountability and the restoration of confidence
- defining racist incidents
- reporting and recording racist incidents
- police practice and the investigation of racist crime
- liaison with families

- treatment of victims and witnesses
- prosecution of racist crimes
- first aid training
- racism awareness and valuing cultural diversity
- employment, discipline and complaints
- stop and search
- recruitment and retention
- the role of education.

In relation to the Macpherson report, it seems the police still have a long way to go. However, they have begun to respond to the Race Relations Act 2000 which was introduced after the report to ensure that the police service are liable for any discrimination by its officers and to create a positive attitude towards race equality.

Responsibilities of the police service

One of the ways that the needs of the community can be met is by creating a more user-friendly service and this has been a priority issue for the police constabularies across England and Wales. Some of the changes that have taken place across the country to create a better police service for its users include:

- **24-hour service** which can be accessed when needed. Many police stations have front counter facilities that are open to the public for longer hours than before and are often staffed by volunteers to help ease the workload of police officers. During the times the front counters are closed an outside telephone link is available at the police station which is connected to a central control room so assistance can still be obtained.
- **Improving the physical accessibility** of all police stations such as
  - clear signposting
  - use of plain English and/or picture symbols
  - wheelchair access
  - disabled toilets
  - automatic doors

A police station

  - dropped and raised kerbing
  - installation of hearing loops
  - minicom systems
  - flashing doorbells and smoke alarms
  - talking police stations
  - low-level front counter
  - Dial-a-Ride.

  It is a legal requirement to meet the needs of disabled people (Disability in Public Places Act 1999)
- **More patrol officers** are on the beat to help police be more involved with the local community and make people feel safer and in some areas local partnerships are paying for street wardens to help combat crime.
- **Better response** times to 999 calls.
- **Communication** is also being improved by the introduction of voicemail systems to ensure follow up and contact is easier to establish and maintain even when officers are not at their desks. The use of email and mobile phones are also being implemented by a number of constabularies.
- **Working with young people** through youth clubs and cadet projects. All police constabularies are actively involved in community groups, which enable discussion of issues of crime and disorder in the area, proved

prevention advice and act as an ideal forum to gain the views of local people with regard to policing issues.

Think about it

Using your knowledge on accessibility, conduct an audit of your college and assess how it caters for the needs of people with disabilities.

Assessment activity 5-P3, 5-P4, 5-M1

Create a short report outlining how one local service such as police, fire or ambulance has become more user friendly and accessible to all sections of the community.

Create a visual display including images and pictures that shows how accessibility has been improved to allow greater integration by the whole community.

In order to get a **merit** your report must analyse and evaluate the 'user-friendly' service provided by your chosen public service.

Policies and procedures

The public services provide many policies and procedures for creating and promoting diversity and equality within the workplace.

Community forums

One of the ways policies are implemented are through community forums. The Police Commission recommended that forums be established in which Chief Constables and other senior officers can discuss ideas that underpin race relations and related policies. Discussion at these forums will hopefully lead to a clarity of action by the police and place ideas for change within wider, societal and organisational contexts. This will also minimise the chance of incorrect policies and procedures being implemented and finally community forums will help to change the 'can't do' culture of the senior ranks.

Training

Training of police officers with regard to diversity issues is focused on making new officers knowledgeable and aware of the needs of minority groups. This is done in a variety of ways as all services have different training procedures. The MET polices service devotes a whole week of its initial recruit training for diversity and equality training which includes academic seminars and practical role plays.

For this kind of training to be effective, there should be clear race relations strategies at divisional levels. These should filter down to enable all officers to distance themselves from the negative perceptions based on race which are part of the police 'culture'. Also, diversity training should cover all ranks of the service and not just new recruits.

Appropriate language

Promoting appropriate language is one of many ideas that constabularies across the country are implementing to tackle negative attitudes. Appropriate language policies are intended to: protect officers from making unintentional mistakes in the language they use; to help them interact better with communities; to specifically set out what language is acceptable and what is not and to provide valuable guidance on how officers should respond to inappropriate language both within and outside of the service. The policies cover many issues such as appropriate language to use with regard to race, ethnicity, gender, disability, sexual orientation and religion. These policies take the view that inappropriate language can seriously impact on recruitment and service delivery within the police service.

Think about it

1 Why might it be better to train police officers outside the force itself?
2 Can you think of a European country whose policing record is more positive in relation to race than the UK force?

Ethnicity

The police now have to demonstrate that they are receptive to change and able to implement reforms that benefit the ethnic minority employees by reforming their policies and practices. We can learn a lesson from the USA as this country has black police associations, which can have a very considerable effect on change within constabularies. Black police associations also act as a pressure for change within constabularies; they offer support to ethnic minority officers and they affirm the presence of ethnic minorities within the police workforce. Currently a National Black Police Association is being established within the United Kingdom to take up such a role.

Disability

Many of the Public Services, in particular the police, will need to make arrangements to meet the Disability Discrimination Act 1995 (see page 51). They will be required to make reasonable adjustments for employees who sustain disabling injuries whilst in employment such as fire-fighters or police officers who are often forced to leave their employment. Under the DDA, public service organisations will have to look at individual assessment of each case and if an employee is unable to work they should receive support in finding alternative employment.

Gender

Women have traditionally been discriminated against in the public services. Currently representation in the police service is around 17% for women and whilst recruitment nationally is running at 27%, this is a clear indication that a new recruitment drive and advertising is encouraging more women to join. This should be the case as women represent 44% of the economically active population and therefore police officer numbers should reflect this.

The Gender Agenda was developed by a number of pressure groups representing women officers' rights and interests and was launched in August 2001

Police officers on duty

A female police officer

with Ministerial support. It identifies a series of problems affecting women officers and seeks to focus the attention of the police service on solving these. The long term aims of the gender agenda are:

- for the police service to demonstrate consistently that it values women
- to achieve a gender, ethnicity, and sexual orientation balance across the rank structure and specialisms
- to have a women's voice in influential policy
- to develop an understanding of the demands in achieving a work/life balance and a successful career
- to have a working environment and equipment of the right quality to enable women to do their jobs professionally.

Grievance procedure

One method of retaining staff is to ensure there is an adequate grievance procedure which staff can use if they feel they are being unfairly treated.

In any organisation, employees may have problems or concerns about their work, working environment or working relationships that they wish to raise and have addressed. The main purpose of grievance procedures is to provide a means for individual members of staff, who feel aggrieved about the way they have been treated, either by management or colleagues, to raise those issues without fear of recrimination and to explore ways of finding a resolution to their sense of grievance. A grievance procedure provides one mechanism for these to be dealt with fairly before they develop into major problems. Each of the public services will have their own written grievance procedure to provide workers with a reasonable and prompt opportunity to obtain redress. Every worker should have a copy of the procedures or be provided with access to it.

Case study

An Employment Appeal Tribunal has upheld a claim by a female Police Inspector that she was discriminated against because of her marriage to the Divisional Commander of the same police force.

In April 1998, Margaret Graham, an Inspector with Bedfordshire Police, married a Chief Superintendent in the same force. The following year, she applied for the post of Area Inspector at Houghton Regis in D Division. Whilst her application was successful, and she was formally appointed to the post, this decision was later withdrawn by the Chief Constable of Bedfordshire Police.

He told Inspector Graham that due to her relationship with the Divisional Commander of Houghton Regis D Division (her husband) he did not feel it was appropriate for her to take the post.

The reasons set out by the Chief Constable related to Inspector Graham's ability to carry out her operational duties competently because of her marriage to a Divisional Commander. Namely: her competence in giving evidence against her husband in any criminal proceedings; the difficulty officers under her supervision could face in any grievance proceedings involving her and the possible problems relating to any underperformance by Inspector Graham, because of her relationship with a Divisional Commander.

In June last year, Inspector Graham took her grievance to an Employment Tribunal claiming that she had been directly and indirectly discriminated against on the grounds of being a woman and married. The tribunal upheld her claim, finding that substantially less married men than married women in the Bedfordshire Force could potentially face the same situation as Inspector Graham did. It also found that the reasons put forward by Chief Constable for rescinding her appointment were based on speculation and could be overcome in other ways.

The tribunal's decision was appealed against by the Chief Constable but the Employment Appeal Tribunal has now dismissed the appeal, upholding the decision of the original tribunal

Source: *Russell Jones and Walker solicitors*

1. What are the key points of the case?
2. Do you agree with the decision?
3. How effective do you believe employment tribunals are?

Police complaints authority

The independent Police Complaints Authority (PCA) supervises investigations into complaints against police officers. As a member of the public, you can make a complaint about the conduct of a police officer towards yourself if you think you have good reason, or you can complain on someone else's behalf if you have their written authorisation.

The PCA is an independent body set up by the Government to oversee public complaints against police officers in the 43 police services in England and Wales, plus the British Transport, Ministry of Defence, Port of Liverpool, Port of Tilbury and Royal Parks.

Assessment activity 5-P6

Explain the working policies and procedures adopted by an identified public service to promote equality. Select a public service and investigate its plans for combating either racism or sexism. Compare its plans with the police objectives outlined above and analyse and evaluate the likely effectiveness of each service's plans.

Issues

Achieving diversity within the workforce is not just something that employers should do because 'it's the right thing to do'. There are many advantages of recruiting a more diverse workforce: it helps a public service to have employees who come from all parts of society as the service will gain a greater operational picture of the needs of the whole society and such officers bring with them there own life experience and views which will help to combat 'canteen culture' within the work place. We must ensure that all the public services are at the heart of every community so their workforce should mirror the diversity of the local population as a diverse workforce enables public services to connect with all sections of the community, increases their positive image and offers greater customer satisfaction to people regardless of age, gender, ethnicity and so on.

Developing a diverse workforce

Much of the above section has focused on the relationship between the police and the public. However all public organisations are employers and this section will consider additional issues in relation to employment in the public sector which needs to have a diverse workforce to represent the community from which it is drawn. The police, Army and Navy have identified recruitment and training as key issues they need to address. The Bain Report (review of the fire service) sets out recommendations for how the service should change in the future to meet the demands of the twenty-first century. One of the changes is 'to encourage a more diverse workforce by developing new national recruitment processes which receive endorsement from the Equal Opportunities Commission and the Commission for Racial Equality.'

- **Positive advertising** has helped boost numbers as the recent 'Could You?' campaign which is the national police recruitment campaign has generated over 143,528 calls and 200,000 online enquires and police forces have received over 81,000 expressions of interest of which 40% of these enquiries have been from women.
- **Attracting disabled people**: the services will also have to attract applications from the disabled. Current recruitment policies need changing as the public services need to be brought into the 21st century and the government is currently reviewing recruitment policies in the fire and police services in preparation for 2004. Any changes will hopefully remove entry requirements that have barred people with conditions that are now largely manageable with modern medicines and wouldn't affect a person who is a police officer from carrying out their day-to-day duties.
- **Recruitment from ethnic minorities**: in 1999, all police constabularies were set employment targets for the recruitment, retention and

progression of minority ethnic officers. These targets need to be met by 2009 and many police services are struggling to meet these targets which has led to the MET recruiting ethnic minority officers from abroad.

Case study

The Metropolitan Police has begun signing up foreign nationals for the first time to help meet ethnic recruitment targets.

The idea of employing officers from abroad was first suggested by Met commissioner Sir John Stevens last year, but could not take place until the Police Reform Bill became law.

Now people from Austria, Belgium, Denmark, Finland, France, Germany, Greece, Iceland, Ireland, Italy, Liechtenstein, Luxembourg, the Netherlands, Norway or Portugal who live in London can apply. Previously only UK and Commonwealth citizens could join.

Candidates must be able to prove that they are competent in written and spoken English and pass current assessment tests.

Chief Superintendent Bob Carr said: 'This will mean that the Metropolitan Police can now take one step closer to being truly representative of all the people that it serves.

Source: Met signs up foreign nationals – Friday, 11 April, 2003 – BBC NEWS

1 Why is it important to attract more recruits from ethnic minority backgrounds?
2 Do you think recruiting people from abroad is a good way to meet recruitment targets?

However, it still seems evident from recruitment figures that ethnic minority groups are still reluctant to join the police service because of informal bias and in particular negative stereotyping and assumptions by ethnic minorities themselves that they are not likely to gain acceptance by the police as members of the Force.

Other possible ways the police could encourage the creation of a diverse workforce could include:

- a public statement from all the police constabularies on how they will promote equality
- diversity training for all current staff
- screening of all policies and procedures to eliminate any element of discrimination especially in the recruitment of new officers
- positive media articles in the press or on the TV
- open days to create awareness of the recruitment procedure
- community events for under represented groups to show them that the police value them
- providing mentors for new recruits
- conduct independent exit interviews, which will assist in building up a picture of why officers are leaving the police
- minority development programmes to encourage recruitment from the local communities
- more opportunities for development and promotion of ethnic minorities to the more senior ranks
- improve the collection, analysis and use of workforce data on age, gender, ethnicity, race and disability so that services are fully aware of how their service reflects the community they serve
- ensure that the proportion of people from ethnic minority communities is reflected at all levels of the workforce including the civilian posts.

Think about it

What steps would you take to encourage more applications to the police force from ethnic minority groups and to ensure they remain in the police?

Assessment activity 5-P5, 5-M2, 5-D1

Create a powerpoint presentation that could be used at local community forums to explain how a public service is going about creating a more diverse workforce to meet the needs of the minority groups within society.

In order to get a **merit**, your presentation must analyse the methodology used by your chosen public service to develop a diverse workforce.

In order to get a **distinction**, your presentation must analyse and evaluate the success or failure of your chosen public service to develop a diverse workforce.

Catering for employees' needs

Public service trade unions are associations which protect the rights of their members whilst at work and their working conditions.

UNISON is the biggest **trade union** in Britain, representing people who work in **public services**, the voluntary and private sectors.

Other trade unions include

Police Federation of England and Wales and The Fire Brigade Union (FBU).

The Police Federation of England and Wales is the representative body to which every police officer below the rank of Superintendent belongs. It was established by the Police Act 1919 to provide the police with a means of bringing their views on welfare and efficiency to the notice of the government and the police authorities. Under the provisions of the Police Act, the police are forbidden to strike and must at all times obey the lawful orders of senior officers. The current membership of the Federation is 136,000.

Once staff have been recruited, all public services need to tackle the real issues of staff wastage and the need for practices and attitudes which are free of discrimination.

As employers, the public services are subject to all the anti-discrimination law discussed previously in this unit and in the citizenship unit. They will have to produce policies and procedures to ensure they are not in breach of the law in relation to ethnicity, gender and disability

Glossary of key terminology

Multiculturalism – the practise of acknowledging and respecting the various cultures, religions, ethnicities, attitudes and opinions within a society. This includes experiences that shape perceptions common to age, gender, religion, socio-economic status as well as cultural, linguistic, and racial identities.

Racism – the belief that some races are superior to others based on the false idea that different physical characteristics such as colour or ethnic origin make some people better than others.

Minority – a culturally, ethnically or racially distinct group living within a larger society.

Ethnic group – a group of people who share a common culture.

Ethnicity – the shared culture (language, religion or beliefs) of a social group, which gives its members a common identity.

Race – people who share a common origin or heritage.

Racial hatred – hatred against a group of people by reference to colour, race, nationality, or ethnic origin.

Institutional discrimination – the result of organisations failing to provide appropriate services because of prejudiced or ethnocentric attitudes of service providers.

Ethnocentricity – the assumption that an individual's viewpoint from their own cultural perspective is normal or superior without considering that there could be other points of view.

Diversity opens people to new experiences and to new ways of looking at things. Being open to other cultures enriches everyone and means that our everyday lives are more interesting, even at such basic levels as the types of food we eat. Fashion often borrows from other cultures and popular music has benefited from diverse cultural influences.

Culture is the term used to describe the norms and values which belong to an identifiable social group. Cultures can vary between different religious, ethnic, class, gender and age groups.

End of unit questions

1 Identify 5 key events that have led to Britain becoming more diverse?

2 What are the main religions in the world?

3 How can body language be a barrier to communication?

4 In what ways do minority groups gain support within their community?

5 How can the army become more accessible to disabled and ethnic minority groups?

6 List five groups of people who may experience discrimination.

7 Describe five negative effects of discrimination.

8 List five pieces of legislation which challenge discrimination.

9 What is the contribution of the Macpherson report to our understanding of unequal access to services?

10 What is the difference between a prejudice and a stereotype?

11 Why might it be necessary to treat people differently in order to treat them equally?

12 Why might the following conditions be indirectly discriminative:

- mobility requirements
- unsociable hours
- height or weight requirements
- full-time work.

13 What is positive discrimination?

14 What is bullying and how does it differ from harassment?

15 How can harassment in the workplace be damaging to the

- aggressor
- victim
- public service.

16 Why do the public services need to increase the employment numbers of minority groups? Identify five ways you believe this could be done.

Resources

Allport G W, *The Nature of Prejudice*, Perseus Books, 1988.

Collins H, *Equality in the Workplace*, Blackwell, Oxford, 1995.

Clements P and Spinks T, *The Equal Opportunities Guide*, Kogan Page, 1996.

Williams A, *Croner's Guide to Discrimination*, Croner Publications, 1995.

A Short Guide to the Equal Opportunities Commission, 1993.

Women and Men in Britain, 1993.

Faces of Britain – A Cultural Guide, Avon & Comerset Constabulary, Trinity Road Police Station, St Phillips, Bristol, BS2 0NW.

Websites

www.eoc.org.uk – Equal Opportunities Commission

www.irr.org.uk – Institute of Race Relations

www.open.gov.uk – Commission for Racial Equality

www.disability.gov.uk – Disability Discrimination Act

INTERNATIONAL PERSPECTIVES

Introduction to Unit 6

This chapter introduces you to the global organisations and international relations that have an impact on the UK. It examines the role of international institutions such as the UN and NATO and their influence on public services in the UK.

This chapter also looks at the causes of war and instability, local and national terrorism and the counter-measures designed to prevent it. The final section of this chapter examines the effect that human rights and its legislation has on the work of the public services in the UK.

Assessment

Throughout the unit, activities and tasks will help you to learn and remember information. Case studies are included to add industry relevance to the topics and learning objectives. You are reminded that when you are completing activities and tasks, opportunities will be created to enhance your key skills evidence. After completing this unit you should be able to achieve the following outcomes.

Outcomes

1. Describe **international institutions** and evaluate how they effect UK public services
2. Investigate the causes and effects of **war and conflict**
3. Investigate the effects of **international terrorism and counter-terrorism**
4. Explain **human rights** and investigate human rights violations.

International institutions

An understanding of international peacekeeping and human rights organisations are crucial to the public services of the 21st century. This is because increasingly national public services are being called upon to deal with international problems and incidents.

This could be in a variety of situations such as offering humanitarian aid in a natural disaster situation, acting as a peacekeeping force in war torn nations or co-operating with other international agencies in crime detection and prevention. In order to understand the role the public services play internationally it is firstly important to examine the major international institutions which can influence and direct their role.

The United Nations (UN)

After the First World War, The League of Nations was established as a mechanism to try and establish international cooperation, peace and security between nations and so prevent another global war. It was established in 1919 by The Treaty of Versailles. However, The League of Nations failed to prevent World War II and with its effectiveness in serious doubt it ceased its activities.

The United Nations was established in very similar circumstances after World War II came to an end. Political and social unity were seen as very important in the post-war climate and as a consequence, representatives from 50 nations met in the United States to debate the creation of a new global organisation to help maintain friendly international relations and promote peace and security. The new United Nations (UN) organisation officially came into existence on 24th October 1945 with 51 members. The UN today has 191 members, all of whom must agree to and be bound by The UN Charter, a treaty which sets out the rights and duties of the member states in the international arena and also sets out fundamental practices in international relations. The UN has many roles and performs many international functions, as shown in Figure 6.1 below.

Think about it

Considering the roles in Figure 6.1. Which of them could apply to a recent UN situation such as the intervention in Iraq?

The structure of the UN comprises of six main divisions:

1 The General Assembly
2 The Security Council
3 The Economic and Social Council
4 The Trusteeship Council
5 The International Court of Justice
6 The Secretariat

All of these divisions are based at the UN headquarters in New York except for The International Court of Justice which is based at The Hague in The Netherlands. Each division of the UN has responsibility for a variety of functions and tasks.

1 The International Court Of Justice

This is the principal judicial arm of the UN and it is located at the Peace Palace in The Hague. It was established in 1946 to fulfil two primary roles:

- settle legal disputes between member states
- provide opinions and advice on international legal issues.

When deciding on issues of dispute amongst the member states, participation in proceedings is done on a voluntary basis but if a country does agree to take part then it must be prepared to abide by the decision of the court. The court consists of fifteen judges who are elected from across all member states by the General Assembly and the Security Council. The judges serve a nine year term of office and no more than one judge from any member state may serve at a time. The judges are expected to be completely independent and do not serve on behalf of their respective governments.

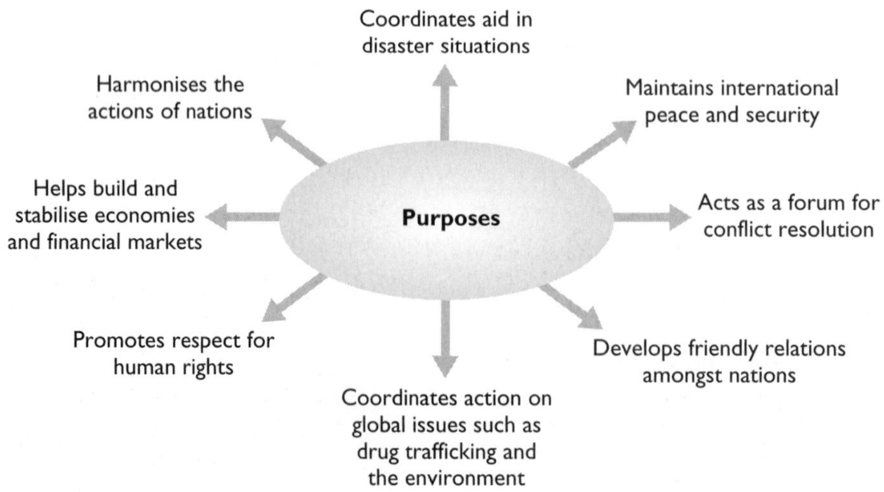

Figure 6.1 Roles and functions of the UN

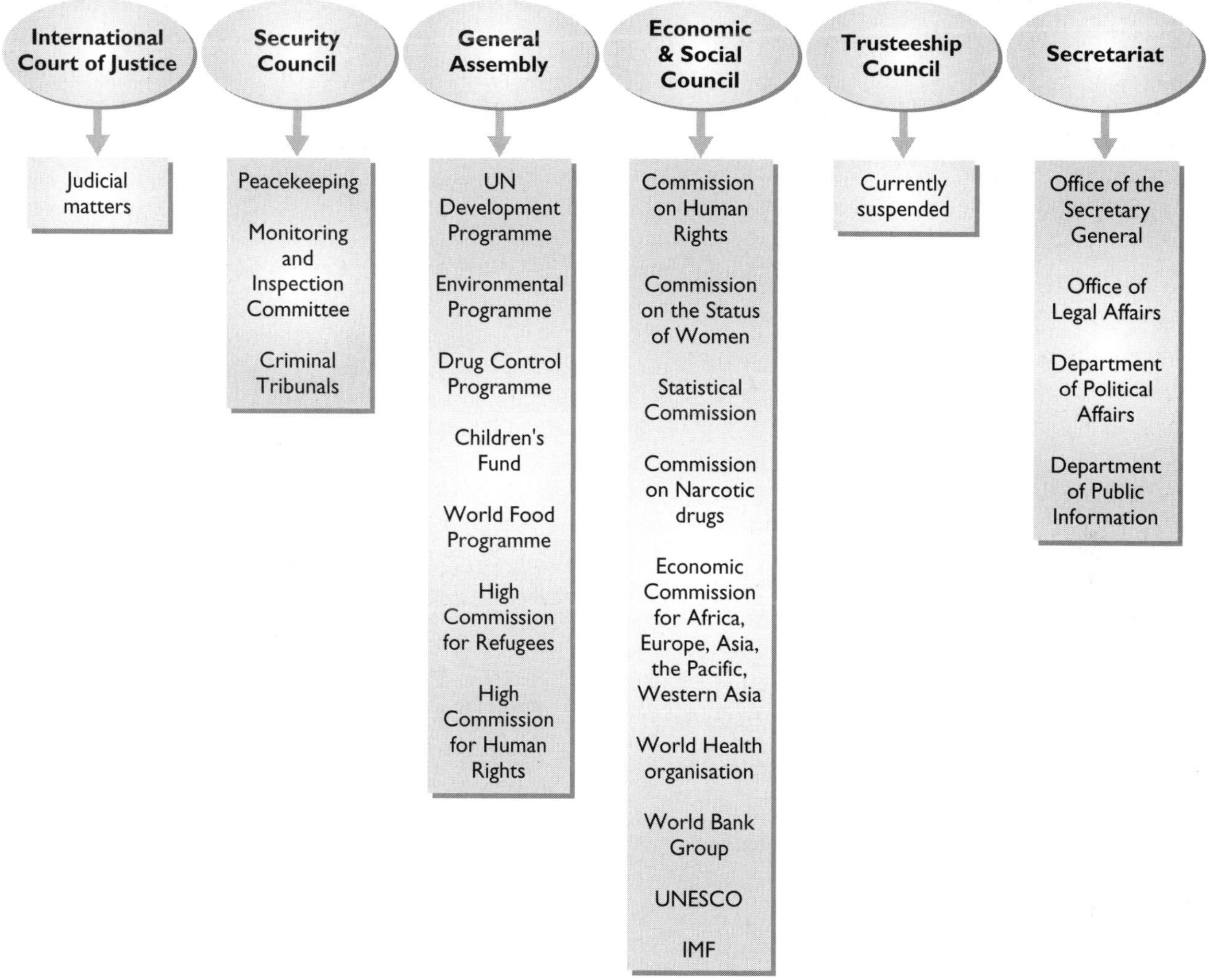

Figure 6.2 The UN structure has six divisions with responsibilities in different areas

It is not just judges from powerful Western nations who are elected to serve the court, all UN nations are eligible to serve. Currently the court has many cases pending, ranging from issues of territorial and maritime dispute, to oil conflict to genocide. An example of an ongoing case is detailed below.

Case study

Islamic Republic of Iran V United States of America

This case arises from the destruction of several offshore oil production complexes by the United States Navy in 1987 and 1988. The oil platforms were owned by the National Iranian Oil Company and were located in a region of the Persian Gulf that belongs exclusively to Iran. The platforms, named 'Result' and 'Reshadat' were subject to a 90 minute attack by four US Navy destroyers, which left one platform totally destroyed and the other carrying 90% damage. This stopped oil production from these oil fields, costing millions to the Iranian oil industry.

The US justified the attacks on the oil platforms as lawful self-defence and as a response to an alleged Iranian attack on a Kuwaiti tanker in the region. The Iranian government dispute these claims arguing that oil platforms have no means of defence and no military value and accuse the United States of a breach of International law. As a consequence of this, the Iranians made an application to the United Nations International

Court of Justice in order to have the matter resolved and seek compensation from the US government.

1 Why couldn't the US and Iran resolve their own difficulties?
2 Is it a good idea to have an international court? Explain your reasons.
3 From the information given above, which country do you think is in the wrong?
4 Do you think Iran ought to receive compensation? If so, how much?

2 UN Security Council

This body has primary responsibility for maintaining international peace and security. Members can bring complaints before it, but the council's first action is usually to encourage the parties involved to reach a peaceful agreement themselves. However, it may act as a mediator in the dispute or appoint a special representative to oversee the process.

If the conflict has led to violence, the Security Council has a responsibility to bring it to an end and it does this by using measures such as: negotiating ceasefires between hostile groups or deploying UN peacekeepers to help reduce tensions in troubled areas. In addition, the council may impose other sanctions such as trade embargoes, as with Iraq during and after The first Gulf War or collective military action such as in Kosovo.

It consists of fifteen members of which five are permanent members and ten are elected for a two-year term. The five permanent members are:

- United Kingdom
- United States
- China
- Russian Federation
- France

Each member has one vote. On simple matters an affirmative vote of nine members is needed for action to take place. On more serious issues, such as military action, nine votes are still needed, but all of the five permanent members must be in agreement. If they are not then the action cannot go ahead. This is called the power of veto.

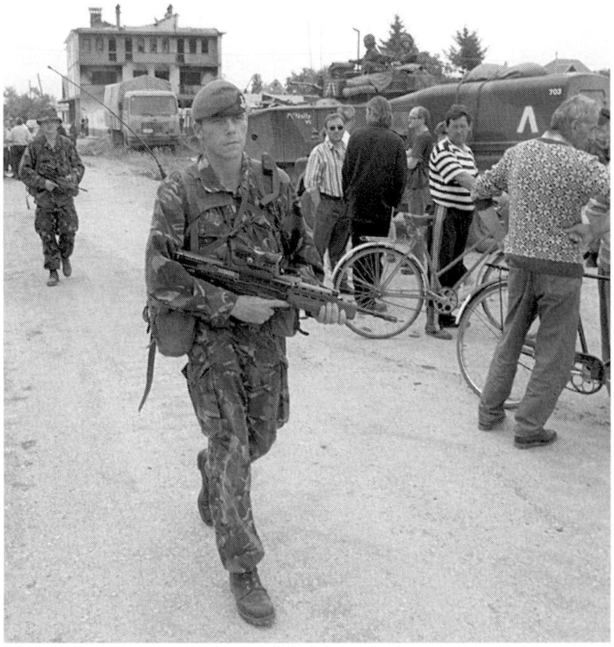

UN peacekeepers help to reduce tension in troubled areas

Think about it

Why is a power of veto important when discussing serious matters like collective military action?

The UN has admitted a large number of new member states since 1995 and membership of the Security Council needs to be reformed as a result. It is difficult to see how 15 representatives can effectively make decisions on behalf of 176 other nations on such serious matters as international security. There are several proposals that the UN could consider:

- increasing the number of permanent and non-permanent members

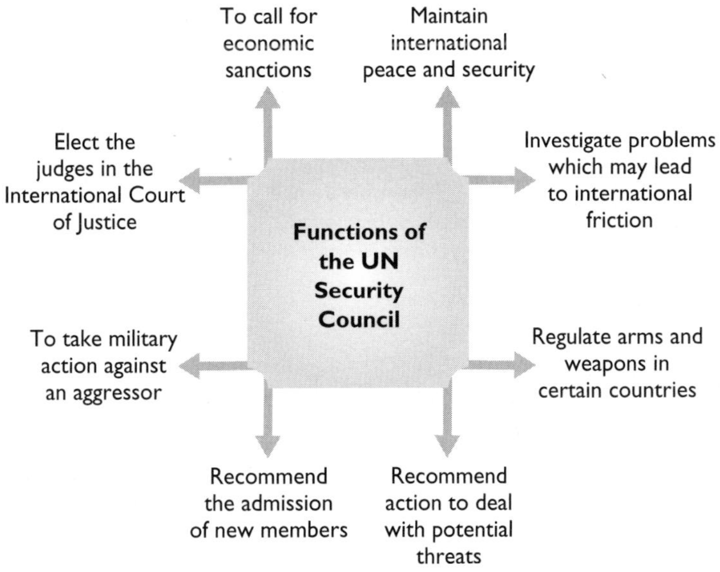

Figure 6.3 Functions of the UN Security Council

- rotating or sharing council seats
- modifying the power of veto
- improving the councils working methods.

Think about it

- Do you think membership of the Security Council needs reform? If so how would you reform it?
- How do you think the five permanent members of the security council secured their places?

3 The UN General Assembly

The General Assembly is like the parliament of the UN in which representatives of the 191 member states sit. The assembly meets to discuss some of the world's most pressing problems such as poverty, human rights and armed conflict. Each member state has a vote and decisions are made on the basis of a majority vote for routine matters and a two-thirds majority on important issues. The assembly cannot force a nation to comply with its resolutions or recommendations. The work of the other main divisions is based on the decisions made at the general assembly. It has a variety of powers and functions:

- to make recommendations on disarmament and arms regulation
- promote international political co-operation
- discuss threats to international peace and security
- to support international respect for human rights
- to approve UN budgets
- to develop international law
- to elect non-permanent members of the Security Council
- to elect members of the Economic and Social Council.

The UN General Assembly deals with a tremendous amount of information and queries from all 191 member states, so rather than debate each issue between the 191 members in open forum which would be very time consuming, the General Assembly has six main subsidiary committees which deal with many of the issues. The six main committees are shown in Figure 6.4 overleaf.

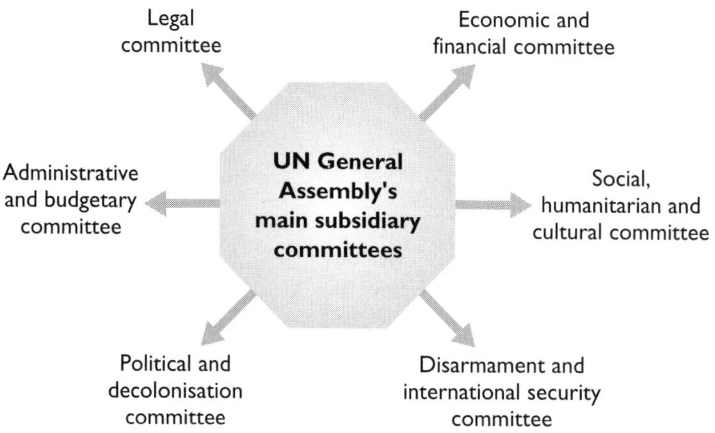

Figure 6.4 Six main committees of the UN General Assembly

4 The UN Economic and Social Council

This body comprises of representatives from 54 member states who are elected for a three-year term of office. Seats on the council are allocated on the basis of geographical region, Africa has 14 seats, Asia has 11, Eastern Europe has 6, Central and South America have 10 and 13 seats go to Western European nations and other states.

The council has responsibility for discussing economic and social issues and developing recommendations and policies. The council coordinates the work of 14 specialised agencies including the following:

- World Health Organisation
- International Monetary Fund
- World Bank

It coordinates 10 functional commissions including:

- Commission on Human Rights
- Commission on the Status of Women
- Commission on Narcotic Drugs

It also coordinates the work of 5 regional commissions including:

- Economic Commission for Africa
- Economic Commission for Europe

These specialised agencies research complex issues such as protecting the global environment and the international status of women. The work of the Economic and Social Council accounts for over 70% of the human and financial resources of the whole UN.

Think about it

Why does the work of the Economic and Social Council take such a large amount of the UN budget?

5 The Trusteeship Council

This council was established so that member countries with other territories could have assistance in preparing them for independence or self-governance. It consists of the five permanent members of the UN Security Council and until 1994 it met annually. However, on November 1st 1994 the Trusteeship Council suspended its operations after Palau became independent. Palau was the last UN trust territory to gain its independence. Today the council meets only as and when required.

Theory into practice

Investigate one area of the UN and list how its decisions affect the UK public services.

6 The UN Secretariat

This is the administrative arm of the UN. It is presided over by the Secretary General who is appointed for a five-year term of office and it conducts the work and operations of the other UN bodies. The Secretariat has about 9,000 staff who are drawn from all of the member nations in the UN. They are expected to be independent of their home country and not be biased towards it. The Secretariat may fulfil tasks such as:

- administering peacekeeping operations
- organising international conferences
- public relations
- survey economic and social trends.

Staff in the Secretariat can be stationed anywhere in the world. Although the UN headquarters are in New York it has offices in many of its member states.

UK service involvement

The UK services play a key role in UN peacekeeping operations and military action which has UN support. For instance, in Afghanistan, Kosovo and Cyprus. Being part of a collective of nations means that our armed and civilian public services can be utilised by the UN to help maintain peace and resolve conflict globally. The decisions of the UN can have a tremendous impact on UK public services. For example, the 2003/4 situation in Iraq, which was initiated by a series of UN resolutions, led to the following impact on the UK services:

- the deployment of thousands of armed services troops, who had to leave their families and loved ones behind to enter a dangerous and potentially life threatening situation
- the death and injury of service men and women

Kofi Annan

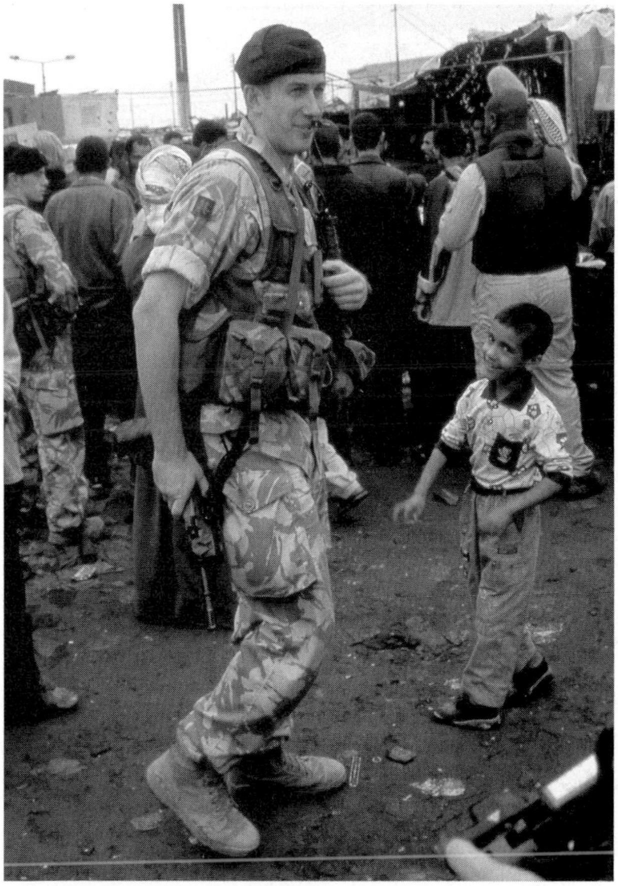

UK service personnel in Iraq

- the potential for post traumatic stress disorder in service personnel
- the deployment of UK emergency services such as the police to retrain and recruit new police officers in Iraq
- increased expenditure
- highlighted a lack of resources available to protect our service men and women.

Case study

Although there have been many cases of the poor quality and lack of equipment issued to our troops in conflict situations, the case of Sergeant Steve Roberts of the 2nd Royal Tank Regiment who died in Iraq aged 33, has particularly highlighted the issue of insufficient resources to protect our troops. Sgt Roberts was told to hand back his flak jacket (body armour) as there were not enough to go around but was later shot dead near Basra trying to stop a riot. Later tests proved that had Sgt Roberts been wearing the body armour the bullet may not have killed him.

1. In your opinion who is responsible for the death of Sgt Roberts?
2. Why are the services short of resources and equipment?
3. What can the government do about this situation?
4. Can you find any other examples of the lack of equipment and resources leading to tragic consequences?

The European Union (EU)

The EU developed from The Treaty of Rome in 1957 which created the European Economic Community (EEC), although Great Britain did not join until 1973. The EEC was established in a post-war climate to try and ensure that there would be no more European based wars like World War I and World War II. It hoped to achieve this through economic and political co-operation between member nations. The EEC changed to the EU in 1994 and it now has 25 members who have a total population in excess of 500 million citizens.

Think about it

Why do you think the UK didn't join the EU until 1973? Do you consider yourself European?

The EU performs a wide variety of functions. For instance, it is the world's largest trade body and is one of the largest providers of funds and humanitarian aid for developing countries. It also sets out rules and guidance for member states on a whole range of important issues such as:

- monetary union
- agriculture
- fishing
- immigration.

Although member states are considered to be sovereign or independent, they can have their national laws overruled by European Union laws in certain cases.

Membership of the EU

The following map highlights the 25 member countries currently in the EU:

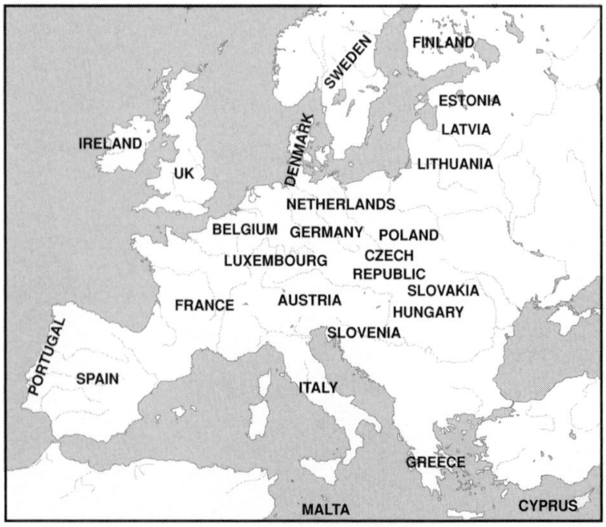

Membership countries of the EU

There are many other countries who wish to join the EU and who have lodged formal applications for entry.

All members who are seeking entry into the EU must comply with a strict set of criteria on issues such as the ability to cope with competitive market pressure and adoption of the main aims of the EU such as monetary, political and economic integration. Some nations are not permitted to enter, even if they fulfil these criteria. Morocco was denied entry on the basis that being located in Africa it did not have European status and Switzerland did not pursue its application after a referendum of its population showed that they did not want to be part of the EU.

Many new candidate countries are not as economically or technically developed as most of the current member nations and many have only recently overcome years of totalitarian regimes which have left lasting economic and cultural scars. As a consequence, the EU will have to adapt its institutions to ensure that including new members do not threaten the existing integration between current members. It can do this by ensuring that nations who are allowed to join are politically and economically stable and are fully committed to playing a part in the mechanisms and organisations of the EU.

There are good reasons to allow new members to join the EU:

- to strengthen the Union
- to strengthen the new democracies of the applicant nations
- to help preserve peace in Europe.

However, there are also concerns about allowing new nations in if:

- they have a history of political and economic instability
- they may take more resources from the EU than they put into it
- they may cause substantial changes to they way the current EU works.

The EU decided to admit 10 new member states on 1st May 2004:

- Czech Republic
- Estonia
- Cyprus
- Latvia
- Lithuania
- Hungary
- Malta
- Poland
- Slovenia
- Slovakia

Think about it

What are the main concerns about letting in 10 new members and what are the main benefits?

Structure of the EU

Like the United Nations Organisation, the EU is made up of several subsidiary organs each of which have specific tasks (see Figure 6.5 overleaf):

We will look at the most important of these in this chapter.

- **The European Parliament:** The Members of the European Parliament (MEPs) are elected every five years. In April 2003 there were 624 of them in total. Each member state elects its own set of representatives to send to the parliament and just like in a British General Election, MEPs come from a variety of political parties. The European Parliament has three main functions:

  1 It shares with the European Council (Council of Ministers) the power to create law which applies to all the member states.

  2 It shares authority for the EU's budget with the European Council and can influence how European money is spent.

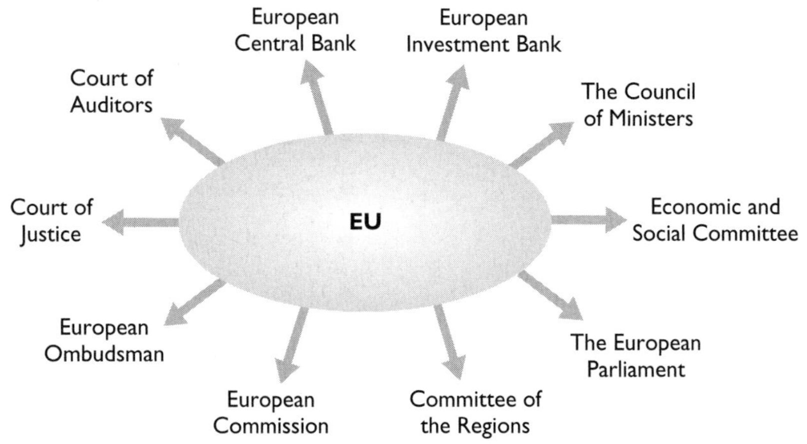

Figure 6.5 Structure of the EU

3 It supervises the European Commission and it has political supervision of the other institutions shown above.

- **The Council of the European Union (Council of Ministers):** This is the main decision making body of the EU. It is made up of one minister from each of the member states who is responsible to their own national parliament and its citizens. It discusses issues such as finance, education, health and foreign affairs. Like the European Parliament it has several key roles:

  1 Shares law making power with the European Parliament.

  2 Co-ordinates the economic policies of the member states.

  3 Shares authority for the EU budget with the parliament.

  4 Takes decisions on common foreign and security policies.

  5 Co-ordinates members states and plays a special role in helping the police and judiciary of member states co-operate in criminal matters. Clearly this is a matter of some importance for the British public services such as the police and customs and excise.

Its main seat is in Brussels in Belgium, but it also sits in Luxembourg for part of the year. Like the United Nations there is often too much information to be discussed in general sessions and so the group is broken down into sub-groups who deal with specific issues such as agriculture, transport, fisheries, justice or the environment.

Each member state is president of the Council for a period of 6 months before it passes to another country. The voting power of member states is weighted in accordance with its population, so that the more populous a country is the more voting power is has. Germany, France, Italy and the UK have 10 votes, Spain has 8, Belgium, the Netherlands and Portugal have 5, Austria and Sweden have 4, Denmark, Ireland and Finland have 3 and Luxembourg has 2. These have changed with the inclusion of the 10 new members from 1st May 2004.

- **The European Commission:** This body of the EU is designed to uphold the interests of the European Union as a whole and not any one particular member state. Commissioners are expected to perform their duties without bias to their own member state. It has several responsibilities:

  1 It drafts laws and proposals for the parliament and council to consider.

  2 It implements European laws.

3 Along with the Court of Justice it makes sure that EU law is followed.

4 Represents the EU in the international arena.

It has its main seat in Brussels and consists of 20 members all of whom are chosen for their general competence and impartiality. All of them have held political office in their own country, sometimes at quite high levels. The Commission is re-elected once every 5 years at around the same time that the European Parliament is elected. This gives the new parliament time to approve the commission and its members.

It normally meets once a week and in most cases a simple majority is enough to secure a decision. The proposals made by the Commission relate to particular fields such as transport, agriculture, energy, trade relations and social policy. The Commission makes proposals where it believes that European wide co-operation would be more effective than national initiatives.

- **The Court of Justice:** This court has the task of ensuring that EU law is applied equally throughout the 25 member states. It sits in Luxembourg and has judges who are appointed by the member states. Their term of office lasts 6 years and they usually consist of one judge per member state. The majority of cases heard by the Court of Justice are referred to it by the national courts of the member states. In order to ensure that European law is followed, the court has wide jurisdiction in the following proceedings:

  1 Preliminary rulings – this guarantees co-operation between the European Court and the national courts. If the national courts are in doubt as to the interpretation of a European law they must ask for clarification from the European Court.

  2 Proceedings for failure to fulfil an obligation – this allows the court to monitor how the member states are fulfilling their obligations to the European community as a whole. If the member state is found to be failing in their legal obligations to either their citizens or other member states they must rectify this at once.

The European court

  3 Proceedings for annulment – this allows the European Court under certain circumstances to annul a piece of law set by the other European community institutions.

  4 Proceedings for failure to act – this is where member states can lodge a complaint against the European union itself for failing to reach a decision on a given issue. If upheld, this is then officially recorded.

When cases are submitted they are followed through by one judge. He or she draws up a report summarising the legal arguments in the case and makes a draft ruling which is then submitted to the other judges of the court for their examination. The lawyers of the parties involved then have the opportunity to present their case to the judges who consider a verdict. In general, judgements of the court are decided by a majority vote. Now the 10 new members have joined they will also be entitled to send a judge to be appointed to the court.

Think about it

When the judges deliver their majority verdict, the views of the judges who disagreed with the decision are not discussed. Do you think the parties involved have a right to hear the views of the judges who did not agree with the final decision?

Case study

- The European Court fined the Greek government for failing to close a waste tip on the island of Crete which was polluting local streams and burning refuse causing air pollution. The government was fined $20,000 dollars a day from the end of the court case to the day it closed the tip.
- The European Commission took the French government to court for failing to comply with EU legislation on the hunting and protection of wild birds.

1. Why does the EU need its own court?
2. Is it appropriate that the Court of Justice steps in to deal with these matters or should it be the responsibility of the EU member states own national courts?
3. How does the Court of Justice help the citizens of the member states?
4. How does the Court of Justice help the governments of the member states?

Decision making in the EU

Decision making in the EU is a complex and lengthy procedure. Many bodies are involved and as the process is supposed to be democratic, the movement of policies and proposals between bodies as they are discussed and amended can be very difficult to track. The three main bodies involved in EU decision making are the European Commission; the European Parliament and the Council of the European Union. The European Commission proposes new legislation, but it is the Council and Parliament that pass the laws.

There are 3 main ways that the EU makes decisions:

- co-decision
- consultation
- assent

Co-decision: in this procedure, Parliament and the Council share the power to make laws. The Commission sends its proposal on law to both institutions and they each read and discuss it

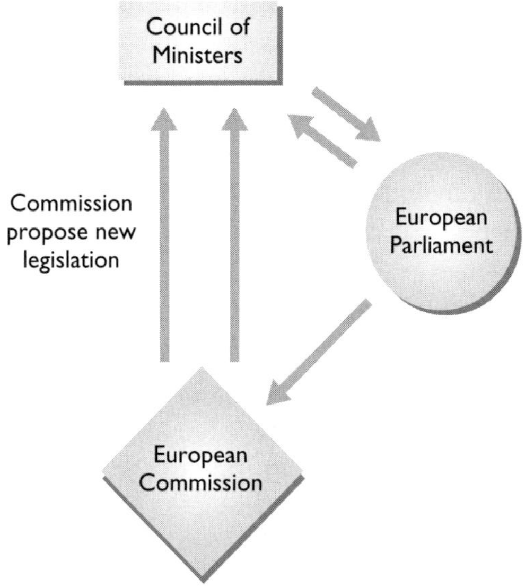

Figure 6.6 The 3 main bodies involved in EU decision making

twice in succession. If for any reason they can't agree on it, it is put before a committee which tries to resolve the difficulties. This committee is composed of equal numbers of Council and Parliament representatives. Commission representatives also attend the committee meetings and contribute to the discussion since they were the ones to propose the law in the first place. Once the committee has reached an agreement, the agreed text is then sent to Parliament and the Council for a third reading, so that they can finally adopt it as law.

Consultation: under this form of decision making procedure, the Commission sends its proposal to both the Council and Parliament as we have described in the co-decision procedure. However, it is then the Council that takes responsibility for consulting with Parliament and other EU bodies such as the Economic and Social Committee and the Committee of the Regions, whose opinions are an important factor in decision making.

In all cases, Parliament can:

- approve the proposal made by the commission
- reject the proposal
- ask for amendments to be made to the proposal.

Assent: this method of decision making means that the Council has to obtain the European Parliament's assent before certain very important decisions are taken. The procedure is the same as in the case of consultation, except that Parliament cannot amend a proposal: it must either accept or reject it.

UK service involvement

As you would expect, Europe must work together on a variety of issues and the decisions made at EU level can have a great effect on UK public services in areas such as:

1 **European Defence**: the European Council meeting in Helsinki in 1999 agreed that a European rapid reaction force to target trouble spots in Europe was needed. The situation in Kosovo in the mid 1990s highlighted the problems of European Armed Forces strategic co-operation and utilisation of equipment as most of the equipment used in Kosovo was American as was most of the telecommunications technology.

   The proposed rapid reaction force would be designed to combat some of these problems. It would aim to establish a 60,000 strong force able to be deployed within 60 days and operate for up to a year. The rapid reaction force also makes sense for economic reasons as it is better value for money to pool military resources across EU nations and split the cost. European armed forces need to think alike if they are to act in common with each other and there have been some suggestions that a European Defence Academy which trains Armed forces' officers from EU nations would promote the convergence of defence structures and policies.

2 **Police and Customs Cooperation**: formal cooperation between the police and customs of differing member states began in 1976. The main focus at that time was terrorism and the problems of training in police departments. By 1989, organised crime and the free movement of persons (illegal immigrants) had also been added to the list of concerns. There are several agreements and EU treaties which promote European public service co-operation:

   - The Schengen Agreements which set up a system of liaison officers in each of the member states who share information on points of concern such as organised crime and terrorism. They also give police the power to pursue a suspect across national borders within the EU.
   - The Maastricht Treaty created the European Police Service (Europol) and also discussed areas of common interest in which the member states could increase cooperation such as drug trafficking and football hooliganism.
   - The Treaty of Amsterdam increased the role of Europol and called upon public services and courts to cooperate fully to ensure the safety of all the citizens of the member states.

   European police and customs cooperation can take many forms, from a simple exchange of criminal intelligence to targeted campaigns to fight international crime. The role of Europol is set to become crucial in this context as it is hoped that it will eventually coordinate all of the cross border police activity in Europe. However the European Parliament has asked the Council not to assign powers to Europol until it is formally accountable to the organisations of the EU.

Think about it

Why is it important that Europol be accountable to the European Parliament and the European courts.

3 **Judicial cooperation**: the European Union has in many ways reduced the importance of national borders between its member states and as a consequence the citizens of the EU have greater freedom to move freely within its borders than ever before. Effective judicial cooperation is therefore vital if life is to be made easier for those citizens who move

throughout the Union frequently or who conduct business in a variety of countries, each with its own particular legal system. In addition, criminals have the same freedom of movement across national borders and so it is in the member states own interests to work together with other nations to bring a halt to their activities regardless of which country they find themselves in. To this end, the courts of the various member states have endeavoured to cooperate in both civil and criminal matters as well as the council which has given its provisional agreement to the creation of Eurojust – a body which will specifically promote cooperation on issues of serious crime where two or more member states are involved.

The North Atlantic Treaty Organisation (NATO)

The North Atlantic Treaty was signed in Washington on April 4th 1949 and it created an alliance of ten European and two North American nations committed to each others defence. It arose because of the growing strength of the Soviet Union after World War II. The Soviet Union had become resurrected under communism and its defensive and offensive capabilities were strong. In contrast, much of Europe in the post-war period was destroyed and vulnerable to external attack. Although the United States implemented 'The Marshall Plan' which aimed to help with the rebuilding of Europe, it was also recognised that any attack which came from the Soviet Union would have to be repelled by the Americans and Canadians until Europe was back on its feet. The treaty itself is not very long and conforms to the United Nations Charter. It states that:

- member countries of NATO commit themselves to maintaining and developing collective defence capabilities.
- if one of NATO's member states is attacked it will be considered to be an attack against them all.
- members must contribute to the development of peaceful and friendly international relations.
- members must eliminate conflict with the economic policies of other member states and encourage co-operation between them.

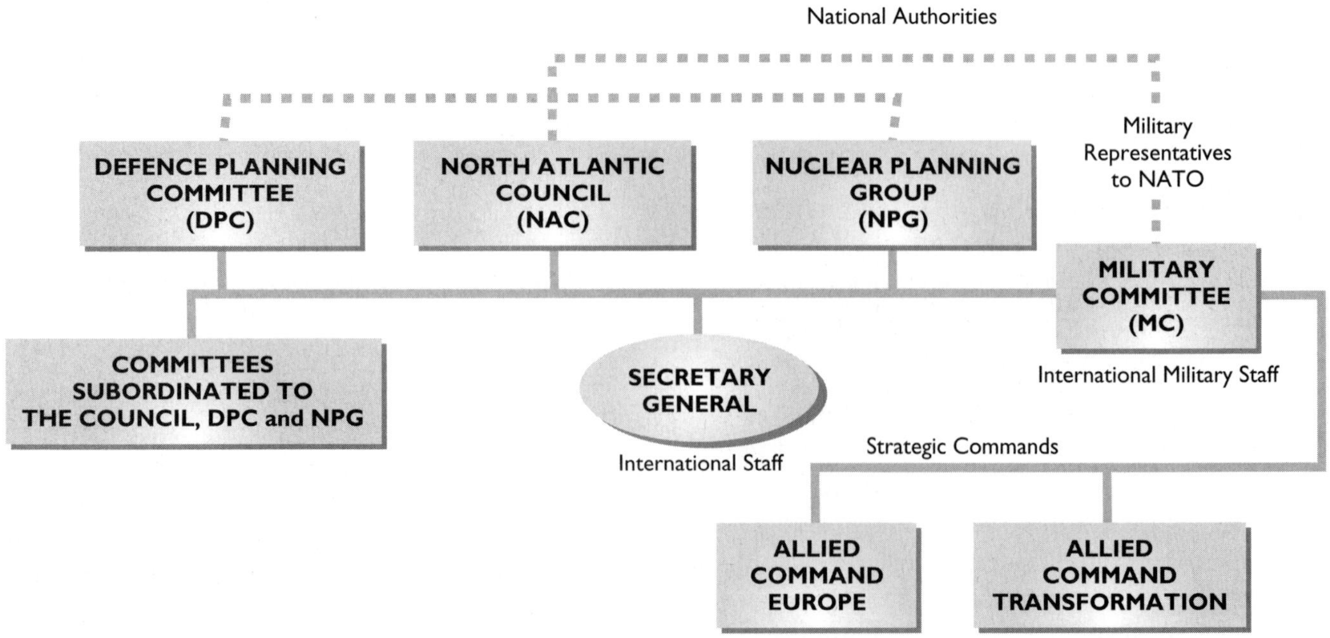

Figure 6.7 NATO's civil and military structure

There are significant questions about the role of NATO in the modern world:

- does it have a future now that the cold War is over?
- since its inception, NATO has been US dominated and this has been questioned by the EU who are considering alternative methods of European defence, such as the Rapid Reaction Force already detailed in this chapter. This is not popular with NATO or the USA.

Effects on UK forces

As Britain is a committed and influential member of NATO, our armed services have to be ready to accede to NATO's commands. This means that the British government must be prepared to send our armed forces personnel and equipment wherever NATO believes there is a need for them.

In NATO headquarters about 14% of the staff are British as was the former NATO Secretary General Sir George Robertson. Only the US has a greater number of personnel than we do. In addition to personnel, the UK government contributes in excess of £100 million to NATO budgets. There are currently two main NATO operations in which UK services are deployed and both of these are in the former Yugoslavia.

UK Armed Services deployed on behalf of NATO

The Stabilisation Force (SFOR) Mission

This NATO operation is designed to deter hostilities and stabilise the peace in Bosnia and Herzegovina in order that the area is safe and secure for the citizens in the region. The total number of troops committed to SFOR is about 18,000.

The Kosovan Force (KFOR)

This is an international operation designed to establish and maintain security in Kosovo. KFOR has a full strength of around 50,000 troops from 30 countries of which around 2,400 are British. The British troops come from a variety of regiments such as:

- The Queens Royal Lancer
- The Queens Royal Hussars
- The Royal Horse Artillery
- The Royal Mechanical and Electrical Engineers
- The Royal Engineers
- Royal Military Police

The World Bank

The World Bank is not a single organisation. It consists of 5 organisations which use their expertise and development specialisms in order to reduce world poverty. The 5 organisations are:

1. International Bank for Reconstruction and Development (IBRD)
2. International Development Association (IDA)
3. International Finance Corporation (IFC)
4. Multi-lateral Investment Guarantee Agency (MIGA)
5. International Centre for the Settlement of Investment Disputes (ICSID)

As with the EU and NATO, The World Bank developed as a consequence of World War II and one of its main roles was post-war reconstruction in Europe. Today, the focus of The World Bank is on poverty reduction. It provides financial assistance in the form of loans to developing economies. Its headquarters are in Washington DC, but it has offices in more than 100 other countries and more than 180 countries are members. The loans it gives out are supposed to finance issues such as:

- education
- agriculture
- industry
- healthcare.

These improvements are designed to establish economic growth in developing countries that is stable and sustainable. However, there are problems associated with improvements made by The World Bank:

- The World Banks own research states that more than 50% of the projects it loans finances to failed to achieve satisfactory sustainable results.
- The World Bank does very little to ensure that loans are spent on their stated purpose.
- The distribution of funds is not equitable. Over the last decade The World Bank lent 70% of its funds to just 11 countries.
- Loans must be repaid. If a country is already in poverty how can they be expected to pay back the loan plus the interest it has accrued. It could cause more poverty in the long term.

Think about it

Do you think the World Bank operates for the benefit of all nations?

The International Monetary Fund (IMF)

The IMF came into existence in 1945 with an original 29 member countries. It now has a membership of 183 states. As with many of the other organisations already discussed it was created in a post-war climate for specific purposes:

- to promote international monetary co-operation
- to promote and expand international trade
- to enable its members to receive short term financial assistance.

It is structured as follows:

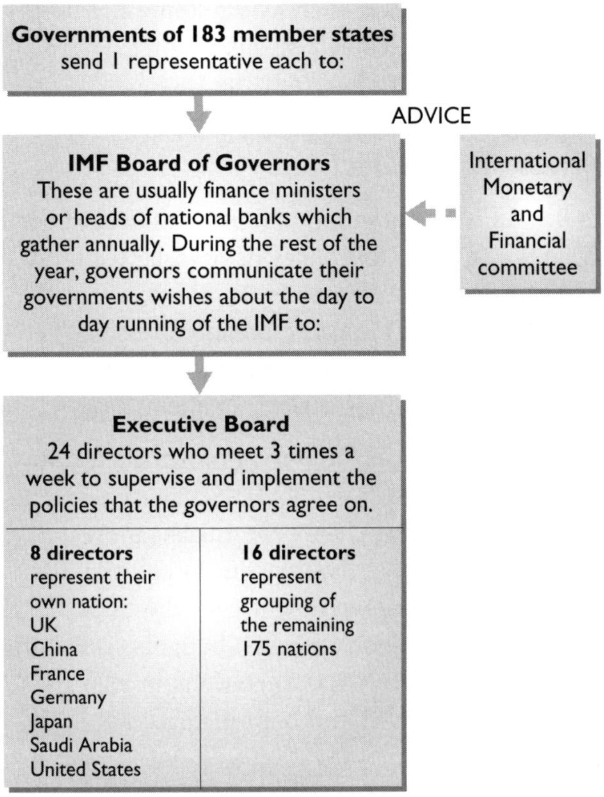

Figure 6.8 Structure of the IMF

The role of the IMF in today's world is to monitor nations exchange rate policies based on the principle that strong and consistent national economies will lead to stable exchange rates and a prosperous world economy. It also provides financial assistance such as credits and loans. In 2001 the IMF had credit and loans extended to 90 countries for a total amount of $65 billion (US). It also seeks to provide technical assistance in developing monetary and financial policies and the establishment of national banks.

The IMF gets its money from its member nations. The amount of money each country pays into the IMF is based on its share of the world's economy so the richest countries pay more and the poorest countries pay much less. The IMF is also one of the largest holders of gold bullion, worth about $27 billion (US).

There are a range of problems associated with the IMF:

- It can be a lengthy process to acquire loans or credit, but financial crises can develop very quickly in poor nations.
- The IMF has been known to bail out insolvent domestic banks which has the effect of softening the consequences for unwise investing.
- Some have argued that IMF money is used by governments such as the US to pay money to poorer countries where they may be a military advantage to do so.
- IMF money lending does not always encourage the monetary reform that would help a country get out of poverty in the first place. Throwing money at a problem will not make it go away, the root cause of it must be addressed.
- The IMF is supposed to provide short-term financial assistance, yet it typically makes long term loans. Some countries have been continually borrowing for the last 30 years.

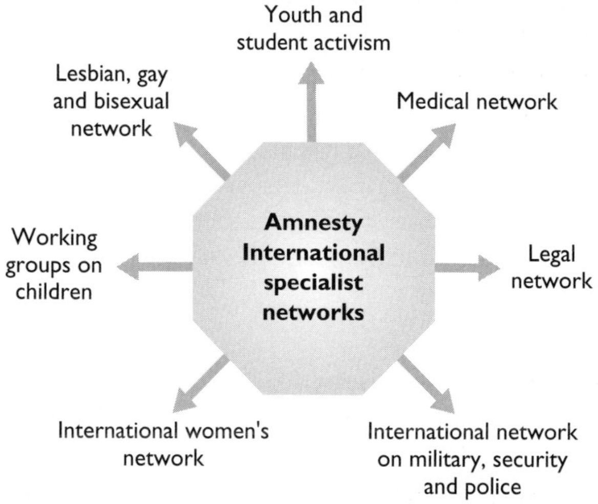

Figure 6.9 Amnesty International specialist networks

Amnesty International (AI)

Amnesty International is a non-governmental organisation (NGO) which was established in 1961 by a British lawyer called Peter Benenson. Its symbol is a lighted candle surrounded by barbed wire which was inspired by the Chinese proverb 'it is better to light one candle than to curse the darkness'. Today AI has branches in over 160 countries and over a million members. The main focus of Amnesty International is:

- **To free prisoners of conscience** – these are people who are illegally detained because of their beliefs, ethnic origin, sexuality, religion or political affiliation. Amnesty only works to free those prisoners who don't use or advocate violence.
- **Ensure fair and prompt trials for political prisoners** – political prisoners are those people who oppose a ruling party or who a ruling party considers to be a threat. Often they may be held in prison for years without trial or access to justice.
- **Abolish the death penalty, torture and other cruel, inhuman or degrading treatment of prisoners.**
- **End extra-judicial executions and disappearances** – extra-judicial executions are where individuals are executed on behalf of the state, but without a trial or hearing. These executions are often conducted by the military or civilian police.
- **To oppose opposition parties who advocate violence to oust a government.**

AI campaigns can take many forms, such as letter writing campaigns on behalf of particular individuals. They also gather information on human rights abuses worldwide. Amnesty pride themselves on their independence and they accept no government funds. Their finances are generated from membership fees and broad public support in the form of fundraising and donations. Amnesty has several specialist networks which investigate and campaign on specific issues. The specialist networks are detailed in Figure 6.9 above.

Think about it

Why is an organisation like AI important on a global scale?

Amnesty International has a superb website at www.amnesty.org which details human rights abuses worldwide. It also gives much greater detail on the origins and purposes of Amnesty.

Greenpeace

The Greenpeace environmental trust was set up in 1982, but it's precursor had been investigating environmental issues for more than a decade prior to this. Like Amnesty International it is another non-governmental organisation (NGO) which uses non-violent confrontation to highlight global environmental social problems and their causes through specific research and bearing witness to environmental events. It was originally established to examine the following issues:

- the effect of human activities on the environment
- making information known to the public
- relieving sickness and suffering of humans and animals caused by environmental issues.

It has also campaigned vigorously on many issues such as:

- genetically modified crops
- international whaling
- promotion of renewable energy sources
- elimination of toxic chemicals
- nuclear disarmament
- driftnet fishing.

Greenpeace does not accept funding from governments and it is independent of any political movement. It raises its funds from donations from the public and grants for research.

Case study

Genetic engineering enables scientists to create plants, animals and micro-organisms by manipulating genes in a way that doesn't exist in nature. Greenpeace are very concerned that these organisms will breed with natural organisms and spread in an uncontrolled and unmonitored way with potentially devastating consequences to natural food stock and the environment.

Greenpeace would like to see an end to genetically modified organisms but they recognise that commercial interests usually override ethical ones and they have called for interim measures such as keeping genetically modified organisms separate from natural ones to discourage cross-breeding and making sure that all food products are labelled as genetically modified so that the public has a chance to avoid them.

1 Why are Greenpeace concerned about GM crops?
2 Why is there a need for environmental groups like Greenpeace?
3 What is your view on GM crops?
4 What kind of power and influence do companies have who produce and develop GM crops?

Assessment activity 6-P1, 6-M1

Produce a magazine aimed at a public service officer such as a fire-fighter or police officer. Your magazine should be visually appealing and contain lots of diagrams and graphics. The topic of your magazine is international institutions and how they affect the services. What you need to do is describe a range of international institutions such as those described above, paying particular attention to the structure and decision making processes of the EU and show how the decisions made by these institutions have affected UK public services.

In order to get a merit your magazine should go further and *analyse* how the decisions made at international levels have affected the operations of UK public services.

Security issues at world summits

World summits are occasions where world leaders can come together to discuss international social and economic issues. There are many different kinds of summit with different nations attending each. For instance, the G8 Summit gathers the 8 most powerful nations on earth together, while the European Union Summit gathers the heads of the 25 member states together. In recent years these summits have been the site of rioting and violence by anti-globalisation and anti-capitalism protestors, who would like to see the world economic system be run in a more equitable manner so that the poorer people of the world have the same opportunities afforded the citizens of rich nations.

Regardless of the moral strength of their argument, protestors can cause tremendous disruption to the towns and cities where the summits are held and cause severe problems for the local public services. The world media really began to take notice of these protesters at the Seattle World Trade Organisation meeting in 1999 and realising that the headlines can bring in more supporters the protesters have demonstrated a strong presence at most summits since then.

Recent examples are The European Union Summit at Gothenburg in Sweden in 2001. The Swedish police were relatively unused to dealing with major civil disturbances and many police officers were injured in the protests to say nothing of the damage done to property and businesses in the city. The G8 summit at Genoa in Italy in 2001 was also the site of large protests despite the action taken by the Italian government and the public services to stop protesters even entering the city by closing airports, train stations and ports. In order to try and stop the protesters, Italy temporarily withdrew from the Schengen agreement (see earlier in this chapter) in the hope that this would stop the free movement of protesters over the Italian border. Similar precautions were taken by Spain who hosted the 2002 EU summit in Barcelona. The cost to the public services in terms of injury, resources and finance runs into the millions of pounds.

Protesters at the European Union Summit 2001

Think about it

Why do people protest at summits such as the ones described above?

War and conflict

One of the main functions of international organisations is to help prevent, manage and resolve conflict wherever it occurs globally. This can be a very difficult job and they are not always successful due to the underlying tensions and long history which can exist in conflict situations.

War has been given many definitions, but loosely it could be considered to be one of the responses a society can take to reduce the capacity of another society to achieve its objectives. Very simply put, war is a clash of interests which results in a violent armed struggle.

War and conflict are of vital importance in understanding the role of domestic and international public services. This is because conflicts of an ethnic, religious, political and cultural nature are continuing to dominate world attention. The United Nations University (UNU) estimates that over 150 wars have taken place since 1990. Although most of these wars occur within countries rather than between countries, the role of the public services is still crucial in a peacekeeping rather than an offensive capacity. UNU also notes that since about 90% of countries are made up of different ethnic and cultural groups this level of conflict shows no sign of decreasing. In fact one of the major changes in conflict over the last 40 years or so has been the tendency of wars and conflict to occur within nations rather than between nations.

Spectrum of conflict

Freedman (2001) comments that two main types of war and conflict have been the subject of contemporary thought as shown in Figure 6.10

High intensity conflicts

High level, high intensity conflicts involve military action in the form of an alliance of nations or a superpower using their military resources to obtain objectives in a highly organised and lethal manner. High intensity conflict tends to have a limited life span and rarely exceeds 6–10 years. With the end of the cold war and the decline in the influence of the superpowers these wars are becoming relatively infrequent. Examples of high intensity conflict over the last 100 years include:

- The Great War (World War I)
- World War II
- Vietnam War
- Falklands War
- Gulf War

Case study

The Persian Gulf War was fought by a United Nations coalition of 39 countries against the invasion of Kuwait by Iraq. The invasion of Kuwait occurred on August 2nd 1990 and by March 3rd 1991, Iraq had accepted a ceasefire and began withdrawing from the region. Iraq had seized control very quickly in Kuwait due to its vastly superior military strength, but within days the United Nations had called for Iraq's immediate and unconditional withdrawal. When it became clear that Iraq was not going to comply, the UN member states began deploying troops to bases in friendly nations in the region such as Saudi Arabia.

As a leading member of the United Nations, Britain was among the first countries to join the coalition. All three armed services were utilised in defence of Kuwait.

By January 1991 there were over 500,000 allied troops in the Persian Gulf region and the coalition had begun to heavily bomb Iraqi forces in Kuwait and also in Iraq itself.

In an attempt to split Arab support for the coalition the Iraqi leader Saddam Hussein began to target Israeli cities such as Tel Aviv with Scud missiles in an attempt to provoke a retaliation. There has been continuous conflict between Israel and the Arab world and an Israeli attack on Iraq might have fractured the coalition. However, the US pledged to protect Israeli cities and a direct Israeli retaliation was unnecessary. The ground war began on February 23rd 1991, but by then many Iraqi troops has been cut off from supply bases by the aerial campaign and were not well equipped to fight for sustained periods.

Type	Detail
Wars of necessity (usually high intensity)	These tend to be major conflicts involving regional and global powers who are mounting challenges to vital interests such as oil pipelines (Gulf War) or territory (Falklands War).
Wars of choice (usually low intensity)	These tend to begin as a civil war within weak countries which then leads global powers to intervene as a stabilising force. They often involve militia's and guerilla's and can be very difficult to bring to a decisive conclusion due to ethnic, cultural and religious divisions, for example the Yugoslavian crisis in 1999.

Figure 6.10 Two main types of war

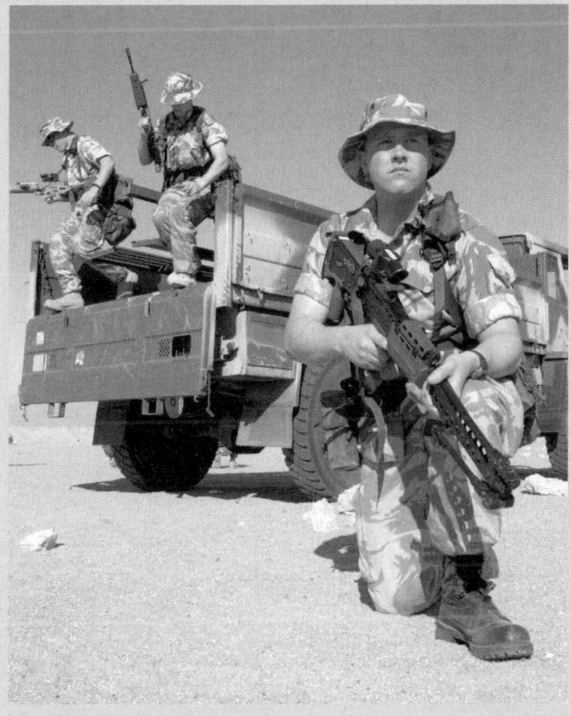

British troops in Kuwait

Causes:

- Iraq had long considered Kuwait to be a part of its nation and this had led to several confrontations before.
- Rich deposits of oil straddle the border of Kuwait and Iraq and control of them means finance can be generated for the economy. The deserts in the region make it difficult to define a border accurately.
- Iraq had recently been defeated in a long and bloody conflict with its neighbour Iran. It could be argued that the Iraqi government was looking for an easier conquest to salvage national pride.

1 What triggered the invasion of Kuwait by Iraq?
2 Why would the global community respond to this particular invasion when other invasions such as China's invasion of Tibet were largely ignored?
3 What was the long term impact of the war on the people of Iraq?
4 What was the impact of the conflict on the UK public services.

Low intensity conflicts

Low level conflict in contrast can last many decades and often has its roots in cultural and religious issues going back hundreds of years. They tend to involve military skirmishes and low intensity attacks and retaliation.

Nations have become increasingly fragmented, with each ethnic grouping asking for recognition or power from the government of the nation concerned. If a government does not want to recognise a group of people or if they are becoming too powerful they may take action against them in the form of propaganda designed to create hatred. They may also seize property or land and ultimately take military intervention against them. Equally, a sub-group of society may take action against the government if they feel they are being ignored or persecuted. This action could take the form of local militia's, guerrilla warfare or terrorist attacks.

Low-level conflict can also occur over a disputed border territory where two or more countries clash over ownership of a territory over a period of many years. Examples of low-level conflict have been seen in the following areas:

- Northern Ireland
- Israel/Palestine
- Kashmir

Case study

The conflict over Kashmir involves 2 of the world's newest nuclear superpowers: India and Pakistan. The tensions in the region have erupted from a cycle of violence and aggression dating back to 1947 when British Colonial Rule ended. The British departure created two new states in the region divided roughly on ethnic and religious lines – Muslims in Pakistan and Hindus in India.

The fate of the region of Kashmir was problematic because the leader at the time was Maharajah Hari Singh, a Hindu, whilst the majority of the population was Muslim. The choice of the Kashmiri leader to accede to India was not a popular one either with the Kashmiri Muslim

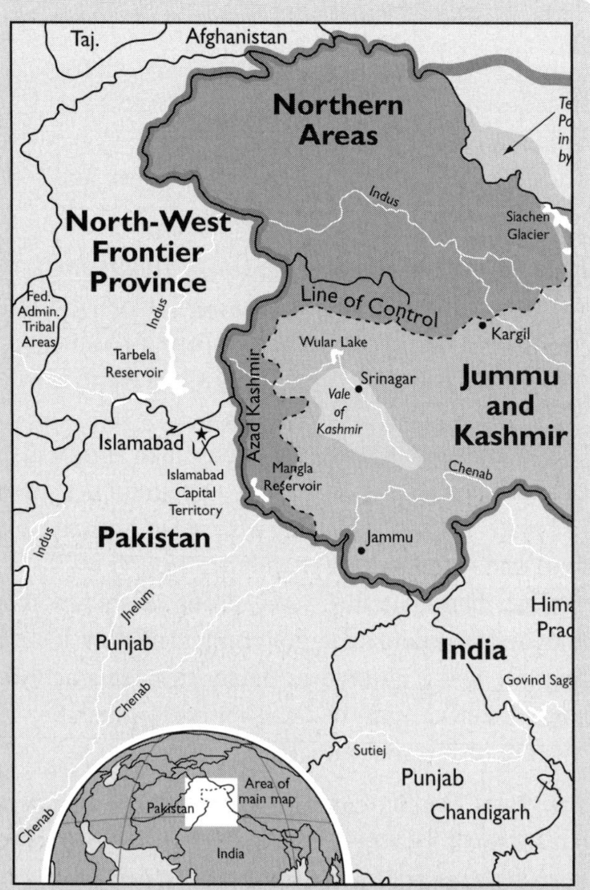

Map of disputed region

population or the Pakistani government who considered Kashmir part of their natural cultural territory. War in the area broke out in 1947 and continued throughout 1948 resulting in Pakistan controlling one third of the disputed region and India two thirds. The border between the disputed regions is called the line of control and it is hotly contested. The situation is also complicated by the involvement of a third nuclear superpower, China, who claim a controlling interest in the Aksai Chin region of Kashmir.

Causes:

- disputed border territory across the line of control
- territorial control over a politically important region
- ethnic, religious and cultural differences
- differing political ideologies.

British involvement:

The area was under British colonial rule for around 200 years with the end of British control being the start of the current conflict. Although British service personnel are not stationed in Kashmir the British government has continually supplied arms to India whilst maintaining an arms embargo on Pakistan. This situation gives the impression that the British government favours India over Pakistan in a conflict in which we should be neutral. In recent years as tensions have escalated, British politicians have mediated between the countries in order to reduce the growing threat of nuclear conflict which would not only devastate the region concerned, but would have widespread repercussions across the globe.

1. What do you think are the main reasons for the Kashmir conflict?
2. What are the implications of a conflict involving 3 nuclear superpowers?
3. How could the conflict be resolved?
4. What is the impact of the conflict on the people of Kashmir?
5. What are the implications on the UK public services?

Theory into practice

Make a list of as many wars and conflicts as you can and decide, based on the information above, whether they are low intensity or high intensity.

Causes of war

What causes war is a very difficult question to address. Many academics and historians have examined why war happens, but there is often much disagreement between them. The first issue that you must be aware of is that war and conflict rarely happens because of a single identifiable cause. Most wars happen because of a combination of the factors we are about to explore. Nitinkin (2000) identifies 4 main causes of war, each with its own sub-divisions.

1 War is natural

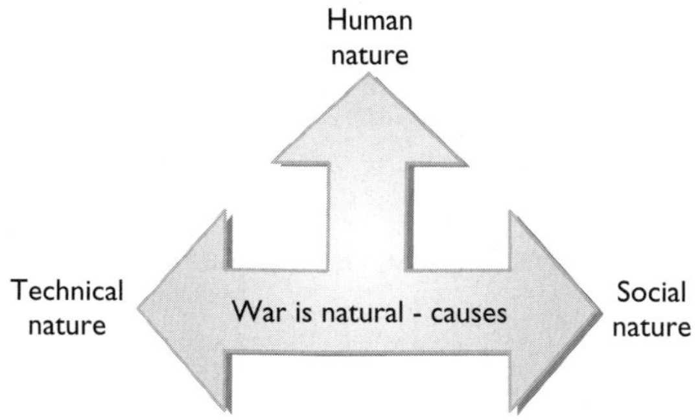

Figure 6.11 Natural causes of war

- **Human nature** – there are those who believe that humans have inborn and inbuilt destructive and aggressive impulses. These aggressive drives must be channelled into the right context and the perfect forum for these drives is war. In essence, war is our biological destiny, we cannot escape from it. The urge to be violent and aggressive is with us from birth and it is a continuation of the struggle for survival that happens between different species or territorial groupings in the animal kingdom.
- **Social nature** – the social nature of humanity can cause wars because we tend to have structured social relationships. These social relationships have divisions and sub-divisions which take the form of race, religion, class, caste or nationality. According to this point of view, war is a natural form of interaction between these groupings and can help societies make social and technological developments.
- **Technical nature** – this theory supposes that war is a natural companion to scientific and technological developments. Modern countries have unprecedented influence over others by virtue of their weaponry computers and media.

2 Resources

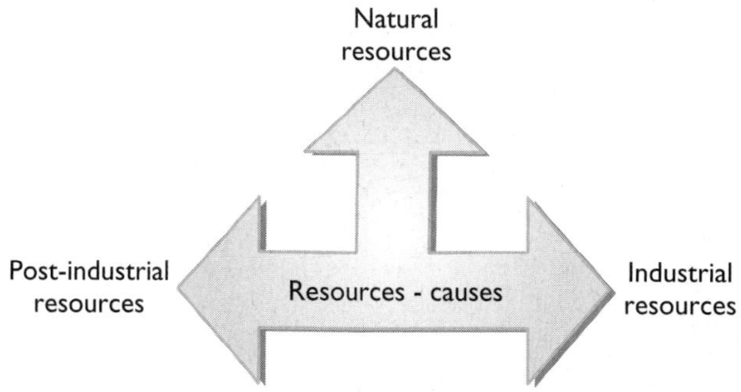

Figure 6.12 Causes of war – resources

- **Natural resources** – nations often involve themselves in war over a variety of natural resources, such as oil, gas and water. These assets are immobile, they cannot be moved to another location so preserving them is a matter of enormous political and economic concern. In some countries the income generated from natural resources can constitute the majority of money entering a country. Without these resources the economy would collapse. Countries that rely on immobile natural resources are often found in the Middle East and Africa where the land is rich in oil and precious stones and minerals. An example of this kind of war is the first Gulf War as Iraq invaded Kuwait in a dispute over oil pipelines.
- **Industrial resources** – wars can be caused because one of the groups desires to acquire the industrial wealth and influence of another. This wealth can take the form of cities or ports, trade routes, manpower, manufacturing industries or financial centres.
- **Post-industrial resources** – we live in an information age and conflict over the control of information is not uncommon. Control of this data is usually in the form of computer technology and scientific advancement. Conflict can develop particularly over the development of military technology.

3 Power

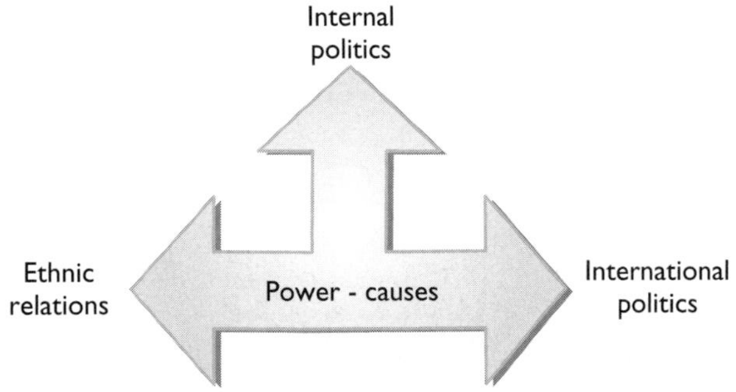

Figure 6.13 Causes of war – power

- **Internal politics** – wars can be caused by internal power struggles between sub-groups and divisions in a society, such as classes and tribes. It may also involve certain geographical regions wanting autonomy and self-determination or even full independence from a larger nation. Conflict can also be caused by the tactics and politics used by a government against those who it seeks to represent.
- **International politics** – the international political arena has many potential sources of war and conflict, such as border disputes and disputes over territory as can be seen by the ongoing conflict between India and Pakistan over Kashmir. It must also be remembered that many countries exist as a part of a greater political and military alliance, such as NATO. An attack on one of these countries may be seen as an attack upon them all. This was the case with the German invasion of Poland which started WWII. Britain had an alliance with Poland and so was obliged to enter into conflict even though it had not suffered an attack.
- **Ethnic relations** – this factor can cause war and conflict if an ethnic group is denied access to resources and the mechanisms of government. There have been instances of some ethnic groups being denied access to facilities that other groups take for granted such as education, healthcare, and political suffrage. Clear examples of this are the Jews under the Nazi regime and non-whites in South Africa. In certain circumstances, relations between ethnic groups can deteriorate to such an extent that genocide and ethnic cleansing can occur. This is where the dominant ethnic group undertakes the wholesale extermination of another group, as happened in the former Yugoslavia and also in Rwanda.

4 Identity

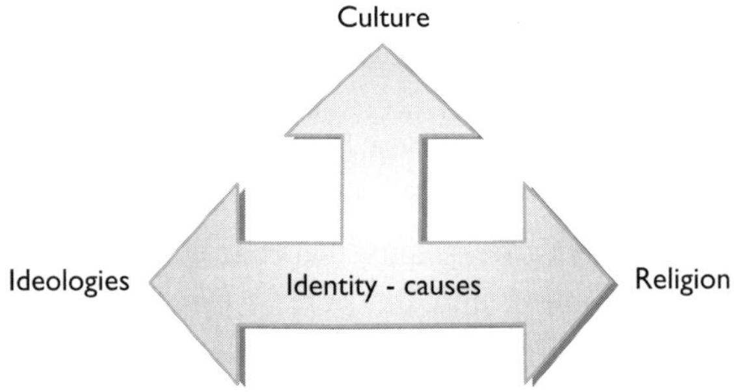

Figure 6.14 Causes of war – identity

- **Culture** – often people feel so passionately about their way of life that they want to protect it against pollution or dilution by the culture of other groups or societies. Sometimes this feeling may apply to a small tribe and sometimes it may apply to a whole country. When it applies to a country it is called 'nationalism' and it can lead to the persecution of people who do not belong to the dominant culture. It can also cause conflict if the leaders of a society have a different cultural background to the population they lead.
- **Religion** – religion can often be a great source of stability and cohesion in society by providing moral and ethical guidelines on appropriate ways to conduct ones day-to-day existence. However, conflicts between different or competing religions can lead to hatred and mistrust and cause political instability. Equally, the distribution of power between civil and religious leaders can be a source of conflict if either are not happy with the balance of power. An example of religious differences being a

contributing factor to conflict is apparent in the Northern Ireland situation.

- **Ideologies** – an ideology is a set of ideas about how things should be organised. For instance, a political ideology is a set of ideas about politics and a religious ideology is a set of notions governing how a belief system may be organised and implemented. Groups of people may have competing thoughts on many different issues. For example, the USA and the Soviet Union had competing political and economic ideologies after the Second World War leading to a state of mistrust and hostility that became known as 'The Cold War'.

Think about it

Using the ideas outlined above and any more that you can think of, what do you think is the single main cause of war in the twentieth century?

Assessment activity 6-P2

Research and deliver a 10-minute presentation which summarises the common causes of war and conflict. In addition, produce a handout for your audience which illustrates the spectrum of conflict and the changing nature of war.

British service involvement in war and conflict

Since 1960, British services have been involved in the following wars or conflicts:

Location	Time period
Malaya	1948 – 1960
Kenya	1952 – 1960
Cameroon	1960 – 1961
Borneo	1962 – 1966
Cyprus	1963 – 1964
Aden	1964 – 1967
Hong Kong	1966 – 1967
Northern Ireland	1969 – present
Oman	1970 – 1975
Falklands	1982
Gulf	1991
Sierra Leone	1991 – present
Bosnia	1992 – present
Kosovo	1999 – present
Afghanistan	2001 – present
Iraq	2002 – present

The role that the British public services play in these conflicts is not always the same. The roles can vary from:

- direct military combat, for example in the Falklands
- peacekeeping, for example in Kosovo
- evacuation of foreign nationals, for example in Sierra Leone
- policing of disputes or riots, for example in Northern Ireland
- training military and civilian personnel, for example in Kosovo and Iraq
- disaster relief, for example in Afghanistan and Iran
- war crimes investigation, for example World War II.

Case study

In 1921, Ireland was partitioned into six Northern counties which remained under British control and 26 Southern counties which were independent. However, this arrangement was seen as a betrayal by some Irish republicans, who were prepared to fight for a united and independent Ireland completely free from British rule. To this end, there were Irish Republican Army (IRA) campaigns in the 1920s, 1940s and 1950s. Constant vigilance was needed by Unionists (supporters of British rule) and the British government to ensure relative

Map of Northern Ireland and Eire

stability, and emergency legislation introduced a predominantly protestant unionist police service and systems of economic discrimination against the Catholic minority in Northern Ireland. It was the dissatisfaction of the Catholics with their treatment that lead to civil rights disorders in the 1960s which were the origins of the modern troubles.

In the 1960s there were many protests by the Catholics such as marches, sit ins and the use of media to publicise grievances. By 1969 the Northern Ireland administration were increasingly unable to handle the disorder and the British government sent in troops to re-establish order. The Provisional Irish Republican Army (PIRA) was formed in 1969 as a consequence of the violence and riots in Londonderry and Belfast in August of that year and began a campaign of violence against the British Army and military targets designed to liberate Northern Ireland from British rule. The violence reached a peak in 1972 when 468 people died. The British government suspended the Northern Ireland government and began direct control of the province from Westminster, a situation which continued into the 1990s. What began as an Anglo-Irish conflict before 1921 developed into an intra-Irish conflict between Protestants and Catholics.

Causes:

- British colonisation and involvement in the province
- political differences between the British and the Irish Republicans and between the Irish Republicans and the Irish loyalists
- religious conflict between protestants and catholics.

British involvement:

Since this is an Anglo-Irish conflict it is expected that British involvement would be high. British public and security services have been operating in

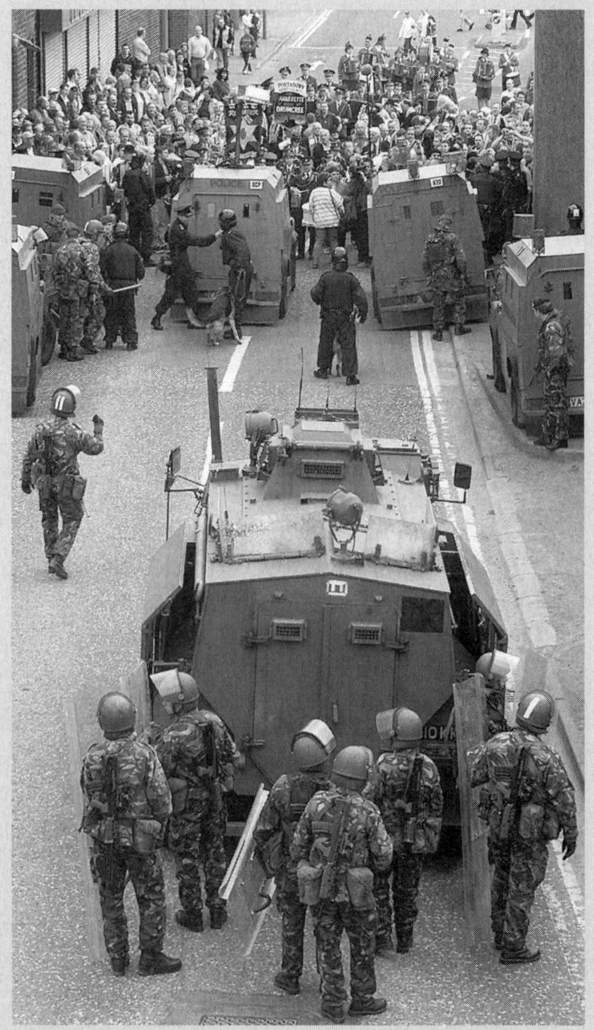

British Troops on the streets of Northern Ireland

Northern Ireland for over thirty years. Essentially they are supposed to act as a support for the police service, The Royal Ulster Constabulary (RUC) in its mission to bring peace and stability to the area. In reality, their presence on the streets of Irish cities has often caused resentment, hatred and violence placing the lives of troops and support staff at risk from terrorist attack. Indeed many British soldiers and intelligence personnel have lost their lives on the streets of Northern Ireland. However, the brutality is not a one-way street and the British public services have been accused of colluding with loyalist terrorist groups in order to assassinate republican terrorists. In addition there have been many instances where the conduct of the British Army has been called into question for their treatment and sometimes killing of Irish individuals.

Case study

In 1971 the British forces put into place operation Demetrius which allowed those suspected of terrorist activity in Northern Ireland to be put in prison without trial. This is called internment which is a gross violation of human rights. However, the process of internment still began, but there were several problems with it. Firstly the intelligence held by the RUC and the British intelligence services was out of date and many of those interned had not been active for many years and secondly only suspected republicans were picked up despite the fact that loyalist terrorists were also active. It was also well documented that those who were interned suffered ill treatment.

Protests against internment grew and it is against this background that the massacre which became known as 'Bloody Sunday' took place. On January 30th 1972 soldiers from the 1st Parachute Regiment opened fire on an unarmed protest in Derry, killing 13 people outright and wounding many others, one of whom later died. A British appointed tribunal found the soldiers not guilty of the murder of those fourteen civilians to the outrage of republicans in Ireland and others across the world. The Saville Inquiry was set up in 1998 to investigate the actions of the British services in this massacre. Six years later it is still ongoing and the results are not expected to be known until 2005.

1. Why are the events of Bloody Sunday still controversial 30 years on?
2. Why might a new inquiry help resolve some of the issues still surrounding this event?
3. Why might the initial inquiry into the event have been biased?
4. How did operation Demitrius breach Human Rights conventions?

It is also important to remember that involvement in some of the conflicts mentioned above is not the sole province of the armed services. During the Hong Kong riots of 1966 and 1967 there were many British police officers serving as part of the Hong Kong police force. Similarly the situation in Northern Ireland has tremendous implications for all of those involved in any public service including people like postal workers who have been recent targets in the troubles.

Case study

Originally Vietnam had been a French Colony, but during World War II it was occupied by Japanese troops who committed atrocities on the civilian population. As a result, a strong anti-Japanese movement developed which had sympathy with communist economic and social ideals. It was led by a man called Ho Chi Minh and the movement was called the 'Vietminh'. After WWII ended and the Japanese occupation withdrew, France wanted to rule Vietnam again, but the Vietminh were fiercely opposed to this and war broke out between them lasting eight years. The Vietminh received aid from communist China and eventually they defeated the French in 1954.

The peace treaty stated that Vietnam would be temporarily split into a communist North and a non-communist South along a position called the 17th parallel. The peace treaty also stated that democratic elections would be held nationally in 1956 which would reunify the country under a single government. The United states were very concerned about communism in North Vietnam

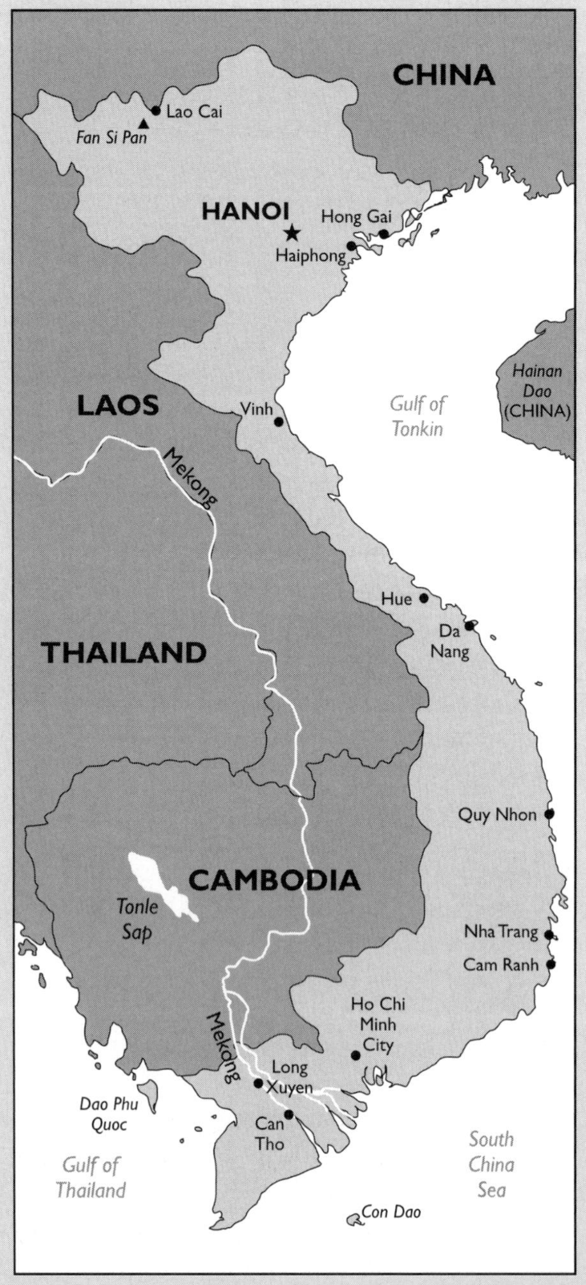

Map of Vietnam and neighbouring nations

and pumped massive amounts of military, political and economic aid into South Vietnam, creating The Republic of Vietnam under the leadership of Ngo Dinh Diem who was fierce anti-communist. Almost immediately Diem began claiming that North Vietnam was attacking his nation. Using US backing he began to retaliate in 1957 and he began arresting thousands of South Vietnamese civilians who were suspected of being communist sympathisers. This caused outrage amongst most South Vietnamese who hated this oppressive US backed regime.

The promised reunification elections did not take place which angered the North Vietnamese government who then embarked on a course of action to 'liberate' South Vietnam. By 1965 or so the South Vietnamese government was on the verge of collapse and the US decided to bolster them by sending in their own military troops. However the US did not fully understand the desire of the people of South Vietnam for a united country free from foreign intervention and they failed to account for the guerrilla tactics used by the South Vietnamese rebels, called the 'Vietcong'. The US began to lose the support of its citizens because of high casualty rates amongst military personnel and highly publicised atrocities against Vietnamese civilians. By 1969 there was no question that the US would have to withdraw, the only problem was how to do it without appearing defeated. By 1973 a ceasefire had been agreed which meant the last US personnel could leave.

Causes:

- the end of the French colonial era created a political vacuum which needed to be filled
- US paranoia over the post-war rise in communism and the belief that if one nation falls to communism, the surrounding nations will also become communist which led to intervention in a situation that was not their concern
- the peace treaty which separated North and South Vietnam against the wishes of the people.

British involvement:

The British declined any official involvement in the Vietnam conflict, but other commonwealth countries such as Australia and New Zealand did send troops and military aid to the region.

1 Why did the US decide to get involved in Vietnam?
2 Why were the Vietcong in a strong military position?
3 What have been the long-term effects on the people of Vietnam?

4 Do you think there were any lessons for the US to learn in this military encounter?
5 What is the 'domino theory' and why is it relevant to this conflict?

Assessment activity 6-M2

Produce an A3 poster which compares the causes and effects of at least two contrasting international conflicts or wars since 1960. Your poster should be visually appealing and make use of graphics and maps wherever possible.

In summary

There are several factors which indicate that war and conflict may appear in a region. Some of these factors are:

- a government had an oppressive and unaccountable regime
- gross human rights violations
- economic distress
- military seize power from a civilian government
- demographic pressures such as an increase in population coupled with limited access to food and water.

International terrorism and counter terrorism

Terrorism can be a difficult concept to define, but it includes the idea of violence against a civilian population to inspire fear for political purposes. The CIA defines terrorism as the use of violence for political ends.

Think about it

New Internationalist journal makes an interesting point by quoting a US ambassador in Central America:

'If they do it, it's terrorism; if we do it, It's fighting for freedom.' NI Issue 161

Consider the above quote by a US ambassador. What are the implications of making a statement like this?

Threats posed by international terrorism

Terrorist groups may be international, operating in many countries and fighting against a perceived global threat or they may be regional in nature operating in one locality. Whether local or international, terrorist groups in general tend to exist for only a few reasons.

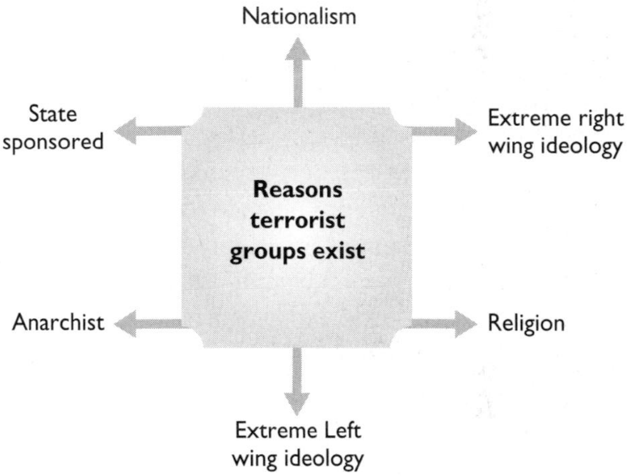

Figure 6.15 Reasons why terrorist groups exist

1 **Nationalism** – this is when a group of individuals feel so strongly about independence and self-determination in their region or country that they are prepared to take up arms against those who govern their 'nation'. Examples of nationalist terrorist groups are the PIRA in Northern Ireland, Euskadi ta Askatasuna (ETA) in Spain and the Palestine Liberation Organisation (PLO) in Palestine.

Case study

HAMAS (Islamic Resistance Movement) is a terrorist group operating primarily in the disputed Israel–Palestine territories of the West Bank and Gaza Strip. It is an outgrowth of a social, religious and educational movement called the Muslim Brotherhood and its aims are to establish an Islamic Palestinian state in place of Israel. HAMAS are a very influential and successful terrorist group in their region.

The occupied territories of the West Bank and Gaza Strip typically have high numbers of refugees and the population suffers from substantial socio-economic hardship and discrimination. This makes the idea of fighting for liberation a very attractive one. HAMAS has been successful in developing a social and political structure based around Islamic principles that operates as an alternative to nationalist structures of other terrorist organisations in the region such as the Palestine Liberation Organisation (PLO) led by Yasser Arafat. Hamas use suicide bombers in attacks against Israeli interests and they have widespread support amongst Palestinians in doing so. Hamas's spiritual and religious leader is Islamic cleric Sheik Ahmed Yasin, but the leaders of the terrorist branch of Hamas prefer to be anonymous since the Israeli government of Ariel Sharon has made a policy of tracking them down and killing them. Sheik Yasin was assassinated by the Israeli government in March 2004.

Its activities are financed through donations from other Islamic states such as Iran and through substantial private donations from Palestinians and other Muslims worldwide. However, Hamas is not just a terrorist organisation, it provides a social, educational and cultural infrastucture for many Palestinians which goes some way to explaining its popularity.

1. Which of the reasons terrorist groups exist described above apply to HAMAS?
2. What are the main aims of HAMAS?
3. Why is HAMAS popular amongst the Palestinian population?
4. Do you think the policy of the Israeli government in dealing with HAMAS is likely to be successful or is it more likely to create increased anger and resentment? Explain your reasons.
5. Why is the Israel–Palestine situation a breeding ground for terrorism?
6. Do you think the assassination of Sheik Yasin is morally or legally defensible?

2. **Religion** – religious groups use terrorism to further divinely commanded purposes. They come from all major faiths or sometimes smaller sects and target individuals or countries who they perceive to be enemies of their faith. Examples of such groups are Hezbollah (Islamic), Aum Shinrikyo (doomsday cult in Japan) and Al-Quaida (Islamic).

Case study

Al-Quaida has become one of the world's best known terrorist groups since it claimed responsibility for the destruction of the twin towers of The World Trade Centre on September 11th 2001. It is an international terrorist group which funds and organises the activities of Islamic militants worldwide. It developed in the early 1980s to support the war in Afghanistan against the Soviet Army. Ironically one of the major sources of funding to Al-Quaida at that time was the United States who gave $500 million to arm and train members of Al-Quaida and other anti-soviet groups. After the war against the Soviets came to a successful conclusion the organisations primary goal became the overthrowing of corrupt governments of Muslim states and their replacement with true Islamic law (Sharia). Al-Quaida is intensely anti-western with particular emphasis on the United States. There are several reasons for this:

- the US support for Israel at the expense of Islamic Palestine
- the US is seen as providing support for Islamic countries that are enemies of the group such as Saudi Arabia and Egypt
- the involvement of the US in Islamic affairs, such as the Gulf war in 1991/2 and Operation Restore Hope in Somalia in 1992/3.

The group is led by Osama bin Laden amongst others, and it was originally based in Afghanistan and the Peshawar region of Pakistan. It moved its base of operations to Sudan in 1991 and returned to Afghanistan in 1996 where it was the subject of a campaign by the US and its allies in 2002 to seek and destroy its infrastructure and operations in response to September 11th.

Al-Quaida is implicated in a whole string of terrorist attacks in many nations such as the killing of US military personnel in Somalia and Yemen, attempted assassinations of the Egyptian president and the Pope and car bombings against US and Egyptian embassies worldwide. It is thought to have several thousand members, but it also acts as a focal point for other Islamic extremist groups. It is well funded, with Osama bin Laden himself estimated to have a personal fortune of 300 million dollars. The organisation also maintains many profitable businesses and collects donations worldwide.

1 What are the reasons Al-Quaida exists?
2 What are its primary aims?
3 Why is the US a particular target?
4 What are the implications of Al-Quaida activity on the British public services?
5 What are the favoured terrorist methods of Al-Quaida?

Collapse of the twin towers

3 **Extreme left wing ideology** – these groups seek to destroy the economic system of capitalism and replace it with a left wing socialist or communist alternative. Examples of left wing groups include Japanese Red Army, the Baader-Meinhoff group in Germany and the Khmer Rouge in Cambodia (Kampuchea).

4 **State sponsored** – this is when a terrorist group forms to attack the enemies of another nation. Although they would seem to be independent they actually receive funds and resources from countries that are sympathetic to their aims. Countries that sponsor terrorism are often found in the Middle East and their targets are usually powerful western nations. Examples of state sponsored groups are the Abu Nidal Organisation (Syria & Iraq) and the Japanese Red Army (Libya). It is interesting to note that Western nations have also been accused of funding terrorist regimes. For instance, the US-funded freedom fighters in Afghanistan in the 1980s in their war against the Soviet Union. These freedom fighters developed into the Mujahadin and Al-Quaida.

5 **Right wing terrorist groups** – these are often quite poorly organised and indulge in street violence and riots with racist and anti-semitic purposes. The breeding ground for this type of activity is Western Europe and there are many small neo-fascist groups in Germany, France and Britain.

6 **Anarchist terrorism** – this is where revolutionary groups seek to overthrow the established government or destroy the established world order by the use of violence, bombings and assassinations. Some academics have argued that the anti-globalisation and anti-capitalist protesters and world summits fall into this category.

Groups such as the ones detailed above often do not fall neatly into one category. Just because a group has a religious motive for its action does not mean it can't be state sponsored. Similarly, a group may also be left wing and nationalist. Just about any combination of the above reasons for terrorism is possible.

Case study

The Basque region is located in the North West corner of Spain and across the border of the South Western French provinces of Labourd, Basse-Navarra and Soule. Euskadi ta Askatasuna (ETA) was established in 1959 with the aim of creating a Basque homeland, independent of Spanish rule, based around Marxist principles. It arose partly as a reaction to the right wing rule of General Franco in the 1950s and 60s. Their activities include political bombing and assassinations of Spanish government officials, including judges and opposition leaders. It finances its activities from the extortion of Spanish businesses and armed robberies. It also claims ransoms on kidnap victims.

ETA has killed more than 800 people since the early 1960s. ETA is also thought to have received training or assistance from Libya and Lebanon, which are countries with a history of sponsoring terrorist activities. It is also possible that it has links with the IRA in Northern Ireland due to the similarity of their political aims and methods. Although many people in the Basque region are in support of self determination for their region, the vast majority of them reject achieving it by terrorist means.

1 Which of the reasons terrorist groups exist described above apply to ETA?
2 What are ETA's main aims?
3 What are ETA's preferred terrorist methods?
4 What are the effects of ETA's actions on the Spanish public services?
5 Why are they often compared to the IRA?

Methods used by terrorists

Terrorist groups use a variety of methods to inspire fear and achieve their political goals, such as bombings, assassinations, suicide attacks and hijacks. These have been the traditional tactics of most terrorist groups in the twentieth century, but increasingly there is the threat of terrorist groups using non-conventional methods such as:

- nuclear terrorism
- biological terrorism
- chemical terrorism
- cyber terrorism.

Nuclear terrorism

Nuclear terrorism is not just the use of a nuclear bomb to cause widespread mass destruction, it is also the use of radioactive materials to cause environmental damage and destroy property. It can also be the use of conventional weapons to damage a nuclear target such as a power station. Nuclear materials are not especially difficult to get hold of on the European black market, particularly since the collapse of the USSR. Terrorist groups can also purchase radioactive material from nations which are sympathetic to their aims and support their terrorist actions. These might be nations such as Libya or Iraq.

Biological terrorism

This is the use of biological organisms such as microbes and viruses spread in civilian populations in order to cause casualties and lower morale. The recent terrorist use of Anthrax spores in the US in 2001 is a perfect example of this particular strategy. Biological terrorism cannot be used for pinpoint attacks and often the results may be unnoticed for many days making it very difficult to track down the perpetrators. However, biological weapons can be rendered almost harmless by a quick and organised medical response and vaccination programme. Biological weapons are weapons of terror and panic rather than mass destruction. Their primary aim is to demoralise and frighten a civilian population and distract a government from other, more effective attacks.

Chemical terrorism

This is the use of a toxic chemical agent released into the atmosphere or water system in order to create casualties and demoralise the population. Chemical terrorism is not a theoretical possibility, it is a concrete reality. In 1995 a terrorist group called Aum Shinrikyo (Supreme Truth) released the chemical nerve agent Sarin on the Tokyo underground killing 12 people and injuring hundreds of others. Chemical substances are much easier to manufacture or obtain than either nuclear or biological substances. They are also more mobile because they are safer to carry meaning they can be carried from country to country in relative safety. However, chemical weapons are very difficult to use effectively because environmental conditions such as wind and rain interfere with its progress. Often, just moving out of the area will be enough to counter the immediate effects of a chemical toxin. To put chemical attacks in context, when Aum Shinrikyo conducted their attack on the Tokyo underground they had perfect environmental conditions, but even so only 10% of the people present were injured and only 1% of the injured died. Chemical attacks are not very effective at mass destruction, but like biological terrorism it succeeds in its primary aim which is to generate fear and panic.

Cyber terrorism

Cyber-attacks have become a pressing concern for counter-terrorism experts in the Western world because most of our critical systems such as defence, communications and finance are computer controlled. If systems such as air traffic control, medical facilities or nuclear power plants were targeted, the loss of lives could be devastating. The potential for cyber-attacks is great because the computer equipment needed to do it is freely available across the world and anyone can possess it without fear of interference. However, as yet there has been no major terrorist cyber-attack on the critical systems of Western Nations.

Case study

The situation which gave rise to the creation of the PIRA (Provisional Irish Republican Army) in the late 1960s is detailed earlier in this chapter. The PIRA seek to create a united Ireland free of British control. The military wing is organised into tightly knit units called 'cells' which work independently of each other and are administered by the army council. Its actions have included most of the conventional terrorist methods such as bombings, assassinations, kidnapping and murder against British and loyalist targets both in Northern Ireland and on the British mainland. It receives funding from criminal activities such as robberies and also overseas aid from countries such as the United States and Libya. The structure of the PIRA is shown in Figure 6.16 on the following page.

The original PIRA established in 1969 has also spawned several splinter groups:

1 **The Real IRA (RIRA)** – formed in 1997 because of objections to the peace process by PIRA hard liners. It continues its activities in the hope of disrupting the peace process. The RIRA claimed responsibility for the Omagh bombing in 1998 which killed 29 people including a woman who was heavily pregnant with twins. It has also been linked to the attack on MI6 Intelligence Headquarters in London.
2 **The Continuity IRA (CIRA)** – this splinter group is not as active as the RIRA but is thought to be responsible for sporadic assassinations and attacks since it was established in 1994 aimed mainly at protestant targets.
3 **Irish National Liberation Army (INLA)** – this is the least active of the groups and has been implicated in some shooting of loyalists in Northern Ireland. It was established in 1974 and is effectively what was left of the original IRA after the PIRA split from them in 1969. The INLA has Marxist roots.

It has been argued that the splinter groups and the PIRA do not get along well and that their relationship is characterised by distrust and dislike. In the past they needed to present a united front against the British, but this did not stop Gerry Adams leader of Sinn Fein (the political wing of the PIRA) from condemning the Omagh bombing in 1998.

1 Why have the IRA splintered during their history?
2 Why do you think IRA terrorist activities receive such a lot of media coverage but attacks by

loyalist terrorist groups in Northern Ireland do not receive as much?

3 Do you think the British should withdraw from Northern Ireland? Explain the reasons for your answer.

4 What is the impact of both loyalist and republican terrorist activity in Northern Ireland on the UK public services?

5 What are the preferred terrorist methods of the IRA?

Effects of terrorism, war and conflict on the British public services

Terrorism has a substantial effect on the British public services in terms of training for biological and chemical attack and disaster management co-ordination between the emergency and armed services. They must be prepared to respond to an attack on the mainland UK or its territories by a

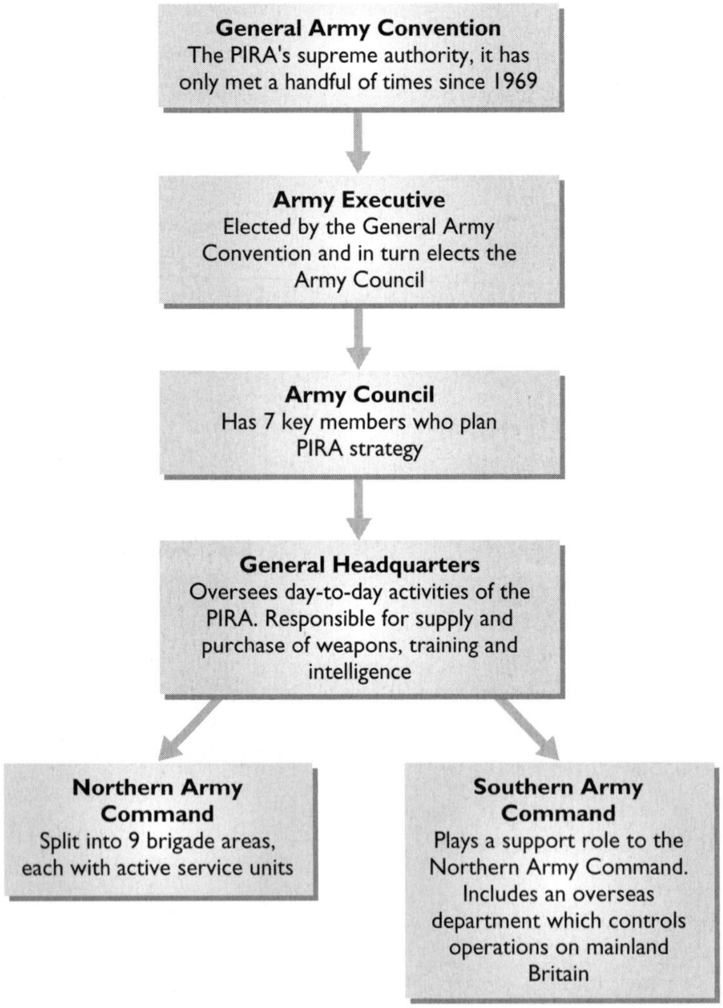

Figure 6.16 Structure of the PIRA

terrorist group. This includes preventing attacks by gathering intelligence on when attacks are likely to take place and acting to prevent such attacks.

There are also substantial new pieces of legislation such as The Terrorism Act (2000) which gives the police increased powers to seize assets and arrest people who may be promoting terrorism outside Britain. However, there are concerns from some civil liberties groups such as Amnesty International that the new legislation could be used to stop legitimate protests such as those against genetically modified crops and road building or unions calling for strike action. There is a delicate balance between combating terrorism and promoting respect for civil liberties. This is where the government and the public services need to caution against 'knee-jerk' reactions to horrors such as the September 11th attack and give careful thought on how to end terrorism without compromising freedom.

In addition to the effects of terrorism directly on the services it also has an indirect effect by creating situations of war and conflict which the services have to respond to, such as in Iraq and Afghanistan. The overall effects of terrorism, war and conflict on the services can be described in summary as follows:

- **Additional specialist training** – needed to be able to respond effectively to any conflict or terrorist situation which may occur.
- **Death and injury** – terrorism and conflict can cost the lives and health of UK service men and women as the current situation in Iraq demonstrates.
- **Post traumatic stress disorder** – this is a long term complication which many service men and women face after dealing with traumatic situations such as those they may be faced with in terrorist and war situations.
- **Loss of equipment and resources** – terrorism and war can lead to the destruction of equipment and resources which the services need to be able to perform their duties effectively. A lack of equipment can have serious implications on the safety of our services and civilians.
- **Training others** – often our emergency and armed services are called upon to train the services of other nations to deal effectively with the aftermath of terrorism and war. This may be in the form of rebuilding a civilian police force such as is ongoing in Iraq or in assisting an existing foreign service to combat terrorism through effective counter terrorism measures.
- **Financial cost** – combating terrorism and responding to conflict is a very expensive business and this money must come from somewhere. The consequence of this is that the services may have to go without some things in order to have others.
- **International institutions** – the UK public services must be prepared to work with other international agencies to respond to conflict or terrorism. This may mean that they are allocated to a peacekeeping force led by the UN or NATO and have to work within a slightly different framework than they are used to.

Assessment activity 6-P3

Produce an A3 poster which describes how British public services are affected by war, conflict and terrorism. Your poster should be visually appealing and be designed to go on display in your classroom.

Counter terrorism

Combating terrorist networks can be a very difficult job. By their very nature terrorist groups operate in secret and often in small groups that cannot implicate the wider organisation if they are apprehended. The British security service spends over half its annual funding allocation on combating domestic and international terrorism. Figure 6.17 (see page 123) shows some of the possible counter-terrorist measures listed by the United Nations which can be implemented by governments and agencies seeking to end terrorism.

Not all groups will respond to all of these methods and not all countries will be prepared to utilise all of these strategies. It takes more than one counter-terrorism measure to disrupt a terrorist organisation and in reality governments will employ multiple tactics to achieve the result they want. It is difficult to assess the effectiveness of many counter-terrorism methods because details about their use may not be available for security reasons. However, where evidence is available the results are mixed.

- Economic sanctions against Iraq put in place after The Gulf war have succeeded only in harming the general population as those who sponsor terrorist attacks have enough money and power to be immune from such sanctions.
- In Northern Ireland, diplomacy and political compromise have brought a measure of security to the region in recent months and it is hoped that the peace process will be ongoing and come to a successful conclusion for all concerned as a result of this.
- The US favoured direct military strikes as a response to September 11th in order to destroy Al-Quaida. This tactic is expensive and time consuming and can cost many lives without any visible results. Al-Quaida is an international terrorist group with independent cells across the world who are well funded and well trained. A military strike against one part of it will not destroy the organisation and it may recruit new members to the cause because of their resentment of US countermeasures.

The effectiveness of counter-terrorist measures is variable and depends largely on the type of strategies employed by a particular government. Negotiation and compromise is generally a far better tool of resolution than direct military action. This is because the root cause of most terrorism lies in the perceived oppression of one group by another and negotiation can help lift this feeling of oppression while violence simply reinforces it. The problem with this is that governments cannot be seen to be forced to the negotiating table by groups who use violence to threaten them and their citizens as it would be a licence for any group with a grievance to commit atrocities simply to get the ear of those in power.

Think about it

What is your view on the fact that most governments refuse to negotiate officially with terrorists?

Assessment activity 6-P4, 6-M3, 6-D1

This is the only distinction level task in the International Perspectives assessment criteria so if you want to get a high grade it is important that you do well on this task.

Write a report that summarises the threats posed by international terrorism and the effectiveness of counter terrorist measures. Your report should be clear and concise and contain a full bibliography. In order to get a merit you should go into further detail and *explain* rather than summarise the threats posed by international terrorism and in order to get a distinction you should *analyse* the threats rather than explain them.

Method	Detail
Combating terrorism through mechanisms of politics and government.	• Address the specific political grievances of the terrorists. • Engage publicly or privately in discussion to resolve conflict. • Offer political concessions to terrorist groups or to the political parties representing them. • Offer amnesty to active terrorists. • Apply diplomatic pressure on the countries sponsoring terrorist groups.
Combating terrorism through economic and social policy.	• Address the specific socio-economic grievances of the group. • Ban terrorist fundraising. • Create a socio-economic climate that disinclines people to violence, by having good standards of living for all. • Apply economic sanctions to countries which sponsor terrorism.
Combating terrorism through psychological and educational strategies.	• Establishing common values with opponents. • Allowing freedom of expression. • Ban interviews and publications by terrorist groups. • Provide training in dealing with terrorist threats. • Media campaigns to condemn the groups methods.
Combating terrorism through the use of military tactics.	• The use of strikes/operations to undermine/ destroy groups. • Use public services to protect potential victims and property. • Recruitment and training of counter-intelligence personnel.
Combating terrorism through the use of the judicial and legal system.	• Agree and abide by international treaties which denounce terrorism. • Expand extradition treaties. • Introduce and update laws prohibiting terrorist activity. • Give harsh sentences to convicted terrorists. • Provide witness protection. • Increase the speed of justice for terrorists.
Combating terrorism through the effective use of the police and prison service.	• Target harden objects or people which might be at risk from attack. • Improve international police relations and co-ordination. • Run training simulations of terrorist attacks. • Encourage informants and infiltrators. • Ensure terrorist networks cannot recruit in prisons.
The use of intelligence and security services to combat terrorism.	• The effective use of technology to monitor terrorist groups. • Improve and maintain links with other intelligence services. • Infiltrate terrorist organisations.

Figure 6.17 Counter-terrorist measures as described by the United Nations

Human rights

Rights are certain things that an individual is entitled to have or do based on principles of fairness and justice. Many rights are written down in the constitution of a country which lists the basic rights a citizen can expect. However, some countries such as Britain do not have a constitution and in these countries it is assumed that people have the right to do anything unless the law expressly forbids it. These are called legal rights. People also claim rights based on general ideas of fairness and equality which are called moral rights and they may or may not be supported by the law of the land. It is also important to remember that legal and moral rights can sometimes be in opposition to each other.

Think about it

Can you think of a situation where a person's legal and moral rights might be in opposition.

There are many organisations which examine human rights and monitor how people are treated across the world, such as Amnesty International and The United Nations. There are also many charters or agreements which set out the rights countries should afford their citizens. We will now examine some of these agreements.

The United Nations Declaration of Human Rights

As with many of the organisations and issues discussed in this chapter the UN Declaration is a post-war initiative and it is easy to see why. Two major global conflicts had been fought in less than thirty years and terrible atrocities had been committed against the European Jewish population, prisoners of war in the Far East and the populations of Hiroshima and Nagasaki in Japan amongst many others. These atrocities had shocked the world and it was felt that a better way must exist for dealing with international problems and treating people in times of both peace and conflict. This was the birth of the United Nations organisation and its charter which emphasises the fundamental importance of human rights. The UN organised a commission to draw up a declaration that would state the importance of civil, political, economic and social rights to all people regardless of colour, religion, nationality, gender or sexuality.

The declaration was agreed in December 1948 and consists of 30 rights or articles. (see appendix on page 356).

Of the 30 articles in the declaration it has been argued that 3 and 5 are key provisions. Article 3 states that all human beings are entitled to life, liberty and security of the person. Article 5 states that no one shall be subjected to torture or to cruel, inhuman or degrading treatment or punishment. These are core political and civil rights ensuring freedom and safety. Article 25 specifies that all people are entitled to an adequate standard of living for themselves and their families. This includes food, clothing, housing and medical care, which would seem to be fundamental rights on which the others are built. Articles 28 and 29 are also crucial although they are not often discussed. They overarch the others in that they emphasise the responsibility of the international community to put into place a political and social framework in which respect for human rights can flourish. Without this foundation the other articles cannot be effectively implemented. The UNDHR has achieved world-wide prominence and is probably the most important document of its type ever written. It has become an influential standard by which nations are measured.

Assessment activity 6-P5 (a)

Conduct a discussion with a colleague in which you explain the key features of the UN Declaration of Human Rights (see appendix on page 356). Record your discussion in the form of a set of minutes.

The Geneva Convention

The Geneva Convention can trace its roots back to 1859 when a Swiss citizen called Henry Dunant witnessed the aftermath of the Battle of Solferino during the Second War of Italian Independence and was horrified at the numbers of soldiers who lay dying and wounded with no-one to help them. This experience led him to call for medical relief societies to be set up to care for wounded soldiers and civilians in times of war. Dunant also called for an international agreement to be established which would protect those agencies and the wounded from further attack. This is how the voluntary relief society of The Red Cross was established.

In 1864 twelve nations signed a treaty in which they agreed to care for all sick and wounded people regardless of nationality and they also agreed to recognise the Red Cross agency as neutral in any conflict. This treaty was called The Geneva Convention. There are now 4 Geneva Conventions which most countries have signed which cover a variety of issues such as armed forces on land and sea, treatment of prisoners of war and the treatment of civilians in times of war.

The 1st and 2nd Geneva Conventions

These 2 conventions are very similar and the main points are:

- the sick, wounded and shipwrecked must be cared for adequately
- each side must treat the wounded as carefully as if he/she were their own
- the dead should be collected quickly
- the dead should be identified quickly and protected from robbery
- medical personnel and establishments should not be attacked.

The 3rd Geneva Convention

This convention outlines what should happen if a member of the armed forces falls into enemy hands and becomes a prisoner of war (POW). Its main points are:

- POWs do not have to provide any information other than their name, rank and service number
- POWs must be treated humanely
- POWs must be able to inform their next of kin and the International Red Cross of their capture
- POWs must be allowed to correspond with their family
- POWs must be supplied with adequate food and clothing
- POWs must be provided with medical care.

The 4th Geneva Convention

This deals with the protection of civilian personnel in wartime and its main points are in Figure 6.18.

Protected civilians MUST be:	Protected civilians MUST NOT be:
• treated humanely • entitled to respect for honour, family and religious practices • allowed to practice their religion • specially protected in safety zones if : – under 15, – sick/wounded, – old, – expectant mothers.	• discriminated against because of race, religion or political opinion • forced to give information • used to shield military operations • raped, assaulted or forced into prostitution • punished for offences they have not committed.

Figure 6.18 The detail of the 4th Geneva Convention

The European Convention on Human Rights

This treaty was signed in 1950 by members of the Council of Europe. It predates the EEC and the EU, but membership of the EU requires that the treaty is signed. The UK was a founding member of the convention and very influential in its content. It was also one of the first countries to sign and agree it. As with the United Nations Declaration of Human Rights it arose from the atrocities Europe had experienced during the Second World War. The convention came into force in 1953 with civil and political rights. Social and economic rights were included in 1961. It is intended to act as the lowest common denominator of rights, which means that it is set at a modest level to encourage compliance with it. It incorporates the right to:

- life
- freedom from torture or inhuman or degrading punishment
- freedom from slavery, servitude, enforced or compulsory labour
- liberty and security of the person
- a fair trial
- respect for private and family life
- freedom of thought, conscience and religion
- freedom of expression
- freedom of assembly and association
- freedom to marry and raise a family.

Until the Human Rights Act 1998 came into force British courts could take note of the convention but could not directly enforce it.

The Human Rights Act 1998

This piece of law is designed to incorporate the European Convention on Human Rights into domestic (British) law. It provides a package of rights based law which is in contrast to the traditional English system based on common law prohibitions (statements about what people cannot do). Under the Act, courts will have to interpret any existing law as being consistent with the convention. This shifts some power away from parliament and towards judges. The impact of The Human Rights Act on the public services will be addressed later in this chapter.

Human rights violations

Here are some examples of human rights abuses committed round the world. Human rights violations are not the sole province of developing nations, they occur in developed Western nations such as the UK and the USA as well.

Case study

The human rights organisation Amnesty International claims that the UK is the only country in Europe that routinely sends children under the age of 18 into armed conflict. The United Nations Convention on the Rights of the Child is being compromised and children could be at risk from serious injury and death. Under 18s have been deployed during the Kosovo crisis, Gulf War and the Falklands war with Argentina. The recruitment of under 18s into the armed forces has seen a sharp increase over the last few years, possibly as a result of the difficulties in recruiting and retaining older staff. The Ministry of Defence has recorded the deaths of 12 under 18s in training activities between 1982–1999.

1. Why is it inappropriate that under 18s fight in wars and conflicts?
2. Should the UK armed services stop recruiting under 18s? Explain your reasons.
3. Why is this a human rights issue?
4. What are the implications to the armed services of only recruiting over 18s?

Case study

The use of the death penalty as a legal punishment is problematic at best. There is no real evidence that it acts as a deterrent to other offenders, it can be more expensive than keeping someone in prison for life and running through it all is the possibility that the wrong person may be executed. In the period since 1990 almost 60 countries have abolished the death penalty and in the same period the US has executed 750 prisoners. The real problem in the US lies in the fact that the death penalty is a political issue not a moral or ethical one and that the system applies the penalty in an arbitrary way. Amnesty International report that since 1977 the US has applied the death penalty in the following cases:

- 18 prisoners for crimes they committed as children which is in direct violation of international law
- people with mental illnesses and severe learning difficulties
- 25 individuals whose guilt was questionable
- 17 foreign nationals who were denied their right to consular assistance.

Racial and geographic bias in the death penalty is still a major issue. 80% of the people executed since 1977 were convicted of killing white victims, which seems to indicate that the murder of a black victim isn't seen to be as serious to the US judicial system. In addition, 80% of the executions were carried out in the southern US states, Texas in particular. So whether a criminal is given the death penalty can depend on the colour of the victim and their geographical location at the time of the crime. This kind of inequality and bias is not consistent with a fair and impartial judicial system.

84 people have been released from death row since 1977, proving conclusively that no criminal justice system is flawless and when innocent people are wrongly convicted in the US it could cost them their lives.

1 What is your view on the death penalty?
2 Why does the application of the death penalty in the US breach Human Rights?
3 Explain how the application of the death penalty in the US could be considered racist.
4 Can any judicial system ever be flawless?

Case study

Australian government policies up until 1970 allowed for the removal of tens of thousands of indigenous children from their families and home in order to prepare them for a place in 'white' society. However, this policy was aimed at the extinguishing of the aboriginal language and culture. Many of the children who were forcibly removed were raised on government and church missions in remote outback locations where living conditions were harsh and abuse, both physical and sexual, were widespread. The policy of taking children has had lasting and devastating consequences on the aboriginal population of Australia. According to a 1997 report on The Stolen Generation:

- 90% of 'stolen' Aborigines have suffered from chronic depression
- an estimated 2/3 suffered physical abuse
- 1/6 had been sexually abused
- in some parts of Australia 90% of Aborigines seeking legal assistance for criminal offences were 'stolen' as children.

The forced extermination of one group of people's language and cultural identity by another is widely considered to be genocide. Successive Australian governments tried to force an indigenous people to assimilate white culture leading to the attempted cultural destruction of the aboriginal people.

1 What are the long-term consequences of the actions taken by successive Australian governments on the aboriginal population?
2 Do you think the actions of the Australian government amounts to cultural genocide? Explain your reasons.
3 How could the Australian government begin to make amends for the situation?

Case study

Although Kenya has not officially executed a prisoner for more than 10 years, there are widespread allegations about extra-judicial killings by prison and police officers. For example, 6 prisoners were shot by prison guards in King'ong'o Prison 150 miles outside Nairobi in September 2000 and in July 2001 7 people were executed by a roadside after the Kenyan police pulled them from a bus. In executions such as this the individuals responsible are rarely held to account and are allowed to continue with their brutality. The excessive use of force used by Kenyan public services also applies to policing of demonstrations and the arrest of criminal suspects. Kenya has been highlighted as a human rights violator both by the United Nations and Amnesty International.

1. What are extra-judicial executions and why are they a breach of human rights?
2. Why is it important that any public service is accountable for its actions?
3. What could the Kenyan government do to bring those responsible to account?
4. Do you think this particular breach of human rights is widespread globally? Explain your reasons.

Assessment activity 6-P5 (b)

Amnesty international has an excellent website at www.amnesty.org where you can find hundreds of examples of human rights abuses in their online library. Use this facility and the information outlined above to produce a factsheet which describes human rights abuses in at least three countries.

Human rights and the public services

The Human Rights Act 1998 makes it unlawful for any public authority to act in such a way that it is incompatible with a right under the European Convention on Human rights. Public authorities include:

- Government departments
- National Health Service
- police.

The Home Office has set up a Human Rights taskforce, with members from both government and non-governments organisations that will monitor the implementation of the Human Rights Act and its consequences for the public services. As the Act only came into force on 2 October 2000 there is little current research available.

The police

Of all of the public services, the police are most likely to be affected by the new legislation. The Association of Chief Police Officers (ACPO) has set up a team to disseminate human rights information and issues of good practice to all 43 forces in England and Wales. Each police service is required to nominate a human rights 'champion' who will regularly meet with other champions to share ideas and experience. ACPO also comments that The Human Rights Act 1998 will help reinforce good policing practice and encourage greater professionalism and ethical behaviour in the ranks. A police human rights working group is currently in the process of assessing the effects of the Act on police policy and procedure which is being completed in conjunction with The Home Office.

In addition to dealing with the challenges of Human rights legislation there are several other human rights issues which are of importance to the police. One of these is the allegations of racism which followed in the wake of the Stephen Lawrence Inquiry (Macpherson report). The commission for racial equality claims that although Afro-Caribbean people make up 2% of the British population they account for 46% of arrests for robbery. It also comments that ethnic minorities in Manchester are 4 times more likely to be stopped by the police than whites. The Greater Manchester police chief at the time Davis Wilmott admitted that his force had 'overt' and 'internalised' racism. The Macpherson report made recommendations regarding police practices:

- ensure that ethnic minorities are encouraged to join the police service
- instigating procedures to allow racist incidents to be reported
- proposals to make 'stop and search' procedures fully accountable so that officers will have to explain why they stop black people more than white.

The issue of racism in the police service also leads to another human rights issue faced by the police which is the issue of police brutality. It has often been claimed that police brutality is a problem in multi-ethnic communities which suffer from economic deprivation. In 1981 the predominantly black neighbourhood of Brixton in London suffered horrific rioting after 13 black people died in a fire that was dismissed by the police as accidental. Allegations of police brutality and paramilitary policing were widespread at the time and were reinforced by the behaviour of certain police forces in the Miners strikes of the early 1980s. Instances of police brutality caught on camera in recent years also add to public concern regarding the issue. It is also worth noting that a paper from the police research group at The Home Office states that 6% of deaths of suspects while in custody could be linked to excessive use of force by the police. This has clear implications under article 2 of the Human Rights Act, the right to life.

The police must also address the fact that the Police Complaints Authority (PCA) is not an independent investigating body and that complaints made against the police are investigated by the police themselves. This does not promote public confidence and it does not ensure that grievances against the police are being investigated in an impartial and unbiased way. Other human rights issues which affect the police include the use of police surveillance which could be challenged under the right to privacy and the stop and search procedure which could be challenged under the right to privacy and the prevention of discrimination.

The Armed Services

The armed services have traditionally been very biased in terms of who it employs to complete its work. Homosexuality was banned in the services and those who were found to be homosexual were dismissed. This was in clear breach of the UN Convention on Human Rights and The Human Rights Act 1998. The ban on homosexuality in the Armed Services was lifted by Defence Secretary Geoff Hoon in 2000, but this was not until the government had been challenged in the European Court of Human Rights by four homosexual ex-military personnel. The four, each from different services, were denied the right to appeal against their dismissal by the Appeal Court in London. They took their case to the European Court arguing that the investigations into their private lives violated their human rights. The European court agreed stating that it was illegal to ban homosexuals in the Armed Services under The European Convention on Human Rights.

A similar debate is currently ongoing regarding the entry of people with disabilities into the Armed Services. Sir Charles Guthrie, one of Britains foremost senior military officers told a royal services institute in London that disabled people had 'no right' to serve in the Army. It has been claimed by some disabled groups that the recruitment of individuals with disabilities would enable the forces and particularly the Army to relieve its recruiting crisis and that people with disabilities could be recruited to work behind the lines in non-combatant roles.

This form of discrimination also applies to the service of women in the Army. Currently women are not permitted to fight in the infantry or in front line positions. This rule may have to be abolished in the light of the new human rights legislation and the changing nature of society that we live in.

The Army must also deal with the human rights issues of sending under 18s into combat situations as outlined earlier in this chapter.

Think about it

What are your views on:

- the inclusion of gays, lesbians, bisexuals and transgendered individuals in the armed services
- the possibility of women serving in front line infantry units
- the opportunity for people with disabilities to serve their country.

Theory into practice

You have been told above about some of the human rights issues that apply to the police and the Armed Services. Choose another service you are interested in and consider how human rights issues apply to that service.

Assessment activity 6-P6

Research and deliver a 10-minute presentation which explains how human rights issues affect the operations of at least 3 public services in the UK. Use visual aids where appropriate.

End of unit test

1 Why did the United Nations Organisation come about?

2 What was the major threat to Europe when NATO was created?

3 What is the impact of EU decisions on the UK public services?

4 What are the principle aims of Amnesty International?

5 Describe the spectrum of conflict.

6 How has war and conflict changed over the past 40 years or so?

7 What are the common causes of war?

8 What is the role of peacekeepers?

9 What roles do UK public services play in war and conflict?

10 What are the common methods used by terrorist groups?

11 What are the common sources of global instability?

12 Describe in detail at least 3 counter-terrorist measures and consider how effective they are.

13 Describe the main principles of the various Geneva Conventions.

14 What is cultural genocide?

15 How are human rights protected in the UK?

16 Why do people engage in terrorist activity?

17 What is the 'stolen generation'?

18 What are extra-judicial executions?

19 What human rights issues affect the UK public services?

20 How are the UK public services accountable for human rights breaches?

Additional resources

Human Rights Act 1998 Her Majesty's Stationery Office

Websites

www.nato.int – NATO

www.un.org – United Nations

www.europa.eu.int – Europa

www.amnesty.org – Amnesty International

www.greenpeace.org – Greenpeace

www.state.gov – US Department of State

www.bbc.co.uk/news – BBC News

DEMOCRATIC PROCESSES

Introduction to Unit 10

The aim of this unit is to develop your awareness of British politics and its relevance to the public services. It examines the importance of democracy to individuals and society and explores the advantages and disadvantages of different voting systems.

You will also gain an understanding of how major British and European political institutions function and the power they have to influence the lives and work of civilians and public services. To fully appreciate the British political system you must also evaluate and understand the ideologies of the political parties, which are represented within it. This unit will also signpost some contemporary political issues and examine in detail their consequences on the public services.

Assessment

Throughout the unit, activities and tasks will help you to learn and remember information. Case studies are included to add industry relevance to the topics and learning objectives. You are reminded that when you are completing activities and tasks, opportunities will be created to enhance your key skills evidence. After completing this unit you should be able to achieve the following outcomes.

Outcomes

1 Examine the importance of a **representative democracy**

2 Describe the functions of **political institutions**

3 Summarise the main features of the **structure of British Government**

4 Investigate a **political issue** and its relationship to the public services.

Politics

This chapter provides you with an overview of British and European politics and examines their impact on individuals, society and the public services. Politics is the study of different opinions or conflicts and the solutions which can be put into place to solve difficulties such as crime, healthcare, education and defence.

If you ever get worked up about an issue you hear on the news or read in a newspaper then you are being political. Even if you don't read a newspaper or watch television news, you are political every day of your life, whether it is negotiating an extension for an assignment or being active in the student union. Even at home you are political from arguing over territory or property with your brothers and sisters to resolving conflict with your parents.

Think about it

What was the last issue you heard on the news which angered you? Explain why you felt this way.

The public services are looking to recruit active citizens (see chapter 4 for further discussion) who are interested in the issues which are going on in wider society and understand how the work of politics affects the duties of the public services directly. Being an active citizen also means being able to understand and analyse the impact of political decisions on how you conduct yourself in uniform.

Political issues

The practice of politics is mainly concerned with the resolution of conflict between various parties on particular issues and the production of an agreement which enables societies to be stable and harmonious. Politics has become increasingly important on a number of levels as shown in the table below.

Think about it

Why is a broad political agreement a desirable aim for a society?

Theory into practice

The British National Party (BNP) have recently made significant political gains in the local elections in Lancashire towns such as Burnley and Oldham. The BNP is an extreme right wing party whose core political beliefs include repatriation of immigrants and a complete ban on any asylum seekers regardless of the situation in their home nation. Some of their beliefs are not consistent with the values of all sections of society.

1 The BNP believe that the political rights of white British people are more important that the political rights of other sections of society. What kinds of conflict are likely to arise from this view?
2 Are the rights of one group ever more important than the rights of another?

Conflict in modern society normally occurs when individuals have conflicting interests or values. Individuals will agree over broad issues such as high quality education and healthcare for all, but

Level	Description
Local	The managing of local resources to benefit local communities.
Regional	Management and distribution of resources and issues of independence in a larger geographical area.
Multi-regional	Several different geographical regions sharing common interests or in conflict about shared resources.
National	Issues which affect an entire nation, such as changes in law and policy or taxation.
International	Issues which affect 2 or more nations, who have shared interests such as the members of NATO or the EU. Equally, issues of dispute between different nations such as border, territory and resources.
Multi-national	Issues which affect many countries such as UN peacekeeping in which over 50 nations participate, declarations of war which activate systems of alliance or disease epidemics.
Global	Issues affecting the majority of nations such as human rights abuses, asylum and involvement in the United Nations which currently has 191 members.

Figure 10.1 The importance of politics at all levels

will disagree on the specifics of how to achieve these goals. For instance, teaching unions such as the National Union of Teachers (NUT) and National Association of Teachers in Further and Higher Education (NATFHE) agree with the government that a good quality education is of fundamental importance, but teaching unions want to achieve this by paying teachers more money whereas the government might achieve it through restructuring. Individuals and groups are keen to protect their own interests and will make decisions which benefit them. Value conflicts can also bring people into opposition, in some instances even if they are not directly affected by it. For example, a person might object to the building of a new nuclear power station even if they don't live close enough to it to be directly affected.

Think about it

What issues do you feel strongly enough about to become political?

Key points

1 The study of politics is very important to any public service career.
2 Most people are political as they have values, beliefs and opinions which they discuss openly.
3 Politics revolves around managing different points of view.
4 Different points of view can lead to conflict.
5 A general political agreement over issues such as morals is advantageous in managing a society.

Democracy

There are many ways of organising a system of government but the one that we are most familiar with in the West is democracy. Democracy is a system of government which involves rule by many. As early as the 4th century BC distinctions had been drawn between democracy and other systems of government. Plato in his political commentary 'Politics' was among the first scholars to try and evaluate different political systems. However, this meaning does not indicate how power should be distributed, who the many rulers are or who they should rule. According to Heywood (2002) many meanings have been attached to the notion of democracy including:

- a society based on equality of opportunity and individual merit
- a system of welfare and redistribution aimed at narrowing social inequalities
- a system of decision making based upon majority rule.

The nature of the relationship between the government and the people is complex; at the forefront of democracy is the notion of political equality. This is the idea that each individual has an equal amount of political power. In the UK we have traditionally had restricted access to political power, for example women did not receive full voting rights until 1928. A similar situation has existed in most nations which claim to be democratic; Switzerland did not get universal suffrage until 1971. It is clear to see from the above examples that democracy – rule by the people – doesn't always include all of the people.

Think about it

Which substantial group of individuals are denied voting rights and access to political representation in the UK and other Western Nations?

The term democracy becomes much more useful in understanding political systems when we examine types of democracy often used in organising societies. There are three main types of democracy that this chapter will examine; direct, representative and liberal.

Direct democracy

This particular form of democracy is sometimes called participatory democracy and according to accepted political views it was established over 2000 years ago in ancient Greece. It is a system based on the direct and continuous participation of citizens in the political process. Direct democracy is a very difficult system to manage with large populations of citizens eligible to vote. How do you ensure that millions of individuals have the same access to political meetings and equal time to speak out on issues?

Direct democracy is still used in certain circumstances such as referendums. A referendum is a system of voting on one particular issue which is then decided on the basis of the will of the majority of people. For example, if there was a referendum in the UK about joining the European single currency, every citizen eligible to vote would have to abide by the majority judgement of the people. In a direct democracy there is no distinction between the government and the governed, the people make the decisions and therefore act as their own government. The advantages and disadvantages of direct democracy are outlined in Figure 10.2 below.

Think about it

Could direct democracy work in the UK?

Representative democracy

This system of democracy is different from direct democracy in that rather than having a direct part to play in the political process, an individual elects a representative to put forward their views and make decisions for them. This system distances the individual from the political process as they are only able to exercise their political power once every few years at election time. One of the major features of representative democracy is that the elected representative must be genuinely accountable to the citizenry; they must put forward the views of the people who elected them or face losing their seat at the next election.

Advantages of direct democracy	Disadvantages of direct democracy
• Each citizen can express their own views on issues that are important to them. • It may help to educate the general public the importance of political issues. • It ensures decisions are accepted as legitimate. The people are more likely to accept decisions they have chosen themselves. • It enables the citizenry to be empowered and responsible for change.	• Cannot be used with large groups of citizens. • Citizens may be ignorant or uninformed about the issues they are expected to decide upon. • Time consuming as organising constant referenda can delay crucial decision making. • The public can be swayed by propaganda and emotional appeals and are therefore unreliable decision makers.

Figure 10.2 Advantages and disadvantages of direct democracy

However, it is often the case that once elected, representatives may choose to follow their own agenda ignoring the wishes of the electorate. Representative democracy and the use of elected individuals with a mandate to speak for the people raises a whole host of issues which do not arise in a direct democracy, such as:

- the role of the representative
- the separation of individual and government
- the role of the citizenry after elections.

The advantages and disadvantages of representative democracy are shown in Figure 10.3 below.

Simulation

The National Democratic party has announced it intends to contest the Witchingham South Constituency when its seat comes up for by election next month. The current MP, 60-year-old Sheila Southall has represented Witchingham South for over 25 years. The new contender is Richard Marks who is a multi-millionaire entrepreneur and has recently bought several large businesses in Witchingham including the local newspaper, the Witchingham Chronicle. Mr Marks, 45 who lived in London until 3 months ago has already begun an aggressive political campaign to win the seat and commented to our reporter yesterday, 'Witchingham needs a new MP for the new Millennium'. Mrs Southall who has lived and worked in the constituency all her life refused to comment on the upcoming battle.

1 What is the role of the MP for Witchingham South?
2 What are the advantages for the people of Witchingham in electing a representative?
3 What are the disadvantages to the people of Witchingham in electing a representative?
4 What impact might Mr Mark's business interests have on the outcome of the election?
5 In your opinion which candidate would be a suitable representative for Witchingham South? Explain the reasons for your choice.

Assessment activity 10-P1

Identify the main concepts of a representative democracy.

Liberal democracy

Liberal democracy is a term often used to describe Western democracies. Ideas about liberal democracy began in the nineteenth century and the main idea behind it is that the state should have minimal involvement in the organisation of society. It should exist to remove barriers to the well being of an individual, but that is all. In a liberal democracy the state provides healthcare, education and security but would not regulate business or personal conduct. Liberal democracies

Advantages of representative democracy	Disadvantages of representative democracy
• It is more practical to have direct democracies in large societies. • Decisions are made by individuals whose job it is to be well informed. • Representatives are directly accountable to the electorate. • Releases the citizenry from the time consuming burden of being involved in politics directly. • Often quicker than going through the processes of organising a referenda.	• Individuals are distanced from the political processes of their society. • Representatives may be self serving or have their own agenda. • Citizenry are only involved in the democratic processes once every few years. • Encourages political apathy in the citizenry. • Representatives with more money to fund a media campaign are often more successful. The best representative isn't always elected. • May not be a choice of candidate or party.

Figure 10.3 Advantages and disadvantages of representative democracy

are capitalist in nature as they believe in the paramount importance of the market, economy and competition. According to Roberts (1995) all of the liberal democracies that have emerged in the last century have been representative democracies where political authority was based on the popular consent of the people and there was a genuine choice between a variety of representatives and parties. Liberal democracy with its notion of a limited state and free market competition cherishes ideals such as civil liberties and political equality.

In the UK we have a parliamentary democracy which is based on liberal democratic principles. The government of the UK is formed from whichever political party commands a majority in the House of Commons. It is the role of the House of Commons and the House of Lords not to run the country but to hold to account those who do. The advantages and disadvantages of liberal democracy are outlined in Figure 10.4 below.

Simulation

A leaked memo from the office of the Chancellor of the Exchequer last night caused a storm of controversy in the Commons. The memo outlines the government's plans to cut taxation for small businesses, while increasing taxation on individuals. The Shadow Chancellor last night commented 'that as much as businesses ought to be encouraged, they should also pay into the treasury in order to fund essential services, just like the rest of us'. Neither the Prime Minister nor the Chancellor were available for comment.

1. Why would the chancellor choose to reduce taxation on small businesses?
2. What are the advantages of minimal state intervention in the running of society?
3. What are the disadvantages in minimal state intervention in the running of society?
4. What are the benefits to society of having a range of political parties and representatives to choose from?
5. Should business interests be of more importance than individual or group interests? Explain your answer.

The role of the elected representative in a democracy

Liberal representative democracies are the kind of political systems we are most familiar with in the West. The system relies heavily on the role of the elected representative.

Jones et al (2001) comments that although the House of Commons may constitute a representative assembly in that the members were appointed in fair and free elections the members of the House are not representative of the population which elects it. The majority of MPs representing constituencies in the UK are white, male and middle class. Jones et al notes the following points about the countries elected representatives:

- in 1945, 85% of Conservative MPs had attended Public school
- in 1997, 66% of Conservative MPs had attended Public school

Advantages of liberal democracy	Disadvantages of liberal democracy
• The citizenry have a choice of representatives and parties. • Civil liberties are protected. • Market competition helps create and sustain a healthy economy. • The state has minimal interference with the private/family life of individuals.	• Market and corporate interests come before the interests of individuals and groups. • Many political parties have similar views and many offer no real choice to the electorate. • Electorate is divorced from the political process.

Figure 10.4 Advantages and disavantages of liberal democracy

- in 1997, the vast majority of all MPs had attended University
- in 1997, women and ethnic minorities were heavily under represented.

Think about it

Can a socio-economically unrepresentative elected body ever represent accurately and fairly the views of its electorate? Explain your answer.

The duties of a Member of Parliament are split between working in the constituency where they were elected and working in the House of Commons itself. The current split is described below:

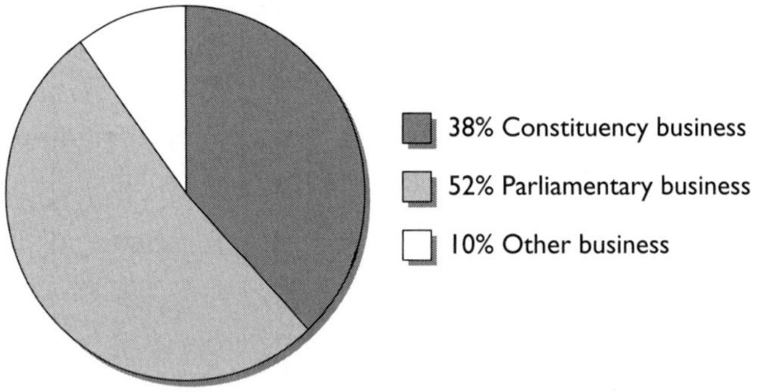

Figure 10.5 Duties of a Member of Parliament

One of the benefits of our current voting system is that MPs are strongly tied to a particular geographical area and a particular local population, which means that they must spend some time in their constituency if they hope to be re-elected. However, MPs are often powerless to address the local concerns which constituents are likely to raise, such as rubbish collection or poor repair of council houses since these concerns are the province of local councillors. Another of the key roles played by MPs is that of advocate. Although they have limited power to directly address individual constituents concerns, they are able to support sectional groups such as business or charities which can raise the business profile and influence changes in law and policy.

Think about it

There have been concerns that some MPs receive money or goods in return for supporting sectional interests. What are the implications of this on their impartiality?

MPs also spend a great deal of time on public business which includes the creation of legislation. As discussed in Chapter 2 Law and the Legal system, the process by which a bill becomes law is long and complicated. MPs in varying numbers are required for all of the first 5 stages and for some matters MPs are required to attend to cast a vote.

Representation

Representation is an issue of crucial importance in understanding the process of democracy. Heywood (2002) argues that there are 4 main theories of representation each of which put forward differing models of the role and purpose of an elected representative. They are as follows:

1 **Trustee model:** this model supports the idea that the role of the representative is to exercise judgement on matters of importance. The MP is a trustee, who by virtue of a better education and a more informed level of understanding has a moral duty to represent the interests of the less fortunate. This view has come under close scrutiny and has been criticised on several fronts. Firstly, it makes the assumption that the general public are ill informed and ill educated which is not necessarily the case. Secondly,

having a high level of education does not particularly help in the resolution of moral problems or make an individual more likely to want to perform citizenship duties for the rest of the population. There is also the concern that if MPs are allowed to exercise their own judgement, they will represent their own interests and not the interests of the electorate.

2 **Delegate model**: the role of the representative in this view of democracy is to act as a delegate. A delegate is an individual who acts on behalf of others on the basis of receiving clear instructions. A delegate does not exercise his or her judgement on a matter; they merely perform as they are instructed. This model of representation has the advantage of restricting politicians who serve their own interests first and ensures that they do as their constituents wish; the problem with this model is that representatives cannot make decisions for the good of the nation, but must act on what is good for their constituency. These two competing interests will make the political life of the representative very difficult. In addition it is difficult for representatives to demonstrate leadership if they are unable to exercise their own will.

3 **Mandate model**: this model reflects the fact that most political representatives are not elected on the basis of their own individual skills or talents, but instead are elected on the basis of the party they represent. In this view the representative is a small part of a large organisation, which by winning a general election receives a mandate from the people to implement policies it outlined in its election manifesto. This view has the advantage that politicians must keep their word and implement the political changes they promised the public. This means that the public have a reliable and valid way of measuring whether politicians achieve their stated objectives and can use this information to evaluate their voting behaviour. The problems with this view are that voters don't always vote on the grounds of political aims and objectives; they can be influenced by the media, the perceived qualities of the party leader and the habitual voting patterns of their family. There is also the point that since a manifesto may contain many aims and objectives, voters will undoubtedly agree with some and not with others. Therefore just because a citizen voted for a particular party it does not mean that the voter endorsed all of its decisions.

4 **Resemblance model**: this model is based on the idea that the role of the MP is to be an example of the group they represent. Representatives should form a representative cross section of the community they serve. In this model the House of Commons would have an even gender split and would constitute about 8% ethnic minorities. If the members of the House of Commons do not form a representative cross section then the interests of the under represented groups such as the working classes and ethnic minorities will not be given adequate consideration. This view of political representation promotes a narrow view, which argues that only people who have a resemblance to a group can represent that group interests. Representatives in this view cannot advance the greater good of society but can only represent sectional interests.

Think about it

Which theory of representation do you think would be the most appropriate to describe our current system?

Simulation

Jamilla Hussein has recently returned as MP for North Reiston after a local by-election. Mrs Hussein is a British citizen by birth with a Pakistani heritage. The constituency of North Reiston is predominately white. During several local surgeries she has conducted to gather the views and concerns of her constituents she has come across several issues of concern. Firstly, it seems that local refuse collection is erratic and unreliable. Secondly, the majority of the constituents she has seen want her to vote against a new education bill which is currently passing through the commons, Jamila is in favour of this bill.

1 What is Jamila's role as an MP?
2 What powers does Jamila have to resolve the issue of unreliable refuse collection?
3 Jamila has a different ethnic background to the majority of her constituents. Which theory of representation argues that she cannot understand or represent the interests of her constituents?
4 Is it likely that Jamila was elected on the basis of her personal skills and abilities or on the basis of the political party she represents? Explain your reasons.
5 Should Jamila respect the views of her constituents and vote against the new education bill or should she follow her own conscience and vote for it? What would the trusteeship and delegate theories have to say about this?

Think about it

How important is the role of the representative in modern politics?

Key points

1 The role of an MP is not laid down and is largely self-defined.
2 Most MPs have very limited powers to help individuals; instead they often represent sectional interests.
3 MPs largely split their time between constituency matters and public matters.
4 Heywood (2002) suggests there are 4 main theories of representation;
   - trusteeship model
   - delegate model
   - mandate model
   - resemblance model.
5 Trustees exist to use their own judgement to benefit their constituency.
6 Delegates perform as instructed by their constituents.

Voting systems and processes

We have examined the role of an MP and discussed the various theories, which describe how representatives may perform the duties required of them. Now we will examine how representatives come to be elected.

The right to vote

In the UK, only individuals who are registered on the electoral register are eligible to vote. However, there are also several other conditions which must be met if an individual is to be granted a vote.

- the individual must have reached the age of 18 years on or before polling day
- the individual must be a British or other commonwealth citizen or an Irish citizen resident in the UK
- the individual must not be a convicted prisoner currently serving a prison sentence.

You are not automatically registered to vote once you reach the age of 18. You must have been entered on the electoral register which arrives at every household periodically. If this is completed you will be put in the electoral register which is a full list of everyone eligible to vote in a particular area. The register is a public document and can be viewed freely at local councils and some large public libraries.

The voting age was lowered to 18 by the Representation of the People Act 1969 and the first time 18 year olds could vote was in the 1970 general election. There have been many arguments recently about reducing the voting age again to 16 in line with other rights that young people acquire at that age, such as the right to live independently, engage in sexual activity, become parents and get married.

Think about it

Consider the implications of reducing the voting age to 16. What are the advantages and disadvantages of such a reduction?

The reason that Irish and Commonwealth citizens who are resident in the UK can vote is due to the long and close ties that exist between the UK and these nations. British citizens who are resident in the Republic of Ireland may also vote in their parliamentary elections. Individuals of other nationalities cannot vote in the UK national elections even if they have been resident in the UK for a long time and pay taxes. If individuals such as this want to vote they must acquire British citizenship.

British citizens who live abroad have the right to vote in UK elections for a period of 15 years after they have left the country. This ensures that individuals who have to work abroad or choose to live in another nation for a while can still have a say in how their home nation is organised and run.

Think about it

Do you think that British citizens who live abroad should have the right to vote for 15 years after they leave the country? Should it be longer or shorter? Explain your reasons.

It used to be the case that individuals who did not have a permanent address were not entitled to vote. This effectively excluded the entire homeless population from voting. As you will have noted earlier in the discussion on types of democracy, one of the major factors of a successful representative democracy is political equality with voting rights for all citizens. The UK could not be considered a true democracy if sections of society were denied the right to access political processes. As a result of pressure from various pressure groups, the Representation of People Act 2000 ensured that homeless people or people without a fixed address can still register to vote by means of a 'declaration of local connection'.

Think about it

Individuals who are patients (voluntary or detained) in a mental hospital may register to vote. What are your thoughts on this?

Individuals who are currently serving prison sentences upon conviction of an offence are not permitted to vote although prisoners detained on remand may still register to vote. This is because remand prisoners have not been found guilty of an offence, they are innocent individuals until a fair and unbiased trial decides otherwise and it would be a breach of their rights to deny them their vote.

Case study

R (Pearson & Others) v Secretary of State for the Home Office

This case involved 3 convicted prisoners: a drug dealer, an arsonist and an individual convicted of manslaughter who took the government of the UK through the judicial process in an attempt to gain voting rights for the nearly 60,000 prisoners held in England and Wales. Convicted prisoners have been denied voting rights since the 1870 Forfeiture Act although remand prisoners had their right to vote returned in 2001. The arguments for disqualifying convicted prisoners from the vote was succinctly summed up as follows:

"A democratic society can reasonably take the view that those who break its laws sufficiently seriously to be sent to prison, forfeit the right to take part in the government of that society while they serve their sentences"

Rabinder Singh, counsel for the Home Secretary 2001

However, the view of the prisoners is that by removing the right to vote the government is breaching the Human Rights Act (1998) and the European Convention on Human Rights. One of the three defendants was quoted thus:

"The ban on prisoners voting means MPs do not have to pay attention to prisons and the issues raised by prisoners. This leads to issues such as the poor state of healthcare for prisoners being neglected. While I accept that criminals must be punished, I cannot accept that it is just for me to die in custody or to be denied the rights of others in democratic society – to vote my MP in or out and to represent me in Parliament".

Anthony Pearson, 2001

The fundamental issue lies in the withdrawal of citizenship rights as a form of punishment versus the rights of prisoners to retain their civil rights.

1. Why does the government want to deny convicted prisoners the right to vote?
2. According to Pearson, what are the implications in denying prisoners the right to vote?
3. If prisoners were given the right to vote what would be the impact on marginal constituencies which contain prisons?
4. Does allowing prisoners voting rights have any impact on public safety? Explain your answer.
5. Should prisoners be afforded full political citizenship rights? Explain your answer.
6. How would the role of an MP change if prisoners had voting rights?

Ballot Secrecy

Until the Secret Ballot Act 1872 voters had to declare their choice of candidate to the presiding officer of the election who recorded it. This had implications in that if a vote is made public the individual may face intimidation from others who voted differently. In addition, the urge to conform is strong when surrounded by peers who are voting a particular way (see unit 12 – Human Behaviour for more detail on conformity). The 1872 Act allowed voters to mark a ballot paper without being observed and place it in a ballot box where it would remain anonymous.

The secrecy of an individual's vote is protected by:

- polling booths which are surrounded by screens to protect privacy
- ballot boxes which are sealed until the count
- prohibition of photographs or TV footage of ballot papers close up.

There are also safeguards against the misuse of a secret ballot system in the UK as ballot papers come in books similar in style to raffle tickets and both the ballot paper and the counterfoil are numbered. This means that suspicious ballot papers can be checked against the counterfoil. Your voter number is written on the counterfoil which enables issues of fraud to be checked. If there is suspicion of fraud, access to ballot papers can only be given by an election court and only accessed for this purpose.

Think about it

If the counterfoil has a matching number to the ballot paper and the counterfoil also has your voter registration number it is theoretically possible to discover how people voted. Does this mean we have a secret ballot system or not? Explain your answer.

Voting systems

As discussed earlier there are a variety of voting systems which can be used in the election of representatives. Some of these are shown in Figure 10.6

Broadly speaking these different voting systems can be classified into 3 categories (see Figure 10.7):

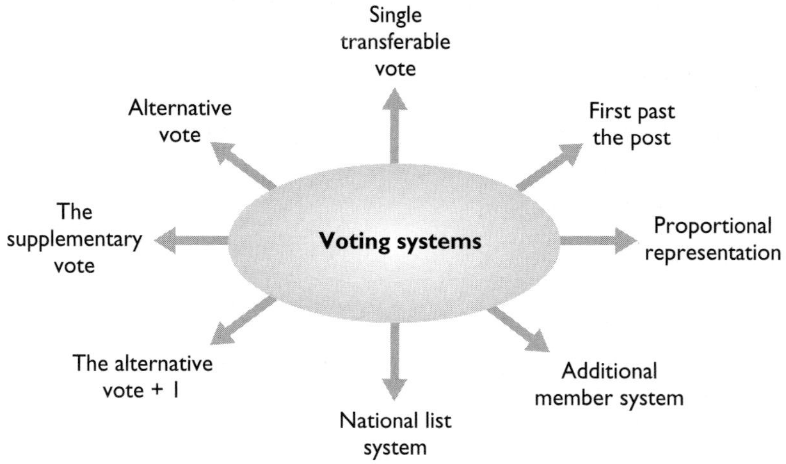

Figure 10.6 Different voting systems

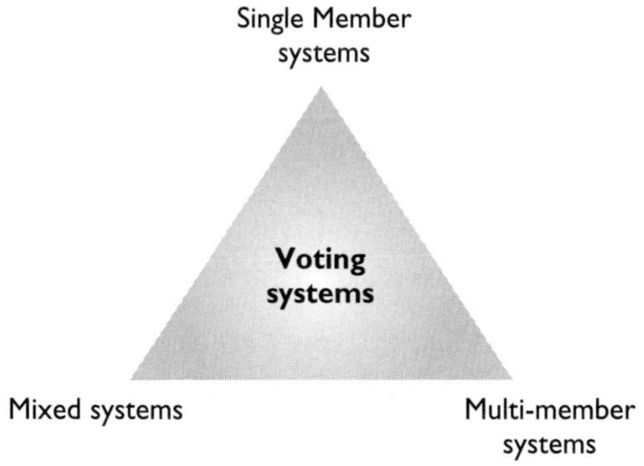

Figure 10.7 Categories of voting systems

Single member systems

Single member systems are also sometimes known as majority systems. These types of system ensure that the elected representative has achieved more than 50% of the votes cast in a constituency. The best known single member systems are:

- first past the post used in the UK, USA, India and Canada
- the alternative vote used by the Australian House of Representatives (see Figure 10.8 on page 145)
- the supplementary vote used in the London Mayoral Elections (see Figure 10.8 on page 145)
- the second ballot system used in France (see Figure 10.8 on page 145).

First past the post: the British electoral system is based on the first past the post (FPTP) system. This system is very clear-cut and definitive as the candidate with the highest number of votes in a constituency wins. In order to vote in a FPTP system you simply mark 'X' next to the name of the candidate of your choosing. If your candidate polls more votes than the others then they win regardless of whether he or she has more than 50% support. For example, a by-election takes place with the following results:

- candidate 1 polled 40% of the vote
- candidate 2 polled 32% of the vote
- candidate 3 polled 18% of the vote
- candidate 4 polled 7% of the vote
- candidate 5 polled 3% of the vote.

This means that candidate 1 is empowered to act as a representative for the constituency despite the fact that only 4 out of every 10 constituents voted for this candidate. When members have been elected in this way, the party with the most elected representatives is invited by the Queen to form the government. The FPTP system is used in both House of Commons elections and local elections.

The advantages of FPTP are:

- it is a cheap and simple way to hold an election
- counting of ballot papers is fast and accurate
- ballot papers are easy to understand

- it allows a new government to either take over the reins or continue as usual with the minimum of upheaval
- it gives a clear mandate to the party in power
- it provides a stable and legitimate political system with usually just 2 parties dominating which enables a party to pass legislation and tackle the countries problems without having to rely on other parties for support
- it provides a close and direct link between the MP and the constituency.

The disadvantages of FPTP are:

- more people in a constituency can vote against a candidate than vote for them and the individual is still elected. The example described previously had the winning candidate on 40% of the vote. This means that 60% of the constituents voted against them. Is this truly democratic?
- individuals may cast negative votes – voting against a candidate they dislike rather than voting for one they like.
- there is a lack of choice of representatives as usually only 3 or 4 will stand for election.
- the government as a whole may not represent the will of the people. For example, in 1997 the Labour Party gained just over 40% of the vote nationally but received over 60% of the seats in the House of Commons.
- the government can change constituency boundaries to affect the results of elections. This is called 'gerrymandering'.
- voters in strong party constituencies may feel their vote is wasted. If you know the other candidate will win why bother to vote? This badly affects smaller parties such as the Liberal Democrats.

Think about it

Is it fair that a party can poll a relatively low percentage of votes and still maintain a strong majority in the House of Commons? Explain your answer.

Assessment activity 10-M1

Write a 500-word report demonstrating your understanding of the importance of a representative democracy and problems with the present voting system.

Multimember systems

Multimember systems are a form of proportional representation. This is when the proportion of votes cast is reflected in the number of parliamentary seats gained. For example, if the Green Party polled 8% of the votes nationally they should be entitled to 8% of House of Commons seats. Proportional representation seeks to ensure that the final tally of elected representatives mirrors as closely as possible the votes cast for each party. There are two main forms of multi- member systems:

- single transferable vote (STV) used in developed assembly elections and Australian Senate (see Figure 10.9 on page 146 for further details)
- list systems used in Israel, across Europe, Russia and South Africa.

Mixed or hybrid systems

There are 2 main mixed voting systems:

- the additional member system (AMS) which is used in Germany and New Zealand
- the Alternative Vote Plus (AV+) which is currently not in use. (See Figure 10.10 on page 147 for further details on mixed voting systems).

Key points

1. There are over 300 different systems of voting available to be used.
2. The UK uses the 'first past the post' system for elections to the House of Commons.
3. Voting systems fall into 3 main categories: single member, multi member and mixed.
4. The Secret Ballot Act 1872 ensures that votes cast are kept secret.
5. Not every one in the UK is entitled to vote. There are voting criteria, which must be met before an individual can vote.

System	Description	Advantages and disadvantages
The alternative vote (AV)	Voters must rank the candidates on the ballot paper in order of preference. If a candidate receives 50% or more of first preferences then they are elected. If not, then the candidate with the lowest number of first choices is eliminated and their second choices are redistributed to the other candidates. This process continues until one candidate has an absolute majority.	**Advantages** ● Ensures the winner has a majority. ● Strong bond between representatives and constituents is maintained. ● Removes issues of wasted votes. ● Extreme left or right wing parties would be unlikely to get enough support to be elected. **Disadvantages** ● Does not give parties the proportion of seats that their votes have earned. ● Does not help change the status of those who have been traditionally under represented in political processes. ● Time consuming and more complex that FPTP.
The supplementary vote (SV)	This is very similar to the AV system described above. If one candidate receives 50% of the vote they are automatically elected. If not then the 2 strongest candidates survive and all of the eliminated candidates are distributed between the 2 survivors. The one with the most votes wins.	**Advantages** ● Strong bond between representative and constituency. ● Removes issues of wasted votes. ● Less time consuming than AV. **Disadvantages** ● Shares all of the disadvantages of AV.
The second ballot system	This system allows for 2 separate ballot days. If on the first ballot a candidate receives 50% or over then they are elected. If there is no winner a second ballot is held a short time later either with all of the original candidates or with just the candidates who scored a certain percentage of the vote in the first ballot.	**Advantages** ● Encourages pacts between parties. ● No sense of wasted votes. **Disadvantages** ● Does not help small parties. ● Time period is longer than FPTP. ● More complex than FPTP.

Figure 10.8 Other single member systems

System	Description	Advantages and disadvantages
Single transferable vote	This system involves multi member constituencies in which parties can field as many candidates as there are seats. Voters then rank the candidates on a ballot paper in order of preference. If a voter's first choice candidate doesn't need their vote because they have already accrued enough votes to be elected then the vote is transferred to the 2nd choice and so on.	**Advantages** ● Power is in the hands of the voters. ● Wide choice of candidates. ● Reflects the views of voters. ● No wasted votes. ● Voters can rank in preference based on things other than party allegiance, such as gender or ethnicity. ● It is a relatively simple procedure. ● Small parties will benefit. **Disadvantages** ● Link between representative and constituency is gone. ● Leads to weak coalition governments. ● Voters have no say in which individuals are chosen. ● Favours big parties. ● Power is in the hands of the party leadership.

Figure 10.9 Additional information on multimember systems

Think about it

Which voting system do you think is the most effective way of electing candidates?

Simulation

Newly elected President Baldur is keen to honour her election promise to reform the current FPTP voting system. The party manifesto clearly laid down the kind of system the President favours. It must be able to form stable governments, constituents must have an effective and accountable representative, votes must not be wasted and the results should be broadly proportional. The voters turned out in their millions and gave the President the mandate she needs to be able to seek change. What she will do with this mandate remains to be seen.

1. What are the disadvantages of the current system of election outlined above?
2. Which voting system best fits the President's vision for the future?
3. What are the advantages and disadvantages of the voting system you have selected?
4. Why might the President decide to keep the existing FPTP system?
5. Should the President seek the views of the voters via a reflection? Explain.

Assessment activity 10-D1

Write a 500-word report evaluating the present voting system and suggest alternatives which are fully justified and valid.

Assessment activity 10-P2

Explain the workings of the voting process and systems.

System	Description	Advantages and disadvantages
Additional member system (AMS)	This is effectively a combination of FPTP and party list systems. It was specifically designed for post war Germany to ensure extremists could not come to power. The nation is divided into single member constituencies and regions. Each voter has 2 votes, firstly for a constituency representative and secondly for a party from the regional list. If the proportion of votes received by a party is not proportional to its share of the vote then this is corrected by the proportional allocation of the regional lists.	**Advantages** • There is an accountable representative for each constituency. • The results are broadly proportional. • Voters have at least 1 effective vote. • Simple and straightforward. **Disadvantages** • Some representatives are not accountable to the voters. • Creates 2 types of MP with differing roles. • May lead to weakened or coalition governments. • If a party wins a disproportionate number of constituency seats they get to keep them.
The alternative vote +1	Although this system is currently unused it was recommended by an independent voting commission as a possible replacement for the FPTP system in the UK general elections. It is a combination of the alternative vote system and the additional member system. Constituency MPs are elected by AV and additional members are selected via the use of party lists. So as with AMS there are 2 types of representative.	**Advantages** • Constituency MP's have at least 50% of the vote. • Votes are not wasted. • It is broadly proportional. **Disadvantages** • Creates 2 types of MP. • More complex than FPTP. • May lead to weaker governments.

Figure 10.10 Additional information on mixed voting systems

Political institutions

Political power

As we have discussed earlier in this chapter the UK is a liberal democracy which encourages competition and the minimal interference of the state. There are 3 forms of power involved in the running of a liberal democracy. The 3 powers work together to ensure the smooth running and stability of the nation.

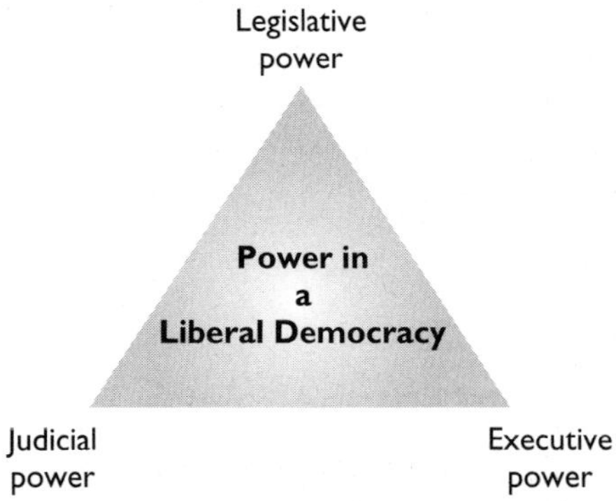

Figure 10.11 Categories of power

1 Legislative power

This is the power to make laws. In the UK the body with legislative power is parliament. Parliament makes laws through a multi-stage process, which is outlined in Unit 2 – Law and the Legal System. In addition to the power to make new laws parliament also has the legislative power to reform old laws.

2 Executive power

This is the power to suggest new laws and ensure existing laws are implemented. This power is invested in government departments and the civil service who deal with the day to day running of the country. Laws are suggested through green papers, which open discussion about potential new laws and white papers, which set out blueprints for potential laws.

3 Judicial power

This is the power to interpret the laws that have been made and make unbiased judgements on whether laws have been broken. This power is given to the court system and is implemented by judges in all courts in the UK.

Assessment activity 10-P3

Research, prepare and deliver a 10-minute presentation on the separation of powers (legislative, executive, judicial), the instructions of power and the role of an elected representative.

Key points

1. The UK is a liberal democracy.
2. Power in the UK democracy is divided into 3 parts.
3. Executive power proposes laws.
4. Legislative power makes and implements laws.
5. Judicial power interprets and judges whether law has been broken.

British institutions

In this section of the chapter we will examine some of the most important institutions in the British political system including the Houses of Parliament and regional assemblies in Northern Ireland, Wales and Scotland. Many political institutions are formed from one or two legislative bodies. The correct term for this is unicameral which is single chamber and bicameral which is a double chamber. The UK has a bicameral system, which means we have 2 legislative chambers – the House of Commons and the House of Lords and the USA also has a bicameral system consisting of the Senate and the House of Representatives.

The unicameral system

One-chambered political systems are more commonly found in nations with a very centralised, unitary structure and sometimes in smaller nations. It is a more common system of organising a primary political institution with well over 100 nations having a unicameral system.

Judicial power is implemented by judges in all courts in the UK.

Generally a unicameral chamber consists of a single publicly elected chamber which creates and approves the law. Examples of countries using unicameral systems are Portugal, New Zealand, Sweden, Finland and Israel.

Advantages of the unicameral system:

- legislation can be created much more rapidly because it doesn't have to pass through a second chamber
- it is less expensive than maintaining 2 chambers
- there is increased accountability as only one chamber is responsible for decisions.

Disadvantage of unicameral system:

- there is no other chamber to question the actions of the unicameral chamber. The chamber has no check on its actions.

The bicameral system

The bicameral legislature has two chambers, which are commonly known as the upper and lower chambers. In the UK, the House of Lords is the upper chamber and the House of Commons is the lower chamber. In general, the lower chambers are filled with the winning representatives from public elections but upper chambers vary widely in how representatives are selected. Some upper chambers have an elected membership who represent certain geographical regions, others such as the UK appoints members to act on behalf of the whole nation rather than just one region. The relationship between the two chambers can also vary. In many bicameral legislatures the upper chamber has limited power and often can only delay or slightly amend legislation. However, in the US both chambers have equal standing and are able to offset each other. Bicameral systems tend to be found in federal political systems. These are political systems in which geographical regions have some autonomy over their own affairs, for example the states of the USA or the counties in the UK.

The House of Lords

Think about it

What are the implications in the UK becoming unicameral? Would it be a benefit or a disadvantage to the nation?

Advantages of bicameral legislature:

- it provides a much more rigorous system of checks and balances on the actions of the government than unicameral systems
- faulty or impulsive laws can be weeded out or amended
- it offers the opportunity for under represented groups to play a part in government. For example, in Botswana the upper house is made up of elected or appointed members of traditional ethnic groups.

Disadvantages of bicameral legislature:

- creating new legislation can be a time consuming process if a piece of law has to pass through both chambers
- the two chambers may hold inflicting opinions causing a stalemate situation
- more expensive to operate than a unicameral system.

Theory into practice

Consider the following nations:

- Portugal
- Canada
- New Zealand
- India
- Germany

1 Find out whether each country has a unicameral or bicameral legislature.
2 Discover the names of the chambers in each country.
3 In the bicameral nations what is the power relationship between the chambers and how are members to the upper chambers elected?

Key points

1 Unicameral legislature means that laws are created by a single chamber of representatives.
2 Bicameral legislature means that 2 chambers of representatives are involved in the legislative process.
3 Usually the upper chamber has less power and influence than the lower chamber.
4 Unicameral legislatures tend to be found in small unitary nations.
5 Bicameral legislatures tend to be found in larger more federal nations.

The House of Commons

The House of Commons is the lower chamber of our bicameral system and it consists of 659 elected members of parliament (MPs) who represent a broad spectrum of political parties. Each of the MPs represents a localised geographical area called a constituency.

Members of Parliament are elected by the 'first past the post system', described earlier in this chapter. There are 2 ways in which an individual can be elected to the House of Commons. Firstly, in a general election which is when representatives from all 659 constituencies are elected simultaneously and secondly, representatives can be elected through a by-election. By-elections happen when the current representatives of a constituency dies, retires or resigns and a new representative is needed for that one constituency only. A general election happens every 5 years or so, but a by-election can occur at any time. The last general election was held on 7th June 2001 and the House of Commons had the following representatives within it (see Figure 10.12 on page 151).

As you can see a whole range of political views and interests are represented in the House of Commons. This enables the House to ensure that legislation and decisions are debated by a variety of individuals holding different political views. As the figures above show the Labour Party has a substantial majority of MPs. This means that they can pass laws almost unopposed so the variety of parties represented does not always mean that unfair or flawed law will be stopped. The majority party is called upon to form the government and this party sits to the right of the speaker while the opposition and smaller parties sit on the left of speaker.

It is important that parties are disciplined as an undisciplined party does not inspire public confidence and does not run the country effectively or conduct an effective opposition. MPs are entitled to vote any way they wish in parliamentary matters but they are usually required to vote the way their party tells them to. Each party has individuals who are responsible for ensuring that MPs vote as they should. These individuals are called 'whips'. The name of these individuals is entirely appropriate as they whip their party members into line. Every week 'whips' send out a list of parliamentary business called The Whip.

Party business is underlined with either 1 line, 2 lines or 3 lines. A 1-line whip means that the matter in question is routine and attendance is requested but not essential, a 2-line whip means that the matter in question is important and the attendance of an MP is particularly requested. A 3-line whip is by far the most important as it

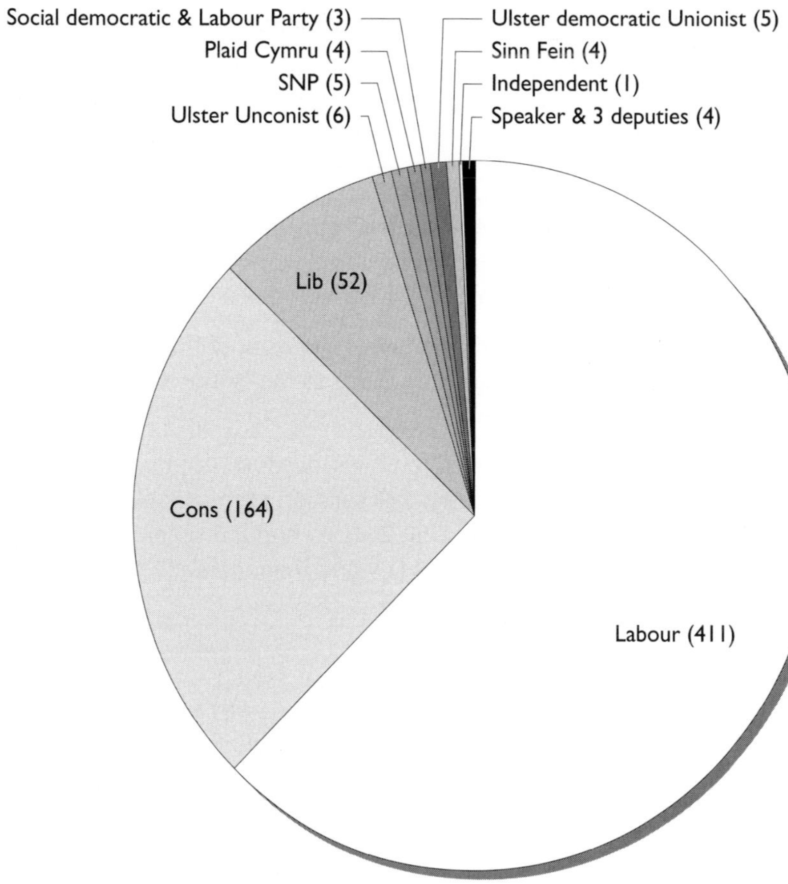

Figure 10.12 2001 Breakdown of parties in House of Commons

House of Commons

indicates that the parliamentary business is very important and that members of parliament must attend.

Whips are very important for a number of reasons:

- they help organise parliamentary business
- they provide party discipline
- they inform MPs about parliamentary business
- they can help members who are promoting a bill
- they act as a channel of communication between ministers and back bench MPs
- they make recommendations to party leaders on MPs who are likely to make good ministers.

Most MPs are happy to abide by the Party Whips because of the benefits they bring. However, if an MP repeatedly disobeys the Whip then they risk losing the affiliation to their party and potentially losing their seat in the Commons.

The House of Commons has several main roles to fulfil as shown in Figure 10.13 overleaf.

Function	Explanation
Making laws	Nearly 50% of the time of the House of Commons is spent on making new laws. More details of how laws are created can be found in Unit 2 – Law and the Legal System.
Controlling finance	The House of Commons controls the raising of finances through taxation and the selling of government assets. It must also give its approval to any plans the government has to spend money. The House can also check up on the spending of government departments through the Public Accounts Committee.
Scrutiny	The House of Commons scrutinises the work of the government. The government must explain its policies to the House and be prepared to accept criticism and questioning.
Delegated Legislation	The House does not have the time it needs to debate, discuss and pass all the laws needed by the country. The solution to this problem is the creation of delegated legislation (see Unit 2 – Law and the Legal System for more details). The house creates the parent law and then monitors how delegated legislation is implemented.
Examining European proposals	The House of Commons must examine all proposed European laws in order to assess their likely impact on the UK.
Protecting the individual	The members of the House of Commons are often contacted by individuals with difficulties. In addition, large petitions are often put forward to the House on a variety of issues of importance to individuals.

Figure 10.13 Roles of the House of Commons

Key points

1 The House of Commons is the lower chamber of our bicameral system.
2 It consists of 659 members of parliament.
3 There are currently 9 parties represented in the House of Commons.
4 Sinn Fein will not take their seats in the House of Commons because they will not swear allegiance to the Queen.
5 Party discipline is kept by the Whips.
6 The House of Commons performs a variety of functions such as making laws, scrutinising the work of the government and controlling finance.

The House of Lords

The House of Lords is the upper chamber of our bicameral system. Its origins date back to the 14th century and it has a long, distinguished and more recently, controversial history. The Lords consists of the following:

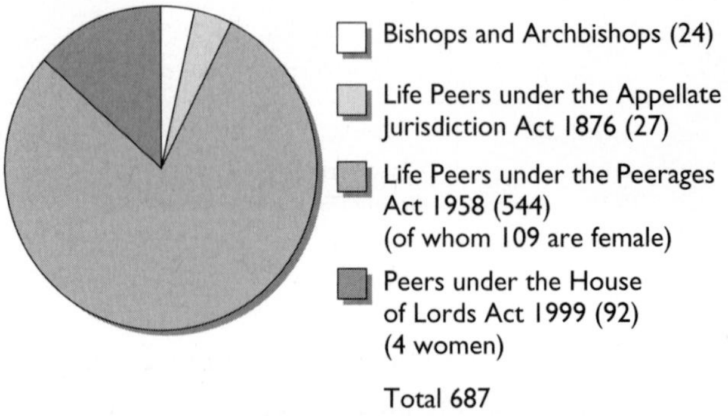

Figure 10.14 Proportions of Lords
Source: (*Crown copyright material is reproduced with the permission of the Controller of HMSO and the Queen's Printer for Scotland.*)

Think about it

The House of Lords used to consist of hereditary life peers. In essence our upper chamber was made up of the aristocracy which is no longer the case. What are the advantages and disadvantages of hereditary life peers?

This creates a total of 687 members of the House of Lords. As with the House of Commons many of these members have a particular political affiliation or belong to a political party. The breakdown is shown in Figure 10.15.

The House of Lords carries out a variety of roles, some of which are similar to the Commons, but some of which are quite different as shown in Figure 10.16.

Party	Life peers	Hereditary: elected by party	Hereditary: elected office holders	Hereditary: Royal office holders	Bishops	Total
Conservative	163	41	9			213
Labour	182	2	2			186
LIB Dem	60	3	2			65
Cross Bench	146	29	2	2		179
Archbishops and Bishops					24	24
Other	7					7
Total	**558**	**75**	**15**	**2**	**24**	**674**

Note: This table excludes 13 peers on leave of absence as of June 2003.

Figure 10.15 Members of The House of Lords 2003
(*Crown copyright material is reproduced with the permission of the Controller of HMSO and the Queen's Printer for Scotland.*)

Role	Description
Judicial work	The House of Lords is the most senior court of law in the UK. See unit 2 – Law and Legal System for more details on this role.
Law creation	The process by which a bill is created is detailed in Unit 2 also. The House of Lords plays a large part in this.
Scrutiny	The House of Lords performs the same function as the Commons in that they act as a form of scrutiny on the government, using questioning and criticism as a form of control on government.
Independent expertise	The Lords conduct a variety of investigations and inquiries. They have a range of expertise which can be used on government business.

Figure 10.16 Functions of The House of Lords

The time of the lords is spent as follows:

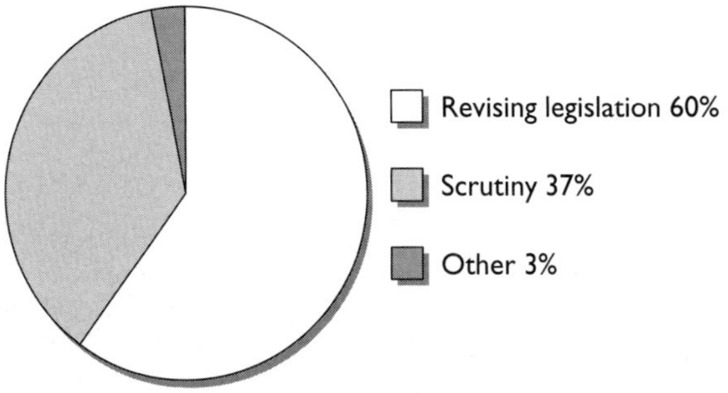

Figure 10.17 How the Lords spend their time

Source: (*Crown copyright material is reproduced with the permission of the Controller of HMSO and the Queen's Printer for Scotland.*)

Key points

1 The House of Lords is the upper chamber of our bicameral system.
2 It consists of 687 members including Law Lords, Bishops and life peers.
3 It acts as a check on the House of Commons.
4 It has a key role in the creation of law.
5 It dates from the fourteenth century.
6 It has seen substantial changes in recent years.

Devolution and the decentralisation of power

Devolution is a process whereby power is transferred from a centralised governmental organisation to a regional organisation. Bagador argues that devolution consists of 3 elements:

1 The transfer of power to a subordinate elected body.
2 The geographical transfer of power.
3 The transfer of functions of government from central to regional assemblies.

The powers of regional assemblies are defined by central government and they rarely include major financial powers or large-scale law making powers. In effect, regional assemblies are very much a junior power in the process of government.

Advantages of devolution

1 Regional assemblies can reflect and take into account cultural and linguistic differences between the region and central government.
2 Regional assemblies are more in touch with the needs of their people; laws will be fairer and more readily accepted by the people.
3 Reduces the burden on central government.
4 As regional assemblies only deal with the work of the region they are more efficient.
5 Central government can concentrate on issues of national importance rather than being concerned about the regions.
6 The combative politics seen in centralised government are reduced in regional assemblies where parties are happier to work towards common goals.

Disadvantages of devolution

1 Establishing regional assemblies is very expensive. Why create an organisation to do what central government already does?
2 Regional assemblies lack the decision-making experience of central government.
3 There may be conflict between regional and central government.
4 May lead to the break up of the UK.
5 Low voter turn out in devolution referendums indicates a lack of popular support for regional assemblies.

Regional assemblies

In the UK there are 3 regional assemblies which have devolved power:

- The Scottish Parliament
- The Welsh Assembly
- The Northern Ireland Assembly.

The Scottish Parliament

Scotland came under the power of Westminster in 1707 with the union of Scotland and England under the rule of James VI of Scotland who became James I of England after the death of Elizabeth I. The Scots had a long and distinguished history which was quite different from England and the Act of Union 1707 ensured that much of this individual character would survive including a separate legal system, education system and church organisation. However, the institutions of Westminster took control of the Scottish political life and Scotland was ruled by the English Parliament. This state of affairs continued for almost three hundred years until the Scotland Act 1998 established the Scottish Parliament.

The Scottish Parliament is empowered to deal with devolved matters such as education, health, civil and criminal law, environment, housing and local government. The Scottish Government is self-contained which means it can pass laws without having to pass through the English Parliament first. The English Parliament has reserved powers, which means it still has jurisdiction on matters that affect the UK as a whole or have an international impact.

The Scottish Parliament is made up of 129 elected Members of the Scottish Parliament (MSP) and, as with the English Parliament, the party which has the most representatives forms the government which is also called the Scottish Executive. The majority party selects a representative from their ranks who is appointed as First Minister by the Queen.

Theory into practice

What are the advantages and disadvantages of the Scottish Parliament? List your answers as fully as possible.

The Scottish Parliament at Holyrood

Think about it

What are the implications of allowing devolution to continue to other regions which have distinctive culture and language such as Cornwall?

The Welsh Assembly

The Act of Union between England and Wales was signed in 1536, almost 170 years before Scotland. This means that England and Wales have traditionally been much closer in terms of culture and institutions than Scotland. The Welsh Assembly was established by the Government of Wales Act 1998 after a Welsh referendum showed public support for the idea.

The Welsh Assembly has 60 members, 40 of whom are elected constituency members and 20 additional members who are elected on a regional basis to ensure that the overall number of seats awarded to a party in an election represents the overall number of votes received by that party. The members of the Welsh Assembly are elected by the additional member system outlined previously in this chapter. Like the Scottish Parliament, the Welsh Assembly has considerable scope to deal with regional issues such as transport, health, education and the environment. Like Scotland, Wales also has a First Minister who is elected by the whole executive and is usually the leader of the largest political party. One substantial difference between the Scottish

Parliament and the Welsh Assembly is that Wales does not have jurisdiction over its own criminal and civil law; it is subject to English Law in this area.

Think about it

Why have Wales and England had a much closer administrative and political relationship than England had with Scotland?

The Northern Ireland Assembly

The Northern Ireland Assembly was created by the Northern Ireland Act 1998. This Act was based on a referendum of the Belfast Agreement (more often referred to as The Good Friday Agreement). A system of proportional representation was used to elect members to the assembly called the single transferable vote. This mechanism allowed for the election of 108 members, 6 representatives from each of the 18 constituencies in Northern Ireland.

As with Scotland and Wales, the Northern Ireland Assembly has responsibility for education, health, agriculture, housing and so on. The Assembly is based at Stormont and there are around 10 political parties represented within it. Like the other regional assemblies it has a First Minister who is elected by all members and is usually a member of the dominant party. The conflict between the different parties in Northern Ireland has led to an unstable Assembly, which has been suspended by the British Government.

The Northern Ireland Assembly at Stormont

European institutions

European institutions have a tremendous impact on British politics. Their role is outlined and discussed in detail in Unit 6 – International Perspectives.

Assessment activity 10-M2

Briefly analyse the functions of the Houses of Parliament.

Structure of British Government

The government in its current form could not work effectively without structures. Some of these structures which assist the British government in the performance of its duties are:

- Prime Minister
- Cabinet
- Opposition
- government departments
- Civil Service.

Features of the governmental system

The Prime Minister

The individual who is appointed to the office of Prime Minster is usually the leader of the political party with the highest number of representatives in the House of Commons. Currently this is Tony Blair who is the leader of the Labour party. The PM is a very powerful figure. The role is complex and difficult, involving a variety of administrative, bureaucratic and public duties such as:

- allocation of duties to Ministers
- appointment and dismissal of Ministers
- appointment of chairs of national industries
- giving out honours

- setting agendas for government business
- control of information released to the Cabinet, Parliament and the public.

The PM also plays a significant role on the European and World stage, meeting with other heads of state to discuss foreign and financial policies, which can have far reaching implications. As a public servant the PM is answerable to the Queen, their party and the public. In addition, they cannot just appoint anyone they like to ministerial posts. They must take account of advice given to them by senior advisors and ensure that the individuals appointed are competent to do the job and do not create substantial political imbalance.

The increased concentration of the media on high profile politicians such as Government ministers and the Prime Minister means that their activities are closely scrutinised and the majority of their choices are in the public domain. This means that PM's must balance their own conscience with the demands of the public. The general public often favour or disfavour issues based on biased media information rather than a real analysis of the facts. Leaders must be aware of this and sometimes be prepared to take a political stance which is in opposition to the wishes of the public.

Tony Blair

Think about it

Can you think of a recent issue where the Prime Minister has made a decision the majority of the population didn't agree with? What are the political implications of doing this?

Cabinet

The Cabinet is the central committee of the British government. It consists of around 20 of the most senior members of the government selected by the Prime Minister. The majority are elected MPs from the House of Commons who have been selected by virtue of their expertise and loyalty to head up particular ministries such as the Ministry of Defence or the Home Office. The Cabinet also consists of a few members of the House of Lords and so it is representative of both chambers of Parliament. Cabinet meetings are chaired by the Prime Minister and are usually held once a week on Thursday mornings.

It has been argued that the Cabinet is informally divided into two layers, the first layer is comprised of 6–10 very senior ministers who carry tremendous authority such as the Chancellor of the Exchequer and the Home Secretary. The remaining 10–12 ministers have much less influence and authority. The role of the Cabinet is to make important government and policy decisions and to review decisions, which have already been made to assess their impact on policy areas. The Cabinet also ensures that key social problems are reviewed such as rising crime rates, inflation and the state of the NHS. It is difficult for a Cabinet to address these social problems in any kind of depth bearing in mind that cabinet meetings only occur once a week and last for just a few hours. What is more likely to happen is that problems may be referred to a cabinet committee which will feedback to the full Cabinet on its findings. The Cabinet also plays a key role in ensuring that all government ministries are able to communicate freely with each other ensuring that decisions taken by one department do not have unintended consequences on another department. Ministers must show public unity and coherence in decisions if they are to retain public confidence. The Cabinet helps reinforce this.

Simulation

After extensive discussions at the Ministry of Defence, the Defence Minister announced yesterday that civilian emergency services would be used to secure civil order in the major cities of Iraq. The decision comes after extensive looting in the past conflict climate of cities such as Basra and Baghdad. The Defence Minister was quoted as saying:

'Our public services are amongst the finest in the world, they have respect for human rights and a great capacity for adaptability. It is right and proper that they are used to help secure post conflict areas and pass on their skills to the fledging emergency serivices in these areas'.

The Home Secretary refused to comment on the situation last night, but was seen emerging from Number 10 after extensive talks with the PM.

Answer the following questions:

1 Does the Secretary of Defence have the right to deploy civilian public services into overseas conflict situations?
2 What would be the implications to the UK of such an action?
3 What would be the likely feeling of the public services themselves towards such a move?
4 Why do you think the Home Secretary refused to comment?
5 How have the functions of the cabinet failed in this situation?
6 How could the PM deal with this situation?

Key points

1 The Prime Minister is Head of the Cabinet.
2 The Cabinet consists of around 20–22 senior politicians who head up government ministries.
3 The Cabinet usually meets on Thursday mornings
4 The Cabinet exists to facilitate inter-department communication, review key social problems and to make and review important political decisions.
5 Although the Cabinet is supposed to be a committeee of equals, it has several layers, with the Prime Minister at the top, senior cabinet ministers below this and other cabinet ministers at the bottom.

The Opposition

The primary opposition party in the House of Commons has a group of senior politicians who shadow government ministers; this opposition group is called the Shadow Cabinet. This 'shadow' system helps prepare opposition politicians for a time when they may be elected into office. The opposition system in parliament performs several main functions:

1 They provide constructive criticism to government policy proposals or suggested legislation and in doing so they help shape the decisions of the government.
2 The opposition can stall government proposals if it has substantial numbers and if it has insufficient numbers it can oppose legislation in order to gain amendments to it.
3 Opposition parties also make a priority of promoting their own policy suggestions in order to gain public support.
4 The opposition acts as a check on the power of the ruling party. By exposing government scandals and mismanagement, they act in the interests of the public and the interests of democracy.

Government departments

The government has many ministries each with differing roles and responsibilities. The main government departments and their duties are described in Figure 10.18.

Government Department	Roles and Responsibilities	Agencies
Department for environment, food and rural affairs (Defra) *www.defra.co.uk*	• Climate change • Access • Water • National Parks • Waste, conservation • Plant Health, floods • Air quality, forestry • Animal health and welfare • Fisheries, farming • Energy efficiency, pesticides	• Central science laboratory • Pesticides safety directorate • Rural payments agency • Vetinary laboratories agency • Centre for environment • Fisheries and aquaculture science
Department for transport *www.dft.gov.uk*	• Railways, shipping • Aviation, ports • DVLA, vehicle safety, Roads, European Policy, Haulage	• DVLA • Driving Standards agency • Highways agency • Maritime and coastguard agency
HM treasury *www.hm-treasury.gov.uk*	• Public spending • Public sector pay • Taxation • Inland revenue • Customs and excise • European tax issues • Monetary union	• Debt management office • Office of national statistics • Royal mint • National savings and investments
Foreign and commonwealth office *www.fco.gov.uk*	• Foreign policy • British trade • Non proliferation • Counter terrorism policy • Drugs and international crime • Human rights policy • UK visas • Overseas territories	
Department of health *www.doh.gov.uk*	• NHS finance and budgets • Prison health services • Maternity services • Mental health services • NHS treatment for asylum seekers • NHS performance and management • Public health • Sexual health and HIV • Foods standards • Ambulance services • Dental services	• Medical devices agency • NHS estates • NHS purchasing and supply • Medicines control agency

Figure 10.18 Government departments and their duties

Government Department	Roles and Responsibilities	Agencies
The Home Office *www.homeoffice.gov.uk*	• Civil emergencies • Security, immigration • Terrorism, citizenship • Crime reduction • Policing, organised crime • Custodial provision • Criminal justice system • Race equality • Community safety	• Criminal records bureau • Forensic science service • Passports and records agency • HM prison service
Department for work and pensions	• New Deal • Child support agency • Employment zones • Jobcentres • Incapacity benefit • Pensions • Maternity pay	
Department for education and skills *www.dfes.gov.uk*	• OFSTED • Teacher training • 14–19 curriculum • Independent schools • Qualification accreditation • Local education authorities • Higher education • Widening participation • National curriculum • Careers service (connextions) • Prison education • Adult education	
Ministry of defence *www.mod.uk*	• Armed Forces • Nuclear policy • NATO, UN, European security • Peacekeeping • Disaster relief • Veteran's issues • MOD police • Reserves and cadets • Military training • Defence technology	

Figure 10.18 ctd Government departments and their duties

There are some issues which overlap many government departments, such as terrorism. On issues such as these ministries try to work in close coordination to ensure that the overall government response to a situation is coherent and provides a good service to the citizens they serve.

All governments are headed up by a secretary of state, who may or may not be part of the cabinet. The secretary of state usually has several junior ministers who are responsible for specific areas of the ministries remit as shown in Figure 10.19.

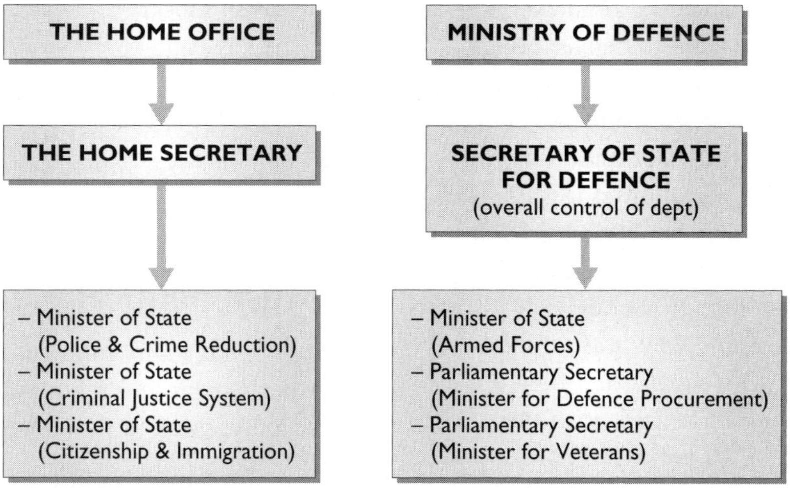

Figure 10.19 The secretary of state may have several junior ministers

It should be apparent that the 659 elected members of parliament cannot run an effective government by themselves. The actual machinery of government, which sees decisions implemented lies with the 500,000 or so civil servants who execute government decisions.

Key points

1. Government is made up of many departments, which have responsibilities for key policy areas. These departments are called ministries.
2. Each department is headed by a Secretary of State, who is supported by several junior ministers of state.
3. Key departments include HM treasury, transport, education, health and media.
4. Departments which has a large impact on the public services are:
   - Treasury which controls public spending, customs and excise
   - Home Office responsible for police, prisons, immigrations, CJS
   - Ministry of Defence responsible for Armed Forces, peacekeeping
   - Ministry of Transport responsible for HM Coastguard
   - Ministry of Health responsible for the ambulance service.
5. The decisions of the cabinet and individual ministries are executed by the Civil Service.

The Civil Service

The Civil Service is a vital mechanism of government which is split into departments and attached to particular ministries. The civil servants in these departments are directly responsible to the Minister in charge of that department and work for them in carrying out government policy. The structure of the Civil Service is very hierarchical and many civil servants make a career from progressing through the ranks. Civil servants perform a variety of roles such as:

- consulting with pressure groups on specific issues
- providing advice to ministers
- preparing speeches for ministers
- dealing with a minister's correspondence
- researching specific issues of ministerial importance
- helping a minister prepare for questions they may face from the media
- costing of government proposals
- technical aspects of implementing policy.

The Civil Service is a very powerful organisation as government would be unable to deliver policy initiatives without it. It has 173 departments and agencies which act to support government. Civil servants are meant to be politically impartial and as a consequence they are not allowed to stand for political office as long as they are civil servants. They are privy to very sensitive information, particularly in the home, foreign and defence ministries and because of this they must abide by the Official Secrets Act. This means that they are forbidden from discussing their work with the general public and media. As you will appreciate from the work they do, they have information which could cause serious embarrassment to the government and possibly compromise national security.

Quangos

Another branch of government which assists in the implementation of policy initiatives are 'public bodies'. Public bodies carry out a wide range of government work and spend many billions of pounds each year. They belong to a government ministry but carry out their functions with a high degree of autonomy and freedom which has led to public bodies being termed QUANGO's. Quango stands for Quasi Autonomous Non-Governmental Organisation. Public bodies include organisations such as:

- national industries, for example The Waterways Board
- public corporations, for example The BBC
- NHS bodies, for example NHS Trusts.

The annual report of the cabinet office on public bodies 2002 identifies 834 public bodies, which over the financial year 2001/2002 spent a staggering £20 billion between them. There are many well-known public bodies which you may come across in the course of completing your national diploma such as:

- The Equal Opportunities Commission
- Independent Television Commission
- Channel 4 Television
- British Library
- British Museum
- English Heritage
- Imperial War Museum
- Royal Armouries.

British political parties

The UK has many political parties represented in its parliament and many more parties who are not yet represented in parliament.

There are 3 main political parties in the UK: the Labour party, the Conservative party and the Liberal Democrats. There are also many other mainland UK political parties that hold seats in the commons such as the Scottish National Party and the Welsh Nationalists.

The purpose of a political party is to put forward a set of beliefs which will be used to run the country. In theory, the party that reflects the views of the public will be elected to form the government and these values and beliefs will be used to change policy on issues which both the government and the public feel strongly about such as:

- asylum
- immigration
- crime
- tax
- sentencing
- health and education systems
- the environment.

Some political parties must also answer to their largest financial supporters such as unions and business interests which can affect the policies they implement. Different political parties tend to have very different ways of wanting to organise and run the country and they usually act in opposition to each other. However, during times of national crisis or war traditional rivalry is suspended and all parties work together towards a common aim.

Kavaugner (2001) comments that political parties share many of the same functions as described in the list below:

1 Political parties reconcile political interests to form a stable government.

2 They provide a forum for citizens to participate in politics.

3 They act as a recruitment facility for future MPs, Ministers and leaders.

4 They allow for democratic control of government.

5 They offer a choice to voters.

6 They provide representation of local areas at national level.

7 Parties provide opportunities for the public to communicate their views back to the MP who represents them.

8 Parties are accountable to the public for their actions.

These functions apply not only to the ruling party which forms the government, but to every party which is represented in parliament and at local level on local councils.

The Labour Party

The labour Party have formed the following governments since the turn of the twentieth century:

- 1924 Ramsey McDonald
- 1929 Ramsey McDonald
- 1945 Clement Atlee
- 1964 Harold Wilson
- 1966 Harold Wilson
- 1974 Harold Wilson/James Callahan
- 1997 Tony Blair
- 2001 Tony Blair

The Labour Party has several core values, which it seeks to promote in its policies when in government and its actions when in opposition. These core values are:

- social justice
- strong community and strong values
- reward for hard work
- decency
- rights matched by responsibilities.

The Labour Party proclaims itself a democratic socialist party. In general, democratic socialists advocate the protection of the basic rights of individuals coupled with constitutional rule. One of the most basic and most controversial aspects of any socialist government, whether democratic or not, is a commitment to redistribute the wealth of a community. In many societies a small minority of individuals hold tremendous wealth, while the large majority live on or below the poverty line. Socialists feel that this situation is unfair and all individuals ought to have the same opportunities in life, such as the chance for a good education and high quality health care.

In order to redistribute wealth, socialist governments believe in the public ownership of industry and commerce. This means that companies and business should be owned and operated by the state and any companies not owned by the state will be subject to regulations. This ensures that all businesses run are for the benefit of the people not for the benefit of a few shareholders. Examples of nationalised industries were British Telecom, British Rail, British Steel and the utilities such as water, gas and electricity. However, Britain today has very few publicly owned industries due to the Conservative regime of 1979–1997 which undertook to sell them off to private investors. Remaining state-owned industries such as Royal Mail are gradually having state control cracked by further involvement with the private sector in the form of PPI's or public-private initiatives.

Think about it

Do public – private initiatives undermine socialist principles? Explain your reasons.

The advantages of democratic socialism are that it balances the needs of business and state with the needs of the individual. It also offers social justice and fairness for the very citizens who need it – the poor. It is arguable whether the current policies of New Labour actually conform to the democratic socialist model outlined above or whether New labour has actually become a politically centralist party.

The Labour party general election manifesto released in 2001 sets out their vision for the public services. The key labour aims were:

- an extra 6000 police recruits
- a bill of rights for victims
- to half the burglary rate
- to double the chance of persistent offenders being caught and punished
- 300 new prosecutors by 2004 for the CPS
- the reform and modernisation of the Criminal Justice System
- support for the European Defence Initiative.

Theory into practice

Choose one of the above Labour party promises and assess how the government intends to implement it and evaluate the progress made on it so far.

The Conservative Party

The Conservative Party have formed the following governments during the 20th century:

• Arthur Balfour	1902–1905
• Andrew Law	1922–1923
• Stanley Baldwin	1923–1924 1924–1929 1935–1937
• Neville Chamberlain	1937–1940
• Winston Churchill	1940–1945 1951–1955
• Sir Anthony Eden	1955–1957
• Harold Macmillan	1957–1963
• Sir Alec Douglas-Home	1963–1964
• Edward Health	1970–1974
• Margaret Thatcher	1979–1990
• John Major	1990–1997

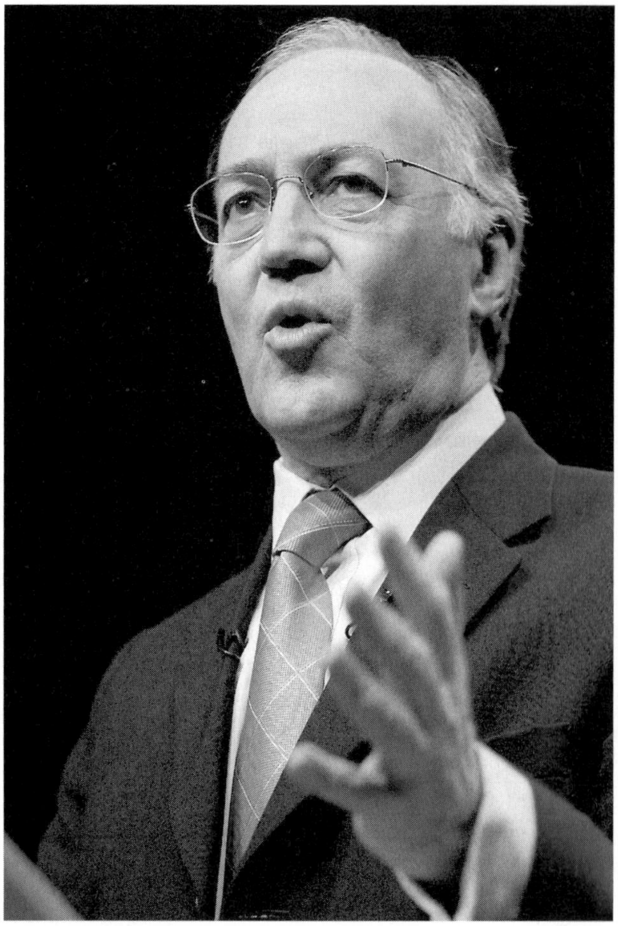

Michael Howard

The Conservative party is built around several major political principles. An 'Introduction to the Conservative Party' by The Conservative Insight Group describes these principles as follows:

- Freedom – this is freedom from state interference. A Conservative state intervenes in personal or business affairs only when absolutely necessary.
- Enterprise – a support for businesses, by reducing taxation.

- Responsibility – support for law and the family.
- Nation – safeguard the interests of the UK.

The current leader of the conservative party is Michael Howard and as of June 2003 the conservatives held 163 seats in the House of Commons. Conservative political ideology is right of the political spectrum. It supports initiatives such as monetarism. Monetarism includes the idea of restraining inflation and control of money supply. Application of monetarism often involves job losses in the short term to ensure economic prosperity in the long term. This policy was promoted vigorously by the successive 1980s Thatcher governments with unemployment peaking at over 3 million during the recession. The principle is that if unemployment is high, wages can be forced lower to benefit businesses and reduce inflation.

Think about it

Why would high unemployment cause wages to be lower?

Conservatives also believe in privatisation of nationalised industries which goes hand in hand with the belief in the minimal state intervention. A Conservative state would not consider it ideologically sound to own state industries and the Conservative government between 1979 and 1997 sold the majority of state owned businesses, freeing them up to be competitive in a global market. Linked with this is the principle of deregulation, which is also supported by conservative ideology. Deregulation removes government checks and requirements from business, such as reducing health and safety regulation or halting price regulation. The idea of this is that businesses have reduced overheads and can therefore be more competitive. Competition is a key element of conservative philosophy.

Conservatives also traditionally oppose trade unions and often introduce policy and legislation designed to reduce their power and influence. Another aspect of conservative political ideology is the principle of nationhood. Conservatives traditionally are anti-European, which is often referred to as 'Eurosceptic'. Conservatives take the view that the UK should be in Europe, but not run by Europe. This view does not support any moves towards a European single currency. The Conservative view of the world lost a great deal of credibility in the 1990s with their economic policies being seen as uncaring and harsh. Many householders were locked into negative equity on their homes and the policies were seen as defending the interests of the rich at the expense of the poor. This led to a landslide Labour victory in 1997 and the Conservative Party has been in opposition since this time.

Assessment activity 10-M3

Demonstrate a detailed understanding of the main ideologies of at least two political parties.

The Liberal Democrats

The Liberal Party currently has only 53 representatives in the House of Commons, so it is difficult to imagine that they were once a major political force, but indeed it was so:

- Sir Henry Campbell Bannerman 1905–1908
- Herbert Henry Asquith 1908–1916
- David Lloyd George 1916–1922

Think about it

Consider the fact that the majority of Liberal and Conservative Prime Ministers were titled. What does this tell you about their social background?

Liberals firmly believe in the freedom of the individual and in a system of government that ensures the rights of the individual are written in law. This includes issues surrounding minority rights and restriction on the oppressive use of majority power. Liberal doctrine also supports notions of equality of opportunity and past Liberal governments have enacted legislation to protect workers, widen education and improve health care.

Charles Kennedy

The aspects of ideology described above show clear commitment to the principles of human rights and support for the idea of intervention in cases where human rights are being breached at home and abroad.

In common with Labour, the Liberal party are also supporters of social justice. Social justice is the principle of equality, democratic government, rights, economic opportunity and respect for the environment although social justice should not be achieved at the expense of individual freedom.

The Liberals argue that some of the most oppressive regimes of this century have pursued equality for all and as a result reduced freedom for everyone. They use communist regimes as an effective example of this. The current leader of the Liberals is Charles Kennedy MP and since the Liberals have not held power since Davis Lloyd George in 1922 he has his work cut out in convincing the British population that the party is ready and able to rule.

Think about it

Communist regimes are built around the principle of equality for all. How do Liberals justify their criticism that communist regimes actually reduce freedom?

The Liberals are making headway against the two main parties but are hindered by the use of the first past the post system (FPTP) of voting employed in the UK. They gain around 20% of the vote at elections, but do not get 20% of the seats in the Commons. It is not surprising that they support the introduction of proportional representation as an alternative voting system as this would provide them with much greater power and influence.

The Liberal Party do not shy away from income tax rises as do the Conservatives, nor do they introduce them by stealth as the Labour Party has been accused of. Instead they are open about the need to increase income tax to fund essential services such as education and they also freely discuss further taxation of societies highest earners.

Assessment activity 10-D2

Critically evaluate the ideology of at least two political parties.

Plaid Cymru (Welsh Nationalist Party)

Plaid Cymru was established in 1925 to promote Welsh culture, language and independence. It is based on socialist principles and has much in common with other socialist parties such as Labour. Plaid Cymru differs from traditional socialism in that it supports decentralisation and the devolvement of power to the regions. The main aims of Plaid (as it is more commonly known) are as follows:

- promote and revive the Welsh language and culture
- attain independent membership of the EU

- attain independent membership of the UN
- promote a sense of community through social justice, citizenship and respect for equality.

The fortunes of Plaid have been mixed over the last few years. Its first representative was elected in 1966, but Plaid has had a chequered history of losing and gaining seats. Their strongest showing was through the late 1990s, but by 2003 only 4 of their candidates had seats in the Commons. They make a stronger showing in Welsh politics in 2003 when they had 12 Welsh Assembly Members (AM's) in the devolved political body of Wales.

Scottish Nationalist Party

The Scottish Nationalist Party (SNP) is another political party with strong socialist tendencies. The SNP has a lot in common with Plaid since devolution, independence from England and recognition as an independent entity on the world stage are high on their agenda. The SNP was formed from a combination of 2 earlier Scottish parties, The National Party of Scotland and The Scottish Party. The first SNP candidate to gain a seat in the House of Commons was Dr Robert McIntyre in 1945. Despite this early victory the SNP had a relatively low profile until the 1970s when North Sea oil was discovered and processed from the rich oil fields off the coast of Scotland and was used as a major political issue by the SNP. The thrust of the campaign was that the Scottish people were not receiving any economic, social or political benefit from what could be considered to be Scottish oil.

The October 1974 general election placed 11 SNP MPs in the House of Commons and prompted the Labour government of the time to seriously consider the issue of Scottish devolution. A referendum on the issue was held in 1979, but an insufficient percentage of the voters supported Scottish home rule. Later that year Labour lost the 1979 general election and conservative ideology did not support notions of Scottish independence. This effectively ended discussions regarding devolution until 1997 when Labour were returned to power. A referendum in 1997 saw the Scottish electorate overwhelmingly support moves towards devolution. This resulted in the creation of the Scottish Parliament at Holyrood. The SNP are currently the second largest party in Holyrood after New Labour with 27 seats. In addition they currently have 5 MPs in the House of Commons and are also represented in the European Parliament.

Other political parties

There are many other political parties whose ideologies can have significant impact on the work of the public services. In Northern Ireland, Ulster Unionists, Democratic Unionists, Independent Unionists and Sinn Fein all have significant impact on the work of the public services. In mainland UK, the British Nationalist Party, which supports an extreme right wing ideology, has gained council seats in Northern towns such as Burnley. The Green Party that has an environmental agenda also gains support from the electorate regarding environmental issues. It is important to understand that even parties without political representation at Westminster can still have substantial impact on the work of the public services.

We have examined the political ideologies of socialism, liberalism and conservatism through the philosophies of the 3 leading parties in the UK, but it is important to acknowledge that there are many other political ideologies that govern parties and nations round the world. Other ideologies include:

- fascism
- communism
- religious fundamentalism.

Assessment activity 10-P4

Summarise the structures of the British governmental system including the European dimension.

Assessment activity 10-P5

Draw a table outlining the principle beliefs of at least 4 political parties.

Political issues

There are many political issues that will have a major impact on the public services, for example:

- racial discrimination
- equal pay
- gender discrimination
- prison reform and sentencing
- Northern Ireland
- international conflicts
- terrorism
- reform of NATO
- Human Rights Act.

Many of these issues are covered comprehensively elsewhere in this book:

- Terrorism – Unit 6 International Perspectives
- Discrimination – Unit 5 Equality and Diversity
- Human Rights Act – Unit 2 Law and the Legal System
- War and Conflict – Unit 6 International Perspectives.

As you can see the Democratic Processes unit cross references to many other units on your National Diploma. For this reason, this chapter will not examine a major political issue, instead you are advised to make links between this unit and the others you are studying to address the following linked assessment activities.

Assessment activity 10-P7, 10-M4, 10-D3, 10-D4

Research a political issue, such as those described above giving your own balanced conclusions. For a higher grade you must include evaluation and analysis of the issue you have chosen, making sure you use appropriate language. Present your findings in the form of a 1,000-word research report.

Influence of the government on the public services

There are many nations in the world where there is no division between the public services and the government. This type of military or security force regime occurs in regions such as Africa and Central and South America. However, generally speaking the rest of the world across Europe, North America, Asia and Oceania have very clear boundaries between the public services and the government.

Think about it

What are the implications of having military rule in a nation?

In effect this means that the public services are subordinate to civilian governments. The public services have no official political role, although they do of course have a large amount of political influence as can be highlighted by the recent firefighters strikes of 2002/2003. The result of this is that civilian governments have a tremendous influence on the work and role of the public services:

- **Public service legislation** that outlines the role and duties of all the public services are made solely by civilian politicians. This means that the operation of all services is dependent of civilian decisions. This could include matters of discipline, such as The Armed Forces Discipline Act 2000, matters of reform such as The Human Rights Act 1998 and matters of practice such as The Crime and Disorder Act 1998. The public services have no right of challenge to any decisions made by civilian government, although they can and do offer expert advice to the government. However, the government can choose to disregard such advice in favour of its own agenda.
- **Civilian governments control** the budgets, staffing and resources of all public services. This means that the operational strength of a service and how much money it has to spend on equipment is entirely in the hands of civilians.
- **Civilian governments set specific objectives** that the public service must achieve regardless of their views on the objective itself. This gives civilian governments the power of life and death over members of the Armed Forces in particular. The objective set could be anything from an order to capture territory or personnel to a directive to reduce street crime by 25%.
- **Civilian authorities can change** the internal political nature of a public service by its actions. Traditionally public services are viewed as right wing, with an emphasis on tradition and duty. The government has changed the political landscape of the public services in terms of racial equality, sex discrimination and discrimination on the grounds of sexual preference. The Macpherson report into the murder of Stephen Lawrence highlighted the issue of institutional racism in the Metropolitan police service which the civilian government acts on its findings to change the underlying political philosophy of the public services.

As you can see the public services are not merely influenced by governments, they are actively directed by them. The public services are politically neutral agents of the government and they must perform as they are instructed. Many services do not even have the right to industrial action. Heywood (2002) notes:

> *'Not since the English civil war of the seventeenth century and the rule of soldier-statesman Oliver Cromwell has the army exerted a direct influence on British political life.'*

Assessment activity 10-P6

Identify the influence on the public services of the government in power.

Public services and the European dimension

The public services can also be affected by EU directives. For example, the problem of cross Europe drug trafficking and computer fraud have both been targeted for action by the EU and the UK has to act on these directives. Other examples of EU policy having an impact on the public services are as follows.

- Proposals for a European Defence force as decided by the European Council in Helsinki in 1999. The UK Armed Services must be prepared to contribute personnel and equipment to this endeavour. In addition, this move will encourage standardisation across Europe's Armed Services possibly leading to common defence structures and policies.
- European integration lends itself to criminals wishing to operate across European borders. The EU has instigated several treaties which encourage police and customs co-operation across nations such as: The Schengen Agreements, The Maastricht Treaty and The Treaty of Amsterdam. All of these agreements are discussed in Unit 6 International Perspectives.

- The EU has also promoted European judicial co-operation in both civil and criminal matters. This includes the creation of Eurojust in 2002, whose role it is to support investigation and prosecution into cross border and trans-national crime.

The public services must be willing to co-operate and support our EU partners, just as they must co-operate with and support us.

The public services must also deal with the implications of their actions in The European Court of Human Rights which exists to investigate human rights breaches in member states. Due to the large amount of power the public services has over the lives of civilians it is important that their activities are monitored and that civilians and serving personnel who feel that their human rights have been breached have an effective recourse.

Assessment activity 10-P4

Produce a newspaper article which summarises the structures of the British government system including the European dimension.

Case study

Finucane v United Kingdom

Patrick Finucane was a solicitor in Northern Ireland who had been involved in several high profile cases which arose from the conflict. Finucane was shot dead in front of his wife and children in February 1989. The cases that he had been involved in included the ill treatment of prisoners by the Royal Ulster Constabulary (RUC). Clients of Patrick's had reported that he had received abuse and death threats from RUC officers while he represented clients in interrogations. The investigation into his death was conducted by the RUC and subsequently there were claims that the RUC had colluded with loyalist paramilitaries and that the investigation was flawed. The European Court of Human Rights concluded that there had been a breach of Article 2 of the European Convention on Human Rights in that Mr Finucane's murder had not been properly investigated by the Northern Ireland security forces and Mrs Finucane was awarded 43,000 EUR to cover costs and expenses.

1 Why do you think Mr Finucane was targeted for assassination by those with loyalist tendencies?
2 Why would British security forces have reason to collude with loyalist paramilitaries?
3 Do you think the RUC should have conducted the investigation into Mr finucane's murder?
4 Was Mrs Finucane right to take the UK government to the European Court of Human Rights?
5 What is your view on the settlement she received?

Case study

Smith and Grady v United Kingdom 1999

This case revolves around the Armed Services dismissing 4 armed forces personnel due to their sexual orientation. The European Court of Human Rights concluded that conducting an intrusive investigation into the private lives of personnel and then dismissing them on the basis of their sexuality breached article 5 of the European convention on Human Rights. The 4 were awarded £19,000 each as compensation for the emotional impact of the dismissal and then varying amounts between £40,000 and £95,000 to cover the loss of earnings. In addition the UK government had to pay the full costs of bringing the case forward. The ban on homosexuals serving in the Armed Services has subsequently been lifted.

1 Should the Armed Services have the right to investigate the sexuality of personnel?
2 Does an individual's sexuality have any impact on how they perform their duties?
3 What is your view on the UK government's decision to repeal the ban on homosexuality in the Armed Services?
4 Do you agree with the amounts awarded by the court?
5 Do you think that UK public services ought to be subject to the European Court of Human Rights? Explain.

End of unit test

1 What is politics?
2 On what levels do politics operate?
3 What is meant by the term 'autocracy'?
4 What is a meritocracy?
5 Define direct democracy.
6 What are the advantages and disadvantages of a representative democracy?
7 Describe the role of an MP.
8 Describe Heywood's (2002) 4 theories of representation.
9 Explain the 'first past the post' voting system.
10 What are the differences between unicameral and bicameral political systems?
11 What are the advantages and disadvantages of the bicameral system?
12 Explain how whips maintain party discipline.
13 What functions does the House of Lords perform?
14 Evaluate the pros and cons of devolution.
15 Where is the Scottish parliament based?
16 What role does the Prime Minister fulfil?
17 Explain the acronym 'Quango'.
18 What influence does the government have on the public services?
19 Describe a recent case where the actions of a UK public service has fallen foul of the European Court of Human Rights.

Resources

Dunleavy P et al, *Developments in British Politics*, 2002, Basingstoke, Palgrave

Gray D et al, *Public Services Book 1*, 2004, London, Heinemann

Heywood A, *Politics 2nd ed*, 2002, Basingstoke, Palgrave

Jones B, *Politics UK*, 2003, London, Prentice Hall

Jones B et al, *Politics UK 4th ed*, 2001, London, Longman

Wilson C, *Understanding Government and Politics*, 2003, Manchester, Manchester University Press.

Websites

www.parliament.uk – The UK Parliament

www.wales.gov.uk – National Assembly for Wales

www.scottish.parliament.uk – Scottish parliament

www.ni-assembly.gov.uk – Northern Ireland Assembly

www.europa.eu.int – Europa

www.bbc.co.uk/news – BBC News

www.labour.org.uk – Labour Party

www.conservatives.com – Conservatives

www.libdems.org.uk – Liberal Democrats

HUMAN BEHAVIOUR

Introduction to Unit 12

The intention of this unit is to provide you with an understanding of the basic principles of psychology and their impact on public service work. This includes understanding the psychological theories and approaches to psychology and how they can be used to benefit the roles of the public services. It discusses different behaviour and possible treatments available.

In addition to a strong introduction to psychology in the public services, this chapter also examines the skills required in interview situations and provides a thorough grounding in various types of communication strategy.

Assessment

Throughout the unit activities and tasks will help you to learn and remember information. Case studies are included to add industry relevance to the topics and learning objectives. You are reminded that when you are completing activities and tasks, opportunities will be created to enhance your key skills evidence. After completing this unit you should be able to achieve the following outcomes.

Outcomes

1 Investigate **approaches to psychology**

2 Examine the **behavioural types**

3 Demonstrate **interview skills**

4 Explore **types of communication**.

Introduction to psychology

The word psychology comes from the Latin terms 'psyche' which means mind and 'logos' which means study. Simply put, this would indicate that psychology is the study of the mind but this is not strictly true. The mind is an imaginary concept. Look on any anatomy chart and see if you can find the mind listed as a body part or organ!

The mind is another word for our brain, our consciousness, our personality and our memory amongst other things. When we call psychology the study of the mind what we are really saying is that we are studying the observable signs of our 'mind' – our behaviour. Our behaviour can tell a psychologist a great deal about an individual's mental state. People who work in the public services see a variety of behaviour every day and an insight into the causes of some of the behaviour they witness has great potential for improving their own safety and the safety of others. It also has wider implications such as resolving conflict with colleagues and superiors.

Psychology is also evident in many other disciplines:

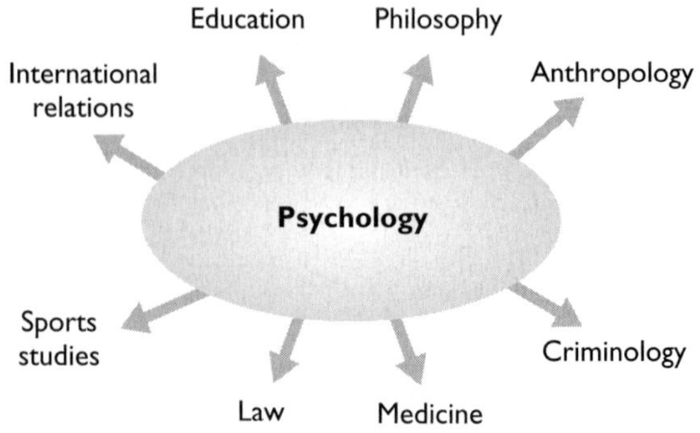

Figure 12.1 Psychology is evident in many other disciplines

Approaches to psychology

There are 4 main approaches to psychology:

PSYCHOANALYTICAL	BEHAVIOURIST
HUMANISTIC	COGNITIVE

Behaviourism

The principles of behaviourism were developed by pioneers in the field such as John Watson. Behaviourism is the study of human behaviour; it uses scientific experimental principles to examine behaviour in response to specific factors such as changes in the environment. Watson's behaviourist manifesto 'Psychology from the Standpoint of a Behaviourist' published in 1913 argued that we could not study the mind because it was not observable – its workings could not be documented or analysed, all that could be studied was an individual's actual physical behaviour.

The theory that Watson proposed revolved around the following principles:

- Behaviourism is concerned with how environmental factors (also called stimuli) affect observable behaviour (also called response).
- The focus of behaviourism is on learning. The interaction between stimulus and response is how learning occurs.
- The ultimate aim of behaviourism is to be able to predict and control behaviour.
- There is no fundamental difference between the behaviour of humans and the behaviour of animals. Each organism learns via the stimulus – response mechanism. Humans will simply display more complex behaviour because they are a more complex organism.

Watson's principles of behaviourism were aided by work from many other psychologists such as B.F. Skinner and Ivan Pavlov and it has made a tremendous contribution to the field of psychology. It enjoyed almost universal acceptance throughout the first half of the twentieth century. Its particular focus lies in the link between behaviour and learning. For behaviourists there are two main forms of learning – classical conditioning and operant conditioning.

Think about it

Can you think of any examples of your own, which you may have experienced where a stimulus produces a reponse?

Classical conditioning

Classical conditioning (also known as Pavlovian conditioning) can best be described with reference to a study in 1927 by Ivan Pavlov. He was a physiologist (a scientist who studies the functions of the body). The principle of classical conditioning is that a stimulus, which wouldn't ordinarily produce a response in an individual, comes to do so by being linked or paired with a stimulus, which does provoke a response. In Pavlov's experiment he noted that dogs salivated when they received their food. He wondered if dogs could be taught to pair their salivation with something that wouldn't normally cause them to salivate – in this case a bell. During the experiment, every time the dogs received food a bell rang. Eventually the dogs associated the sound of the bell with their food and would salivate at the sound of it.

Bowl of dog food → Dog salivating

Bell and Bowl of dog food → Dog salivating

Bell → Dog salivating

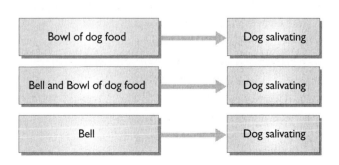

Process of classical conditioning

Although the dog's behaviour doesn't change, the reasons for which it salivates do. At the first point the dog naturally salivates to food (as do we and many other organisms). This is called an unconditioned response – it is something we do quite naturally like scratching an itch. At the second point the bell is linked with the food. The bell is not a natural stimulus to the dog and is called a conditioned stimulus. The dog, however is still salivating at the food in an unconditioned response. By the last stage, the dog has associated the conditioned stimulus of the bell with the food and will salivate at the sound of the bell alone. This is called a conditioned response. The dog has moved from an unconditioned response to the food to a conditioned response to the bell.

Humans can be conditioned in much the same way although in experimental conditions this is difficult because humans understand that the experimenter is making the unconditioned stimulus (such as a bell) occur and this changes the level of conditioning. However, there is an example of a study of classical conditioning conducted on a baby by Watson and Rayner (1920) outlined in the case study below.

Case study

Watson and Rayner 1920 – Little Albert

This study was conducted on a child of eleven months old called Albert and its principle was very much the same as the one described in Pavlov's dogs. The child was given a white rat to stroke but as the child reached out to pet the animal one of the researchers brought a hammer down on a metal bar causing a sudden and extremely loud crashing noise. This was repeated on a number of occasions so that eventually the sight of the rat alone was enough to terrify the child. Watson and Rayner had artificially created a phobia in a baby through classical conditioning.

1 This study has been described as ethnically unsound. What do you think this means?
2 Why was it wrong to conduct an experiment like this?
3 What were the possible long-term implications for the child?
4 Could the child's phobia have been removed in the same way it was created?

Key points

1 Classical conditioning was pioneered by Ivan Pavlov.
2 One of the most important studies is Pavlov's 1927 study of conditioned stimulus in dogs.
3 The principle of classical conditioning is that organisms can be taught or conditioned to associate various stimuli with reward or punishment in order to produce a desired behaviour.
4 Classical conditioning is able to create phobias in humans.
5 Paired with operant conditioning it forms learning theory, a fundamental principle on which behaviourism stands.

Think about it

Do you think experiments into human classical conditioning such as the one outlined earlier by Watson and Rayner 1920 should be conducted today? Explain your reasons.

Operant conditioning

Operant conditioning is the process of changing behaviour through rewards and punishments. Although operant conditioning is often considered to be the brainchild of B.F. Skinner, in actual fact much of Skinner's work is based on the research of Edward Thorndike conducted at the end of the nineteenth century and the early decades of the twentieth century. Like Pavlov, Thorndike also experimented with the learning or conditioning of animals.

Thorndike (1898 and 1911) put a hungry cat into a box; the cat had to find its way out and was rewarded by food when it did so. After the cat had escaped and eaten its reward it was placed back in the box and the process began again. What Thorndike noted was that each time the cat was placed in the box it took less time for it to escape. Thorndike was able to plot a learning curve for the cat's behaviour.

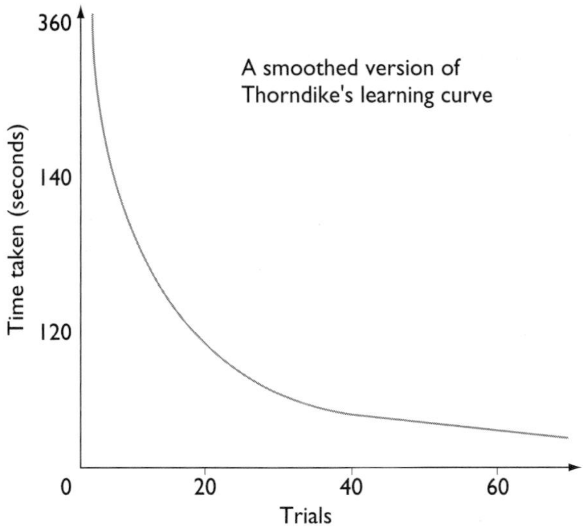

Figure 12.2 Thorndike's learning curve

Thorndike's learning curve shows that the cat was making an association between pushing a lever and being able to escape from the box to get a reward. Skinner built upon these findings of animals being rewarded or punished to reinforce and encourage learning. Skinner argued that behaviour is moulded by the consequences of that behaviour; therefore if behaviour is rewarded or positively reinforced, the animal will repeat it. If behaviour is punished, or negatively reinforced the animal is less likely to repeat the behaviour. This is the process of operant conditioning.

Think about it

Describe circumstances where you were positively or negatively reinforced. What impact did it have on your behaviour?

Skinner used a puzzle box similar to Thorndike, but instead of cats he used rats and pigeons. The process of operant conditioning is as follows:

Rat presses a lever, food tumbles out of tube. Rat is more likely to repeat lever-pressing behaviour.

Rat press a lever and receives a mild electric shock. Rat is less likely to repeat lever-pressing behaviour.

The use of rewards and punishments has long had a place in the behavioural shaping of humans from childhood through to adulthood and beyond. The rewards of humans are more likely to be praise and respect and the punishments physical discipline or loss of privileges, but the principles remain the same. Hayes (1996) points out that one of the first clinical applications of operant conditioning on humans were used to create a token economy system in highly institutionalised patients of psychiatric hospitals.

> *"Since these people had often been in psychiatric hospitals for many decades, teaching them to become self reliant rather than passively dependent on ward staff was a complex job. In some hospitals a token economy system was introduced in which patients were rewarded for showing the appropriate behaviours with tokens which could be exchanged for additional privileges or sometimes goods at the hospital shop".*
>
> *Hayes (1996) Chapter 9, 307*

Think about it

How could operant conditioning be applied to criminal behaviour in adults?

Evaluation of behaviourist theory

1 Watson argued strongly that there is no difference between the behaviour of humans and other animals. However, other psychologists have argued that this is simplistic as humans have a capacity for thought, language and deduction not shared by other animals. Much of what drives us to action is

not merely external environmental factors, but thought processes which occur out of observable sight. For example, a human, put in a situation by a researcher may respond in a variety of different ways rather than simply perform as their environment dictates.

2 Behaviourist theory promotes the beliefs of philosopher John Locke 1632–1704 who argued that at birth humans are a blank slate waiting to be taught. Other research suggests we are born with many genetic traits and abilities which will emerge whether we are taught them or not.

3 Behaviourism relegates humans to the level of a test tube experiment whereas human behaviour is complex and often unique to the individual. Not all humans respond the same way to the same stimuli so it is simplistic to reduce it to a form of observable natural phenomena.

4 Most behavioural experiments are conducted in a laboratory environment which is in accordance with behaviourisms scientific principles of objectivity. However, this setting strips away the natural environment and context within which different behaviour may occur.

5 The use of positive and negative reinforcement and punishment is flawed as what one person considers a punishment may be a reward for another; there is no universal reward that all humans would change their behaviour for and no universal punishment which would induce an individual to avoid a certain behaviour. Although Skinner makes the point that what is defined as a reward or punishment cannot be decided until the effect on behaviour is monitored this pushes behaviourism down a value laden route which is at odds with its claim to scientific objectivity.

6 Another criticism of behaviourism lies in the idea that not all animals can be conditioned in the same way. Seligman (1970) developed the concept of 'preparedness' which is the idea that biological organisms are instinctively prepared to learn actions related to survival in their natural environment, but cannot easily learn actions which are not part of these natural learning tendencies. Gross (2001) comments that pigeons can be trained very easily to fly from one perch to another but it is extremely difficult to train them to peck a disk to avoid a shock. This calls into question whether conditioning is simply an animal building on its instinctive and genetic survival behaviours rather than true learning.

Think about it

What are your views on the behaviourist approach to psychology?

Key points

1. Operant conditioning began with the work of Thorndike and was built upon by Skinner.
2. It involves the use of positive and negative reinforcement and punishment as ways of changing behaviour.
3. Positive reinforcement is a reward such as pushing a lever to get food.
4. Negative reinforcement is a removal of a painful situation, such as pushing a lever to turn off an electric shock.
5. Punishment is a sanction to deter certain behaviour such as an electric shock when an animal presses the wrong button.
6. Skinner argued that all behaviour is shaped by its consequences and the best way to modify behaviour in humans is to couple positive reinforcement for appropriate behaviour with punishment for inappropriate behaviour.

Psychoanalytic theory

This approach to the study of human thought and behaviour is based on the work of Sigmund Freud. Freud pioneered the use of psychological therapy called psychoanalysis, which is still widely used today in helping people identify the causes of their psychological problems and suggesting ways in which they could be overcome. Freud's theory suggests that the majority of our behaviour is influenced by factors we are not consciously aware of.

The conscious is the part of your mind that is currently aware of itself. It knows you are reading this book, it knows when you are due in class and it knows your circumstances and feelings right at this moment. Our conscious mind, the thoughts and memories we are currently aware of are only the tip of the iceberg that is our mind. The preconscious mind is the short-term storehouse for memories and thoughts. It contains information, ideas and beliefs that are not currently on your mind or are temporarily forgotten, but can be recalled easily when they are needed. The unconscious mind according to Freud is the most substantial part of this equation; it contains emotional experiences, ideas and memories that are 'repressed' by the individual. Repression is the process whereby information or significant experiences are buried deep in the mind and the individual concerned will not even be aware of their existence. Freud's theory is that the contents of the unconscious mind influences the actions and behaviour of the individual even though the individual themselves may be unaware of it.

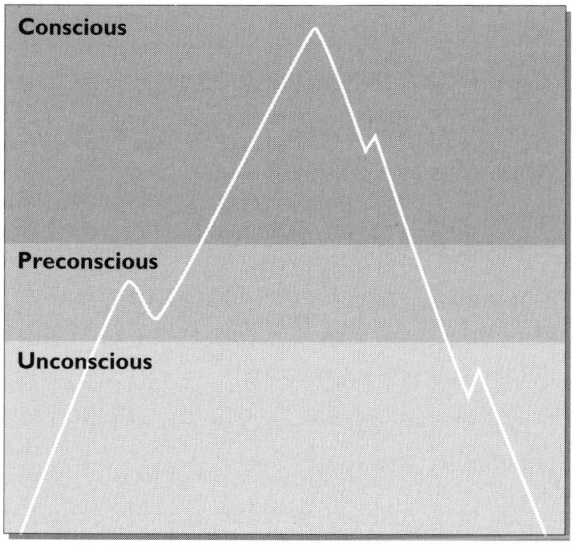

Figure 12.3 Our conscious mind is just the tip of the iceberg

Psychoanalytic theory also greatly stresses the importance of early childhood experience on the eventual mental state of adults and this will be covered later in this chapter. One of the most influential developments to come from Freud's theory is the treatment of psychological problems through a method of therapy called 'psychoanalysis'. Psychoanalysis is the process of uncovering the root causes of psychological problems in order to resolve them. This is also discussed in further detail later in this chapter.

Think about it

You have probably heard terms like 'Freudian slip' or a 'Freudian remark'. From what you have read so far, what do you think these expressions mean?

Think about it

What are your views on Freud's impression of the mind as an iceberg?

Theory into practice

Keep a dream diary for one week. At the end of the week use a Freudian based dream interpretation dictionary to see what your unconscious mind is trying to tell you.

Evaluation of psychoanalytic theory

1 Psychoanalytic theories have been regarded as unscientific because they cannot be disproved. If they predict a certain kind of behaviour and that particular behaviour occurs then they have gathered supporting evidence for their theory. If however the behaviour does not occur then the individual is repressing the instinct to perform that behaviour and the psychoanalysts have still gained evidence to support their theory.

2 Eysenck (1952) pointed out that the recovery rates for patients undergoing psychoanalytic treatments was virtually the same as patients who got better on their own.

3 Eysenck (1985) further noted that the patients opting to undergo psychoanalysis were often young, wealthy and intelligent and therefore were the type of patients most likely to recover anyway.

4 The role of the analyst is questionable. The analyst is supposed to remain completely detached and unemotional. However, Gross (2001) argues that Freud himself often engaged in conversation with his patients and often explained his reasoning to them.

5 In order to be effective, a traditional course of psychoanalysis takes place several times a week for several years and is usually provided by private clinicans. This is clearly extremely expensive and puts it out of the reach of the majority of the population.

Key points

1 The inspiration of psychodynamic theories is the work of Sigmund Freud.

2 Freud's psychoanalytic approach has had a substantial impact on the evolution of psychology from the beginning of the twentieth century.

3 Freud believed that only a small fraction of the mind is directly accessible. He called this the 'conscious'.

4 The rest of the mind is not immediately accessible. It consists of the pre-conscious, which holds information we might need at a moments notice and the unconscious where we repress information we would rather not deal with.

5 The unconscious has a large impact on our behaviour even if we are unaware of it.

Humanism

The humanistic approach emerged in the 1950s and 1960s from the work of Abraham Maslow and Carl Rogers. It differs significantly from the behaviourist and psychoanalytic approaches already examined in that it believes individual's are responsible for choosing their own behaviour rather than simply responding to environmental or unconscious forces which act upon them.

Maslow's theory is outlined in detail in Unit 3 Leadership and so will not be covered here. Carl Rogers (1961) provided a similar but alternative point of view. He suggested that humans have two basic needs. The first is the same as the ultimate goal proposed by Maslow: 'self actualisation' which is the striving for personal development and the aim of achieving ones potential. Rogers saw the other need as the requirement for positive regard. This is the love, respect, trust and affection of others.

Rogers saw individuals very differently from psychoanalysts and behaviourists. He saw an individual as a whole person rather than a group of component parts and he differed from his psychoanalytic training in that he didn't believe an individual had tendencies towards destructiveness and neurosis automatically. Instead, he and Maslow emphasised the essential healthiness of the mind and a natural tendency to grow and develop rather than repress.

Rogers developed a treatment for psychological problems called person centred therapy (PCT). It differs from psychoanalytic therapy in that the therapist is encouraged to engage in the problems of the client and use their own personal qualities to understand the world, as the client perceives it.

Evaluation of the humanistic approach

1 As has already been mentioned it is hard to see humanism as a coherent approach to psychology, it is best described as a way of thinking instead.

2 Many of its concepts are difficult to test scientifically as they are vague and difficult to define and test objectivity.

3 It doesn't provide an explanation of how personality develops.

4 It has been labelled by some as a self-indulgent theory. It focuses too much on the individual's feelings and needs in an introspective spiral.

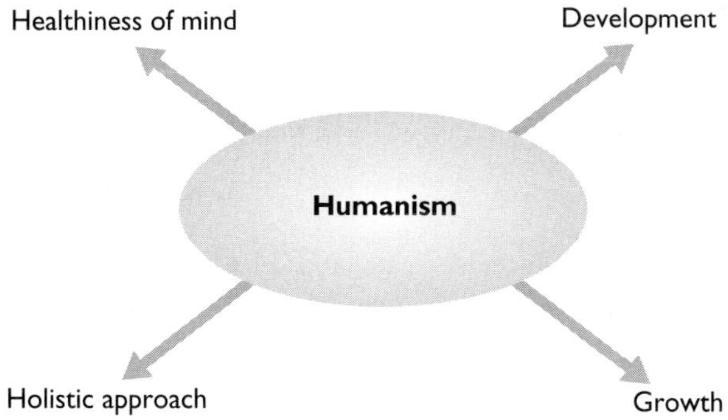

Figure 12.4 The humanistic approach to psychology

5 Psychoanalysts argue that the introspective approach favoured by humanists cannot be effective because individuals cannot see into their own unconscious.

6 PCT relies on the individual discussing how they feel with a therapist. However, many individuals may not be discussing what they really feel, but what the therapist wants to hear.

Key points

1 Humanism is more a way of thinking than a hard and fast scientific approach to psychology.
2 It developed in the mid twentieth century from the work of Maslow and Rogers.
3 It treats the person as a whole recognising and respecting individuality.
4 It argues that individuals have a natural tendency for growth and development. Individuals develop difficulties when this growth and development is halted by external forces.
5 It developed person centred therapy from which most forms of counselling have developed.

Think about it

The humanistic approach to psychology was often called the third way. Can you think why this was?

Cognitive psychology

Cognitive psychology was developed between the 1950s and 1970s. Its origins lie in the focus during and after World War II on subjects such as human performance, attention and memory. It is also linked to developments in computer science and linguistics.

Cognitive psychology is concerned with the mental processes within an individual and the consequences of these processes on behaviour. It focuses on aspects of the individual such as perception, motor control, memory, language and decision-making. Like behaviourism and psychoanalytic theories, cognitive psychology relies upon scientific methods to support its case. The dominant view in cognitive psychology is that the brain is an information processing system similar to a computer where information is input and behaviour is output. This has lead to an over reliance on laboratory experiments as a method of providing evidence for the theory, as the example below highlights.

Case study

Tolman's cognitive behaviourism

Working in the early part of the twentieth century, Tolman examined the process by which learning takes place. The experiments were conducted with rats in a laboratory who had to find their way through a maze. The rats were split into 3 groups: group 1 received food every time they made their way successfully through the maze, group 2 never received food and group 3 received food only after 10 days had gone by. The result of the study is relatively predictable as group 1 navigated the maze most effectively, group 2 were the least effective and group 3 made improvements after day 10. It is interesting to note that cognitive experiments such as this are often used to form parts of theories designed to explain human behaviour.

Cognitive psychology proposes how a person thinks will largely affect how they feel and behave. Although there is no primary 'spokesperson' or pioneer in the field, several researchers have made significant contributions to our understanding of cognition such as Bruner who developed a theory based on principles of categorisation. This theory argues that individuals perceive the world in terms of similarities and differences. Depending on the similarities and differences individuals, objects and events are categorised by information processing and decision-making which is a cognitive process.

Cognitive psychology has become strongly associated with computer science and the study of artificial intelligence. It explores whether computers are capable of problem solving in similar ways to humans and examines the parallels between the human brain and the computer. Cognitive psychology like other approaches we have examined has had a substantial impact upon developments in the field such as cognitive behavioural treatments for mental health difficulties.

Evaluation of the cognitive approach

1 One of the main criticisms of the cognitive approach is that the use of lab experiments on humans alters their behaviour and thought processes. By taking an individual out of a natural setting and placing them in an artificial environment their thought processes may be changed.

2 The cognitive approach also neglects individual differences to some extent. It generalises across all humans in terms of how they perceive, receive, process, store, retrieve and use information.

3 The likening of the human mind to a computer neglects culture, history and interaction with others and the environment.

4 A cognitive approach doesn't address the process of remembering or learning things in groups. It emphasises the individual mental processes without reference to others.

5 Some of the experiments conducted by cognitive psychologists are unrealistic which can result in incorrect results. For instance, a cognitive psychologist may wish to study short-term memory and provide a list of words for subjects to memorise. However, this is not a normal procedure for most people who remember things through imagery or prose.

Freewill vs determinism

Freewill is the idea that an individual has the freedom to choose how they will act and develop whereas determinism puts forward the idea that everything that you do is already predetermined. Freewill embraces the concept of freedom of choice and responsibility for your actions. It maintains that peoples actions are not solely determined by their genetic or environmental circumstances. Determinism on the other hand puts forward the idea that a person's behaviour and actions are a direct result of their genetic inheritance and their past life experiences which come together to form a predicable course of action which cannot be changed or avoided.

In order to have freewill a person must have choices available to them and not be pressured or forced to make any particular decision. As individuals, many people support the view that they are free to choose what they do and they are the ones who must take responsibility for poor decisions. In fact our criminal justice system is based on the fact that citizens have freewill and can choose the course of their actions.

Think about it

What are the implications on our criminal justice system if the principle of determinism is true? Could we hold people responsible for their actions when effectively they had no choice?

The perceived lack of responsibility in determinism is one of the major problems with examining it in relation to behaviour. If a person is not responsible for their actions because of their genes or because of how they have been treated in their environment and the people who treated them badly are not responsible for their behaviour and so on you get a spiral of non-responsibility. However, it is very important to note that to simply put freewill on one side of the debate and determinism on the other over simplifies the situation. There are many different kinds of determinism each of which has a different perspective on why people act the way they do.

Theory into practice

What kinds of determinism exist? Research and explain as many as you can find.

The debate on freewill and determinism is not actually part of psychology at all, it belongs to psychology's parent discipline of philosophy. It usually finds its way into the subject of psychology through the nature v nurture debate which revolves around whether a person's behaviour is caused by genetics or by their environment.

Key points

1. Cognitive psychology is not a cohesive theory and has no particular spokesperson.
2. It studies the mental processes involved in perception, motor control and memory, etc.
3. It is particularly concerned with how we perceive, receive, process, store, retrieve and use information.
4. Cognitive psychology draws parallels between the human brain and computers, seeing them both as information processing systems.
5. Developed from the 1950s onwards as a result of performance testing on humans and developments in computer science.

Assessment activity 12-P1

Considering all of the information you have read on the various approaches to psychology, act out the role play/presentation below 4 times, each time from the point of view of a different psychological perspective. The approaches are summarised in Figure 12.5.

Role play/presentation: you are a serving police officer who must explain to a group of police cadets how their behaviour has developed and what they can do to improve their performance.

Biographies of important psychologists

Sigmund Freud

Sigmund Freud was born on May 6th 1856 in Moravia in what is now the Czech Republic. The Freud family moved to Vienna in Austria when Sigmund was around 4 years old. Freud was a brilliant student and did exceptionally well at school. He opted to progress to medical school and studied medicine at the University of Vienna concentrating on the study of physiology and neurology. Vienna at this time was a breeding ground for anti-semitic feeling and as a Jew, Freud began to feel this discrimination.

He married in 1886 and over the next 9 years he and his wife had 6 children. The change in his family status did not put a halt to Freud's research; he continually published papers and books from dream interpretation to sexuality. The theory of psychoanalysis was to become very popular until the outbreak of the First World War

Approach	Developed	Type	Contribution	Strengths	Weaknesses
Behaviourism	Late (19th early 20th century) by Watson, Pavlov, Skinner.	Deterministic. Positivist.	Behaviour therapy. Behaviour modification. Biofeedback. Computer assisted learning.	Objective and scientific. Highlights importance of learning and association.	Draws interferences from animal behaviour to human behaviour. Does not contextualise behaviour.
Psychoanalytic	Late (10 and early 20) by Freud.	Deterministic. Positivist.	Psychoanalysis. Dream interpretation. Free association. Verbal analysis.	Coherent theory of mind.	Psychoanalysis does not produce recovery rates higher than other therapies. Assumes humans are innately destructive.
Humanism	Mid 1950s and 60s by Rogers, Maslow.	Freewill. Phenomenological.	Person centred therapy. Counselling.	Emphasises choice. Considers the social context of behaviour.	Concepts are vague and lack objectivity. Labelled as narcissistic and self indulgent.
Cognitive	1970s and 1980s.	Freewill. Positivist.	Social learning theory. Rational, emotive. Behaviour therapy.	Popular. Combined scientific rigour with an emphasis on mental processes. Now have a greater appreciation of our complexity.	Relies on artificial experimentation. Ignores issues of culture, emotion and history in its computer analogy.

Figure 12.5 Approaches to psychology summary table

when millions died and all 3 of Freud's sons fought in the army. These experiences led him to conclude that all humans have an instinct which drives them towards death and destruction – he called this instinct 'Thanatos'.

It was often thought that the Great War (WW1) was the war to end all wars, but during the 1930s Nazism began to move through Austria and found it receptive to its ideology. This placed Jews like Freud in a very difficult and dangerous position.

Sigmund Freud

He chose to escape and immigrated to England where he died in September 1939.

Freud is famed for his neurological research into hysteria, development of a major approach to psychology and development of the treatment technique of psychoanalysis.

Key texts:

The Interpretation of Dreams	1900
Beyond the Pleasure Principle	1920
Studies of Hysteria	1895 (with Joseph Brever)
The Ego and the ID	1923
Three essays on the theory of Sexuality	1905

B.F. Skinner

Burrhus Frederick Skinner was born on March 20th 1904 in Pennsylvania in the United States. His initial education was not in the field of psychology at all. He received a degree in English from Hamilton college in New York and for a significant period of time he had aspirations to be a writer. Although he published several newspaper articles, he didn't achieve any real writing success and he decided to return to university. This time he went to Harvard and completed a Masters Degree in Psychology and a PhD in 1931. He

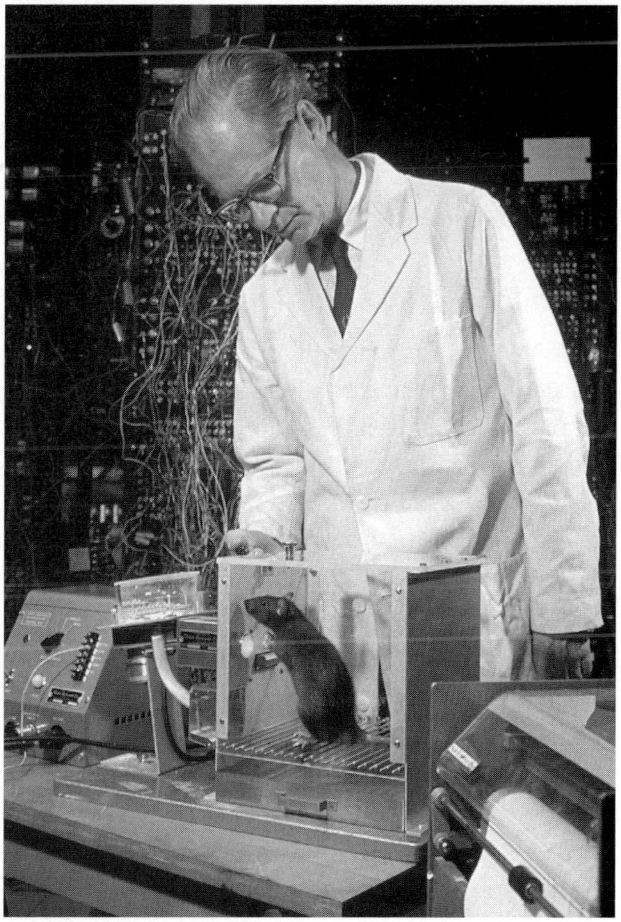

B F Skinner

stayed at Harvard performing research until 1936 when he moved to the University of Minnesota.

When Skinner began his psychology studies the dominant theme at Harvard was introspectionism, but Skinner found himself more and more favouring the behavioural approach developed by Watson and Pavlov. He developed the use of Skinner boxes (based on Thorndike's puzzle box outlined earlier in this chapter), which allowed him to test the behaviour of animals when presented with stimuli.

Skinner is famed for his work on operant conditioning and behavioural shaping and developed teaching machines, which helped students learn by breaking down tasks and rewarding students for correct answers. In 1948 he was invited to return to Harvard where he remained for the rest of his professional life. Skinner died in August 1990.

Key texts:

Walden II	1948
The Behaviour of Organisms	1938
Science and Human Behaviour	1953
About Behaviourism	1974

Abraham Maslow

Maslow was born on April 1st 1908 in New York to a very poor Russian immigrant family. He was the first of 7 children. His parents believed education was the only way for their children to become successful in their new nation and they pushed Maslow hard academically. Like Skinner, Maslow did not set out to be a psychologist, he initially began to study law at the City College of New York but following a transfer of his studies he became interested in psychological research and spent time working under the direction of Harry Harlow who researched maternal attachment in baby monkeys.

Maslow did not graduate with the law degree he initially started, but got his degree in psychology in 1930, his masters in psychology in 1931 and his PhD in 1934. After he achieved his PhD he returned to New York where he began research on sexuality at the University of Columbia. Maslow had a distinguished teaching and theoretical career and is best known for his work on self-actualisation and the promotion of the humanistic approach to psychology. He died in June 1970 after years of ill health.

Abraham Maslow

Key texts:

Motivation and Personality	1954
Towards a Psychology of Being	1962
The Farther Reaches of Human Nature	1971 (Posthumous)

John Watson

John Broadus Watson was born in Greenville, South Carolina in a farming community in 1878. He received a Masters degree in 1901 and proceeded to the University of Chicago to complete a PhD in Psychology. By 1908 he was Professor of Experimental and Comparative Psychology at the prestigious Johns Hopkins University.

John Watson

Watson is best remembered for his tremendous contributions to the development of the behaviourist approach to psychology. However, he spent the latter half of his career outside academia by applying his knowledge of psychology to the field of advertising. He retired in 1945 and died in 1958.

Key texts:

Psychology from the Standpoint of a Behaviourist	1919
Behaviourism	1925
Behaviour: An introduction to Comparative Psychology	1914

Think about it

From what you have read so far, what do you think advertising has to do with psychology? Discuss with your colleagues and list the impact psychology might have on advertising.

Carl Rogers

Carl Rodgers

Rogers was born in 1902 in Chicago, part of a large family with a successful civil engineer at its head. Like Skinner and Maslow, Rogers's education began in a completely different direction. Although he was to end up one of the founding fathers of humanism he began university as an agriculture student and then switched to theology. He graduated, married and moved to New York. While training to enter a religious ministry Rogers questioned his religious beliefs and decided on another change in direction, this time towards psychology. He returned to education, enrolling on a Masters Degree at Columbia University and he received his PhD in 1931. He taught at various academic institutions such as Ohio State University and the University of Chicago and The University of Wisconsin.

Rogers is best known for pioneering the humanistic approach to psychology which contrasts sharply with the deterministic view of psychoanalytic theory and behaviourism which led to humanism being described as 'the third way'. Rogers's theory is based around a human's need for self-actualisation; his theory spawned the huge growth in counselling and therapy seen throughout the latter half of the twentieth century. Rogers was active in the field of psychology right until his death in 1987.

Major texts:

Client Centred Therapy	1957
On Becoming a Person	1961
A Way of Being	1980

Benefits of psychology for individuals and organisations

As you can see from the diagram below there are lots of reasons to use psychology within large organisations such as the public services. These uses benefit both the individual themselves and the organisation as a whole. We will now examine these reasons in more detail.

Dealing with stress

Performing public service work whether uniformed such as the police, fire-fighters or nurses or non-uniformed such as teachers, lecturers and probation officers can come with a certain amount of stress attached to the job. Psychology can be used by a particular organisation to try to reduce the impact of stress on the workforce. This may take the form of actively reducing stress by actions such as limiting working hours or providing mechanisms to help the workforce deal with stress more effectively such as sports facilities or in-house counselling. Millions of pounds are lost every year due to staff absences from stress and it is in the interests of an organisation to realise that lowering levels of stress will make them more efficient. Psychology can help by identifying psychological and physiological stressors such as:

- Continuously high noise levels – linked to ulcers and high blood pressure. This understanding can inform employers on how to reduce high noise levels in order to make a better working environment for public service employees.
- Levels of light – generally the better the levels of light the better the work performance. Psychology in this instance can be incorporated into the design of buildings so that light levels are bright enough to motivate and encourage enhanced work performance.
- Temperature – both extremes of high and low temperature cause stress and inability to perform work. The Health and Safety at Work etc Act acknowledges the importance of a good working temperature, but optimum working temperatures are evaluated and examined by psychologists and can save companies a great deal of money by helping to maximise the productivity of employees.
- Space – lack of personal space, overcrowding and lack of privacy can cause stress in individuals. Discoveries in this field by psychologists are incorporated into the design of buildings and the structuring of offices to help workers feel more comfortable in their environment.
- Shift work – Sparks & Cooper (1997) found that the longer the hours worked the less productive an individual is and the more likely they are to suffer from stress related illness. Tepas et al (1985) found that divorce was 50%

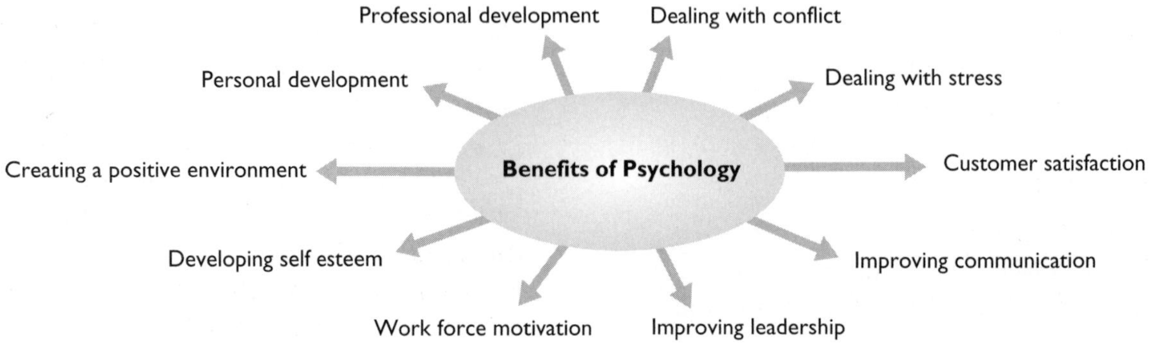

Figure 12.6 Benefits of psychology

more common amongst night shift workers than others. Having knowledge such as this can help employers change shift patterns to a less damaging format and offer support mechanisms for employees who find it difficult to adjust.

It is important to note that many public service workers actually thrive on stress factors such as these because they add variety and excitement to the nature of the work. Although there is no doubt that public service life can be stressful at times it is also personally rewarding and professionally fulfilling.

Case study

Environmental satisfaction in open-plan environments: effects of workstation size, partition height and windows by Charles and Veitch 2002

This study examined some of the characteristics of open plan offices to see if they made any difference on the productivity and general satisfaction of employees. The study examined each individual's workstation area (their desk and surrounding environment), their partition height (which indicates how much privacy they have) and the presence of windows near to the persons work environment. It found that the larger the persons workspace the better they felt about performing their role, the presence of a window close by improved a persons satisfaction with their environment and that the more privacy they had the better they felt about working in the environment.

1. If you were a psychologist how would you use the results of this study to improve the working areas in a police station?
2. Why do you think that the amount of space a person has to work in matters to them?
3. Why might the presence of a window make people feel better about their work environment?
4. Why is privacy in the workplace important? Consider this in a public service office particularly.

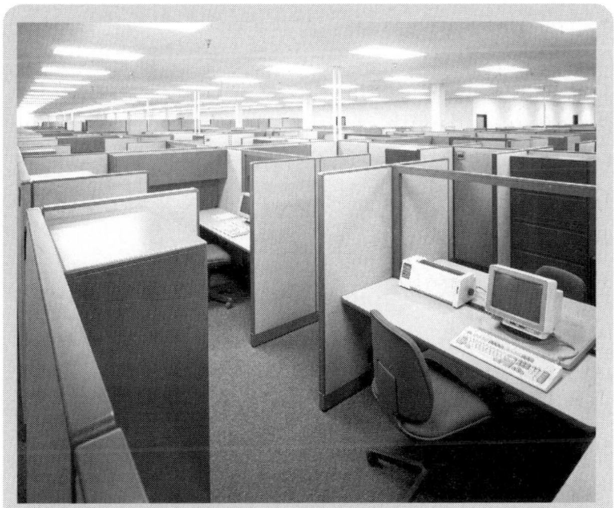
An open plan office

Improving communication

Psychology has spent a great deal of time researching communications in organisations and between individuals. It forms a large part of a later section of this chapter and will therefore not be discussed here.

Workforce motivation

Psychological studies have focused greatly on the issue of motivation, analysing how and why individuals can be motivated to perform better and be more positive. These studies are outlined in Unit 3: Leadership.

Creating a positive environment

Customers, clients and staff need a positive environment in which to interact and perform their respective roles. A negative environment harms productivity. For example, if a police station reception was dirty and intimidating less people may be inclined to go in to report a crime. Equally, if the offices of a building are dirty and intimidating there may be increased absenteeism from staff who dislike the environment. Psychological studies have found optimum conditions which are likely to be conducive to the productivity and comfortableness of all and they are able to highlight the benefits of good working conditions. This can help with the physical design of buildings and with training for managers on how to deal with members of staff.

Professional development

Psychology has a role to play in the effectiveness of appraisal systems, which have a direct impact on the professional development undertaken by an individual. Appraisals outline an individual's strengths, areas that require development and organise training to address areas of development. This may mean the difference between promotion and standing still within an organisation.

Dealing with conflict

Dealing with conflict is a daily part of the professional life of most individuals. However this is more pronounced in the lives of public service workers who may deal with conflict from:

- the public
- colleagues
- superiors
- government
- media
- pressure groups
- the family.

Grounding in psychology can provide useful tools to avoid, minimise and resolve conflict as employers will have a larger range of coping techniques and an deeper understanding of what motivates people to act the way they do. They will also understand themselves better and control their response to difficult situations.

Simulation

PC Jensen and PC Dev have been called out to respond to calls from the public about a disturbance in a local shopping centre. When they arrive on the scene they find a man in a state of disarray shouting abuse to passers by and bleeding heavily from a head wound. One of the local shopkeepers has left his shop and is behaving very aggressively towards the injured man who he believes to be drunk. Neither of the police officers can smell alcohol on the injured man and attempt to resolve the situation.

1 How could the police officers use psychology to diffuse the situation?
2 Considering your own knowledge of psychology what advice would you give to the officers on why the man who is shouting abuse might be behaving this way?
3 How do you think psychology would explain the actions of the shopkeeper?
4 If you were one of the police officers in this situation what would your first action be?
5 How important is an understanding of psychology and why people behave the way they do in resolving conflict?

Personal development

The humanistic approach to psychology argued by Maslow and Rogers puts an individuals need for self-development and self-actualisation at the forefront of psychological theory. People have a natural urge to try and reach their full potential and an understanding of psychology can help them understand and overcome barriers to this self fulfilment and achieve their goals more quickly and efficiently.

Improving leadership

Confident and effective leadership skills are of vital importance in a public service organisation and many people at various ranks have these skills. Unfortunately some do not and this is where problems can occur. Psychology can help good leaders become better and help poor leaders understand and overcome the challenges they face. Effective and ineffective leadership is discussed in detail in Unit 3: Leadership, but consider the simulation below.

Simulation

Penny is the leader of a tightly knit and highly effective team of workers who are widely respected within the educational organisation they inhabit. Penny's team sits within a larger management structure headed by Rhys who is Penny's line manager. Rhys has poor relations with Penny's team largely because he accords them no professional respect, constantly criticises them and ensures Penny does a great deal of the work that is actually within his remit to do.

Penny is justifiably proud of her team and the achievements they have earned and she understands their resentment as she has also had to deal with unfounded criticism from Rhys. Penny suspects that Rhys feels threatened by the success of the team and is trying to consolidate his own leadership position by putting others down.

1. How could an understanding of psychology help Penny understand and deal with Rhys behaviour?
2. How could an understanding of psychology be used by Rhys himself to understand his actions?
3. What aspects of psychology could Penny use to motivate her disgruntled team?
4. How could psychology improve the flow of communication between all concerned?
5. What aspects of psychology could help Penny deal with the conflicts she faces?

Developing self-esteem

An understanding of psychology can be used by organisational managers to improve the self-esteem of their employees. Equally, individuals themselves can use psychology to promote their own self-esteem. Self-esteem and self-confidence are important components in performing stressful and difficult jobs effectively.

Customer satisfaction

Although it is not often thought about, the public services have a customer base of 60 million individuals – the entire UK population. In addition, they service numerous other thousands of individuals abroad in delivering humanitarian aid and engaging in UN backed military action such as recently in the Balkans, Afghanistan and Iraq. Like any other organisation, the public services must keep their customers satisfied with their performance or the government would be forced to change, reform or even replace the functions that the public services currently call their own. Psychology can offer techniques on how to deal with customers effectively and sensitively regardless of how angry, upset, grief stricken or drunk they may be. This is vital in training officers to deal with the public courteously and respectfully.

People approach everyday situations very differently to each other, as one person's approach to a violent situation may defuse it, while another person's approach may escalate it. For example, if you refer back to the simulation on page 188 on using psychology to deal with conflict, you will see that if PC Dev and PC Jensen had approached the situation in an aggressive manner they might have arrested a man with a head injury for being drunk when in actual fact his head injury could have caused his bizarre behaviour and he might have been a victim of a violent crime. Taking a more considered approach would have calmed down the situation and ensured that the man received medical treatment. This shows the usefulness in having a considered understanding of how psychology can enhance the professional role of public service officers. It is a useful skill to be able to assess how your colleagues and your potential customers (the general public) approach situations from a psychological standpoint.

Assessment activity 12-M1/12-D1

Give the questionnaire on page 191 to 5 of your colleagues on your public service course and to 5 members of the public. Using the scale described at the end, analyse the approaches to psychology you find in your colleagues and the members of the general public. What do these approaches mean in terms of how you should deal with them in everyday situations and the effect these individuals will have on other individuals and organisations?

The following questionnaire is designed to find out which psychological approach you favour in your day-to-day activities and attitudes. Examine the following statements and place a ring around the number that best describes your response. The responses are as follows:

1 Strongly Disagree
2 Disagree
3 No firm opinion/Don't know
4 Agree
5 Strongly Agree

How to interpret the results

If questions 1–10 has the highest score then this person views the world through the eyes of a behaviourist. This means that they believe in the importance of the environment on how we behave and that poor behaviour can be unlearned by a similar process to the way it was learned in the first place. They believe that all human behaviour is learned rather than inborn. This kind of person will reward good performance in an organisation and may punish ineffective performance; they may not take into account individual differences and expect the same performance from all members of their team. In addition, they may place emphasis on individuals learning new skills creating a culture of professional development in an organisation.

If questions 11–20 has the highest score then this person approaches the world in a psychoanalytic frame of mind. This means that they believe that people have hidden depths and are influenced by very early childhood experiences. This individual may be unlikely to use rewards and punishments to motivate individuals and may instead prefer to ask an individual to explain their behaviour. They may expect the worst in people as Freudian psychology emphasises the innate destructiveness of humans. They may pay particular attention to slips of the tongue, which could be a useful skill in interview and appraisals in that it provides an insight to the person's unconscious mind in which much of our behaviour is rooted.

If questions 21–30 has the highest score then this person will have humanist tendencies. This means that they acknowledge the individuality of the people around them and they may not look at an example of poor performance in isolation, but looks at the person as a whole. An individual who has strong humanist tendencies may believe that the behaviour of another person is a choice they have made. that people have free will in their actions and are basically good. An organisation with a humanist approach will provide ample opportunities for its employees to reach their potential and will have respect for the home lives of individuals because it understands that individuals need love and affection to perform their roles well.

If questions 31–40 has the highest score then the person favours a cognitive approach to the world. This means that they may view humans like computers in the way they perceive, receive, store, retrieve and use information. They are not necessarily interested in the fact that an individual completed a task, they may want to know how the individual completed the task and the process they went through to achieve an outcome. A person with a cognitive approach may value reason and logic and use these skills to overcome difficulties.

Approaches to psychology questionnaire

STATEMENT	ANSWER				
1. I believe that people can be trained to do anything.	1	2	3	4	5
2. I believe that you can predict human behaviour by experimenting with animal behaviour.	1	2	3	4	5
3. I believe the best way to understand a person is to observe their behaviour.	1	2	3	4	5
4. I believe that people are heavily influenced by contact with aspects of their environment.	1	2	3	4	5
5. The only way to understand the behaviour of another is to analyse it in a scientific, detached manner.	1	2	3	4	5
6. Individuals who behave poorly can learn to behave better.	1	2	3	4	5
7. Punishment can deter poor behaviour.	1	2	3	4	5
8. Good behaviour can be encouraged by rewards.	1	2	3	4	5
9. There is always a direct environmental cause for a person's behaviour.	1	2	3	4	5
10. With enough information the behaviour of individuals can be predicted and controlled.	1	2	3	4	5
11. People can't often explain their behaviour.	1	2	3	4	5
12. Humans are aggressive and destructive by nature.	1	2	3	4	5
13. Individuals may reveal what they are thinking by accident.	1	2	3	4	5
14. Individuals can choose to forget and repress information they don't want to deal with.	1	2	3	4	5
15. An individual's poor behaviour stems from their treatment as a child.	1	2	3	4	5
16. Individuals often make excuses and justifications for poor behaviour rather than facing up to it.	1	2	3	4	5
17. The causes of all our behaviour, both good and bad are very deep rooted.	1	2	3	4	5
18. Dreams can tell an individual a great deal about their fears and worries.	1	2	3	4	5
19. Most people don't know themselves very well.	1	2	3	4	5
20. Behaviour is caused by internal conflict rather than external environmental factors.	1	2	3	4	5
21. People are individuals, it is difficult to generalise from one person to another.	1	2	3	4	5
22. People are basically good by nature.	1	2	3	4	5
23. Individuals have free will and choose how to behave.	1	2	3	4	5
24. Scientific study isn't the best way to examine human behaviour.	1	2	3	4	5
25. Humans are constantly trying to improve themselves and reach their potential.	1	2	3	4	5

STATEMENT	ANSWER				
26. You can't explain behaviour by simply watching it from a distance.	1	2	3	4	5
27. The best way to understand a person's behaviour is to try and see things from their point of view.	1	2	3	4	5
28. It is silly to look at certain bits of an individual's behaviour; you have to see the whole picture.	1	2	3	4	5
29. People need to have love and affection in their lives.	1	2	3	4	5
30. Each of us sees the world through individual eyes and with a unique perspective.	1	2	3	4	5
31. Humans have a lot in common with computers.	1	2	3	4	5
32. Rather than studying behaviour we should study the thought processes behind the behaviour.	1	2	3	4	5
33. Changing a person's thoughts can change their behaviour.	1	2	3	4	5
34. Humans process information like machines.	1	2	3	4	5
35. You have to examine specific bits of behaviour in order to generalise about the whole.	1	2	3	4	5
36. A person's irrational beliefs are responsible for their irrational behaviour.	1	2	3	4	5
37. Individuals learn by putting the pieces of a problem together like a jigsaw.	1	2	3	4	5
38. Individuals don't need rewards in order to learn.	1	2	3	4	5
39. The more complex the behaviour that individuals show the wider the variety of differences between them.	1	2	3	4	5
40. An understanding of language and communication is crucial in understanding behaviour.	1	2	3	4	5

Collect the results of your questionnaire together and analyse the results as follows:

Score for Questions 1–10 __________

Score for Questions 11–20 __________

Score for Questions 21– 30 __________

Score for Questions 31–40 __________

The highest scoring section gives an indication of that persons approach to psychology (see page 190).

Behaviour and personality

This section looks at defining behaviour and examining attitudes which affect behaviour. It also examines personality theories before concluding with an examination of abnormal behaviour and possible treatments for it. An examination of attitudes is crucial in understanding how the public services operate because attitudes have a direct impact on how individuals treat each other in terms of prejudice, discrimination and persuasion. It is here that we will begin our analysis of behaviour and personality.

Attitudes

There is no hard and fast definition of what an attitude is because a behaviourist definition of what an attitude is would differ greatly from a humanist view or a psychodynamic view.

Think about it

How would you describe or define an attitude?

Consider what the following definitions of attitude actually mean. How do they compare with the definition you came up with earlier?

> "An attitude is a mental and neural state of readiness, organised through experience, exerting a directive or dynamic influence upon the individuals response to all objects and situations with which it is related."
>
> *Allport, 1935*

> "A learned orientation, or disposition towards an object or situation which provides a tendency to respond favourably or unfavourably to the object or situation. . ."
>
> *Rokeach, 1968*

> "An attitude is an evaluative disposition towards some object"
>
> *Zimbardo & Leippe, 1991*

What these definitions have in common is the idea that an attitude revolves around how you feel about something. It is a positive, negative or neutral view of an object, person or situation. Attitudes help us to make sense of the world around us as they provide us with a framework from which we can react and respond to situations. Attitudes provide us with standards of behaviour from which we determine what we consider to be right or wrong and what we agree with and disagree with. Hayes (1996) comments that attitudes allow our past experience to guide our reactions, so that we don't have to go through the process of learning how we should react each time.

Our attitudes towards certain things help us bond with like minded individuals to form a group and help us identify with other individuals who feel as we do – this process is called social identification. Attitudes can directly affect our behaviour and can have an impact on how we speak to people and how we treat them. However, just because we hold a particular attitude doesn't always mean we will show it publicly. In a famous study by Lapiere in 1934 it was found that although people hold a particular attitude they don't always let it affect their behaviour.

Case study

Lapiere 1934

This is a key study on attitude and behaviour. Over a 2-year period a researcher travelled around the USA with a young Chinese couple to see how much discrimination they would face. They visited 251 establishments such as hotels, guesthouses, restaurants and cafes. They were only discriminated against once. However the researcher sent a letter out to all of the establishments they had visited asking if the proprietors would be prepared to accept Chinese guests. Of the establishments that replied to the letter 91% said they would not accept Chinese guests. This study highlights a clear inconsistency between the attitudes of the owners of the establishments and their actual behaviour when confronted with a situation.

1. Why do you think Lapiere expected to find discrimination against the Chinese couple?
2. Is there any evidence to suggest that the USA in the 1930s was a particularly racist society?
3. Do you hold any attitudes which are inconsistent with your actual behaviour? How do you explain this?

Lapiere's study is just one instance of the difficulty in finding a direct link between attitude and behaviour. It is generally agreed that attitudes do not predict behaviour but according to Gross (2001) attitudes act as a pre-disposition to behaviour. They might make us more inclined to behave in a particular way but they do not guarantee that we will do so. The diagram below highlights why attitudes do not automatically influence our conduct directly.

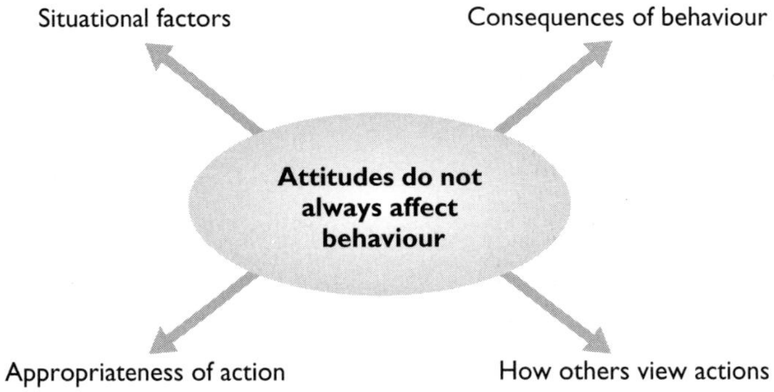

Figure 12.7 Why attitudes do not always affect behaviour

1 **Consequences of behaviour**

The immediate and long-term consequences of our behaviour can have a direct impact on whether we translate our attitudes into behaviour. The short-term consequences of displaying our attitudes in the form of behaviour may include any or all of the following:

- confrontation
- embarrassment
- loss of respect
- loss of business.

The long-term consequences could be any of the following:

- guilt
- disciplinary proceedings
- loss of business.

If you consider Lapiere's 1934 study it is clear that the racist attitudes of the establishment owners were not put into practice. It is possible that they wished to avoid any angry confrontation this may cause or avoid any embarrassing explanations as to why the Chinese couple were not welcome. It is also possible that the Chinese couple in Lapiere's study challenged racist stereotypes held by the proprietors since they were middle class and accompanied by a white researcher – this may have made it more difficult for racist attitudes to become behaviour.

2 **How others view actions**

It may be the case that our behaviour is influenced by how we perceive that others view our actions. For instance if we hold racist or homophobic attitudes and we put those into practice through our behaviour we may face disapproval by our friends and colleagues. If the attitude a person holds places them in a minority they may be more inclined to conform to the group's attitude rather than express their own.

3 **Appropriateness of action**

It may be that expressing our attitudes through our behaviour may not be the appropriate course of action to take in a particular situation. For example, if you are a member of a public service you are required to treat all individuals fairly and with respect regardless of which section of the community they belong to. To show prejudicial and discriminatory attitudes would be highly inappropriate.

4 **Situational factors**

Situational factors can be highly influential in how attitudes affect behaviour. For example, a person who holds racist attitudes might find himself or herself in the position of having an employer who belongs to an ethnic minority. This situational factor would clearly help to prevent racist sentiment converting into behaviour. Equally if an individual with racist attitudes had a vehicle breakdown and the roadside recovery mechanic had an ethnic minority background, the individual would hardly be likely to refuse assistance.

Think about it

Do you hold any strong attitudes, which influence your behaviour?

Attitudes which are very strongly held may have more likelihood of predicting the behavioural responses of an individual – such attitudes may include:

- racism
- sexism
- homophobia
- educational elitism
- social elitism
- cultural elitism.

Attitude change

Attitudes can change very quickly or they can stay the same for decades. There are many methods which can and have been used in order to change the attitudes of individuals or groups such as:

- persuasion
- advertising
- religious conversion
- indoctrination
- brainwashing
- propaganda.

In order for these techniques to be successful they must fulfil several factors:

1 The person delivering the attitude change message or communication must be respected and carry a certain amount of authority, power or influence. The sender of the message must be a credible and reliable source.

2 The message itself must be clear and consistent. The language used must be definite in tone rather than half hearted and it cannot induce too much fear or it will be counter productive.

3 The receiver of the message is unique and how they are influenced by an attitude change message will depend largely on individual factors such as their level of education, their pre-existing values and beliefs and their level of personal involvement with an issue.

4 The situation or context of the message is also important. For example if a humorous advertisement is placed between segments of a serious or emotional drama it may have less influence than if it was placed between segments of an action/adventure film. Essentially the situation must be appropriate for the message or the message will not contribute towards attitude change.

Assessment activity 12-P3

Produce an A3 size poster which explains the evolution of behaviour, using diagrams where possible.

Personality

As with most aspects of psychology there is no single unified approach to the study of personality and similarly no single definition of what a personality is. Gross 2001 argues that personality is:

> *"those relatively stable and enduring aspects of individuals which distinguish them from other people, making them unique, but which at the same time allow people to be compared with each other"*

Allport (1961) defines personality as:

> *"The dynamic organisation within the individual of those psychological systems that determine his characteristic behaviour and thoughts"*

Allports trait theory

A trait is a name for a personal characteristic. Allport describes traits in the following way (see Figure 12.8 overleaf).

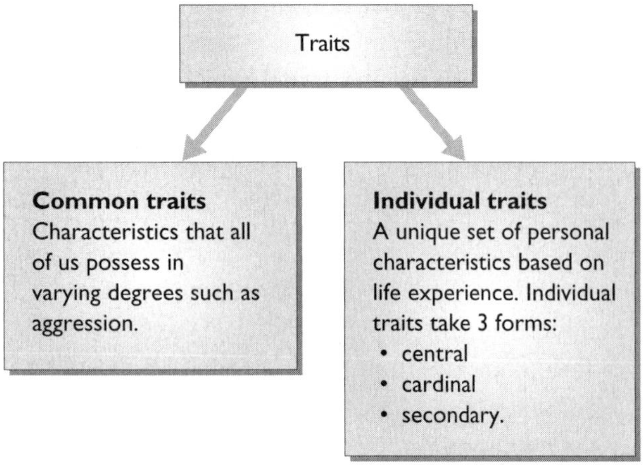

Figure 12.8 Allports description of traits

There are 3 forms of individual traits:

Central: this trait is very important and forms the core of our personality and how a person copes with their everyday experience of the world.

Cardinal: this trait dominates an individual's behaviour almost to the exclusion of other traits, for example, lust, greed.

Secondary: these traits are less important and influences aspects of personality such as tastes or preferences.

Think about it

Consider your own personality. What are your central, cardinal and secondary traits? Compare them with those of your colleagues.

The balance between central, cardinal and secondary traits is what makes an individual unique. Although the use of the word 'trait' assumes that behaviour and personality is stable and consistent over time. However, there is evidence to suggest that individuals can often behave in very different ways. Mischel (1968) found very little evidence of behavioural consistency from situation to situation; he argued that situational factors are more important than common or individual traits in explaining behaviour. It is more and more accepted that neither traits nor situation are the only cause of behaviour, in fact it is likely to be a combination of the two that causes a particular response.

Eysenck's theory of personality

Eysenck's approach to personality begins from a physiological standpoint; he believes that the majority of our personality comes from inherited physiological tendencies with social or situational factors playing a very minor role. His theory revolves around the idea that the most distinctive aspects of personality could be grouped into two major trait categories and that these categories could be measured using psychometric tests (psychometric testing will be discussed later in this chapter).

By the use of personality questionnaires Eysenck came to the conclusion that there were a number of personality traits which naturally seemed to link with each other. He called these 'first order personality traits'. Upon further examination Eysenck decided that first order personality traits could be categorised into two main groups which are called second order traits. Eysenck's second order traits are introvert – extrovert and neuroticism – stability.

Introvert and extrovert:

This pair of second order traits refers to how sociable and outgoing a person is, but the introvert – extrovert traits are more than just a reflection of how shy or outgoing an individual might be. Eysenck believed that the causes of introversion and extroversion were physiological and stemmed from a part of the brain called the reticular activating system (RAS). The type of RAS that an individual has may lead to the following characteristics:

Introvert	Extrovert
Quiet	Easily bored
Reserved/distant	Stimulation seeking
Serious	Sociable
Cautious	Friendly
Controlled	Impulsive risk taker

Introvert	Extrovert
Ethical	Optimistic
Reliable	May have aggressive tendencies
Bookish	Active
Calm	Emotionally open
Passive	Easy going

Of course, most people do not conform directly to an ideal type such as those described above. Most people may be introvert or extrovert depending on the situation.

Think about it

Think of a situation where you have behaved like an extrovert and a situation where you behaved in an introverted manner – why did you behave differently in the two situations?

Neuroticism and stability:

This pair of second order traits revolves around an individual's response to stressful or threatening life events. Again, Eysenck argues that the root cause of an individual's neuroticism or stability is physiological in nature but rather than revolving round the RAS as with extroversion and introversion, this pair of second order traits are thought to be a function of the autonomic nervous system.

Neurotic	Stable
Moody	Calm
Overreacts	Even tempered
Excitable	Constant
Changeable	Reliable
Anxious	May underreact
Touchy	Leadership qualities
Restless	
Potentially aggressive	

Type A/B personality

Another way to classify personality type was devised by Friedman and Rosenman (1959). Unusually Friedman and Rosenman were not psychologists, they were cardiologists. These are doctors who specialise in the health and well being of the heart. The personality typology that the doctors developed has become known as Type A personalities and Type B personalities. The doctors were conducting research into the development of heart problems and discovered that many of their patients with heart problems shared similar personality characteristics.

Type A personality: an individual with a type A personality may have many or all of the following characteristics:

- ambitious
- aggressive
- competitive
- impatient
- sense of time urgency
- fast speech
- tense
- determined
- free floating hostility
- apprehensive
- cynical
- suspicious
- multi-taskers.

Type A personalities cause themselves substantial amounts of stress which increases heart rate and blood pressure making heart attacks and related heart problems highly likely.

Type B personality: an individual with a type B personality may have some or all of the following characteristics:

- less competitive
- less rushed
- patient

- easy going
- sociable
- relaxed
- even tempered
- operates at normal speed
- moderately ambitious.

Type B personalities have a much more relaxed attitude to life which leaves them less prone to heart problems in later life.

Type C personality: more recently the notion of Type A and Type B personalities has been built upon, Temashak helped develop the idea of a Type C personality which denotes an individual who is the exact opposite of a Type A personality. Type Cs are passive, self-sacrificing, helpless, obedient and accepting of the situations they find themselves in. Whereas Type As are more prone to heart problems, Type Cs appear to be more prone to cancer. Type Bs who are the well-balanced group tend to live longer and healthier lives in comparison. However, it is important to note that almost everyone falls somewhere between all of these three types. To find a true type A, B or C is relatively rare.

What personality type are you?

This brief questionnaire (shown below) is designed to ascertain which personality type you must closely resemble. Tick in the most appropriate box.

If you have answered the majority of the questions with 'always/often' you may be more likely to have a Type A personality. If you answered mostly 'sometimes' it may be that you are more similar to a type B personality and if you answered 'never' you may have more in common with a type C personality.

Assessment activity 12-P2

Using the information you have already received on personality traits conduct an assessment of your own personality and associated traits. Write a 100 word report which describes you and let someone close to you assess it for accuracy.

Abnormal psychology

Abnormality implies that certain behaviour is out of the ordinary but this definition is not much help to us when we consider the value of such abnormality. Clearly the selfless ideals of Mother Theresa are a positive aspect of abnormal or atypical behaviour while the actions of Hitler are at the extreme opposite of the spectrum of morally accepted behaviour.

Statistical deviation from behaviour which is considered the norm is an unreliable test of whether an individual's behaviour could be considered to be abnormal since most people

Question	Always/Often	Sometimes	Never
Do you evaluate your own performance by comparing it against the performance of others?			
Do you worry about the future?			
In a stressful situation do you lose your temper?			
Do you speak quickly?			
Do you eat quickly and do something else immediately?			
Do you often read or watch TV while you are eating?			
Does it bother you if you have to wait in a queue?			
Do you find it difficult to fall asleep because you are upset about something a person has done?			

deviate from what is considered to be normal or average in many aspects of our lives. The study of abnormal behaviour is also problematic because as society changes certain behaviours become acceptable and other behaviours fall out of favour. How abnormality is defined depends very much on the social and cultural thoughts of the times.

Think about it

In which areas of your life do you consider yourself to be different from the average person.

There are many ways of exploring the concept of abnormal or atypical behaviour. Usually this is done through an examination of the various psychiatric and psychological perspectives which exist:

- psychoanalysis
- behaviour therapy
- humanistic and existential perspectives
- cognitive therapies.

However, before we begin it is important to mention that diagnosing and treating abnormal behaviour is not as straightforward as diagnosing and treating physical illness.

Case study

An extremely famous study into mental health diagnoses was conducted by Rosenhan (1973). In this study 8 normal and average individuals were instructed to present themselves at the admissions offices of various mental health institutions. Other than presenting a false name and one false symptom of hearing a voice saying the word 'thud' the 8 behaved perfectly normally. All were admitted to the hospitals for treatment and 7 of the 8 were diagnosed as schizophrenic despite the fact that none of Rosenhan's helpers 'heard' voices after they were admitted to hospital. It took one unfortunate subject 52 days before the hospital discharged him.

The fact that perfectly normal and healthy individuals could be so universally misdiagnosed on the basis of one erroneous (and in reality non-existent) symptom intrigued Rosenhan so much that he conducted a follow up study to see if the idea would work in reverse – whether individuals with genuine symptoms could be classified as healthy. Rosenhan (1975) informed a hospital dealing with mental health problems of the findings of his previous study and told them that several 'false' patients would arrive at the hospital over a specified period of time. In actual fact Rosenhan sent no false patients to the hospital, all of the patients who attended the hospital were genuine. However of the 193 new patients seen in the specified period almost 25% were alleged to be normal by at least one member of staff.

1 What does Rosenhan's 2 studies say about the diagnosing abilities of the medical profession with regard to psychological problems?
2 Why do you think the diagnosis of mental health difficulties is so difficult?
3 What are the problems with the diagnosis of mental illness being made on the basis of subjective judgements?
4 Are there any ethical problems with Rosenhan's studies?
5 Rosenhan's studies were conducted 30 years ago. Do you think a similar study would have similar findings today?

Psychoanalysis

The psychoanalytic approach to psychology was outlined earlier in this chapter. Its approach to mental illness and the study of atypical behaviour is quite similar. Abnormality is rooted in the unconscious mind and is the result of deeply seated inner conflict. If these inner conflicts can become recognised by the person displaying the abnormal behaviour then it is likely they can begin to resolve the conflict and display alternative behaviour.

For example, in psychoanalysis a phobia (an extreme irrational fear of a situation or object), is caused by conflict between the id, ego and super ego originating in childhood. The id, ego and super ego work together to define the personality of an individual and the balance between the 3

Figure 12.9 Relationship between id, ego and super ego

parts determines what an individuals personality will be. The id is the first part of the personality to develop, it is the childish and demanding and instinctual part of us which is most dominant in early childhood. The ego is the part of the personality which tries to regulate the demands of the id by satisfying what the id wants in a socially acceptable way. The super ego acts like an internalised parent and is worrying and neurotic in nature. The 3 of them fit together in a structure like Figure 12.9. The phobia develops as a response to anxiety being displaced from its original cause onto an external object.

The techniques developed by the psychoanalytic approach to treatment illness are described in Figure 12.10.

Behaviour therapy

Behaviour therapy revolves around several techniques described in Figure 12.11.

Psychoanalytic treatments	
Technique	**Description**
Psychoanalysis	This is a form of therapy in which the aim is to resolve inner conflict and change the personality and behaviour through contact with an analyst who helps the unconscious fears and conflicts come to the surface. Traditional psychoanalysis can continue for many years, but this can prove extremely expensive and as a result many therapists offer abridged versions ranging from 6 to 30 weeks which focus on one or two issues rather than the personality of the individual overall.

Figure 12.10 Psychoanalytic treatments for atypical behaviour

Behaviour therapy	
Technique	**Description**
Systematic desensitisation	This treatment involves a series of graded interactions with an object or situation, which may provoke fear or anxiety. For example, if an individual had arachnophobia their therapy may progress from simply being able to say the word 'spider' to examining a picture of one to allowing one to crawl over their hand. These graded interactions are normally supported by the learning of relaxation techniques based on the principle that an individual cannot be relaxed and anxious at the same time. Systematic desensitisation is most useful for the treatment of specific phobias such as arachnophobia rather than other more general fears such as agoraphobia (fear of the outdoors).
Implosion therapy (flooding)	This behavioural technique operates on the principle that maintaining high levels of anxiety and fear demands a lot of effort and it cannot be sustained indefinitely. Flooding is the exposure of the individual to a real and active source of their fear without the build up of systematic desensitisation and studies have found flooding to be more effective than SD.
Aversion therapy	This is a therapy that pairs the behaviour which requires change with a negative stimulus. For example, in this form of conditioning an individual with an alcohol problem would have alcohol paired with sickness and vomiting. This is achieved by the use of a drug which triggers nausea and vomiting if alcohol is ingested. The effects of the drug can last several weeks and by the end of the treatment the individual will have learned to associate alcohol with vomiting and illness and will therefore avoid it.
Token economy	This is a system whereby bizarre behaviour is ignored and 'good' or appropriate behaviour is rewarded with a token, which can be exchanged for something the individual wants. This has been trialed extensively and effectively in the treatment of patients in long term psychiatric care. The use of rewards encourages positive behaviour and eventually the positive behaviour becomes sustained even without the rewards.

Figure 12.11 Treatments for atypical behaviour in the behaviourist perspective

Humanistic and existential perspectives

As you will recall from the introduction to humanism found earlier in this chapter, this perspective views individuals as essentially healthy and striving for self-fulfilment. Mental illness and abnormal behaviour can arise when the paths to reaching ones potential for growth and development are blocked or denied to us. This may include a lack of positive regard or love from others leaving an individual unable to express their 'true' self for fear of the disapproval of others. Humanists such as Rogers (1961) argue that the positive regard of others allows an individual to become more confident and autonomous moving away from behaviour which is depressive or neurotic. The main technique humanists use as therapy is described in Figure 12.12 overleaf.

Humanist approach	
Technique	**Description**
Client centred therapy (CCT)	This type of therapy creates a situation of warmth and security where an individual can develop positive self-regard and become less self-critical. This therapist takes an active role in the therapy unlike psychoanalysis where the therapist must be impassive and professional. The therapist in CCT must be genuine, non judgemental and empathetic to the client. In this supportive and secure environment clients who feel strong, assertive and liked will be able to help themselves, since they are the only people who can. Like many forms of therapy the effectiveness of CCT is open to question. In a study by Truax & Mitchell (1971) it was found that a good therapist who embodied the principles of empathy and positive regard were more likely to have clients with positive changes whereas poor therapists could actually make the condition of their clients worse.

Figure 12.12 Humanist treatments for atypical behaviour

Cognitive approach

The cognitive approach to psychology emphasises the importance of thought processes and how humans process information from the surrounding environment. Since the focus of the cognitive approach lies in the thought process of individuals it is safe to assume that abnormal behaviour and mental illness stem from faults in the thought and information processing systems an individual has. As a result the cognitive approach is based on changing thought process as a mechanism to changing behaviour.

This approach sees an individual displaying abnormal behaviour not as a passive recipient of treatment, but as the primary agent of change. If the individual can develop and change their thought patterns they will be better equipped to cope with difficult situations and challenge situations they find unbearable. The strategies developed by those who advocate the cognitive approach are described in the table below.

Cognitive approach	
Technique	**Description**
Cognitive therapy	This form of therapy attempts to change the way individuals with mental health difficulties perceive the world around them and the situation they find themselves in. It encourages an individual to re-evaluate the way they see the world. There are two main forms of cognitive therapy; rational emotive therapy (RET) and personal construct therapy (PCT).
Rational-emotive therapy (RET)	These techniques endeavour to challenge irrational beliefs held by individuals with neurotic tendencies. These beliefs can be very destructive since they are almost always highly unrealistic, such as 'I must always succeed' or 'I must be liked by everyone'. RET challenges unrealistic beliefs by addressing them logically and highlighting the faulty reasoning behind them and showing the individual more positive thought processes. This technique can be very difficult for individuals with problems to deal with since it confronts the problems head on.

Cognitive approach	
Technique	**Description**
Personal construct therapy (PCT)	All individuals have a certain way of viewing the world, which helps them make sense of situations and experiences. As we encounter new situations and experiences our constructs must change as new information may challenge our views and beliefs. Neurotic individuals are said to have very rigid personal constructs and do not adapt well to change or uncertainty. PCT encourages an individual to change their personal constructs of the world in a positive manner showing them that new information, which changes the way we perceive the world, does not need to be a threatening or challenging experience.

Figure 12.13 The cognitive treatments for atypical behaviour

Assessment activity 12-P4

Using the information you have received so far in this chapter produce an information leaflet for a public service of your choice which describes personality types and related behaviour and the treatment of abnormal behaviour types.

Classification of disorders

Psychology relies heavily on the diagnosis of mental illness and the grouping together of related disorders in a formalised classification system. In the same way that medicine might group physical illnesses such as respiratory diseases or sexually transmitted infections together, psychiatry attempts to do the same with mental illness and abnormal behaviour. There are two primary classifications systems used in Western Nations. DSM and ICD.

DSM

DSM stands for the Diagnostic and Statistical Manual of mental disorders. It was developed by the American Psychiatric Association and is now in its fourth incarnation, so it should be properly termed DCM-IV. This code of classification is primarily used in the US.

The DSM-IV classification system operates on the basis of around 11 major groupings of disorders although others such as Gross (2001) divide it into 16 categories. Since this system is used primarily in the US we will not examine it here, but it is important you are aware of its existence.

ICD

ICD stands for the International Classification of Diseases which was developed by the World Health Organisation (a subsidiary of the Economic and Social Council of the United Nations). The ICD is currently in its tenth revision and should properly be termed ICD-IO. This code of classification is popular across Europe including the UK.

The ICD-IO classification system revolves around a 100-point categorisation beginning with F00 and progressing to F99. Not all of the F categories are filled to allow for the growth of the system as new disorders are recognised. ICD-IO categories can be broadly condensed into 11 sections as follows:

- F00-F09 – Organic, including symptomatic mental disorders
- F10-19 – Mental and behavioural disorders due to psychoactive substance use
- F20-29 – Schizophrenia, schizotypal and delusional disorders
- F30-39 – Mood disorders
- F40-48 – Neurotic, stress related and somatoform disorders
- F50-59 – Behavioural syndromes associated with physiological disturbances and physical factors

- F60-69 – Disorders of adult personality and behaviour
- F70-79 – Mental retardation
- F80-89 – Disorders of psychological development
- F90-98 – Behavioural and emotional disorders with onset usually occurring in childhood and adolescence
- F99 – Mental disorder not otherwise specified

An understanding of these classification systems is important in understanding how certain disorders are linked with others and the signs and symptoms which indicate particular examples of abnormality.

Each of the ICD-IO sections is further subdivided, for example:

F65 Disorders of sexual preference:

- F65.0 Fetishism
- F65.1 Fetishistic transvestism
- F65.2 Exhibitionism
- F65.3 Voyeurism
- F65.4 Paedophilia
- F65.5 Sadomasochism

As you can imagine these subdivisions ensure ICD-IO is a very comprehensive classification system. ICD-IO and DSM IV have a lot of information in common as the diagnostic symptoms used to identify the disorders are virtually identical. The primary difference is simply in the groupings of some disorders with others.

Interview skills

Interview skills play an important role in job recruitment for the public services as well as throughout your professional chosen career and an understanding of psychology can help you perform better. There are many types of interview you are likely to encounter such as the ones described in the diagram below.

Job recruitment

This interview is designed to assess your suitability for a particular job or role. It is not just about getting an initial offer of employment, it is also about trying out new roles within the same organisation. For example, if a Police Constable wanted to join CID and become a Detective Constable they would still have to be assessed for their suitability to perform the new role even though they are already successfully employed within the same organisation.

Discipline

There may be occasions when your professional conduct is called into question and you are

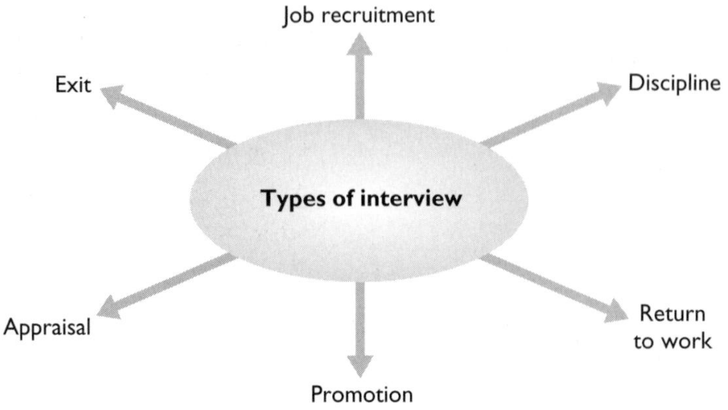

Figure 12.14 Types of interview

required to account for your actions or the actions of your colleagues in a formal interview setting. The sad fact is that complaints are often made against members of the uniformed public services, some are justified and others are not. It is a hazard of the job that by the simple act of wearing a visibly identifiable uniform and engaging with individuals and communities it becomes more likely that at some point your conduct will be examined.

Return to work

These interviews are commonplace in most public sector workplaces and involve an employee returning from sick leave and having an informal interview with their line manager. This interview is to ascertain the nature of the sick leave and the steps taken by the individual to improve their health, such as seeing a doctor. A good employer will also check that support is put in place to help a sick member of staff return to the workplace without further detriment to their health.

Promotion

In the majority of organisations professional advancement does not come automatically at each stage of your career. There may be further training, testing and interviewing before you are promoted. Often this interview process can be much more rigorous than the initial recruitment interview which brought a person into an organisation in the first place. In addition, it is likely there will be as much competition for the promotion as there was to get the original job. The reason promotion interviews can be more rigorous is that a higher level of skills and qualities are needed as you may have management responsibility for personnel and finance and it is crucial that the organisation promotes only those who are able and competent to do the job.

Appraisal

This is one kind of interview you can be almost certain of encountering in a public sector workplace. Appraisals can range from very informal chats with a manager to a formal interview with your line manager. It is an opportunity for both parties to assess the professional progress of an employee and to set goals against which your future performance can be measured. In effect it is an evaluation of your workplace performance. According to Kane and Lawler (1979) cited in Bull et al (1985), an appraisal serves 4 primary purposes.

- It is a source of information on which to base decisions about where a person will work most effectively and whether they should be promoted
- It is a basis on which to allocate rewards
- It enables selection methods and training programmes to be evaluated
- It enables managers to tell staff how well they are performing and offer opportunities to improve.

Exit

An exit interview is not always conducted but it is an opportunity to draw together a particular strand of a career before you move on to a new job or role. You may be asked why you decided to leave and what could have been changed to encourage you to stay. It is very expensive to fully train public service officers and it costs the government when you leave because you will be taking that training with you and someone else will have to be trained to take your place. Any sensible far sighted organisation will want to know why you are leaving and consider those reasons carefully so that they know what to do to keep the rest of the workforce happy.

Assessment activity 12-P5

Considering the information above, explain to a colleague the kinds of interview they are likely to face during a full public service career. Make a record of your discussion.

Interview formats

Interviews can take many forms from an informal chat to a multi-day selection procedure. It is important to know what kind of interview you will face so you can prepare appropriately for it. Figure 12.15 highlights the possible interview formats you could encounter.

Psychometric testing

Psychometric tests are used to measure the characteristics of people, such as intelligence, ability and personality. They are used as a screening process to ensure that the applicant is suitable for the job. The public services make extensive use of psychometric testing as part of their interview procedure. This may take the form of the Police Initial Recruit Test (PIRT) or the British Army Recruitment Board (Barb) and may involve tests such as:

- verbal checking
- spatial awareness
- decision making
- numerical reasoning
- observation
- spelling/dictation
- writing skills.

Psychometric tests can generally be broken down into two main areas shown in Figure 12.16 overleaf.

Aptitude and personality tests can be very intimidating, but they are actually considered a great deal fairer than a traditional interview because they have no bias and cannot treat people differently based on stereotypes or prejudice. Psychometric testing can be culturally biased however and great care must be taken to ensure the test itself is fit for its purpose. Testing also does not provide an employer with a face to face picture of a candidate and for this reason you are unlikely to face psychometric testing alone, it is much more likely to occur before a formal interview as a method of weeding out unsuitable or poorly qualified candidates.

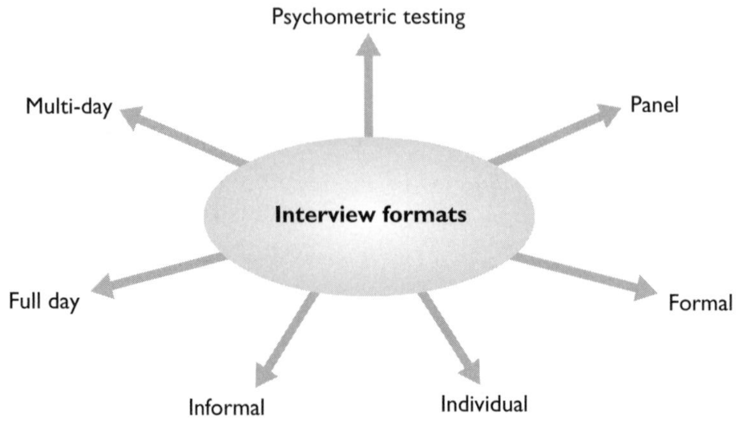

Figure 12.15 Types of interview formats

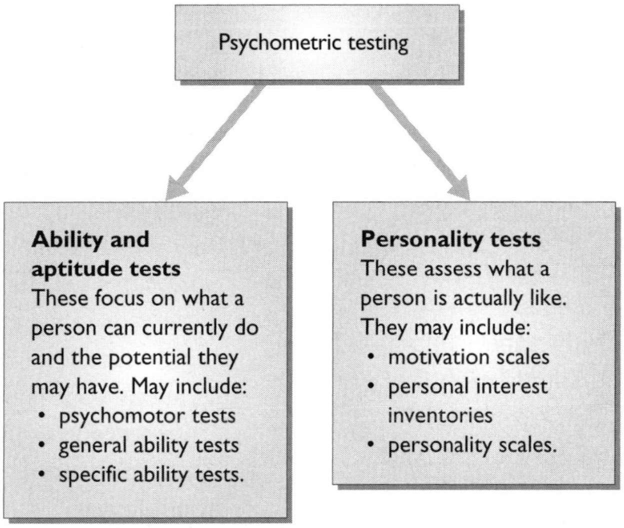

Figure 12.16 Psychometric testing

Other interview formats

Format	Detail
Formal	This is a structured interview in which you are likely to be asked a set series of questions in a formal or rigid environment. It is likely that more than one person will interview you and you may be asked to produce a presentation or report as part of the procedure.
Informal	More relaxed and in a less formal setting than in a formal interview. May be only one or two individuals conducting the interview rather than a panel.
Full day	Some interviews can last anything up to 10 hours. These can be exhausting and it is likely that you will interact with the others who are competing for the job.
Multi-day	These are common in the public services and you may have to be interviewed on 3 or more days over several weeks.
Panel	Many interviews are conducted by a panel of up to 6 or 7 individuals. Each individual may assess you on different aspects of your performance and then discuss their findings to form a picture of you as a whole.
Individual	Sometimes a single individual may interview you although this is not considered to be good practice because they have no second opinion or expertise to reinforce or challenge the conclusions they draw.

Figure 12.17 Interview formats

Planning for interview

It is amazing how many people do not prepare adequately for an interview and are then disappointed when they don't get the job they want. A burning desire to be a police officer isn't enough! You must be able to prove that you are more suitable for the job than any of the other 100 applicants which is a tall order. Interview planning plays an essential part in maximising your chances of being offered a job in the public services.

1 **Take care with personal appearance:** you must dress appropriately – usually a suit is appropriate for both men and women. Jewellery and make up must be subtle and discreet and you should be free from any facial piercing such as eyebrow, nose or lips. Men should consider removing earrings. Your clothing should be clean and pressed and you should get a friend or family member to check you over before you set off. Your shoes should be polished and your clothing should aim to give off a message about you and your ability to perform the job. You should ensure that you are clean and tidy and project an air of confidence and professionalism.

2 **Be punctual:** there is no excuse for being late and it gives an impression that you are unreliable. Instead aim to arrive around 10 minutes early. If necessary practice your journey beforehand to ensure you have your timings right.

3 **Be gracious to other candidates:** part of the assessment process in public services interviews revolves around your interaction with others. If you are unpleasant or uncooperative to your competitors you do not have the interpersonal skills to work in a close-knit team or work with the public.

4 **Do your research:** it does you no credit if you turn up to an interview without knowing the first thing about the public service in question. If you are completing a public service qualification you will have an advantage, but don't become complacent. Research your chosen public service, be familiar with its structure and principles and ensure you have read its annual reports and its literature. If you want the job be prepared to learn everything you can about the local, national and international issues which affect it.

5 **Be confident, not dominant:** if you try and dominate an interview it screams 'NOTICE ME!!' – your interviewer will notice you but for all the wrong reasons. You should project an image of a confident team player, not a dominant leader.

6 **Be genuine:** public service interviewers are usually officers of many years standing and they will have seen hundreds of hopeful candidates just like you. Don't think that flattery or humour will sway them in their choice and don't be tempted to exaggerate or lie about your skills and abilities. Recruiting officers read people very well and the last thing you want is to be considered false or fraudulent.

7 **Stay calm:** interviews can be nerve racking but make sure you stay calm and in control. This means not fidgeting, paying close attention to questions and making sure you understand the question before you answer as people who are nervous tend to say inappropriate things. The interviewer expects a certain amount of nervousness but someone who appears very edgy will give the impression of not coping well in stressful situations which is clearly not a desirable quality in the public services.

Key points

1 Interview skills are of crucial importance throughout a public service career.

2 Interviews are conducted for a variety of reasons, such as appraisal, leaving jobs, getting a new job etc.

3 You have to work hard at interviews if you are to succeed.

4 You must research the job role and the organisation thoroughly.

5 You must pay attention to issues of equal opportunities.

6 You must listen carefully to the questions you are asked and make sure you answer them.

Assessment activity 12-P6

Engage in a role play public services with fellow students acting as the interviewing panel and you as the interviewee. Conduct a formal interview and afterwards evaluate your own interview techniques. Compare your own evaluation with how your colleagues assessed your performance to see if your evaluation was accurate.

Think about it

If your interview performance is weak it is well worth drawing up an action plan for improvements.

Interview questions

Most interview questions are fairly standard in employment interviews and you can expect to be asked in some form or other any or all of the following questions:

- Why do you want this job?
- What can you bring to the job?
- Describe how your previous experience makes you suitable?
- What do you hope to gain from the job?
- What do you know about the job?
- Do you know about current developments affecting the job?
- Are you able to work as an individual and a team member?
- What are your long-term career goals?
- What training and education do you have which would enable you to tackle this job effectively?
- What are your views on equal opportunities?

In addition to these questions you may be asked to take part in role-play scenarios designed to test your practical coping skills in a variety of circumstances which are likely to be unfamiliar to you. The response you give to the questions and scenarios are crucial in the interview procedure and you must be ready to deal with unexpected questions. Consider the following examples below.

Interview question 1

Q The police are trying to recruit more ethnic minority officers into the ranks. What is your view on this?

Good answer	Poor answer
It's important that the police service is representative of the communities it serves. This means having an inclusive recruitment procedure, which encourages all sections of the community to apply. Without this the service could be seen as racially exclusive which doesn't help the police to develop an understanding of cultural awareness and doesn't improve community relations. The Macpherson report highlighted many potential steps forward in building community relations and eliminating racism and I think this is a positive recommendation to come from that report.	People should get into the police on the basis of their own ability. If ethnic minority people can't get in any other way than because of their colour it's not fair is it? They should not be given any special treatment.

Interview question 2

Q Why do you want to be a police officer?

Good answer	Poor answer
It's a decision I've thought long and hard about because I know that it is a stressful and potentially dangerous job. I've done a great deal of voluntary community work and I find it immensely rewarding to give something back to the community. I'd like to think that the job I do makes a difference to the community and the individuals within it. I also like the idea of a job which combines this with the challenge of learning and developing skills on an ongoing basis.	I have wanted to be a policeman since I was a young boy. I always watch The Bill and I've really got into CSF lately. Besides, it's good money isn't it?

Interview question 3

Q The regiment you are hoping to join is currently serving with the UN as peacekeepers in Kosovo. What do you know about this situation?

Good answer	Poor answer
I know that peacekeeping is one of the primary roles of the British Army today. I think that it is crucial that the UN and NATO are able to deploy forces to protect civilians and offer humanitarian aid in situations of conflict across the world. The British Army play a key role in this, particularly in Kosovo where they serve in KFOR and SFOR.	Is Kosovo abroad? Is it about that Al Keyda bloke?

Question analysis

In an interview, you must ensure you are answering the question they are really asking you. This means you should be able to see through the language they use to phrase their question and see the real question beneath it. For example, consider the 3 interview questions looked at earlier (see the table below).

Some of the questions asked by interviewers require a little more analysis before you rush into an answer – you must be sure you know what each answer is designed to find out before you address it.

What makes a good interviewer and interviewee?

The table opposite (Figure 12.19) highlights those areas which make a good interviewer and interviewee.

Assessment activity 12-M2

Get 2 of your colleagues to conduct a mock interview. Observe them and assess what qualities they had which made them good at their particular role.

Communication

Another aspect of human behaviour which is particularly relevant for individuals wishing to have a career in the public services is the field of communication. Communication is an integral part of all our lives and is a critical factor in most areas of employment, particularly when the job involves substantial contact with the public and teamwork situations with colleagues, both of which occur almost all the time in public service work.

Question	Real questions being asked
The police are trying to recruit more ethnic minority officers into the ranks. What is your view on this?	• Do you support equal opportunities? • Are you racist? • Have you been bothered enough to research this issue?
Why do you want to be a police officer?	• Do you have any idea what the job is really about? • Are you more bothered about the money and security than the job itself?
The regiment you are hoping to join is currently serving with the UN as peacekeepers in Kosovo. What do you know about the situation?	• Do you understand what it means to be a modern soldier? • Do you keep up to date with global political issues which affect us? • Have you been bothered to do your research?

Figure 12.18 Language used in interview questions

Interviewer	Interviewee
A good interviewer will: • put the candidate at ease • be dressed appropriately • have read your CV and application form • ask one question at a time • listen carefully to your answers • make notes and records of your answers • control and structure the interview • probe areas of your personal life sensitively • show interest in your comments and answers • answer questions you ask them • demonstrate good body language and project confidence • uphold equal opportunities • treat all candidates equally and fairly • ask intelligent and pertinent questions • not interrupt • inform the candidate of the interview structure.	A good interviewee will: • dress smartly • be punctual • show good body language • project confidence and enthusiasm • make eye contact • ask sensible and insightful questions • treat the interviewer with respect • research the organisation and the job role • smile • shake hands firmly • have practiced the interview with friends or family • speak clearly • anticipate likely questions and be prepared to answer them fully • **not** interrupt • be sincere • **not** answer with yes or no • support the principles of equal opportunities • be courteous to other candidates.

Figure 12.19 Signs of a good interviewer and interviewee

Senses

All of our senses are involved in communication:

- sight
- hearing
- touch
- taste
- smell.

We use all of these senses when we communicate with others. Communication is not just about being understood, it is a mechanism to both give and receive messages which we need in order to interpret the situation and environment around us and act accordingly.

When we communicate with others we do not simply speak to them. In fact, studies suggest that the actual literal content of our communication is much less important than how we say it, the tone of our voice, the facial expression of the speaker and the body language involved. Our senses are involved in giving and receiving communication all the time although we may often not be directly conscious of it.

Hearing

Studies such as Rankin (1926) and Barker et al (1981) found that when an average individual communicates, between 42% and 53% of the time is spent listening. This shows that the auditory sense is very important when receiving messages. When you hear communication you are not simply hearing and understanding the spoken word, you are listening to the tone of the communication and the sentiment behind it. Listening is made up of a behavioural process involving the following components (see Figure 12.20 overleaf).

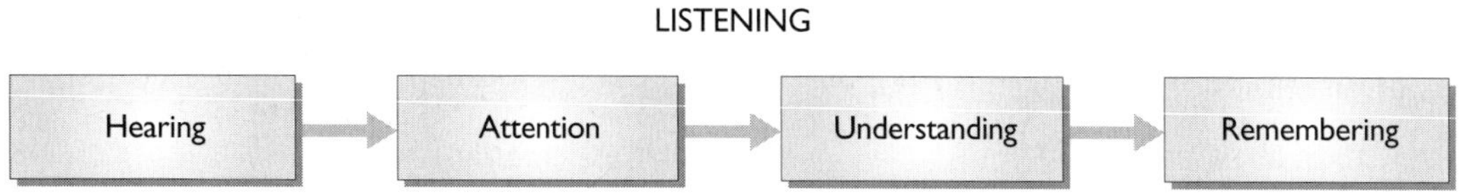

Figure 12.20 Listening is made up of many components

You must hear what is being said, pay attention to the speaker, understand the content of the message and be able to remember it. This process is very important on several levels. Firstly if you don't listen you are placing yourself at risk and increasing your vulnerability. For example, if you are told not to touch a piece of electrical equipment which carries live electricity and you do not listen the consequences could be fatal. In a public service situation it is of vital importance that you listen to the commands of your senior officers as failing to do so may compromise the safety of yourself, your colleagues and the general public. Listening and paying attention are also crucial factors in job success.

Listening can be divided into two main categories:

- active
- passive.

Active listening: this can be summarised as listening with a purpose. It involves paying attention to what is being said and questioning the speaker to ensure real understanding has been achieved. Active listening requires as much energy as speaking and it is a skill which requires practice and development if it is to be perfected.

Active listeners generally possess the following skills:

- do not finish other peoples sentences
- do not daydream or 'wander' while others speak
- do not talk more than they listen
- may make notes to help them remain focused
- ask questions for clarification.

Think about it

You are a public service employee and a complaint has been made against you by a member of the public. You are anxious to defend yourself and go to see your line manager at the earliest opportunity. Your line manager hears what you say but her eyes continually wander and she stifles a couple of yawns. Explain how this makes you feel and explain why it is important that she actively listens.

Passive listening: this type of listening simply involves hearing what has been said. The listener is not motivated to respond or check understanding. This type of listening occurs when you are watching TV or listening to music.

Think about it

Are you generally an active or passive listener?

Sight

This is a very important sense when communicating as about 80% of the information we receive is perceived visually. We use sight to understand and interpret words and images and to help us evaluate the social world. For example, if someone is injured you may see the blood before you hear an auditory cue such as a groan of pain. We also use our sight to interpret facial expressions and non-verbal communication such as body language. As well as receiving messages visually, we also send them as our own posture, expression and appearance tell others a great deal about our emotional state and our likely conduct.

Smell

Our sense of smell is much more important than people realise. A familiar smell can communicate safety and security, such as a particular home cooked meal or a parent's favourite perfume or aftershave. Equally, an unfamiliar smell can communicate danger such as the smell of gas or chemicals. It is possible to communicate fear and attraction through a sense of smell.

Touch

The skin is the largest organ of the human body and it is designed to understand and respond to communication through the sense of touch. Touch can mean support, affection, concern, curiosity, attraction, hostility and dislike amongst many other feelings.

Think about it

Consider how many people you touch during the day and how many touch you – list the range of messages you are communicating.

Taste

Although taste may not have the importance of some of the other senses such as sight and hearing, with regard to public service work it does have more general uses. For example, it can communicate whether food or drink is safe to consume. The sense of taste also works in harmony with the sense of smell, one enhances the other.

Verbal communication

It is easy to assume that a verbal message will mean the same thing to everyone who hears it. However, this is not the case as the words are interpreted by the receiver of the message and the interpretation of the words depends upon factors such as culture, age and gender. Consider the word 'gay'. Its use has changed over the last 50 years, so a pensioner describing someone as gay might mean someone was particularly lively and happy whereas today the word has a far different association. This tendency of people to interpret words differently can have tragic consequences.

Case study

Derek Bentley was hanged on 28th January 1953, aged 19 for the murder of PC Sidney Miles who had stopped Derek and his accomplice Christopher Craig after an abortive break in. Chris Craig pulled a gun on PC Miles and Derek Bentley allegedly said 'Let him have it, Chris'. Chris Craig then shot and killed PC Miles. This case became well known because of the possible interpretation of the words. He was sentenced to hang on the premise that 'let him have it, Chris' meant shoot him. However Bentley's defence and the campaign for his posthumous pardon revolved around the phrase 'let him have it, Chris' being taken to mean that Chris Craig was to give the police officer the gun. Bentley was pardoned in 1998, 46 years after his execution.

1. How does this case study highlight communication problems?
2. What do you think caused the communication problems?
3. What is your view on what Derek said?

Verbal communication is of paramount importance in the operation of the public services as the majority of instructions are given verbally so the potential for misunderstanding is high. In addition, radio based communication takes away any non-verbal cues such as body language or facial expression which might help a public service operative interpret the verbal message in the way it was intended. There are many ways to improve your verbal communication skills and completion of your National Diploma/Certificate/Award is one of them. The list below describes other ways to improve this skill:

- be sure you know what you want to say before you say it
- speak clearly so that you can be heard and understood

- get into the habit of having general conversations with your family and friends
- be sure what you say is what you mean
- be conscious of the fact that people interpret words differently and use techniques such as questioning to ensure understanding
- try to be polite and respectful in verbal communication
- in a work situation consider using a written back up such as a memo or email to reiterate and clarify the verbal message.

Barriers to communication

There are many barriers to communication which come between the sender of the message and the intended recipient:

- Noise can prevent us from receiving a full message or distract us from the message itself. Imagine you are a fire-fighter at a blaze or a member of an artillery unit on the firing line, it would be very difficult to concentrate on the communication rather than on the noise in the wider environment.
- The status of the speaker can be a barrier to verbal communication. Generally we pay more attention to those who have more or equal status to ourselves and pay less attention to those who are lower down the social or employment ladder to ourselves.
- Stress can be a barrier to verbal communication as it is easier to misunderstand and misinterpret a verbal message when we are stressed. In addition, we are more likely to take offence, not listen and not respond appropriately.

Non-verbal communication

The use of non-verbal communication is very important when sending and receiving messages. We use non-verbal communication all the time, often without being aware of it. Consider the following examples:

- putting your hand out for a bus
- putting your hand up in class
- giving someone a thumbs up sign
- rolling your eyes when being told gossip
- blushing
- fidgeting.

All these are examples of non-verbal communication (NVC) and without a single word being spoken you know exactly what the message is. It has been suggested that the majority of human communication is non-verbal in nature. Mehrabian (1972) argues that 93% of all face to face communication is non-verbal and although studies have found different percentages with different groups of subjects there is no doubt that NVCs make up significantly more than half of all face to face interaction. Consider the following NVCs:

- **Eye contact and general eye movement:** it is important to engage in eye contact with the person or people you are communicating with as it is considered to be the mark of sincerity. People who avoid our gaze are often considered with suspicion. Some psychologists argue that the way your eyes dart left or right in communication denotes whether you are lying or not. A flick to the left indicates a person is gathering information from memory where a flick to the right denotes information being constructed or imagined. However, humans are far too complex for information such as this to be completely accurate.
- **Facial expression:** your face is an accurate indicator of your moods and humans are very adept at reading facial expression. Smiling, raising your eyebrows, pursing your lips and frowning are just a few of the possible ways of communicating with your face. Reading a person's expression acts as back up for a verbal message and also acts as a message in its own right. It helps us know how to respond in any given situation.

Communicating through sign language

- **Gestures:** these can convey a great deal of information if they are interpreted correctly. Nodding our head is a gesture of agreement which is almost universally understood; the same is true for shaking our head to indicate disagreement. Each culture is likely to have its own gestural communication and in the case of sign language the gestures themselves make up the entire message.
- **Posture:** the way you hold yourself and move around can convey a great deal of information. It can indicate confidence and authority; equally it can denote shyness or even anger. If a person holds themselves very rigid it can indicate they are nervous or tense. If they slouch it can mean anything from boredom to relaxation. In public service work reading a person's posture can be a first indicator of potential aggression or that a person has been a victim of crime.
- **Proximity:** the distance you maintain when involved in face-to-face communication is called proximity. It is important not to evade another's personal space when communicating as this can make them feel uncomfortable or threatened.
- **Our physical appearance and the appearance of others:** this can be a useful form of communication. Some public service students are required to wear a uniform. Consider what it communicates if they refuse to do so.

Assessment activity 12-P7

Research and deliver a 10-minute presentation which explains the differences and similarities between verbal and non-verbal communication and highlights the importance of the senses in each. Make a point of using visual aids and produce a handout for your audience.

Written communication

Written communication is widely used in most employment situations and includes the use of:

- memos
- e-mails
- letters
- notices
- newsletters
- intranet.

Written communication is often used as a back up for verbal communication as well as a communication source in its own right. Written communication can present difficulties such as loss of the communication document, poor spelling and grammar leading to loss of the message, the communication not being perceived as relevant and the message being unclear and difficult to isolate from the rest of the text. In addition, some forms of communication such as texting and e-mail have their own etiquette and protocol which can be difficult for individuals unfamiliar with the medium to decipher. It is also difficult to check the understanding of a written document since you cannot question it for clarification as is possible with verbal communication.

Assessment activity 12-M3

Consider a public service of your choice and write a brief report which analyses the different types of communication used within it. Highlight the uses and effectiveness of each.

RESTRICTED

S/TGB/121

2LI
AN Army Barracks
Soldierville
Armyshire

AN Army Barracks ext 222

5 Sep 2003

Internal Information
Captain BE Alert

Training Ammunition

Reference our telephone conversation of 4 Sep 2003.

1 The allotment of training ammunition for 51mm mortars has been delayed until 20 Sep 2004
2 Your unit will now use Field Firing Range 2 on 22 Sep 2004 instead of Field Firing Range 1 on 16 Sep 2004.

Captain SNA Glass

Distribution
External:
Internal:
Captain BE Alert
Action:
QM
Wpn Trg Offr
Information:
2IC
RSM

Figure 12.21 An example of a formal letter sent out by the Army

Communication style

Regardless of whether a message is written, verbal or non-verbal there are a range of styles which it can be delivered in. Communication style depends on the situation an individual finds themselves in and a good communicator will adapt their style to suit their circumstances.

Aggressive communicators

Communicators who use an aggressive style may be generally disliked because they intimidate others. It may be that their body language is threatening, they are loud and abrupt in verbal communication and they may often interrupt and shout over others. As a public service employee it is likely that you will encounter this communication from members of the general public as you conduct your duties. More rarely you may encounter it in a colleague or a boss. This form of behaviour can be considered bullying and should never be accepted.

Responding to aggression with aggression simply leads to a worse situation for all concerned. In addition to which you should never behave in an aggressive manner to the public even on occasions where you may be called upon to restrain someone or otherwise stop certain behaviour. A good public service officer will maintain a calm temperament and take action based on the situation rather than act on the basis of anger or resentment.

Submissive communicators

A submissive communicator generally adheres to the opinions of those with more power than them and can be very hesitant in putting across their own message. A submissive approach to communication is unlikely to command authority and respect making it an inappropriate choice for the majority of public service work.

Many people use submissive communication in their daily lives without being aware of it. It may appear when you are speaking to your tutor or your boss at work or it may even be apparent when you communicate with your friends and parents. Submissive communicators have body language designed to make them appear smaller and may avoid eye contact which is the opposite reaction to aggressive communicators.

Assertive communication

Assertive communication strikes a balance between the previous two styles we have examined. It ensures communication is direct and clear, but still has room for other aspects of communication such as sympathy, empathy and negotiation. Body language may be relaxed, but alert and eye contact is maintained but it does not

Communication styles		
Style	**Advantages**	**Disadvantages**
Aggressive	• You will be heard. • You may get what you want.	• You will be feared not respected. • You may cause aggression in others. • You may be personally and professionally disliked. • May cost job prospects. • You may be labelled a bully.
Submissive	• You may be able to keep out of trouble and away from conflict. • Requires less effort and commitment.	• You will not be respected. • You may be ignored. • You are not likely to be placed in positions of leadership or responsibility. • You may be considered weak.
Assertive	• You will be heard and are more likely to be respected. • Actions are more likely to come from your message. • You are more likely to be put in positions of responsibility and leadership. • You can respect yourself. • You will develop confidence. • You will be less stressed.	• Requires you to be firm and polite even when others are not. • Requires energy and commitment.

Figure 12.22 Communication styles

generate an uncomfortable feeling in those being communicated to. It has the capacity to calm a tense situation and it commands authority through respect, not fear. A key component of assertive communication is confidence as a genuinely confident person does not need to shout and scream to make a point, nor do they agree with others for the sake of a quiet life.

Assessment activity 12-M4

Evaluate communication styles in relation to speech and behaviour.

Key points

1. There are various styles of communication.
2. Good communicators ensure they can adapt their style to the situation.
3. The most productive form of communication in the public services is assertive communication.
4. Aggressive communication styles can be considered bullying and usually show an individual has little confidence.
5. A submissive communicator is unlikely to be given positions of responsibility and leadership.

End of unit questions

1. What is behaviour?
2. What is psychology's parent discipline?
3. Who developed the psychological approach of behaviourism?
4. Which approach is Sigmund Freud associated with?
5. Explain the process of classical conditioning.
6. Explain the process of operant conditioning.
7. Which approach sees humans as information processors?
8. Describe the relationship between the id, ego and superego.
9. Which theorists are associated with humanism?
10. Describe the introspectionist approach.
11. How is an understanding of psychology useful in public service life?
12. What treatments are associated with the behaviourist approach to abnormality?
13. Which two classification systems are widely used to categorise atypical and abnormal behaviour?
14. What is a personality?
15. How do attitudes influence behaviour?
16. Describe the main principle of the medical model.
17. Describe 3 communication styles.
18. How could you prepare for a promotion interview?
19. Why is non-verbal communication important?
20. Describe the role of the 5 senses in communication.

Resources

Gray, D. *Public Services Book 1*, 2004, London, Heinemann

Gross, R, *Psychology: The Science of Mind and Behaviour* 4th edition, 2001, London, Hodder and Stoughton

Harrower, J, *Applying Psychology to Crime*, 1998, London, Hodder and Stoughton

Hayes, N, *Foundations of Psychology*, 1994, Surrey, Thomas Nelson and Sons

MEDIA AND THE PUBLIC SERVICES

Introduction to Unit 13

The media in all its forms has become increasingly important to the public services over the last 100 years. This unit highlights this importance by exploring a variety of media forms, such as television, radio, newspapers and the Internet. It also examines how information is gathered and transmitted and the developments in modern technology, which allows information to be transmitted instantly from remote areas.

The influence and effect of the media on public perceptions of the services is also covered in this unit as well as how the public services use the media to suit their own purposes. It is also important to consider the impact of media ownership on the practice of generating the news and the implications this brings in terms of media bias. Codes of conduct and legislation which have an effect on the media are also looked at.

Assessment

Throughout the unit activities and tasks will help you to learn and remember information. Case studies are included to add industry relevance to the topics and learning objectives. You are reminded that when you are completing activities and tasks, opportunities will be created to enhance your key skills evidence. After completing this unit you should be able to achieve the following outcomes.

Outcomes

1 Investigate the role of the media in the **reporting of information**.

2 Examine the **control and regulation** of the media.

3 Analyse **how the public services are portrayed** in the media.

4 Investigate **case studies** of public services portrayal in the media.

Reporting of information

On first analysis, an examination of the media does not seem to have particular relevance to a career in a uniformed service but in fact this could not be further from the truth. The media is a central social institution, which stands alongside other key institutions such as the family and education as a fundamental part of a social structure. Skeggs & Mundy (1992) make the following point:

> *"Listening to the radio, playing records, tapes and compact discs, going to the cinema, reading newspapers, comics and magazines, watching television and video cassettes are central activities, not just in terms of the time and money spent on them and their importance as leisure activities but also because they are the prime site through which human beings, as active social participants construct meanings, beliefs and values".*
>
> *Skeggs and Mundy (1992) Chapt1, Pg1*

This quote highlights the importance of the media not just as a leisure activity but as a primary means of communication and information. The role of the media in information transmission should not be underestimated. The tabloid newspaper The Sun has an estimated daily readership of 11 million people in the UK and is considered to be the most widely read newspaper in Britain which means it has tremendous impact and influence on the beliefs and actions of a sizable proportion of the British public.

Think about it

Where do you get your information on local, national and international events from? Do you automatically believe all the information you get from the media? If not, why not?

Even more people watch particular television programmes such as Coronation Street and Eastenders which regularly achieve an audience of 12–19 million people. This means that in some cases an entire third of the country can be watching a particular transmission. The importance of this becomes apparent when we consider that for the majority of people the media is their only source of information on a particular issue. If you only receive one point of view or one side of a story it can be difficult to form a balanced opinion. The media has a tremendous amount of power which it can bring to bear on individuals and groups, including the public services. This power can be used by unscrupulous media corporations and politicians who want the general public to react in a particular way. A good example of this is 'The News of the World's' naming and shaming campaign against paedophiles.

Think about it

Consider the News of the World's naming and shaming campaign against paedophiles in 2000. Was this a genuine attempt by a powerful newspaper to help with community safety or a cynical attempt to provoke an emotional response in the readership and therefore ensure more people bought the newspaper?

It is precisely because the media have the power to create civil unrest, topple governments and create prejudice that they ought to be closely scrutinised by any prospective member of a public service.

Although it is generally agreed that the media are a powerful social institution, there is a wide variety of views on how, why and when (if at all) they use their power. Much of the evidence on media influence is contradictory and it can be difficult to come to any firm conclusions about the media based on this. This chapter seeks to explore some of these issues and provide you with enough information for you to begin to analyse media content and actions for yourself.

The information age

The majority of the mass media today, such as radio, television and cinema are actually very recent inventions and belong almost entirely to the technological revolution of the twentieth century. Although the printing press was invented in the fifteenth century, the mass production of books and newspapers did not really begin until the seventeenth century. Written media could not enjoy mass popularity until the majority of the population had basic literacy skills which is why the development of the modern written media saw a large growth in the nineteenth century as more and more people learned to read. The oldest English newspaper still in existence is The Times which was first published in 1785. This was followed by The Observer in 1791, The Guardian in 1821, The News of the World in 1843 and The Telegraph in 1855.

As more people became literate the demand for material to read increased. Early newspapers were generally targeted at the educated and financially wealthy minority and these kind of newspapers (with the exception of the News of the World) are generally referred to as 'broadsheets'. This name comes from their size as the pages are substantially larger than tabloid newspapers (although tabloid size versions of broadsheets are now available). Broadsheets tend to concentrate primarily on news issues without reference to entertainment and excitement that tabloid newspapers include alongside their version of the news.

The changes to education in the late nineteenth and early twentieth century saw a need develop for popular newspapers. These newspapers more commonly called 'tabloids' are designed to appeal to the majority of the population by combining news with a combination of other issues such as humour, entertainment and titillation. Many of the early tabloid newspapers are still with us, such as the Daily Mail established in 1896, The Daily Express first published in 1900 and the Daily Mirror in 1903.

Think about it

It is important to keep up to date with current national and international current affairs if you are to be successful in a public service interview. One of the best ways of doing this is to read a broadsheet newspaper such as The Guardian or The Times at least once a week and more often if you can.

New forms of media such as radio and cinema started to take precedence in the early years of the twentieth century. Nicholas (1996) notes that the first British cinemas were opened in 1908 and by 1910 cinema was firmly established as a form of mass media.

The uses of radio waves as a form of communication were first identified by Marconi at the end of the nineteenth century and the British Broadcasting Corporation (BBC) was formed in 1926. Television as a form of mass media is more recent still; the first television broadcast was made in 1936 at the Berlin Olympic Games.

Television did not become a dominant force in the communication industry until after the Second World War in the 1950s and 1960s. Although television is still the most popular form of mass media, newspapers and radio are still read and listened to by millions of people each day. Over the last 10 years access to news and information over the Internet has also become increasingly commonplace. This has been facilitated by the increased availability and decreased price of home computers and the increasing use of computers in the workplace. News on the Internet is up to date and interactive giving it distinct advantages over other forms of media.

Developments in media over the last decade

It can be difficult to discuss media technology as it changes and evolves at a phenomenal rate. However some of the main media developments over the last decade are listed below.

- development of desktop publishing
- moves from analogue to digital communications technology
- fibre optic communications technology
- satellite technology
- mobile phones and video phones
- development of the Internet and World Wide Web (WWW)
- development of multi-media technology such as CD-Roms and DVDs
- e-mails
- wind up radios
- satellite video phones
- blue tooth
- satellite uplink
- broadband
- microwave transmitters.

Some of the most important developments are discussed in further detail below

Desktop publishing (DTP)

DTP is a system whereby the layout of documents intended for publication can be arranged on a computer. It co-ordinates text, pictures, graphics and charts in a readable and useable format. DTP became widely used in the production of books, journals and newspapers from the late 1980s and throughout the 1990s. Prior to the development of DTP, publishers had to use mechanical or electronic typesetting which were more expensive and more specialised. DTP packages such as Microsoft Publisher and Quark Xpress allows anyone with computer skills to quickly and efficiently produce printed and electronic documents. It allows the user to play around with a variety of designs and formats before committing to an expensive print run.

The advantages of DTP are:

- easy to use
- accessible to all computer users with the right software
- saves time and money when including graphics and artwork
- easy and inexpensive to correct errors
- can be directly input to a printing company
- process of publication is faster and more efficient.

The disadvantages of DTP are:

- enables anyone with the appropriate hardware and software to produce publication materials which means that mediocre and poor publications may be produced by untrained individuals
- loss of jobs in the print industry and the adaptation to new technology
- does not reduce the burden of time spent proofreading and deciding on layout.

Analogue to digital

Most media transmissions used to be analogue by nature. Analogue signals are transmitted via a continuous wave-like form but the further the wave travels the more it degrades. This means that unless the signal is only travelling a short distance it needs to be amplified at regular intervals. This amplification also amplifies any faults in the signal as well as the signal itself. Over the last ten years analogue signals have been replaced with digital signals.

Digital signals are much better quality, degrade less and the transmission capacity of digital communications networks is so much greater than analogue. This change has affected television, radio and mobile phones because they are less subject to interference and require less power to transmit therefore reducing the need for signal boosting.

Fibre optics

Increasingly over the last decade or so fibre optic cables have been used for media and communications transmissions rather than old style copper wire coaxial cable. The traditional cables transmit media signals in electrical form as a flow of electrons. Fibre optic cables differ significantly in that they use light pulses to transmit signals. Optic fibres are made from plastic or glass and bundled together to form cable. There can be up to 1000 fibres in a single cable. The light transmitted down fibre optic cables is confined to the cable due to total internal reflection which means light cannot escape the glass fibre due to the angle at which it hits the external barrier of the fibre. It also allows cables to bend and twist without losing the signal or having signals crossover between different fibres in a cable.

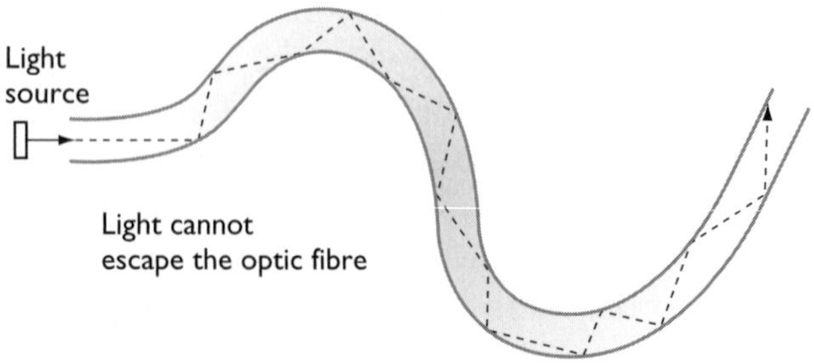

Figure 13.1 Total internal reflection in fibre optic cable

The usual form of light used in optic fibre transmissions is infrared, as infrared light is a low frequency form of light and therefore requires less energy to travel further. The first transatlantic fibre optic cable was laid in 1988 and they have become widespread throughout the 1990s and into the new millennium. They have several distinct advantages over old style copper cable:

- a large data carrying capacity which is a distinct benefit in a global society
- they are not subject to electrical interference
- they are lightweight and easy to deploy
- the signals degrade less, removing the need for boosting and amplification.

However, optical cables can be very expensive to produce and there is a need for transmitting and receiving devices at each end of the cable.

Satellite communication

The introduction of satellite communication dates back to the late 1920s and the work of Herman Potocnik, a Slovenian scientist in the Austrian army. Potocnik's book 'The Problem of Space Travel – The Rocket Motor' published in 1929 introduced the concept of communications satellites and influenced many later thinkers on the subject. For example, Arthur C Clark who published an article in 1945 in a journal called 'Wireless World' which effectively described a satellite communications network used to transmit television signals around the globe. Of course in 1945 the space race was not significantly developed enough to allow for such an ambitious project. It wasn't until the launch of Sputnik1, an unmanned Russian aircraft in 1957 that humans managed to put technology into orbit. After this, developments were rapid and world's first communications satellite 'Telstar' was launched in 1962.

'US Strategic Command' the tracking body responsible for monitoring satellites and debris in earth's orbit, estimate there are now almost 9000 man made objects circling the earth. Earth orbiting satellites have a variety of functions such as:

- **Communications** – there are over 100 communications satellites orbiting the earth used for sending TV signals, telephone calls, Internet connections.
- **Earth remote sensing** – these are used to gather data about the earth's surface.
- **Weather** – there are several weather satellites in orbit round the earth, many of them operating as an integrated system so that weather across the entire globe can be monitored.
- **Global positioning** – this was developed by the Military to determine the exact location of an object or person in terms of latitude and longitude.
- **Scientific research** – some satellites exist simply to conduct research into scientific phenomena. This is particularly true in astronomy as earth based telescopes can be distorted by the atmosphere and in space this difficulty is removed.

The height at which a satellite orbits the earth depends on many factors, such as its task or speed. The majority of communications satellites use a geostationary or geosynchronous orbit. This is when a satellite is placed directly above the equator at a height of just over 22,000 miles. These satellites travel around the globe every 24 hours, keeping pace with the Earth. From an earthbound point of view the satellite appears to stay in the same spot. Geosynchronous communications satellites have revolutionised the media industry. This is because a smaller number of communications satellites moving in high orbit can provide global satellite coverage.

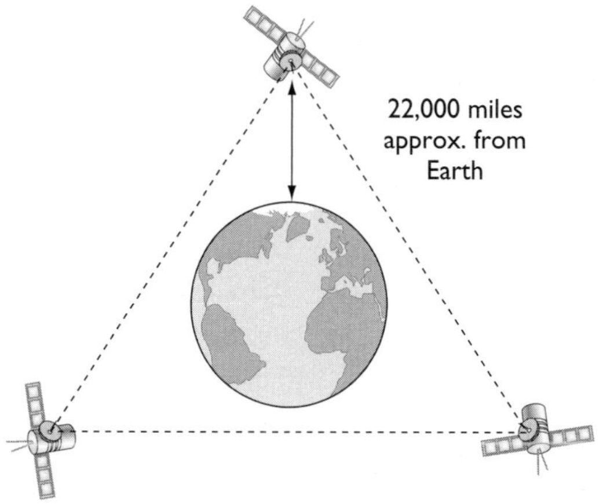

Figure 13.2 With as little as 3 geosynchronous satellites total coverage of the earth can be achieved.

The practical application of this is that communications and media signals can be beamed around the world in a matter of seconds ensuring news and current events happening in one part of the world can be seen almost instantly across the globe. Geosynchronous communications satellites need transmitters and receivers which can sometimes be large and expensive. The alternative to this, which has been developed in recent years, is the Low Earth Orbit (LEO) satellite which operates in a very close orbit of around 500 miles from the earth. LEO satellites are able to send and receive information much more quickly because they are closer to the source of the signal. However because they are so close, many more of them are needed to provide global coverage.

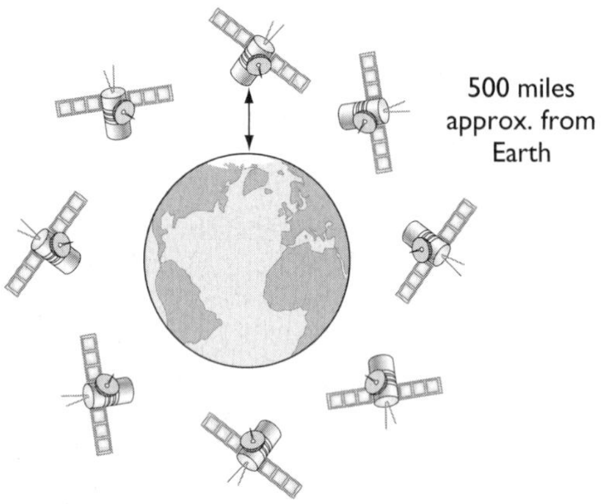

Figure 13.3 Low earth orbit satellite system

The developement of LEO systgems will enable media reporters to transmit news regardless of their location and it will also mean global coverage for mobile phone networks. The media already makes extensive use of satellites for reporters on remote or challenging locations, such as during conflict and so on. Reporters are able to transmit their story via a satellite uplink, which is then relayed to a receiver which may be thousands of miles away. There are satellite systems which do not need expensive central receiving equipment in which a signal is sent from a satellite to a receiving centre and then transmitted around the country using transmitters located at height such as Emley Moor near Huddersfield in West Yorkshire. These newer systems bypass this form of transmission and are called Direct Broadcast Systems (DBS). The first DBS was Sky in 1989, which originated as a signal from the Astra satellite. DBS Systems require a small satellite dish to be placed at a high point (usually a roof or high wall) before signals can be received; they then receive direct transmission from a satellite.

Assessment activity 13-P1, 13-M1

Explain and analyse how changes in technology in the last 10 years have affected the gathering and presentation of information in different types of media and its ability to affect events. Produce a 10-minute presentation on your findings.

Types of media

The media is any form of communication which is intended to be viewed by many. This includes shows, plays, music performances and leaflets as well as the more traditional media with which we are more familiar, such as:

- newspapers
- magazines
- television
- radio
- journals
- Internet.

Media effects

Concern about the influence of the media on the behaviour and conduct of the public is often discussed in both academic and media circles. However, the scientific research conducted into the effects of the media on the behaviour of the public, particularly in relation to the use of violence is contradictory and unclear. The reasons that there seems to be no clear consensus on the effects of the media on violent or delinquent behaviour lie in problems with media research itself. Martinez (1994) examined the reasons for this lack of consensus and came up with the following issues.

Media violence is extremely difficult to define and measure. For example, some media researchers exclude cartoon violence while others include it, equally some researchers include verbal violence such as shouting and obscenities while others do not. As you can appreciate if different studies are using different definitions of violence, the results of the studies will be difficult to compare.

The data produced by these media researchers can be interpreted in very different ways. Some researchers argue that a particular set of data highlights a causal link between media violence and violent behaviour in an individual. Other researchers examining exactly the same data may decide that there is no evidence of a link at all.

Martinez looked at a variety of media violence experiments and concluded that many studies highlighted a positive correlation between exposure to violent imagery and increased aggression in individuals. However, she also notes that this correlation was usually weak and sometimes not present at all. This would seem to indicate that the relationship between the media and violence is not straightforward and is certainly not as casual as some researchers and politicians maintain.

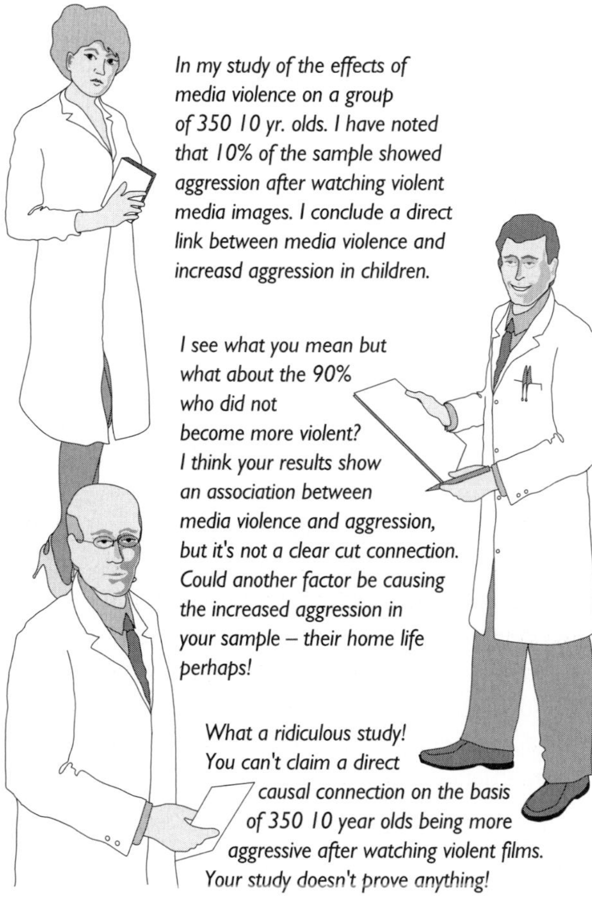

In my study of the effects of media violence on a group of 350 10 yr. olds. I have noted that 10% of the sample showed aggression after watching violent media images. I conclude a direct link between media violence and increasd aggression in children.
I see what you mean but what about the 90% who did not become more violent? I think your results show an association between media violence and aggression, but it's not a clear cut connection. Could another factor be causing the increased aggression in your sample – their home life perhaps!
What a ridiculous study! You can't claim a direct causal connection on the basis of 350 10 year olds being more aggressive after watching violent films. Your study doesn't prove anything!

Three researchers with differing views on media violence

Case study

Transmission of Aggression through Imitation of Aggressive Models, Bandura, Ross, Ross (1961)

This study conducted by the famous Albert Bandura was designed to see if very young children would imitate violence they had seen in 3 different mediums. The subjects were 96 nursery children with an average age of just over 4 years. The children were divided into 4 groups of 24.

Group 1 This group saw a real life aggressive model of behaviour. This involved an adult behaving aggressively towards an inflatable doll, which included punches, kicks and verbal aggression. The aggression was carefully designed to be unusual so that if the children imitated the behaviour they would be unlikely to have seen this distinctive behaviour elsewhere.

Group 2 This group of children saw exactly the same performance as group 1 did, but this time they did not observe it in real life, they saw it on a film which ran for approximately 10 minutes.

Group 3 This group again saw exactly the same events as the first 2 groups but instead of real life or film versions they saw an animated cartoon depiction of the aggression towards the inflatable doll.

Group 4 This group was the control group. This means they were used as a standard to compare the behaviour of the other 3 groups against. Accordingly they were not exposed to violent images and spent 10 minutes playing with non-aggressive toys.

Each of the individuals in each of the 4 groups was monitored for an increase in aggressive play. The results demonstrated several significant differences:

- overall boys were significantly more aggressive than girls.
- the exposure of children to an aggressive scene led to a significant increase in aggressive play.
- the children who saw the real life and film aggression demonstrated similar levels of aggression.
- children who saw the cartoon aggression showed slightly less aggression.
- the control group showed the least aggressive behaviour.

This study appears to suggest a link between observation of violence and imitation of violence. Children who observed violent behaviour, whether real or media based were more likely to behave aggressively in their play.

1 Why did the control group demonstrate the least aggression?
2 Why do you think there was a significant difference in the aggression of boys and girls?
3 What are the implications of this study on the media?
4 What are the implications of this study on the public services?
5 Do you think that media violence has an impact on you?

Think about it

Recent films such as Terminator 3, Rise of the Machines and The Lord of the Rings Trilogy have a high violence content. Do you think these films or similar ones that you have seen recently have an impact on your levels of aggression when you leave the cinema?

The case study described above highlights the likelihood of a relationship between media depicted aggression and increased aggression in the audience, but this is only one of the possible impacts of viewing media violence. Another possible effect is a process called 'desensitisation' whereby exposure to violent scenes on television or in the cinema makes individuals less sensitive to violence in real life, they may demonstrate less concern about the pain and suffering caused to the victim of violence and be prepared to tolerate more violence in real life. Desensitisation, it has been argued, is particularly prevalent among children who see a great deal of violence on TV which has no discernable consequences. For example, most children's cartoons such as Tom and Jerry or Roadrunner show brutal acts of violence where the victim walks away slightly singed or flattened, but otherwise unharmed. The principle of desensitation means that in theory, individuals are less concerned about violence and less aware of the consequences of committing it.

There have been several major cases over the last decade or so in which graphic violence on TV and in the cinema has been blamed for the murderous actions of individuals.

Think about it

Terrestrial television channels have a 9pm watershed and some encrypted satellite channels have an 8pm watershed. What is a watershed and why is it used?

Case study

The 1993 murder of two-year-old James Bulger by 10-year-old killers John Venables and Robert Thompson shocked the nation and reopened the debate on media violence. The media images in question were those belonging to the horror film 'Childs Play 3' in which a possessed doll called 'Chucky' commits violent murders. The murder of Jamie was said to imitate a certain part of one of the murders that Chucky commits in the film and from this the tabloid newspapers claimed a direct connection between the film and the crime. Despite a lack of any real evidence the media ran with this story and created a 'moral panic' (this will be discussed in more detail later in this chapter).

The moral panic incited public emotion and forced the government to respond by creating new legislation. The Amendment to the Video Recordings Act was contained in section 5.88–91 of The Criminal Justice and Public Order Act 1994.

1 Do you think that if the killers of James Bulger watched horror films, it had an effect on them?
2 Is the increase in 'video nasties' responsible for violent juvenile crime?
3 How common are murders committed in the UK by under 14s?
4 What other factors could have influenced John Venables and Robert Thompson in their decision to commit murder?
5 Why would the tabloid media choose to blame the murder on violent films?

The media frenzy whipped up by the media after the tragic events in 1993 was so powerful that you could've been forgiven for believing that the diet of sex and violence on TV was breeding a generation of young people with no sense of right or wrong. Clearly this was not the case but sometimes it is easier to blame a scapegoat like the media than look at the real structural causes of juvenile crime such as poor parenting, poverty, social exclusion, poor education and inner city deprivation. The arguments against media influence are just as compelling as the evidence suggested by researchers such as Bandura. David Gauntlett (1998) suggests the following arguments against the media effects model. (See Figure 13.4)

It is clear from Gauntlett's work that the effect of the media is not as clear cut as some researchers would lead you to believe, at least in the area of increased aggression. However, this is not to say that the media doesn't influence us in other ways. The portrayal of fictional violence on TV and cinema while gaining lots of public attention may be the least of the ways in which the public are influenced. Consider the case study on page 228.

Criticism	Detail
The media effects model tackles social problems backwards.	The argument here is that instead of using individual and group aggressive behaviour as a starting point and analysing the patterns behind it and the characteristics of those who commit it, the media effects model uses the media as a starting point and works backwards from there.
The effects model treats children as inadequate.	Researchers studying the impact of media violence tend to concentrate on the impact on children. The perception of children is that they are unable to understand the difference between media violence and real violence.
Media effects model is underpinned by Conservative ideology.	Gauntlett comments that the critical attitude towards aspects of the media by conservative politicians seeks to divert attention from other threats to social stability such as poverty.
The effects model inadequately defines its own objects of study.	The definition of violence and aggression varies between studies. Gauntlett is arguing that what is considered aggressive or violent relies upon the value judgement of the watcher. To one person, slamming a book in frustration may be seen as aggression, to others it would not be. The definition of violence is too poorly defined to produce high quality data.
The effects model is based on artificial studies.	Experiments such as the one conducted by Bandura, Ross and Ross (1961) outlined earlier takes place in artificial environments. The scenarios are stage managed rather than naturally occurring and therefore the evidence is artificially created.

Figure 13.4 Arguments against the media effects model

Criticism	Detail
The effects model is selective in its criticism of media depiction of violence.	Gauntlett makes the point that media effects researchers condemn fictional accounts of violence in cartoons, dramas and soaps, but do not condemn factual accounts in news and documentaries.
The effects model assumes superiority over the masses.	Gauntlett argues that the media affects model is rife with snobbery and cultural elitism. The researchers look upon their subjects as 'others' and make assumptions about them based on their media habits.
The effects model is not grounded in theory.	The media effects model is largely unsubstantiated, the evidence is contradictory and it leaves many important questions unanswered such as how does the media create the motive for aggression or why the media should want to influence people.

Figure 13.4 ctd. Arguments against the media effects model

Case study

Rwanda is located in Central Africa, bordering countries such as Tanzania and the Democratic Republic of the Congo. It is a small nation with a population of around seven and a half million. The population was made up of 3 distinct cultural groups: the Twa who were traditional forest hunters and made up 1% of the population, the Tutsi who were traditionally cattle breeders and made up 16% of the population and the Hutu's who constituted 80% of the population and traditionally were involved in land cultivation. Intermarriage was common and all 3 cultural groups spoke the same language.

However, relations between the Tutsi's and Hutu's deteriorated in the period from the nineteenth century and the colonisation of Africa by white Europeans. The white settlers considered the Tutsi's to be racially superior to the other 2 groups and accorded them more rights and privileges. This bred discontentment among the much larger group of Hutu's and created a sense of superiority in the group of Tutsis. In 1994 this continually simmering racial conflict erupted and in a 100-day period from April to June 1994 an estimated 800,000 Tutsi men, women and children were murdered by Hutu's who were often neighbours, friends and family of the victims.

It should also not be forgotten that part of the genocide was a systematic rape and sexual mutilation of surviving Tutsi women, many of whom were infected with HIV in order to ensure that exiled Tutsi men who had fled the genocide would not be able to marry and have a family when they returned.

Rwanda has a high illiteracy rate and radio is the only mass form of communication in the country. Rwanda had no independent radio stations until just prior to the genocide so the population received all of their information from just one government owned radio station – Radio Rwanda.

In 1993 another radio station was established Radio Tele Libre Mille Collines (RTLM). Both of these radio stations served as vehicles for incitement to racial hatred against the Tutsi, who were often described as snakes and cockroaches. The impact of this ongoing racial propaganda should not be under estimated.

Genocide in Rwanda

"In a country with a high degree of illiteracy and where TV is confined to a minority of homes in the capital, radio was enormously important."

Alison Des Forges, Human Rights Watch (2002)

Media actions included providing false information about Tutsi's and obscene cartoons and jokes. The newspaper 'Kangura' published 10 commandments which Hutus should follow. The 10th Commandment read:

"Any Hutu must know that a Tutsi woman, wherever she is works for her Tutsi ethnic group. Therefore is a traitor any Hutu who marries a Tutsi woman or who has a Tutsi concubine or who hires a Tutsi secretary, or protects a Tutsi woman"

IMS Report, 2003

In the Rwandan example the media did not merely report the news, by its message of hatred and violence it made the news and almost one million people lost their lives in the ensuing bloodshed.

1. Why is radio an influential medium in Rwanda and many other African nations?
2. How did the media in Rwanda encourage the bloodshed?
3. Why did the media distribute propaganda?
4. Why do you think Rwandan Hutis believed the propaganda printed in newspapers such as Kangara?
5. What level of responsibility do you think Rwandan media sources should bear for the genocide?

Moral panic

The Rwandan case study clearly outlines how the media can influence public perceptions and generate or escalate civil unrest. Although Rwanda may seem far removed from the UK, the British media also has the capacity to create a 'moral panic'. A moral panic is the public expression of concern which results from media coverage of an event. It is generally a media hyped public overreaction, which leads to more newspaper sales and therefore higher revenue for media corporations. Moral panics

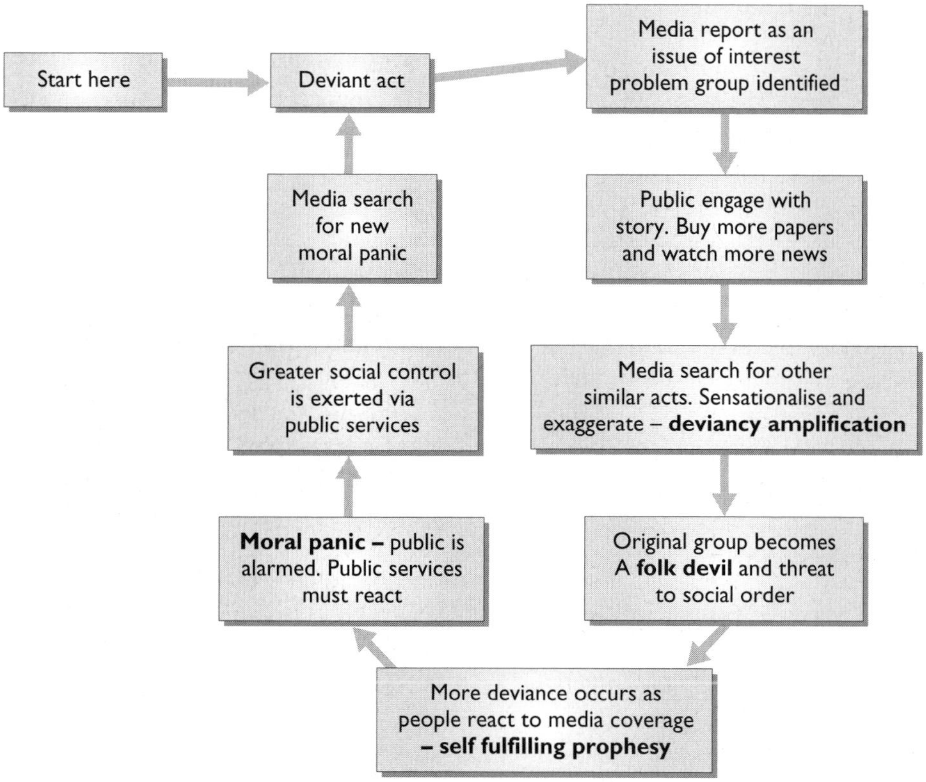

Figure 13.5 How a moral panic occurs

typically involve an incident or a group of people who may threaten perceived social order. Examples of moral panics include: paedophiles on the internet, asylum seekers, SARS virus, drug abuse, football hooligans, street crime and youth crime.

The media demonise these acts or groups making them seem much worse than they are – creating a 'folk devil'.

A folk devil is a particular group which is seen as a threat to social order. In a moral panic it is important to remember that the folk devil in question has not changed or grown larger, the media has simply chosen to focus on it almost exclusively for a particular period of time. The SARS outbreak is a good example of this.

Case study

Severe acute respiratory syndrome (SARS) was brought to media attention in March 2003, but cases were appearing in the Far East as early as November 2002, almost 6 months earlier. The media gloried in comments from 'experts' who argued that SARS could spread like the 1918 flu epidemic which killed 50 million. However, this contradicted the evidence which showed that the vast majority of individuals with SARS recovered quickly and according to the World Health Organisation there have been less than 1,000 deaths from SARS globally amongst a world population approaching 7 billion. By June the panic had subsided not because the threat of SARS had disappeared, but because the media moved their attention elsewhere.

1. Why would the media create a moral panic out of the SARS outbreak?
2. Why would the media readership be interested in a medium scale outbreak of a disease thousands of miles away?
3. Why do the media create moral panics in the first place?
4. Do you think the public actually believe these moral panics?
5. Read a tabloid newspaper, and find out if there are any current moral panics.

Media manipulation

The media have several tools which they can use to manipulate the audience. Michael Parenti in an article entitled 'Methods of media manipulation' discusses some of these tools. This is summarised in Figure 13.6 below.

Think about it

What does manipulation mean? Discuss in small groups what manipulation is and how it can happen.

Method	Explanation
Suppression by omission	The media can choose to manipulate the news by omitting aspects of a story or even the story in its entirety. Parenti argues that stories which reflect badly on those with power do not often make the news. Examples of this include US backed political regimes in right wing countries such as Turkey, Indonesia and Saudi Arabia which have poor human rights records and have been implicated in large scale human rights abuses.
Attack and destroy the target	If a media story cannot be suppressed by omission then the media can attack the story as a fabrication and discredit evidence or witnesses.
Labelling	The media can attach a label to an individual or an occurrence, which puts it in a positive or negative light. For example, individuals who fight for freedom and justice for all may be despairingly called 'do-gooders' which instantly demotes them to the status of busybody rather than social activist.

Figure 13.6 Tools used by the media to manipulate the audience

Method	Explanation
Pre-emptive assumption	Media coverage makes assumptions about the way things are and does not encourage debate around these issues. For example, the media often refer to a 'flood' of asylum seekers who cost the nation millions of pounds. What they do not question is the fact that the UK takes far less asylum seekers than most other nations in the EU and that many asylum seekers are repatriated if their claim is found to be bogus or their country becomes stable again.
Face value transmission	This is when the media accept at face value official lies and pass them on to the public unquestioningly. The Rwandan case study highlights the dangers of this.
Slighting of content	The media may ignore the actual content of a story in favour of other factors. Parenti provides the example of an election campaign which is reduced to a 'who will win' race. The actual policies and political philosophy behind the campaigns is almost forgotten.
False balancing	The media are supposed to provide a fair and balanced account of events, according equal weight to each side of the story. In actual fact the media often provide biased coverage and promote a balanced view where in fact there is no balance. Parenti gives the example of a BBC World News Report (Dec 11 1997), which spoke of a history of violence between Indonesian Forces and Timorese Guerrillas. Parenti notes that no mention is made of the fact that the Timorese were facing a genocide by Indonesian forces which killed over 200,000 of their countrymen.

Figure 13.6 ctd. Tools used to manipulate the audience by the media

All of the methods that Parenti highlights can be used to manipulate public perceptions, provide sympathy or provoke social unrest. The media can provoke positive and negative emotional responses in us, such as great outpourings of grief in the aftermath of Princess Diana's death, great surges of sympathy for individual's caught up in war or famine and great waves of hatred such as those demonstrated in Rwanda.

Assessment activity 13-P2

Give three examples of how the media has affected events as well as reported them.

Control and regulation

Regulation of the media

The Broadcasting Standards Commission (BSC)

The role of the Broadcasting Standards Commission was established by the Broadcasting Act 1996. Its main functions are to produce codes of conduct regarding broadcasting standards, to evaluate and assess complaints made against TV and radio programmes and it also conducts research into issues of standards in TV and radio broadcasting. It is currently chaired by Lord Dubs of Battersea who is a former Labour MP for the constituency of Battersea.

The Independent Television Commission (ITC)

The ITC is a regulatory body independent of the government and also independent of television broadcasting companies. It is funded by fees paid by broadcasting companies such as Carlton or Yorkshire Television who must purchase a license to broadcast their programs. The ITC sets standards for the content of programmes and the commercials which appear between them and like the BSC it also investigates and adjudicates on complaints made by the public on programme tone and content. It is chaired by Sir Robin Biggam who was appointed in 1997.

The Office of Telecommunications (Oftel)

Oftel regulates the UK telecommunications industry and was established by the Telecommunications Act (1984). It exists to ensure that telecommunications companies such as British Telecom honour their obligations to customers in the service they provide. Oftel also exists to formulate telecommunications policies which assist telecommunications companies in providing high quality services to customers. It also instructs companies on appropriate use of technology and services. For example, Oftel ensures that communications services provide public call boxes, directory information and access to emergency services. It is chaired by David Edmonds.

The Radio Authority (RAu)

The Radio Authority was created by the Broadcasting Act (1990). It exists to licence and regulate independent and commercial radio stations which includes regional and local stations, national stations and cable/satellite stations. The current chair of the RAu is David Witherow. The RAu has 3 main functions:

- to plan frequencies
- to provide licenses to operate radio stations which improve listener choice
- to regulate standards in programmes and adverts.

The Radiocommunications Agency (RA)

This agency belongs to the Department of Trade and Industry and its role is to manage the non-military radio spectrum across the UK. One of the main roles of the RA is to keep the radio spectrum 'clean'. This involves tracking and prosecuting individuals who are broadcasting without a license. These 'pirate' stations can interfere with other channels and cause problems for legitimate radio stations and also interfere with legitimate broadcast transmissions such as those made by public service radio frequencies.

Ofcom

All of these agencies currently work together to ensure media TV and radio broadcasts are of high standards and that customers are dealt with fairly. However, the management of 5 individual agencies to do similar jobs is not in the best interests of cost effectiveness and efficiency. The government proposed a merger of all 5 of these agencies into a single large regulatory body called The Office of Communications (OFCOM). Although the Office of Communications Act 2002 created OFCOM, its powers come from The Communications Act 2003 which is when it was created.

OFCOM's main functions are as follows:

- to promote the interests of consumers
- to manage and promote the best use of the radio spectrum
- to ensure a wide range of high standard television and radio services
- to ensure the public is protected from any offensive or potentially harmful effects from radio or television.

The merger of OFTEL, RAu, RA, ITC and BSC creates an extremely powerful and wide ranging agency in OFCOM. It provides a 'one stop shop' for broadcast media regulation including TV, radio, phones, mobiles and Internet. The creation of OFCOM is not without controversy as it has been argued that the agency is too large and unwieldy to perform efficiently and effectively. Particularly, there are concerns that OFCOM will spend most of its time and budget monitoring TV and radio to the detriment of telecommunications and Internet.

Think about it

Do you think combining 5 regulatory bodies into a super-regulator is a good idea for the broadcasting industry? What are the arguments for and against?

Press Complaints Commission (PCC)

OFCOM only regulates broadcast media whereas the Press Complaints Commission responds to issues regarding the written media. The PCC is an independent body which deals with complaints about the content of newspapers or magazines. All national and regional magazines are bound by a code of conduct that covers issues such as accuracy of reporting and invasion of privacy. The PCC provides a free service to the public who may have concerns about the accuracy or editorial comment of a news story which concerns them or their organisation. The PCC itself claims that there are many benefits to the way the organisation is run (see Figure 13.7).

According to Furneaux and O'Carroll (2001) the Press Complaints Commission has adjudicated (decided on) over 23,000 complaints in its 10 year history. In their article entitled 'The Press Complaints Commission Greatest Hits' printed in the Guardian they highlight some of the most memorable and important adjudications.

2000 – HRH Prince of Wales v The Sunday Times

The Sunday Times printed a story claiming that Prince Charles and Camilla Parker Bowles had been in talks with the church and planned to marry. Prince Charles complained to the PCC on the grounds that the story was a fabrication. The PCC upheld the complaint and the Sunday Times was forced to apologise.

1988 – George Michael v The Sun

This complaint was made by George Michael when The Sun published an article about his new home including a map and photos. The Sun was forced to issue an apology.

Benefit	Detail
Accessibility	The PCC is free and available to all citizens. They operate a 24 hour service in a variety of languages to facilitate enquiries from all sections of the community.
Speed	The average time taken to investigate and adjudicate is 32 days. This is a very speedy service. Compare it to an average County Court case as outlined in unit 2 'Law and the Legal System' which takes an average of around 80 weeks to be resolved.
Raising standards in the industry	The PCC argue that their presence and powers ensure high standards in the written media. This is because it pursues newspapers who have breached the industries code of practice.
Independence from the industry	Although the PCC is funded by the newspaper and magazine industries and although many industry personnel sit on the PCC it has a majority of lay representatives who are not connected to the industry and are therefore not biased towards it.
Freedom of the press	The PCC is a self regulatory body which means that through this agency the press regulate themselves. This is seen as an advantage because government regulation of the press may restrict or undermine press freedom.

Figure 13.7 Benefits of the PCC

1999 – Tony and Cherie Blair v The Mail on Sunday

The Prime Minister complained when the Mail on Sunday printed a front page story which alleged his daughter had gained a place at a local comprehensive school by virtue of her parents connections and at the expense of other children. The PCC found that there had been no special treatment and agreed that the newspaper had misrepresented the situation.

However, the PCC has received substantial criticism that it does not act strongly enough against blatant breaches of the industry code of conduct. Greenslade (2003) highlights the following case study in which he labels the actions of the PCC 'feeble in the extreme'.

Case study

Shortly before Easter 2003 the Sunday Telegraph ran an in-depth story entitled 'Hot cross buns: councils decree buns could be offensive to non-Christians'. The story claimed that 5 councils had banned schools from serving hot cross buns due to their religious significance. Other newspapers such as The Times, The Express and The Sun also published the story as did many radio stations. The story even made it onto several Internet sites. In actual fact the story was utter fabrication. None of the councils had ever served hot cross buns at mealtimes and there was no ban in force. Even the picture which accompanied the story of 3 schoolgirls eating buns was a stage managed affair. The journalist in question had bought a bag of buns for the schoolchildren of Hathaway Primary School and then photographed them eating it without informing the school of the use to which it would be put. One of the councils concerned complained to the PCC which resulted in the Sunday Telegraph and other newspapers who had published the story withdrawing the story and offering an apology. Greenslade criticises the PCC in this instance on several counts.

- it did not approach the other councils who had been misrepresented to see if they wished to complain after the story was admitted to be fictitious
- it did not ensure that the apology in the Sunday Telegraph was large and prominently placed
- it did not ensure that all of the newspapers who printed the story apologised to all of the councils named
- the PCC did not criticise the Sunday Telegraph for clear breaches of the editor's code of practice
- the PCC did not address the issue of misrepresentation in the staged photo that accompanied the story.

1. Do you think the media often fabricate information – explain your answer
2. Why was the behaviour of the media unethical in this situation?
3. What are Greenslades criticisms of the PCC?
4. What should the punishment be for media fabrications?

Greenslade's analysis highlights concerns that the PCC has a long way to go if it is to gain the trust of the public. The debate surrounding the PCC is part of a wider debate about press regulation in general. In addition, although the PCC claims to deal with issues very quickly and with no bias towards the press, the Campaign for Press and Broadcasting Freedom (CPBF) highlights that of the 2360 complaints received by the PCC in 2002, it filtered out 2326 and made judgements on just 34.

Self-regulation

The media regulation debate is concerned with whether the government should oversee regulation through legislation designed to restrict and monitor media conduct or whether the media industry should have the power to regulate itself. The new Communications Act 2003, which provides Ofcom with its powers, promotes the idea of self regulation amongst the industry. The idea behind self regulation is that encouraging the press to draw up their own policies and standards and handle complaints themselves offers increased flexibility and adaptability. It is seen as more user friendly for the industry and it is argued that the media industry will be more likely to accept criticism and censure from a regulatory body it has a hand in shaping.

There is also the issue of freedom of the press. In any democratic society it is vital that the press are free to discuss current political issues away from the control of the government who may apply restrictions on what can be covered in a news story. Governments often have their own agenda in terms of what the media broadcast and it would be easy for them to restrict stories which criticised their policies in order to protect their position at the next election.

It is also argues that self regulation offers a much better service to the public who make complaints. Self regulatory bodies such as the PCC are able to offer a fast, accessible and free service to anyone making a complaint. Government regulation could lead to expensive court cases to resolve complaints increasing the length of time spent dealing with complaints and the cost which could lead to less well off individuals being unable to make a complaint.

In addition, a system of self regulation is funded by the industry itself and is not an additional burden on taxpayers. A government system would be funded from the government treasury which may take money away from more vital services such as education, health and the public services such as police, fire, paramedics and Armed Forces.

One of the arguments against self regulation is that a self regulatory body is funded by the organisation it polices, therefore it cannot be free from bias. Higham (2003) comments:

> *"The PCC's modest achievements may be down to the fact that as a voluntary body paid for by the organisations it polices, it cannot criticise newspapers too robustly for fear that they will simply walk away".*
>
> *BBC News 21/1/03*

The issue of accountability is also important as a system of self regulation has no accountability to the government or the general public in the way that a government regulated system does. Accountability is important because it allows the regulatory system to be monitored for effectiveness and efficiency by independent individuals with no vested interest in the outcome. The police have an independent complaints commission which investigates complaints made against officers and constabularies.

It is also important to note that current self regulatory bodies such as the PCC do not always appear to have public trust and confidence. The fact that in 2002 they decided on only a small percentage of the complaints they received and they have current and former newspaper editors serving on the commission harms their claim to independence and impartiality.

Assessment activity 13-P3

Produce a factsheet which explains regulation and de-regulation of the media in the UK.

Voluntary codes of practice

The media do adopt voluntary codes of practice which are often conducted successfully. An example is the voluntary code of practice which protects Prince William and Prince Harry from media intrusion until they have completed their education. This includes allowing the Princes to be free from harassment, checking that stories about them are correct prior to publication and not publishing photos which infringe the Princes' privacy. However, some publications are prepared to push these guidelines to the limits. In 2000 OK magazine published photos of Prince William in the Chilean Jungle. OK magazine argues that this was a public place and therefore their photographic coverage was entirely legitimate. Representatives for the Prince took the matter to the PCC who decided that the prince was not in a location where the press would have normally been and therefore his privacy had been invaded by the photographer.

Human Rights Legislation

As you will have seen from many other units in this book, the Human Rights Act (HRA) 1998 is a very important piece of legislation. It sets out the rights that individuals can expect to enjoy in the UK. The HRA initially caused confusion amongst the press particularly around 2 of the 18 articles highlighted in the Act:

Article 8 – Everyone has the right to respect for his private and family life, his home and correspondence.

Article 10 – Everyone has the right to freedom of expression.

These 2 rights appear contradictory and the press were concerned with the relationship between the 2 which would be established in test cases by the judicial system. The HRA was adapted from the European Convention of Human Rights (UCHR) and across Europe Article 10 had taken precedence over Article 8 giving the press a much strengthened position when the law came into effect in the UK. However, the provisions of the act do not seem to be being applied equally across the courts. Jaffa (2000) argues that the higher courts are interpreting the legislation in the way that Europe intended, with freedom of expression taking precedence over the right to privacy but the lower courts are favouring individual privacy over freedom of expression. This highlights discrepancies in the way the law is applied.

Think about it

Do articles 8 and 10 of the Human Rights Act 1998 contradict each other? If so which should take precedence and why?

Another aspect of the HRA with the potential to impact the press is Article 12 which outlines issues regarding injunctions on information about to be published. It makes it more difficult for a court to grant an injunction to prevent publication of a story which supports the principle of freedom of expression and works in favour of the press.

One article which has been a disadvantage to the press is Article 6 which states that everyone is entitled to a fair trial. By publishing stories about notorious crimes or paying witnesses for their stories the press can put the idea of the defendants guilt in the minds of the public even before a trial has taken place. Clearly this compromises the defendants right to a fair trial and the courts have recognised this and have used Article 6 a number of times across the country to restrict how the press report a case.

The HRA is generally a support to the press as it ensures their freedom of expression, but increasingly the press must be wary of breaching articles such as the ones described above, for fear of sanctions and censure by the PCC and the courts.

Think about it

Using chapters such as Unit 4 – Citizenship find out if the Human Rights Act 1998 might affect the press in any other way.

Libel and slander

Libel and slander are two forms of 'defamation'. According to Denham (1999) a defamatory statement is one which injures the reputation of another person or organisation. Libel is a defamatory statement that has a permanent nature, such as writing, printing, pictures, films and broadcasts made on the radio or TV. Slander is slightly different in that it is an impermanent form such as the spoken word. Clearly defamation has tremendous impact on the operation of both the broadcast and written media. The case study below highlights the impact on the press and the individual concerned if they are defamatory in their actions.

Case study

The Daily Mail published a story on March 6th 2003 which alleged that actress Nicole Kidman had engaged in an affair with married actor Jude

Law in the set of a film they were jointly working on called 'Cold Mountain'. Ms Kidman's repeated denials of the allegations were labelled dishonest by the Daily Mail. The Mail further claimed that the affair had led to the breakdown of Mr Law's marriage to his wife Sadie Frost. Nicole Kidman sued the Daily Mail for libel on the grounds that the allegations were a fabrication and that they harmed her reputation. Ms Kidman's solicitor commented in court:

> *'The publication of this article has caused grave damage to the claimants personal and professional reputation and she has suffered considerable embarrassment and distress'*
>
> *Gideon Benaim (2003)*

The editor of the Daily Mail, Paul Dacre and the journalist who wrote the story, Nicole Lambert

Nicole Kidman

accepted that the story was untrue. They were ordered to pay costs and substantial damages to Ms Kidman as well as tender an unreserved apology.

1. Why were the Daily Mail's allegations defamatory?
2. Why is this case libellous rather than slanderous?
3. Is it important that celebrities such as Ms Kidman are able to be protected in law from false allegations? Explain your answer.
4. Do you think the newspaper concerned was punished appropriately?

Think about it

Paul Dacre, the editor of the newspaper involved in the Kidman case outlined above sits on the press complaints commission. What are your views on editors whose publications have been found guilty of making false allegations sitting in judgement of press complaints?

Censorship

Censorship is the ability of individuals or groups in power to restrict freedom of expression. Censorship criminalizes or suppresses the production of certain information and access to that information. It is often explicitly defined in law, for example the Obscene Publications Act 1959 and 1964 or it may rely on unspoken intimidation by government officials which leaves people frightened to speak out on an issue for fear of losing their job or in some countries their life. There are arguments for and against censorship of the media which are outlined in Figure 13.8 below.

The censorship debate	
For	**Against**
Censorship of violence can reduce levels of violence in society – people will not commit copycat crimes.	Censorship in any form is an attack on freedom of expression.
Protects society from offensive material.	Censorship is conducted by the powerful against the powerless.

Figure 13.8 Arguments for and against censorship of the media

The censorship debate	
For	**Against**
Sometimes the media needs to be censored to protect the public good, for example ensuring media coverage does not harm criminal or civil trials.	Censorship rejects the notion that people should be able to decide for themselves what they see and read.
Censorship can be crucial in maintaining national security.	Censorship can be used by governments to prevent information becoming known which may harm their election prospects or public image.
Censorship can help respect the privacy of individuals.	An effective democracy relies on the free flow of information, discussion and debate. Censorship therefore harms democracy.
It can help protect some of the most vulnerable individuals in our society – children.	Censorship in many cases lacks scrutiny. It is merely one group of individuals wishes being imposed on others without checks and balances.

Figure 13.8 ctd. Arguments for and against censorship of the media

Think about it

What is your view of censorship? Do you think it is a necessary or unnecessary step for government to take?

There is no doubt that censorship can be misused by the powerful to prevent information coming to light which may cause political embarrassment. The case study below highlights this.

Case study

In 1987 former MI5 agent Peter Wright wrote his memoirs about his time in the security agency. The book outlined abuses by MI5 including a plot to undermine Prime Minister Harold Wilson in the 1970s. The Prime Minister of the time, Margaret Thatcher decided that publication would harm the credibility of the UK security services and proceeded to instigate a legal action to secure a ban on the book 'Spycatcher' being published in the UK. The problem with this censorship was that 'Spycatcher' became a bestseller in both the US and Australia while remaining banned in the UK. The British government lost its fight to keep Spycatcher banned in 1988.

1 Why did the British government wish to see 'Spycatcher' banned?
2 Peter Wright was a former MI5 agent and therefore subject to The Official Secrets Act. In view of this should he have written his memoirs at all?
3 Which is more important in your opinion: freedom of information or protection of national security? Explain your reasons.
4 Why was censorship of Spycatcher in the UK ineffective?
5 Do the public need to know about abuses conducted by the public services regardless of the consequence?

The censorship and age classification of films and videos in the UK is conducted by the British Board of Film Classification (BBFC). The BBFC was established by the film industry in 1912 as a result of local authorities applying widely varying standards to the matter of film classification. The BBFC brought standardisation to the classification of films to be shown in UK cinemas. Local authorities can still overrule the BBFC and reclassify films if they wish, but in practice this happens extremely rarely. The BBFC classifies films in the following ways:

- U
- PG

- 12
- 12A
- 15
- 18
- R18 (Applies to material supplied through licensed sex shops)

Think about it

Find out what each of the cinema ratings means. Do you think that these classifications are valid?

Ownership and revenue generation

Media empires

The media is dominated by a few giant global media corporations who own the majority of the western media. The moves towards deregulation and privatisation in the US and UK in the 1980s lead to increased opportunities for media companies to buy up other media assets which directly lead to the growth of trans-national media companies. The size, scope and reach of these trans-national media companies is very important because the media are one of the main sites for the discussion and dissemination of ideas and philosophy.

One of the main issues when examining these trans-national corporations is the fact that by their very size they can dominate virtually all news coverage in a country. It is important to remember that the news you see on TV is not just an accurate reporting of events, it is a news companies view on what you should see and what you shouldn't see. There are thousands of news stories occurring world wide every hour of every day – a typical news bulletin may cover half a dozen stories in 10 minutes. Someone makes the choice as to which stories make the news and which do not. This is a dangerous situation as a global media group can effectively silence some stories or portray them in an entirely different way than they occurred in reality. For example, one of the largest media corporations is The Walt Disney Corporation. It owns, amongst other things the ABC news network in the US. Recently ABC has decided not to air several reports that were critical of Disney. The question is were these stories pulled from the news for sound reasons or because ABCs parent company exerted influence? Disney is not the only company to come under scrutiny for what it *doesn't* air as well as what it does. News Corporation, the media empire owned by Rupert Murdoch which owns such newspapers as The Sun, The Times and The 'News of the World and Sky chose not to gossip about his private life when he and his wife split after 31 years of marriage. Is this because the situation wasn't newsworthy or because he happens to own them?

There are currently 10 very large media corporations:

- AOL Time Warner
- Viacom Inc.
- Walt Disney Company
- News Corporation
- Bertelsmann
- Vivendi Universal
- General Electric
- Liberty Media
- AT&T
- Sony.

Think about it

Do you think that media owners exert influence over what the media publishes or chooses to report on?

Theory into practice

The James Bond film 'Tomorrow Never Dies' gives a fictional account of what could happen if a media giant decided to manipulate the news to his own benefit. Watch it and consider the implications for global media ownership. Write a 200 word report summarising your findings.

Theory into practice

Consider the 10 largest media corporations. Research at least 3 of them and find out how much they are worth and what they own.

Influence of advertisers

The impact of advertisers cannot be overstated. They create tremendous wealth and revenue for newspapers and magazines.

> *"The influence of advertising on magazines reached a point where editors began selecting articles not only on the basis of their expected interest for readers, but also for their influence on advertisements. Serious articles were not always the best support for ads. An article that put the reader in an analytical frame of mind did not encourage the reader to take seriously an ad which depended on fantasy or a trivial product."*
>
> *Bagdikian (2000) pg 138*

The point that Bagdikian is making is that the stories you read in newspapers and magazines are designed to put you in a buying mood. Therefore they emphasise entertainment interest as opposed to controversy and serious issues. For example, the Chrysler Corporation had a policy of previewing the editorial content of magazines before it bought space in them in the 1990s. This was to keep its car advertisements away from anything it considered controversial such as stories on car safety or global warming. Another example is the fashion and beauty industry refusing to be associated with stories connected to anorexia. Since a publication or commercial TV/radio station relies extremely heavily on advertiser revenue they often bend to demands to change content. Soley (1997) comments that 65 years ago a reporter and press critic called George Seldes wrote that advertisers, not government are the principle news censors in the UK. Today this comment could be applied across most western nations.

Case study

The British Broadcasting Corporation is a well respected and influential member of the national and international media community. However, it is owned in its entirety by the British government and questions have been raised recently regarding its independence from the government. In theory the BBC is completely independent as it has no advertisers who can influence the news or programming and it is not supposed to receive any political pressure from the government. In September 2002 the government produced a dossier which argued Iraq could deploy weapons of mass destruction within 45 minutes. These claims strengthened the argument to go to war against Iraq. In May 2003 on The BBC's Today programme broadcast journalist Andrew Gilligan's reported that the dossier was in fact 'sexed up' and included information the intelligence service did not think was valid. The government denied the reports and heavily criticised the BBC for broadcasting the report. It also named Andrew Gilligan's source of information as Dr David Kelly a well respected intelligence expert who worked for the government. Dr Kelly's name was made public on the 10th July, by the 17th July he had committed suicide. The Hutton Inquiry into the incident blamed the BBC almost entirely as a result. Andrew Gilligan resigned as did Director General of the BBC Greg Dyke and BBC Chairman Gavyn Davies.

1. The government appointed Lord Hutton to investigate the circumstances surrounding Dr Kelly's death. Can a government appointed Inquiry ever be independent?
2. What impact did the government Inquiry have on the BBC?
3. Do you think the government applied pressure to the BBC. If so can the BBC be considered independent?
4. Do you think it is fair that the BBC bears the brunt of the responsibility in the Hutton Inquiry?
5. What could the BBC do to make itself more independent from the government?

Assessment activity 13-P4, 13-M2, 13-D1

Produce a written report of at least 500 words which evaluates and analyses the independence of the media from owners, revenue generators and politicians. Use graphics, statistics and case studies to provide evidence for your conclusions.

How the public services are portrayed

The public services are portrayed in a variety of ways by the media depending on the situation they find themselves in. The coverage can be both 'real' in that it highlights actual members of the public services performing the job that they are employed to do or it can be a fictional portrayal which may not be grounded in the experience of many public service officers.

In the UK, Williams and Dickinson (1993) found that tabloids portray more crime than broadsheets. The Sun had 30.4% of crime news, compared to 5.1% in the Guardian. What this highlights is that a substantial proportion of media time and energy goes on the portrayal of public services. In addition, the number of crime dramas and public service related TV shows form a large proportion of our day to day TV viewing. The figures below from a single week in August 2003 highlight the range and frequency of fictional media portrayal (see Figure 13.9).

Week commencing Mon 11th August – Fri 15th August 2003		
BBC1 Diagnosis Murder Spooks Watching the Detectives Film: Charley Varick Film: Two Minute Warning	**BBC 2** The Thin Blue Line Film: Two Days in the Valley	**ITV** Quincy Film: Last Rites Police! Crossing Jordan The Bill Bad Girls Dragnet A Touch of Frost The Rockford Files
Channel 4 Pet Rescue Film: Double Team The Man from the Met Film: Lost	**Channel 5** Charlie's Angels CSI Miami CSI The Shield Film: Murphy's Law Battlefield Detectives Film: The Deadly Look of Love Film: Nothing to Loose Fred and Rose – The West Murders Film: Route Nine	**Sky One** Road Wars Americas Dumbest Criminals

Figure 13.9 Fictional media portrayal

As you can see, portrayals of the public services take up a great deal of air time, but how are the services themselves actually portrayed? A US based National Television Violence study found that over a 4-year period every reality based police show contained acts of visual violence including shoot outs, dangerous car chases and assaults. It also includes portrayals of murder, sexual assault and robbery at a much higher rate than actually happens in real life.

The study also found that police shows depicted 33% of police officers using or threatening physical aggression compared with only 10% of criminals. This clearly highlights the medial portrayal of police officers as aggressive or brutal.

Think about it

Conduct your own content analysis along the lines of the one above. How many crimes and crime related programmes did you count?

However, the findings of the US National television Violence study also found that the media portrayal of the police was positive in some regards. For example, it found that on the reality based police shows around 60% of the crimes were solved. In reality the number of crimes solved by the police is generally a great deal lower. Police work is also portrayed as a job which involves continual excitement as TV audiences often see dramatic snapshots of the police capturing a suspect, executing a warrant or receiving calls to mobilise on the radio. This gives a false impression of real police work which can be routine and involves a great deal of paperwork.

Negative images of the public services

The police in the UK face a great deal of media coverage on issues such as:

- racism
- compensation
- canteen culture
- corruption.

Racism

Racism has long been a charge levelled at the police service by the media, such as the Brixton riots in the early 1980s, the stopping and searching of black youths in the 1990s or the lack of recruitment of ethnic minority officers across all 43 police force areas in England and Wales.

However, it took the murder of a black teenager called Stephen Lawrence to put the subject firmly on the political and media agenda.

Case study

Stephen Lawrence was an 18 year old A-Level student who was attacked and killed by a gang of white youths in April 1993. The investigation (or lack of) which followed led to one of the most tense situations between the police and urban ethnic communities since the early 1980s. It also led to the most damning report on the activities of the metropolitan police ever published. As the case progressed it became clear that the media saw the Lawrence situation as a potentially explosive situation with the potential to rock British race relations. In fact the murder of Stephen Lawrence and the ensuing investigations and reports, including the Macpherson Report which claimed the Metropolitan Police were institutionally racist, continually made newspaper headlines throughout the mid to late 1990s.

The media made great use of the Macpherson report and highlighted the failings of the Met in the Lawrence case as well as highlighting many other racist allegations made against the police. The media coverage ensured that the inadequate investigation could not be swept under the carpet and that the recommendations from the Macpherson report would be seen to be acted upon.

The results of the media examination into this case have been largely positive even though it was a negative portrayal of the police themselves. This is because it has encouraged and fostered change within the service and put the issue of police racism firmly in the public domain. However it did have a direct effect on police morale as the force as a whole came under heavy political and media criticism. This affected many officers who had worked hard building up community and ethnic relations and felt like the time and effort they had put in had been dismissed. Equally the accusation of racism left police officers uncertain of how to approach black individuals who they suspected might have committed a crime as the media attention on the issue at the time meant any genuine error might be reported in the press as a racist incident.

1 Why was the investigation of the murder of Stephen Lawrence flawed?
2 Why did the media cover this story in detail?
3 Do you think the media has helped improve the situation for reporting racist incidents to the police?
4 What were the negative impacts of the media coverage of this case?

Think about it

Why was the media a useful tool in highlighting race relation's issues during the Lawrence inquiry?

Compensation

The issue of compensation for police officers who are injured in the line of duty is one that the media felt very strongly on. Particularly after officers who attended the Hillsborough football stadium disaster were able to claim hundreds of thousands of pounds after they developed post traumatic stress disorder (PTSD) in response to the events they witnessed at Hillsborough. The media had a field day with this and were scathing in their response, noting that the families of the victims received 100 times less than one of the officers who claimed PTSD. The media in this instance opened the debate as to whether public service workers should be entitled to any compensation at all since the activities which are likely to cause PTSD are an integral part of the job that they sign on to do. However, the issue of PTSD is not the only police compensation issue to appear in the papers. There have also been headlines surrounding pension fraud and malingering in order to claim sick pay.

The media have portrayed the issue of police compensation very negatively but officers, just like any other employee up and down the country are entitled to compensation for workplace injuries. In fact due to the hazardous nature of public service work it is even more important that they are able to claim compensation.

Think about it

Why would the media choose to portray the image of police compensation so negatively?

Canteen culture

Canteen culture is a term applied to describe the attitudes of rank and file police officers in the UK. It is white male dominated and has been accused of spreading racist, sexist and homophobic notions throughout the service.

The media has increasingly targeted these areas for criticism particularly singling out the Police Federation, the representative body of the police service in the UK, as a major culprit in the perceived discriminatory attitudes of police officers. The media has called for canteen culture and its attitudes to be stamped out, making way for newer more liberal ideas to enlighten the police service making it more user friendly and community centred. This view portrays a very negative view of the police as unwilling or unable to change. In actual fact by the very nature of its job it must be more adaptive than many other organisations but it is impossible to change the culture of an organisation over 120,000 strong overnight regardless of media pressure.

Think about it

The media often highlights the negative aspects of canteen culture. Can you come up with a list of the advantages you think it might bring to serving officers?

Corruption

The recent criminal trial of four former Flying Squad detectives for corruption put this issue firmly in the media spotlight. The allegations were that Flying Squad officers siphoned off cash from the recovered proceeds of bank robbers. The main witness in the case was a former police officer who turned 'supergrass' to report his colleague for years of corrupt practises. Several officers were given jail sentences for their part in the activities while others were acquitted when a key witness became too ill to testify. The media sensationalized these events with a detrimental effect on other flying squad officers.

Think about it

If accusations are made against some officers, does it undermine the reputations of their colleagues as well? Explain your answer.

Police corruption is a relatively rare occurrence but intense media coverage which sensationalises the few occurrences which do occur give a false impression to the public and have a negative effect on police morale.

Case study

During the 1970s and 1980s the West Midlands Serious Crime Squad gained confessions to crimes from suspects by brutal and corrupt interview techniques. Allegations against them included writing out false statements and putting plastic bags over suspects heads, suffocating them until they signed the confession. The squad was disbanded in 1989 and 30 of the convictions which were secured by the squad were found to be unsafe and were quashed by the court of appeal. These include such notable cases such as 'The Birmingham Six', 'The Bridgewater Four' and Keith Twitchell. One of the appeal judges in the Twitchell case commented:

'Birmingham Six' on 'release day'

"A significant number of officers in that squad, some of whom rose to a very senior rank, behaved outrageously and in particular extracted confessions by grossly improper means, amounting in some cases to torture."

Lord Justice Rose 1999

1 Do you think increased pressure on police officers to achieve crime fighting targets may lead to actions such as those described above? Explain your answer.
2 How would you propose to tackle police corruption?
3 Why does police corruption make headline news?
4 Does media publicity on police corruption and miscarriages of justice create an inaccurate picture of police conduct?

Positive images of the public services

The public often only hear about the negative aspects of the public services. The outstanding contribution of the vast majority of the public services to social order, stability and personal safety on a day to day basis is not something you often read about. The public services operate 24 hours a day, 7 days a week, 365 days a year performing acts of tremendous courage, bravery and self sacrifice. For example, the death of Firefighter Rob Miller from Leicester fire and rescue service who died in 2002 while searching a burning factory to see if anyone was trapped, Fleur Lombard a firefighter in Avon who died in a supermarket blaze in 1998, PC Andrew Jones of South Wales Police who was fatally injured by a car while chasing a burglar in 2003 or the 6 Royal Military Police officers who were killed in 2003 in Majar al-Kabir in Iraq. The list of public service officers who have given their lives for the protection and safety of others is long and distinguished. Although the press doesn't often comment on the excellent day to day performance of the public services they do pay respect to remarkable acts of bravery such as those described above which helps create admiration and respect in the public for the services.

Assessment activity 13P-5, 13-M3, 13-D2

Using all the information you have received in this chapter so far coupled with your own research produce a newspaper article written in broadsheet style which evaluates, analyses and compares using examples how positive and negative images affect public perceptions of the public services as well as service practice and morale.

How public services use the media

In addition to being portrayed in the media the public services also increasingly are using the media to further their own ends. Some of the ways in which they use the media are listed below:

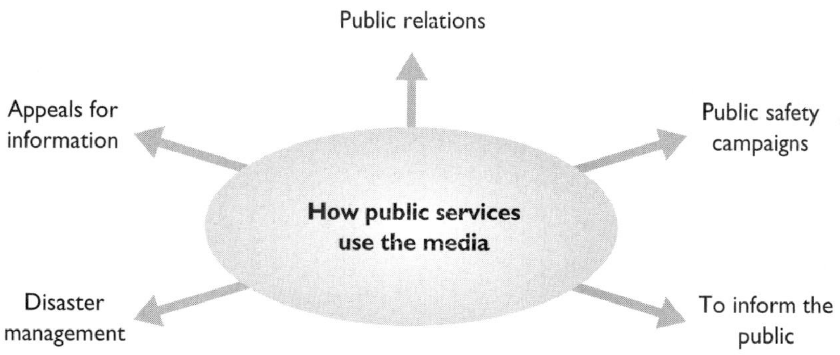

Figure 13.10 Public services and the media

Public service press and public relations departments are becoming increasingly professionalised and media aware. As a consequence the services are being proactive in their approach to the media.

Public safety campaigns

The public services support government public safety campaigns. Good examples of this are the drink driving campaigns, road safety for children and crime prevention campaigns. These come in the form of billboards, posters, newspaper advertisements, TV and radio commercials. A large scale publicity campaign can help the public be aware of the issues surrounding drink driving and the consequences of it. These campaigns extend to children as well as traffic is one of the largest killers of children under the age of 14. Government safety campaigns can help make children more aware of the dangers that face them when they encounter traffic. These campaigns are supported by police officers who go into schools to promote the message behind the campaign.

It is not just the police who advise on and support public safety campaigns, the fire service are heavily involved in promoting the governments fire safety campaigns on issues such as smoke alarms, kitchen fires, careless smoking, fire evacuation plans and hoax callers.

Improve public relations

All of the public services rely on civilian support to help them do their jobs. Whether this takes the form of dialling 999, pulling over to let an emergency vehicle pass or working in a paid or voluntary capacity for them. Services which come into contact with the public on a frequent basis need to be particularly aware of their public image. A negative image of a service can harm recruitment and retention of officers and it can also cause tremendous resentment among the public with the possibility of civil disorder or attacks on officers. Public relations can be harmed by many things such as service corruption, incompetence and poor treatment of members of the public. The services use the media for damage limitation in circumstances like this and to promote the positive aspects of their work. The current scandal of prisoner abuse in Iraq is a good example of this.

Appeals for information

The services, particularly the police, may call upon the media to help solve crimes by publicising the crime to the general public and appealing for information on it. This may take the form of a press conference, a news story or a programme such as 'Crimewatch' which exists purely to help the police connect with the public on a large scale. There are many occurrences where the police need to inform the public to be vigilant, perhaps in the case of a sighting of a dangerous criminal or the abduction of a child. Equally many crimes have witnesses who don't even know that they are witnesses until an appeal for information goes out.

To inform the public

The public services use the media to inform the public on a whole range of issues such as crime prevention, dealing with emergencies and traffic congestion.

Disaster management

The public services use the media extensively in a disaster management situation for any or all of the following reasons:

- to inform the public to stay indoors in the event of a chemical or biological contamination
- to make a call for off-duty medial professionals to report to their hospitals
- to provide information on casualties and fatalities
- to warn the public to stay away from a disaster site
- to publicise helpline numbers for concerned individuals
- to reassure the public that a disaster is being dealt with quickly and efficiently
- to coordinate evacuation plans
- to call for specialised assistance such as counsellors or utility workers.

As you can see, the services use the media extensively. In effect they have a mutually advantageous relationship as the media relies on the services for inspiration for drama, entertainment, comedy and news while the public services use the media as a vehicle to connect with the public.

Assessment activity 13-P6

Produce an A3 poster which illustrates how the public services make use of the media.

Assessment activity 13-P7, 13-M4

Examine and analyse at least 2 cases of media portrayal of the public services including at least one factual and one fictional. When you have done this prepare and present a presentation which highlights your findings.

End of unit test

1 What is the mass media?

2 Describe how satellite technology has changed reporting of the news.

3 What have been the major changes in media technology in the last 10 years?

4 What is OFCOM?

5 How does censorship work in the UK?

6 Why do we have censorship?

7 What is the PCC and what does it do?

8 How does the Human Rights Act impact upon the media in the UK?

9 Explain libel and slander and why they are important in studying the media?

10 What is media self regulation?

11 What are the names and holdings of the worlds top media corporations?

12 How do advertisers influence the media?

13 How can politicians influence the media?

14 How does the media portray positive aspects of the public services?

15 Give an example of when the media have portrayed negative aspects of the public services?

16 In what ways do the public services make use of the media?

17 How has the growth of the internet changed the media?

18 How do negative images of the media affect public service morale?

19 Should the government impose regulation on the media?

20 Do you think the public services could use the media more effectively? Explain your answer.

Resources

Bagdikian, B, *Media Monopoly*, 2000, London, Beacon Press

Denham, P, *Law A Modern Introduction*, 4th edition, 1999, London, Hodder and Stoughton

Gauntlett D, *Ten Things Wrong with the Effects Model*, 1998

Greenslade R, *Press Gang: The True Story of how Papers make Profits from Progaganda*, 2003, London, Macmillan

Leishman, F and Mason, P, *Policing and the Media*, 2003, Devon, William Publishing

Skeggs, B and Mundy J, *Issues in Sociology*: The Media, 1992, London, Nelson Thomas

Websites

www.ofcom.org.uk – Office of Communications

www.pcc.org.uk – Press Complaints Commission

TEAMWORK IN THE PUBLIC SERVICES

Introduction to Unit 17

This unit will help you gain an understanding and subject knowledge of the importance of teamwork within the public services. The main focus of the unit is on the importance of individuals being able to work within public service organisations including involvement in teams and mechanisms for co-ordinating with teams.

It will also help you develop your own teamwork skills and to appreciate the importance of effective teamwork within the public services. You will also gain an understanding of the range of team activities that happen within public service organisations and between the emergency services when working together at major incidents.

The final part of this chapter looks at how public service organisations function in multi-disciplinary situations and how they offer their expertise in these situations.

Assessment

Throughout the unit activities and tasks will help you to learn and remember information. Case studies are included to add industry relevance to the topics and learning objectives. You are reminded that when you are completing activities and tasks, opportunities will be created to enhance your key skills evidence. After completing this unit you should be able to achieve the following outcomes.

Outcomes

1. Investigate how the **development of teams** in public service organisations has been assisted by the supporting theory
2. Review the **types of teams** used in the public service organisations
3. Explore the **characteristics of effective teams** in public service organisations
4. Examine the impact of **barriers of effective teamwork** that may arise in a work situation.

What is a team?

A team is two or more people with complementary skills who coordinate their efforts to accomplish a goal or common purpose. The way they meet this goal or common purpose and coordinate with each other is what makes them a team. This means that teamwork is more than just a group of people getting together, it is a working unit where there is dependence on each other and mutual respect for each other, a sense of shared ownership and a common approach in achieving the goal. Individual talent and knowledge is encouraged and used to complete the task along with open communication between every member. The team also needs to be able to deal with conflict and disagreement effectively. If any of these elements are missing then the group is unlikely to succeed, whether it is playing a team sport or solving a mathematical problem.

Think about it

Why do we work in teams? Think of the teams you are involved in and discuss with your colleagues.

Think about it

What public service teams are you aware of? Can you think of a public service where teams are not a vital part of the organisation.

Working as a team is important for team sports

Teams or individuals?

There are a number of good reasons for assigning tasks to teams rather than individuals. Firstly, it allows for distribution of the workload as sometimes a task is too big or complex for a single individual to handle in the time allowed. For example, building a stationary catapult is difficult as it consists of a number of different components, so a number of people are needed to build it. Each team member will contribute in different ways as they will have different skills and in some cases may possess expert knowledge.

Think about it

Think of 3 examples of winning teams? What have those winning teams done to be successful?

When a group is formed a group leader will often be chosen on the grounds that he or she is perceived by other members as the most competent at meeting the requirements of the leadership role. The remaining group members will accept the other group roles which we will look at during this chapter

Development of teams

To work effectively in teams, an individual needs to understand what advantages are offered by teamwork and what kind of role within the team is likely to be appropriate for them. One of the keys to an effective team is to understand what strengths, skills, and motivations each individual brings to the team and the issue of group diversity will help to make a team strong and flexible.

Stages of team development

The cohesiveness of groups has a major impact on their functioning and generally groups go through 4 stages. Bruce Tuckman published his 'Forming, storming, norming, performing, model in 1965 and this theory remains a good explanation of team development and behaviour still today. The theory on team development predicts that teams must go through the whole sequence to be successful.

Everyone who works in a team needs to know what the various growth stages of a developing team are and they should know how best to move the team through these stages. Knowing that it is normal for a team to go through a roller coaster ride to achieve their goal will help you understand and anticipate the team building process and take action to be more productive when working in groups in the future. Some teams will go through the 4 recognized stages fairly rapidly and move from forming through to performing in a short space of time. It all depends on the composition of the team, the capabilities of the individuals, the tasks at hand and the leadership style.

Teams that go through these stages successfully should become effective teams and display:

- clear objectives and agree goals
- openness

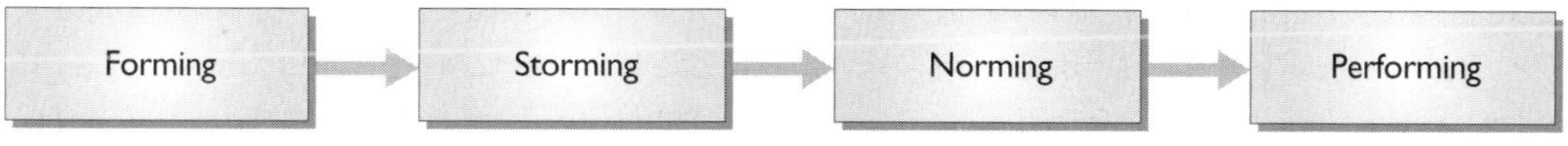

Figure 17.1 Forming, storming, norming and performing model

- support and trust towards each other
- co-operation
- good decision-making skills
- appropriate leadership
- ability to review team performance
- sound inter-group relationships
- individual development
- understanding on how to deal with confrontation and conflict.

Stage 1: forming

The forming stage is the first stage of team development and happens when a newly formed team comes together with individuals who they may not know. This often means that these people may feel anxious and uncomfortable. It is a difficult time and a lot of things can happen at this stage. This stage is when team members will explore the boundaries of acceptable behaviour along with determining their individual role with the team. They will discuss the task and decide how it will be accomplished, they will identify the resources or skills needed and begin to communicate openly about individual likes and dislikes and strengths and weaknesses.

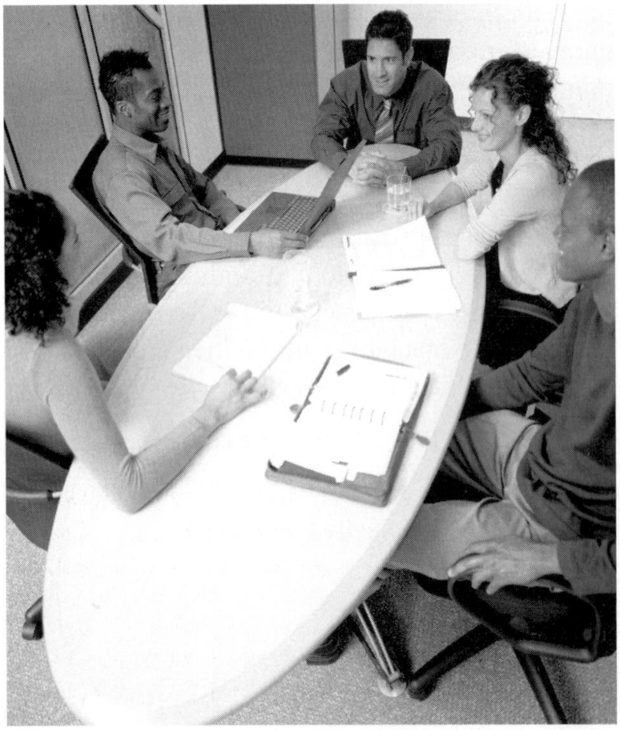

Open discussion is an important part of team development

A key tip for anybody taking a group through this stage is to ensure that open discussion takes place at the start of the task. This ensures that people get the chance to air their views, concerns and queries, because if its not done at this stage then it could result in failure later.

The following points highlight what you can do as a team to ensure this stage goes well:

- outline the task the team has to complete
- identify each person's role in the task by identifying peoples strengths and weaknesses
- encourage each team member to perform
- ensure that the team form a set of rules and guidelines
- decide on how decisions will be made
- decide how the team are going to give feedback on each other's performance.

Stage 2: storming

This stage is when team members start to 'jockey' for position and when control struggles take place. The storming stage is a critical stage as this is where things may start to go wrong. If members have not become acquainted then the team members may still feel uncomfortable with their roles. For example, some team members may think the task is too hard and others may distance themselves from the group because they feel excluded. Communication may be poor as the team is not listening to each other. Conflicts may begin as simple disagreements which then lead to more fundamental differences of opinion, meaning that the group can become divided. Although conflict may damage or destroy a team, conflict is a natural consequence of team membership and it may, in fact, strengthen the team as the members learn to accept and constructively resolve their differences.

Storming is a challenging phase and this is where the leadership qualities are tested as the storming usually arises as a result of goals, roles and rules becoming unclear. This can lead to conflicts with the potential of creating separate parties within the team and decreased productivity. To deal with this problem you must go over the agreements made by the team during the forming stage and ensure that the understanding is uniform across the team. If necessary rules may need to be modified and roles or responsibilities may need to be renegotiated. The earlier in the storming stage this is revisited the more likely the outcome will be successful.

Stage 3: norming

This stage is when rules are finalised and accepted and when team rules start being adhered to. The norming stage is where team members accept the team and its ground rules along with their individual role within the team. The team works cooperatively with a willingness to confront issues and solve problems and constructive criticism replaces conflict. There is a sense of team spirit and identity which ensures everyone is working together. Members are highly involved and member satisfaction is at it highest. Not only are members pleased with the team, but they themselves may experience higher self esteem and lower anxiety as a result of their participation in the team. At this stage the group will look at more detailed planning for completing the task.

Norming is the calm after the storm. The team is calm and focused on the goal, roles and rules are clarified and understood by all and relationships become stronger as people are more aware of each others strengths and weaknesses.

Stage 4: performing

This stage is when the team starts to show productivity through effective and efficient working practices. This occurs late in the developmental life of the team as team members at this stage have a clear understanding of each other's strengths and weaknesses and are able to avoid conflict as they are aware of how to resolve differences by utilising each persons individual talents and opinions.

It is at the performing stage where team members really concentrate on the team goals and this is a period of potential personal growth among team members as there is a good deal of sharing of experiences, feelings and ideas together.

Not every team makes it to the performing stage. Many get stuck at the norming stage because there is often a lack of momentum and motivation towards achieving goals.

Stage 5: adjourning

This stage is when team dissolution occurs. This may happen for a number of reasons, for example when the team has completed its task, when the team has exhausted its resources/ideas, when they are unable to resolve conflicts, team members have grown dissatisfied and depart or when repeated failure makes the team unable to continue.

As teams perform it is almost inevitable that fatigue, tension and conflict will develop. Fatigue will set in if the task is physically demanding or boredom will develop if it is too easy. Tension and conflict will develop when alternative approaches need to be considered and applied because the first approach was unsuccessful.

> ***Assessment activity 17-P2***
>
> Explain clearly the stages of team development using the forming, storming, norming, performing and adjourning model

Roles of team members

No one individual can combine all the qualities of a good team but a team of individuals can. This is why strong teams are the instruments of sustained and enduring success.

A team is a complex system. For groups to function as a team, a number of different roles and tasks must take place. Too often team members assume someone else or the group leader will take care of things. There are many individual roles within a team and people often take up roles naturally as they reflect their personality. For example, some people will look to lead a group from the front while others will be hands on and happy to follow instructions.

No matter what role you take within a team, there are some general factors that each team member should follow including abiding by ground rules and fully participating in tasks by working to an agreed agenda. Each team member should look to generate ideas, insights, solutions and recommendations whenever possible and encourage others by building on their ideas. They should always share available information, experience and expertise and take responsibility for the team's success and failure.

Think about it

What type of team member are you. Identify your strengths and weaknesses and discuss these with a fellow learner.

The need for good teamwork is recognised in every type of organisation, whether it be public or private, large or small and many public service organisations can only achieve success by combining their talents and energies as a group, such as fire-fighters tackling a major blaze or the police dealing with football hooligans causing disorder in a town centre.

Think about it

Some teams work very well, whilst others do not and the difference cannot always be explained by the absence of particular skills or specialist knowledge within the team. Some teams simply don't seem to gel as well as others. Why do you think this happens?

Major theorists

MJ Belbin

Dr Meredith Belbin has developed an understanding of how teams work and how to make them work better. Through extensive research at Henley Management College, Belbin isolated and identified 9 key roles as the ones available to team members. He spent over 20 years researching why some teams succeed whilst others fail and his work on team role theory has been found to have great practical application for people seeking to improve the performance of teams.

Belbin describes a team role as 'a tendency to behave, contribute and interrelate with others in a particular way.' There are

- 3 action oriented roles – shaper, implementer and completer finisher
- 3 people oriented roles – co-ordinator, teamworker and resource investigator
- 3 cerebral roles – plant, monitor evaluator and specialist.

To create this theory, Meredith Belbin and his team of researchers studied the behaviour of managers from all over the world for a period of 9 years. Managers taking part in the study were given psychometric tests and put into teams while they were completing a complex management exercise. The teams different core personality traits, intellectual styles and behaviours were assessed during the exercise. As time progressed different clusters of behaviour were identified as underlying the success of the teams which are now known as the 9 team roles shown in Figure 17.2.

Dr Merideth Belbin has extensively researched why some teams succeed and others fail. He has demonstrated that the perfect team must have the correct mix of different types of roles in order for a team to be balanced. However, the roles of any team are varied and each team member is likely to fill more than one role and roles can change as the team progresses. The secret of building perfect

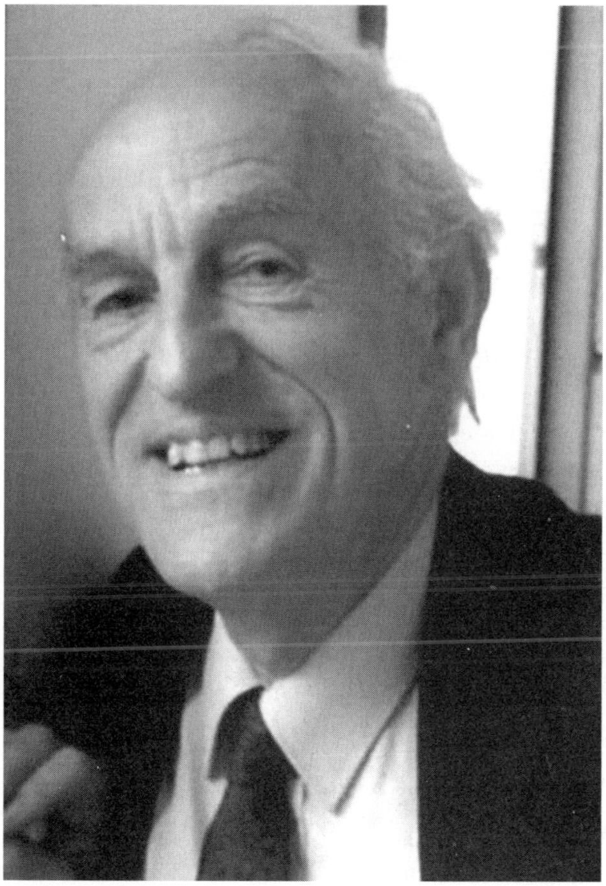

MJ Belbin

teams is for the group of people concerned, however many they may be, to play to their own strengths and both tolerate and compensate for one another's weaknesses.

An understanding of team roles can help us to pick the best teams and work more effectively together as team players and leaders. A well-balanced team of competent people will almost always outperform an unbalanced team full of star players.

Belbin's team roles:

The way people behave and act within a group is central to Belbins research as he identified 9 very different team roles. Dr Belbin believes that if all the 9 roles are present in a team, it will have a good chance of success.

The 9 key roles are as follows:

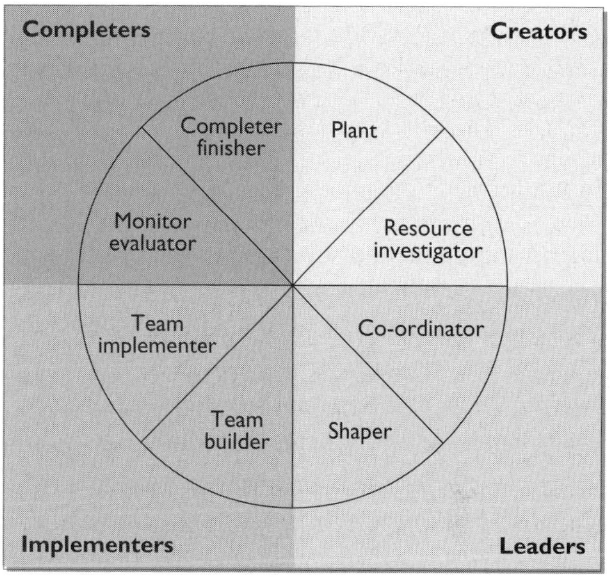

Figure 17.2 Belbin's team roles

Plant: the plant is the one who scatters the seeds which the others nourish until they bear fruit. The plant was named when it was found that one of the best ways to improve the performance of an ineffective and uninspired team was to 'plant' one of this role in it.

The plant is the team's source of original ideas, suggestions and proposals: the ideas person. The plant tends to be the most imaginative as well as the most intelligent member of the team and the most likely to start searching for a completely new approach to a problem or to bring a new insight to a line of action already agreed.

Positive qualities: genius, imagination, intellect, knowledge.

Negative qualities: up in the clouds, inclined to disregard practical details or protocol.

Resource investigator (RI): this person is probably the most immediately likeable member of the team. Relaxed, sociable and gregarious and easy to interest and enthuse, RI's responses tend to be positive and enthusiastic, though they can dismiss things as quickly as they take them up. The RI's ability to stimulate ideas and encourage innovation can lead people to mistake them for an ideas person but the RI does not have the originality that distinguishes the plant. They are, however, quick to see the relevance of new ideas.

Positive qualities: a capacity for contacting people and exploring anything new, an ability to respond to challenge.

Negative qualities: liable to lose interest once the fascination has passed.

Co-ordinator: this person is best suited to lead the team even though that may not be their 'formal' role. The Coordinator is the one who presides over the team and co-ordinates its efforts to meet external goals and targets. They are the social leader; calm; self-confident; controlled.

Positive qualities: a capacity for treating and welcoming all potential contributors on their merits and without prejudice; a strong sense of objectives.

Negative qualities: no more than ordinary in terms of intellect or creative ability.

Shaper: the Shaper is full of nervous energy: outgoing and emotional, impulsive and impatient and sometimes edgy and easily frustrated. Quick to challenge, and quick to respond to a challenge, the shaper is the task leader of the team. The principal function of the shaper is to give a shape to the application of the team's efforts, always looking for a pattern in discussions and trying to unite ideas, objectives and practical considerations into a single feasible project which the shaper seeks to push forward urgently to decision and action.

Positive qualities: drive and a readiness to challenge inactivity, ineffectiveness, complacency or self-deception.

Negative qualities: proneness to provocation, irritation and impatience and most prone to paranoia. Quick to sense a fight and the first to feel that there is a conspiracy afoot and he is the object or the victim of it.

Team builder: the team builder is the most sensitive of the team; the most aware of individuals' needs and worries and the one who perceives most clearly the emotional undercurrents within the group. If you want to know the mood of the team ask the team builder. Supportive; uncompetitive; mediator; socially oriented; rather mild; sensitive.

Positive qualities: an ability to respond to people and situations and to promote team spirit.

Negative qualities: Indecisiveness at moments of crisis.

Team implementer: the implementer is the practical organiser; the one who turns decisions and strategies into defined and manageable tasks that people can actually get on with. If anyone does not know what has been decided and what they are supposed to be doing they will go to the team implementer first to find out. A practical organiser; conservative; dutiful and predictable, research has shown that a high proportion of team implementers end up in leading roles in industry.

Positive qualities: organising ability, practical common sense, hard-working, self-disciplined.

Negative qualities: lack of flexibility, unresponsive to unproved ideas.

Monitor evaluator (ME): in a balanced team it is only the plant and the monitor evaluator who need a high IQ, but by contrast with the plant, the monitor evaluator has a serious temperament. The ME's contribution lies in measured analysis rather than creative ideas. Analytically rather than creatively intelligent; sober; unemotional; prudent.

Positive qualities: judgement, discretion, hard-heartedness.

Negative qualities: lacks inspiration or the ability to motivate others.

Completer finisher: the completer finisher worries about what might go wrong and is never at ease until they have personally checked every detail and made sure that everything has been done and nothing has been overlooked. Checks details; worries about deadlines; painstaking; orderly; conscientious; anxious.

Positive qualities: a capacity for follow through, perfectionism.

Negative qualities: a tendency to worry about small things, a reluctance to 'let go'.

The specialist: is slightly different to the rest as this is a person within a team who has prior knowledge or specialist skills that are suited to the task at hand. For example, if you were making a rope bridge for a river crossing the specialist is the kind of person who has done it before or has an extensive knowledge of rope tying and levering.

Theory into practice

In groups, watch a video or film or view a real event where a public service team is working together. Identify as many activities as you can which relate to the Belbin theory in the chapter and explain in terms of team theory who is doing what.

Summary of the team roles

The **co-ordinator** clarifies group objectives, sets the agenda, establishes priorities, selects problems, sums up and is decisive but does not dominate discussions.

The **shaper** gives shape to the team effort, looking for patterns in discussions and practical considerations regarding the feasibility of the project. Can steamroller the team, but gets results.

The **plant** is the source of original ideas, suggestions and proposals that are usually original and radical.

The **monitor evaluator** contributes a measured and dispassionate analysis and, through objectivity, stops the team committing itself to a misguided task.

The **implementer** turns decisions and strategies into defined and manageable tasks, sorting out objectives and pursuing them logically.

The **resource investigator** goes outside the team to bring in ideas, information and developments to it. They are the team's salesperson, diplomat, liaison officer and explorer.

The **team worker** operates against division and disruption in the team, particularly in times of stress and pressure.

The **finisher** maintains a permanent sense of urgency with relentless follow-through.

The **specialist** has expert knowledge which is relevant to the task.

Think about it

Look at the first 8 team roles above and score each one from one to five with relation to how much they describe you. The ones that score highly will give you an idea of your strengths and likely behaviour within a team situation.

An ideal team should have a healthy balance of all 9 team roles. Strong teams normally have a strong co-ordinator, a plant, a monitor evaluator and one or more implementers, team workers, resource investigators or completer finishers. A shaper should be an alternative to a co-ordinator rather than having both. In practice, the ideal is rarely the case, and it can be beneficial for a team to know which of the team roles are either over represented or absent and to understand individual's secondary roles. It is not essential that teams comprise people each fulfilling one of the roles above, but people who are aware and capable of carrying out these roles should be present. In small teams, people can, and do, assume more than one role.

There is a tendency in many teams is to have for too many 'shapers' and 'plants' with few if any 'completer finishers'. This means that everyone likes to talk, wants their own ideas to be accepted by all and relies on others to take the follow-through actions. Another role that is often lacking in many teams is that of 'monitor evaluator' – this person is often seen as trying to prevent things from happening by introducing balance and reality into the discussions.

Belbin's (1981) research showed that effective teams were comprised of between 5 and 7 members and contained a blend of team role types. As there are 9 team role types people need to use more than one type, for instance a person may act as a plant at the beginning of a task but as a specialist later on. A team of plants might be very creative but be unlikely to implement the ideas, conversely a team of implementers might be very practical but would lack the creativity to break new ground.

If you are working in a team and you are suffering any of the problems below then by using Belbin this is how you could resolve them.

Margerison and McCann

Apart from Belbin, the other major theorists on team roles are Margerison and McCann who have spent many years working with teams and along with Belbin are the most influential people in this field. Through their experience they have found that many teams fail because they have no clear picture of where they are heading or do not understand what their purpose is. They created the model shown in Figure 17.4 overleaf which illustrates the different types of work that are conducted in any team.

This model is very much a business model but can be used by all types of teams and for an organisation to be successful they need to be aware that each of these functions must be carried out effectively.

Margerison and McCann also created a number of techniques that would help to improve team performance which are shown on their Team Management Wheel shown in Figure 17.5. Margerison and McCann determined that everyone fits somewhere on the wheel depending on their personality. For example, a thruster organiser is a person who likes to make things happen and organise others. This team management wheel has been tested worldwide and has been actively endorsed by a number of major corporations, including Hewlett Packard, Unigate, Dupont and many others.

Margerison and McCann (1985) saw roles in terms of those who were most happily suited to innovating, promoting, developing, organising, producing, inspecting, maintaining and advising as follows:

Reporter advisers: these people are good at generating information and gathering it together so that it can be understood. They are patient and prepared to hold decisions until the situation is understood. They can often be perceived to be delayers but the reason for this perception is that they like to be accurate and won't make wild suggestions. They are valuable to a group because they offer support to other members but don't try to organise them. They ensure that the job is done correctly and are often very knowledgeable and well-liked.

Creator innovators: these people create ideas which may contradict and go against existing ideas. They are independent and look to experiment and develop their ideas regardless of others. They will work at an idea until it comes to fruition so often need time to develop ideas and like to talk through and air their views even if this goes against what the group is doing.

Problem	Solution
Underachievement	Needs a good co-ordinator or finisher.
Conflict	Needs a team worker or strong co-ordinator.
Poor performance	Needs a resource investigator, innovator or shaper.
Error prone teams	Needs an evaluator.
New teams	Needs a strong shaper to get started.
Uncompetitive	Needs an innovator.

Figure 17.3 Solving team problems using Belbin

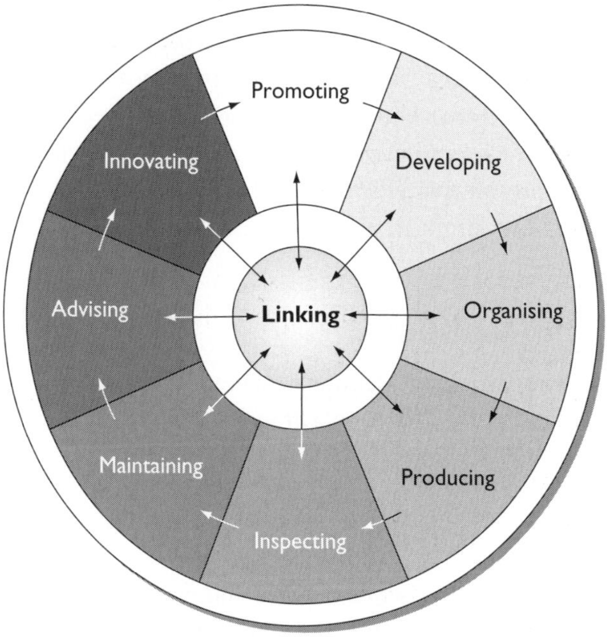

Figure 17.4 Margerison and McCann's different areas of work conducted in a team

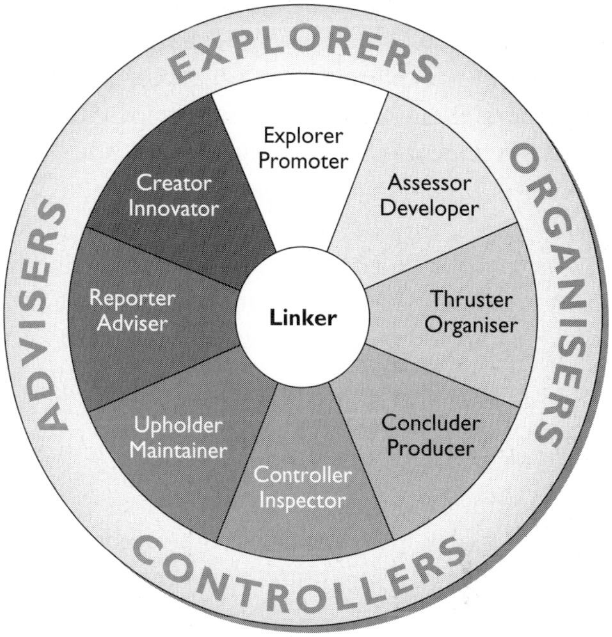

Figure 17.5 Margerison and McCann's team management wheel

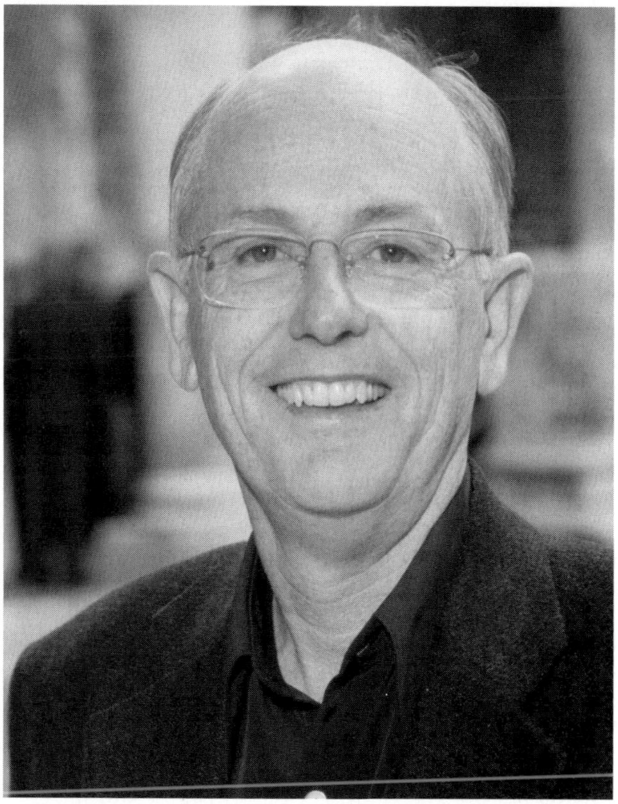

Margerison and McCann team theorists

Explorer promoters: these people are good at taking up an idea and generating enthusiasm for it. They enjoy exploring what people from other groups are doing so that they can compare their ideas. They are good at making contacts and finding information and resources to help the team or task. They are capable of pushing an idea but are not the best at organising or controlling it. These people are often influential and will act as the voice for the group when giving feedback.

Assessor developers: these people like new ideas to experiment and test. They work best at analysing different options and developing proposals prior to a decision. They also like organising activities by pushing other people's ideas forward and organising time keeping by creating a schedule.

Thruster organisers: these people make things happen as they enjoy getting the groups ideas into practice. This can mean that they are sometimes prone to impatience and may rush into putting an idea into action when it is not the best approach. These are the ones who may cause conflict as they sometimes ruffle feathers.

Concluder producers: these people take pride in completing tasks to a good standard on a regular basis. They feel fulfilled if plans and schedules are met and like to work to procedures and routines. They are the complete opposite to the creator innovators who dislike routines and want variety and different challenges. When working in a team they will look to use their existing skills in preference to learning new ones.

Controller inspectors: these people enjoy detailed work and are careful and meticulous. They will spend a lot of time concentrating on the task at hand. They like ideas to be well thought out before being implemented as they look for quality not quantity of ideas. They are very different to explorer promoters who need variety and spend very little time concentrating.

Upholder maintainers: these people are good at ensuring that the team is operationally sound. They take pride in maintaining the physical and social sides of work and are often the team's 'conscience' by providing support/help to other team members. They will have strong views on how the team should be run and if they become upset they can become rather obstinate. When they are motivated in the task they are a great source of strength and energy.

Think about it

Margerison and McCann's roles are similar to Belbin's roles. Try to match up the roles of team members suggested by both theorists.

Different team roles

Belbin's theory is only one of many such theories with relation to teamwork and below is a more general look at teamwork roles. The general team roles are the ideal roles needed for getting the team task completed or the team problem solved. As a team member, you will likely find yourself engaging in many of these roles during your time at college or within a work based team.

Simulation

Frank, the health and fitness lecturer has asked Alan, Jill, Mohammad, Nick, Kate and Nell to create a fitness programme for the whole group to last for one month. Unfortunately they are struggling to come up with a fitness programme as they are unorganised and this has led to conflict. They ask you for help as your team has created a similar programme. You suggest that they identify their individual strengths and characteristics and assume this role within the team.

Alan – is very assertive and considerate towards other people's views and will ensure that everyone has the opportunity to speak. Alan is a very motivated person and believes in setting an example for people to follow.

Jill – enjoys taking notes which helps her to understand and offer input. She also dislikes time wasting and will always keep track of the time during a team activity.

Mohammad – dislikes conflict and will always act as a mediator as he hates bad feeling within teams. He does this by airing out the conflicts to find a solution and will never take sides. Mohammad is also a good listener and will always remember the key points mentioned during group discussion and mention them throughout the task.

Nick – is often seen as a bit of a problem causer as he always questions the validity of peoples ideas and will always offer alternative solutions. This can cause conflict at times, even though he is always the first to acknowledge a good idea.

Kate – has good listening skills and will ensure that the team stays focused on the task which this makes her a good team leader. She also ensures that no one person will dominate and prevent others from taking part.

Nell – likes to take a back seat when doing tasks but will support the actions of others.

Decide which role each of the team members should be assuming within the group to achieve their goal. Relate the roles to Belbin's 9 divisions of team roles.

Think about it

Using the team roles below identify which divisions they fit under within Margerison and McCann's division of team roles. Note they are likely to fit under more than one heading and people can assume more than one role within a team.

Team scribe: this role involves recording the major points, actions and decisions of the team. Having a record of what was accomplished or decided is important for the team. This role of scribe should be rotated amongst team members.

Timekeeper: one problem teams have is wasting time or not getting through everything they need to do to complete the task. The team should decide how much time it plans to spend on each element of the task and it is the timekeeper's responsibility to inform and alert the team as time passes. Often, the timekeeper may give the team updates after every few minutes depending on the time given for the task and the nature of the exercise.

Information/opinion seeker: this role involves asking other team members for their ideas or opinions.

Clarifier/summarizer: this role requires someone to be a good listener and to be able to identify the important points raised during the discussion stages of the task. The clarifier/summarizer will sum up what has been said by all team members to give the team the opportunity to reflect on what has been said and decide if the team is progressing. Continued talking without some sort of summarisation will often be frustrating to a team and unproductive.

Orienter: this role also requires good listening skills as the orienter is the person who speaks up when it appears that the team is straying from the task. Teams can find that their discussion and ideas drift away from the main focus of the activity and this may be irrelevant to the task. The orienter is the person who notices this and points out to the team that the discussion may be going in the wrong direction.

Reality tester: when new ideas are proposed, the reality tester asks the team if the ideas will work. The reality tester may be the person who will say, 'Yes, it is a great idea, but do we have the time to accomplish it.' or 'I think that idea has merit, but how are we going to find the tools to implement the idea.' The reality tester focuses the team on discussing the feasibility of ideas that are generated.

Team maintenance roles

These roles aid the team in maintaining the right attitude for getting the task completed. If you have been in a team where the team just doesn't seem to have the right 'chemistry' or can't work together, then it is likely that some of these team maintenance roles have gone unfilled.

Harmoniser: conflict and disagreement in a team is natural and a successful team will often have had some disagreement amongst its team members. The harmoniser is a levelheaded team member who tries to reconcile these differences and ensure they don't get personal. When discussions get heated, the harmoniser is the person who steps in to sort it out.

Gatekeeper: have you ever been on a team where someone dominates the discussion or some people never say anything? The gatekeeper is the person who tries to ensure that all members participate. If someone is dominating the conversation, the gatekeeper may say, 'let's hear what other members of the team have to say'. The gatekeeper focuses on getting all team members involved and preventing any one team member from dominating the team to the point that others are no longer interested in participating.

Encourager: like the harmoniser, the encourager is the person who tries to keep the team moving. The encourager offers praise to help maintain team unity and is the person who offers reinforcement when appropriate.

Compromiser: this is the mediator for the team. When a team finds itself with opposing positions, the compromiser is the person who understands the different viewpoints and has the ability to find common points within each position. The compromiser focuses on resolving conflicts so the team can get back on track and move toward some middle position that will satisfy all team members.

Standard setter: the role of the standard setter is to be the role model for team member behaviour. This is the person who shows through his or her own behaviour what is expected of a team member. The standard setter also ensures that the team strives for success through good co-ordination.

Devil's advocate takes a position opposite to that held by the team to ensure that all sides of an issue are considered.

Assessment activity 17-P3, 17-M1, 17-D1

Refer back to a team activity you have done during your studies and analyse and evaluate the roles of each of the team members.

Other major theorists

Lewin

Kurt Lewin was an American psychologist. Born in Germany he was concerned with problems of motivation of individuals and of groups. His work opened up a new realm of psychological investigation. His writings include A Dynamic Theory of Personality (1935), Principles of Topological Psychology (1936), The Conceptual Representation and Measurement of Psychological Forces (1938) and Resolving Social Conflicts (1947).

Kurt Lewin is universally recognised as the founder of modern social psychology. He pioneered the use of theory within teamwork, using experimentation to test hypothesis and created an entire discipline called group dynamics and action research.

He is well known for his term 'life space' and his work on group dynamics as well as t-groups. Lewin's commitment to applying psychology to the problems of society led to the development of the Research Centre for Group Dynamics. From this centre the following six major program areas were tackled.

1 Group productivity: why it is that groups are so ineffective in getting things done?
2 Communication: how influence is spread throughout a group.
3 Social perception: how a person's group affected the way they perceived social events.
4 Intergroup relations.
5 Group membership: how individuals adjust to these conditions.
6 Training leaders: improving the functioning of groups (t-groups).

Lewin's group dynamics has been utilised in areas such as educational facilities, industrial settings and communities. It is also relevant to the public services as they all work in teams and by applying Lewin's theories, public services will have an idea of what motivates them and what they need to do to work effectively. They also gain an understanding of how important communication is to do their job in the community along with how bad teamwork and communication will be perceived by the public and the consequences this will lead to (loss of faith in public services). The theories of Lewin state that group dynamics can be improved or even learnt through effective training and this type of training is core to all public services workers at the beginning of their careers.

Adair

John Adair understood that for any team to respond to leadership, it needed a clearly defined task, and the achievement of that task is related to the needs of the team and the individuals within that team.

This means that the team leader needs to identify the needs of the individuals along with what motivates them and what they want from the task against the teams needs of achieving the task.

The team leader must concentrate on the small central area in the model shown in Figure 17.6 where the 3 circles overlap – the 'action to change' area. To do this, the team leader must perform the following funtions:

Planning – define the team task or purpose and make a workable plan.

Initiating – explain why the plan is necessary, allocate tasks to team members and set team standards.

Controlling – influence the pace of activities by ensuring all actions move towards the objective, keeping discussions relevant and guiding the team to a decision.

Supporting – encourage and discipline the team and individuals by creating team spirit, relieve any tension and reconcile disagreements.

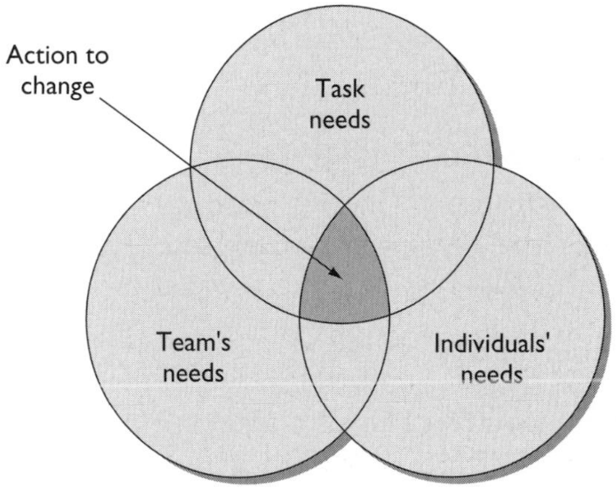

Figure 17.6 Adair's team model

Informing – share any new information with the team, receive information from the team and summarise suggestions and ideas.

Evaluating – discuss the consequences of a proposed solution, evaluate the team performance on completion and ensure that the team members evaluate their own performance.

Other models

The main theorists with relation to other models are:

Wilfred Bion stated that groups operate on two levels, the work level where concern is for completing the task and the unconscious level where group members act as if they had made assumptions about the purpose of the group such as dependency, flight, fight and pairings.

Bennis focused on the difference between a manager and a leader as he believes a manager administers, maintains and controls whilst a leader innovates, develops and focuses on the needs of the team. He also identified two clear types of leadership which were transformational leadership (doing the right thing) and transactional leadership (doing things right).

Kurt Lewin focused on the behaviour of leaders and identified 3 leadership styles. These were autocratic as in directing someone, democratic as in facilitating the ideas of others and laissez-faire leadership. More information on leadership styles can be found in the leadership chapter (Chapter 3).

Much of this work from the theorists above helped Joseph Luft and Harry Ingham to develop the human interaction model known as Johari window (see below)

	Known to self	Not Know to Self
Known to others		
Not known to others		

This window divides personal awareness into four different types, as represented by its four quadrants: open, hidden, blind, and unknown. The lines dividing the four panes are like window shades, which can move as an interaction progresses.

The four panes of the window represent the following:

Open: The open area is that part of our conscious self – our attitudes, behaviour, motivation, values, way of life – of which we are aware and which is known to others.

Hidden: Our hidden area cannot be known to others unless we disclose it. There is that which we freely keep within ourselves, and that which we retain out of fear. The degree to which we share ourselves with others (disclosure) is the degree to which we can be known.

Blind: There are things about ourselves which we do not know, but that others can see more clearly; or things we imagine to be true of ourselves for a variety of reasons but that others do not see at all. When others say what they see (feedback), in a supportive, responsible way, and we are able to hear it; in that way we are able to test the reality of who we are and are able to grow.

Unknown: We are more rich and complex than that which we and others know, but from time to time something happens – is felt, read, heard, dreamed – something from our unconscious is revealed. Then we "know" what we have never "known" before.

Assessment activity 17-P1

Produce a fact sheet which explains in detail the major theories, which support the development of teams in public service.

Types of teams

There are many different types of teams within the workplace and teams are essential for any type of business or agency to function effectively. Teams can help increase individual performance and creativity and give employees ownership and control of their work and a higher commitment to the objectives of the workplace. This will ultimately lead to greater job satisfaction because employees are motivated to work which leads to less absenteeism and a decrease in staff turnover.

Theory into practice

For each of the key words below identify one public service team that would fit under the following headings. The first one has been filled in for you:

- Geographical – one example of a geographical team is the CID within the police service when they combine their effects and work together to detect a criminal such as a murderer who has committed murders in a number of different constabulary areas. They will be required to work together and share vital information such as evidence gathered and witness statements along with any significant leads. This is commonly seen on programmes such as Crime Watch.
- Divisional
- Sub-divisional
- Departmental
- Sectional
- Specialist
- Multi-disciplinary
- Multi-agency (multiple public services working together)

Assessment activity 17-P4, 17-M2

In the form of a short report, describe the types of teams, which operate within two public services

In order to get a **merit** your report must present a logical and well structured analysis of the types of teams operating within the public services.

Shift/watch team

The shift watch system is unique to the public services and involves a work pattern that means enough people are working at any given time to deal with the demand from the public.

An excellent example of this is fire-fighters on duty, as a fire station needs to be staffed 24 hours per day. In order to do this, the fire services adopt a system of watches. Each watch has a designated colour such as red. Each of these watches works with a rotation period of 8 days, comprising of 2 days, 2 nights and 4 days off duty. The day shift is 9 hours and the night shift is 15 hours averaging at 42 hours a week.

Fire-fighters rely on each other on a day to day basis when putting out fires or rescuing people and for them to carry out their duties they need to work as a team. When a fire engine is called out to respond to an incident there will be a team of fire-fighters with different roles and responsibilities:

Station officer: this person is in charge of the other fire-fighters and when arriving at the scene will weigh up the situation and give out instructions on how to deal with the incident.

Engine driver: the primary role of this person is to get the rest of the crew to the scene of the incident in a quick and safe manner. This allows the other fire-fighters to fully prepare for the incident they are attending. It is also the driver's job to look after the engine whilst at the incident.

Fire-fighters in action

Pump operator: another fire-fighter will have the job of pump operator. This person must ensure that there is enough water to tackle the fire. The pump operator must find the nearest water hydrant on arrival and then ensure that hose pressure is suitable for the situation.

Fire-fighters: the standard fire-fighters have the role of 'kitting up' whilst the engine driver takes them to the scene. On arrival it is their job, under the guidance of the station officer, to prevent the fire or incident getting any worse. If they have to enter a building with poor visibility or when tackling a blaze they will always work in at least pairs.

So far we have looked at the fire-fighters who can be found on the scene of a incident. However there are other members of the team who will often not be at the scene:

Station commander: this person is in overall charge of running the fire station. When the other fire-fighters are responding to the incident it is the job of the station commander to check response times and will be in radio contact with the crew to give them any advice or information that they may need to know.

Duty person: this person is in charge of communication at the fire station and receives all emergency calls (via a call slip). It is this person's job to inform the other fire-fighters of a call by sounding the alarm. This person will try and give the responding crew as much information as possible with regard to the incident so the fire-fighters can prepare and collect any specialist equipment that they may need. This person will also log all calls during the shift in a logbook.

The sub-officer: this person will investigate the cause of every incident that the firefighters respond to. This could involve interviewing witnesses or examining the scene of the incident. This person will record the findings of the investigation in the form of a report and store it for future reference.

Think about it

Read the scenario below and think about the roles of each of the police officers likely to be part of the team in charge of catching the robbers. What other services are likely to be involved and what is their role?

It is 3.30 pm on the 10th of May and a call has just come through to the communication centre that a bank robbery has taken place. One of the robbers who is armed has been trapped in the building when the emergency shutters came down after the alarm was activated, along with 3 civilians and 3 members of staff. The other robber managed to escape by rolling under the shutters and is now fleeing north bound out of the city in a stolen car.

Assessment activity 17-P6

Produce examples of good practice in relation to two teams within a specified public service.

Characteristics of effective teams

Roles and norms

All teams develop a set of roles and norms. It is essential that the role structure enables the team to cope effectively with the requirements of the task and assignment of roles should be to members who can perform them effectively. Norms will develop in a team, whether or not they are actively discussed.

Group norms: norms represent the expectations within the group for appropriate behaviour of group members. Guirdham (1995) suggests there are 4 norms that are generally expected by team members in every team. These are:

- fairness
- reciprocity
- reasonableness
- role expectations.

Team culture

For a team to be successful you need to create a team culture – a group identity and ethos. The main way to create a team culture is through valuing other people in the group which leads to increased trust, increased self-esteem of the team members, a positive attitude towards the task and increased productivity through the development of expertise and quality.

Team identity

A team can create its own identity through working together and agreeing common goals

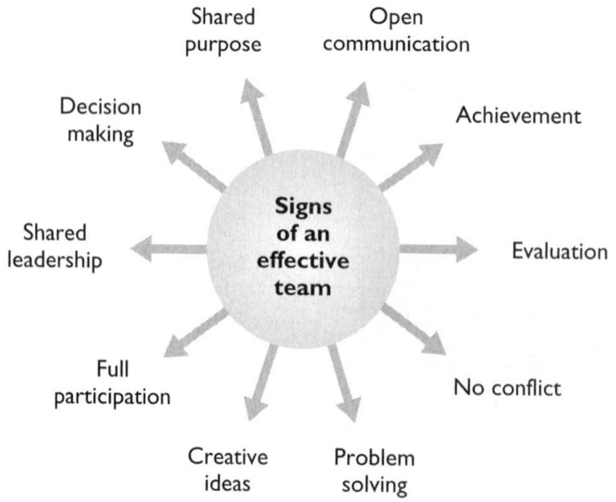

Figure 17.7 Characteristics of effective teams

along with a shared purpose such as agreeing on what to do and who should do what. Team identify can also be visual in the sense that a team may have a name or wear the same kit.

A team will not be successful if they are divided and unequal as there will be no stability in the long term. To ensure this does not happen and cohesion is created we need to consider the following.

Communication: Team members must engage in open interactions amongst other team members to avoid conflict and enable the decision-making process to take place. It is important for a team to develop an effective communication network so team members feel they can state their opinions, thoughts and feelings without fear and everyone can communicate.

Listening is considered as important as speaking as teams need to be able to listen and respond to others in an objective and productive way. Effective communication provides an atmosphere of trust and acceptance and a sense of community and group cohesion is high.

Trust: Before anyone will fully open up they need to trust and have faith in each other and feel that you trust them. This can be done in a number of ways such as showing a person respect by valuing everybody's opinion within the group and being open and honest with ideas and concerns. It is also done by supporting each other as team work can be stressful and different team members will want help at different stages of a task and on a particular type of task. Support is an important element because it means any problems are dealt with sensitively and not aggressively. You must also look for dependability on different peoples strengths (see Belbin's theory) so each circumstance can be handled with good judgment and thoroughness. Loyalty can also lead to trust as showing loyalty to a member of your team or the whole team shows you value them. This is important as it will eliminate potential conflict and prevent frustration.

Morale: Morale has a large effect on a team and when morale is high a team will be enthusiastic about the work of the team and function better. Good morale makes communication easier and clearer and when a team is happy, team members will feel a sense of pride in being a member of that team. Good morale gives your team a good mindset and good team spirit which often means team members become friends.

If team morale is low or needs building you can try offering treats or incentives. If multiple tasks are being done throughout a day, morale can be maintained by celebrating when a task is completed. You need to remember that it only needs one member of the team to drop their morale to effect the rest of the team.

Co-operation: Team co-operation develops when the group identity has emerged. A sign of a co-operative team is a team which is involved in an active decision-making process. Commitment is very important as team members need to feel that they belong to a team rather than just individuals within a team as effective teamwork can only be achieved when individuals work together for the success of the group rather than the success of the individual.

Role identification and responsibilities

Team members need to know their roles as this gives them a sense of ownership and they can see how they make a difference. For a team to be successful every team member needs to be involved by having a role in the team and having their contributions respected and appreciated. In certain circumstances team members may have to take on more than one role in the group in order to accomplish the task. An effective team will be clear about why they need to work as a team and develop mutually agreed goals for completing the task.

Flexibility

Group members should be flexible and perform different tasks as needed. A successful team is fluid, open to opinions and feelings, hard working, fun and adaptive to changing conditions.

Empowerment

Empowerment is when team members are confident about the team's ability to overcome obstacles to complete the task. A sense of mutual respect enables members to share responsibilities, help each other out and take initiatives to meet the challenges of the task. Members have opportunities to grow and learn new skills. There is a sense of personal as well as collective power.

Achievement

Effective teams produce significant results through a commitment to high standards, effective decision-making and problem-solving methods that result in optimum results and encourage participation. To achieve this, teams will need to set goal specifications. It is very important for team members to have common goals for team achievement and shared goals is one of the definitions of the concept 'team'. After goals have been set then a process or plan which involves a successful solution to a problem or adequate planning techniques will need to be put into action to complete the task.

Recognition and appreciation

Individual team accomplishments are frequently recognised by the team leader, and team members by celebrating milestones, accomplishments, and events. Members feel highly regarded within the team and valued by the organisation. They experience a sense of personal satisfaction in relation to their contributions.

Think about it

How could you actively recognise and reward the efforts of a team and its members?

Create a list of 5 possible ways.

Team profiling

By raising people's awareness of their role within a team, team members will be able to handle conflict positively as they will gain a better understanding of what motivates other team members. It will also help team members realise when they may need to modify their behaviour for the good of the team. This behaviour may not be a natural response.

Think about it

So far we have looked at the various aspects of a successful team. Decide which ones you think are the most important by listing the following aspects in order from the most important to the least important. Explain the reasons for your chosen order.

- communication
- trust
- morale
- co-operation
- role identification
- flexibility
- empowerment
- achievement
- recognition
- team profiling.

Can you give an example of a time you failed as a team because one of your top 5 aspects was missing?

Being an effective team member

So far we have looked at what makes a successful team but you can do a lot to ensure team success by fully contributing to the task, actively listening to other peoples opinions and ideas along with providing your own ideas when appropriate. You should maintain a good sense of humour and provide help and support to other team members and seek help and support when you need it. An effective team member will be accountable for their actions and the team as a whole and co-operate with the other team members to achieve the team goals. An effective team member should look to avoid conflict but if conflict occurs they should use their interpersonal skills to help resolve the conflict. Finally they should also seek feedback from the other members of the group on their performance after a task is over and act upon any suggestions made when doing future tasks.

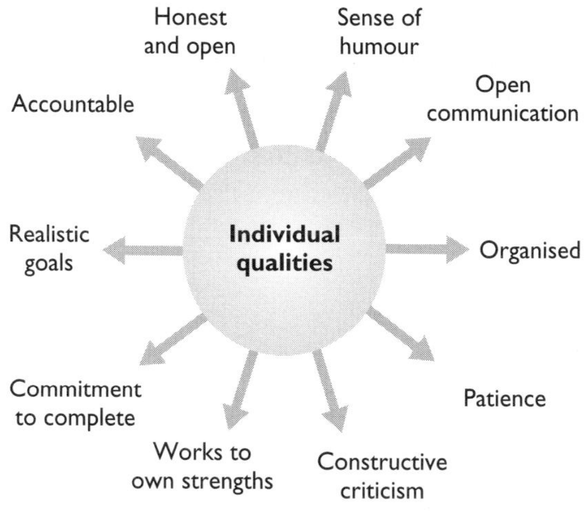

Figure 17.8 Being an effective team member

Being an effective team leader

Think about it

What do you think are the roles and qualities of a good team leader?

A team is a group of people with different backgrounds, varied skills and abilities and different experiences. It is the job of the team leader to bring these different people together to work as a cohesive group. The team leader is the person who manages the team and correct use of authority and delegation of responsibility along with the ability to understand each member of the team are vital qualities for a team leader. The list below hightlights the range of qualities a good team leader should possess:

- making sure that all team members are clear on the goals and purpose of the team
- inspiring other members of the team by being an active participant of the team
- the ability to listen to the opinions of team members and not dominate
- the ability to encourage team members to give their best
- the ability to handle conflicts with tact and firmness and find resolutions to team conflict
- being flexible enough to accommodate others' opinions and ideas
- accessible to all members of the team
- being able to make appropriate decisions
- being able to deal with people by possessing good interpersonal skills
- getting the team to respect the authority of the team leader
- getting the task done with maximum efficiency and minimum fuss
- maintaining a clear focus on the goals and purposes of the team
- being able to promote teamwork within their group and value diversity
- giving praise and thanks when tasks are well done.

A team leader is not a supervisor but a member of the team who is willing to take on the coordination functions for the team. The team leader is more like a facilitator, taking each member's input and ideas, helping team members to coordinate their tasks and schedules and helping and supporting all team members. The team leader is the contact point for communication between the team members and should encourage and maintain open communication.

Think about it

Write 10 words that describe a good leader and 10 words that describe a poor leader

Who can be a team leader?

Any person can be a team leader and everyone should have the opportunity to fulfil this role. Admittedly some people will make better leaders than others but as long as a person is interested and willing with an idea of how to communicate well, understands the needs of others, knows how to offer support and is flexible then they have the basis to develop their leadership skills.

Often the role of a team leader will be rotated between the members of the team. The advantages of this are that it helps everyone in the team to get a chance to experience the leadership role and realise their leadership potential. This experience will make them a better team member and leader. It also encourages leadership development among less dominant, introverted and shy members and facilitates the development of the whole team.

Advantages of effective teams

Effective teams are more successful in implementing complex plans, they develop more creative solutions to difficult problems, they have a higher level of commitment and have more people who are prepared to help implement an idea or plan.

Another advantage of effective teams is overall achievement of objectives on time. To ensure that a team you are involved in is successful at meeting its objectives, focus on one clear goal for the team and break down the goal to define a role and one objective for each team member. To do this, ask team members for ideas on how the goals could be refined and ensure that they are clear of their role to prevent overlap and conflict. When putting an agreed objective into place the team leader should always ensure that it has SMART targets – Specific, Measurable, Agreed, Realistic and Time limited.

The following list highlights the advantages of effective teams:

- more likely to achieve results within the time set
- more likely to find the solutions to complex tasks by pooling expertise and knowledge
- collective decision-making leads to less conflict and makes implementation of possible solutions easier
- higher level of morale and ownership through participative decision-making
- more likely to have good efficient communication which is not fragmented or problematic
- problems are exposed to a greater diversity of perspectives, knowledge, skill and experience.

Case study

The Armed Forces involvement in the overthrowing of Suddam Hussain in Iraq is an example of effective teamwork for the following reasons. Firstly, it was a multi-agency effort as the Army, RAF and Navy were all involved and had to work together to control the land, air and sea in and around Iraq. Secondly, they took control of the country in a very short space of time and with minimal casualties. The main reason for this was that they shared their expertise and knowledge on combat tactics along with working closely with troops from other countries such as USA and Australia. Thirdly, the success of the Armed Forces in Iraq was also helped by people power as the amount of troops in and around Iraq were great and these troops believed in what they were doing and therefore took the ultimate risk of willingly putting their life on the line.

Teamwork was also made easier because of clear leadership and clear objectives from the government and senior officers. One of the British forces key objectives was to take control of Basra.

However, as with all teams, the Armed Forces didn't always get it right and poor communication on a number of occasions lead to a number of incidents where their own troops were killed in what the Armed Forces term friendly fire.

Think about it

If Britain suffered a terrorist attack on a similar scale to September 11th how would the various public services work together and what would be their roles?

Skills and abilities of effective teams

Communication

When speaking in a group, you should ensure that communication is short and concise and focused on the task. It should be as simple as possible and always be honest. Don't pretend to be an expert if you are not and always ask questions for clarification. When someone else is speaking you should listen and be an active receiver. There is a difference between hearing and listening. Hearing is purely physical whereas listening involves not only hearing sounds but also responding.

The cornerstones to effective speaking are clarity, simplicity, vividness, preparedness, naturalness and conciseness. To ensure that communication is active in your teams consider the following points.

- be open and responsive to problems when they occur and be prepared to talk about them as a group
- respect and seek the opinion of all members of the group or communication will break down as people feel alienated
- compassion: always exhibit concern, empathy, sympathy, remorse as required as this puts people at ease
- generosity: go beyond what is expected or required of you
- honesty: learn from your mistakes and talk with the group about what you've learned.

Inter-personal skills

Inter-personal skills are the skills and abilities you have to help you deal with situations and behave in the right manner. Inter-personal skills are important for personal and professional reasons and are necessary for relating and working with others such as verbal and non-verbal communication, listening and giving and receiving feedback.

When preparing to listen, the first step is to avoid external and internal distractions. These can be external environmental noises or internal distractions such as thinking about how you are going to respond rather than concentrating on what is being said. To demonstrate you are actively listening to the speaker you should face the speaker squarely, have an open posture, maintain eye contact and acknowledge them by nodding your head or smiling.

Another inter-personal skill is assertiveness. Being assertive involves stating your point clearly and positively. When developing an assertive approach, firstly think of how you would like to be treated. Most people respect someone who is honest and direct, but you should be respectful of others rights and feelings as well as your own. By showing respect for your own feelings and those of others you can achieve your desired goals.

Being able to understand and work with others in teams or groups is another important aspect of interpersonal skills. One of the best ways of developing these skills is through small group work which provides the opportunity to share ideas, hear other perspectives, to benefit from the experience and expertise of others and to receive help and support.

We all interact with other people on a day-to-day basis so it is worth reviewing and constantly improving our interpersonal effectiveness. For people who are going into the public services these skills are crucial. All employers demand people who can communicate well and work with others.

The following tips will help you improve your inter-personal skills:

- understand effective communication and identify barriers that prevent it
- assess your own communication style
- learn how certain behaviours affect others
- use body language to help get your message across
- learn how to give and receive constructive feedback
- sharpen up your listening skills.

Management skills

The key management skills that a person needs to develop are

- presentation skills
- time management
- delegation
- managing people/leadership
- communication
- planning.

Presentation skills: usually working with others involves some form of presentation that may even be assessed. Giving presentations is a key employment related skill that needs to be learned. Effective speaking is a skill that can be taught and practised.

For many, making a presentation or giving a talk is a daunting prospect. This may be a result of limited experience or a fear of being the centre of attention or a worry that they may not give a perfect performance.

Presentation skills are important in a public services role

The key to a good presentation is to find a balance between too much information and poor preparation. The latter may be due to a lack of or inaccurate information. The presentation should be clear, accurate and analytical. Remember it must be relevant to the audience. Good knowledge of the subject provides confidence for getting up and delivering the presentation. It is a good idea to consult several types of sources, such as newspapers, journals, periodicals, government publications, Internet and reference books for a higher quality presentation.

The structure of a presentation should start with an introduction to catch the audience's attention. The middle or main portion of the presentation is where the argument or explanation is provided which should consist of key points. Finally, the closing or conclusion summarises the main points. It is also useful to include a concluding statement, perhaps related to the objectives stated in the introduction.

Remember to rehearse the presentation to help reduce feelings of nervousness and increase feelings of control.

Think about it

Why are the following aspects an important part of a presentation.

- clear voice
- relevant information
- eye contact
- gestures
- posture
- clothes.

Time management: a successful team is one that manages its time. Time can be managed effectively by determining which task or element of a task is most important. A well-managed team will also look to control the distractions that waste time and break your flow.

Delegation: the key to delegation is to delegate as much as possible so team members feel empowered and to delegate it equally by identifying people with prior experience. Apart from giving a person responsibility for the completion of the task you should also give them ownership. For example, you may say something along these lines 'Tom I want you to tie all the rope ends to form the sides of the rope bridge and once that has been done can you ensure that it is secure and safe. If you are unsure give me a shout or call over Tim as he his good at this kind of stuff'.

Managing people: the main way of managing people is through motivation. This can be done in a number of ways from achievement of the task, recognition of individual contribution, the role and responsibilities given to the team members and finally making the team members feel valued and trusted.

Planning: you can't always plan for every eventuality as there may be unexpected difficulties, but planning the most effective way of completing the task helps a group to achieve when others around are failing. Just think about the group exercises you have done – if you discussed the possible solutions to the problem and what you need to do, then you have shown some planning.

The planning process helps you to:

- take stock of your current position
- identify precisely what is to be achieved
- detail precisely who will do what, when and where it will be done and why and how the task will be achieved
- assess the impact of your ideas to solving the problem
- evaluate the success of the task and what you could have done differently.

Problem solving

The following tips should be followed when solving a group problem:

Suspend judgment: this is by far the most important as the team needs to create a supportive environment where judgment and criticism are not allowed.

Brainstorm: the philosophy behind brainstorming is that the more ideas there are on the table, the more likely a suitable solution will emerge. This stage of the process is a 'freewheeling' exchange of ideas to get together a list of as many possibilities as you can. Remember to write all ideas down, no matter how far-fetched they may seem and to maintain an open mind at all times.

Develop a positive attitude: the team need to be enthusiastic and optimistic for success which can be achieved by encouraging all team members to be involved in ideas. This can be done by developing a positive attitude towards all the ideas presented by the various team members even if some seem wild and unrealistic.

Use checklists: it is always a good idea to write down the possible solutions and ideas to solving a problem as it sends a clear message to the team that everyone's ideas are valued which helps to create a supportive environment. Secondly, recording all ideas will ensure that nothing of importance is forgotten and it gives the team an opportunity to go back and combine parts of one idea with parts of another.

Be confident: as a team be confident in your ideas and have faith in your creativity as many great ideas are met negatively in the first instance.

Encourage others: praise and encouragement are the fuel for creative ideas; it enable ideas to flow freely and motivates team members. Never just criticise or reject an idea, instead offer praise and encourage your fellow team members to keep up the good work.

Decision-making

We make decisions every day of our lives and when making a decision you need to consider many factors, for example you may have to make a decision to change something or a decision may be based on an opinion from another person. When we make these changes we will often weigh up the pros and cons of a decision by looking at it from different perspectives and predicting the outcome. This is no different from when we make decisions within a team or during employment.

Decision-making can be a difficult area for any type of team as it involves power issues and offers potential conflict. Decisions are best made by consensus as this allows all team members to be involved in the process but it also takes more time. The consensus approach will ensure that all team members have had time to express their opinions or if they have not expressed an opinion then they can back an idea presented by another team member. A consensus decision is not a majority vote as a consensus decision is one that each team member agrees on, even if it is not their first choice idea. This may take longer to achieve than a straight majority decision but a consensual decision will ensure that everyone is committed to seeing the idea prevail and be successful.

The other way that decisions can be made within a team is randomly by one member, either by the group leader or the team member who has prior knowledge or expertise.

The diagram below illustrates the stages of making a decision.

Assessment activity 17-P5, 17-M3

Create a charter that could be used by public service personnel to help them identify the characteristics, skills and attributes of effective teams.

Conduct a short presentation that shows actual examples of how the teams within various public services work effectively together.

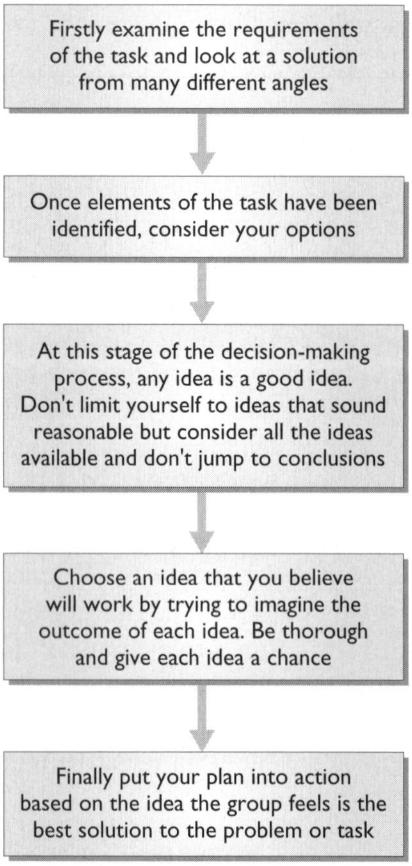

Figure 17.9 Steps to making a decision

Barriers to effective teamwork

Theory into practice

Describe 10 possible barriers to effective teamwork and create an A4 poster that could be placed either in the workplace or on the classroom wall to remind people of the possible barriers before they undertake a team task.

Whenever a group of people get together in a team they each bring different values, beliefs, expectations, history, education, agendas, goals, personality style and communication style. The key to effective teams is recognising these differences and a willingness to be flexible by accepting and understanding other people's views, opinions or communication style.

Role ambiguity

Group dynamics can be a barrier to an effective team if the group are suffering from role ambiguity. This is likely to occur if the team have not yet decided on roles and responsibilities to suit their strengths and character. It could also be down to certain members assuming dysfunctional team roles such as:

- asserting authority or superiority in manipulating the team or certain members to his or her own agenda; domination usually takes the form of asserting higher status, giving directions authoritatively, using expert knowledge or interrupting the contributions of others.
- seeking attention to himself or herself through such things as boasting, reporting on personal achievements, acting in unusual ways (arriving late or leaving early) or volunteering for all presentations.
- being negative and stubborn, resistant to all team actions, disagreeing and opposing without or beyond reason and attempting to maintain or revive an issue after the team has rejected it.
- bringing down other team members by deflating the status of others, expressing disapproval of the values, actions or feelings of others, attacking the team or the team's problem area, joking in a negative or sarcastic manner or attempting to take credit for the work of others.
- trying to do the least amount of work possible by not getting involved in team discussions, sitting quietly (or doing other work) during meetings, not volunteering for team assignments, presentations or action items and never accepting any leadership responsibilities.
- making cynical remarks, adopting a nonchalant attitude, using an excessive amount of humour or engaging in horseplay with other members.

Think about it

The following group members behaviour is causing a barrier to effective teamwork. What can be done to improve the group dynamics in this team:

Ann – enjoys being the centre of attention and will constantly interrupt other team members to get her point across.

Bryan – likes working in a team but can easily become upset if the group does not implement his point of view or ideas and this can make Bryan very difficult to work with.

Clare – spends much of her time during teamwork tasks de-motivating other team members with derisory comments when someone suggests an idea that she thinks is ineffective. However, when someone comes up with an idea she agrees with she will do her best to take over the idea and make it her own.

Desmond – believes he is a natural leader and will always try and assume this position when conducting a task even if someone else has been asked to take on the role of group leader.

Ellen – is very quiet and clearly lacks confidence and interpersonal skills. During group tasks she often works on her own and will never volunteer to help others

Fred – sees himself as the class clown and he acts no differently when working in small groups. This means that he is easily distracted and would rather have a laugh than complete the task.

Communication

Communication can be a barrier to effective teamwork if instructions given are poor (look back to the section on effective communication). Other communication barriers will occur if:

- you label or make assumptions about other team members especially if this leads you to not being able to work with them
- you try to dominate a person by ordering or lecturing them then you may find yourself meeting resistance or a cold shoulder. This is also true for people who constantly interrupt conversations or finish another person's sentences within the group. There are also the people who demoralize and criticize others
- your body language is giving incorrect signals, for example if your arms are crossed and you are not engaged with the group then it may be assumed that you are unwilling to participate.

Less obvious barriers to communication may include language, cultural, educational differences external influences such as a noisy environment as people become distracted or if a person has physical or emotional problems.

Poor leadership

Certain types of leaders can create barriers to effective teamwork. These are the people who see leadership as a dictatorship and will settle for nothing more than full control. Other aspects of poor leadership are:

- someone who has low standards and expectations of the team and its success which is likely to lead to disrespect and poor performance of the team
- lack of accountability for the performance of the team and the actions of the leader, for example a poor leader might say ' it's not my fault we failed to get across as you wouldn't listen to my instructions'
- someone who is inconsistent, for example someone who says one thing but does another
- someone who is not 'hands on' as a leader
- someone who shows little encouragement as this can lead to a drop in motivation and team members become discouraged and fragmented
- someone who doesn't have a clear goal or doesn't work towards the goal of the team/task.

Other barriers to effective teamwork

Other barriers to effective teamwork include: teams that lack commitment to completing the task, team members who have hidden agendas or individual interests, people who refuse for what ever reason to co-operate with the rest of the team and teams who lack focus and waste time.

Conflict resolution

Conflict amongst team members can create many barriers to effective teamwork as it effects motivation, lowers morale and reduces co-operation. Conflicts can arise for a variety of reasons such as different needs, values or motivations and it is important to deal with these before they fester. Conflict is not a bad thing as it can allow people to air issues that affect the teams success. However the important thing is how the conflict is managed and how people respond to conflict, which determines if the outcome is positive or negative.

Early indicators of conflict can be recognised such as poor communication and body language, a team member who is looking to use power to control others or desires power, a team member who is not satisfied with the team leader or another team member for some reason which leads to constant disagreement and when the team lacks focus on the team goals and individual objectives.

The following list shows ways in which you can try and avoid conflict:

- recognize individual differences and respect and value them
- change your attitude from a focus on 'me' to 'we'
- agree to disagree – understand healthy disagreement will build better decisions

- be open to changing your position based on new information and changed attitudes
- accept that each person has a unique point of view
- communicate frequently, openly and honestly
- get rid of individual ego
- attack the problem, not the person
- always stay calm and listen
- consider the needs of the group.

Conflict is natural and should be expected from time to time and confrontation is almost always the most effective path of action. Resolving conflict requires special skills, which can be practiced and learned. The following 3 methods are good for managing conflict:

- The first way of resolving conflict is through negotiation which is done by talking calmly and trying to resolve the situation by compromising. For example, this can be done by saying 'I respect your point of view on the subject and I expect you to respect my views'.
- The second way of resolving conflict is by being assertive and clearly stating what you want or need. An assertive person will seek external support from another person to resolve a situation and ultimately be the one who walks away if the situation can't be resolved.
- The third way of resolving conflict is by highlighting the consequences of the conflict and the problems faced if the conflict continues.

Each of the 3 methods above are good for managing conflict. However, knowing at bit more about assertiveness is vital for dealing with people in a group situation and can help to avoid conflict in the first place.

Assertiveness is expressing our thoughts, feelings, and beliefs in a direct, honest, and appropriate way. It means that we have respect both for ourself and for others. An assertive person effectively influences, listens and negotiates so that others choose to cooperate willingly.

Assertiveness is very different from aggressiveness. Aggressiveness involves expressing our thoughts, feelings, and beliefs in a way that is inappropriate and violates the rights of others. It can be either active or passive, but no matter which, it communicates an impression of disrespect. By being aggressive, we put our wants, needs and rights above those of others. We attempt to get our way by not allowing others a choice. Where assertiveness tries to find a win-win solution, aggressiveness strives for a win-lose solution.

Assertiveness is also different from non-assertiveness. Non-assertive behaviour is passive and indirect. It permits others to violate our rights and shows a lack of respect for our own needs. It communicates a message of inferiority. It creates a lose-win situation because the non-assertive person has decided that his or her own needs are secondary and opts to be a victim.

Think about it

Situation: You have just been introduced to your new team members who you have never worked with before. You are introduced to them all by their first name but unfortunately you have forgotten one of their names.

Assertive response: As soon as possible, ask, 'What is your name again?'

Non-assertive response: avoid any type of conversation where you need to use his/her name

Aggressive response: blame him/her, by saying 'You didn't speak clearly earlier, what's your name again?'

Assessment activity 17-P7, 17-M4

Create a script and act out 2 scenarios that analyse and evaluate the barriers to teamwork that may exist in 2 public services.

End of unit questions

1 Explain the importance of teamwork in an organisation and its advantages and problems.

2 Explain the functions of the team leader.

3 Describe the skills needed in a team to be effective.

4 Define and explain the key factors in team development.

5 Describe two reasons for group formation.

6 What feelings are team members likely to feel at each of these stages?

- forming
- storming
- norming
- performing

7 As team leader, how would you manage the team at each stage?

8 What do you belive is the goals of a public service team such as the fire service?

9 What are your strengths as an individual that you can bring to a group situation?

10 What is Belbins theory all about?

11 What do you think about John Adairs team model?

12 If you were a recruitment officer what would you say are the main qualities needed by a public service worker to enable them to work with others?

13 Why is communication so critical to the public service workers?

14 How do we go about making an effective decision?

15 What are common barrierss to effective teamwork?

16 When is conflict likely to occur in team situations – how can it be resolved?

Resources

Adair J, *Effective Team Building*, Gower Publishing, 1987

Adair J, *Effective Leadership*, Pan Books, 1988

Adair J, Motivation: *How to Make a Winning Team*, Pan Books, 1996

Belbin M, *Team Roles at Work*, Butterworth–Heinemann, 1996

Guirdham M, *Interpersonal Skills at Work*, Prentice Hall, 1990

Murdock A, *Personal Effectiveness*, Butterworth–Heinemann, 1993

Sallis E, *People in Organisations*, Macmillan, 1990

Website

www.homeoffice.gov.uk – Home Office

HEALTH AND FITNESS

Introduction to Unit 18

This chapter aims to highlight the importance of health and fitness generally and in the public services.

The public services need individuals who are able to think quickly and respond to a challenge and a good state of health and a reasonable level of fitness are crucial to this. In addition, if you want to be recruited into the public services you must reach certain levels of health and fitness by passing medical and fitness tests. This unit will explore the major body systems and their relationshp to health and fitness, the impact of lifestyle and nutrition and the general physical fitness tests of the public services.

This chapter has substantial links with Unit 9: Physical preparation for entry to the uniformed services which you will find in Book 1. These chapters enhance and complement each other.

Assessment

The unit is assessed internally and you may be able to use a range of assessment methods (presentations, practical activities, assignments) to produce the evidence you require. Within this unit there are lots of different activities and opportunities for discussion which will help you work to the desired grade.

Outcomes

1 Examine the main **body systems** in relation to health and fitness
2 Examine the effects of **lifestyle and nutrition** on health and fitness
3 Describe the **principles of fitness**
4 Investigate and demonstrate a range of **fitness testing** methods.

Health and fitness is an important subject to study in the public services as it will underpin much of the work you will need to do if you put on a public service uniform. The nature of public service work is such that your body may be subjected to a variety of stressors such as:

- stress
- extremes of temperature
- shift work
- physical exertion
- lack of time leading to poor diet
- disturbed sleep patterns
- physical attack or injury
- fatigue.

Body systems

Anatomy and physiology of the main body systems

Anatomy is the science of body structures; it examines how the body is organised and interconnected and what the body is made up of. Physiology is the science of body functions; it examines how tissues and organs work and the role that they fulfil. Before we examine our first body system it may be helpful for you to have some definitions of commonly used anatomical terms:

Term	Meaning	Example
Superior	Upper or above	Superior vena cava is a vein which emerges at the top of the heart.
Inferior	Lower or below	Inferior vena cava is a vein which emerges from the bottom of the heart.
Anterior or ventral	The front	The sternum (breastbone) is anterior (in front of) the heart.
Posterior or dorsal	The back	The oesophagus is posterior to (behind) the trachea.
Distal	Furthest from source	The fingers are distal from the wrist.
Proximal	Nearest to the source	The palm is proximal to the wrist.
External	Outer	The nose is an external organ.
Internal	Inner	The heart is an internal organ.

Figure 18.1 Commonly used anatomical terms

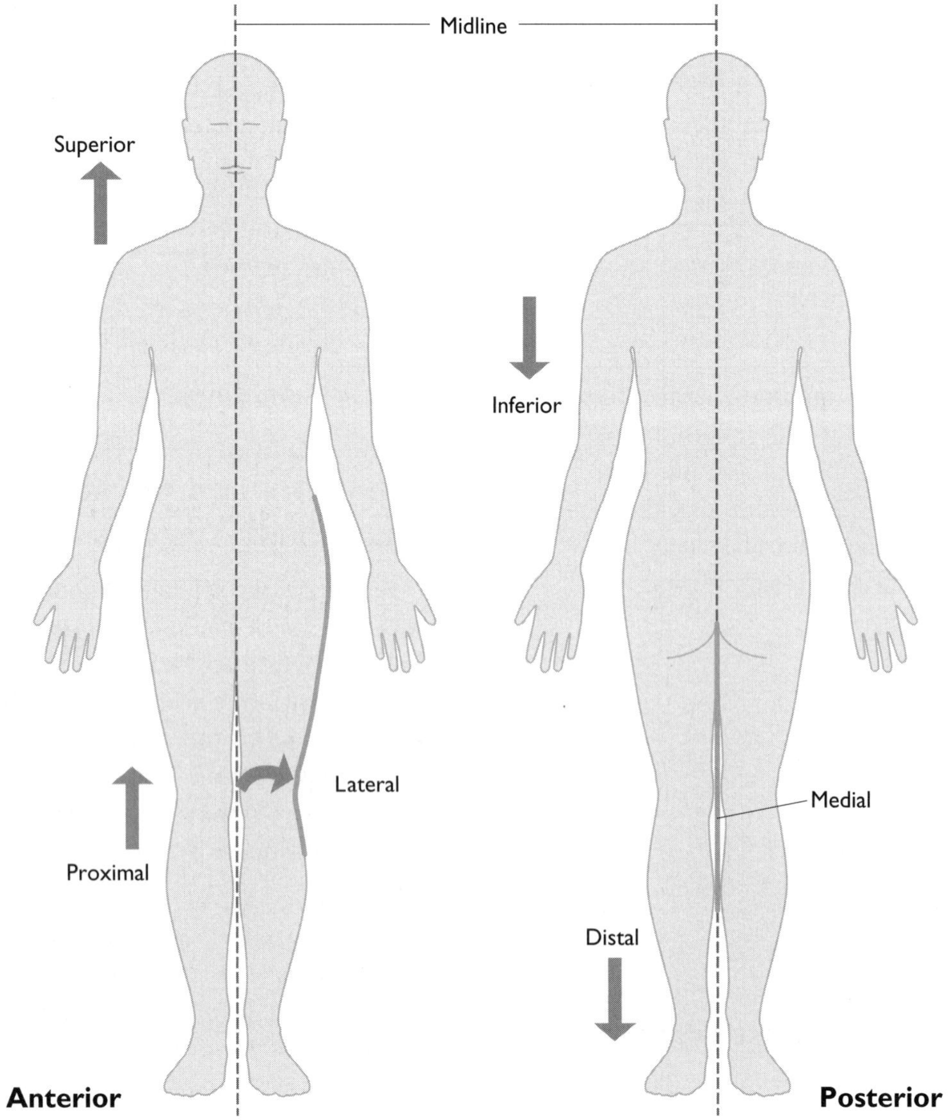

Figure 18.2 Body positions

The first part of this unit will examine the anatomy and physiology of 4 main body systems:

- the skeletal system
- the muscular system
- the cardiovascular system
- the respiratory system.

It is also important to remember that although we will examine only 4 body systems in detail there are many more which are crucial to our survival and can have a tremendous impact upon health and fitness. In brief, these are shown in Figure 18.3.

Before we proceed on to the skeletal system it is very important that you recognise that all of the body systems are integrated and interrelated. They operate in a dependent partnership which makes up an entire organism. If a system fails to operate correctly, the organism may become very ill and possibly die without corrective treatment.

The skeletal system

The skeletal system forms the bony supportive framework of the body. With the muscular system it brings about movement. You will see that these 2 systems work closely together to enable you to carry out daily functions including exercise.

The skeleton can be divided into 2 parts

- the axial skeleton
- the appendicular skeleton.

The axial skeleton

The axial skeleton consists of 80 bones concentrated in the upper central part of the body.

- **The skull** is divided into the cranium and the face.
- The **vertebral column** consists of 33 small bones connected by strong ligaments. These bones are called vertebrae:

Name	Component parts	Role
Nervous system	Brain, spinal cord, nerves	To interpret and respond to changes in the environment.
Endocrine system	Glands	Regulates body activities by using hormones (chemical messengers).
Reproductive system	Testes or ovaries and associated organs	Production of eggs and sperm, production of reproductive hormones.
Urinary system	Kidneys, bladder	Produces, stores and eliminates urine.
Digestive system	Mouth, stomach, intestines, anus	Absorbs nutrients from foods and eliminates waste material.
Immune system	Lymphatic fluid and vessels and organs containing a lot of white blood cells	To produce and direct white blood cells which defend the body against infection.
Integumentary system	Skin, hair, nails, etc	Detects sensation, protects the body and regulates body temperature.

Figure 18.3 Body systems

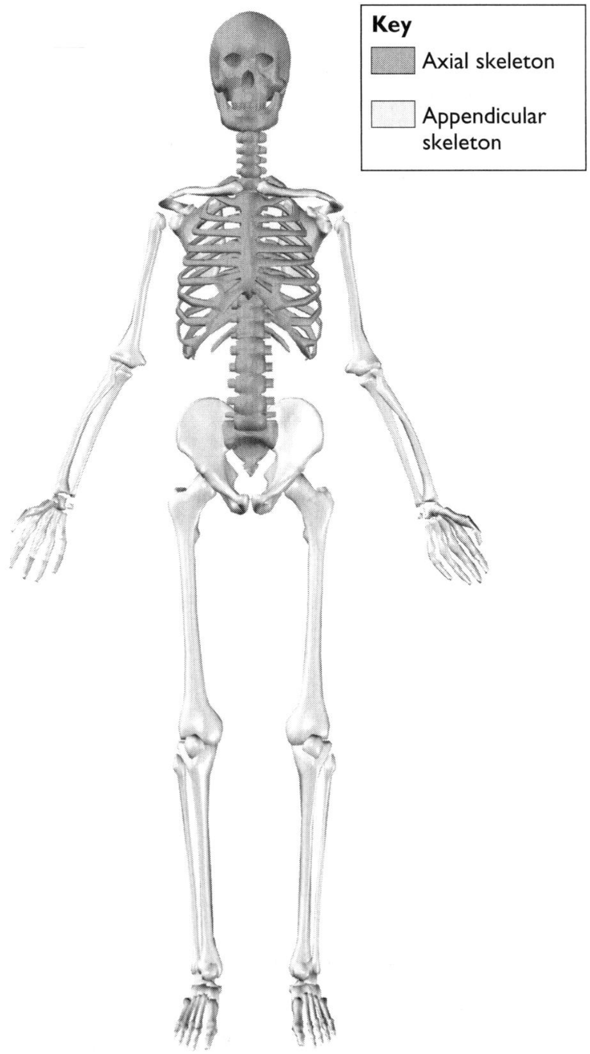

Figure 18.4 The axial and appendicular skeleton

- 7 cervical vertebrae (moveable)
- 12 thoracic vertebrae (moveable)
- 5 lumbar vertebrae (moveable)
- 5 sacral vertebrae fused together to form the sacrum
- 4 coccygeal vertebrae fused together to form the coccyx.

The moveable vertebrae are separated by intervertebral disks which are padded and act as shock absorbers.

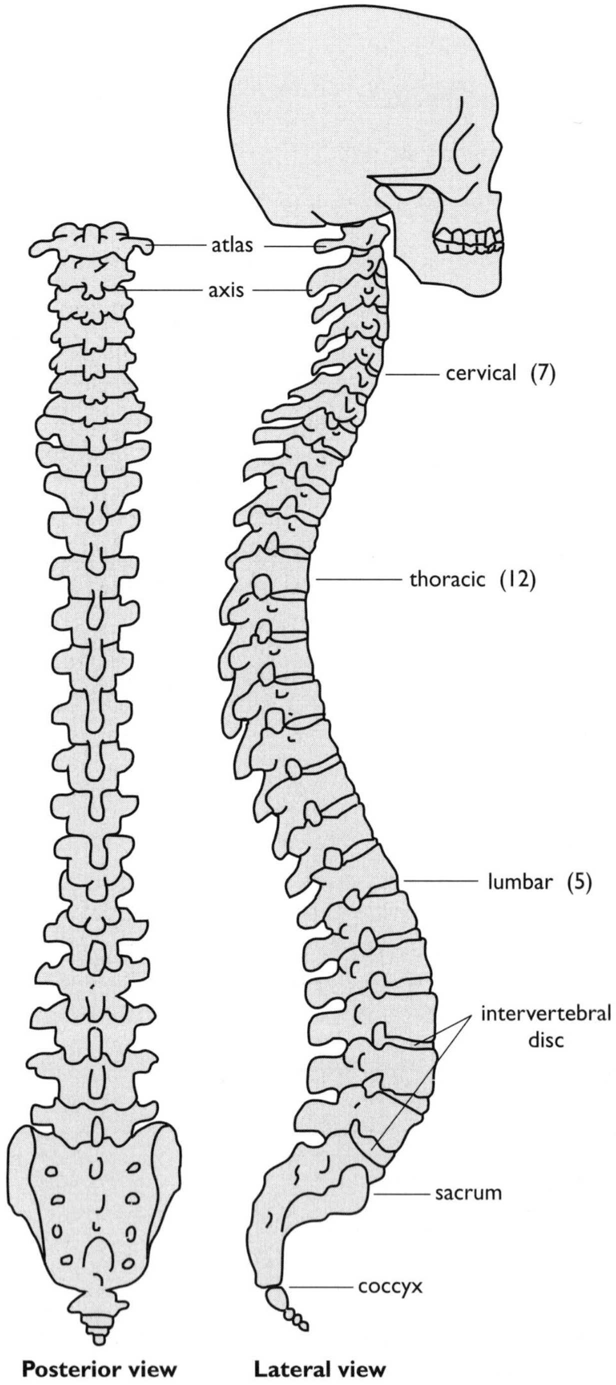

Figure 18.5 The vertebral column

Think about it

The cervical and lumbar vertebrae are most likely to be injured in sport or while taking exercise. Can you work out why this is?

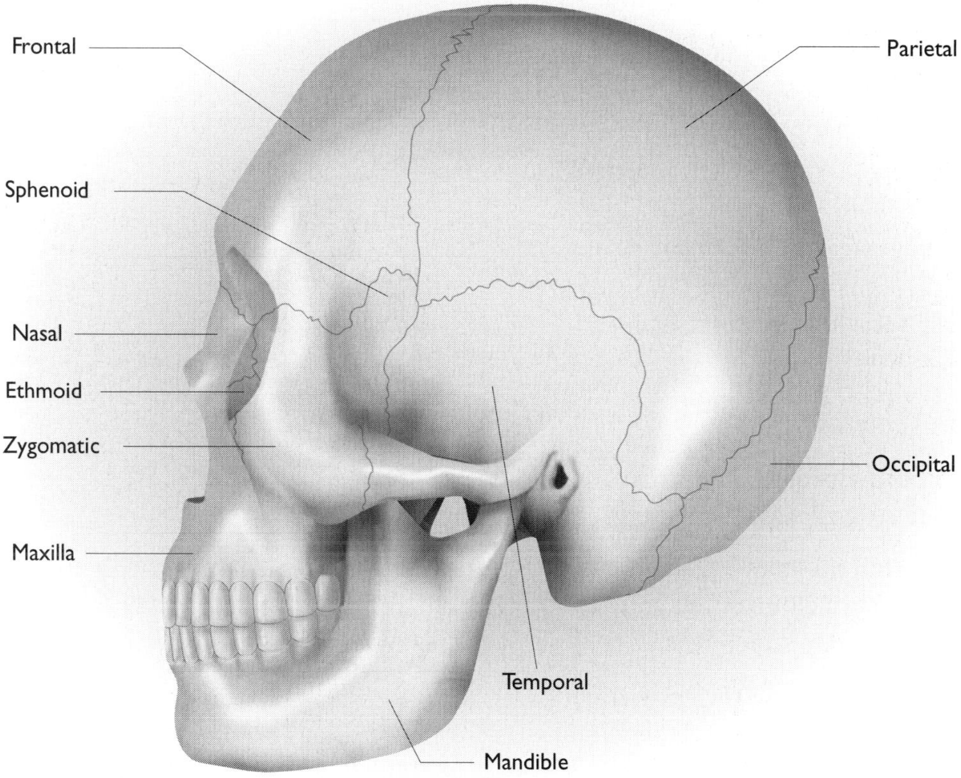

Figure 18.6 The skull

The vertebral column gives flexibility, height and shape to the body. It also has many functions which are similar to the function of the skeletal system:

- **protection** of the spinal cord
- **support** to the rib cage
- **support** to body weight
- **attachment** of muscles
- **movement** of the body.

The sternum is also known as the breast bone and forms the structure for the centre of the chest.

There are 12 pairs of ribs made up of long flat bones.

Think about it

What internal structures of the body do the ribs protect?

Appendicular skeleton

- **The shoulder girdle and arms:** the clavicles (collar bones) and scapulae (shoulder blades) form the bones of the shoulder girdle. The arms are made up of the humerus, radius and ulna which are long bones. The hands are made up of 5 metacarpals and 14 phalanges. There are 8 carpal bones in the wrist.
- **The pelvic girdle and legs**

Theory into practice

1. Working with a partner see if you can identify as many bones as possible of the appendicular skeleton that we have described so far. Give each other a spot test.
2. Why do you think the appendicular skeleton is called that?

Key points

1 The skeletal system supports and protects the body.
2 There are 206 bones in the adult human body.
3 The skeletal system is divided into two sections: axial and appendicular.
4 Bone is made from organic tissue and mineral compounds.
5 Bones generally occur in pairs on the right and left sides of the body.

Function of the skeletal system

The skeletal system consists of bone, cartilage and joints which provide several major functions:

- **Support:** the skeleton provides a shape for the body – a framework which takes the body's weight and supports body structures.
- **Protection:** bones help protect the body from injury, for example the skull protects the brain and the sternum and ribs protect the heart.
- **Movement:** bones provide attachment points for muscles. The bones provide a structure for the muscles to work against. As muscles can only contract, the bones are used as levers against which one muscle contracts in order to extend another.
- **Storage:** the bones serve as storage areas for minerals such as calcium and phosperous which are used by your body.
- **Production of blood cells:** red blood cells which carry oxygen around the body and some white blood cells which fight infection are produced in long bones.

Bone

A living bone consists of about 35% organic tissue, such as blood vessels and 65% minerals, such as calcium compounds.

There are 2 types of bone tissue:

- compact bone tissue which are strong and are found on the outside of bones
- spongy or cancellous tissue.

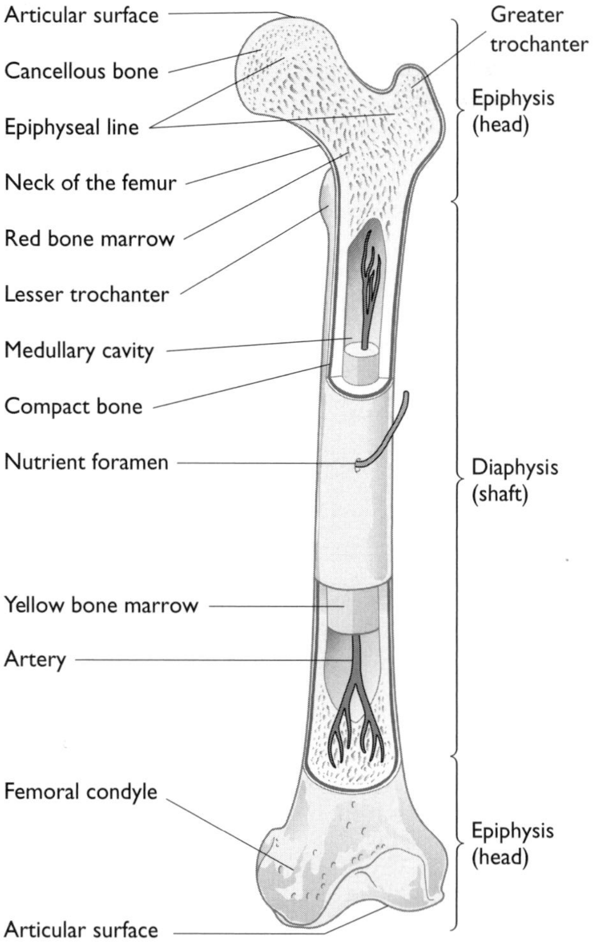

Figure 18.7 Structure of a long bone

The bone illustrated above is called a long bone. It is covered by the periosteum which is like the skin of the bone. The periosteum contains the cells that make new bone. The bone itself is divided in to 2 parts: the epiphysis, which are the 2 rounded end parts and the diaphysis which is the central, straight part of the bone. The end of the epiphysis is covered with cartilage which makes it connect and articulate smoothly with any bones that it meets in a joint. The inside of the epiphysis is made up of cancellous bone which is spongy; the spaces in the spongy cancellous bone are filled with bone marrow. The diaphysis has a hollow centre which is filled with bone marrow; the walls of the diaphysis are made of compact bone which is much tougher than the cancellous bone on the epiphysis. Bones are not dead structures but living tissue that is capable of being renewed.

Think about it

If bone was dead tissue, how could broken bones ever be mended?

There are several classifications of bone as shown in Figure 18.8 below.

Cartilage

Cartilage is dense tissue that is similar to bone but not as hard. Cartilage is a very important substance in the skeletal system as it acts like a shock absorber between bones. It is a type of gristly connective tissue, which performs functions such as:

- preventing bones knocking together and becoming worn and damaged
- forms a cushion for bones in slightly moveable joints
- acts as a shock absorber

Classification	Examples	Purpose
Long bones	Clavicle, humerus, radius, ulna, femur, tibia	To provide support and to act as levers for muscles.
Short bones	Carpals, tarsals	Provide movement, elasticity, flexibility and shock absorption.
Flat bones	Ribs, sternum, scapula	Protection, attachment sites for muscles.
Irregular	Skull, pelvis, vertebrae	Protection, support, movement.
Sesamoid	Patella	Protection of tendons, change the pull of a tendon improving mechanical advantage of a joint.

Figure 18.8 Classification of bones

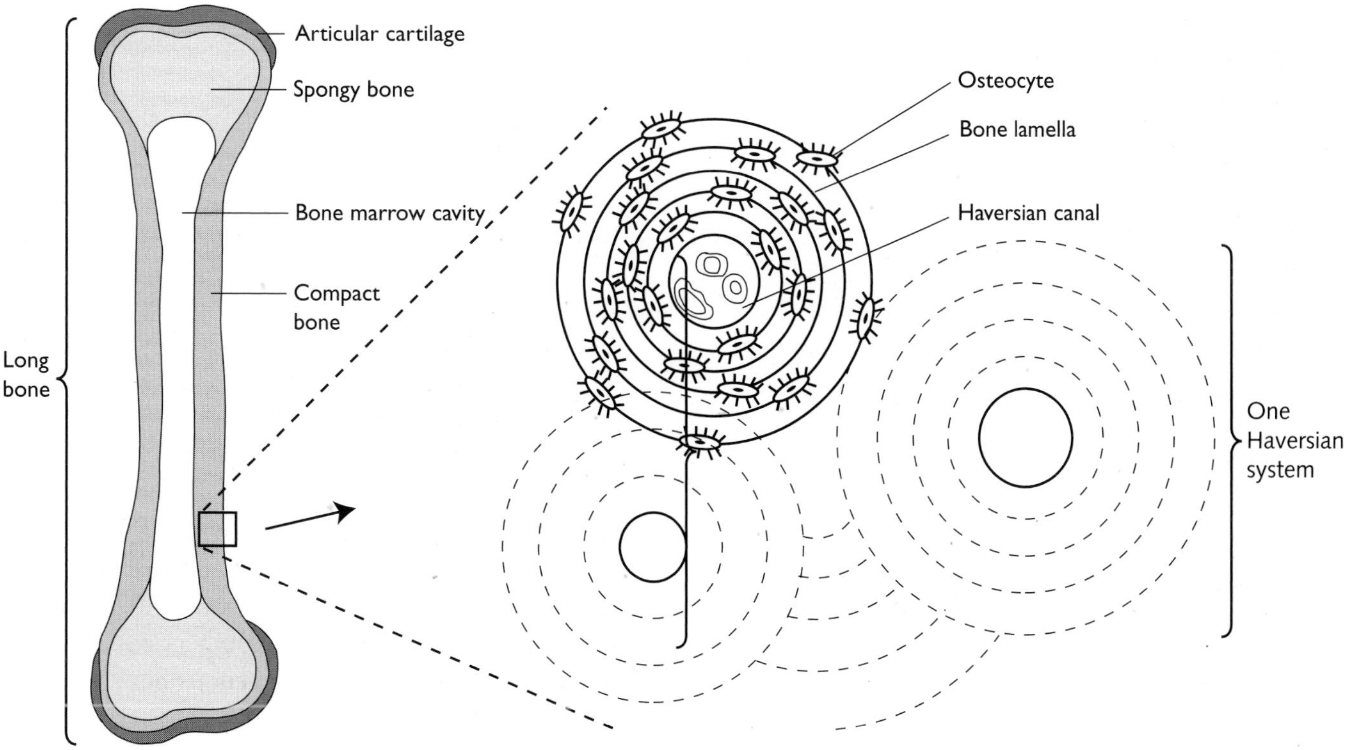

Figure 18.9 A long bone and the microscopic structure of compact bone

- aids freedom of movement by providing a slippery surface for bones to move against.

The cartilage and ligaments hold the joint together tightly and only permit small movements.

Theory into practice

There are 3 types of cartilage as follows. For each type, list one characteristic and one example of where it can be found:

- hyaline
- fibrous
- elastic.

Joints

At points in the body where bones come together, joints occur. Joints are areas where flexible connective tissue holds bones together while still allowing freedom of movement. Joints are also called articulations or arthroses. Since the skeleton is not naturally flexible, joints are crucial for movement.

Think about it

What problems would having damaged joints pose for a member of the public services?

Joints are classified as shown below in Figure 18.10.

- **Fixed joints (also called fibrous or synarthroses):** these bones are held together by fibrous connective tissue that is rich in collagen fibres. An example of this is the joints sutures' in the skull or the connection between the teeth and the jaw. In adults these joints are not designed to be mobile. They serve their function best when held immovable and firm, for example, chewing food, protection of the brain.
- **Slightly moveable (also called cartilaginous or amphiarthroses):** these are joints that are connected by cartilage.
- **Freely moveable (also called synovial or diarthroses):** these joints have cavity called the 'synovial cavity' between articulating bones. The cavity is filled with synovial fluid held in place by a synovial membrane. The fluid acts as a lubricant and reduces friction between the ends of the bone. When at rest the fluid is gel like but as the joint moves it becomes more liquid. A warm up before exercise stimulates the fluidity and production of synovial fluid and so acts as a benefit for the joints.

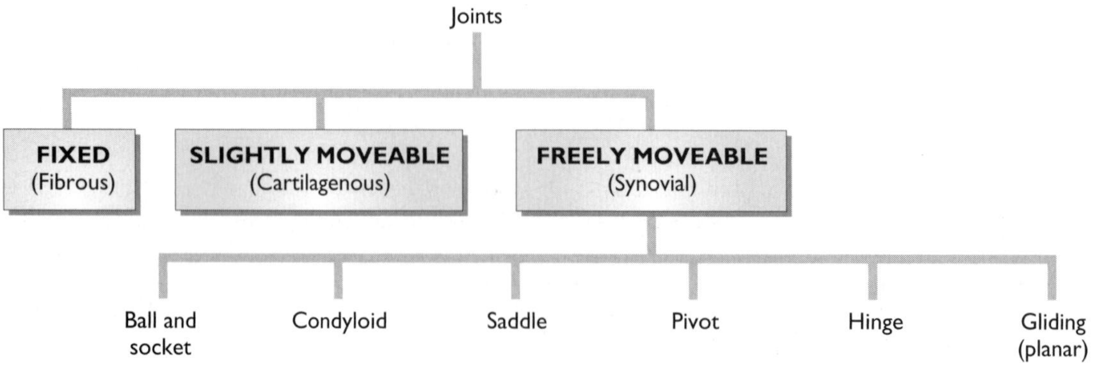

Figure 18.10 Body joints

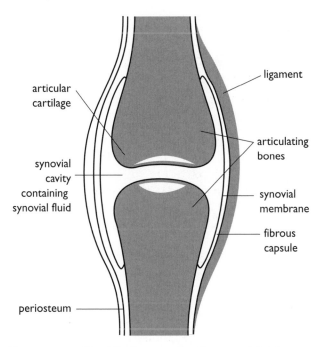

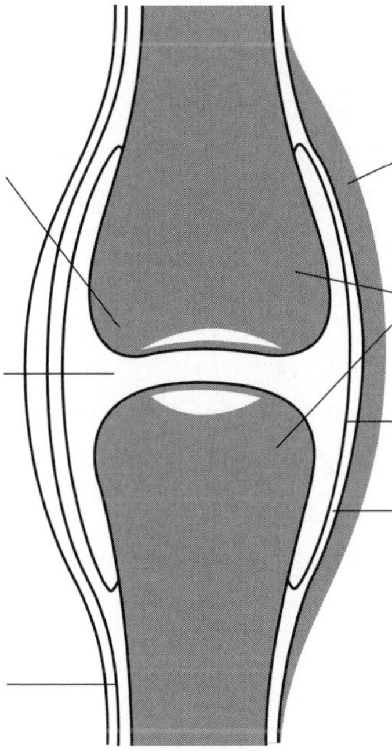

Figure 18.11 Simplified structure of a synovial joint

Most of the major joints in the human body are freely moveable. They fall into 6 categories shown in Figure 18.12 below:

Different joints allow for different kinds of movement. There are 17 kinds of movement that joints help the human body to make:

- **Flexion** – bending.
- **Extension** – straightening.
- **Dorsiflexion** – the foot bending upwards at the ankle.
- **Plantorflexion** – pointing the toes away from the ankle.
- **Abduction** – the arm or leg moving outwards away from the body's midline.
- **Adduction** – the movement of a bone towards the midline.
- **Circumduction** – movement of a distal end of a body part in a circle (moving a finger in a circular motion without moving the hand).
- **Rotation** – a bone revolves around its own long axis – such as turning the trunk from side to side while keeping the hips and legs stationary.

Type	Anatomy (structure)	Example physiology function	Part of body
Ball and socket	A ball shaped end of one bone fits into a cup shaped end of another bone.	Wide range of movement including rotation. Multiaxial.	Shoulder Hip
Condyloid	An oval shaped projection of one bone fits into an oval shaped depression in another.	Bioxial movement (side to side and up and down).	Metacarpals Phalanges Metatarsals Phalanges
Saddle	Part of the bone is saddle shaped and the bone it articulates with sits on it.	Wide range of movement.	Thumb
Pivot	The round or pointed surface on one bone fits into a ring formed by bone and ligament.	Monaxial movement. Movement around one axis only.	Axis and atlas in the neck (shaking your head to signify no)
Hinge	A convex projection on one bone fits into a concave depression in another bone.	Monoaxial movement. one direction only.	Knee, elbow, ankle
Gliding (planar)	Flat or slightly curved surfaces moving against each other.	Nonaxial, side to side and back to front, gliding movements. Limited movements.	Ribs and vertebrae carpals and metacarpals

Figure 18.12 Major joints fall into 6 categories

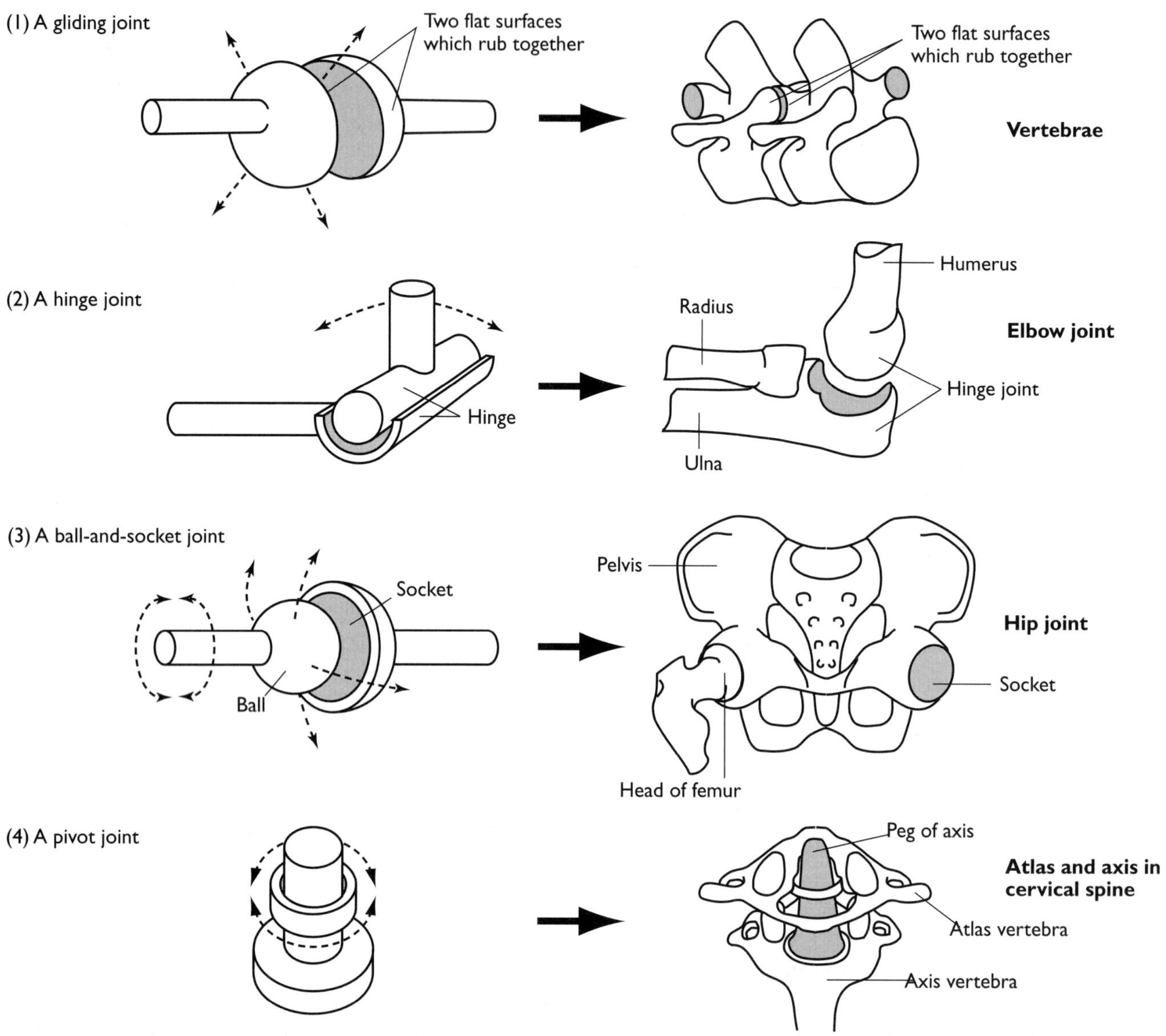

Figure 18.13 Types of joint

- **Pronation** – a movement of the forearm which results in the palm of hand facing up.
- **Supination** – a movement of the forearm which results in the palm facing down.
- **Inversion** – a movement of the soles of the feet so that they face inwards (towards each other).
- **Eversion** – a movement of the soles of the feet so that they are facing outwards (away from each other).
- **Protraction** – anterior movement of a body part forwards (thrusting out your lower jaw or making your shoulder blades stick out).
- **Retraction** – posterior movement of a protracted piece of the body back into its correct anatomical position (relaxing your shoulder blades or jaw back into its natural position).
- **Elevation** – upward movement of a body part such as shrugging your shoulders.
- **Depression** – downward movement of a body part such as drooping the shoulders or opening your mouth.
- **Hyper extension** – continuation of an extension beyond the anatomically correct position, such as bending the head backwards

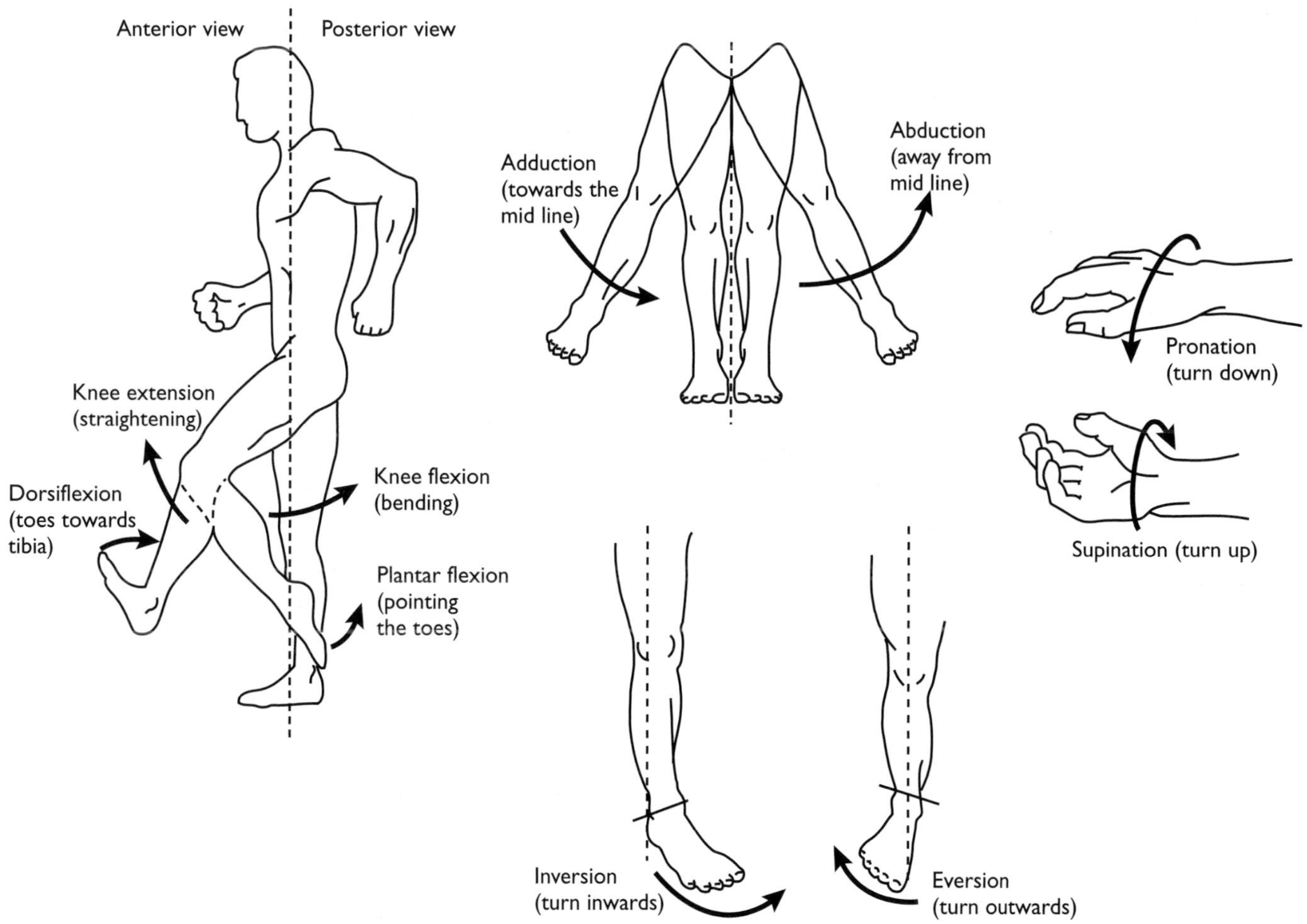

Figure 18.14 Examples of joint movements

or moving the palm backwards at the wrist joint. Hyper extension is usually prevented by a network of tendons and ligaments or the actual arrangements of bones themselves.

> ***Theory into practice***
> Think of an activity like cleaning your teeth, dancing, eating or shopping in a supermarket. How many of the different types of motion have you used? List and describe them.

The skeletal system in health and fitness

The skeleton is one of the few systems in the body that cannot be trained to improve directly. You cannot increase or reduce bone length and you cannot make a bone move faster, it is the muscles which are responsible for this. The use of regular load bearing exercise such as walking or weightlifting can help strengthen your bones. It does this by increasing the activity of osteoblasts which are cells in your body which create bone cells. This means that some naturally occurring bone degeneration or degeneration caused by diseases such as osteoporosis can be helped by regular activity.

However, the skeletal system is very important in terms of playing sports and there has been a lot of research conducted on bone and skeletal dimensions in terms of how they can impact athletic performance. This branch of sports science is called 'kinanthropometrics' and it proposes that there are 3 main characteristics of the skeleton, which can affect athletic performance. These are:

1 Size of the skeleton – the total height of the body.

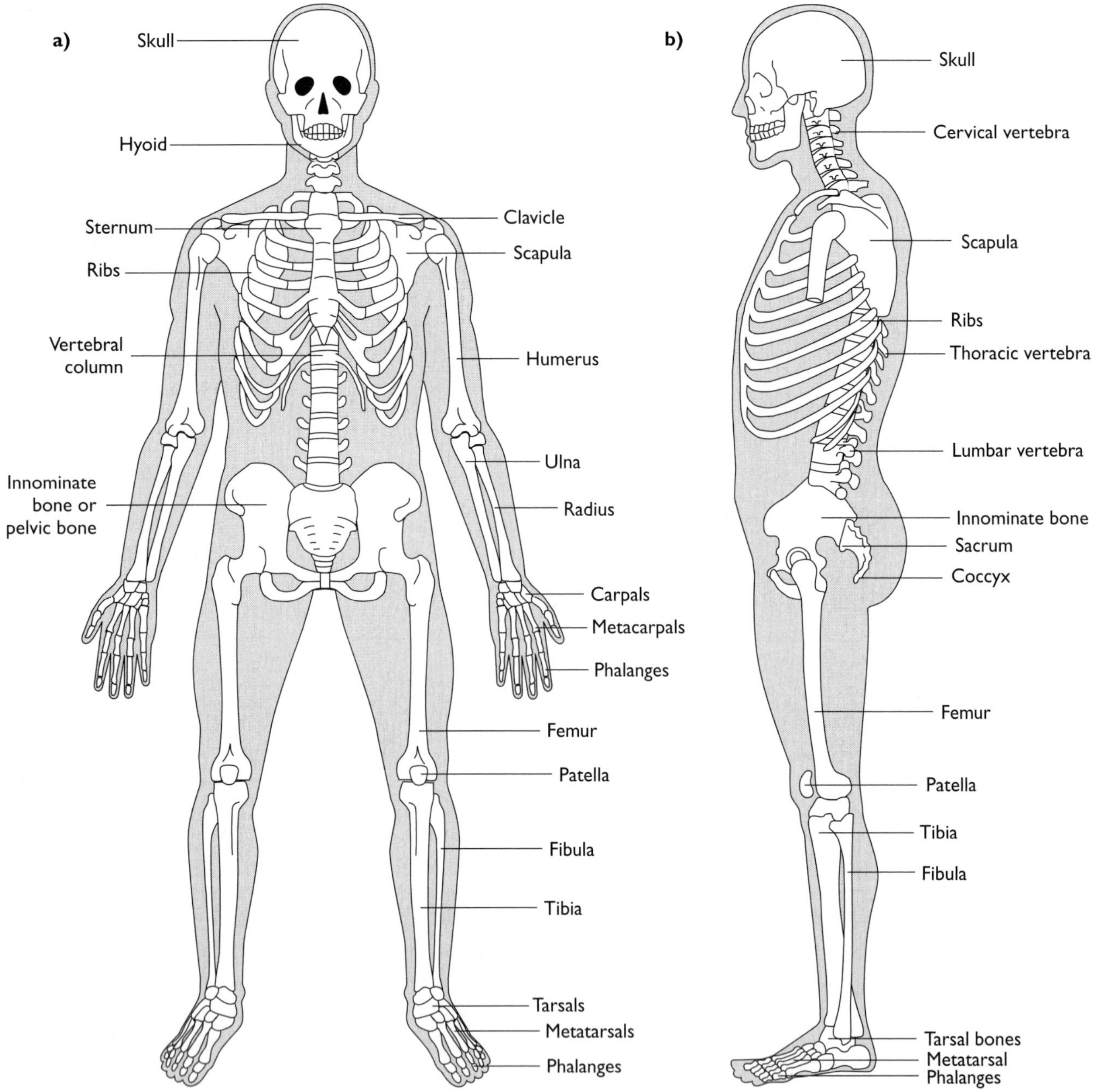

Figure 18.15 The skeletal system (a) anterior view (b) lateral view

2 Proportions of the skeleton – the size of the upper body in relation to the lower.

3 The size of certain individual bones.

The overall height of the skeleton is important since height is a crucial factor in many sports such as high jump and basketball. Too great a height would be a disadvantage however in some physical activities such as ballet or being a jockey.

Equally important is the size of the upper body in relation to the lower body. This 'proportion' is a large factor in determining an individual's centre of gravity. The longer your upper body is in relation to your lower body, the lower your centre of gravity. A low centre of gravity is important in sports such as skiing where upright balance is necessary. A high centre of gravity is a good characteristic for a runner to have. Lastly, there are a variety of sports where the size of particular bones in an individual's body can provide them with an advantage over their competitors. For instance a long humerus and ulna/radius would improve the 'reach' of a boxer, long distance runners are advantaged by having long femurs whereas sprinters gain an advantage if they have a narrow pelvis because it provides a more direct line for the legs to follow.

Think about it

Why is a high centre of gravity an advantage for some runners?

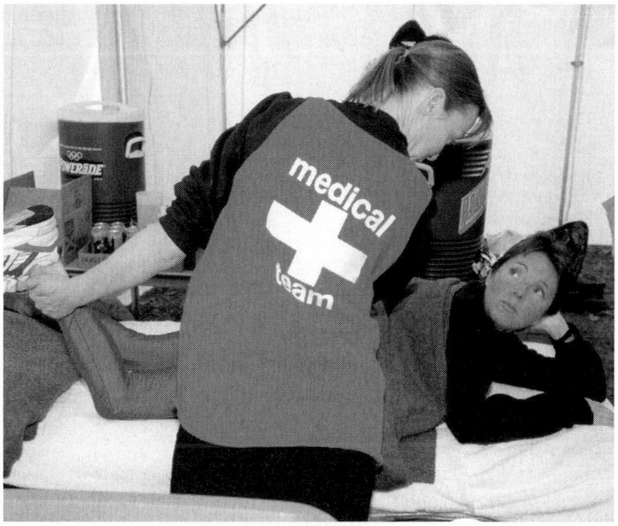

Treatment of a sports injury

Problems with the skeletal system

There can also be many problems with the skeleton, which can have a negative effect on health and fitness. Joints can be damaged by accidents and sports leading to sprains, dislocations and strains. A dislocation is when a bone comes out of its socket, which is quite common in ball and socket joint such as the shoulder and hip and also in joints such as the jaw and fingers. Some joint problems can be very easy to treat by use of the RICE method for soft tissue injuries.

R – Rest

Rest the injured joint as continued movement is likely to damage the soft tissue of the joint further.

I – Ice

The application of ice is used to reduce swelling and alleviate some of the pain. Ice should never be applied directly to the skin, it should be wrapped in a towel or cloth so that it doesn't cause damage to the skin. In addition, ice should not be applied to very sensitive body parts such as the eyes.

C – Compression

This is the application of a compression or elasticated bandage, which helps to reduce swelling or bleeding. It is important to ensure that any compression bandage still allows free circulation of blood flow otherwise the limb could be permanently damaged.

E – Elevation

This involves raising the injured limb above the level of the heart if possible to reduce swelling and bleeding.

Think about it

What would be the consequences of failing to follow the RICE procedure?

There can also be problems with disorders of the joints such as osteoarthritis, which is thought to be caused by wear and tear on the skeleton and consequently tends to be more common in older people. Some autoimmune disorders such as rheumatoid arthritis can also have a negative effect on the skeleton because the tendons and ligament of joints are attached by the person's own immune system. This can severely restrict mobility and cause tremendous pain.

Fractured bones

A fracture is the correct name for a broken bone. Although bones are very strong they can break for many reasons, such as hyper extension, disease and injury. There are several types of fracture, these are:

Type	Detail
Impacted fracture	The bone is broken into two pieces and the ends are crushed together.
Complete fracture	The bone snaps into two pieces.
Partial fracture	The bone is broken, but not all the way through.
Comminuted fracture	The bone breaks into more than two pieces.
Greenstick fracture	The bone doesn't break cleanly. The ends are jagged and possibly still connected in places.
Simple fracture	The broken ends of the bone don't poke through the skin
Compound fracture	The broken ends of the bone split the skin and protrude out.

Figure 18.16 Types of fractures

There are also environmental factors, which can affect the skeletal systems relationship to health and fitness. A poor diet with insufficient calcium can lead to a condition called osteoporosis where the bones lose mass and density and are consequently more fragile and susceptible to breaks and fractures. This can occur in post menopausal women particularly.

A lack of sunshine can cause a condition called 'rickets' which used to be a relatively common disease. Sunlight is a crucial factor in the body's manufacture of vitamin D as this vitamin moves calcium compounds into the bones which helps strengthen them. Without it calcium is lost from the body. Rickets occurs primarily in children but can occur in adults during pregnancy or breast-feeding when it is called osteomalacia.

Diet and the skeletal system

It is also important to remember the importance of diet on skeletal health, for instance:

- White sugar products, chocolate, caffeine, alcohol and cola remove calcium and minerals from the body. The more of these products that are consumed the higher the amount of important minerals that are excreted in urine. The worst culprits are colas which are high in sugar and caffeine.

Think about it

How much chocolate, tea and cola do you drink everyday? What impact might this have on your skeletal health.

- Smoking may lead to osteoporosis as there appears to be a link between prolonged tobacco use and loss of bone density. Again this seems particularly true in post menopausal women. It has been suggested that smoking interferes with calcium absorption ultimately leading to weaker bones.
- A high meat diet can lead to bone problems. Many people are turning to high protein diets as a reasonably quick way to lose weight. However, a high protein meat diet produces high levels of acidity in the blood which is called ketoacidosis. This suppresses the function of osteoblasts which are the cells that help produce new bone.

How to help your skeleton stay healthy

1 Ensure that your diet is rich in:
   - Vitamin A – increases rate of bone growth.
   - Vitamin B – helps bone mass formation and connective tissue strength.
   - Vitamin K – participates in a procedure which attracts calcium to the bones.
   - Vitamin C – helps maintenance and development of bones.

2 Do not smoke.

3 Avoid drinking too much tea, coffee and cola.

4 Limit your intake of chocolate and other foods which contain high levels of oxalic acid.

5 Limit your intake of meat. Have fish instead especially tinned tuna, salmon or sardines.

6 Eat plenty of raw and steamed vegetables.

Assessment activity 18-M1

Draw and label a diagram of the skeletal sysytem. Use this diagram as the basis for a five minute presentation which analyses the role of the skeletal system in relationship to health and fitness.

Did you know

A tooth placed in a glass of cola will eventually melt and dissolve.

The muscular system

Bones and joints form the framework of the body, but they move by the co-ordinated action of muscles on bones. Muscles are bundles of protein filaments which work together to produce motion in the body. A muscle fibre is a long thin strand of protein, within that strand are even smaller strands called myofibrils which are perfectly aligned and give the muscle its characteristic striations (stripes).

The human body is made up of 3 different types of muscle tissue, each with a different function.

1 Voluntary or skeletal muscle

2 Involuntary or smooth muscle

3 Cardiac muscle.

As you can see from the summary table in Figure 18.17, muscles have several main functions.

Muscle type	Muscle structure	Muscle function	Muscle location
Voluntary or skeletal muscle	Striped or striated	To provide movement for the body, maintain posture and produce body heat.	Attached to bones
Involuntary	Smooth	To maintain functions of many vital organs of the body.	In arteries and visceral organs
Cardiac muscle	Combination of smooth and striped	To allow the pumping action of the heart.	Forms the walls of the heart

Figure 18.17 Summary table of muscle location and function

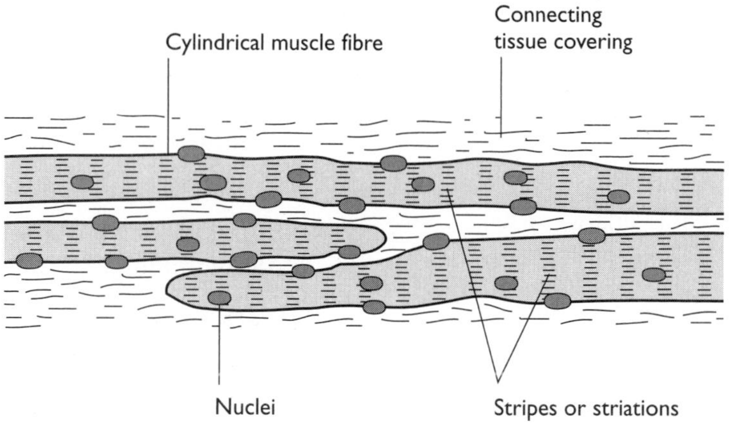

Figure 18.18 The microscopic structure of skeletal muscle

1 **Movement** – the actions of muscles allow you to change position and move around.

2 **Maintain posture** – believe it or not standing upright is a very difficult thing to do as gravity is always pulling at you. The reason you don't fall to the ground is due to the actions of your muscles.

3 **Produce heat** – the action of muscles produces heat which is why you get hot when you are doing physical activity. If you are cold and inactive your muscles will start to rhythmically contract in an effort to keep you warm, which is called shivering.

4 **Regulate blood flow** – your heart is a muscle which pumps blood around your body in accordance with your needs. If you need more oxygen to get to the muscles to enable them to work harder your heart rate will increase.

5 **Digestion and waste removal** – the digestive system moves food through it and eliminates waste due to muscle action in the rectum. Equally the bladder holds on to your urine until you relax the muscles which allow it to be eliminated.

6 **Supports the skeleton** – muscles act as a way to tie the skeleton together. There are muscle attachment points at all joints and this ensures the bones stay in position.

Muscle tissue typically composes 40–50% of body weight and the human body contains well over 600 skeletal muscles, which usually work in pairs. These pairs consists of the agonist, which is the prime mover and the antagonist which works against it. For example, your arm moves by the bicep muscle (agonist) working against the triceps muscle (the antagonist).

Muscle tissue has several characteristics, which identify it:

- Excitability – the ability to respond to stimuli
- Contractility – the ability to shorten
- Extensibility – the ability to stretch
- Elasticity – the ability to return to original shape and length.

Skeletal muscles can only pull, they cannot push. This is why they usually work in pairs. One muscle pulls a limb into the required position and the other muscle pulls it back when required.

Cardiac muscle

Cardiac muscle is found only in the heart and makes up the walls of the heart or myocardium. It has a branching network of cells which form layers of overlapping spirals. It acts as a single sheet of muscle, which operates on an involuntary basis and has its own blood supply. The heart generates its own impulse to beat and so is 'myogenic' and unlike many muscles in the body the cardiac muscle is attached together rather than to a bone and is designed to resist fatigue.

Think about it

Why is it important to have cardiac muscle which is able to resist fatigue?

Smooth muscle

Smooth muscle makes up a large part of our internal organs such as the bladder, veins and digestive tract. It is involuntary which means that it works without conscious thought on an automatic basis. Smooth muscle demonstrates two kinds of inervation (movement).

1 Multi unit innervation – rapid co-ordinated contraction, for example iris of the eye

2 Visceral innervation – a wave of contraction, for example peristalis (movement of food through the gut).

Smooth muscle contracts very slowly and so it is able to resist fatigue. In addition it can stay contracted for relatively long periods of time.

Skeletal muscle

This is the most common type of muscle found in the human body and can make up about 40% of an adult males body weight. It has stripe like markings called striations and it is composed of large cells bound together in bundles or sheets. The muscles are served by a system of nerves, which connect them to the spinal cord and the brain that controls the activation of a muscle.

Muscle attachment and movement

Skeletal muscles are attached to bones by tendons. It is attached at 2 points which are known as the origin and the insertion. To bring the body into action, different parts of the muscular skeletal system work under the influence of the nervous system to produce voluntary movement. Skeletal muscles contract when stimulated by impulses from the nervous system. At the point of contraction, muscles shorten and pull on the bones to which they are attached. When a muscle contracts, one end remains stationary while the other is drawn towards it. The end that remains stationary is called the origin and the one that moves is called the insertion.

Remember

Tendons attach muscles to bone.

Ligaments attach bone to bone.

Key points

1. Muscles are bundles of fibres.
2. Muscles usually work in pairs.
3. The muscular system provides support and movement to the body.
4. Muscles comprise 40–50% of body weight.
5. There are 3 types of muscle – cardiac, smooth and skeletal.

Muscle contraction

Muscle contraction is powered by a chemical molecule called adenosine triphosphate or ATP. ATP is synthesised from the food you eat and it provides energy for cells to use in performing their function. Muscles need a constant supply of ATP in order to contract. There is only a limited supply of ATP in muscles which means it needs to be regenerated quickly. During long periods of muscular contraction body fat becomes the main source of energy to power contractions. There are 3 main methods of muscle contraction:

Isometric (or static) contraction: a muscle produces force without changing its length (without movement). Examples of static contraction include maintaining your posture standing upright or hanging from a chin up bar with your arms at a ninety degree angle. At its maximum level static contraction can only be maintained for about 10 seconds. This is because as force on the muscle increases, blood flow to the muscle is proportionally reduced causing fatigue. However, low-level static contraction can be maintained for a long period of time.

Isotonic contraction: this kind of muscle contraction is a controlled shortening of the muscle. For example, a bicep curl is a simple example of a contraction that shortens the bicep. Equally, bending at the knee produces an isotonic contraction in the hamstring.

Eccentric contractions: this is when a muscle actively lengthens, such as the quadriceps (knee extensors) during walking.

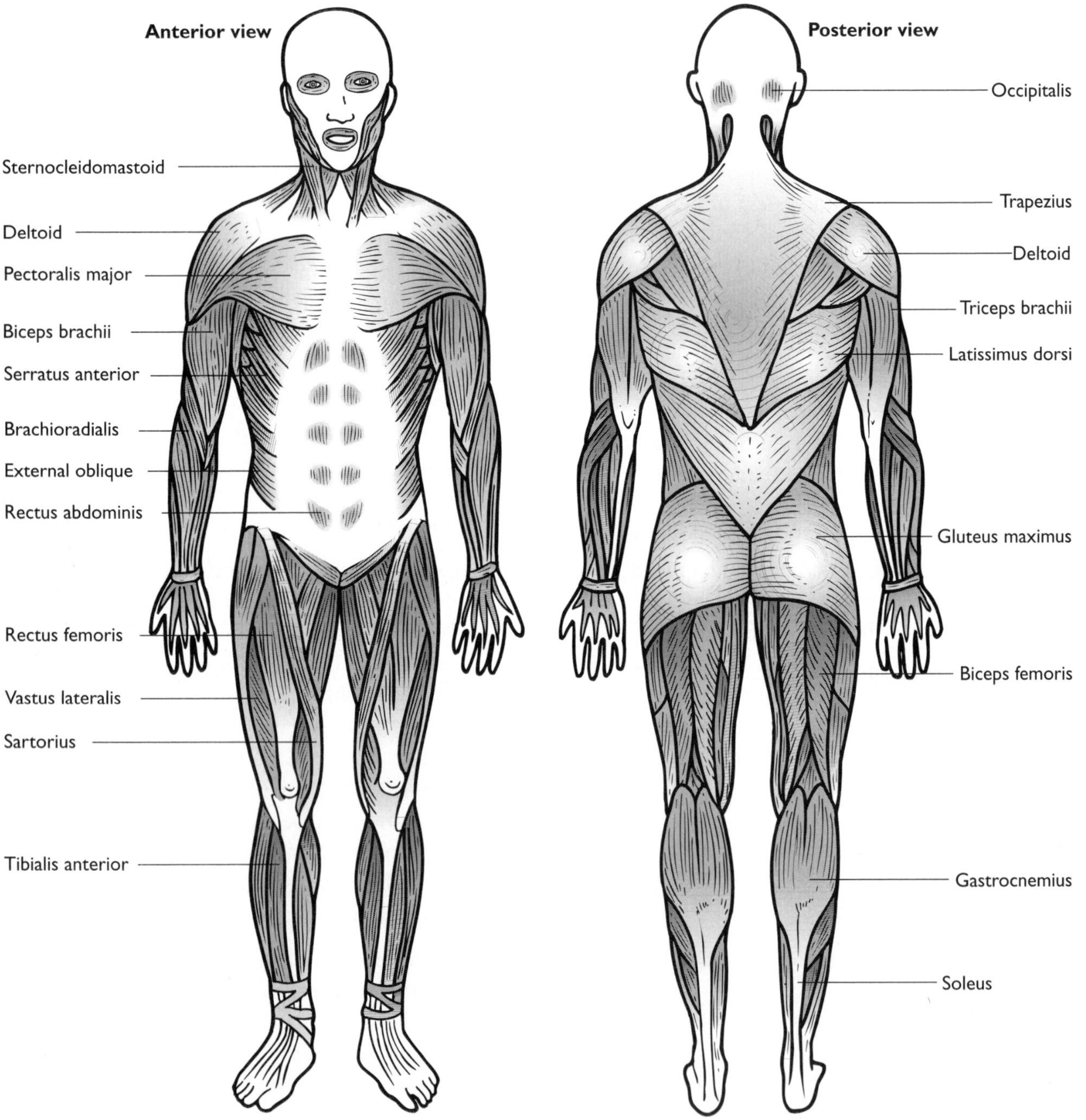

Figure 18.19 The muscular system

The relationship of the muscular system to health and fitness

- Muscles determine whether you can perform your daily functions: the better your level of muscular fitness, the greater your ability to complete the tasks in your life without fatigue or injury.
- Enhanced muscular fitness will enhance athletic performance both in terms of capacity to perform a particular sport but also in terms of performing that task for an extended period. This is useful in public service professions which can be physical in nature such as the armed and emergency services.

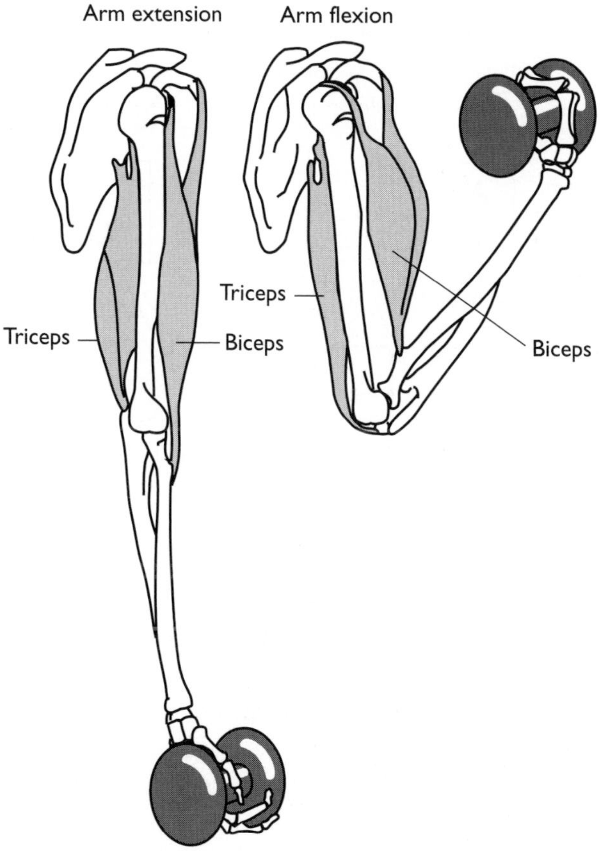

Figure 18.20 Bicep curl action

- Strong abdominal and lower back muscles can help prevent lower back pain which can be a significant problem in many public service professions such as nursing, fire fighting and the police.
- A good muscular system can help control your weight. The amount of lean muscle you have determines your resting metabolic rate (how quickly you can burn calories).
- An enhanced muscular system can help your psychological health by improving your body image and self-confidence.

Think about it

Can you think of any other benefits to having a healthy muscular system.

Problems with muscles

Muscular injuries can cause problems with performance by increasing stress on other muscles which compensate for the injury, decreasing endurance and limiting biomechanical movement. There are also significant psychological issues associated with muscle injuries such as the inclination to protect the injury long after the injury itself has healed and a loss of confidence in sporting ability.

There are also many diseases which can affect the muscular system such as muscular dystrophy. Muscular dystrophy is characterised by weakness and wasting away of muscle tissue. There are many types of muscular dystrophy, but all of them involve a loss of muscular strength, increasing levels of disability and possible deformity.

Keeping your muscular system healthy

Keeping your muscular system healthy is very important if you are to be effective as a member of the public services. There are several things you can do to keep your muscles in optimum shape:

- eat a balanced nutritious diet
- exercise regularly
- always warm up prior to exercise and cool down after
- perform stretching and flexibility exercises.

Key points

1 ATP provides energy to fuel muscle contraction.
2 There are 3 types of muscle contraction.
3 Muscle injuries increase stress on other muscles which have to compensate for the injury.
4 Muscular dystrophy causes weakness and wasting of the muscular system.

The cardiovascular system

The cardiovascular system consists of the heart, blood vessels and blood. Oxygen and waste products are carried to and from the tissues and cells by blood. The heart is the mechanism which allows this by pumping blood around the body through tubes called veins and arteries. The heart pumps continually throughout your life to the tune of around 30 million beats per year and even when you are asleep it pumps approximately 10 litres of blood a minute through the 60,000 miles of blood vessels which make up the transport system of your body. The cardiovascular system is one of the most important of all the body systems.

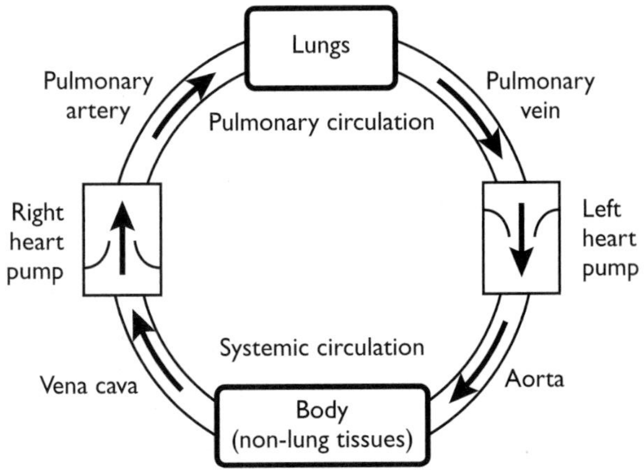

Figure 18.21 Double circulation of blood through the heart

The heart

The heart is about the size of a clenched fist and is located in the chest between the lungs with its apex slightly tilted to the left. It is made up of cardiac muscle (myocardium) and is surrounded by the pericardium, which is a fluid filled bag which reduces friction when the heart beats. It is not really heart shaped at all, it more closely resembles a cone shape. It contains 4 chambers, the left and right atria which are the upper chambers of the heart and the left and right ventricles which are the lower chambers. These form the basis for the two distinct transport circuits of the body, both of which begin and end at the heart:

- the pulmonary circuit which carries blood to and from the oxygen exchange surfaces of the lungs
- systemic circuit which involves blood flow to the rest of the body.

The blood collects initially in the atria which then pumps it to the ventricles. The walls of the atria are relatively thin as they are only passing the blood to the lower chambers, but the ventricles have to have enough power to send the blood around the circuits. As a result, the cardiac muscle in the ventricles is much thicker because more muscular power is needed. The right atrium receives deoxygenated blood from the rest of the body which it then pumps into the right ventricle. The right ventricle pumps this deoxygenated blood to the lungs where it drops off any waste gases and picks up a fresh load of oxygen in a system of gaseous exchange. This newly oxygenated blood now returns to the heart where it is pumped into the left atrium. This has completed the pulmonary circuit. The left atrium pumps the blood to the left ventricle which then pumps the oxygen rich blood to the organs and tissues of the body. The systemic circuit around the body is much larger than the pulmonary circuit so the left ventricle is the most powerful chamber in the heart with a thicker muscle wall than the other three chambers.

The heart is divided into left and right by a central wall called the septum and two thirds of its mass lies to the left of the body's midline. The heart weighs about 250 grams in adult females and 300 grams in adult males. It is able to contract rythmatically independent of a nerve supply because it is stimulated by an area of specialised tissue in the right atrium called the sino-atrial node.

Think about it

How many times will a heart beat in an average lifetime?

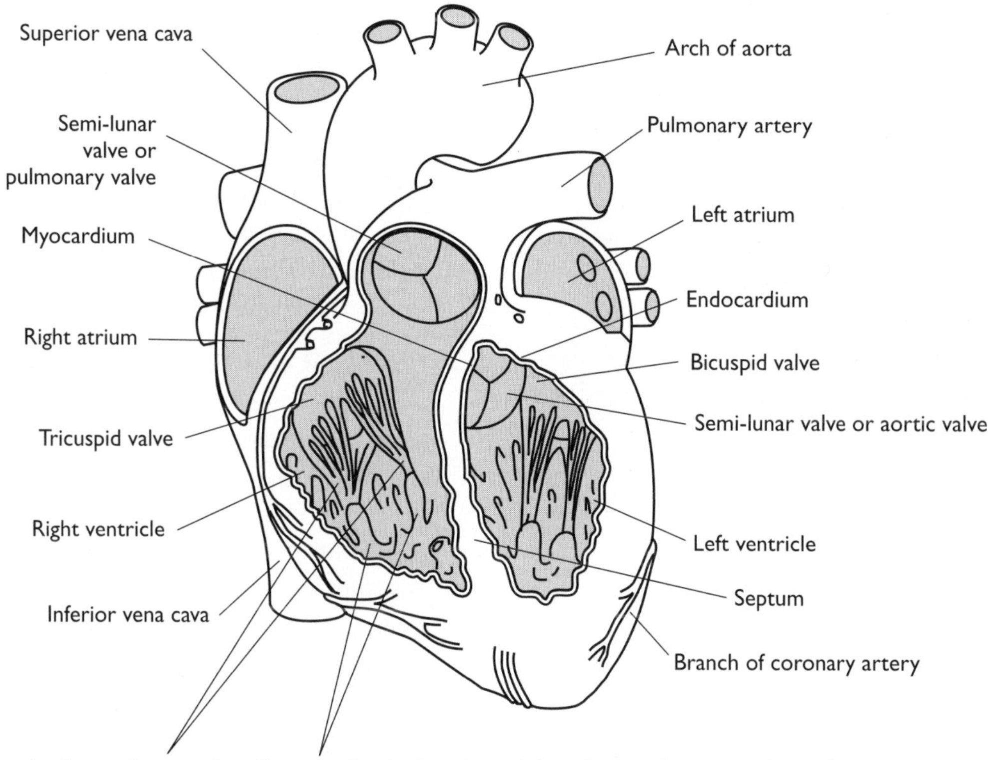

Figure 18.22 A section through the heart

Key points

1. The cardiovascular system consists of the heart, blood vessels and blood.
2. The heart pumps blood through the pulmonary and systemic circuits.
3. The heart is a cone shaped muscular organ.
4. The heart weighs around 250–300 grams.
5. The heart is situated in the thoracic cavity slightly to the left of the mid line.

Both of the blood flow circuits described above rely not only on the heart, but also on the blood and blood vessels, it is these aspects of the cardiovascular system that we will now explore.

Blood vessels

The blood vessels are the body's transport network as they allow blood to travel to every part of the body and return to the heart. The system of vessels consists of:

Arteries: these are large vessels which usually carry oxygenated blood away from the heart to the rest of the body (the exception being the pulmonary artery). They subdivide to form smaller vessels called arterioles which then branch off again to form capillaries. These vessels are cylindrical and muscular and are able to contract and dilate in order to regulate blood flow.

Veins: these vessels are usually responsible for the movement of deoxygenated blood back towards the heart so that it can be sent on the pulmonary circuit once more. Vessels called venules connect the capillaries where the oxygen has just been deposited to the veins which then return it to the heart. The blood flow in the veins is under less pressure than the arteries therefore they tend to be slightly less muscular than the arteries.

Capillaries: these are the smallest blood transportation vessels in the body. They are incredibly thin which allows the exchange of gases through them. Organs and tissues which need a high amount of oxygen and nutrients, such as muscles and the brain will have lots of capillaries, while other organs which are not so dependent may not have as many.

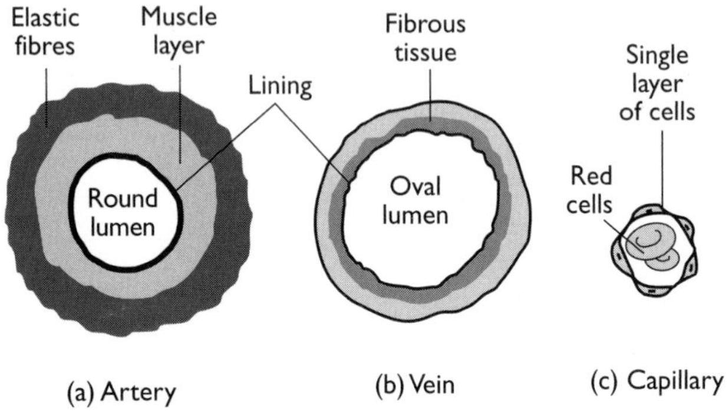

Figure 18.23 Major blood vessels

Think about it

How many miles of blood vessels are in your body?

Blood

Blood is a red fluid which carries oxygen, nutrients, hormones and disease fighting agents around the body. The typical human has around 5 litres of blood in their body. Blood is made up of several different substances:

- plasma 55%
- cells } 45%
- platelets. } 45%

Plasma: plasma is what makes the blood a liquid. Without it the cells in the blood would be solid and therefore not travel around the body. It is a pale yellow fluid made predominantly from water and a small amount of protein.

Red blood cells (erythrocytes): these are the most numerous cells in the blood. They are disc shaped with a depression in the centre at each side. They are created by the marrow in the bones and have a life span of approximately 3 months. They carry a substance called haemoglobin which helps transport oxygen around the body and it is haemoglobin that gives the blood its red colour.

White blood cells (leucocytes): white blood cells are the soldiers of the body as they are the cells that fight off bacteria and viruses. They are much bigger than red blood cells and they are irregular in shape. There are several different kinds of white blood cell as shown in Figure 18.24 below.

Platelets: platelets play a crucial role in the repair system on the body. They secrete serotonin which restricts blood flow to a damaged part of the body and they also stick together at the site of an injury

Type of white blood cell	Function
Neutrophils	These are the most common sort of white blood cell. They are found at wound sites where they try to engulf and destroy foreign particles such as dirt and bacteria which have entered at the wound site.
Eosinophils	These cells attack parasites and are also responsible for triggering allergic reactions to irritants.
Basophils	These cells are involved in fighting off germs in the body. It is part of the immune response to illness.
Monocytes	These are the largest of the white cells which deal with particles and germs that the neutrophils cannot cope with.
Lymphocytes	These are involved in the immune response of the body and they help produce antibodies to disease.

Figure 18.24 Types of white blood cells

to plug gaps in broken blood vessles. They activate proteins found in blood plasma which then create a basket like structure which captures red blood cells forming a natural wound covering called a scab. The scab prevents foreign particles entering the bloodstream and stays in place until the tissue underneath is repaired, after which it falls off.

Key points

1 Blood vessels are the body's transport system.
2 The transport system consists of arteries, veins, arterioles, venules and capillaries.
3 Blood consists of plasma, cells and platelets.
4 Red blood cells transport O_2.
5 White blood cells fight off infection.

Cardiovascular system and health and fitness

The cardiovascular system can be improved with regular exercise. For instance, aerobics activity for a period of 20 minutes elevates cardiac output and accelerates an individual's metabolic rate. 3×20 minute sessions a week are usually recommended for improving the health of the cardiovascular system. After several weeks of training, an individual can alter their maximal cardiac output increasing overall oxygen delivery to the tissues. Regular exercise can also help reduce blood pressure, anxiety, depression, control weight and increase the body's ability to dissolve blood clots.

Think about it

Do you do enough exercise to keep your cardiovascular system healthy? If you don't, consider drawing up an action plan which details how you could improve.

Diet is an important issue in cardiovascular health. Being overweight or obese places an additional strain on the system leading to increased risk of high blood pressure, strokes and heart attacks. In addition, the fatty diet eaten in most western countries deposits cholesterol on the walls of the arteries leading them to become narrower, which can lead to a condition called angina. This is characterised by acute chest pain and shortness of breath. If the arteries become blocked it can cause a heart attack which may prove fatal.

Anaemia occurs when the number of red blood cells is decreased. Without an efficient and plentiful supply of the nutrients the blood carries, processes such as cell repair slow down and become less efficient. It may also cause dizzy spells and fatigue. Anaemia is very common, particularly in women and can usually be rectified by an iron rich diet.

The respiratory system

Cells continually use oxygen (O_2) in their reactions and release carbon dioxide (CO_2) as a waste product. The body therefore needs a system which provides O_2 for the body and gets rid of CO_2 before it builds up and causes damage. This system is the respiratory system. The exchange of O_2 and CO_2 is completed in 3 stages.

1 **Pulmonary ventilation:** this is the process of breathing in air (inspiration) and breathing out CO^2 (expiration).

2 **External respiration:** this is the exchange of O_2 and CO_2 between the air spaces in the lungs and the blood in the pulmonary capillaries. O_2 is picked up and CO_2 dropped off.

3 **Internal respiration:** this is the exchange of gases between the blood in the capillaries and the tissues in the body. O_2 is dropped and CO_2 picked up.

The Respiratory System comprises:

The nose The pharynx The larynx The trachea	Leading to the lungs
The bronchi The bronchioles The alveoli	Within the lungs

Inspiration and expiration happens because of changes in air pressure inside the lungs caused by the action of the diaphragm and intercostal muscles. Inspiration happens when the muscular action of the respiratory system expands the chest causing a decrease in air pressure, which makes air rush into the lungs. Expiration happens when the muscles return to their resting position causing an increase in air pressure which forces air out of the lungs.

Inspired air contains:

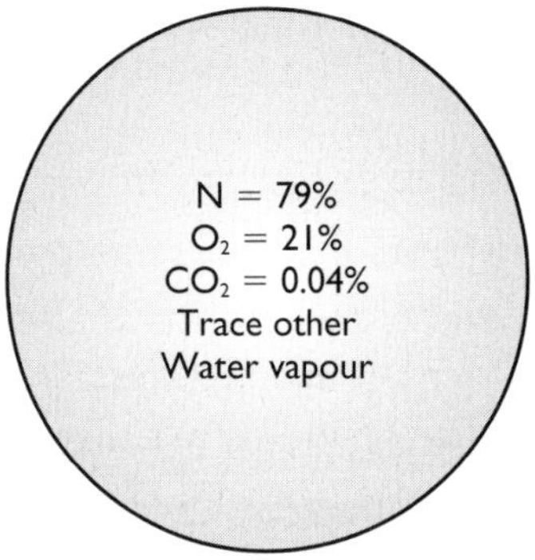

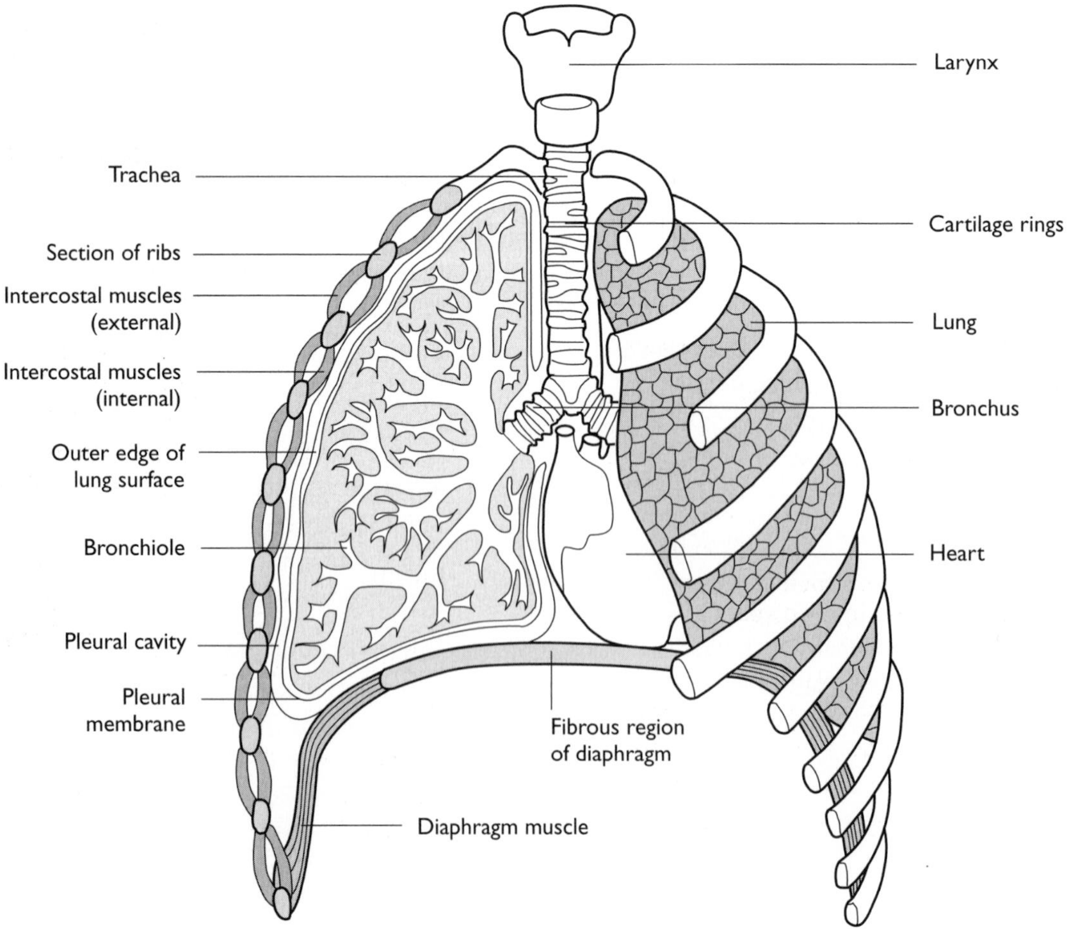

Figure 18.25 Cross-section through the thorax to show respiratory organs

Expired air contains:

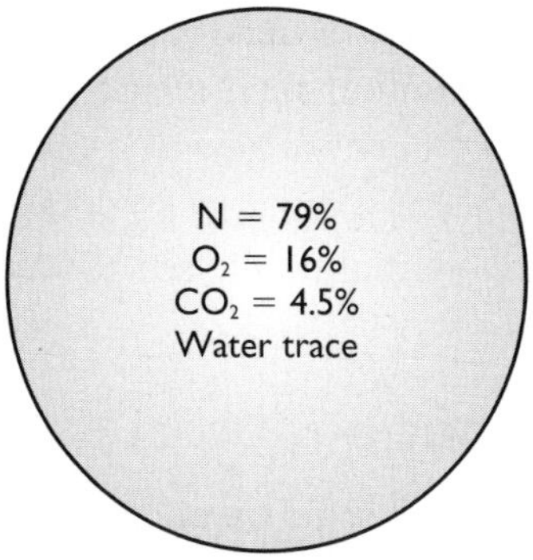

At rest a typical healthy adult will take 12 breaths per minute with each inspiration and expiration which moves about half a litre of air. The function of the respiratory system is therefore to supply O_2 to the tissues and remove harmful waste products before they can build up and cause damage to the body. In order to do this effectively the respiratory system works in partnership with the body's transport mechanism which is the circulatory system in order that O_2 can reach tissues all over the body and CO_2 can be bought back.

Think about it

Why is a healthy respiratory system a requirement of many public services occupations?

The main parts of the respiratory system

The nose: air usually enters through the nostrils and proceeds to open space within the nose called nasal passages and nasal cavity. The air is filtered by small hairs and mucus in the nostrils and warmed before it reaches the lungs. The mucus also helps to moisten the air which is why it is better to breath through the nose rather than the mouth.

Pharynx and larynx: moving on from the nose air moves through the pharynx (throat) and larynx (voice box). Air vibrates the vocal chords, which are on either side of the larynx enabling us to make sounds.

Trachea: the larynx connects with the trachea (windpipe) which is a tube approximately 12cm in length and 2.5cm wide in adults. It is held open by rings of cartilidge and is covered with tiny hairs (cilia) and mucus which help filter the air and remove obstructions back up to the throat.

Bronchi: the trachea divides into 2 bronchi which lead into the lungs and further subdivide and spread like tree branches into bronchial tubes.

Bronchioles: the bronchial tubes further divide and spread becoming smaller and thinner tubes called bronchioles.

Alveoli: each bronchiole ends in a tiny air chamber containing cup shaped cavities called alveoli. The alveoli are very thin and this allows O_2 and CO_2 to be exchanged through their walls.

Key points

1 The respiratory system supplies the body with O_2 and eliminates some waste products.

2 The average adult takes around 12 breaths per minute.

3 It works in conjunction with the circulatory system.

The respiratory system and health and fitness

During exercise the respiratory system must adjust and work harder in response to the intensity of the activity. This is because the muscles produce more CO_2 and consume more O_2. This is fulfilled by:

- increases in breathing – quicker and deeper breaths
- increases in cardiac output – blood pumped around the body faster due to increased heart rate
- increases in oxygen and CO_2 exchange – more O_2 is deposited in tissues and more CO_2 is extracted

- increased blood flow – working tissues such as muscles have more blood directed towards them than less active muscles such as kidneys or intestines.

You can see that a healthy respiratory system is crucial to all physical activity whether it is a 3-day decathlon or simply walking up a flight of stairs. However, there are many problems which can affect the respiratory system and therefore undermine an individual's capacity for sports, exercise and public service work.

Smoking

Smoking can have a serious impact on athletic performance for several reasons:

- nicotine restricts bronchioles which decreases airflow in and out of lungs
- carbon monoxide in smoke reduces the blood's ability to carry 0_2 to tissues
- irritants and particles in smoke cause increased mucus production which again reduces airflow
- smoke destroys and damages cilia which allows foreign bodies to enter the lungs more easily
- long term smoking destroys the elasticity of the lungs which can lead to the collapse of broncioles, reducing gas exchange capacity.

Think about it

If you smoke you are inhibiting your body's ability to utilise the O_2 you breath in.

Asthma

Asthma is a disorder of the respiratory system which is characterised by an inflammation of the airways. This can lead to obstruction of the airways and reduced oxygen consumption or in extreme circumstances death. Individuals with asthma may react to irritants such as pollen, dust mites and cigarette smoke. Other triggers can be emotional or psychological upset. Asthma is becoming increasingly common and is usually treated with a ventolin inhaler. An individual with asthma has to monitor their respiratory system carefully during exercise ensuring that their inhaler is on hand. Asthma is a common cause of rejection for potential public service recruits.

Think about it

See if you can find some up to date information on asthma and its growing increase in the UK and why this might be. Why is asthma a common cause of rejection in the public service recruitment process?

Emphysema

Emphysema is generally caused by long-term exposure to an atmospheric irritant such as cigarette smoke or pollution. It is characterised by a reduced capacity for 0_2 exchange in the alveoli. Any mild activity can leave an individual breathless.

Lung cancer

Lung cancer is one of the leading causes of death for adults in the UK. About 85% of cases of lung cancer are smoking related and it is up to 30 times more common in smokers than non-smokers. The symptoms include coughing up blood, shortness of breath, chest pain, hoarseness, weight loss and difficulty swallowing.

Pneumonia

Pneumonia is an acute inflammation of the alveoli caused by microbes entering the lungs. The alveoli and bronchial membranes are damaged which interferes with gas exchange and leads to a reduced capacity for physical activity if the individual recovers.

Theory into practice

Tuberculosis or (TB) is a bacterial infection which affects the lungs. It is spread via droplets from sneezing or coughing and had almost disappeared until a few years ago but is now reappearing. Carry out some research into this disease and make a presentation to your group focussing on:

- the disease process
- its relationship to poor living conditions including homelessness
- drug therapies for TB and why they might be difficult to maintain
- any other issues surrounding TB which you come across in your research.

Keeping your respiratory system healthy

The body needs oxygen in order to survive so it is crucial that your respiratory system can exchange gases efficiently. In order to do this the system needs to be healthy and disease free. There are several ways to help this:

- don't smoke
- avoid atmospheric irritants
- seek medical advice for any shortness of breath or chest infections
- get vaccinated against diseases such as influenza if you are in a high risk group.

A strong respiratory system is important in many public services, but the fire service place a premium on it due to the atmospheric irritants such as smoke you are likely to encounter and the need for you to be able to use specialist breathing apparatus.

Assessment activity 18-P1

Considering the information you have received on human body systems produce a leaflet aimed at potential recruits to the public services which describes in detail the role of the muscular, respiratory and cardiovascular systems and their relationship to health and fitness.

Body types

William Sheldon (1898–1997) was an American psychologist who examined the relationship between human bodies and temperament. Using over 4000 photographs of young men he concluded that all of us are made up of 3 elements which when combined together form our physique. This now commonly used method of classification is called somatotyping. The 3 elements are:

- the endomorph – centred on the abdomen
- the mesomorph – centred on the muscles
- the ectomorph – centred on the brain.

However, there have been problems applying Sheldon's body type theory to the body types of women and body shape can change with age as well as metabolic disease such as hyper/hypothyroidism. In addition, ideal types are relatively uncommon.

The endomorph 7–1–1

The extreme endomorph physique has the following features:

- the body is round and soft
- arms and legs are short and tapering
- hands and feet are comparatively small
- upper arms and thighs more developed than lower arms or calves
- body has smooth contours
- a high waist
- breast development in males
- tendency to premature baldness
- head is large and the face is broad and relaxed.

The mesomorph 1–7–1

The extreme mesomorph physique has the following distinct features:

- body is square and hard
- large bones and well-defined muscles

- narrow, low waist
- clearly defined cheekbones and a heavy jaw
- lower and upper limbs are well developed
- wrists and fingers are large.

Ectomorph 1–1–7

The extreme ectomorph physique has the following distinct features:

- physique is fragile and delicate with light bones and slight muscles
- limbs are relatively long and shoulders droop
- ribs are visible
- thighs and upper arms are weak
- baldness is rare
- fingers, toes and neck are long.

Think about it

Using the above criteria, which body type do you most closely resemble? Do you think that it is helpful to have these kinds of classifications? What problems can be associated with our perceptions of body image?

Body types and exercise

Somatotyping can be helpful in helping to develop exercise and lifestyle programmes to gain or lose weight or to become more physically fit. It has been suggested that the different body types respond best to different forms of exercise as shown in Figure 18.26 below.

Body type	Possible training suggestions
Endomorph	Strength training to improve the muscle to fat ratio using moderate weights at a reasonably fast training pace. Lower calorie intake. Cardiovascular activities such as walking or cycling.
Mesomorph	Strength training to maintain naturally occurring muscular shape and aerobic activity. Muscle is gained easily. This body type must be careful not to over train unless muscle bulk is required.
Ectomorph	Strength training with heavier weights than an endomorph, but at a slower pace. Diet should be high in calories (but not junk food). Limited aerobic exercise so as not to lose weight.

Figure 18.26 Appropriate exercises for different body types

Lifestyle and nutrition

Effects of lifestyle on health and fitness

Each of us makes lifestyle choices, which can affect our levels of health and fitness. Lifestyle is the way we choose to conduct our lives from what we eat, to the jobs we do, to the types of relationships we choose to have. The following lifestyle choices impact upon our health and fitness.

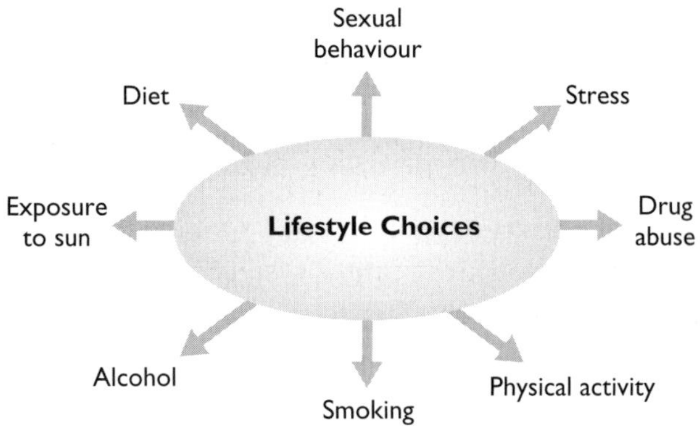

Figure 18.27 Lifestyle choices

Stress

Stress is a constant part of our lives, whether its worrying about getting assignments in on time or more serious worries such as divorce or bereavement. The kind of stress that is really damaging to your body is a long-term stress, which can be caused by things such as family problems, financial difficulties or being unhappy in your workplace.

Stress can manifest itself physically and emotionally in signs such as indigestion, fatigue, insomnia, feeling irritable or headaches. These symptoms are caused by the increased activity of the nervous system as it responds to your stress and the production of hormones such as adrenaline and cortisol which trigger your 'fight or flight' response. These hormones stimulate the heart to beat faster and redirects blood to the brain, heart and muscles. This causes an increase in blood pressure, which can lead to the heart and blood vessels being placed under stress. If a blood vessel bursts in the brain it is called a 'stroke' and can have fatal consequences. In addition the blood becomes 'sticky' with sugars and fats released from the liver in order to give the muscles more energy to power the fight or flight response, but if you are sitting at a desk fuming at your boss these fats and sugars are not utilised by the muscles and they can stick to artery walls clogging them up with fatty deposits which put you at greater risk of heart disease.

Stress has been linked with many other problems such as eczema, stomach ulcers and depression. The obvious way to deal with this problem is to tackle the cause of the stress so that it no longer exists or to change the way you react to stress. Techniques such as meditation and exercise can help an individual cope with stress more effectively.

Think about it

What are the sources of stress in your life? What strategies do you have for coping with these sources of stress?

Level of physical activity

It is a well known fact that individuals who exercise regularly either as part of their job or in their leisure time have less heart attacks than those who don't. Exercise builds up the strength of the heart which means it can cope better if you put a sudden physical demand on it. Exercise will also:

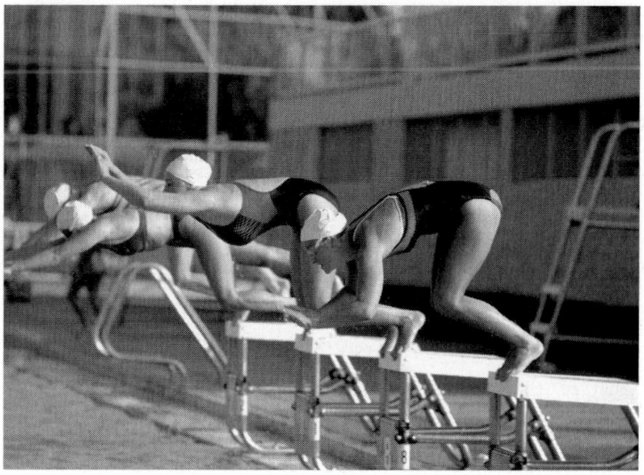

Sport or exercise is important for health and fitness

- help reduce blood pressure
- keep weight in check
- slow down the bone deterioration in older people (particularly important for women)
- keep muscles strong and joints flexible
- help you deal with stress and depression in more productive ways
- decrease the amount of bad cholesterol in the blood helping keep the heart and blood vessels healthy
- promote psychological well being and positive self image.

Diet

Healthy eating is vital for all our body systems since they rely on the energy from food to run effectively. Diets in the western world tend to contain too much fat, sugar, salt and dairy products, which can cause problems such as obesity, high blood pressure, coronary heart disease and dental decay. Food such as fresh fruit and vegetables, cereals, rice and pasta can help fight against diseases such as bowel cancer and gum disease. Diet and nutrition will be discussed in more detail later in this chapter.

Alcohol

Alcohol has impacts on all of the major body systems and abuse of alcohol can lead to death. Some of the main effects of excessive alcohol are: blackouts, liver cancer, liver disease, diarrhoea, heartburn, cancer of the oesophagus, malnutrition, high blood pressure, loss of libido, reduced fertility, impaired decision making and increased risk of accidents. However, it is important to note that recent studies have concluded that alcohol in moderation is actually good for you, helping protect against heart disease. In terms of public service work the abuse of alcohol can directly affect your working performance.

Many public service jobs require the operation of complex equipment such as breathing apparatus, weapons and vehicles and the presence of alcohol in your system will impair your judgement, placing yourself and others at risk.

In addition, alcohol is very high in calories and without proper exercise this will lead to a gain in weight. Carrying excess weight places an additional strain on systems such as the cardiovascular and respiratory systems which have to work harder to perform their functions.

Smoking

Smoking is a major danger to your health. It can cause heart disease, numerous cancers and bronchial disorders. Over 100,000 people every year die from smoking related diseases. Smokers have double the heart attack risk of non-smokers and linked with the contraceptive pill in women the risk may even be higher. The body becomes addicted to nicotine, which is a stimulant, and makes the heart beat faster and the blood vessels narrow causing a strain on the cardiovascular system. In addition, the blood becomes more 'sticky' with fats and sugars leading to a 'furring up' of the arteries. Carbon monoxide in cigarette smoke can drastically reduce the capacity of the blood to carry O_2 to the tissues which means again the heart must work harder.

Sexual behaviour

Unprotected sexual activity can lead to the transmission of sexually transmitted infections (STI) such as chlamydia, herpes, genital warts, venereal disease and HIV. Although many STIs are easily treatable with antibiotics they can do severe damage before symptoms begin to show. For instance, pelvic inflammatory disease in women can lead to permanent infertility. There are some STI's which there is still no cure for such as herpes and HIV. In addition, there is some evidence to suggest a link between unprotected sexual intercourse and a virus which may cause cervical and anal cancer.

The risk increases with the number of unprotected sexual partners an individual has had. To combat some of these problems the use of a condom is crucial and can protect against many (though not all) STIs. It is recommended that women should have regular cervical smears from the time they become sexually active. Your choice of sexual lifestyle can have long term implications for your health so it is important to be responsible.

Think about it

The excessive use of alcohol can lead to unwise and unsafe sexual behaviour. Why do you think this is?

What risks to the person or to health can excessive alcoholic intake give?

Exposure to the sun

In moderation the sun is beneficial to our health, promoting a sense of psychological well being and helping in the manufacture of Vitamin D, a substance crucial for the health of the skeletal system. However, too much exposure to the sun's ultraviolet radiation can burn the skin and lead to the development of skin cancer.

Drug use (abuse)

The abuse of different drugs will lead to a variety of effects on the short and long term health and fitness of an individual:

- **Opiates (heroin) effects:** constipation, loss of libido, drowsiness, respiratory distress, an overdose is fatal. It is also linked to the spread of HIV and hepatitis through the sharing of contaminated needles.
- **Amphetamines (speed, whiz) effects:** sleeplessness, anorexia.
- **LSD effects:** sensory distortions, hallucinations, a feeling of panic or anxiety.
- **Ecstasy effects:** hallucinations, heatstroke, dehydration, panic attacks and depression.
- **Cocaine effects:** damage or loss of nasal septum, may cause paranoid psychosis

Drug abuse may also lead to unwise sexual behaviour or involvement in crime.

Think about it

What do you as a group or as an individual feel about the lowering of the classification of cannabis?

Do you think that this will lead to less addictive drug taking or more?

Key points

1. Your lifestyle choices can seriously affect your health and fitness
2. Stress can raise blood pressure and increase cholesterol
3. Regular exercise will help to keep you healthy
4. Healthy eating can enhance your general health
5. Smoking can lead to respiratory disease.

Nutrition

Nutrition is the study of how the body uses foods and nutrients vital to health in promoting growth, maintenance and reproduction of cells. In essence it is how what we eat and drink affects our health. An understanding of nutrition is important as it helps us understand how our body uses the food we eat. There are 7 essential foodstuffs the body must be supplied with:

- protein
- carbohydrate
- fats
- water
- mineral salts
- vitamins
- fibre.

Protein

Protein is composed of chains of amino acids which are the building blocks of cells. They provide cells with material with which to grow and maintain their structure. The human body contains around 20 amino acids.

There are two types of amino acids: essential and non-essential. Non-essential amino acids are made for you by your body, so they don't come from the food you eat. Essential amino acids described below must be acquired through your food, so it is important to have a diet that contains adequate amounts of these proteins.

Essential amino acids (proteins)

- **Histidine:** involved in the creation of histamines which invoke allergic reations. Essential for absoption of zinc and involved in red and white blood cell production.
- **Isoleucine:** promotes recovery after exercise. Also involved in the formation of haemoglobin and in the regulation of blood sugar levels and formation of blood clots.

- **Leucine:** involved in the regulation of blood sugar levels and energy production, also growth and repair of tissue and muscle building.
- **Lysine:** involved in the growth and development of children, tissue repair and the production of hormones and antibodies.
- **Methionine:** involved in the breakdown of fats and cholesterol, assists detoxification of the livers and plays a role in the digestive system.
- **Phenyalanine:** involved in the nervous system, increases chemicals involved in neurotransmission, may have a role in memory and learning.
- **Threonine:** involved in the creation of collagen and elastin in the skin, liver function and the immune system.
- **Tryptophan:** involved in the production of vitamin B_3 niacin, and the production of the neurotransmitter serotonin.
- **Valine:** involved in muscle metabolism, repair and growth of tissue.

The digestive system breaks down protein in the food we eat and allows it to be absorbed into the bloodstream where it is then utilised for growth. Protein is found naturally in foods such as fish, milk and bread, pulses and meat. Protein is also important as it is responsible for making haemoglobin which as you will have read earlier in this chapter is responsible for the transportation of oxygen in the blood. Protein is also a prime ingredient in the white blood cells that fight off infection and repair wounds.

Theory into practice

More and more people are becoming vegetarian and certain religions, for example those of the Hindu faith, have a wholly vegetarian diet. Carry out some research into vegetarian diets looking at sources of non meat protein and present your findings to your group.

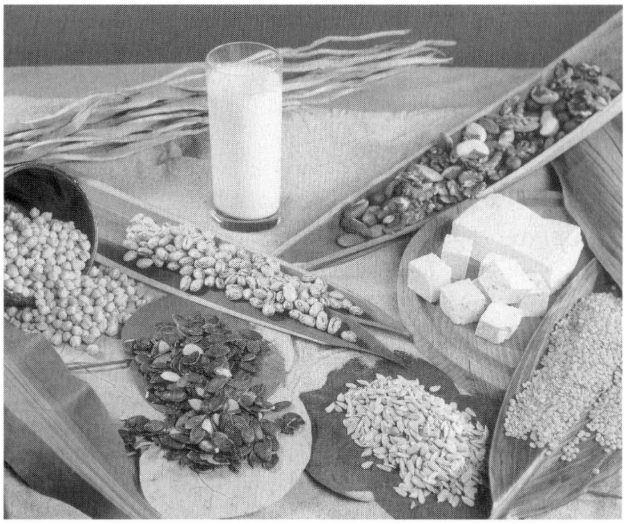

The typical UK diet includes adequate protein

Carbohydrates

Carbohydrates provide fuel for the body. The digestive system enables the absorption of the 'sugars' and 'starches' that make up carbohydrates and allows them to be carried in the bloodstream to every cell in the body where they are converted into a substance called adenosine triphosphate (ATP) which powers the functions of a cell. Sugars such as glucose, fructose (found in fruit) and lactose (found in milk) are called simple carbohydrates (monosaccharides and disaccharides), they are easily digested and enter the bloodstream quickly. There are also complex

Carbohydrate foods include bread, rice, pasta, potatoes and cereals

carbohydrates (polysaccharides), which are commonly called starches. This is when simple carbohydrates are bonded to form a chain. Complex carbohydrates are found in food stuffs such as potatoes, wheat, corn, pasta and rice. The digestive system breaks down the complex carbohydrates into their simple sugars but it takes longer for it to do this. As a result they are released into the bloodstream at a much slower pace therefore keeping you going for longer. If you have an excess of sugars such as glucose they are stored by the body in the liver as a product called glycogen. Additional sugars are also stored as fat. When you are exercising for short periods of time the body uses the energy source from the liver but if you exercise for a long time your body will begin to burn fat instead.

Fats

Fats are also called 'lipids'. A high fat diet can lead to obesity, heart disease, heart attacks and strokes. However, fat is essential to the body in insulating its systems from the cold and cushioning our hardworking organs against jolts and knocks. It also helps process some vitamins and minerals and is the major source of the bodies energy storage. Generally speaking there are 3 kinds of fat.

1. **Saturated fat:** the most harmful type of fat to the body as it can cause clogged arteries leading to coronary disease. They are normally solid at room temperature such as butter and lard and are found primarily in animal products such as meat, eggs and milk, but also in vegetable products such as coconut milk and palm oil. The excessive use of saturated fat in the diet has links with obesity, high levels of cholesterol, breast cancer, strokes and heart disease.
2. **Polyunsaturated fat:** has fewer fatty acid molecules than saturated fat and is generally liquid at room temperature, such as sunflower oil and oily fish. It is thought to be less damaging to the body systems than saturated fats.
3. **Monounsaturated fats:** considered to be the best of all three fats as it actively helps to lower cholesterol levels, they are generally found in food such as olive oil, rapeseed oil, and nuts and seeds.

Fats that you eat in your food are broken down in the digestive system by an enzyme called 'lipase' which ensures they are ready for transport in the bloodstream; the fats are then either used in muscles as fuel or stored for later in 'adipose tissue'. When we consider ourselves 'fat' it is usually because we have too much adipose tissue. It is important to remember that although some fats have a more damaging effect on our body systems than others, there is no difference in their calorie content. Eating too much monounsaturated fat will make you overweight just as quickly as saturated fat will.

Water

The human body is about 60% water and it constantly needs to be replaced as we lose a great deal through respiration, sweating and urine. At rest a person loses approximately 40 ounces of water per day. Without water no system in the body could survive. Many people do not drink enough water to replace the losses which occur naturally in the body. This can lead to inattention, headaches and irritability.

Mineral salts

These are inorganic substances the body must have in order to regulate processes or manufacture specific molecules. They are involved in all body systems and some of the most well known are described in Figure 18.28 overfleaf.

Other minerals include chloride, copper, chromium and fluorine. If these minerals are over abundant in the body then they can have a negative effect. For instance, too much sodium has been linked with high blood pressure. Equally, if mineral levels are low these can be a negative effect, for instance too little iron can lead to anaemia.

Mineral	Function	Sources
Calcium	Bone formation	Milk, dairy produce, green vegetables, nuts and seeds
Iron	Formation of red blood cells	Meat, cereals, vegetables
Iodine	Metabolism and body weight	Fish, seaweed, dairy produce
Magnesium	Bone support, activation of vitamins, production of cholesterol, relaxing effect on muscles	Cereals, green vegetables, potatoes, nuts and seeds
Manganese	Activation of vitamins and enzymes, neutralise poisons in blood, antioxidant	Cereals, nuts, fruit, vegetables
Phosphorus	Provides strength to bones and teeth, transportation of fats, activation of vitamins, cell membranes	Dairy produce, bread, red meat and poultry
Potassium and sodium	Sodium/potassium pump, transmission of nerve impulses, control of body pH, control blood pressure	Vegetables, fruit, sodium in table salt
Selenium	Enzyme activation, recycle iron from red blood cells, joint lubrication, bonds to hazardous heavy metals in the body to facilitate ease of elimination	Cereals, meat, fish, shellfish, brazil nuts
Zinc	Aids calcium absorption, role in sexual maturity, helps in blood sugar regulation	Meat products, shellfish, bread, dairy products

Figure 18.28 Common mineral salts

Fibre

Fibre is important in maintaining health by assisting in eliminating waste products from the bowel. Food high in fibre are those such as whole grain cereals, vegetables, nuts and fruit. Breakfast cereals such as muesli, branflakes and oats are good sources of fibre. Eating a diet rich in fibre is now believed to be crucial in helping to prevent diseases such as bowel cancer, diabetes, irritable bowel syndrome and cancer of the colon.

Theory into practice

Research amounts of fibre in food from any book on nutrition or from the Internet and look at your own diet. You should have around 18g per day – do you?

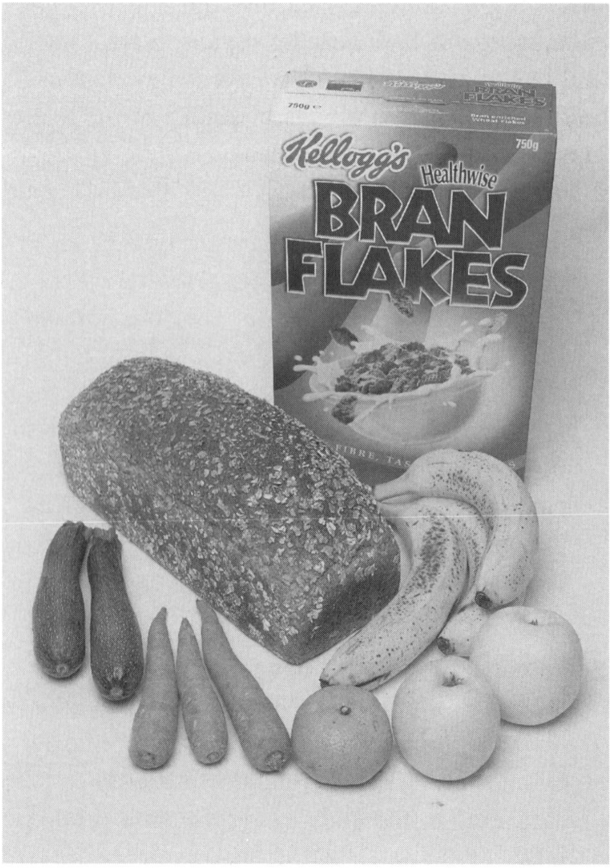

A healthy diet should be high in fibre-rich foods

Key points

1. Nutrition is the study of how the body uses nutrients
2. The body needs protein, carbohydrates, fats, water, minerals and vitamins
3. Proteins are the building blocks of the body
4. Carbohydrates provide energy
5. Fats stores energy and cushions and protect organs.

Vitamins

Vitamins are organic compounds which can provide energy for the body and help assist chemical reactions within the cells of your body and help regulate metabolic processes. The human body needs 13 different vitamins. Vitamins are divided into fat soluble (A D E K) and water soluble (vitamins from the B group and Vitamin C).

Think about it

You may have heard about scurvy as a disease once suffered by sailors on long voyages. Do some research and find out who discovered a cure for scurvy and what it was. Who would be at risk from scurvy these days?

Fruit and vegetables are a rich source of vitamins, particularly Vitamin C

Balancing a diet

A well balanced diet should contain enough of the five food components to keep the body running smoothly (see Figure 18.30 on page 313).

As you can see a well balanced diet would consist of enough of each of these components to satisfy the needs of the body. The portions outlined in Figure 18.31 on page 314 are only an indication of the amount of food you should eat to stay healthy as it depends on your current weight, level of physical activity and current health. As a general guide a 10 stone woman should be aiming for

Vitamin	Source	Function	Deficiency	Excess
A (retinol)	Animal foods only: fish liver oils, liver, kidney, eggs, carrots, red vegetables, spinach, also added to margarine.	Essential for vision and healthy growth of skin	Night blindness	Excess can kill
D (calciferol)	Action of sunlight on human skin. Dairy produce, liver, oily fish.	Helps absorption of calcium and builds strong bones	Deficiency causes a disease called rickets and other diseases related to soft bones	Too much vitamin D is dangerous: calcium excess if deposited in the kidneys
E	Most foods especially oily foods, wholegrain cereals and eggs.	Antioxidant	Rare	
K	Manufactured in the intestine. Also green leafy vegetables.	Essential for blood clotting	Rare	

Figure 18.29 Functions of vitamins

Vitamin	Source	Function	Deficiency	Excess
Vitamin B1 ● thiamin	Milk, offal, pork, eggs, fruit, vegetables, cereals and yeast extract.	Release of energy from carbohydrates, functioning of the central nervous system	Disease called beri-beri	
Vitamin B2 ● riboflavin	Dairy produce, offal, red meat, eggs, green vegetables, cereals and yeast extract.	Energy release from proteins, carbohydrates and fat	Sores at the corners of the mouth	
Vitamin B6 ● pyrixodine	Meats, fish, eggs, wholecereals and some vegetables.	Metabolism of protein and formation of haemoglobin	Rare	
Vitamin B12 ● cyanobalamin	Liver, eggs, meat, milk, fish, cheese, cereals and yeast extract.	Required for healthy red blood cells. Metabolism of proteins, carbohydrates and fats and helping cell growth. It is also vital for the normal functioning of the central nervous system	Disease called pernicious anaemia. Also degeneration of nerve cells	
Biotin	Cereals, dairy foods, meat and eggs.	Release of energy from proteins, carbohydrates and fats	Hair and skin disorders	
Niacin	Meat, fish, dairy produce, cereals and yeast extracts.	Relase of energy from proteins, carbohydrates and fats	A disease called pellagra which causes painful skin lesions	
Folic Acid	Offal, raw green leafy vegetables, cereals and yeast.	Developing healthy red blood cells	Anaemia. Pregnant women require folic acid to help prevent foetal abnormalities developing	
Pantothenic Acid	Offal, meat, nuts, vegetables and yeast extracts.	Metabolism of protein, carbohydrates and fats	Rare	
Vitamin C (ascorbic acid)	Fresh fruit and vegetables especially citrus fruit.	Maintain healthy connective tissues, absorption of iron, wound healing. Antioxidant	Scurvy, slow healing of wounds bleeding gums	

Figure 18.29 ctd. Functions of vitamins

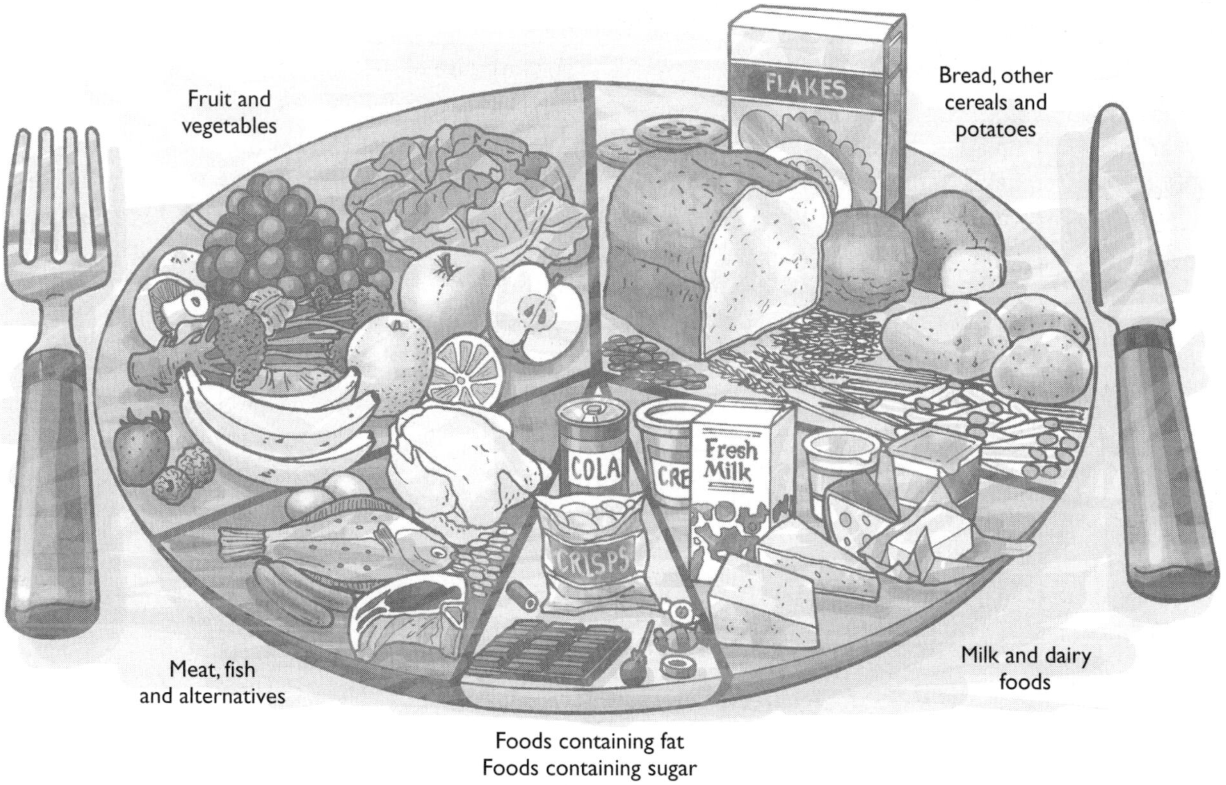

Figure 18.30 The Balance of Good Health model

around 2300kcals per day and a 11.5 stone man around 3000kcals per day.

A balanced diet can help to improve health and reduce the incidence of heart disease and cancer. A study by the National Audit Office published in February 2001 found that nearly two thirds of adults in England are overweight or obese. This costs the health services over £2.5 billion per year. Obesity is a growing problem across the Western world. It is on the increase due to the availability of high fat and sugar foods and snacks and a decrease in the amount of exercise we take.

Key concept

Obesity is a state in which the weight of a person is at a level where it can seriously endanger their health.

Think about it

Why does having an obese population cost the health service so much money?

Assessment activity 18-P2, 18-M2

In the following role play you take the part of a public services physical fitness instructor having a 1–1 discussion with a potential recruit. You must advise them on how they can best prepare themselves physically for a career in the public services. Describe and analyse to them the effects of lifestyle, balanced diet and good nutrition on health and fitness and how following your advice might improve their public service job prospects.

Assessment activity 18-D1

Justify the need for a healthy lifestyle and a balanced diet to ensure health and fitness.

Suggested proportions of different foods groups in the UK National Food Guide				
Food group	**Food types**	**Serving size**	**Amount recommended**	**Main nutrients supplied**
Bread, cereals and potatoes	Bread, rolls, muffins, bagels, crumpets, chapattis, naan bread, pitta bread, tortillas, scones, pikelets, potato cakes, breakfast cereals, rice, pasta, noodles, cous cous and potatoes	3 tbsp breakfast cereal, 1 Weetabix or Shredded Wheat, 1 slice of bread, $\frac{1}{2}$ pitta, 1 heaped tbsp boiled potato, pasta, rice, cous cous	These should form the main part of all meals and snacks About a third of total volume of food consumed each day	Carbohydrate, NSP – mainly insoluble, calcium, iron and B vitamins
Fruit and vegetables	All types of fresh, frozen, canned and dried fruits and vegetables except potatoes, and fruit and vegetable juices	1 apple, orange, pear, banana, 1 small glass of fruit or vegetable juice, 1 small salad, 2 tbsp vegetables, 2 tbsp stewed or tinned fruit in juice	At least 5 portions each day About a third of total volume of food consumed each day	NSP – especially soluble, vitamin C, folate and potassium
Milk and dairy products	Milk, yoghurt, cheese and fromage frais	$\frac{1}{3}$ pint milk, $1\frac{1}{4}$ oz cheese, 1 small carton of yoghurt or cottage cheese	2–3 servings per day About a sixth of total volume of food consumed each day	Protein, calcium, vitamins A and D
Meat, fish and alternative protein sources	Meat, poultry, fish, eggs, pulses and nuts Meat and fish products such as sausages, beefburgers, fish cakes and fish fingers	2–3 oz of lean meat, chicken, or oily fish, 4–5 oz white fish, 2 eggs, 1 small tin baked beans, 2 tbsp nuts, 4 oz Quorn or soya	2 servings per day About a sixth of total volume of food consumed each day	Protein, iron, zinc, magnesium and B vitamins Pulses provide a good source of NSP
Foods containing fat and sugar	Fat-rich: butter, margarine, cooking oils, mayonnaise and salad dressings, cream, pastries, crisps, biscuits and cakes Sugar-rich: sweets, jams, honey, marmalade, soft drinks, biscuits, cakes and pastries	1 tsp butter or margarine 1 tsp vegetable or olive oil 1 tsp mayonnaise	These should be eaten sparingly and where possible lower fat options selected Extra energy provided by sugars may be useful in meeting carbohydrate requirements for active individuals	Fat-rich: fat, essential fatty acids and some vitamins Sugar-rich: carbohydrate and some vitamins and minerals

Figure 18.31 Food groups and their recommended intake

Principles of fitness P3

Strength

Strength can be defined as the maximum muscular force we can apply against resistance. It can be demonstrated in 3 ways:

Static strength: this involves isometric resistance against a stationary load. For example, pushing as hard as you can against a wall or pulling against an equal force as in a 'tug o war'.

Dynamic strength: uses isotonic muscle contractions to move heavy loads such as in weight training or power lifting.

Explosive strength: the use of fast and powerful muscular reactions. An example of this would be the static long jump, which is present in some public service fitness tests.

Fitness centres have a number of fixed resistance machines

There are several important strength training principles which are essential if you are to improve your strength. Firstly, in order to see gains in strength, your muscles must be stimulated more than they are used to which is called overload. Secondly, muscles must continually work against a gradually increasing resistance in order to maintain overload. This is called the principle of 'progression'. Thirdly, there is the principle of 'specificity' which is that the strength gains you receive from training depend on the particular muscle groups used and the particular movement performed. There are many benefits to increasing muscular strength, such as:

- Increased strength of tendons and ligaments which may help prevent strains and sprains while taking part in physical activity. This increases strength in an individual's joints which may also have the potential to help him or her become more flexible.
- Reduced body fat and increased lean muscle mass which helps the body's metabolic system run more effectively and enables food to be utilised more efficiently.
- May help to reduce resting systolic and diastolic blood pressure.
- May help reduce the amount of LDL cholesterol in the body thus offering some protection from the 'furring' up of arteries, which can lead to coronary heart disease.

Stamina

Stamina is also known as aerobic endurance, which put simply is the ability to repeat an activity for a length of time without becoming fatigued. This is crucial to performance in many sports whether it is a 90 minute football match or a 3 hour long distance run. Stamina depends on the efficiency of your cardiovascular system (heart, blood, blood vessels, lungs) in terms of how well they provide the muscles with oxygen. There are different forms of stamina:

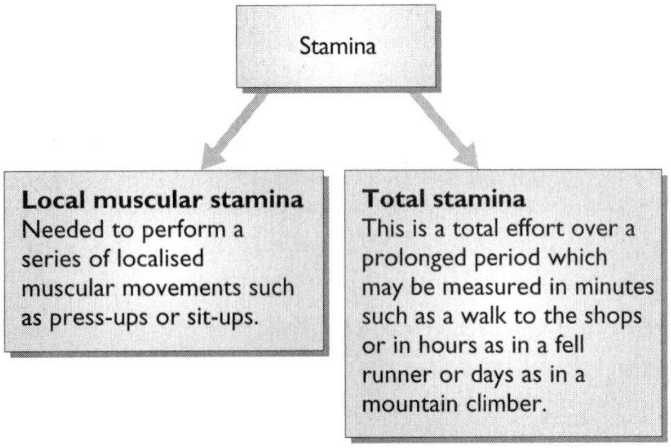

Stamina
Local muscular stamina
Needed to perform a series of localised muscular movements such as press-ups or sit-ups.
Total stamina
This is a total effort over a prolonged period which may be measured in minutes such as a walk to the shops or in hours as in a fell runner or days as in a mountain climber.

As with strength training, the efficient and effective use of our oxygen transport system can protect us against heart disease in later life. In addition, the ability to perform physical tasks over sustained periods with minimum fatigue is crucial in sports performance.

Speed

Speed is the ability to move a part of the body or the whole body quickly. Speed can be crucial in many sports where the activity is timed or you may be required to outpace an opponent. Speed is not just important for athletes, it is also important in a public services role as a quick physical reaction time might help you avoid injury at work or perhaps chase and run down criminal suspects.

It is possible to improve our speed with speed training methods such as fartlek training or speed play. These techniques are based upon constant changes in speed.

Suppleness

Suppleness and flexibility is defined as the range of movement possible at joints. Up until the age of 40, ligaments, tendons and muscles are relatively elastic but after this age, movement that is not used frequently can be decreased and eventually lost. This can cause problems and injuries if the body is suddenly asked to do something it has not done for a while.

In terms of sports performance, suppleness will help reduce the risk of injury, improve the execution of sports skills and reduce the likelihood of muscle soreness. Suppleness can be developed and maintained by stretching exercises or activities such as yoga and swimming. It is recommended that an individual should employ 5 or 10 minutes of stretching prior to beginning any sport or a physical activity in order to prepare the muscles for what is to follow. Stretching should also be conducted after physical activity since it helps to initiate the recovery process. There are several methods of stretching:

- **Active stretching:** where an individual moves a part of their body slightly beyond the usual range and holds for a few seconds.
- **Passive stretching:** an individual's body is moved beyond the normal range of movement by a partner and held there for a few seconds.
- **Ballistic stretching:** involves moving the body well beyond the normal range of motion by way of swinging or bouncing movements. It is not recommended for use at all.
- **Proprioceptive neuro-muscular facilitation (PNF):** an individual moves the body beyond the usual range of movement, contracts and releases the muscle involved and then moves a little further.

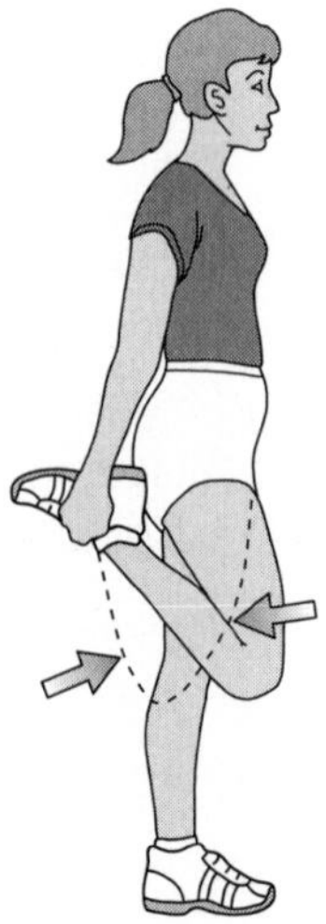

Figure 18.32 Active stretching gives increased flexibility and strength

Skill

Skill is the coarse and fine motor control that is required to perform specific abilities. It is a measure of how proficient an individual is at a particular physical ability which is vital to sports performance. For instance, it doesn't matter it you have strength, stamina and suppleness if you can't hit a tennis ball with a racquet. Skill can be improved by repetition and practice.

Sleep

Sleep is a period of unconsciousness which the body uses to perform vital functions such as:

- repair and replace damaged or aged tissues
- archive and organise memories and information in the brain
- reduce energy consumption
- recharge the brain.

A lack of sleep can severely affect mental and physical performance:

- Missing one night – irritable, fatigued or may experience adrenaline surges.
- Two nights – poor concentration and attention, increases in mistakes and error, extreme fatigue.
- After 3 days – possible hallucinations and other distortions of perception, loss of sense of reality.

Individuals with disturbed sleep patterns may experience these symptoms developing over a period of time. This has a particular consequences for the public services who often rely on rotating shift patterns for effective operation.

Agility

This is the ability to move with quick fluid grace and it is critical for improving sports performance. It involves rapid changes in speed and direction while maintaining balance and skill. Like skill it can be developed with practice and is improved by developing strength, stamina and suppleness.

Assessment activity 18-P3

Produce an A3 poster with a public services theme which describes the principles of fitness and how they might apply to your performance in a public service of your choice.

Fitness testing P4+5

There are many benefits to undertaking a series of fitness tests, for instance:

- to establish the strengths and weaknesses of an individual in order to design an appropriate training programme
- to provide a baseline initial fitness level against which future progress can be measured
- to ascertain level of fitness loss after injury, illness or pregnancy
- to allow medical practioners to recognise and assess some specific health problems such as coronary heart disease.

Methods

If you wish to examine the physical fitness tests for a particular public service you are advised to read Unit 9: Physical Preparation for the public services in the Award book (Book 1) which considers specific uniformed services tests and pass rates. This chapter will examine some of the tests used by the public services in general.

- multi stage fitness test (MSFT)
- step test
- push ups test
- sit ups test
- sit and reach test
- body fat percentage
- body mass index
- vertical and horizontal jumps
- grip strength

MSFT

This test involves continuous running between two markers 20m apart in time with a set of pre-recorded bleeps (often called the bleep test for this reason). The start speed of this test is about 8.5km/hr which is really just a fast walk, but the time between the bleeps increases every minute or every level which means that running speed must increase by 0.5km/hr each time the level changes if the individual is to keep time with the bleeps.

One advantage of this test is that large numbers of people can be tested at the same time but the disadvantage is that you need to be highly motivated to run until you can't go any further. Many people drop out earlier than this. Also audio tapes can stretch which may distort an individual's score. Scoring is based on the number of levels and shuttles completed, for example 7/2 means level 7 has been reached and 2 shuttles completed.

The scoring levels for both male and female participants are shown in Figure 18.32 below

Step test

The 3-minute step test is an aerobic assessment which measures the heart rate in the recovery period following 3 minutes of stepping. The stepping is conducted at a set rate of 24 steps per minute for 3 minutes. Immediately upon completion, a 60 second pulse rate is taken at the carotiol pulse in the neck. This recovery heart rate is the measure of an individual's fitness.

Push ups test

This is an assessment of the muscular endurance of the chest, shoulders and arms. The total number of press ups completed in one minute is the score. Traditionally, the press ups for males and females differ as men should be in contact with the ground at their hands and toes while women should be in contact with the ground at their hands and knees or on a slightly raised bar. The resting position is up with elbows locked.

Sit ups test

Like the previous test, this is also an assessment of muscular endurance but this time the muscles involved are the abdominals and hip flexors. The test involves the number of sit ups completed in one minute.

Sit and reach test

This test is a flexibility and suppleness assessment. The individual sits down with their legs straight out in front of them and the soles of their feet flat against a box with a measuring device such as a ruler or distance gauge on top of it. They then reach forward with the fingertips to see how far past their toes they can reach. The movement should be smooth and continuous rather than lunging. The test is very easy to administer but it only assesses hamstring flexibility rather than the flexibility of the whole body. The test is usually measured in centimetres and as a rough guide females tend to be slightly more flexible than males.

Body fat percentage

This is a measure of a person's distribution of fat in the body. It is usually measured with skinfold callipers although many gyms now measure it electronically with a device very similar to weighing scales but which measures electrical resistance in the body. Callipers can pose a problem in that they can be difficult to use accurately. Measurements are normally taken in 4 places:

- bicep
- tricep

Gender and age	Excellent	Good	Average	Fair	Poor
Female 17–20	10/11	9/3	6/8	52	<4/9
Male 17–20	12/12	11/6	9/2	7/6	<7/3

Figure 18.33 Scoring levels for the multi stage fitness test

- subscapula (below shoulder blade)
- supraillia (just above the waist)

The measurements in millimetres are then calculated to give a body fat percentage. Generally a reading of 12–20.9% in males is acceptable and 17–27% for women.

Body mass index (BMI)

This is another test of body composition and it is very easy to calculate using a simple formula. Multiply your height in metres by itself and then divide it into your mass in kilograms. For example, a female with a height of 1.6m and a mass of 66kg

$$1.6 \times 1.6 = 2.56\text{m}^2 \quad = \frac{66\text{kg}}{2.56\text{m}^2}$$

This female has a BMI of 25.7, which is very slightly overweight. Generally a BMI of 20–25 is ideal.

Think about it

Calculate your own BMI using the calculation above. What does your BMI say about your level of health and fitness?

Vertical and horizontal jumps

Jumps in fitness testing are designed to measure explosive power in the legs. An example of a vertical jump is the sergeant jump when an individual marks the full extent of their normal reach on a wall or vertical measuring board and then tries to touch a point as far beyond the initial mark as possible using the power of their legs. An example of a horizontal test is the standing long jump where an individual stands at the edge of a horizontal measuring board and with both feet together jumps forward as far as they can.

Grip test

This test measures the strength of an individual's grip by use of a grip strength dynamometer. The dynamometer is set at 0 and the handle adjusted to fit the size of the palm. Then the dynamometer is simply squeezed as hard as possible. The reading on the gauge tells you how strong your grip is. Generally most people find the hand that they use frequently is usually the stronger.

Reliability of fitness tests M3

It is important to remember that fitness tests can be influenced and distorted by several factors, such as the individuals health, their emotional state, the temperature, lack of sleep, the time of day and the time since the individual last ate or drank. In selecting tests to measure fitness you must take into account issues of reliability, validity and accuracy:

- **Reliability:** is the test able to repeatedly measure the same physical component?
- **Validity:** does the test actually measure what you want it to?
- **Accuracy:** how accurate are the results. What are the possibilities of error?

As with any physical fitness activity, the safety and well being of the participants must be of paramount importance. For further information on health and safety please see Unit 9: Physical preparation for the uniformed services.

Assessment activity 18-P4, 18-P5, 18-P6

Take part in a number of fitness tests as described above and record your results. Once you have completed at least four of them review, explain and compare the different tests you used. Present your findings to a group of your colleagues and explain the principles behind fitness testing methods. Do you think your performance could have been improved? If so, tell your colleagues how.

Assessment activity 18-M3, 18-D2

After you have comleted the four different testing methods described in the previous assessment activity write a brief report which analyses and evaluates the reliability, validity, accuracy and safety of each test you did. Conclude this report with a closing statement that justifies the use of fitness testing methods for entry into the public services.

End of unit questions

1. What is the study of anatomy?
2. What is the study of physiology?
3. What are the functions of the skeletal system?
4. Describe how bones can be classified.
5. List and describe joint types.
6. What are the functions of the muscular system?
7. Describe the types of muscle found in the body.
8. Identify types of muscle contraction.
9. What are the benefits of a healthy muscular system?
10. Describe the flow of blood in the pulmonary and systemic circuits.
11. Describe the main parts of the respiratory system.
12. What is the impact of smoking on athletic performance?
13. Describe the anatomy of the heart.
14. What are the names of the vessels involved in blood transport?
15. Describe the types and functions of white blood cells.
16. Describe Sheldon's body types and possible exercise regimes for each type.
17. What effect does stress have on the body?
18. What components make up a healthy, balanced diet?
19. What are the consequences of vitamin C deficiency?
20. List and describe the principles of fitness.

Resources

Gray, D et al, *Public Services Book 1*, 2004, London, Heinemann

Galligan, F et al, *Advanced PE for Edexcel*, 2000, London, Heinemann

Morton, D et al, *Advanced PE Through Diagrams*, 2000, Oxford, Oxford University Press

Woods, B and McIlveen, R, *Applying Psychology to Sport*, 1998, London, Hodder and Stoughton

Website

www.policecouldyou.co.uk

CRIMINOLOGY

Introduction to Unit 21

This is the criminology unit of this textbook. It will assist you in developing an awareness and understanding of the theories of crime and deviance. You will have the opportunity to explore crime trends and the effect of crime on the community in terms of finance, emotional trauma and the social impact. It will examine fear of crime and the role played by the media in portraying crime.

The chapter will then proceed to examine how crime is reported to the police and the problems with reported and recorded crime. We will then look at the courts and crime prevention issues. By the time you have examined these topics you should have a clear idea of the criminology you are required to understand in order to pass your National Award, Certificate or Diploma.

Assessment

The unit is assessed internally and you may be able to use a range of assessment methods (presentations, practical activities, assignments) to produce the evidence you require. Within this unit there are lots of different activities and opportunities for discussion which will help you work to the desired grade.

Outcomes

1 Research the theories associated with **criminal** and deviant behaviour, exploring the **effects of crime** on society

2 Investigate and evaluate the methods of **reporting** and **recording crime**

3 Examine and provide an overview of the **judicial system**

4 Explore the multi-agency approach to **crime reduction** and devise effective strategies to improve community safety.

Criminal and deviant behaviour and the effects of crime

Crime has become a national preoccupation over the last few decades. News programmes comment on it every day and our entertainment consists of programmes such as The Bill, A Touch of Frost and numerous true crime documentaries. The study of criminology seeks to examine crime from every angle. It discusses what crime is, how it can be explained and how it may be controlled. Television shows and public attention aside, the concept of crime is more complicated than you might think.

Criminology is a multi-disciplinary subject which draws much of its evidence and research from related subject areas such as:

- sociology
- psychology
- biology
- geography
- law
- anthropology.

The information from these subject areas can help us address the first 2 issues we need to discuss: What is crime and how can it be explained?

Think about it

Write down in 2 sentences or less your own definition of crime.

If you have completed the above task you might have defined crime as:

- an act punishable by law
- something a person does that is illegal
- behaviour which is contrary to the laws of society.

These answers are not wrong but neither are they entirely right.

These definitions do not reflect the fact that what constitutes a crime differs from time to time, place to place and culture to culture. Crime is not a rigid concept, it is not always the same wherever you go – it is constantly changing. For example:

- until 1908 incest was not regarded as a criminal offence in the UK
- until 1967 homosexuality was against the law
- until 1991 there was no crime of rape within marriage.

The above examples relate to our own country, but laws are different in every country you go to, for instance:

- in the Netherlands the age of sexual consent is 12, here it is 16
- in the Republic of Ireland abortion is illegal, here it is legal.

Think about it

What acts are considered criminal now, but might be legal in 5 years?

Can you think of any actions which are now legal but may be illegal is 5 years?

Think about it

If rules of what is considered to be right and wrong are so changeable can anything really be considered to be a crime? Discuss this in pairs.

Theories of crime

There are 3 broad approaches to explaining why people commit crime:

- **Biological or genetic**: this view argues that crime is due to biological inheritance. Criminals are born with a propensity to commit crime.
- **Sociological**: this group of theories see crime as a result of social processes and pressures on individuals and groups. Crime is created by society.
- **Psychological**: these theories see crime as linked to the personality of the individual. Faulty socialisation produces personality disorders which lead to criminal behaviour. Criminals are not truly 'normal' people.

Biology – nature Vs nurture argument

The nature vs nurture debate discusses this issue of whether criminals are born or made.

Think about it

Do you think criminals are born or made? Explain your reasons.

Nature

The nature side of the debate concentrates on the genetic inheritance we are given by our parents and the role of these genes in the personality and intellectual development of an individual. This view enjoyed great popularity in the early part of the last century and it was heavily influenced by the work of biologists such as Charles Darwin whose research highlighted the importance of hereditary in the ability to survive and be biologically successful.

Genetic determinism argues that our personality and intellectual characteristics are inherited from our parents which includes the tendency to commit crime. The evidence for this side of the debate lies in the results of scientifically controlled experiments such as twin studies and family studies, which examine crime and delinquent behaviour in groups of genetically related individuals.

Twin studies: identical twins (also called monozygotic or MZ twins) share exactly the same genes. Pairs of twins have been studied to test whether if one becomes a criminal, the other is also likely to be criminal. This is called 'concordance'. The concordance for non-identical twins should be lower as they only have about half their genes in common. There does seem to be some evidence to support this, such as studies of Goldman and Cottesman (1995) which showed that if a twin committed a crime, the likelihood of the other twin committing a crime was higher for identical twins than amongst non-identical twins. However, other researchers have pointed out that most identical twins also share the same environment and argue this plays a more important role in the commission of crime.

Identical twins share the same genes

Family studies: if crime is a product of genetic determinism then it should show concordance in related individuals (crime should 'run in the family'). This form of study has a long history: Dugdale (1875) inspected a prison in the US and realised that 6 of the prisoners were related. He eventually traced hundreds of relatives in an attempt to assess the pattern of criminality in this family who were nicknamed 'The Jukes'. There is more modern evidence which highlights that criminal parents are more likely to have children who become involved in criminal behaviour than parents who are law abiding. Farrington (1991) carried out a thirty year study based on following a group of working class boys to examine if, when and why they became delinquent. It was found that 6% of families were responsible for 50% of the criminal acts reported. This appears to indicate that crime does have some kind of familial link and geneticists argue that this is a result of genetic transmission of genes which will cause anti-social behaviour and crime.

Nurture

The nurture side of the argument believes that our lived experiences are the main influences on our behaviour. For example, the Farrington study described above identifies that many crimes are committed by just a few families, but it also highlighted that some of the primary factors associated with crime amongst working class boys are:

- **Low family income**: although poverty does not itself cause crime, the economic deprivation which goes along with it may lead to individuals wanting a standard of life they cannot afford, which may in turn lead them to get this standard of life through illegitimate means.
- **Poor child-rearing techniques**: not all parents are effective in their child-rearing role. If parents do not care or do not show an interest in the behaviour of their children then the children may be more likely to become delinquent. Equally if children are raised in a

violent home or with inconsistent discipline they may be less likely to have a clear understanding of social boundaries and be more likely to commit a crime.

- **Large families:** Farrington discovered that families with many children had more of a likelihood of having some of those children become delinquent. This may be because large families are very demanding and children may not always get the attention and guidance they need.
- **Low educational achievement:** education is the key to economic success and low educational achievement can mean poverty or unemployment in adult life.

These factors would seem to support the notion that criminal behaviour is acquired rather than inherited.

Conclusion to nature v nurture debate

The debate surrounding Nature/Nurture is unlikely to be resolved any time soon as the evidence that each side of the argument produces often does not show the full picture of crime and leaves many questions unanswered. The current debate centres not around Nature or Nurture alone, but how these 2 different perspectives could be combined to explain criminal behaviour.

Simulation

Saara and Sureya are non-identical twins who are raised in the same home environment, with their younger brother Parvis and mother and father. When the twins are 16 their younger brother who is 14 begins to get into trouble at school. This trouble eventually becomes more serious and Parvis is sent to a young offender institution at the age of 15. The twins father also had a history of petty crime in his youth, but is a responsible and upstanding citizen now. The twins mother has never had involvement in crime.

1. Explain how supporters of the nature argument would explain how Parvis became involved in breaking the law.
2. Explain how supporters of the nurture argument would explain Parvis's criminality.
3. What is the likelihood that the twins will engage in criminal activity?
4. How might Saara and Sureya differ in concordance from identical twins?
5. Is the twins mother likely to become criminal?

Think about it

If crime is linked to genetic inheritance, how might this affect:

- the way criminals are sentenced?
- the way crime is prevented?

Key points

1. Nature is the argument that criminals are born.
2. Nurture is the argument that criminals are made.
3. There is evidence on both sides of the debate.
4. The real relationship between nature and nurture is still unknown.

Sociological theories

Sociological theories focus on society as the primary cause of crime. This unit examines 4 main theories:

- Functionalism
- Marxism
- Labelling theory
- Chicago School (this has links with geography)

Functionalism

Functionalism developed from the work of Emile Durkheim (1858–1917) who was an active social theorist at the end of the nineteenth century. Durkheim believed that for societies to exist and work effectively there had to be a strong sense of social order. In other words, there had to be an agreement among the members of society about values and rules or norms. He called this agreement in society a 'collective conscience'. A collective conscience is the collective feeling in a group of people about what is wrong or right. Crime and deviance is therefore any behaviour which breaks key social rules or laws. Most people, most of the time, abide by the rules of society but some people break the rules and become criminals. Durkheim agrued that:

1 **Crime is universal and normal**: Durkheim and later functionalists have argued that crime exists in every single community and society you will find across the globe. In every group of people there will be those who break the rules and transgress the law. Functionalists argue that because crime happens everywhere it can be considered to be a normal part of any given society.

2 **Crime is relative**: this means that crime is not constant and it has changed throughout history, from culture to culture and place to place. The acts which contribute breaches of the law are not fixed and static, they change and shift in response to the needs of the time period, the needs of the culture and the changing morality of a society.

3 **Crime is functional and necessary**: Durkheim believed that crime and deviance was both useful and necessary for society as long as it did not reach excessive amounts. Crime was seen as necessary for society for 2 reasons:

- The punishment of rule breakers marks what is considered acceptable behaviour. It lets us know the boundaries of what we can and can't do.
- Crime and deviance can contribute towards social change by providing a constant test of the boundaries. If laws are tested often enough sometimes a change can be made.

Think about it

Do you think it would ever be possible to have a crime-free society?

Theory into practice

The legislation of abortion is a social change which was brought about by people campaigning to change the law. Can you think of a more recent example of changes in society which have resulted from people challenging the law?

Functionalism and anomie

In times of rapid social change the collective conscience of society can be weakened. This means that the shared values of a community become less important and people may be left without clear norms, rules or guidelines on how they should behave. This is a state called 'anomie'. Anomie is discussed in one of Durkheim's most famous books 'Suicide' (1897) in which he asserted that in times of economic upheaval society cannot put controls on peoples dreams and aspirations. In an economic depression people may have to lower their sights and they may not be able to cope with this and in times of prosperity people may set their sights so high that they have no sense of achievement. This leads to the controls society puts on people breaking down, which ultimately leads them into crime and deviant behaviour.

Think about it

Do you think people behave worse when they are free of clear guidelines for behaviour?

Do you think our society today has clear guidelines for behaviour or do we suffer from anomie?

Evaluation of functionalism

The following criticisms have been made about Durkheim's functionalism theory:

- some have argued that crime rates don't increase during times of great social change
- Durkheim based many of his ideas on official statistics which were flawed
- the concept of 'collective conscience' is vague and relatively undefined.

Think about it

Do you think you are part of a collective conscience? Explain your reasons.

Key points

1 Crime is universal and normal.
2 Crime is relative.
3 Crime is functional and necessary.
4 Anomie is a state of normlessness caused by rapid social change.
5 Individuals are encouraged not to commit crime by the existence of the collective conscience.

Merton's strain theory

Heavily influence by Durkheim, Robert Merton (1938) took on board and developed the concept of anomie further. He called this development Strain theory. Although Merton built upon the work of Durkheim, they differ in that Durkheim argued that anomie was caused by rapid social change leading to social disorganisation and a state of normlessness. For Merton, anomie was caused by a social structure which encourages all people to strive for the same cultural goals, such as wealth, but does not provide individuals with equal means to achieve them.

The goals that people strive for in Merton's analysis are things such as economic affluence, a nice home, a car or a rewarding job. Since Merton's view was predominantly US based it focussed around the goal of the pursuit of wealth known as 'The American Dream'. According to society these goals can only be achieved via socially acceptable means such as dedication and hard work. However, Merton argues that the system does not operate a level playing field and some individuals will achieve the goal with very little effort while some will never achieve it no matter how hard they try. Merton was keen to understand how people coped with being given these culturally defined goals, but not the means to achieve them – he called this 'strain'.

Merton described 5 ways that individuals can adapt to conditions of strain:

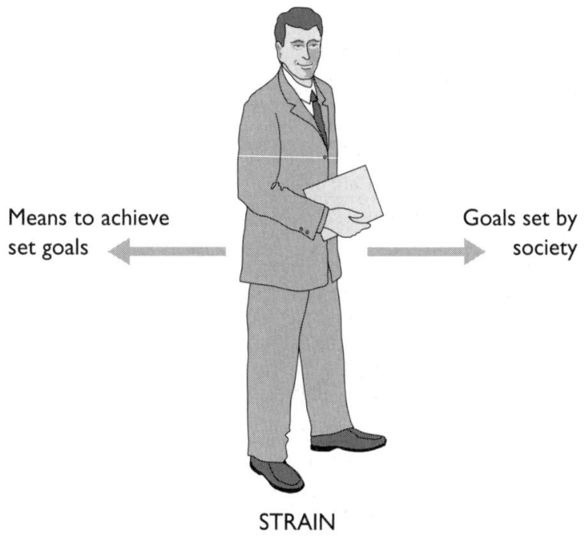

Figure 21.1 Merton's strain theory

- **Conformity**: conformists accept the goals given to them by society and accept the means of achieving them by hard work and dedication.
- **Innovation**: innovators also accept the cultural goals given to them by society, but they reject the traditional ways of achieving them. Instead they may resort to illegitimate means of acquiring wealth such as crime or deviant behaviour
- **Ritualism**: a ritualist rejects the goals of society and lowers his or her sights to a more achievable goal. However, they accept the traditional means of achieving them. Merton argued that this adaptation to strain was more

likely to occur in the middle classes and he provided the example of a bureaucrat or jobsworth.

- **Retreatism**: retreatists reject the goals of society and also the methods of achieving it. These people may drop out of society altogether, Merton gave the examples of drug abusers and vagrants.
- **Rebellion**: the rebel does not accept societies goals and instead creates his/her own goals and also creates new methods of achieving them. Terrorists are a good example of this adaptation.

Merton argues that crime is caused by the adaptation individuals make to try and resolve the 'strain' they feel between the goals they are required to strive for and the tools they have to achieve the goals.

Evaluation of Merton

The following criticisms have been made about Merton's strain theory:

1. **Reliance on official statistics**: Merton believed that most crime was committed by the working classes, who had more reason than most to innovate, retreat or rebel. This was based on official data which is often flawed and is a weak foundation for a theory of crime.
2. **Concentration on crimes of the lower classes**: since Merton belived that the lower classes experienced most strain he focussed much of his work here. However, this means that white collar crime, corporate crime and crimes of the powerful were largely ignored.
3. **Not everyone has the same goals**: it may be the case that not everyone in the US aspired to achieve 'The American Dream'. Different cultures, societies and communities may set their own goals. This predominantly US based theory does not translate well to many other nations.
4. **Merton doesn't explain how an individual chooses one adaptation over another**: why be an innovator instead of a rebel?
5. **Merton does not explain crimes that are not financial in nature and do not seek to enhance the status of the individual**: for example, how does 'The American Dream' apply to crimes such as common assault or vandalism?

Think about it

Do you think Merton's theory that society is obsessed with material success is convincing in explaining:

- property crime
- drug addiction
- terrorism.

Marxist theory of crime

Marxist perspectives in criminology have proved very influential and the original ideas of Karl Marx (1818–1883) have lead to the development of several different Marxist views on crime. It includes theories such as:

- The new criminology
- Critical criminology
- Radical criminology
- Left realism
- Conflict theory

Considering how influential the Marxist school of thought has been it may appear surprising that Marx himself did not have a great deal to say on the subject of crime. Marx put forward a theory of society not a theory of crime. In the Marxist view of the world, economics and ownership of the means of production are of ultimate importance and economic power influences everything else in society. The means of production are factories, farms and industries which create the basic needs for people's existence and employ the workers in a society. It is your relationship to the mean of production which defines your social class, Marx identified two social classes, the bourgeoisie (owners of the means of production) and the proletariat (working classes).

In the traditional Marxist view these two social classes are in constant conflict with each other and this process leads to social change. The cause of this conflict between classes is economic. The proletariat create wealth by working in factories and industry and the bourgeoisie take all the profit for themselves. The proletariat does not protest at this because they are led to believe that society is fair and just and the social order is based on personal merit and hard work. This is the collective conscience discussed by the functionalists earlier. Functionalists take the notion of collective conscience for granted, but Marxists believe the collective conscience is manufactured by the bourgeoisie and given to the proletariat in order to keep them docile and maintain the status quo.

This collective way of thinking is created by agencies such as the media, school and the family. Louis Althusser a follower of Marx, called agencies such as this Ideological State Apparatus (ISAs). The role of ISAs is to socialise the proletariat into submission, it creates acceptance of the way things are. If ISAs fail in their role and members of the proletariat try to change society they are stopped by what Althusser calls Repressive State Apparatus (RSA's). This includes agencies such as the police and army who act as the muscle of the bourgeoisie as they repress the proletariat.

Think about it

Althusser argues that the police exist to keep the bourgeoisie in power – what do you think?

The bourgeoisie therefore impact on crime in the following ways:

Manipulation of morality: We are taught our views on right and wrong by a variety of agencies such as our family, school and the media. The bourgeoisie control each of these agencies and can use them to manipulate what we view as crime and what we do not view as crime to benefit themselves.

In essence the bourgeoisie decide whether we should view an act as a crime and the proletariat believe what they are told.

Theory into practice

Which set of crimes does the media devote more negative attention to? Why do you think this is?

Crimes of the bourgeoisie	Crimes of the proletariat
Tax fraud	Benefit fraud
Embezzlement	Theft
Pollution	Assault
Corporate crime	Vandalism

The Creation of the Law: the bourgeoisie create laws which are designed to protect their own position and prevent the proletariat from becoming powerful. Up until recently in the UK all laws were passed through the House of Lords which comprised of the aristocracy and the most wealthy and powerful people in the land. In recent times the House of Lords has been reformed, but Marxist criminologists would point to the fact that many individuals in the House of Commons and House of Lords have a bourgeoisie background having attended private school and being part of families which own the means of production. The law therefore is not a reflection of the will of the people, it is the reflection of the will of the powerful.

Think about it

The police and the armed services are forbidden to strike by law. What would Karl Marx have to say about this?

Differential law enforcement: law enforcement does not operate across society equally. Some kinds of crimes are policed more heavily than others and some groups of people are targeted more by law enforcement agencies than others.

For example, street crimes such as robbery and assault are more likely to be targeted by the police than 'white collar' crime such as fraud or embezzlement, even though the white collar crimes may cost the economy far more money than the street crime. Groups such as the working class or ethnic minorities are far more likely to be heavily policed than the middle or upper classes. In essence, the bourgeoisie control who is policed and those with the most to gain from a change in society such as the poor, the ethnic minorities and the working class are more heavily policed than others.

Differential sentencing practice: it has been argued by Marxists that the bourgeoisie controlled legal system favours the rich and powerful and does not seek to punish them harshly if they end up in court. Conversely, the justice system behaves harshly towards the proletariat giving them longer sentences in order to send a message to the rest of the proletariat to behave themselves.

Individual motivation: the criminal according to Marx is something of an urban hero, striking a blow in the class war between the bourgeoisie and the proletariat. The nature of capitalism means that competition and financial profit are driving forces in the lives of most people and if they cannot be achieved by legitimate means then an individual may resort to criminal means instead.

Evaluation of Marxist analysis

- If crime is a direct result of capitalism then crime should not occur in societies which use alternative systems such as communism. However there are high crime rates in communist societies also, Marxist views do not explain this problem.
- Marxism has been accused of romanticising working class crime, it ignores the fact that the victims of these 'urban heroes' are often also working class and suffer considerably as a result of the crimes committed against them.
- Marx concentrates on financial motivations for crime and ignores the fact that individuals may have other motivations for committing a crime, such as revenge or addiction.
- In criticising the bourgeoisie for making laws which oppress the proletariat, it is largely ignored that many laws actually benefit everyone regardless of which class they belong to.

Think about it

Marxist theories lost some of their popularity in the late 1980s. Can you suggest any reasons for this?

Key points

1 Marx developed a theory of society, not of crime.
2 There are two social classes, the bourgeosie, who own the means of production and the proletariat who are the workers.
3 The two classes are in constant conflict.
4 Crime is a response of the proletariat to its oppression by the bourgeiouse.
5 The bourgeoisie create an illusion of a just and fair society to keep the proletariat in its place.

Labelling theory

Unlike the previous 2 theories which explain crime as arising out of the way society is organised, this theory sees crime as a result of people labelling an act or a person as criminal. In other words, an act is not wrong or criminal until society says it is. Labelling turns common sense ideas about crime and deviance upside down. It is not the criminal who is responsible, but society:

Think about it

Consider the following quote. What exactly do you think it means?

> *"Social groups create deviance by making the rules where infraction constitutes deviance, and applying those rules to particular people and labelling them outsiders"*
>
> *(Becker 1966)*

Becker points out that most people at some point will commit an act which some would see as deviant. However, it is not committing the act which is significant, it is being caught and labelled a deviant that matters. For labelling theorists the only difference between criminals and everyone else is that they have been caught and labelled and we have not.

Think about it

What consequences are there in judging individuals differently based on their physical or social characteristics?

Labelling theorists argue that being stigmatised and labelled because you have broken the rules encourages an individual to begin to see themselves as deviant and behave in an increasingly deviant manner.

The process of labelling is influenced by an individual or groups sex, class, race, religion and age and not everyone is subject to labelling equally. We all have ideas of the type of person who is most likely to be a criminal (this idea links to the work on stereotyping considered in the Diversity unit) and labelling theorists argue that the people most likely to be labelled criminal are young, male, working class and probably of ethnic minority origin.

Think about it

Can you think of an example where you were given a label you didn't like or didn't agree with? Have you ever given a label to someone else and realised you were wrong after getting to know them?

Evaluation of labelling

The following criticisms have been made about the theory of labelling:

1 Labelling tends to view the offender as a victim of society and loses sight of the fact there may be a 'real' victim that the offender has hurt.

2 The theory lacks evidence to back up its ideas.

3 Marxist criminologists say that labelling doesn't acknowledge the fact that those in control of power in a society can use it to label people for political and economic reasons.

4 Labelling does not explain why some people become criminal and others do not.

Key points

1 Acts are only criminal because we say they are.
2 Criminals are ordinary people who have simply received a label.
3 Societies reaction to the act is more important than the act itself.
4 Once individuals are labelled they become stigmatised.
5 Not everyone is equally subject to labelling.

The Chicago School

The Chicago School developed in 1930s America in Chicago. It is often referred to as Urban Ecology because it studied the effect of the urban environment on the human population. Robert Park, the founder of this theory, saw the city as an organism whose inhabitants responded to ecological changes in the environment such as, competition for space, invasion of territory and dominance over other groups. At this time many large US cities, such as New York and Chicago were subject to migration. New immigrants would move into cheaper areas of cities and immigrants who had been there a while would move out into better areas as their economic circumstances improved. One of the most influential ideas to come from the Chicago School was the concentric zone theory shown below. Burgess (1928) proposed that cities expand radially (in a circular fashion).

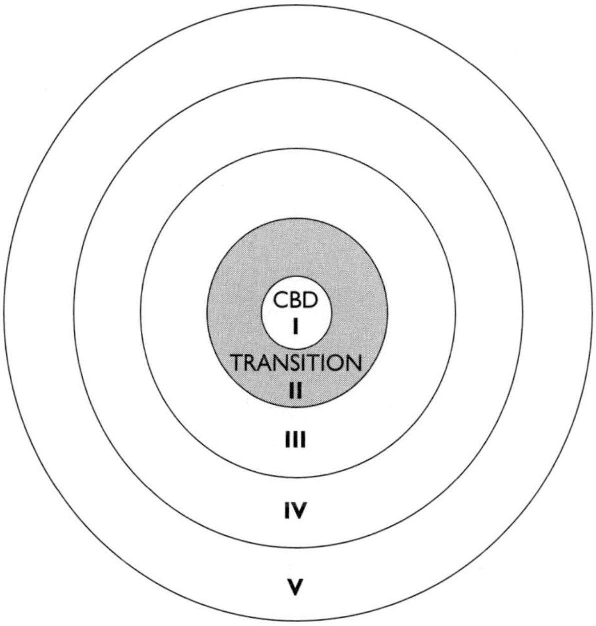

Figure 21.2 Concentric zone theory

Each of these concentric zones had a distinct ecological make up:

Zone I: 'the loop', or 'central business district' if you have studied geography. This zone contains shops, banks and local government buildings. Not many people live in the city centre itself.

Zone II: this is called the 'zone in transition'. It is a largely residential area, but with some businesses and industry encroaching on it from the loop. It has the poorest housing and is often economically deprived and run down.

Zone III: this is what Burgess called the 'zone of working mens homes'. It is made up of manual or semi skilled workers who had moved out from zone II as their economic position improved.

Zone IV: the residential zone has a much more middle class appearance and culture and it contains more expensive and desirable homes.

Zone V: the commuter zone for people who can afford to travel to work in the city live here. It has a middle/upper class culture and homes are expensive.

Theory into practice

Get a map of your town or city and draw concentric circles out from the town centre at 2-mile intervals. Match your set of concentric zones to the descriptions above. Does your city match what Burgess found in Chicago?

Burgess's concentric zone theory was built upon by two other Chicago school theorists, Shaw and McKay (1942). They used the theory to try and examine juvenile crime in large cities. They found that higher crime rates were concentrated in 'the loop' and 'the zone in transition' and that the further out from the city centre you were the lower the crime rate was. In essence, Shaw and McKay were making the claim that crime was a consequence of the area you lived in and once people moved away from zones I and II they became law abiding.

They also put forward the idea that crime in the inner zones was worse because of a problem they termed 'social disorganisation'. In these inner zones there was a mixture of languages, cultures and religions coupled with poor housing and truancy leading to a lack of a sense of community. Residents did not stay in these zones for long so they took less of an interest in the quality of their surroundings and did not get to know one another. Social controls such as the family, church and school may be less effective and juveniles began to become undisciplined and more likely to learn criminal habits. In essence, crime becomes almost normal behaviour in an area where so many people are doing it.

Theory into practice

1. Is crime an environmental as well as a social problem?
2. Is crime linked to migration in modern Britain?
3. How would you suggest crime rates are reduced in inner city areas?
4. Do you think the theories of the Chicago School apply to modern day Britain?

Psychological theories

Psychological theories examine the reasons individuals become criminal. They do not look at the problem from the perspective of society, but from the perspective of the individual. This might mean examining a persons mental health, how they learned to be criminal or how they were raised by their parents. Although there are many psychological theories, we will examine only two:

- psychoanalytical theory
- social learning theory.

Psychoanalytic theory

Sigmund Freud (1856–1939) argues that all humans have natural urges and drives which could develop into criminal tendancies unless they are repressed. Children are socialised to repress their instinctive impulses by their carers (usually their parents). Freud claims that the human personality consists of 3 parts: the id, the ego and the superego.

The id: the childlike, demanding side of a person. The id responds directly to instincts such as hunger, thirst and need for sexual gratification. It wants its needs satisfied NOW! This is the part that must be repressed.

The ego: this is the rational logical part of us and it is governed by reality. It is the part of the id that has been modified by the world around us. It tries to satisfy the id in a socially acceptable way.

The super-ego: this is the moral part of our personality. It judges things as right or wrong or good and bad and it is often referred to as an internalised parent.

Crime can occur when parents do not socialise a child effectively. The result is a poorly developed super-ego which lacks control over the id, leading to anti-social and destructive behaviour. If the anti-social behaviour is directed inwards the person may become neurotic and if it is directed outwards it may lead to criminal behaviour.

Evaluation of psychoanalytic theory

The following criticisms have been made about psychoanalytic theory:

1. The assumption that crime stems from unresolved childhood conflicts does not take into account the effects of poverty or drugs on individual behaviour.
2. Freud's subjects were mainly white middle class Europeans. How can his theories be applied to crime in other racial or socio-economic groups?
3. Freud only studied adult patients although he proposed a theory of child development. This makes it difficult to credit his theory.
4. By its focus on the individual it ignores wider social issues such as power and control which can influence crime.

Social learning theory

Social learning theory is based around the principles of behavioural psychology, which states that an individuals behaviour is learned and maintained by rewards or sanctions. From this perspective, crime can be seen either as learned behaviour or a failure of the socialisation process which teaches children right from wrong. Sutherland (1939) explains how crime can be normal learned behaviour in his theory of 'Differential Association'.

- criminal behaviour is learned through interaction with others
- most of this learning takes place in intimate or close personal groups
- individuals become criminal when they receive more information favourable to lawbreaking than unfavourable to it.

In essence, crime is learned behaviour which does not differ from any other learning experience we might have. Learning theorists argue that deviant or criminal behaviour can be reduced by taking away the reward value for the behaviour and replacing it with a punishment. Hans Eysenck, a learning theorist, states that a child who is consistently punished for inappropriate or deviant behaviour will develop an unpleasant association with the behaviour such as anxiety or guilt which may prevent them from doing it again.

Think about it

Do people only learn behaviour through rewards and punishments or are their other ways of learning?

The following criticisms have been made about the theory of social learning:

1 People are very different and you cannot predict how they will react to negative sanctions (punishments). Some individuals may never commit the behaviour again, while in others it may cause aggression and resentment leading to further deviant behaviour.

2 This theory assumes individuals are passive and unquestioning of what is happening around them. They just soak up information like sponges without using their own judgement.

3 By stating that most learning is conducted in intimate groups such as peers or family it neglects the influence of the media and wider culture.

4 Radzinowicz and King (1979) criticised Sutherland by saying that his theory doesn't allow for the fact that an individual might commit a crime without learning it from anybody.

Other contributing factors to crime

Now that we have examined some of the formal theories of crime we will briefly consider what other factors might have an influence on criminal behaviour.

Family

Farrington and West (1990) noticed that a small proportion of families tend to account for a large proportion of criminal activity. So it is possible that the family of an individual has a part to play in their criminal behaviour. It may be that the family is so large that children do not receive the individual attention they need from their parents and instead rely on friends and peers as models of appropriate behaviour. It may be that the stress and disruption involved in family breakdown may lead the young person into a delinquent career.

Economic factors

There has been much controversy surrounding the links between economic status and criminal activity. Some studies such as Benyan (1994) and Wells (1995) have claimed that there are clear links between low economic status and criminal activity, but Harrower (1998) correctly asserts that the exact nature of the relationship between poverty and crime is still unexplored.

Peer pressure

The influence of a persons friends and peer group is of vital importance when considering the beginnings of a criminal career. There is evidence to suggest that juveniles commit most of their offences in a group of peers who have regular interaction with each other. It may be that committing criminal or deviant activity is a way of gaining acceptance or status within a group.

Education

Poor experiences in education may be linked to juvenile delinquency. If a school does not engage or interest a student they may opt to play truant and become involved in low level criminal activity such as graffiti, criminal damage and causing a nuisance. Persistent truancy increases the likelihood of poor academic performance which means a young person may not achieve the qualifications they need in order to move away from their criminal activity.

Assessment activity 21-P1

In groups of 4 produce a television style role play in which 3 'experts' provide detailed explanations of at least 3 theories of crime and the host of the programme opens up a discussion with the audience on other contributing factors in criminal behaviour such as peer pressure or poverty.

Effects of crime

Public perceptions

Public perceptions of crime can come from a variety of sources such as personal experience, classroom study, hearing about the experiences of others and the media. All of these sources can have a substantial impact on how we view crime and what effect crime can have on our daily lives.

How crime is portrayed by the media

The mass media includes television, radio, newspapers, Internet and magazines. Most provide us with information on happenings outside our social groups and geographical areas and so become a major source of our information. In dealing with crime news, the media often presents a distorted view of reality.

Emphasis on violent crime: the media sift all stories for 'newsworthiness' and will tend to choose crime stories which are the most shocking since that is what will grab the attention of the public and therefore make the media companies more money. It is obvious that a story about a stolen car is not as newsworthy as a brutal murder therefore the media tend to concentrate on crimes of interpersonal violence. This means the public may come to believe that these crimes are much more common than they really are.

Sensationalising events: Williams (1991) comments that the media simplify and sensationalise events and present the story as a simple division of good versus evil regardless of the actual facts. The media has a function to inform, entertain and produce profit for its shareholders and as such it presents stories in a biased way. Criminals are presented as very different from the upright citizen reading the newspaper.

Theory into practice

View 3 different crime programmes, such as The Bill, A Touch of Frost or CSI. Analyse whether these programmes oversimplify and sensationalise crime or actually portray crime honestly. Produce a report on your findings.

Effects on public opinion: the media distort the way crime is portrayed and the public rely on that information to form their picture of crime, criminals and the impact of crime on themselves. Therefore the media can cause moral indignation or outrage in the public.

Case study

The media can even help cause vigilante action as happened in 2001 when The News of the World disclosed information relating to known paedophiles. Several people, some of them completely unconnected with any cases of child abuse, were injured in the public backlash.

1. Do you think the News of the World was right to disclose details of paedophiles? Explain your reasons.
2. What are the implications to society of these kind of disclosures?
3. What are the implications of vigilante action on the criminal justice system?
4. Why is vigilante action counterproductive to society?
5. Should the News of the World be held responsible for vigilante action occurring as a result of a news story?

Deviancy amplification and moral panics: sometimes the press reaction to a crime is so intense and sustained that it can actually set in motion a spiral of increasing deviance. This is best illustrated by Stanley Cohen's well-known work 'Folk Devils and Moral Panics' (1972). Cohen examined the phenomena of Mods and Rockers in the 1960s. Routine incidents involving young people became interpreted as gang warfare between the previously mentioned groups by the press and it was hyped up into something it was not. By amplifying small routine incidents the press created a 'moral panic' about the activities of the younger generation which then lead to heavier policing of the young which in turn caused tensions to escalate further. The process of deviancy amplification is as follows:

- Over reporting of a deviant event, exaggerating it to engage the public interest.
- Identification of those involved with a particular youth culture, involving a style of dress or music.
- A strong reaction by the public in response to the media exaggeration.
- The police and courts become alert to deal with the initial problem and take action swiftly and sometimes harshly. This in turn creates more media interest and seems to validate the original exaggeration of the media.
- Publicity encourages others people to join the deviant acts and the reporting of this leads the public to believe the crime wave is escalating.
- More police action and more arrests.
- The media use emotive language and staged photographs to incite public opinion causing a moral panic.

Eventually, the panic subsides, but usually only when a new one takes its place.

Think about it

Recent examples of moral panics includes the SARS outbreak and paedophiles on the Internet. Can you think of any other moral panic in the news recently?

Fear of crime

Fear of crime is a reaction to real or perceived environmental threats which are felt by the person involved. Fear may not be the result of an immediate danger such as an attack, it could be as a result of sensational media coverage or of environmental issues such as graffiti or poor street lighting. People's fear of crime varies depending on the company they are in, their location, the time of day and their own personal experiences of crime.

Fear of crime is not constant. Some offences cause more fear than others and some people feel more fear than others. According to Hough (1995), people in general worry most about burglary, rape and vehicle crime. Other key points in this study are:

- residents of towns and cities have more fear of crime than people in rural areas
- people aged 60+ tend to worry more about personal safety than younger people
- Individuals with an asian cultural background tend to worry more than the white population.

Fear of crime can have a tremendous impact on lifestyle such as stress related poor health, anger and resentment towards the perpetrators and a withdrawal from social contact with others. Hough notes that between 1–2% of the population **never** go out at night because they are frightened of crime. He also found that:

- 5% of people carried personal attack alarms
- 5% of people in his study chose to carry weapons
- 30% of the sample usually travelled with groups of friends for safety reasons
- 35% organised special transport arrangements rather than walk home or use public transport
- 40% avoided walking near people who they thought might be a threat.

Think about it

What crime prevention precautions do you take in your day-to-day activities?

Theory into practice

Consider the points that Hough (1995) makes on fear of crime. Do you recognise yourself of any of your family in this crime avoidance behaviour? Why do people take such extreme and often unnecessary measures?

Victims of crime

The study of victims of crime is a relatively new area of research. Up until about thirty years ago the majority of criminological literature focused almost entirely on the offender, ignoring the victim totally. However, recently pressure groups such as victim awareness movements have drawn attention to the role of the victim in a criminal interaction and the services which exist for their care after they have been victimised.

The notion of being a victim is historically connected with ideas of passivity and helplessness and victims are assumed to be especially in need of protection such as: children, the elderly or people with disabilities. Their perceived vulnerability is said to make them easier targets for crime. However, these views have increasingly been challenged as stereotypical and inaccurate. In actual fact the real indicator of whether someone will be vulnerable to crime is a person's lifestyle. People who never go out are unlikely to have to deal with crime, whereas those people who live, work or spend leisure time in public places are at increased risk. Ironically the people who we see as being more at risk may actually be safer than you.

Theory into practice

The following groups are vulnerable to criminal behaviour:

- women
- prostitutes
- police officers
- casualty nurses
- teenagers
- individuals with mental health difficulties
- members of ethnic minority communities
- members of the gay, lesbian, bisexual and transgendered community
- publicans
- teachers

Consider the groups above. Why is each group particularly vulnerable to crime and which kinds of crime are they most vulnerable to?

The 1982 British Crime Survey showed that the person with the highest risk of being a victim was:

- male
- under 30
- spends several evenings a week out
- drinks heavily
- assaults others.

The study of victims and others vulnerable to crime is discussed in a branch of criminology called victimology.

Why are people so frightened?

There are many reasons why people tend to be frightened of crime. The Home Office has produced a Crime Reduction Toolkit that contains the following reasons why individuals and communities tend to have strong concerns about crime.

1 **They live in a high crime area**: the area they live in is subject to a great deal of interpersonal and property crime which causes people to have genuine concerns about their risk of becoming a victim.

2 **They have already been a victim of crime**: once a person has been a victim of crime they are more likely to be targeted again. Having a crime committed against you makes you much more frightened and concerned and this fear can affect every aspect of a persons life.

3 **They feel vulnerable**: if a person feels that they are particularly vulnerable to crime they will be much more frightened than usual.

4 **They are poorly informed**: most people do not know their real risk of being a victim. The majority of the population has a very low risk of being a victim of crime, but they think they are at high risk because of the things they hear in the media and the stories they hear in the community.

5 **They feel powerless and isolated**: if people feel that they are alone and can do nothing to defend themselves or their property they will feel more afraid of crime.

6 **They have been subject to anti-social behaviour**: verbal abuse, nuisance neighbours or young people can frighten many people and make them feel more vulnerable to crime especially because putting a stop to the anti-social behaviour of others can put a person at more risk of crime.

7 **State of the local environment**: if a local environment looks run down, has lots of graffiti, poor street lighting or boarded up windows it gives an impression of a crime ridden area and so increases peoples fear of crime.

8 **Poor public transport**: if public transport runs infrequently then it can leave people feeling isolated and unable to escape from their local community unless they have their own transport. In addition, a lack of public transport might leave people with a very long walk home leaving them feeling very vulnerable during the journey, especially if it is at night.

Think about it

What do you think are the main reasons people become frightened of crime? Can you add any reasons to the above list?

What types of crime have people experienced?

A large factor in understanding fear of crime is a knowledge of which crimes are more common than others and the kinds of crime people have experienced in their own life. There are several ways of finding out the kinds of crime individuals and communities are subject to:

- Police statistics are the official figures of crime collected by the police and published by the Home Office
- Victimisation surveys which can be a large scale or small scale and involve asking people what crimes they have been a victim of in the last year. The most famous large-scale survey in the UK is the British Crime Survey which is conducted every year and asks around 40,000 individuals over the age of 16 about their experience of crime in order to build a picture of crime overall in the UK.

Police figures and British Crime Survey statistics often differ in terms of how much crime they show and what kinds of crime appear to be the most frequent. There is now a report which combines the 2 sets of figures: Crime in England and Wales 2002/3 (Simmons et al) highlights the following information about fear of crime:

- 73% of people surveyed believed that crime had risen in the previous 2 years. This is despite the fact that the crime figures have shown an overall decrease in crime rates every year since 1995.

- Many people greatly overestimate the risks of being a victim of crime. The table below shows how likely people thought they were to be a victim of crime compared with the actual risk.

Crime	Percieved risk	Actual risk
Theft from a car	25%	6.8%
Burglary	19%	3.4%
Violent attack	13%	4.1%

Theory into practice

Write down your movements for an entire week and then assess your lifestyle to evaluate your risk of becoming a victim. Consider issues such as the amount of time you spend in public places and whether you have been victim of crime before.

Assessment activity 21-P2

Using the information above produce a leaflet for public service workers which identifies the vulnerable members of society and describes the factors which may increase their fear of crime.

Key points

1. Some individuals are more vulnerable to crime than others.
2. One of the main indicators of whether you will be a victim of crime is your lifestyle.
3. Fear of crime is often based on incorrect information provided by the media.
4. Some criminal offences cause more fear than others.
5. Fear of crime can prevent individuals from living a full and enjoyable life.

Services for crime victims

Services for victims largely fall into 2 categories.

- **Statutory**: these are provided by the government and delivered formally through the criminal justice system.
- **Voluntary**: these are not usually government funded and rely on charitable donations and the work of volunteers.

Statutory services

The emergency services

The emergency services are often a victim's first port of call once they have had a crime committed against them. It may be that they require an ambulance to treat their injuries and transport them to hospital, they may require the fire service to rescue them from an accident caused by criminal behaviour or it may be that they need to report a crime to the police so that it can be investigated. Their full roles and functions are discussed in Unit 8: The Uniformed Services.

Theory into practice

Select a uniformed service such as the police or fire service and list and describe the things they can do to support victims of crime.

The Criminal Injuries Compensation Authority (CICA)

This government body administers the compensation scheme for victims of crime. It was set up in 1964 as the Criminal Injuries Compensation Board (CICB) to compensate individuals who had been injured as a result of a criminal action against them. The role of the CICA is to decide how much compensation an injury is worth and provide an appropriate amount of money. Since 1996 the CICA has operated on a tariff system which means that each individual injury is worth a set amount of money only. The list below details some of the amounts available on the current tariff system. The CICA pays out around £200 million every year to injured victims of crime.

- fatal injury £11,000
- paraplegia (paralysis of lower limbs) £175,000
- severe burns to head £16,500
- permanent deafness in both ears £44,000
- loss of sight in both eyes £110,000
- fracture/dislocation of thumb which causes ongoing disability £4,400
- sprained wrist (causes disability 6–13 wks) £1,000
- severe permanent damage to genitalia £11,000
- sprained ankle lasting more than 13 wks £2,500
- fractured big toe on one foot £2,500
- quadraplegia (paralysis of all 4 limbs) £250,000

Think about it

Do you think the amounts of compensation set up by the CICA are fair?

Simulation

Akhtar was walking home from college one evening when a gang of white youths started shouting racial abuse at him. Akhtar ignored them and continued in the direction of his home. The white youths followed and began pushing and shoving him, Akhtar had no choice but to defend himself. He suffered a broken arm, sprained ankle and extensive bruising. He was unable to return to college for several weeks and missed some vital exams. He will now have to repeat a whole years worth of work.

1 What amount of compensation might Akhtar be awarded?
2 What factors would influence the CICA to make a full payment?
3 Should the attackers be able to claim against Akhtar for the injuries they received?

Clearly this scheme is of great benefit to victims of crime. However, this scheme does have several disadvantages:

- it keeps a low profile – many victims do no claim because they don't know about it
- the tariff system is rigid and does not allow for flexibility.

Reparation

Reparation is the idea that the offender will repay the victim in the form of working for them. A limited system of reparation exists in the UK under community service orders. This is indirect reparation because the offender is helping the community at large, not just his or her actual victim.

Think about it

What are your views on reparation? Conduct a group discussion on whether criminals should have to work for their victims and society to make amends for their actions.

Mediation

This aims to remove the hostility which exists between victim and offender by bringing them together using a mediator such as a social worker in order to discuss the situation face to face. It can be enforced through a court order or remain a less formal arrangement. This method does not suit all victims, some of whom are very frightened at the thought of meeting an offender and like reparation it is not widely utilised in the UK.

Think about it

Why is mediation unpopular in the UK? What are its advantages and disadvantages?

Case study

Restorative justice is a government initiative which was announced by Home Secretary David Blunket in 2003. The main principle of restorative justice is that victims can meet the offenders who committed a crime against them and question them about their actions and tell the offender about the long-term effects of their actions. Restorative justice is designed as an alternative to prosecution and is less expensive than traditional ways of dealing with offenders as it saves on court costs. There are several ways in which mediation can take place:

- **Restorative conferencing**: the victim and offender meet directly, accompanied by others such as parents and loved ones who offer support.
- **Victim offender mediation**: victim and offender meet with an independent mediator, but are unaccompanied by others.
- **Indirect mediation**: the offender and victims do not meet face to face, but communicate through a third party.

1. Is restorative justice a viable alternative to prosecution? Explain your reasons.
2. How could restorative justice benefit victims of crime?
3. How could restorative justice benefit criminal offenders?
4. What do you think is the government's main reasons for piloting mediation?
5. Why would mediation and restorative justice not be suitable for all victims and offenders?

Compensation

The idea of the offender compensating their victim directly for injury caused has become very popular over the last 20 years or so and is supported by the government under legal statutes such as The Criminal Justice Act 1982. Compensation orders can be given instead of or as well as any other sentence of the court, but as with the CICB, victims often do not know how to apply for a compensation order.

Video links

Video links are a particularly useful option for child victims in violence and sexual misconduct cases as a courtroom can be a very frightening place for children. Allowing them to give video-linked evidence rather than face their attacker can remove some of the trauma involved in giving evidence.

Non-statutory services

The voluntary sector – Victim Support

As a registered charity, Victim Support has a low political profile and does not seek to pressure the criminal justice system into change. Instead, it focuses on helping victims of crime in terms of emotional support and practical tasks such as helping with insurance or compensation claims. Victim Support receives support from the police and funding from central government. It relies on the police to notify them of people who need their aid, but the police do not refer every victim to them, which means that many victims receive no help at all.

The Witness Service

The Witness Service exists to ensure that the process of giving evidence in court is as comfortable an experience as possible. It was established in 1989 and is managed and organised by its parent charity Victim Support. There is a Witness Service in every crown court in England and Wales which performs several functions:

- to provide information on courtroom procedure to witnesses
- to accompany witnesses into the courtroom
- to help and reassure victims and witnesses.

Many witnesses may be very intimidated at the thought of giving evidence, but without their testimony many prosecutions would fail and offenders would be able to continue to commit crime without fear of punishment. It is therefore in the government's interests to encourage the growth of the witness service since better supported witnesses can lead to more convictions which may in turn lead to fewer active criminals on the street. Witness volunteers are not permitted to discuss the case itself or discuss the evidence the witness will give. This can only be discussed with the police or legal representatives.

Think about it

Should the Witness Service be a government funded public service rather than a charity which relies on donations and volunteers? Explain your reasons.

Simulation

Alison is a 13 year old girl who was a witness to a brutal attack in a newsagents shop which left the newsagent hospitalised for 3 weeks and 2 customers slightly injured. Alison lives on the same street as the attacker and recognised her immediately as a local drug user and dealer. The attacker knows where Alison and her family live and has a previous history of intimidating witnesses.

1 What support could the Witness Service provide for Alison if she has to give evidence?
2 Why is it in the government's interests that Alison testifies?
3 How do you think Alison will feel if she is called upon to give evidence?
4 What form might any intimidation of Alison by the defendant take?

Assessment activity 21-M3

Using the information above and your own research produce a 10-minute presentation which provides a clear explanation of the support which can be given to a witness in court.

Women's Aid Federation

This organisation was created in 1974 and provides for over 400 refuges nationally. It supports the survivors and families of domestic violence by providing them with a place to live in a refuge with others in similar situations and offering practical and emotional support through volunteers and trained support workers. As with all charities it has limited funds and often struggles to cope with the demand for its services. If fulfils several functions:

- providing refuges and support for women and dependent children who have experienced domestic violence or who are in fear of domestic violence
- to raise awareness of the issues surrounding domestic violence
- to lobby government for changes in law and policy to protect victims of domestic violence
- to train outreach workers to support victims and act as advocates for them
- to share knowledge and techniques with other public services such as the police.

The police traditionally did not take issues of domestic violence seriously and women had little support from the law if they were victimised by their husbands or partners. The overwhelming aim of the Women's Aid Federation is to empower victims of domestic violence and enable them to determine their own lives and the lives of their children. Each year over 50,000 women and children seek safety in women's aid refuges and many more seek help through telephone support lines such as the National Domestic Violence Help-line, which is also part of the Women's Aid Federation.

Think about it

Why were the police traditionally unresponsive to issues of domestic violence?

Citizens Advice Bureau (CAB)

Another volunteer agency which seeks to help victims of crime, amongst others, is the Citizens Advice Bureau (see also Citizenship Unit). The CAB began as an emergency measure during the second world war and has now evolved into a much relied upon national agency. The CAB deals with around six million queries per year on a wide range of issues and can help victims of crime by referring them to legal agencies such as the police or helping them find a civil or criminal solicitor to help represent them. They can also refer people to the Witness Service and Victim Support and give expert advice to victims on their legal rights.

There are over 2000 CAB's in England, Wales and Northern Ireland staffed with almost 25,000 workers of whom 20,000 are unpaid volunteers. Like many other agencies in the non-statutory sector they are almost entirely dependent on government grants and charitable donations for their continued survival. The CAB also acts as a social policy lobby group. As the CAB sees so many problems faced by the public each year they are well placed to advise the government on changes to law and policy which would make the lives of citizens easier.

Rape Crisis

The first Rape Crisis centre was established in London in 1976 as a response to the fact that female victims of rape and sexual assault were often treated unfairly by the police and criminal justice system. There are now many Rape Crisis centres around the country operating 'drop in' centres and telephone support and providing legal and medical information in a safe and emotionally supportive environment.

The Samaritans

Often victims can experience significant emotional trauma. In the aftermath of a crime being committed against them they may develop depression, feelings of anxiety, irrational fears or even more serious problems such as post traumatic stress disorder (PTSD) – for a fuller discussion of PSTD see unit 24 Major Incidents in Book 1.

The Samaritans are a voluntary organisation which operates a 24-hour service designated to help and support individuals who feel desperate or suicidal. This help is given primarily through a telephone support line which operates on the principle that being listened to in confidence and accepted without prejudice can help alleviate the desperate feelings and thoughts of suicide which can plague victims of abuse and crime.

Think about it

What qualities would a person need to be an effective volunteer for the Samaritans?

Think about it

- Do you think more support should be made available to victims of crime from the public sector?
- What advantages and disadvantages are there for victims of having so many support services run by voluntary organisations?

Assessment activity 21-P3

Considering the information you have read so far about services to victims, produce an audit of your own local area which explains the role of the public services and other agencies in assisting victims of crime. Give examples of which services operate in your area and what role they fulfil.

Cost of crime

Crime costs individuals and society a tremendous amount. Current estimates (Home Office Research Report 217) put the cost of crime at 60 billion a year, therefore the potential savings which could be made by effective crime prevention strategies are significant. This 60 billion is broken down approximately as follows:

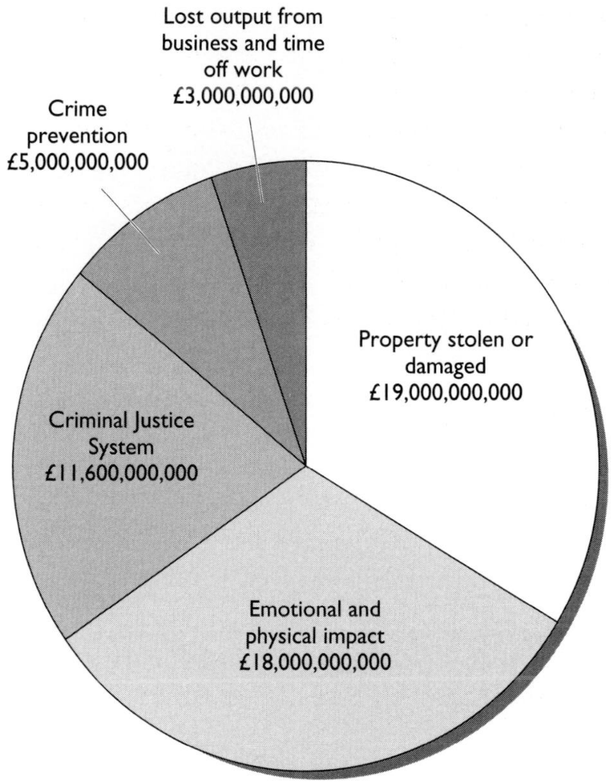

Figure 21.3 Costs of crime

Think about it

If there were no crime what else could this money be spent on?

There are many people who have to bear the enormous cost of crime:

Victims: victims will suffer financial losses. It may be through having property stolen or having to take time off work to recover from an attack. Victims also have to deal with the emotional and social costs of crime in terms of trauma and the changes to lifestyle discussed earlier in this chapter.

Potential victims: the majority of the population are potential victims. Most of us spend a great deal protecting ourselves from crime by purchasing things such as house alarms, window locks, double-glazing, crook locks, immobilisers and insurance.

Society as a whole: we all pay taxes which fund the police, prisons, courts and CPS.

Some crimes cost society more than others, for instance wounding only accounts for around 1% of crime but it costs an estimated 15.6 billion per year. This loss has been calculated on the basis of medical help, criminal justice costs and the pain and suffering of the victim. Each individual wounding costs around £19,000 to society.

Average costs of other crimes per offence	
Vehicle crime	£4,800
Sexual offences	£18,902
Homicide	£1,122,000
Burglary	£2,320
Criminal damage	£510
Common assault	£540
Robbery/mugging	£4,700

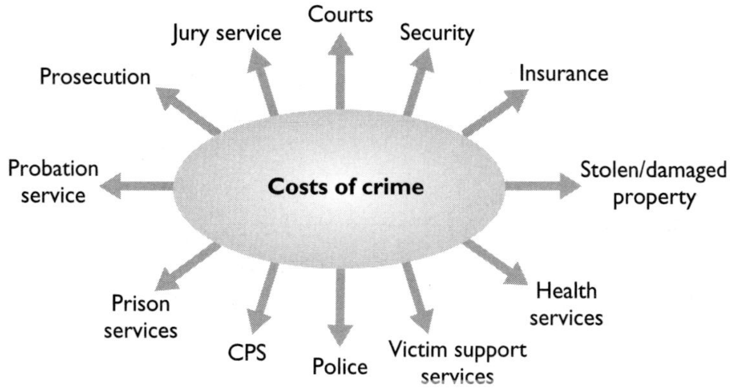

Figure 21.4 The costs of crime impact on many areas

These costs include money spent on law enforcement, medical fees, custodial care and prosecution. It is clear to see that even a relatively minor crime can be expensive.

Types of crime costs

The government identified 3 types of crime costs:

1 **Costs in anticipation of crime**: these are costs incurred by taking precautionary measures to reduce the risk of victimisation. This includes increased security of potential targets and insurance cover.

2 **Costs as a consequence of crime**: these are costs incurred by the actual commission of the crime, such as health care, replacing damaged or stolen property or lost output in the workplace.

3 **Costs in response to crime**: the costs incurred here are huge and include police time, the CPS, the courts, legal aid, prison, probation and compensation. All of these costs happen as a direct response after the crime has been committed.

The following table gives a breakdown of the costs of crime for some of the incidents looked at previously.

Wider economic costs of crime

In addition to the costs above there are much wider costs of crime to individuals and societies. Home Office Research Study 217 'The social and economic costs of crime' (2000) describes the following economic consequences of crime:

Social and economic costs of crime can impact on local amenities

- reduced amenities such as libraries and parks in high crime areas, because the cost to the council of continuous repair is prohibitive
- fewer businesses and shops in high crime areas, which leaves individuals with less choice and higher prices
- fewer businesses means fewer job opportunities in the area encouraging socio-economic decline
- extra taxation on wages to cover the costs of the criminal justice system.

Assessment activity 21-D1

Once again you will use your own local area to complete this assessment activity. Collect your local crime statistics from your local police station (if they cannot help you request them by letter from your force police headquarters). In addition, complete a visual survey of your area noting the amenities it has and does not have. Using this independent research explain the financial implications of the cost of crime to your local community.

Costs	Assault	Criminal damage	Burglary	Homicide	Sexual offences
Anticipation	£0	£30	£430	£0	£2
Consequence	£270	£420	£1,400	£1,100,00	£15,000
Response	£270	£60	£490	£22,000	£3,900
Totals	£540	£510	£2,320	£1,122,000	£18,902

Figure 21.5 Breakdown of the costs of crime

Key points

1 Crime costs society approximately £60 billion pounds per year.

2 The cost is borne by everyone.

3 The Home Office breaks this cost into 3 parts: anticipation, consequence and response.

4 There are many wider financial implications to crime in addition to the figure outlined above, such as loss of jobs and amenities.

Reporting and recording crime

Crime reporting and recording are crucial sources of statistical data for criminologists and for the government to examine the problem of crime control and prevention. Without sources of official data most ideas about crime could never be investigated.

Reporting crime

There are several ways in which the public can report crimes to the police:

- **in person**: at the local or central police station or directly to a police officer.
- **by telephone**: the public can contact the police station on a local number. Only if this incident is an emergency should you dial 999. An emergency situation is when a crime is currently happening or there is immediate danger.
- online: for non-emergency crime notification the Internet can be used. The police service has a web site www.online.police.uk where minor crimes can be reported in about 10 minutes.

Problems with reporting crime

A large proportion of crime never gets reported to the police. This may be because some crime is considered to be 'invisible'. This is where the victim is unaware of the crime and so cannot report it to the police for example white collar or corporate crime. More likely it is because the public may choose not to report a crime for the reasons shown in Figure 21.6 below.

Recorded crime

Recorded crime is the amount of crime that the police choose to record into official statistics. It used to be the case that less than half of the crimes that were reported to the police made it into the official statistics. However, in April 2002 new National Crime Recording Standards (NCRS) were introduced by the government which meant that the police had to record a great deal more crime. In the past for instance a pub fight where neither person wanted to press charges would not have made it into the statistics, but the NCRS

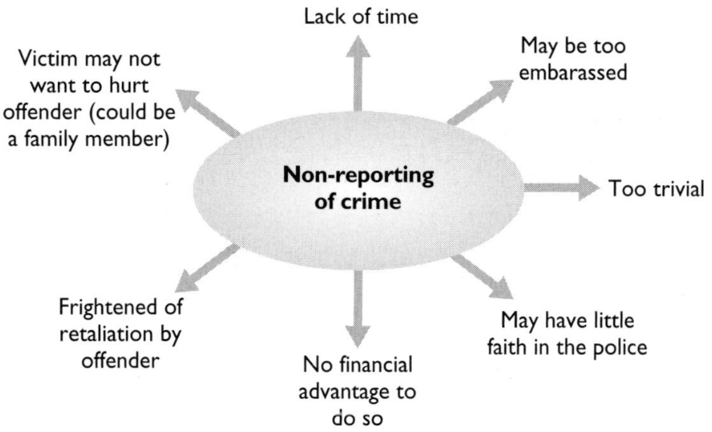

Figure 21.6 Reasons for non-reporting of crime

means it now has to be recorded as a violent crime. The NCRS was introduced to make it easier to compare the figures that each police service produces and to be more supportive to victims of crime. It also highlights the true volume of work police officers have to deal with. Recording a crime can be a time consuming and complex business as the information below will highlight.

Police crime systems

Many police services use simple multi-page crime recording forms which are then faxed or scanned and sent to police HQ. At HQ many forces have a centralised data capture unit which employs specialist software to process the forms automatically using intelligent character recognition (ICR) which can recognise handwriting and ticks or crosses and creates statistics based on the forms that it processes. Often this data is put into a database which is available to officers to help them detect and solve crimes. Examples of such databases are:

Scottish intelligence database (SID): this is a new database being developed in Scotland to help Scottish officers track and monitor offenders. It is likely to contain photos of offenders, fingerprints, aliases and the MO of offenders (how they commit particular crimes).

Police national computer (PNC): this database was created in 1974 and is one of the main sources of information for officers. It contains information on criminals, property and vehicles and can be used in a number of ways, for example:

- Automatic number plate recognition (ANPR): this allows thousands of number plates to be scanned on roads and motorways and suspect cars to be identified.
- Names index: this contains over 6 million records on criminals and missing persons.
- Stolen property index: this contains over 100,000 records of stolen property so that if the police seize it in a raid they can trace it back to its owner.
- Sex offenders register: allows the police to track and monitor convicted six offenders.

Assessment activity 21-P4

Produce an A3 poster for the general public which explains the various methods of reporting and recording crime.

Crime statistics

Crime statistics have been gathered since 1857. The tools which are used today to measure trends in crime are:

- **Police statistics**: these are the notifiable (more serious) offences which are recorded by the police.
- **British crime survey**: this is a national victim survey which is conducted every 2 year. It asks 40,000 people if they have been victims of crime in the last 12 months.
- **Local crime surveys**: these are smaller, localised victim surveys such as the Islington and Merseyside crime surveys. They are often conducted by academics.

Official police records

Police recorded crime statistics are produced on a quarterly and annual basis. Recorded crime refers to the notifiable offences recorded by the police in accordance with Home Office guidelines. They provide a summary of the crimes that the police have recorded over a given period (see Figure 21.7 on page 347.

In 2001 the police in England and Wales recorded 5.5 million crimes, with property offences making up 80% of all recorded crime. However, crime figures recorded by the police are not always a reliable guide to the amount of crime. Home Officer Research (John Burrows, 2000) identified the following issues:

- Police forces do not record all of the crime that is reported to them. One half of personal offences and one quarter of property offences

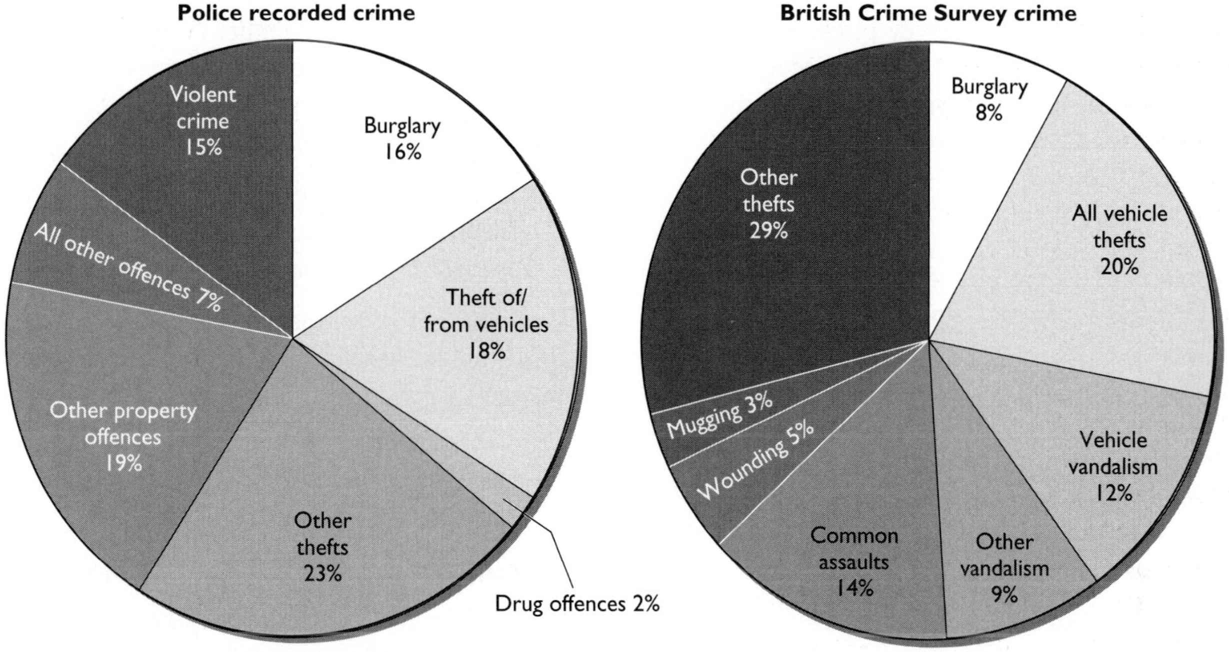

Figure 21.7 Police recorded crime and BCS by type of crime, 2001/2
Source: Home Office

reported are not recorded as crime. This is primarily because the police officer does not perceive there to be enough evidence.

- In about one fifth of cases where a crime was reported to the police it was recorded in a different category to the original allegation.
- On average only 47% of crime allegations were actually recorded as crime.
- Many of the crimes reported to the police are not notifiable (not serious enough to appear in recorded data).

The British Crime Survey (BCS)

This has been used by the Home Office since 1981 to track levels of crime in society. It involves a survey every other year of a large representative sample of the population and asks whether they

Advantages of using police records	Disadvantages of using police records
• Free and easily available.	• Only shows around one half of all offences reported to the police.
• Enables tracking of trends over a long period of time.	• Cannot show crimes which were unreported.

Advantages of BCS	Disadvantages of BCS
Provides a more accurate reflection of actual amount of crime than police records.	Ignores victimless, invisible and very serious crime, for example murder.
Can be used to study trends in actual crime.	People may forget or exaggerate offences committed against them.

have been victims of certain crimes in the previous 12 months. This survey produces much higher levels of crime that the police records. In 2002 BCS reported 13 million crimes while the police recorded 5.5 million crimes.

Trends in crime

The analysis of current crime trends depends largely on the source of data. However, generally crime is falling:

- the 2002 BCS figures show a 14% overall decrease in crime
- crime has fallen ever year since 1995 – over the last 5 years 1997–2002 crime has dropped 22%
- the rates for some offences are decreasing more quickly than others, for example vehicle theft fell by 14%, violence by 17% and burglary by 23%.

Think about it

What factors might explain the recent decline in crime shown by BCS? Why is this decline greater than the decline in recorded crime?

Using crime data to tackle crime

Crime data can be incredibly useful to the public services in targeting and co-ordinating their response to it. For example, the fire service might learn from the statistics that arson is on the increase and develop a strategy for education in schools to highlight the dangers of lighting fires. They can also ensure the availability of staff with fire investigation expertise if the statistics show the need. The implications for the police are even more profound.

- Crime data tells the police which crimes are increasing and which are decreasing so that they can target certain types of crime for heavier policing.
- It tells the police which areas in their constabulary have higher crime rates, thus allowing manpower and resources to be deployed to the areas in most need.
- It helps the police assess the effectiveness of their current crime fighting strategies to ensure they are getting a return on their crime prevention investment.

In addition to this, the crime figures also allow the government to compare the effectiveness of each of the 43 police services in England and Wales. This can affect issues such as funding for facilities, resources and recruitment.

Assessment activity 21-M1

Using the information provided above write a 300 word report which gives a detailed description of how data analysis can be used to tackle crime.

Key points

1. The police figures show a general rise in crime, whereas the BCS shows a decline in crime.
2. Crime statistics vary from source to source.
3. Crime statistics can contain bias.
4. Statistics should be used as a starting point only.

The judicial system

An understanding of the judicial system is vital for anyone interested in understanding crime. Many of the institutions in the system such as the Magistrates Court, Crown Court, High Court and the Court of Appeal are looked at in detail in Chapter 2 Law and Legal System, and it is not considered necessary to discuss them again here. However, the courts are not the only players in the criminal justice system as we will now see.

The Crown Prosecution Service (CPS)

The CPS was created by the Prosecution of Offences Act 1985 and became fully operational the following year. The Phillips Report (1981) stated that it was undesirable for the police to both investigate and prosecute crime due to issues of bias and differing practices in police force areas. The CPS operates between the police and the courts:

The police are responsible for deciding on the charge an offender receives and for preparing a case file for the CPS. The CPS then takes over the prosecution from that point and reviews the case files in order to check that the evidence presented justifies the charge given. If it does not, the reviewing lawyer may discontinue proceedings or charge the offender with a lesser offence. This power to discontinue or downgrade prosecutions is intended to save money by not proceeding with cases that cannot be proved, but in practice it can cause tension and alienation between the CPS and the police. In addition to this role the CPS prepares cases for court, prosecutes cases in magistrates court and instructs counsel in Crown Court.

The decision the CPS makes on whether to prosecute is based on 2 main 'tests':

1 **The evidential test**: is there enough evidence that the case is likely to succeed? If there isn't then the CPS are likely to discontinue a case. This happens in about 12% of cases where the police have charged a defendant.

2 **The public interest test**: if the CPS's reviewing lawyer thinks that there is enough evidence for the case to have a reasonable chance of success he or she will then consider whether a prosecution is in the public interest (will it benefit the public for a prosecution to be continued). The factors which influence the CPS decision on the public interest test are laid out in a document called 'The Code for Crown Prosecutors'.

The present Director of Public Prosecutions is Ken McDonald QC and he is head of the CPS. The CPS employs about 7,700 people with $\frac{1}{3}$ of those being lawyers and the rest legal officers and administrative staff. They deal with 1.3 million cases a year in the magistrates court and approximately 120,000 in the Crown Court. The CPS unfortunately has very little control over its workload. They receive files from the police who have already agreed a hearing date with the court which can place tremendous pressure on the staff of the CPS to prepare cases for court. The Glidewell Report in 1998 made recommendations that the CPS, not the police, should arrange initial hearings in a magistrates court. If this recommendation is implemented it is possible that the caseload of the CPS will become a bit more manageable.

Witnesses

The role of a witness is vital to the judicial system, and they may be required to perform several functions:

- provide a statement of what they saw, usually at a police station
- pick out a suspect in an identity parade
- examine photographs of suspects to assist in identification
- provide testimony in court.

Often without a witness testimony there is no case. Standards for services to witnesses are set out in the 'Victims Charter' and the National Standards for Witness Care, both published in 1996. There is a witness service in every branch of the crown court in England and Wales. It is run by the charity Victim Support and is discussed on page 340. 97% of criminal cases are dealt with in magistrates courts which do not have the witness service on site. Responsibility for witness care lies with:

- Home Office
- Lord Chancellors Department
- The police
- CPS
- Victim Support.

Despite all of these agencies working to help witnesses, Plotnikoff and Woolfson (1998) are not convinced that witness support is as good as it ought to be. They make several key points in their study of the subject.

1. 46% of witnesses did not give evidence on the day they were called to appear and the 54% that did give evidence waited an average of 3 hours before they were called into court.
2. There is no separation of prosecution and defence witnesses which can lead to intimidation of prosecution witnesses.
3. Over 33% of witnesses were not told how to get to court and 50% were not told what to do once they had arrived in court.
4. Prosecution witnesses received more information than defence witnesses.

Theory into practice

This is a paired activity, so first get yourself a partner. Walk round your college for 10 minutes observing the goings on around you. Your partner should make notes on everything they see. Return to your class and get your partner to ask you 20 questions about the things you saw. Based on your answers how good a witness would you be?

Defence solicitors

It is the role of defence solicitors to provide advice, assistance and representation to individuals who are suspected or accused of committing a crime. There are several ways of finding a defence solicitor.

- you can pay for and employ a solicitor of your own choosing
- if you cannot afford to pay for the services of a solicitor the government will provide one for you.

If you need to rely on a government defence solicitor one will be provided for you under the Criminal Defence Service (CDS) which replaced the old criminal legal aid system in 2001. The CDS must approve all solicitors who provide government funded criminal defence and it even employs its own solicitors who are called 'public defenders'. There are 3 levels of assistance that the CDS can provide.

1. **Advice and assistance**: this service includes writing letters, negotiating, providing general legal advice and consulting a barrister on your behalf. In order to qualify for this service your assets and income must be below a certain level.
2. **Advocacy assistance**: this level of service covers the cost of a solicitor preparing a case and initial representation in court. It does not cover a full court defence and once again it is means tested.
3. **Representation**: this is the top level of assistance which is provided by the CDS. It covers the cost of a solicitor to prepare the case, defend you in court and also the cost of a barrister if you need defending in Crown Court for a more serious offence. There is no financial limit on your earnings in this level of assistance. This is because it may involve more serious cases such as rape and murder which can be very complex and time consuming and therefore much more expensive. It is not in the interests of justice to have people pay for their own defence in cases such as this unless they are extremely wealthy.

Think about it

Why is it in the interests of justice to provide criminal defence representation to all people involved in serious cases?

Key points

1 Information on the court system can be found in Unit 2 Law and the Legal system.

2 The CPS is responsible for prosecutions in England and Wales. It was established by the Prosecutions of Offences Act 1985.

3 Witnesses play a key role in the criminal process and they are assisted by the witness service.

4 The system for criminal aid changed in 2001. There are now three levels: advice and assistance, advocacy assistance and representation.

5 The role of defence solicitor is crucial in ensuring all people charged with a crime are able to have a fair trial.

Assessment activity 21-P5

Using information in this chapter and information on the courts found in Unit 2 Law and the Legal System produce a series of factsheets for public service workers which describes clearly the role of the courts, the CPS and other agencies such as the legal profession.

Crime reduction

Multi-agency partnerships

The Crime and Disorder Act 1998 placed a new duty on local authorities, police and other agencies to work together in the development and implementation of strategies to reduce crime and disorder. This partnership involves statutory, voluntary, community and business groups working together to reduce crime, fear of crime and victimisation.

The Crime and Disorder Act created 376 local crime and disorder reduction partnerships in England and Wales. These partnerships have had to develop and implement strategies to tackle crime in three year cycles, the first cycle ran from 1999–2002 and the second cycle is currently operating from 2002–2005. These strategies must reflect local needs and priorities which means that different crime and disorder partnerships around the country will be aiming to tackle different areas of crime depending on what is a problem locally. The partnerships are made up of many different organisations such as:

- police
- community safety officers
- drug action teams
- youth offending teams
- local authorities
- health trusts
- probations service
- NACRO
- Victim Support
- educational establishments
- businesses
- housing associations.

The priorities addressed by a multi-agency partnership could be any of the following issues depending on local needs:

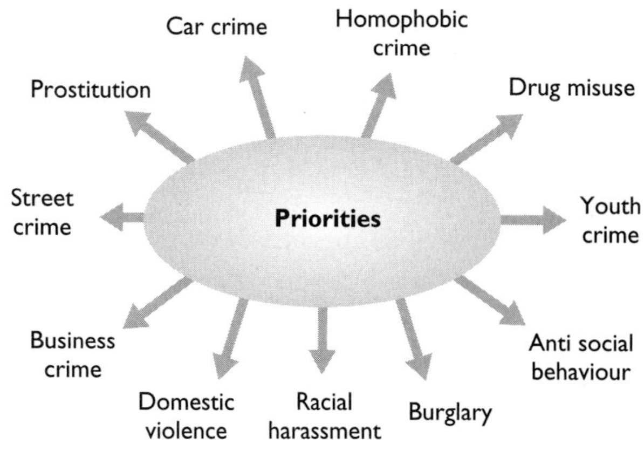

Figure 21.8 Multi-agency partnership priorities

An example of a possible local crime and disorder reduction partnership according to the Home Office would look something like Figure 21.9.

Figure 21.9 A local crime and disorder reduction partnership

The first step a multi agency partnership must take is a crime and disorder audit. The audit is a formal assessment of the needs of a particular partnership area. This audit may contain a number of key stages and actions such as:

- producing a profile of crime and disorder in a particular locality
- a household survey to assess the concerns and experiences of the public
- an examination of existing crime reduction strategies
- carry out discussions with groups vulnerable to crime
- identify key crime and disorder reduction priorities
- working parties established to examine specific key priorities and develop strategies to address them.

According to the Home Office the audit serves several key purposes:

- it ensures that all the participants in the partnerships are aware of the type of crime and disorder which is being committed in their area.
- it identifies the needs of communities and addresses their concerns
- it examines the wider impact of crime on communities
- it helps to identify methods of reducing crime and disorder.

The crime audit is also another effective way for public service agencies to to use and analyse crime statistics in order to target areas of high crime locally and to predict future crime trends. Reducing crime and disorder in a local community can have a tremendous impact on the quality of life for residents. For example, reducing drug abuse in a local area can reduce the numbers or burglaries and street robberies committed by individuals who need to steal in order to feed their habit. This in turn can improve the number of community activities in an area because people feel safe to leave their homes and it may also encourage businesses into the area bringing employment and jobs.

The priorities outlined earlier can be translated into specific schemes or initiatives to reduce crime. Such initiatives might be:

- working with Housing Associations to improve estate management and remove persistent offenders from certain areas
- prioritisation of drug treatment programmes for offenders with a history of drug related offending

- addressing problems caused by prostitution, including multi-agency tactics to keep prostitutes away from residential areas and deter kerb crawlers.

The setting of measurable targets like the ones suggested above are a key issue for multi-agency partnerships. This ensures that projects to reduce crime are continually striving for success and that they are value for money. As you can see from the selection above, these targets can be on virtually any aspect of crime and disorder. Two real life examples from partnerships currently trying to achieve targets are highlighted below:

Manchester Crime and Disorder Reduction Strategy 2002–2005:

- Reduce recorded crime in the city by 10% over 3 years.
- Increase of 6% in the number of residents who feel safe alone after dark over 3 years.
- 15% reduction of violent offences in public places over 3 years.
- 15% reduction in youth nuisance over 3 years.

These are just some of the targets prioritised by Manchester in their strategy for 2002–2005. They were identified by the effective use of a crime and disorder audit.

Charnwood Crime and Disorder Reduction Strategy 2003–2005:

- Reduce burglaries of dwellings by 23% over 3 years.
- Reduce the incidence of theft from vehicles and damage to vehicles by 21% over 3 years.

Many crime and disorder partnerships make their strategy available on the Internet. These strategies are a valuable source of information in understanding the government's overall strategy on crime.

Funding of multi-agency partnerships

Multi-agency partnerships are funded by the government who make an allocation of money available and distributes it to around 10 Home Office Crime Reduction Directors who then administer these funds regionally. These officers are based in each of the 9 government offices for England and one in the Welsh Assembly. They have to:

- build links between partnerships and central government
- provide guidance and training to partnerships
- identify and share good practice
- monitor the effect of the initiatives for crime reduction.

Funding for each of the regions in 2002/2003 was as follows:

North East	£0.929 million
North West	£2.820 million
Yorkshire and Humberside	£1.869 million
East Midlands	£1.621 million
West Midlands	£2.194 million
Wales	£1.114 million
South West	£1.620 million
East	£1.583 million
South East	£2.550 million
London	£3.694 million

Some of the money is directly awarded to partnerships, but if they require extra funds they must develop schemes and initiatives (such as the ones already discussed) and use them to bid for money to run them. If the bid isn't good enough the Home Office will reject it and the money will go elsewhere. In addition, partnerships may bid for European funding or generate funds from local businesses. Most large towns and cities have their own crime reduction partnership website containing very specialised local information.

Evaluation of multi-agency partnerships

The initiatives and partnerships must be evaluated to assess how successful they have been and to see if they are providing the government with value for money. Evaluation is the process of checking whether the strategies achieved their intended outcomes. It is usual for the evaluator to be independent from the project being examined.

The government provides advice to crime and disorder partnerships on evaluation in line with the guidelines laid out in the Crime and Disorders Act 1998. It proposes a formal and structured way of evaluating schemes comprising of the following stages:

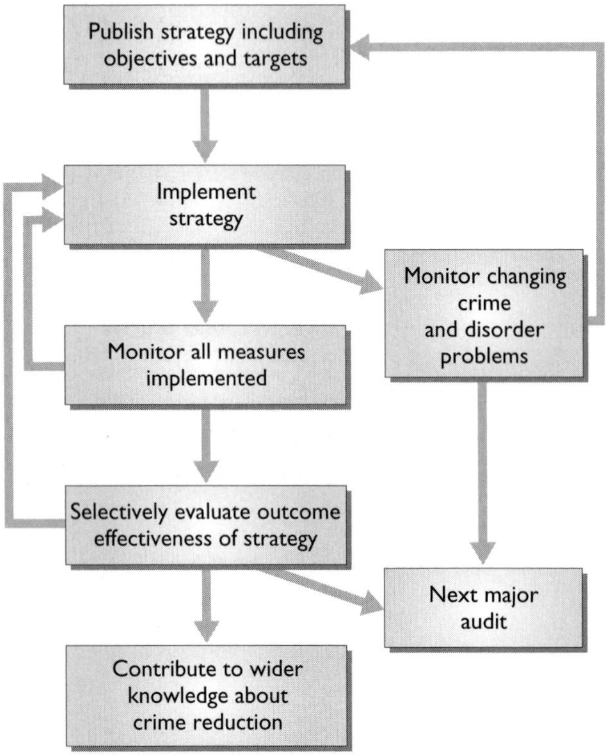

Figure 21.10 Monitoring and evaluation of multi-agency projects

Effective monitoring and evaluation identifies successful projects which can then be shared with other partnerships as examples of good practice. It also helps identify where strategies are ineffective so that they can be redesigned to perform better or further resources can be allocated to them. The process of monitoring is ongoing and a successful partnership will make a priority of checking their progress towards the targets they set in their crime and disorder audit.

Key points

1. Multi-agency partnerships were created by the Crime and Disorder Act 1998.
2. All agencies must work in partnership to reduce crime.
3. The Partnership needs to conduct an audit.
4. The next step is to prioritise targets and monitor and evaluate performance.
5. Target choice depends on local needs.

Assessment activity 21-P6 21-M2, 21-D2

Produce a project which identifies and describes in detail local crime reduction initiatives put into practice by your local multi-agency partnership and analyse how effective these methods are in tackling crime. In addition, summarise the structure and funding of your local crime and disorder partnership.

End of unit test

1. What is meant by the term 'crime is relative'?
2. Who was the founding father of functionalism?
3. Which theory supports the idea of the collective conscience?
4. Which theory argues that there are only 2 social classes in society?
5. Name these 2 social classes and describe their relationship.
6. How do labelling theorists define crime?

7 Describe Merton's adaptations to strain.

8 What is Anomie from both Durkheim's and Merton's point of view?

9 What is normlessness?

10 How do the media manipulate fear of crime?

11 How does fear of crime impact on peoples lifestyle?

12 Which social groups are considered to be more vulnerable to crime?

13 On average how much does crime cost annually?

14 What is the difference between reported and recorded crime?

15 Why do people choose not to report crime?

16 What is the role of the defence solicitor?

17 What does CPS stand for?

18 What are the advantages and disadvantages of the witness service?

19 Which Act created multi-agency partnerships?

20 Why is it important to monitor and evaluate crime and disorder initiatives?

Resources

Ashworth A, *The Criminal Process*

Croall H, *Crime and Society in Britain*, 1998, London, Longman

Doherty M, *Criminology*, 1997, London

Gray D et al, *Public Services Book 1*, 2004, London, Heinemann

Harrower J, *Applying Psychology to Crime*, 1998

Maguire M et al, *The Oxford Handbook of Criminology 3rd edition*, 2002, Oxford, Oxford University Press

Martin J, *The English Legal System 3rd edition*, 2002, London, Hodder and Stoughton

William K, *Criminology*

Websites

www.homeoffice.gov.uk/rds – Home Office research development statistics

www.victimsupport.org.uk – Victim Support

www.cps.gov.uk – Crown Prosecution Service

www.crimereduction.gov.uk/toolkits – Crime Reduction Toolkits

www.legislation.hmso.gov.uk – Her Majesty's Stationery Office

APPENDIX 1

Integrated Vocational Assignment (IVA)

What is an IVA?

The IVA is an assignment set by your awarding body EDEXCEL. It is not an examination, it is a normal assignment and will probably look a lot like the ones you are used to doing throughout your BTEC National Certificate or Diploma.

It is set externally to ensure that your qualification has equivalency with other level three qualifications such as A-Levels and which have external tests. The IVA is marked by your tutors and then checked by experts at EDEXCEL to ensure that your tutors are marking in the way they ought to be. You should not have to worry about an IVA any more than you would worry about another assignment.

You must remember that your IVA is a compulsory part of your course and if you do not complete it you may not be eligible to pass your qualification.

Which subjects are covered by the IVA?

On the BTEC National Certificate and Diploma in Public Services your IVA will be set on Unit 3 Leadership and Unit 4 Citizenship and Contemporary Issues.

How will I get my IVA?

A new IVA is issued every year which ensures that you cannot copy the work of the previous years class. Your college or school will issue you with the IVA at a time they choose, but usually between September and January. However, the IVA is released to the public on the EDEXCEL website earlier than many centres may give it to you. This means that you can go to the EDXCEL website www.edexcel.org.uk and print it off from there if you want to have extra time to consider it or work on it. Be careful to ensure you are downloading the latest version. The IVA for your year group is usually available at the end of June.

How long will I get to complete my IVA?

Completion time for the IVA depends on how long your centre gives you as centres can be flexible when they give their assignment out and when they expect it in. Your tutors may provide you with the IVA at any point from September onwards and the final deadline for submission of your work is usually at the end of May. If you want to get a head start then there is nothing to stop you accessing the assignment direct from the website. However you must remember that your IVA has to be marked by your tutors before it goes off to EDEXCEL so it is likely they will want it in by April at the very latest.

What help will my tutors give me?

Your tutor should help and guide you in exactly the same way that they would for other units on your course. This means that they may point you in the direction of useful resources, such as books, journals or websites. They may give you guidance on structure and presentation of your work and some tutors may be happy to check your notes or drafts for spelling and grammar errors. It is important to remember that all the work you submit should be your own. Your tutors cannot and will not complete the work for you.

What does the IVA consist of?

Your IVA consists of :

- A set of general instructions – this is a list of around ten bullet points which provide you with guidance on how to complete the IVA. Read them thoroughly as they will help you approach your assignment in the correct way.

- Your assignment scenario and tasks – these should be similar to assignments you already complete. The scenario will consist of a hypothetical, but realistic situation involving the public services and a series of tasks or questions you must complete which are based on the scenario. The work you have done in class should help you address these tasks, as will this book and your own research.
- A summary of your tasks and what you should hand in – this is a description of what should be in your final package of work. Make sure you check this through to be certain you don't miss parts of your assignment out or forget to hand it in.
- The assessment criteria for the unit – always reference your answers to this set of criteria as it will provide you with as much guidance on what the assignment requires as the assignment brief itself. Look at the criteria and make sure that your assignment answers the set criteria as well as the assessment tasks.
- Your IVA coversheet – this is the front cover of your assignment which must be placed at the start of your assignment.

What happens if my IVA is late?

It is your responsibility to ensure you plan your academic workload sufficiently well so that none of your assignments are late and this is especially true for the IVA. Each college makes a decision as to whether it will accept late work and the grounds on which they will permit extensions. Your centre can submit your late work for re-marking but it may delay your achievement.

You cannot resit your IVA. However if you take your IVA in year one and wish to improve your grade in year two of your course, you can choose to complete the following year's IVA but you must pay a supplementary remarking fee. Your centre is the best place for this to be arranged.

There may be some occasions where a student is eligible for an extension to allow more time for work to be completed, such as bereavement or a serious illness. If you feel you qualify and would like to be awarded an extension you should speak to your tutors as soon as you become aware of the situation. Equally, you may feel your work should receive special consideration because of your personal circumstances and in this instance your college has an EDEXCEL form wich they can complete on your behalf. Speak to your tutors as soon as you can about this if you feel it applies to you.

How can I do well on my IVA?

You can achieve a high grade on your IVA in much the same way that you would achieve a high grade on any other assignment. The following points will help you work towards a successful outcome for all of your work, including the IVA.

1 Make sure you start your assignment as soon as you get it. Don't underestimate the length of time you will need to understand, research and write your work. It is likely that you will need several months to be able to do a creditable job of it. Leaving it until the last minute and rushing through it is a recipe for disaster.

2 Read your assignment thoroughly and ensure you understand what is required of you. If you just skim the assignment it is highly likely you will miss many relevant points which could have improved your grade. If you don't understand a question you must ask your tutors for clarification.

3 Do not be tempted to take the easy way out and simply reproduce work you have found in textbooks or on the Internet. All of your work must be your own. You may not copy anything you find and if you do use work from external sources you must reference it within the body of your work and again in the bibliography. It is wholly unacceptable for you to submit copied work.

4 If you complete any aspect of your assignment as part of a group you must record your achievement individually. This

means all of your contributions to the group task must be identified and your individual contribution must show that you have met all the outcomes.

5 It is important that you use a wide variety of resources in order to complete your work. Using one or two sources of information will not provide you with the depth and detail required for a high grade. Remember that you may use textbooks, journals, magazines, newspapers, Internet, first hand accounts from public services officers or other professionals, your own primary research and public service promotional information to name but a few. The more sources you use the fuller your answers are likely to be and this will be reflected in your grade.

6 Try to produce work as professionally as possible. It is extremely difficult to mark work where the writing is illegible, so if you know your handwriting is poor then it is in your interests to word process it. If your spelling and grammar is poor then have a dictionary handy or use the spelling and grammar checker on your computer. Your work should be focused and well organised with each task clearly labelled.

7 Pay attention to the key words in your tasks, such as analyse, explain or describe. These key words mean different things and it is important to know what these words mean and how to interpret them in your assignment. (see page viii in the Introduction).

8 Consider creating an action plan that details your plan of how you will approach your assignment with timescales. This will help you monitor how well you are doing and whether you are falling behind schedule in producing your work.

9 If you are having any kind of difficulty with the assignment such as problems managing part-time work and study, health problems or home life difficulties you should tell your tutor immediately so that they can offer you the support you need.

10 Before you hand your work in, check that you have included everything and not left any parts out by accident. This last check and read through may pick up other mistakes on your assignment you didn't spot while you were writing it.

11 If you use a word processor you should ensure you back up your work onto a hard drive or the college network if you are allowed access to your own network area. Don't just rely on a floppy disk to save your work as they can be damaged very easily and your assignment may be lost.

APPENDIX 2

The United Nations Declaration of Human Rights

1 All human beings are born free and equal in dignity and rights. They are endowed with reason and conscience and should act towards one another in a spirit of brotherhood.

2 Everyone is entitled to all the rights and freedoms set forth in this Declaration, without distinction of any kind, such as race, colour, sex, language, religion, political or other opinion, national or social origin, property, birth or other status. Furthermore, no distinction shall be made on the basis of the political, jurisdictional or international status of the country or territory to which a person belongs, whether it be independent, trust, non-self-governing or under any other limitation of sovereignty.

3 Everyone has the right to life, liberty and security of person.

4 No one shall be held in slavery or servitude; slavery and the slave trade shall be prohibited in all their forms.

5 No one shall be subjected to torture or to cruel, inhuman or degrading treatment or punishment.

6 Everyone has the right to recognition everywhere as a person before the law.

7 All are equal before the law and are entitled without any discrimination to equal protection of the law. All are entitled to equal protection against any discrimination in violation of this Declaration and against any incitement to such discrimination.

8 Everyone has the right to an effective remedy by the competent national tribunals for acts violating the fundamental rights granted him by the constitution or by law.

9 No one shall be subjected to arbitrary arrest, detention or exile.

10 Everyone is entitled in full equality to a fair and public hearing by an independent and impartial tribunal, in the determination of his rights and obligations and of any criminal charge against him.

11.1 Everyone charged with a penal offence has the right to be presumed innocent until proved guilty according to law in a public trial at which he has had all the guarantees necessary for his defence.

11.2 No one shall be held guilty of any penal offence on account of any act or omission which did not constitute a penal offence, under national or international law, at the time when it was committed. Nor shall a heavier penalty be imposed than the one that was applicable at the time the penal offence was committed.

12 No one shall be subjected to arbitrary interference with his privacy, family, home or correspondence, nor to attacks upon his honour and reputation. Everyone has the right to the protection of the law against such interference or attacks.

13.1 Everyone has the right to freedom of movement and residence within the borders of each state.

13.2 Everyone has the right to leave any country, including his own, and to return to his country.

14.1 Everyone has the right to seek and to enjoy in other countries asylum from persecution.

14.2 This right may not be invoked in the case of prosecutions genuinely arising from non-political crimes or from acts contrary to the purposes and principles of the United Nations.

15.1 Everyone has the right to a nationality.

15.2 No one shall be arbitrarily deprived of his nationality nor denied the right to change his nationality.

16.1 Men and women of full age, without any limitation due to race, nationality or religion, have the right to marry and to found a family. They are entitled to equal rights as to marriage, during marriage and at its dissolution.

16.2 Marriage shall be entered into only with the free and full consent of the intending spouses.

16.3 The family is the natural and fundamental group unit of society and is entitled to protection by society and the State.

17.1 Everyone has the right to own property alone as well as in association with others.

17.2 No one shall be arbitrarily deprived of his property.

18 Everyone has the right to freedom of thought, conscience and religion; this right includes freedom to change his religion or belief, and freedom, either alone or in community with others and in public or private, to manifest his religion or belief in teaching, practice, worship and observance.

19 Everyone has the right to freedom of opinion and expression; this right includes freedom to hold opinions without interference and to seek, receive and impart information and ideas through any media and regardless of frontiers.

20.1 Everyone has the right to freedom of peaceful assembly and association.

20.2 No one may be compelled to belong to an association.

21.1 Everyone has the right to take part in the government of his country, directly or through freely chosen representatives.

21.2 Everyone has the right of equal access to public service in his country.

21.3 The will of the people shall be the basis of the authority of government; this will shall be expressed in periodic and genuine elections which shall be by universal and equal suffrage and shall be held by secret vote or by equivalent free voting procedures.

22 Everyone, as a member of society, has the right to social security and is entitled to realization, through national effort and international co-operation and in accordance with the organization and resources of each State, of the economic, social and cultural rights indispensable for his dignity and the free development of his personality.

23.1 Everyone has the right to work, to free choice of employment, to just and favourable conditions of work and to protection against unemployment.

23.2 Everyone, without any discrimination, has the right to equal pay for equal work.

23.3 Everyone who works has the right to just and favourable remuneration ensuring for himself and his family an existence worthy of human dignity, and supplemented, if necessary, by other means of social protection.

23.4 Everyone has the right to form and to join trade unions for the protection of his interests.

24 Everyone has the right to rest and leisure, including reasonable limitation of working hours and periodic holidays with pay.

25.1 Everyone has the right to a standard of living adequate for the health and well-being of himself and of his family, including food, clothing, housing and medical care and necessary social services, and the right to security in the event of unemployment, sickness, disability, widowhood, old age or other lack of livelihood in circumstances beyond his control.

25.2 Motherhood and childhood are entitled to special care and assistance. All children, whether born in or out of wedlock, shall enjoy the same social protection.

26.1 Everyone has the right to education. Education shall be free, at least in the elementary and fundamental stages. Elementary education shall be compulsory. Technical and professional education shall be made generally available and higher education shall be equally accessible to all on the basis of merit.

26.2 Education shall be directed to the full development of the human personality and to the strengthening of respect for human rights and fundamental freedoms. It shall promote understanding, tolerance and friendship among all nations, racial or religious groups, and shall further the activities of the United Nations for the maintenance of peace.

26.3 Parents have a prior right to choose the kind of education that shall be given to their children.

27.1 Everyone has the right freely to participate in the cultural life of the community, to enjoy the arts and to share in scientific advancement and its benefits.

27.2 Everyone has the right to the protection of the moral and material interests resulting from any scientific, literary or artistic production of which he is the author.

28 Everyone is entitled to a social and international order in which the rights and freedoms set forth in this Declaration can be fully realized.

29.1 Everyone has duties to the community in which alone the free and full development of his personality is possible.

29.2 In the exercise of his rights and freedoms, everyone shall be subject only to such limitations as are determined by law solely for the purpose of securing due recognition and respect for the rights and freedoms of others and of meeting the just requirements of morality, public order and the general welfare in a democratic society.

29.3 These rights and freedoms may in no case be exercised contrary to the purposes and principles of the United Nations.

30 Nothing in this Declaration may be interpreted as implying for any State, group or person any right to engage in any activity or to perform any act aimed at the destruction of any of the rights and freedoms set forth herein.

INDEX